INSTRUCTOR'S MANUAL

FINITE MATHEMATICS WITH APPLICATIONS

FOR BUSINESS AND SOCIAL SCIENCES
FIFTH EDITION

ABE MIZRAHI
INDIANA UNIVERSITY NORTHWEST

MICHAEL SULLIVAN
CHICAGO STATE UNIVERSITY

JOHN WILEY & SONS
NEW YORK • CHICHESTER • BRISBANE • TORONTO • SINGAPORE

Also available for the instructor:

Student Solutions to Accompany Finite Mathematics With Applications for Business and Social Sciences, Fifth Edition – 0-471-63437-9

Tests to Accompany Finite Mathematics with Applications for Business and Social Sciences, Fifth Edition – 0-471-63434-4

IBM Test Disk to Accompany Finite Mathematics with Applications for Business and Social Sciences, Fifth Edition
(Please contact M. Van Hise, Editor)

Apple Disk to Accompany Finite Mathematics with Applications for Business and Social Sciences, Fifth Edition
(Please contact M. Van Hise, Editor)

Finite and Discrete Software to Accompany Finite Mathematics with Applications for Business and Social Sciences, Fifth Edition – 0-471-63465-4

ISBN 0 471 60163 2

Printed in the United States of America

10 9 8 7 6 5 4 3 2 1

PREFACE

This manual contains worked-out solutions to all problems contained in the textbook Mizrahi and Sullivan: Finite Mathematics with Applications for Business and Social Sciences, Fifth Edition

For more information regarding the following supplements, or to request complimentary copies, please contact your local Wiley sales representative:

Tests to accompany Finite Mathematics with Applications for Business and Social Sciences, Fifth Edition. 0471-60163-2

Testing Disks for IBM and Macintosh to accompany Finite Mathematics with Applications for Business and Social Sciences, Fifth Edition.

Student Solutions to accompany Finite Mathematics with Applications for Business and Social Sciences, Fifth Edition. 0471-63437-9 To order, contact your bookstore directly.

Computer Explorations in Finite/Discrete Mathematics is available for the IBM PC, list price $24.95 (subject to change without notice). Preview demo-disks are available through your local Wiley sales representative. To order, contact your bookstore directly.

CONTENTS

Solutions to Odd-Numbered Problems

CHAPTER 1

Exercise 1.1 (page 11)

1. 0.5 **3.** 1.625 **5.** 1.333... **7.** 0.1666... **9.** 45% **11.** 112% **13.** 6%

15. 0.25% **17.** 0.42 **19.** 0.002 **21.** 0.00001 **23.** 0.734

25. $\frac{2}{40} = \frac{1 \cdot 2}{20 \cdot 2} = \frac{1}{20}$ **27.** $\frac{6}{8} = \frac{3 \cdot 2}{4 \cdot 2} = \frac{3}{4}$ **29.** $0.15 \cdot 1000 = 150$

31. $0.18 \cdot 100 = 18$

33.
$$\begin{aligned} 2x + 5 &= 7 \\ 2x &= 7 - 5 \\ 2x &= 2 \\ x &= 1 \end{aligned}$$

35.
$$\begin{aligned} 6 - x &= 0 \\ 6 &= x \\ x &= 6 \end{aligned}$$

37.
$$\begin{aligned} 3(2 - x) &= 9 \\ 2 - x &= 3 \\ x &= 2 - 3 \\ x &= -1 \end{aligned}$$

39.
$$\begin{aligned} 4x + 3 &= 2x - 5 \\ 2x &= -8 \\ x &= -4 \end{aligned}$$

41.
$$\begin{aligned} \frac{4x}{3} + \frac{x}{3} &= 5 \\ 4x + x &= 3 \cdot 5 \\ 5x &= 15 \\ x &= 3 \end{aligned}$$

43.
$$\begin{aligned} \frac{3x - 5}{x - 3} &= 1 \\ 3x - 5 &= x - 3 \\ 3x - x &= -3 + 5 \\ 2x &= 2 \\ x &= 1 \end{aligned}$$

45.
$$\begin{aligned} x^2 - x - 12 &= 0 \\ (x - 4)(x + 3) &= 0 \\ x = 4 \text{ or } x &= -3 \end{aligned}$$

47.
$$\begin{aligned} x^2 - 5x + 6 &= 0 \\ (x - 3)(x - 2) &= 0 \\ x = 3 \text{ or } x &= 2 \end{aligned}$$

49.
$$\begin{aligned} x^2 - 16 &= 0 \\ (x - 4)(x + 4) &= 0 \\ x = 4 \text{ or } x &= -4 \end{aligned}$$

51. $x = 9$ **53.** $x = \frac{1}{2^3} = \frac{1}{8}$ **55.** $x = -9$ **57.** $x = 2$ **59.** $x = 2$

61. $x = 5$ **63.** $\frac{1}{3} > 0.33 \left(\frac{1}{3} = 0.333\ldots \right)$ **65.** $3 = \sqrt{9}$

67.
$$\begin{aligned} 3x + 5 &\le 2 \\ 3x &\le 2 - 5 \\ 3x &\le -3 \\ x &\le -1 \end{aligned}$$

69.
$$\begin{aligned} 3x + 5 &\ge 2 \\ 3x &\ge -3 \\ x &\ge -1 \end{aligned}$$

71.
$$\begin{aligned} -3x + 5 &\le 2 \\ -3x &\le -3 \\ 3x &\ge 3 \\ x &\ge 1 \end{aligned}$$

73.

$$6x - 3 \geq 8x + 5$$
$$6x - 8x \geq 5 + 3$$
$$-2x \geq 8$$
$$x \leq -4$$

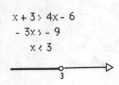

75.

$$x + 3 > 4x - 6$$
$$-3x > -9$$
$$x < 3$$

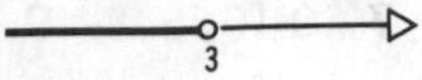

77.

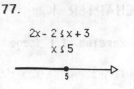

$$2x - 2 \leq x + 3$$
$$x \leq 5$$

Exercise 1.2 (page 15)

1. A = (4, 2); B = (6, 2); C = (5, 3); D = (−2, 1); E = (−2, −3); F = (3, −2); G = (6, −2); H = (5, 0)

3. $\dfrac{f_2 - a_2}{f_1 - a_1} = \dfrac{-2-2}{3-4} = \dfrac{-4}{-1} = 4$

5. $\dfrac{a_2 - c_2}{a_1 - c_1} = \dfrac{2-3}{4-5} = \dfrac{-1}{-1} = 1$

7. $y = x - 3$

x	0	3	2	-2	4	-4
y	-3	0	-1	-5	1	-7

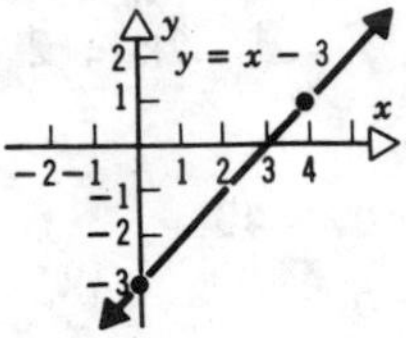

9. $2x - y = 6$

x	0	3	2	-2	4	-4
y	-6	0	-2	-10	2	-14

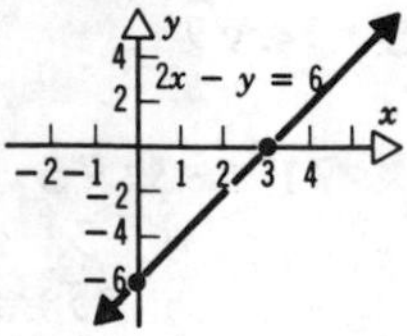

11.

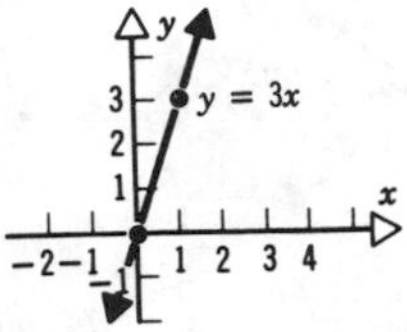

13.

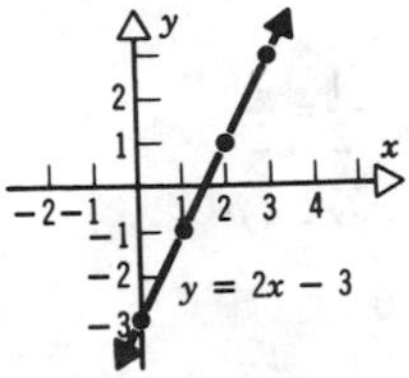

15.

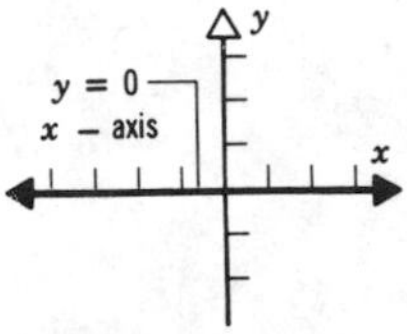

17.

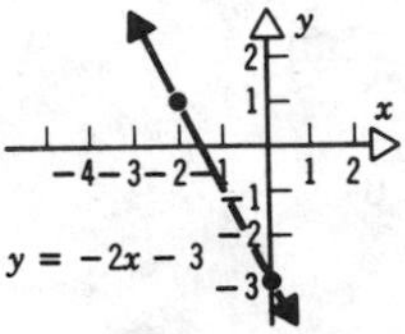

19.

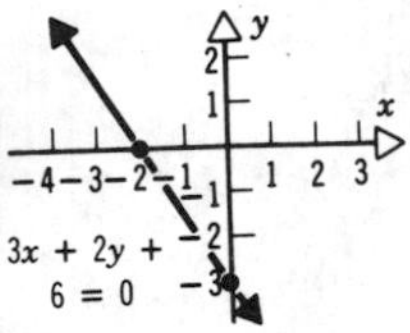

21.

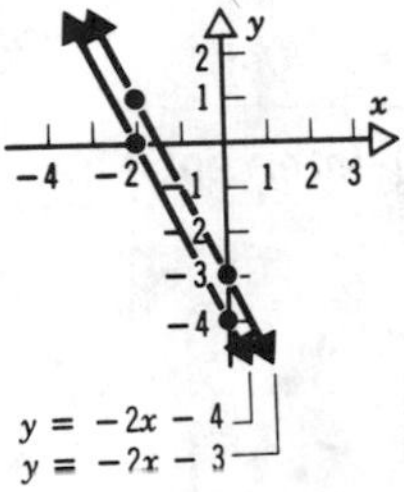

The lines are parallel.

Exercise 1.3 (page 23)

1. $\frac{1-3}{0-2} = \frac{-2}{-2} = 1$

3. $\frac{-4-0}{-5-(-3)} = \frac{-4}{-2} = 2$

5. $\frac{4.0-0.3}{1.5-0.1} = \frac{3.7}{1.4} = \frac{37}{14}$

7.

$$y - 3 = 2[x - (-2)]$$
$$y - 3 = 2(x + 2)$$
$$2x - y + 7 = 0$$

9.

$$y - (-1) = -\frac{2}{3}(x - 1)$$
$$y + 1 = -\frac{2}{3}x + \frac{2}{3}$$
$$2x + 3y + 1 = 0$$

11.

$$m = \frac{2-3}{-1-1} = \frac{-1}{-2} = \frac{1}{2}$$

$$y - 3 = \frac{1}{2}(x-1)$$

$$x - 2y + 5 = 0$$

13.

$$y = -3x + 3$$

$$3x + y - 3 = 0$$

15.

$$m = \frac{-1-0}{0-2} = \frac{-1}{-2} = \frac{1}{2}$$

$$y = \frac{1}{2}x - 1$$

$$x - 2y - 2 = 0$$

17. $x - 1 = 0$

19.

Slope $\frac{3}{2}$, y - intercept -3

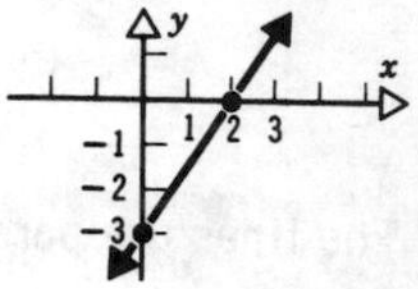

21.

Slope $-\frac{1}{2}$, y - intercept 2

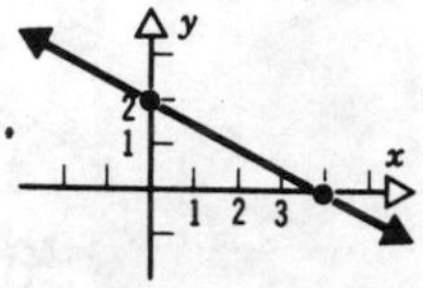

23. Slope undefined, no y-intercept

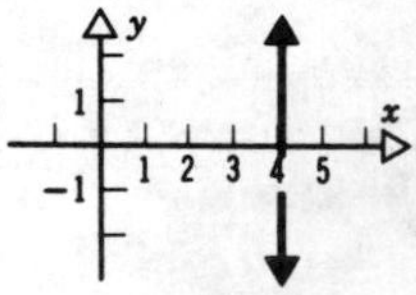

25. $x = 2y$ **27.** $x + y = 2$

29.

$$°F = \frac{9}{5}°C + 32 \text{ or } °C = \frac{5}{9}(F - 32);\ \frac{5}{9}(70-32) = \frac{190}{9} = 21.111\ldots$$

Exercise 1.4 (page 30)

1. $m_1 = m_2 = -1$

3. $m_1 = m_2 = \frac{2}{3}$

5.
$$\begin{aligned} y &= 5 - x \\ 3x - (5 - x) &= 7 \\ 3x - 5 + x &= 7 \\ 4x &= 12 \\ x &= 3 \\ y &= 5 - 3 = 2 \\ (x, y) &= (3, 2) \end{aligned}$$

7.
$$\begin{aligned} x &= 2y - 4 \\ 3(2y - 4) - 4y &= 1 \\ 6y - 12 - 4y &= 1 \\ 2y &= 13 \\ y &= \frac{13}{2} \\ x = 2\left(\frac{13}{2}\right) - 4 &= 9 \\ (x, y) &= \left(9, \frac{13}{2}\right) \end{aligned}$$

9.
$$\begin{aligned} y &= 2 - 3x \\ 3x - 2(2 - 3x) + 5 &= 0 \\ 3x - 4 + 6x + 5 &= 0 \\ 9x + 1 &= 0 \\ x &= -\frac{1}{9} \\ y = 2 - 3\left(-\frac{1}{9}\right) &= \frac{7}{3} \\ (x, y) &= \left(-\frac{1}{9}, \frac{7}{3}\right) \end{aligned}$$

11.
$$\left.\begin{aligned} 2x - 3y + 4 &= 0 \\ 3x + 2y - 7 &= 0 \end{aligned}\right\} \quad \begin{aligned} 4x - 6y + 8 &= 0 \\ 9x + 6y - 21 &= 0 \\ \hline 13x - 13 &= 0 \\ x &= 1 \end{aligned}$$
$$\begin{aligned} 2(1) - 3y + 4 &= 0 \\ y &= 2 \\ (x, y) &= (1, 2) \end{aligned}$$

13.
$$\left.\begin{aligned} 3x - 4y + 8 &= 0 \\ 2x + y - 2 &= 0 \end{aligned}\right\} \quad \begin{aligned} 3x - 4y + 8 &= 0 \\ 8x + 4y - 8 &= 0 \\ \hline 11x &= 0 \\ x &= 0 \end{aligned}$$
$$\begin{aligned} 3(0) - 4y + 8 &= 0 \\ y &= 2 \\ (x, y) &= (0, 2) \end{aligned}$$

15.
$$\left.\begin{aligned} -2x + 3y - 7 &= 0 \\ 3x + 2y - 9 &= 0 \end{aligned}\right\} \quad \begin{aligned} -6x + 9y - 21 &= 0 \\ 6x + 4y - 18 &= 0 \\ \hline 13y - 39 &= 0 \\ y &= 3 \end{aligned}$$
$$\begin{aligned} 3x + 2(3) - 9 &= 0 \\ x &= 1 \\ (x, y) &= (1, 3) \end{aligned}$$

17.
$$\begin{aligned} 3x + 2y + 6 &= 0 \\ 5x - 2y + 10 &= 0 \\ \hline 8x + 16 &= 0 \\ x &= -2 \\ 3(-2) + 2y + 6 &= 0 \\ y &= 0 \\ (x, y) &= (-2, 0) \end{aligned}$$

19.

L: $2x - 3y + 6 = 0$

$-3y = -2x - 6$

$y = \frac{2}{3}x + 2$

M: $4x - 6x + 7 = 0$

$-6y = -4x - 7$

$y = \frac{2}{3}x + \frac{7}{6}$

No solution; the lines L and M are parallel; same slope; different y-intercepts.

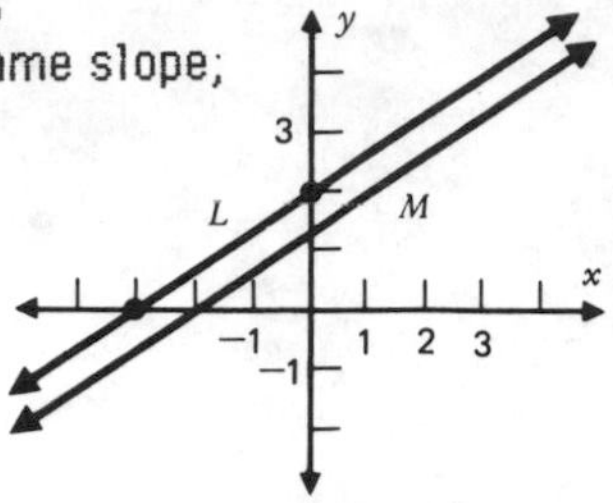

21.

L: $-2x + 3y + 6 = 0$

$3y = 2x - 6$

$y = \frac{2}{3}x - 2$

M: $4x - 6y - 12 = 0$

$-6y = -4x + 12$

$y = \frac{2}{3}x - 2$

Infinitely many solutions; the lines L and M are identical; same slope; same y-intercept.

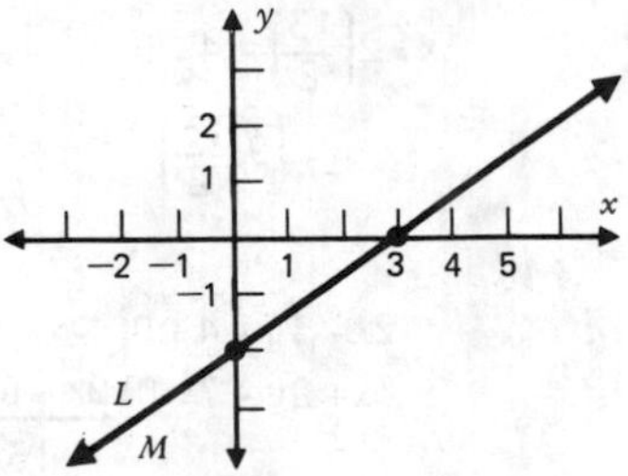

23.

L: $3x - 3y + 10 = 0$

$-3y = -3x - 10$

$y = x + \frac{10}{3}$

M: $x + y - 2 = 0$

$y = -x + 2$

One solution; since the slopes are different, the lines intersect.

$$x_0 + \frac{10}{3} = -x_0 + 2$$

$$2x_0 = -\frac{4}{3}$$

$$x_0 = -\frac{2}{3}$$

$$y_0 = \frac{2}{3} + 2 = \frac{8}{3}$$

L and M intersect at $\left(-\frac{2}{3}, \frac{8}{3}\right)$.

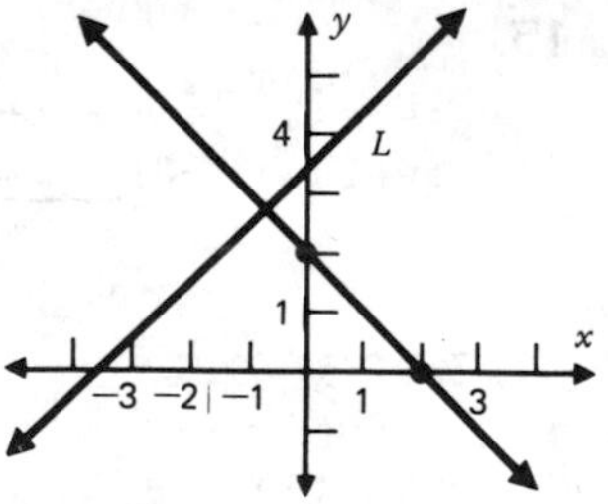

25.

L: $3x - 2y - 4 = 0$
$-2y = -3x + 4$
$y = \frac{3}{2}x - 2$

M: $-6x + 4y - 7 = 0$
$4y = 6x + 7$
$y = \frac{3}{2}x + \frac{7}{4}$

No solution; the lines L and M are parallel; same slope; different y-intercepts.

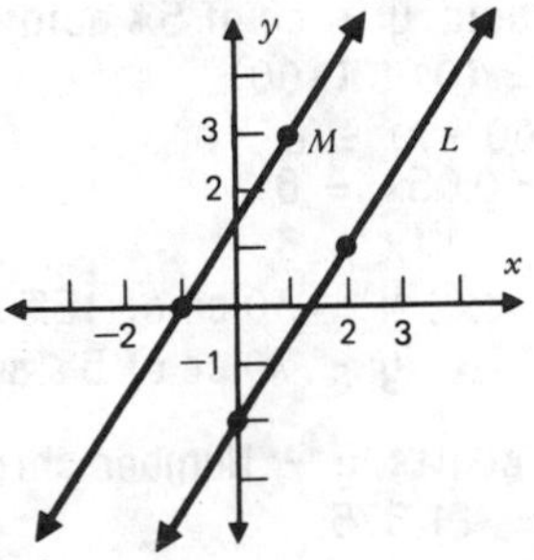

27. $2x - y = 6$
$-y = -2x + 6$
$y = 2x - 6$

A line parallel to this line must have slope 2:

$y - 2 = 2(x - 1)$
$y = 2x$

29. Let x = Number of caramels, y = Number of creams; then $x(0.05) + y(0.10) = 4.0$ and $x + y = 50$:

$5x + 10y = 400$
$5x + 5y = 250$
$5y = 150$
$y = 30$
$x = 20$

20 caramels, 30 creams; increase the number of caramels to increase profits.

31. Let x = Bond investment; y = Savings; then $x + y = 50{,}000$ and $0.15x + 0.07y = 6000$:

$0.15x + 0.07(50{,}000 - x) = 6000$
$0.15x + 3500 - 0.07x = 6000$
$0.08x = 2500$
$x = \$31{,}250$ in bonds
$y = \$18{,}750$ in savings certificates

33. $x + y = 13$ and $5x + 25y = 165$; solving by substitution:

$5(13-y) + 25y = 165$
$65 - 5y + 5y = 165$
$20y = 100$
$y = 5$ quarters
$x = 8$ nickels

35. x = cc of 15% acid; y = cc of 5% acid; then $y = 100 - x$ and $0.15x + 0.05y = (0.08)(100)$:

$0.15x + 0.05(100 - x) = 8$
$0.15x + 5 - 0.05x = 8$
$0.1x = 3$
$x = 30$ cc of 15% acid
$y = 70$ cc of 5% acid

37. x = Number of adults; y = Number children; then $y = 5200 - x$ and $2.75x + 1.50y = 11{,}875$:

$2.75x + 1.50(5200 - x) = 11{,}875$
$1.25x + 7800 = 11{,}875$
$1.25x = 4075$
$x = 3260$ adults
$y = 1940$ children

Exercise 1.5 (page 38)

1. (a) $A = 1000(1 + 0.18t) = 1000 + 180t$ (b) $1000 + 180 \cdot 1/2 = 1090$
(c) 1180 (d) 1360

3. $C = \$10x + \$600$, $R = \$30x$

$10x + 600 = 30x$
$600 = 20x$
$30 = x$

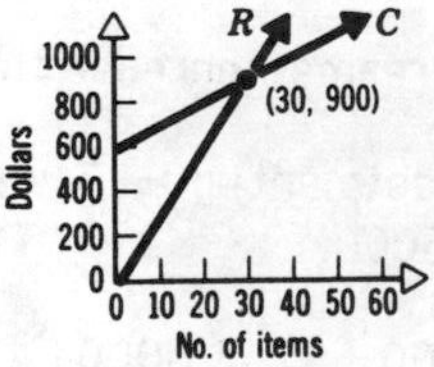

5. $C = \$0.2x + \$50$, $R = \$0.3x$

$0.2x + 50 = 0.3x$
$2x + 500 = 3x$
$500 = x$

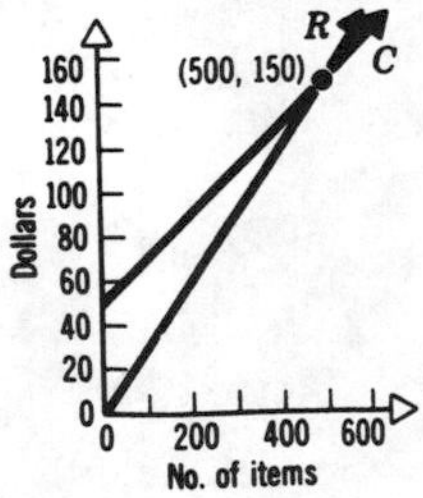

7. $R = \$1x$, $C = 0.75x + 300$

$x = 0.75x + 300$
$0.25x = 300$
$x = 1200$ items

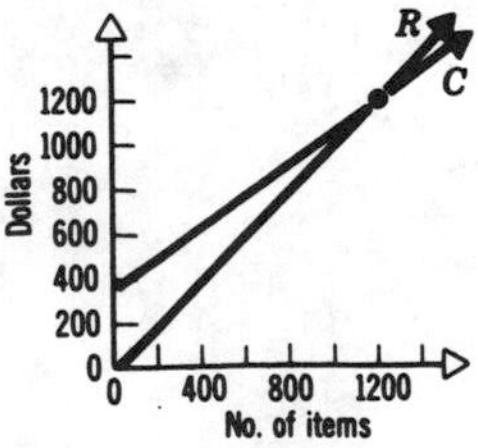

9. (a) \$80,000 (b) \$95,000 (c) \$105,000 (d) \$120,000

11. $S = p + 1,\ D = 3 - p$
$p + 1 = 3 - p$
$2p = 2$
$p = \$1$

13. $S = 20p + 500,\ D = 1000 - 30p$
$20p + 500 = 1000 - 30p$
$50p = 500$
$p = \$10$

15. $S = 0.7p + 0.4,\ D = -0.5p + 1.6$
$0.7p + 0.4 = -0.5p + 1.6$
$1.2p = 1.2$
$p = 1$

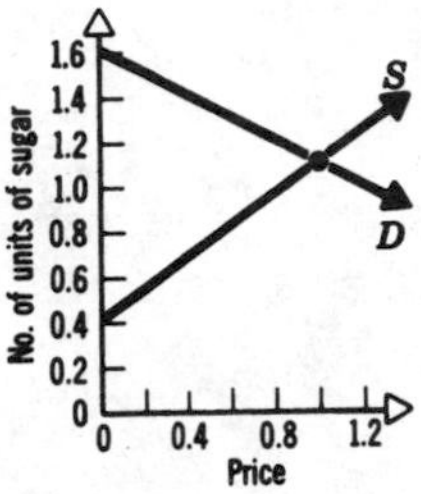

CHAPTER REVIEW

Review Exercises (page 40)

1. $3x + 6 = 2x - 1$
$x = -7$

3. $-2(x + 3) = x + 5$
$-2x - 6 = x + 5$
$-3x = 11$
$x = -\frac{11}{3}$

5. $\frac{4x - 1}{x + 2} = 5$
$4x - 1 = 5(x + 2)$
$4x - 1 = 5x + 10$
$-x = 11$
$x = -11$

7. $2x - 1 \le 5$
$2x \le 6$
$x \le 3$

9. $3x + 7 \ge -2x + 2$
$5x \ge -5$
$x \ge -1$

11.

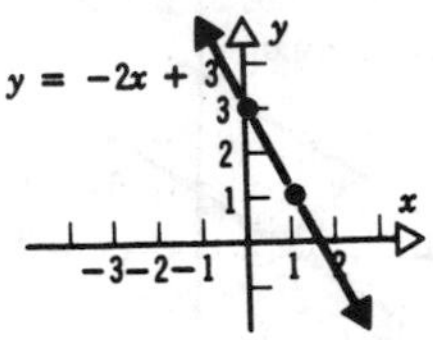

13.

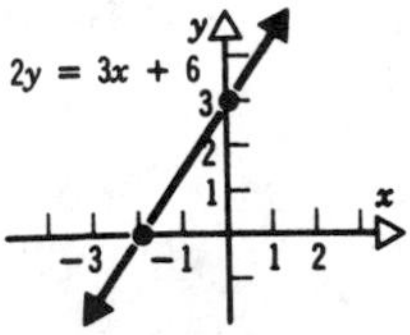

15.

$\text{Slope} = \dfrac{4-2}{-3-1} = \dfrac{2}{-4} = \dfrac{-1}{2}$

$y - 2 = -\dfrac{1}{2}(x-1)$

$2y - 4 = -x + 1$

$x + 2y - 5 = 0$

17.

$\text{Slope} = \dfrac{3-0}{-2-0} = \dfrac{-3}{2}$

$y - 0 = -\dfrac{3}{2}(x-0)$

$2y = -3x$

$3x + 2y = 0$

19. $y = 2(x+1)$

$2x - y + 2 = 0$

21. $y - 3 = 1(x-1)$

$x - y + 2 = 0$

23. $-9x - 2y + 18 = 0$

$2y = -9x + 18$

$y = \left(-\dfrac{9}{2}\right)x + 9$

$\text{Slope} = -\dfrac{9}{2}$

y-intercept = 9

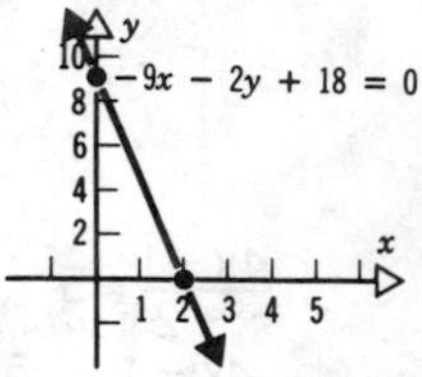

25. $4x + 2y - 9 = 0$

$2y = 4x + 9$

$y = -2x + \dfrac{9}{2}$

Slope = −2

$\text{y-intercept} = \dfrac{9}{2}$

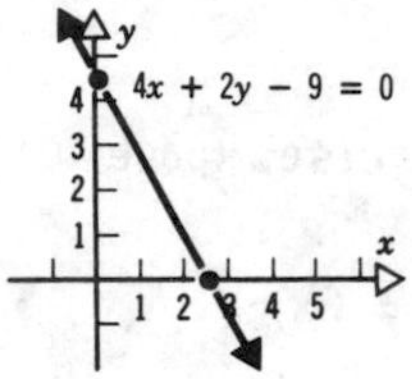

27. $3x - 4y + 12 = 0$

$-4y = -3x - 12$

$y = \dfrac{3}{4}x + 3$

$6x - 8y + 9 = 0$

$-8y = -6x - 9$

$y = \dfrac{3}{4}x + \dfrac{9}{8}$

No solution; the lines are parallel.

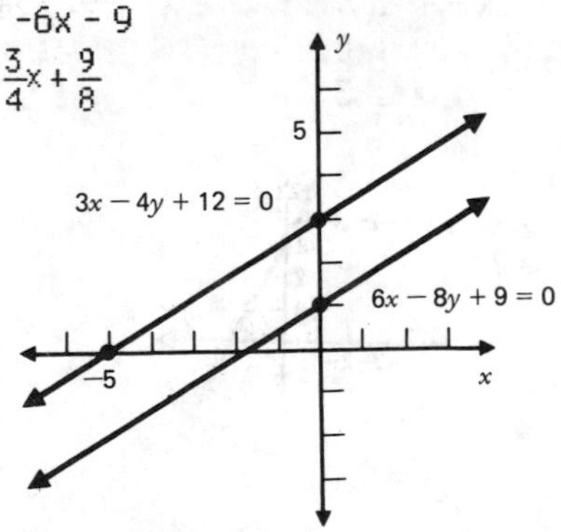

29. $x - y + 2 = 0$

$y = x + 2$

$3x - 4y + 12 = 0$

$-4y = -3x - 12$

$y = \left(\frac{3}{4}\right)x + 3$

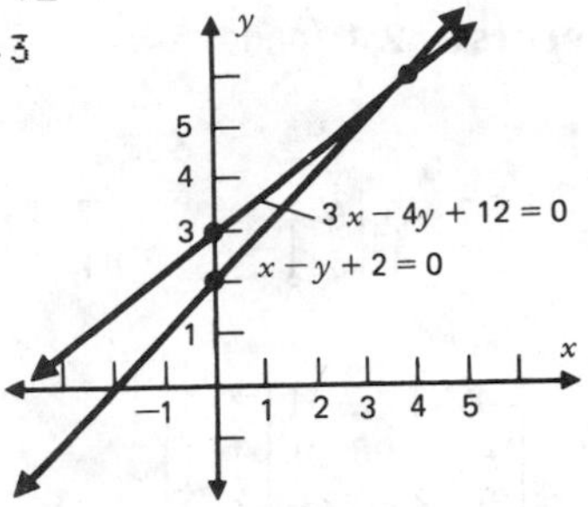

The lines intersect.

$3x - 4y + 12 = 0$

$x - y + 2 = 0$

$$\begin{aligned} 3x - 4y + 12 &= 0 \\ 3x - 3y + 6 &= 0 \\ \hline -y + 6 &= 0 \\ y &= 6 \end{aligned}$$

$x = 6 - 2 = 4$

One solution; the lines intersect at (4, 6).

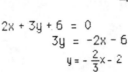

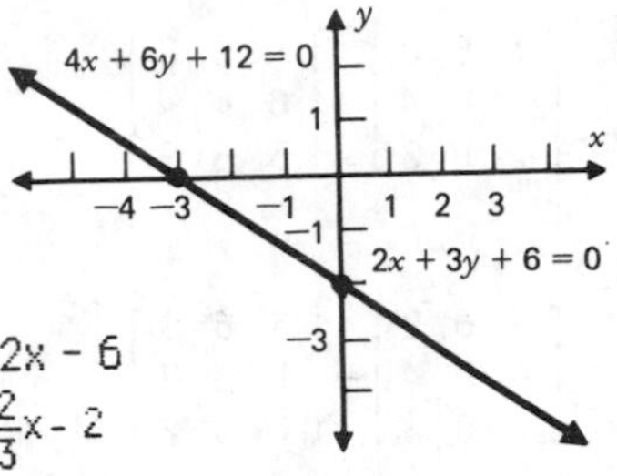

31. $4x + 6y + 12 = 0$

$6y = -4x - 12$

$y = -\frac{2}{3}x - 2$

$2x + 3y + 6 = 0$

$3y = -2x - 6$

$y = -\frac{2}{3}x - 2$

Infinitely many solutions; the lines are identical.

33. Let x = Amount in bonds, y = Amount in bank; then $y = 90{,}000 - x$ and

$0.16x + 0.06y = 10{,}000$:

$$\begin{aligned} 0.16x + (0.06)(90{,}000 - x) &= 10{,}000 \\ 0.16x - 0.06x + 5400 &= 10{,}000 \\ 0.10x &= 4600 \\ x &= \$46{,}000 \text{ in bonds} \\ y &= \$44{,}000 \text{ in bank} \end{aligned}$$

35. (a)

(b)

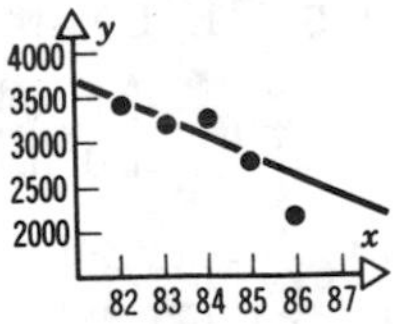

(c) We used the points (80, 2800) and (77, 3400). If you chose two different points, your answer may be different.

$$m = \frac{3400 - 2800}{77 - 80} = \frac{600}{-3} = -200$$

$$y - 2800 = -200(x - 78)$$

(d) $y = -200(82 - 78) + 2800 = 2000$

(Using only the last two digits of the date)

CHAPTER 2

Exercise 2.1 (page 54)

1. $\left[\begin{array}{cc|c} 2 & -3 & 5 \\ 1 & -1 & 3 \end{array}\right]$

3. $\left[\begin{array}{cc|c} 2 & 1 & -6 \\ 1 & 1 & -1 \end{array}\right]$

5. $\left[\begin{array}{ccc|c} 2 & -1 & -1 & 0 \\ 1 & -1 & -1 & 1 \\ 3 & -1 & 0 & 2 \end{array}\right]$

7. $\left[\begin{array}{ccc|c} 2 & -3 & 1 & 7 \\ 1 & 1 & -1 & 1 \\ 2 & 2 & -3 & -4 \end{array}\right]$

9. $\left[\begin{array}{cccc|c} 4 & -1 & 2 & -1 & 4 \\ 1 & 1 & 0 & 0 & -6 \\ 0 & 2 & -1 & 1 & 5 \end{array}\right]$

11. $R_1 = r_2$, $R_2 = r_1$ Interchange rows

13. $R_1 = 4r_1$

15.

$$\begin{bmatrix} 3 & 6 & 9 \\ 0 & 1 & 4 \\ 1 & 0 & 2 \end{bmatrix} \rightarrow \begin{bmatrix} 1 & 0 & 2 \\ 0 & 1 & 4 \\ 3 & 6 & 9 \end{bmatrix}$$

17.

$$\begin{bmatrix} 3 & 6 & 9 \\ 0 & 1 & 4 \\ 1 & 0 & 2 \end{bmatrix} \rightarrow \begin{bmatrix} 0 & 6 & 3 \\ 0 & 1 & 4 \\ 1 & 0 & 2 \end{bmatrix}$$

19.

$$\begin{bmatrix} 3 & 6 & 9 \\ 0 & 1 & 4 \\ 1 & 0 & 2 \end{bmatrix} \rightarrow \begin{bmatrix} 3 & 6 & 9 \\ 1 & 3 & 7 \\ 1 & 0 & 2 \end{bmatrix}$$

21.

$$\left[\begin{array}{cc|c} 1 & 1 & 6 \\ 2 & -1 & 0 \end{array}\right] \xrightarrow[-2r_1+r_2]{} \left[\begin{array}{cc|c} 1 & 1 & 6 \\ 0 & -3 & -12 \end{array}\right] \xrightarrow[-\frac{1}{3}r_2]{} \left[\begin{array}{cc|c} 1 & 1 & 6 \\ 0 & 1 & 4 \end{array}\right] \xrightarrow{-r_2+r_1} \left[\begin{array}{cc|c} 1 & 0 & 2 \\ 0 & 1 & 4 \end{array}\right]$$

$x = 2$
$y = 4$

23.

$$\left[\begin{array}{cc|c} 2 & 1 & 5 \\ 1 & -1 & 1 \end{array}\right] \rightarrow \left[\begin{array}{cc|c} 1 & -1 & 1 \\ 2 & 1 & 5 \end{array}\right] \xrightarrow[-2r_1+r_2]{} \left[\begin{array}{cc|c} 1 & -1 & 1 \\ 0 & 3 & 3 \end{array}\right] \rightarrow \left[\begin{array}{cc|c} 1 & -1 & 1 \\ 0 & 1 & 1 \end{array}\right] \rightarrow \left[\begin{array}{cc|c} 1 & 0 & 2 \\ 0 & 1 & 1 \end{array}\right]; \; x = 2, \; y = 1$$

25.

$$\left[\begin{array}{cc|c} 2 & 3 & 7 \\ 3 & -1 & 5 \end{array}\right] \xrightarrow{\frac{1}{2}r_1} \left[\begin{array}{cc|c} 1 & 1.5 & 3.5 \\ 3 & -1 & 5 \end{array}\right] \xrightarrow[-3r_1+r_2]{} \left[\begin{array}{cc|c} 1 & 1.5 & 3.5 \\ 0 & -5.5 & -5.5 \end{array}\right] \rightarrow \left[\begin{array}{cc|c} 1 & 1.5 & 3.5 \\ 0 & 1 & 1 \end{array}\right] \rightarrow$$

$$\left[\begin{array}{cc|c} 1 & 0 & 2 \\ 0 & 1 & 1 \end{array}\right]; \; x = 2, \; y = 1$$

27.

$$\left[\begin{array}{cc|c} 5 & -7 & 31 \\ 3 & 2 & 0 \end{array}\right] \xrightarrow{\frac{1}{5}r_1} \left[\begin{array}{cc|c} 1 & -1.4 & 6.2 \\ 3 & 2 & 0 \end{array}\right] \xrightarrow[-3r_1+r_2]{} \left[\begin{array}{cc|c} 1 & -1.4 & 6.2 \\ 0 & 6.2 & -18.6 \end{array}\right] \rightarrow$$

$$\left[\begin{array}{cc|c} 1 & -1.4 & 6.2 \\ 0 & 1 & -3 \end{array}\right] \xrightarrow{1.4r_2+r_1} \left[\begin{array}{cc|c} 1 & 0 & 2 \\ 0 & 1 & -3 \end{array}\right]; \; x = 2, \; y = -3$$

29.

$$\left[\begin{array}{cc|c} 2 & -3 & 0 \\ 4 & 9 & 5 \end{array}\right] \xrightarrow[-2r_1+r_2]{} \left[\begin{array}{cc|c} 2 & -3 & 0 \\ 0 & 15 & 5 \end{array}\right] \to \left[\begin{array}{cc|c} 2 & -3 & 0 \\ 0 & 1 & \frac{1}{3} \end{array}\right] \to \left[\begin{array}{cc|c} 2 & 0 & 0 \\ 0 & 1 & \frac{1}{3} \end{array}\right] \to \left[\begin{array}{cc|c} 1 & 0 & \frac{1}{2} \\ 0 & 1 & \frac{1}{3} \end{array}\right]; \quad \begin{array}{l} x = \frac{1}{2} \\ y = \frac{1}{3} \end{array}$$

31.

$$\left[\begin{array}{cc|c} 4 & -3 & 4 \\ 2 & 6 & 7 \end{array}\right] \xrightarrow{-2r_2+r_1} \left[\begin{array}{cc|c} 0 & -15 & -10 \\ 2 & 6 & 7 \end{array}\right] \xrightarrow[\frac{1}{2}r_2]{-\frac{1}{15}r_1} \left[\begin{array}{cc|c} 0 & 1 & \frac{2}{3} \\ 1 & 3 & \frac{7}{2} \end{array}\right] \to \left[\begin{array}{cc|c} 1 & 3 & \frac{7}{2} \\ 0 & 1 & \frac{2}{3} \end{array}\right] \xrightarrow{-3r_2+r_1}$$

$$\left[\begin{array}{cc|c} 1 & 0 & \frac{3}{2} \\ 0 & 1 & \frac{2}{3} \end{array}\right]; \quad \begin{array}{l} x = \frac{3}{2} \\ y = \frac{2}{3} \end{array}$$

33.

$$\left[\begin{array}{cc|c} \frac{1}{2} & \frac{1}{3} & 2 \\ 1 & 1 & 5 \end{array}\right] \to \left[\begin{array}{cc|c} 1 & 1 & 5 \\ \frac{1}{2} & \frac{1}{3} & 2 \end{array}\right] \xrightarrow[-\frac{1}{2}r_1+r_2]{} \left[\begin{array}{cc|c} 1 & 1 & 5 \\ 0 & -\frac{1}{6} & -\frac{1}{2} \end{array}\right] \xrightarrow[-6r_2]{} \left[\begin{array}{cc|c} 1 & 1 & 5 \\ 0 & 1 & 3 \end{array}\right]$$

$$\xrightarrow{-r_2+r_1} \left[\begin{array}{cc|c} 1 & 0 & 2 \\ 0 & 1 & 3 \end{array}\right]; \quad \begin{array}{l} x = 2 \\ y = 3 \end{array}$$

35.

$$\left[\begin{array}{cc|c} 1 & 1 & 1 \\ 3 & -2 & \frac{4}{3} \end{array}\right] \xrightarrow[-3r_1+r_2]{} \left[\begin{array}{cc|c} 1 & 1 & 1 \\ 0 & -5 & -\frac{5}{3} \end{array}\right] \xrightarrow[-\frac{1}{5}r_2]{} \left[\begin{array}{cc|c} 1 & 1 & 1 \\ 0 & 1 & \frac{1}{3} \end{array}\right] \to \left[\begin{array}{cc|c} 1 & 0 & \frac{2}{3} \\ 0 & 1 & \frac{1}{3} \end{array}\right]; \quad \begin{array}{l} x = \frac{2}{3} \\ y = \frac{1}{3} \end{array}$$

37.

$$\left[\begin{array}{ccc|c} 2 & 1 & 1 & 6 \\ 1 & -1 & -1 & -3 \\ 3 & 1 & 2 & 7 \end{array}\right] \to \left[\begin{array}{ccc|c} 1 & -1 & -1 & -3 \\ 2 & 1 & 1 & 6 \\ 3 & 1 & 2 & 7 \end{array}\right] \xrightarrow[\substack{-2r_1+r_2 \\ -3r_1+r_3}]{} \left[\begin{array}{ccc|c} 1 & -1 & -1 & -3 \\ 0 & 3 & 3 & 12 \\ 0 & 4 & 5 & 16 \end{array}\right] \to$$

$$\left[\begin{array}{ccc|c} 1 & -1 & -1 & -3 \\ 0 & 1 & 1 & 4 \\ 0 & 4 & 5 & 16 \end{array}\right] \xrightarrow[-4r_2+r_3]{} \left[\begin{array}{ccc|c} 1 & -1 & -1 & -3 \\ 0 & 1 & 1 & 4 \\ 0 & 0 & 1 & 0 \end{array}\right] \xrightarrow[-r_3+r_2]{r_2+r_1} \left[\begin{array}{ccc|c} 1 & 0 & 0 & 1 \\ 0 & 1 & 0 & 4 \\ 0 & 0 & 1 & 0 \end{array}\right]; \quad \begin{array}{l} x = 1 \\ y = 4 \\ z = 0 \end{array}$$

39.

$$\left[\begin{array}{ccc|c} 1 & 1 & -1 & -2 \\ 3 & 1 & 1 & 0 \\ 2 & -1 & 2 & 1 \end{array}\right] \xrightarrow[\substack{-3r_1+r_2 \\ -2r_1+r_3}]{} \left[\begin{array}{ccc|c} 1 & 1 & -2 & -2 \\ 0 & -2 & 4 & 6 \\ 0 & -3 & 4 & 5 \end{array}\right] \xrightarrow[-\frac{1}{2}r_2]{} \left[\begin{array}{ccc|c} 1 & 1 & -1 & -2 \\ 0 & 1 & -2 & -3 \\ 0 & -3 & 4 & 5 \end{array}\right] \xrightarrow[3r_2+r_3]{-r_2+r_1}$$

$$\left[\begin{array}{ccc|c} 1 & 0 & 1 & 1 \\ 0 & 1 & -2 & -3 \\ 0 & 0 & -2 & -4 \end{array}\right] \xrightarrow[-\frac{1}{2}r_3]{} \left[\begin{array}{ccc|c} 1 & 0 & 1 & 1 \\ 0 & 1 & -2 & -3 \\ 0 & 0 & 1 & 2 \end{array}\right] \xrightarrow[2r_3+r_2]{-r_3+r_1} \left[\begin{array}{ccc|c} 1 & 0 & 0 & -1 \\ 0 & 1 & 0 & 1 \\ 0 & 0 & 1 & 2 \end{array}\right]; \quad \begin{array}{l} x = -1 \\ y = 1 \\ z = 2 \end{array}$$

41.

$$\left[\begin{array}{ccc|c} 2 & 1 & -1 & 2 \\ 1 & 3 & 2 & 1 \\ 1 & 1 & 1 & 2 \end{array}\right] \to \left[\begin{array}{ccc|c} 1 & 3 & 2 & 1 \\ 2 & 1 & -1 & 2 \\ 1 & 1 & 1 & 2 \end{array}\right] \xrightarrow[-r_1+r_3]{-2r_1+r_2} \left[\begin{array}{ccc|c} 1 & 3 & 2 & 1 \\ 0 & -5 & -5 & 0 \\ 0 & -2 & -1 & 1 \end{array}\right] \xrightarrow[-\frac{1}{5}r_2]{}$$

$$\left[\begin{array}{ccc|c} 1 & 3 & 2 & 1 \\ 0 & 1 & 1 & 0 \\ 0 & -2 & -1 & 1 \end{array}\right] \xrightarrow[2r_2+r_3]{-3r_2+r_1} \left[\begin{array}{ccc|c} 1 & 0 & -1 & 1 \\ 0 & 1 & 1 & 0 \\ 0 & 0 & 1 & 1 \end{array}\right] \xrightarrow[-r_3+r_2]{r_3+r_1} \left[\begin{array}{ccc|c} 1 & 0 & 0 & 2 \\ 0 & 1 & 0 & -1 \\ 0 & 0 & 1 & 1 \end{array}\right]; \quad \begin{array}{l} x=2 \\ y=-1 \\ z=1 \end{array}$$

43.

$$\left[\begin{array}{ccc|c} 1 & 1 & -1 & 0 \\ 2 & 4 & -4 & -1 \\ 2 & 1 & 1 & 2 \end{array}\right] \xrightarrow[-2r_1+r_3]{-2r_1+r_2} \left[\begin{array}{ccc|c} 1 & 1 & -1 & 0 \\ 0 & 2 & -2 & -1 \\ 0 & -1 & 3 & 2 \end{array}\right] \xrightarrow[\frac{1}{2}r_2]{} \left[\begin{array}{ccc|c} 1 & 1 & -1 & 0 \\ 0 & 1 & -1 & -0.5 \\ 0 & -1 & 3 & 2 \end{array}\right] \xrightarrow[r_2+r_3]{-r_2+r_1}$$

$$\left[\begin{array}{ccc|c} 1 & 0 & 0 & 0.5 \\ 0 & 1 & -1 & -0.5 \\ 0 & 0 & 2 & 1.5 \end{array}\right] \xrightarrow[0.5r_3]{} \left[\begin{array}{ccc|c} 1 & 0 & 0 & 0.5 \\ 0 & 1 & -1 & -0.5 \\ 0 & 0 & 1 & 0.75 \end{array}\right] \xrightarrow[r_3+r_2]{} \left[\begin{array}{ccc|c} 1 & 0 & 0 & 0.5 \\ 0 & 1 & 0 & 0.25 \\ 0 & 0 & 1 & 0.75 \end{array}\right]; \quad \begin{array}{l} x=0.5 \\ y=0.25 \\ z=0.75 \end{array}$$

45.

$$\left[\begin{array}{ccc|c} 3 & 1 & -1 & \frac{2}{3} \\ 2 & -1 & 1 & 1 \\ 4 & 2 & 0 & \frac{8}{3} \end{array}\right] \xrightarrow{\frac{1}{3}r_1} \left[\begin{array}{ccc|c} 1 & \frac{1}{3} & -\frac{1}{3} & \frac{2}{9} \\ 2 & -1 & 1 & 1 \\ 4 & 2 & 0 & \frac{8}{3} \end{array}\right] \xrightarrow[-4r_1+r_3]{-2r_1+r_2} \left[\begin{array}{ccc|c} 1 & \frac{1}{3} & -\frac{1}{3} & \frac{2}{9} \\ 0 & -\frac{5}{3} & \frac{5}{3} & \frac{5}{9} \\ 0 & \frac{2}{3} & \frac{4}{3} & \frac{16}{9} \end{array}\right] \xrightarrow[-\frac{3}{5}r_2]{}$$

$$\left[\begin{array}{ccc|c} 1 & \frac{1}{3} & -\frac{1}{3} & \frac{2}{9} \\ 0 & 1 & -1 & -\frac{1}{3} \\ 0 & \left(\frac{2}{3}\right) & \frac{4}{3} & \frac{16}{9} \end{array}\right] \xrightarrow[-\frac{2}{3}r_2+r_2]{-\frac{1}{3}r_2+r_1} \left[\begin{array}{ccc|c} 1 & 0 & 0 & \frac{1}{3} \\ 0 & 1 & -1 & -\frac{1}{3} \\ 0 & 0 & 2 & 2 \end{array}\right] \xrightarrow[\frac{1}{2}r_3]{}$$

$$\left[\begin{array}{ccc|c} 1 & 0 & 0 & \frac{1}{3} \\ 0 & 1 & -1 & -\frac{1}{3} \\ 0 & 0 & 1 & 1 \end{array}\right] \xrightarrow[r_3+r_2]{} \left[\begin{array}{ccc|c} 1 & 0 & 0 & \frac{1}{3} \\ 0 & 1 & 0 & \frac{2}{3} \\ 0 & 0 & 1 & 1 \end{array}\right]; \quad \begin{array}{l} x=\frac{1}{3} \\ y=\frac{2}{3} \\ z=1 \end{array}$$

47.

$$\left[\begin{array}{cccc|c} 1 & 1 & 1 & 1 & 4 \\ 2 & -1 & 1 & 0 & 0 \\ 3 & 2 & 1 & -1 & 6 \\ 1 & -2 & -2 & 2 & -1 \end{array}\right] \xrightarrow[\substack{-3r_1+r_3 \\ -r_1+r_4}]{-2r_1-r_2} \left[\begin{array}{cccc|c} 1 & 1 & 1 & 1 & 4 \\ 0 & -3 & -1 & -2 & -8 \\ 0 & -1 & -2 & -4 & -6 \\ 0 & -3 & -3 & 1 & -5 \end{array}\right] \xrightarrow[-r_3]{} \left[\begin{array}{cccc|c} 1 & 1 & 1 & 1 & 4 \\ 0 & -3 & -1 & -2 & -8 \\ 0 & 1 & 2 & 4 & 6 \\ 0 & -3 & -3 & 1 & -5 \end{array}\right] \xrightarrow[(r_2)]{(r_3)}$$

$$\left[\begin{array}{cccc|c} 1 & 0 & 0 & -1 & 0 \\ 0 & 1 & 0 & 0 & 2 \\ 0 & 0 & 1 & 2 & 2 \\ 0 & 0 & 0 & 7 & 7 \end{array}\right] \xrightarrow[\frac{1}{7}r_4]{} \left[\begin{array}{cccc|c} 1 & 0 & 0 & -1 & 0 \\ 0 & 1 & 0 & 0 & 2 \\ 0 & 0 & 1 & 2 & 2 \\ 0 & 0 & 0 & 1 & 1 \end{array}\right] \xrightarrow[-2r_4+r_3]{r_4+r_1} \left[\begin{array}{cccc|c} 1 & 0 & 0 & 0 & 1 \\ 0 & 1 & 0 & 0 & 2 \\ 0 & 0 & 1 & 0 & 0 \\ 0 & 0 & 0 & 1 & 1 \end{array}\right]; \quad \begin{array}{l} x = 1 \\ y = 2 \\ z = 0 \\ w = 1 \end{array}$$

49. $\left[\begin{array}{cc|c} 1 & -1 & 5 \\ 2 & -2 & 6 \end{array}\right] \to \left[\begin{array}{cc|c} 1 & -1 & 5 \\ 0 & 0 & -4 \end{array}\right]$; no solution

51. $\left[\begin{array}{cc|c} 2 & -3 & 6 \\ 4 & -6 & 12 \end{array}\right] \to \left[\begin{array}{cc|c} 2 & -3 & 6 \\ 0 & 0 & 0 \end{array}\right]$; infinitely many solutions $(2x - 3y = 6)$

53. $\left[\begin{array}{cc|c} 5 & -6 & 1 \\ -10 & 12 & 0 \end{array}\right] \to \left[\begin{array}{cc|c} 5 & -6 & 1 \\ 0 & 0 & 2 \end{array}\right]$; no solution

55. $\left[\begin{array}{cc|c} 2 & 3 & 5 \\ 4 & 4 & 8 \end{array}\right] \to \left[\begin{array}{cc|c} 1 & 0 & 1 \\ 0 & 1 & 1 \end{array}\right]$; unique solution $(x = 1, y = 1)$

57. $$\left[\begin{array}{ccc|c} 2 & -1 & -1 & 0 \\ 1 & -1 & -1 & 1 \\ 3 & -1 & -1 & 2 \end{array}\right] \to \left[\begin{array}{ccc|c} 1 & -1 & -1 & 1 \\ 2 & -1 & -1 & 0 \\ 3 & -1 & -1 & 2 \end{array}\right] \xrightarrow[-3r_1+r_3]{-2r_1+r_2} \left[\begin{array}{ccc|c} 1 & -1 & -1 & 1 \\ 0 & 1 & 1 & -2 \\ 0 & 2 & 2 & -1 \end{array}\right] \xrightarrow[-2r_2+r_3]{r_2+r_1}$$

$$\left[\begin{array}{ccc|c} 1 & 0 & 0 & -1 \\ 0 & 1 & 1 & -2 \\ 0 & 0 & 0 & 3 \end{array}\right]; \text{ no solution } (3 \neq 0)$$

59. $$\left[\begin{array}{ccc|c} 2 & -1 & 1 & 6 \\ 3 & -1 & 1 & 6 \\ 4 & -2 & 2 & 12 \end{array}\right] \xrightarrow{\frac{1}{2}r_1} \left[\begin{array}{ccc|c} 1 & -0.5 & 0.5 & 3 \\ 3 & -1 & 1 & 6 \\ 4 & -2 & 2 & 12 \end{array}\right] \xrightarrow[-4r_1+r_3]{-3r_1+r_2} \left[\begin{array}{ccc|c} 1 & -0.5 & 0.5 & 3 \\ 0 & 0.5 & -0.5 & -3 \\ 0 & 0 & 0 & 0 \end{array}\right] \xrightarrow{2r_2}$$

$$\left[\begin{array}{ccc|c} 1 & -0.5 & 0.5 & 3 \\ 0 & 1 & -1 & -6 \\ 0 & 0 & 0 & 0 \end{array}\right] \xrightarrow{\frac{1}{2}r_2+r_1} \left[\begin{array}{ccc|c} 1 & 0 & 0 & 0 \\ 0 & 1 & -1 & -6 \\ 0 & 0 & 0 & 0 \end{array}\right]$$; infinitely many solutions $(x = 0, y = -6 + z)$

61. x = Amount invested at 6%
y = Amount invested at 7%
z = Amount invested at 8%

$$\begin{aligned} x + y + z &= 5000 \\ 0.06x + 0.07y + 0.08z &= 358 \\ 0.06x + 0.07y - 0.08z &= 70 \end{aligned}$$

$$\left[\begin{array}{ccc|c} 1 & 1 & 1 & 5000 \\ 0.06 & 0.07 & 0.08 & 358 \\ 0.06 & 0.07 & -0.08 & 70 \end{array}\right] \to \left[\begin{array}{ccc|c} 1 & 1 & 1 & 5000 \\ 0 & 0.01 & 0.02 & 58 \\ 0 & 0.01 & -0.14 & -230 \end{array}\right] \to \left[\begin{array}{ccc|c} 1 & 1 & 1 & 5000 \\ 0 & 1 & 2 & 5800 \\ 0 & 1 & -14 & -23{,}000 \end{array}\right]$$

$$\to \left[\begin{array}{ccc|c} 1 & 0 & -1 & -800 \\ 0 & 1 & 2 & 5800 \\ 0 & 0 & -16 & -28{,}800 \end{array}\right] \to \left[\begin{array}{ccc|c} 1 & 0 & -1 & -800 \\ 0 & 1 & 2 & 5800 \\ 0 & 0 & 1 & 1800 \end{array}\right] \to \left[\begin{array}{ccc|c} 1 & 0 & 0 & 1000 \\ 0 & 1 & 0 & 2200 \\ 0 & 0 & 1 & 1800 \end{array}\right]$$

\$1000 invested at 6%; \$2200 invested at 7%; \$1800 invested at 8%

Exercise 2.2 (page 64)

1. $\begin{bmatrix} 1 & 2 & 3 \\ 0 & 0 & 0 \\ 0 & 0 & 1 \end{bmatrix}$ **Not in reduced row-echelon form. It violates the rule that states any rows containing all zeros are at the bottom.**

3. $\begin{bmatrix} 1 & 1 & 0 \\ 0 & 1 & 0 \end{bmatrix}$ **Not in reduced row-echelon form. The leftmost 1 in the second row does not have a zero above it.**

5. $\begin{bmatrix} 0 & 1 \\ 1 & 0 \end{bmatrix}$ **Not in reduced row-echelon form. The leftmost 1 of row 2 is not to the right of the leftmost 1 in the row above it**

7. $\begin{bmatrix} 0 & 0 & 1 \\ 0 & 0 & 0 \end{bmatrix}$ In reduced row-echelon form.

9. $\begin{bmatrix} 1 & 0 & 0 & 0 & 0 \\ 0 & 0 & 1 & 2 & 0 \\ 0 & 0 & 0 & 0 & 1 \\ 0 & 0 & 0 & 0 & 0 \end{bmatrix}$ **In reduced row-echelon form.**

11. $\left[\begin{array}{cc|c} 1 & 1 & 1 \\ 0 & 0 & 0 \end{array}\right]$ Infinitely many solutions

$x_1 = 1 - x_2$

13. $\left[\begin{array}{ccc|c} 1 & 0 & 0 & 0 \\ 0 & 1 & 0 & 0 \\ 0 & 0 & 1 & 6 \end{array}\right]$ One solution

$x_1 = 0,\ x_2 = 0,\ x_3 = 6$

15. $\left[\begin{array}{ccc|c} 1 & 2 & 0 & 1 \\ 0 & 0 & 1 & 2 \\ 0 & 0 & 0 & 0 \end{array}\right]$ Infinitely many solutions

$x_1 = 1 - x_2$

$x_3 = 2$

17. $\left[\begin{array}{cccc|c} 1 & 0 & 1 & -1 & 0 \\ 0 & 1 & 2 & 1 & 1 \\ 0 & 0 & 0 & 0 & 0 \end{array}\right]$ Infinitely many solutions

$x_1 = x_4 - x_3$

$x_2 = 1 - 2x_3 - x_4$

19. $\left[\begin{array}{ccc|c} 1 & 0 & -1 & 1 \\ 0 & 1 & 2 & 1 \end{array}\right]$ Infinitely many solutions

$$x_1 = 1 - x_3$$
$$x_2 = 1 - 2x_3$$

21. $$\left[\begin{array}{cc|c} 1 & 1 & 3 \\ 2 & -1 & 3 \end{array}\right] \to \left[\begin{array}{cc|c} 1 & 1 & 3 \\ 0 & -3 & -3 \end{array}\right] \to \left[\begin{array}{cc|c} 1 & 1 & 3 \\ 0 & 1 & 1 \end{array}\right] \to \left[\begin{array}{cc|c} 1 & 0 & 2 \\ 0 & 1 & 1 \end{array}\right];\ x = 2,\ y = 1$$

23. $$\left[\begin{array}{cc|c} 3 & -3 & 12 \\ 3 & 2 & -3 \end{array}\right] \to \left[\begin{array}{cc|c} 1 & -1 & 4 \\ 3 & 2 & -3 \end{array}\right] \to \left[\begin{array}{cc|c} 1 & -1 & 4 \\ 0 & 5 & -15 \end{array}\right] \to \left[\begin{array}{cc|c} 1 & -1 & 4 \\ 0 & 1 & -3 \end{array}\right] \to \left[\begin{array}{cc|c} 1 & 0 & 1 \\ 0 & 1 & -3 \end{array}\right];\ x = 1,\ y = -3$$

25. $$\left[\begin{array}{cc|c} 3 & -4 & 1 \\ 5 & 2 & 19 \end{array}\right] \to \left[\begin{array}{cc|c} 3 & -4 & 1 \\ 2 & 6 & 18 \end{array}\right] \to \left[\begin{array}{cc|c} 1 & 3 & 9 \\ 3 & -4 & 1 \end{array}\right] \to \left[\begin{array}{cc|c} 1 & 3 & 9 \\ 0 & -13 & -26 \end{array}\right] \to$$

$$\left[\begin{array}{cc|c} 1 & 3 & 9 \\ 0 & 1 & 2 \end{array}\right] \to \left[\begin{array}{cc|c} 1 & 0 & 3 \\ 0 & 1 & 2 \end{array}\right] \quad x_1 = 3,\ x_2 = 2$$

27. $$\left[\begin{array}{cc|c} 2 & 3 & 5 \\ 2 & -1 & 7 \end{array}\right] \to \left[\begin{array}{cc|c} 1 & \frac{3}{2} & \frac{5}{2} \\ 2 & -1 & 7 \end{array}\right] \to \left[\begin{array}{cc|c} 1 & \frac{3}{2} & \frac{5}{2} \\ 0 & -4 & 2 \end{array}\right] \to \left[\begin{array}{cc|c} 1 & \frac{3}{2} & \frac{5}{2} \\ 0 & 1 & -\frac{1}{2} \end{array}\right] \to \left[\begin{array}{cc|c} 1 & 0 & \frac{13}{4} \\ 0 & 1 & -\frac{1}{2} \end{array}\right];$$

$$x_1 = \frac{13}{4},\ x_2 = -\frac{1}{2}$$

29. $$\left[\begin{array}{ccc|c} 1 & -1 & 0 & 1 \\ 0 & 1 & -1 & 6 \\ 1 & 0 & 1 & -1 \end{array}\right] \to \left[\begin{array}{ccc|c} 1 & -1 & 0 & 1 \\ 0 & 1 & -1 & 6 \\ 0 & 1 & 1 & -2 \end{array}\right] \to \left[\begin{array}{ccc|c} 1 & 0 & -1 & 7 \\ 0 & 1 & -1 & 6 \\ 0 & 0 & 2 & -8 \end{array}\right] \to \left[\begin{array}{ccc|c} 1 & 0 & -1 & 7 \\ 0 & 1 & -1 & 6 \\ 0 & 0 & 1 & -4 \end{array}\right] \to \left[\begin{array}{ccc|c} 1 & 0 & 0 & 3 \\ 0 & 1 & 0 & 2 \\ 0 & 0 & 1 & -4 \end{array}\right];$$

$$x_1 = 3,\ x_2 = 2,\ x_3 = -4$$

31. $$\left[\begin{array}{cccc|c} 1 & 1 & 0 & 0 & 7 \\ 0 & 1 & -1 & 1 & 5 \\ 1 & -1 & 1 & 1 & 6 \\ 0 & 1 & 0 & -1 & 10 \end{array}\right] \to \left[\begin{array}{cccc|c} 1 & 1 & 0 & 0 & 7 \\ 0 & 1 & -1 & 1 & 5 \\ 0 & -2 & 1 & 1 & -1 \\ 0 & 1 & 0 & -1 & 10 \end{array}\right] \to \left[\begin{array}{cccc|c} 1 & 0 & 1 & -1 & 2 \\ 0 & 1 & -1 & 1 & 5 \\ 0 & 0 & -1 & 3 & 9 \\ 0 & 0 & 1 & -2 & 5 \end{array}\right] \to$$

$$\left[\begin{array}{cccc|c} 1 & 0 & 0 & 2 & 11 \\ 0 & 1 & 0 & -2 & -4 \\ 0 & 0 & 1 & -3 & -9 \\ 0 & 0 & 0 & 1 & 14 \end{array}\right] \to \left[\begin{array}{cccc|c} 1 & 0 & 0 & 0 & -17 \\ 0 & 1 & 0 & 0 & 24 \\ 0 & 0 & 1 & 0 & 33 \\ 0 & 0 & 0 & 1 & 14 \end{array}\right];\quad x_1 = -17,\ x_2 = 24,\ x_3 = 33,\ x_4 = 14$$

33. $$\left[\begin{array}{cccc|c} 1 & 2 & 3 & -1 & 0 \\ 3 & 0 & 0 & -1 & 4 \\ 0 & 1 & -1 & -1 & 2 \end{array}\right] \to \left[\begin{array}{cccc|c} 1 & 2 & 3 & -1 & 0 \\ 0 & -6 & -9 & 2 & 4 \\ 0 & 1 & -1 & -1 & 2 \end{array}\right] \to \left[\begin{array}{cccc|c} 1 & 2 & 3 & -1 & 0 \\ 0 & 1 & -1 & -1 & 2 \\ 0 & -6 & -9 & 2 & 4 \end{array}\right] \to$$

$$\left[\begin{array}{cccc|c} 1 & 0 & 5 & 1 & -4 \\ 0 & 1 & -1 & -1 & 2 \\ 0 & 0 & -15 & -4 & 16 \end{array}\right] \to \left[\begin{array}{cccc|c} 1 & 0 & 5 & 1 & -4 \\ 0 & 1 & -1 & -1 & 2 \\ 0 & 0 & 1 & \frac{4}{15} & -\frac{16}{15} \end{array}\right] \to \left[\begin{array}{cccc|c} 1 & 0 & 0 & -\frac{1}{3} & \frac{4}{3} \\ 0 & 1 & 0 & -\frac{11}{15} & \frac{14}{15} \\ 0 & 0 & 1 & \frac{4}{15} & -\frac{16}{15} \end{array}\right]$$

There are

infinitely many solutions, and we can solve for x_1, x_2, and x_3 in terms of x_4:

$$x_1 = \frac{4}{3} + \frac{1}{3}x_4, \quad x_2 = \frac{14}{15} + \frac{11}{15}x_4, \quad x_3 = -\frac{16}{15} - \frac{4}{15}x_4$$

35.

$$\left[\begin{array}{ccc|c} 1 & -1 & 1 & 5 \\ 2 & -2 & 2 & 8 \end{array}\right] \rightarrow \left[\begin{array}{ccc|c} 1 & -1 & 1 & 5 \\ 0 & 0 & 0 & -2 \end{array}\right] \rightarrow \left[\begin{array}{ccc|c} 1 & -1 & 1 & 0 \\ 0 & 0 & 0 & 1 \end{array}\right]$$ The system is inconsistent.

37.

$$\left[\begin{array}{ccc|c} 3 & -1 & 2 & 3 \\ 3 & 3 & 1 & 3 \\ 3 & -5 & 3 & 12 \end{array}\right] \rightarrow \left[\begin{array}{ccc|c} 0 & -4 & 1 & 0 \\ 1 & 1 & \frac{1}{3} & 1 \\ 0 & -8 & 2 & 9 \end{array}\right] \rightarrow \left[\begin{array}{ccc|c} 1 & 1 & \frac{1}{3} & 1 \\ 0 & -4 & 1 & 0 \\ 0 & -8 & 2 & 9 \end{array}\right] \rightarrow$$

$$\left[\begin{array}{ccc|c} 1 & 1 & \frac{1}{3} & 1 \\ 0 & 1 & -\frac{1}{4} & 0 \\ 0 & -8 & 2 & 9 \end{array}\right] \rightarrow \left[\begin{array}{ccc|c} 1 & 0 & \frac{7}{12} & 1 \\ 0 & 1 & -\frac{1}{4} & 0 \\ 0 & 0 & 0 & 9 \end{array}\right] \rightarrow \left[\begin{array}{ccc|c} 1 & 0 & \frac{7}{12} & 0 \\ 0 & 1 & -\frac{1}{4} & 0 \\ 0 & 0 & 0 & 1 \end{array}\right]$$ The system is inconsistent.

39. $x_1 + x_2 + x_3 = 100$

$0.1x_1 + 0.3x_2 + 0.5x_3 = 25$

$$\left[\begin{array}{ccc|c} 1 & 1 & 1 & 100 \\ 0.1 & 0.3 & 0.5 & 25 \end{array}\right] \rightarrow \left[\begin{array}{ccc|c} 1 & 1 & 1 & 100 \\ 0 & 0.2 & 0.4 & 15 \end{array}\right] \rightarrow \left[\begin{array}{ccc|c} 1 & 1 & 1 & 100 \\ 0 & 1 & 2 & 75 \end{array}\right] \rightarrow \left[\begin{array}{ccc|c} 1 & 0 & -1 & 25 \\ 0 & 1 & 2 & 75 \end{array}\right]$$

$x_1 = x_3 + 25, \; x_2 = 75 - 2x_3$

No. of liters 10% solution	No. of liters 30% solution	No. of liters 50% solution
55	15	30
50	25	25
45	35	20
40	45	15
35	55	10
30	65	5

Exercise 2.3 (page 73)

1. 2 X 2 **3.** 2 X 3 **5.** 2 X 1 **7.** 1 X 1

9. False; the matrices are not of the same dimension.

11. True; number of rows equals number of columns.

13. True; corresponding entries are equal.

15. True; corresponding entries are equal.

17. Corresponding entries must be equal so $x = 4$ and $z = 3$.

19. $x - 2y = 3$ and $6 = x + y$, so $x = 5, y = 1$

21. $\begin{bmatrix} 2 & -3 & 4 \\ 0 & 2 & 1 \end{bmatrix} + \begin{bmatrix} 1 & -2 & 0 \\ 5 & 1 & 2 \end{bmatrix} = \begin{bmatrix} 3 & -5 & 4 \\ 5 & 3 & 3 \end{bmatrix}$

23. $2\begin{bmatrix} 2 & -3 & 4 \\ 0 & 2 & 1 \end{bmatrix} - 3\begin{bmatrix} -3 & 0 & 5 \\ 2 & 1 & 3 \end{bmatrix} = \begin{bmatrix} 4 & -6 & 8 \\ 0 & 4 & 2 \end{bmatrix} - \begin{bmatrix} -9 & 0 & 15 \\ 6 & 3 & 9 \end{bmatrix} = \begin{bmatrix} 13 & -6 & -7 \\ -6 & 1 & -7 \end{bmatrix}$

25. $\left(\begin{bmatrix} 2 & -3 & 4 \\ 0 & 2 & 1 \end{bmatrix} + \begin{bmatrix} 1 & -2 & 0 \\ 5 & 1 & 2 \end{bmatrix}\right) - 2\begin{bmatrix} -3 & 0 & 5 \\ 2 & 1 & 3 \end{bmatrix}$

$= \begin{bmatrix} 3 & -5 & 4 \\ 5 & 3 & 3 \end{bmatrix} - \begin{bmatrix} -6 & 0 & 10 \\ 4 & 2 & 6 \end{bmatrix} = \begin{bmatrix} 9 & -5 & -6 \\ 1 & 1 & -3 \end{bmatrix}$

27. $3\begin{bmatrix} 2 & -3 & 4 \\ 0 & 2 & 1 \end{bmatrix} + 4\left(\begin{bmatrix} 1 & -2 & 0 \\ 5 & 1 & 2 \end{bmatrix} + \begin{bmatrix} -3 & 0 & 5 \\ 2 & 1 & 3 \end{bmatrix}\right) = \begin{bmatrix} 6 & -9 & 12 \\ 0 & 6 & 3 \end{bmatrix} + 4\begin{bmatrix} -2 & -2 & 5 \\ 7 & 2 & 5 \end{bmatrix}$

$= \begin{bmatrix} 6 & -9 & 12 \\ 0 & 6 & 3 \end{bmatrix} + \begin{bmatrix} -8 & -8 & 20 \\ 28 & 8 & 20 \end{bmatrix} = \begin{bmatrix} -2 & -17 & 32 \\ 28 & 14 & 23 \end{bmatrix}$

29. $2\left(\begin{bmatrix} 2 & -3 & 4 \\ 0 & 2 & 1 \end{bmatrix} - \begin{bmatrix} 1 & -2 & 0 \\ 5 & 1 & 2 \end{bmatrix}\right) - \begin{bmatrix} -3 & 0 & 5 \\ 2 & 1 & 3 \end{bmatrix} = 2\begin{bmatrix} 1 & -1 & 4 \\ -5 & 1 & -1 \end{bmatrix} - \begin{bmatrix} -3 & 0 & 5 \\ 2 & 1 & 3 \end{bmatrix}$

$= \begin{bmatrix} 2 & -2 & 8 \\ -10 & 2 & -2 \end{bmatrix} - \begin{bmatrix} -3 & 0 & 5 \\ 2 & 1 & 3 \end{bmatrix} = \begin{bmatrix} 5 & -2 & 3 \\ -12 & 1 & -5 \end{bmatrix}$

31. $[2 + x \quad 3 + y \quad -4 + z] = [6 \ -8 \ 2]$

$2 + x = 6 \qquad 3 + y = -8 \qquad -4 + z = 2$

$x = 4 \qquad y = -11 \qquad z = 6$

33. (a) $U + V = \begin{bmatrix} 2 \\ -1 \\ 3 \end{bmatrix} + \begin{bmatrix} \frac{1}{2} \\ 0 \\ 1 \end{bmatrix} = \begin{bmatrix} \frac{5}{2} \\ -1 \\ 4 \end{bmatrix}$ (b) $U - V = \begin{bmatrix} 2 \\ -1 \\ 3 \end{bmatrix} - \begin{bmatrix} \frac{1}{2} \\ 0 \\ 1 \end{bmatrix} = \begin{bmatrix} \frac{3}{2} \\ -1 \\ 2 \end{bmatrix}$

(c) $\frac{1}{2}(U + V) = \frac{1}{2}\begin{bmatrix} \frac{5}{2} \\ -1 \\ 4 \end{bmatrix} = \begin{bmatrix} \frac{5}{4} \\ -\frac{1}{2} \\ 2 \end{bmatrix}$ (d) $U + V - W = \begin{bmatrix} \frac{5}{2} \\ -1 \\ 4 \end{bmatrix} - \begin{bmatrix} -3 \\ -7 \\ 0 \end{bmatrix} = \begin{bmatrix} \frac{11}{2} \\ 6 \\ 4 \end{bmatrix}$

(e) $2U - 7V = \begin{bmatrix} 4 \\ -2 \\ 6 \end{bmatrix} - \begin{bmatrix} \frac{7}{2} \\ 0 \\ 7 \end{bmatrix} = \begin{bmatrix} \frac{1}{2} \\ -2 \\ -1 \end{bmatrix}$ (f) $\frac{1}{4}U - \frac{1}{4}V - \frac{1}{4}W = \frac{1}{4}\left(\begin{bmatrix} \frac{3}{2} \\ -1 \\ 2 \end{bmatrix} - \begin{bmatrix} -3 \\ -7 \\ 0 \end{bmatrix}\right) = \begin{bmatrix} \frac{9}{8} \\ \frac{3}{2} \\ \frac{1}{2} \end{bmatrix}$

35.

$$\begin{array}{r} \\ \text{Steel} \\ \text{Aluminum} \end{array} \begin{array}{c} \begin{array}{ccc} 1/2" & 1" & 2" \end{array} \\ \begin{bmatrix} 25 & 45 & 35 \\ 13 & 20 & 23 \end{bmatrix} \end{array} \qquad \begin{array}{r} \\ \frac{1}{2} \\ 1" \\ 2" \end{array} \begin{array}{c} \begin{array}{cc} \text{Steel} & \text{Aluminum} \end{array} \\ \begin{bmatrix} 25 & 13 \\ 45 & 20 \\ 35 & 23 \end{bmatrix} \end{array}$$

37.

$$\begin{array}{r} \\ \text{Dem} \\ \text{Rep} \\ \text{Ind} \end{array} \begin{array}{c} \begin{array}{cc} <\$15{,}00 & >\$15{,}000 \end{array} \\ \begin{bmatrix} 351 & 203 \\ 271 & 215 \\ 73 & 55 \end{bmatrix} \end{array} \quad \text{or} \quad \begin{array}{r} \\ <\$15{,}000 \\ >\$15{,}000 \end{array} \begin{array}{c} \begin{array}{ccc} \text{Dem} & \text{Rep} & \text{Ind} \end{array} \\ \begin{bmatrix} 351 & 271 & 73 \\ 203 & 215 & 55 \end{bmatrix} \end{array}$$

39. $K(a_{ij} + b_{ij}) = Ka_{ij} + Kb_{ij}$

Exercise 2.4 (page 80)

1. (3 X 3) (3 X 4) Dimension BA = 3 X 4
Equal

3. (3 X 4) (3 X 3) AB is not defined.
Not equal

5. (3 X 4) (2 X 3) (BA)C is not defined.
Not equal

7. (3 x 4) + (3 X 4) BA + A is defined, since dimensions are equal.
Dimension is 3 X 4.

9. (3 X 3) + (3 X 3) DC + B is defined, since dimensions are equal.
Dimension is 3 X 3.

11.

$$\begin{bmatrix} 1 & 2 \\ 0 & 4 \end{bmatrix}\begin{bmatrix} 1 & 2 & 3 \\ -1 & 4 & -2 \end{bmatrix} = \begin{bmatrix} -1 & 10 & -1 \\ -4 & 16 & -8 \end{bmatrix}$$

13.

$$\begin{bmatrix} 1 & 2 & 3 \\ -1 & 4 & -2 \end{bmatrix}\begin{bmatrix} 3 & 1 \\ 4 & -1 \\ 0 & 2 \end{bmatrix} = \begin{bmatrix} 11 & 5 \\ 13 & -9 \end{bmatrix}$$

15.

$$\left(\begin{bmatrix} 1 & 0 & 4 \\ 0 & 1 & 2 \\ 0 & -1 & 1 \end{bmatrix} + \begin{bmatrix} 1 & 0 & 0 \\ 0 & 1 & 0 \\ 0 & 0 & 1 \end{bmatrix}\right)\begin{bmatrix} 3 & 1 \\ 4 & -1 \\ 0 & 2 \end{bmatrix} = \begin{bmatrix} 2 & 0 & 4 \\ 0 & 2 & 2 \\ 0 & -1 & 2 \end{bmatrix}\begin{bmatrix} 3 & 1 \\ 4 & -1 \\ 0 & 2 \end{bmatrix} = \begin{bmatrix} 6 & 10 \\ 8 & 2 \\ -4 & 5 \end{bmatrix}$$

17.

$$\left(\begin{bmatrix} 1 & 0 & 4 \\ 0 & 1 & 2 \\ 0 & -1 & 1 \end{bmatrix}\begin{bmatrix} 3 & 1 \\ 4 & -1 \\ 0 & 2 \end{bmatrix}\right)\begin{bmatrix} 1 & 2 & 3 \\ -1 & 4 & -2 \end{bmatrix} = \begin{bmatrix} 3 & 9 \\ 4 & 3 \\ -4 & 3 \end{bmatrix}\begin{bmatrix} 1 & 2 & 3 \\ -1 & 4 & -2 \end{bmatrix} = \begin{bmatrix} -6 & 42 & -9 \\ 1 & 20 & 6 \\ -7 & 4 & -18 \end{bmatrix}$$

19.

$$\begin{bmatrix} 3 & -1 \\ 4 & 2 \end{bmatrix}\begin{bmatrix} 1 & 0 \\ 0 & 1 \end{bmatrix} = \begin{bmatrix} 3 & -1 \\ 4 & 2 \end{bmatrix}$$

21.

$$2\begin{bmatrix} 3 & -1 \\ 4 & 2 \end{bmatrix}\begin{bmatrix} 1 & 2 & 3 \\ -1 & 4 & -2 \end{bmatrix} = \begin{bmatrix} 6 & -2 \\ 8 & 4 \end{bmatrix}\begin{bmatrix} 1 & 2 & 3 \\ -1 & 4 & -2 \end{bmatrix} = \begin{bmatrix} 8 & 4 & 22 \\ 4 & 32 & 16 \end{bmatrix}$$

23.

$$-5\begin{bmatrix} 3 & -1 \\ 4 & 2 \end{bmatrix} + \begin{bmatrix} 1 & 2 \\ 0 & 4 \end{bmatrix} = \begin{bmatrix} -15 & 5 \\ -20 & -10 \end{bmatrix} + \begin{bmatrix} 1 & 2 \\ 0 & 4 \end{bmatrix} = \begin{bmatrix} -14 & 7 \\ -20 & -6 \end{bmatrix}$$

25.

$$3\begin{bmatrix} 3 & 1 \\ 4 & -1 \\ 0 & 2 \end{bmatrix}\begin{bmatrix} 1 & 2 & 3 \\ -1 & 4 & -2 \end{bmatrix} + 4\begin{bmatrix} 1 & 0 & 4 \\ 0 & 1 & 2 \\ 0 & -1 & 1 \end{bmatrix}$$

$$= \begin{bmatrix} 9 & 3 \\ 12 & -3 \\ 0 & 6 \end{bmatrix}\begin{bmatrix} 1 & 2 & 3 \\ -1 & 4 & -2 \end{bmatrix} + \begin{bmatrix} 4 & 0 & 16 \\ 0 & 4 & 8 \\ 0 & -4 & 4 \end{bmatrix}$$

$$= \begin{bmatrix} 6 & 30 & 21 \\ 15 & 12 & 42 \\ -6 & 24 & -12 \end{bmatrix} + \begin{bmatrix} 4 & 0 & 16 \\ 0 & 4 & 8 \\ 0 & -4 & 4 \end{bmatrix} = \begin{bmatrix} 10 & 30 & 37 \\ 15 & 16 & 50 \\ -6 & 20 & -8 \end{bmatrix}$$

27.

$$AB\begin{bmatrix} 1 & -1 \\ 2 & 0 \end{bmatrix}\begin{bmatrix} 3 & 2 \\ -1 & 4 \end{bmatrix} = \begin{bmatrix} 4 & -2 \\ 6 & 4 \end{bmatrix} \qquad BA\begin{bmatrix} 3 & 2 \\ -1 & 4 \end{bmatrix}\begin{bmatrix} 1 & -1 \\ 2 & 0 \end{bmatrix} = \begin{bmatrix} 7 & -5 \\ 7 & 1 \end{bmatrix}$$

29.

$$\begin{bmatrix} a & b \\ c & d \end{bmatrix}\begin{bmatrix} 0 & 1 \\ 2 & -1 \end{bmatrix} = \begin{bmatrix} 2b & a-b \\ 2d & c-d \end{bmatrix} = \begin{bmatrix} 2 & 1 \\ -1 & 0 \end{bmatrix}$$

$2b = 2 \quad a - b = 1$

$2d = -1 \quad c - d = 0 \quad a = 2, b = 1, c = -1/2, d = -1/2$

Hence, $A = \begin{bmatrix} 2 & 1 \\ -\frac{1}{2} & -\frac{1}{2} \end{bmatrix}$

31.

$$\begin{bmatrix} 1 & 2 & 5 \\ 2 & 4 & 10 \\ -1 & -2 & -5 \end{bmatrix}\begin{bmatrix} 1 & 2 & 5 \\ 2 & 4 & 10 \\ -1 & -2 & -5 \end{bmatrix} = \begin{bmatrix} 0 & 0 & 0 \\ 0 & 0 & 0 \\ 0 & 0 & 0 \end{bmatrix}$$

33.

$$\begin{bmatrix} a & b \\ b & a \end{bmatrix}\begin{bmatrix} a & b \\ b & a \end{bmatrix} + A = \begin{bmatrix} a^2+b^2 & 2ab \\ 2ab & a^2+b^2 \end{bmatrix} + \begin{bmatrix} a & b \\ b & a \end{bmatrix} = \begin{bmatrix} a^2+b^2+a & 2ab+b \\ 2ab+b & a^2+b^2+a \end{bmatrix} = 0$$

$2ab + b = 0 \Rightarrow b(2a + 1) = 0 \Rightarrow b = 0$ or $a = -\frac{1}{2}$

If $b = 0, a^2 + b^2 + a = 0 \Rightarrow a^2 + a = 0 \Rightarrow a(a+1) = 0 \Rightarrow a = 0$ or $a = -1$

If $a = -\frac{1}{2}, a^2 + b^2 + a = 0 \Rightarrow b^2 = \frac{1}{4} \Rightarrow b = \frac{1}{2}$ or $b = -\frac{1}{2}$

The possibilities are $a = 0, b = 0$; $a = -1, b = 0$; $a = -\frac{1}{2}, b = \frac{1}{2}$; $a = -\frac{1}{2}, b = -\frac{1}{2}$

35.

$$\begin{bmatrix} x_1 & x_2 \end{bmatrix}\begin{bmatrix} \frac{1}{2} & \frac{1}{2} \\ \frac{1}{4} & \frac{3}{4} \end{bmatrix} = \begin{bmatrix} \frac{1}{2}x_1 + \frac{1}{4}x_2 & \frac{1}{2}x_1 + \frac{3}{4}x_2 \end{bmatrix} = \begin{bmatrix} x_1 & x_2 \end{bmatrix}$$

$$\left.\begin{array}{l} \frac{1}{2}x_1 + \frac{1}{4}x_2 = x_1 \\ \frac{1}{2}x_1 + \frac{3}{4}x_2 = x_2 \end{array}\right\} \begin{array}{l} x_2 = 2x_1 \\ x_1 + x_2 = 1 \end{array}\Bigg\} \; x_1 = \frac{1}{3}, x_2 = \frac{2}{3}$$

37. (a) PQ represents the matrix of raw material needed to fill order:

$$\begin{bmatrix} 7 & 12 & 5 \end{bmatrix}\begin{bmatrix} 2 & 3 & 1 & 12 \\ 7 & 9 & 5 & 20 \\ 8 & 12 & 6 & 15 \end{bmatrix} = \begin{bmatrix} 138 & 189 & 97 & 399 \end{bmatrix}$$

(b) QC represents the matrix of costs to produce each product:

$$\begin{bmatrix} 2 & 3 & 1 & 12 \\ 7 & 9 & 5 & 20 \\ 8 & 12 & 6 & 15 \end{bmatrix}\begin{bmatrix} 10 \\ 12 \\ 15 \\ 20 \end{bmatrix} = \begin{bmatrix} 311 \\ 653 \\ 614 \end{bmatrix}$$

(c) PQC represents the total cost to produce the order:

$$\begin{bmatrix} 138 & 189 & 97 & 399 \end{bmatrix}\begin{bmatrix} 10 \\ 12 \\ 15 \\ 20 \end{bmatrix} = 13{,}083$$

Exercise 2.5 (page 90)

1.

$$\begin{bmatrix} 1 & 2 \\ 2 & 3 \end{bmatrix}\begin{bmatrix} -3 & 2 \\ 2 & -1 \end{bmatrix} = \begin{bmatrix} 1 & 0 \\ 0 & 1 \end{bmatrix} = I_2$$

3.

$$\begin{bmatrix} -1 & -2 \\ 3 & 4 \end{bmatrix}\begin{bmatrix} 2 & 1 \\ -\frac{3}{2} & -\frac{1}{2} \end{bmatrix} = \begin{bmatrix} 1 & 0 \\ 0 & 1 \end{bmatrix} = I_2$$

5.

$$\begin{bmatrix} 1 & 2 & 3 \\ 2 & 3 & 4 \\ 1 & 2 & 1 \end{bmatrix}\begin{bmatrix} -\frac{5}{2} & 2 & -\frac{1}{2} \\ 1 & -1 & 1 \\ \frac{1}{2} & 0 & -\frac{1}{2} \end{bmatrix} = \begin{bmatrix} 1 & 0 & 0 \\ 0 & 1 & 0 \\ 0 & 0 & 1 \end{bmatrix} = I_3$$

7.

$$\left[\begin{array}{cc|cc} 2 & 5 & 1 & 0 \\ 1 & 3 & 0 & 1 \end{array}\right] \rightarrow \left[\begin{array}{cc|cc} 1 & 3 & 0 & 1 \\ 2 & 5 & 1 & 0 \end{array}\right] \rightarrow \left[\begin{array}{cc|cc} 1 & 3 & 0 & 1 \\ 0 & -1 & 1 & -2 \end{array}\right] \rightarrow \left[\begin{array}{cc|cc} 1 & 0 & 3 & -5 \\ 0 & 1 & -1 & 2 \end{array}\right];$$

$$\begin{bmatrix} 2 & 5 \\ 1 & 3 \end{bmatrix}^{-1} = \begin{bmatrix} 3 & -5 \\ -1 & 2 \end{bmatrix}$$

9.

$$\left[\begin{array}{cc|cc} 1 & -1 & 1 & 0 \\ 3 & -4 & 0 & 1 \end{array}\right] \rightarrow \left[\begin{array}{cc|cc} 1 & -1 & 1 & 0 \\ 0 & -1 & -3 & 1 \end{array}\right] \rightarrow \left[\begin{array}{cc|cc} 1 & 0 & 4 & -1 \\ 0 & 1 & 3 & -1 \end{array}\right]; \quad \begin{bmatrix} 1 & -1 \\ 3 & -4 \end{bmatrix}^{-1} = \begin{bmatrix} 4 & -1 \\ 3 & -1 \end{bmatrix}$$

11.

$$\left[\begin{array}{cc|cc} 2 & 1 & 1 & 0 \\ 4 & 3 & 0 & 1 \end{array}\right] \rightarrow \left[\begin{array}{cc|cc} 2 & 1 & 1 & 0 \\ 0 & 1 & -2 & 1 \end{array}\right] \rightarrow \left[\begin{array}{cc|cc} 2 & 0 & 3 & -1 \\ 0 & 1 & -2 & 1 \end{array}\right] \rightarrow \left[\begin{array}{cc|cc} 1 & 0 & 1.5 & -0.5 \\ 0 & 1 & -2 & 1 \end{array}\right];$$

$$\begin{bmatrix} 2 & 1 \\ 4 & 3 \end{bmatrix}^{-1} = \begin{bmatrix} 1.5 & -0.5 \\ -2 & 1 \end{bmatrix}$$

13.

$$\left[\begin{array}{ccc|ccc} 0 & 0 & 1 & 1 & 0 & 0 \\ 0 & 1 & 0 & 0 & 1 & 0 \\ 1 & 0 & 0 & 0 & 0 & 1 \end{array}\right] \rightarrow \left[\begin{array}{ccc|ccc} 1 & 0 & 0 & 0 & 0 & 1 \\ 0 & 1 & 0 & 0 & 1 & 0 \\ 0 & 0 & 1 & 1 & 0 & 0 \end{array}\right]; \quad \begin{bmatrix} 0 & 0 & 1 \\ 0 & 1 & 0 \\ 1 & 0 & 0 \end{bmatrix}^{-1} = \begin{bmatrix} 0 & 0 & 1 \\ 0 & 1 & 0 \\ 1 & 0 & 0 \end{bmatrix}$$

15.

$$\left[\begin{array}{ccc|ccc} 1 & 1 & -1 & 1 & 0 & 0 \\ 3 & -1 & 0 & 0 & 1 & 0 \\ 2 & -3 & 4 & 0 & 0 & 1 \end{array}\right] \rightarrow \left[\begin{array}{ccc|ccc} 1 & 1 & -1 & 1 & 0 & 0 \\ 0 & -4 & 3 & -3 & 1 & 0 \\ 0 & -5 & 6 & -2 & 0 & 1 \end{array}\right] \rightarrow$$

$$\left[\begin{array}{ccc|ccc} 1 & 1 & -1 & 1 & 0 & 0 \\ 0 & 1 & -0.75 & 0.75 & -0.25 & 0 \\ 0 & -5 & 6 & -2 & 0 & 1 \end{array}\right] \rightarrow \left[\begin{array}{ccc|ccc} 1 & 0 & -0.25 & 0.25 & 0.25 & 0 \\ 0 & 1 & -0.75 & 0.75 & -0.25 & 0 \\ 0 & 0 & 2.25 & 1.75 & -1.25 & 1 \end{array}\right] \rightarrow$$

$$\left[\begin{array}{ccc|ccc} 1 & 0 & -025 & 0.25 & 0.25 & 0 \\ 0 & 1 & -0.75 & 0.75 & -0.25 & 0 \\ 0 & 0 & 1 & \frac{7}{9} & -\frac{5}{9} & \frac{4}{9} \end{array}\right] \rightarrow \left[\begin{array}{ccc|ccc} 1 & 0 & 0 & \frac{4}{9} & \frac{1}{9} & \frac{1}{9} \\ 0 & 1 & 0 & \frac{4}{3} & -\frac{2}{3} & \frac{1}{3} \\ 0 & 0 & 1 & \frac{7}{9} & -\frac{5}{9} & \frac{4}{9} \end{array}\right];$$

$$\begin{bmatrix} 1 & 1 & -1 \\ 3 & -1 & 0 \\ 2 & -3 & 4 \end{bmatrix}^{-1} = \begin{bmatrix} \frac{4}{9} & \frac{1}{9} & \frac{1}{9} \\ \frac{4}{3} & -\frac{2}{3} & \frac{1}{3} \\ \frac{7}{9} & -\frac{5}{9} & \frac{4}{9} \end{bmatrix}$$

17.

$$\left[\begin{array}{ccc|ccc} 1 & 1 & -1 & 1 & 0 & 0 \\ 2 & 1 & 1 & 0 & 1 & 0 \\ 1 & 0 & 1 & 0 & 0 & 1 \end{array}\right] \to \left[\begin{array}{ccc|ccc} 1 & 1 & -1 & 1 & 0 & 0 \\ 0 & -1 & 3 & -2 & 1 & 0 \\ 0 & -1 & 2 & -1 & 0 & 1 \end{array}\right] \to \left[\begin{array}{ccc|ccc} 1 & 0 & 2 & -1 & 1 & 0 \\ 0 & 1 & -3 & 2 & -1 & 0 \\ 0 & 0 & -1 & 1 & -1 & 1 \end{array}\right] \to$$

$$\left[\begin{array}{ccc|ccc} 1 & 0 & 0 & 1 & -1 & 2 \\ 0 & 1 & 0 & -1 & 2 & -3 \\ 0 & 0 & 1 & -1 & 1 & -1 \end{array}\right]; \quad \begin{bmatrix} 1 & 1 & -1 \\ 2 & 1 & 1 \\ 1 & 0 & 1 \end{bmatrix}^{-1} = \begin{bmatrix} 1 & -1 & 2 \\ -1 & 2 & -3 \\ -1 & 1 & -1 \end{bmatrix}$$

19.

$$\left[\begin{array}{cccc|cccc} 1 & 1 & 0 & 0 & 1 & 0 & 0 & 0 \\ 0 & 1 & -1 & 1 & 0 & 1 & 0 & 0 \\ 1 & -1 & 1 & 1 & 0 & 0 & 1 & 0 \\ 0 & 1 & 0 & -1 & 0 & 0 & 0 & 1 \end{array}\right] \to \left[\begin{array}{cccc|cccc} 1 & 1 & 0 & 0 & 1 & 0 & 0 & 0 \\ 0 & 1 & -1 & 1 & 0 & 1 & 0 & 0 \\ 0 & -2 & 1 & 1 & -1 & 0 & 1 & 0 \\ 0 & 1 & 0 & -1 & 0 & 0 & 0 & 1 \end{array}\right] \to$$

$$\left[\begin{array}{cccc|cccc} 1 & 0 & 1 & -1 & 1 & -1 & 0 & 0 \\ 0 & 1 & -1 & 1 & 0 & 1 & 0 & 0 \\ 0 & 0 & -1 & 3 & -1 & 2 & 1 & 0 \\ 0 & 0 & 1 & -2 & 0 & -1 & 0 & 1 \end{array}\right] \to \left[\begin{array}{cccc|cccc} 1 & 0 & 0 & 2 & 0 & 1 & 1 & 0 \\ 0 & 1 & 0 & -2 & 1 & -1 & -1 & 0 \\ 0 & 0 & 1 & -3 & 1 & -2 & -1 & 0 \\ 0 & 0 & 0 & 1 & -1 & 1 & 1 & 1 \end{array}\right] \to$$

$$\left[\begin{array}{cccc|cccc} 1 & 0 & 0 & 0 & 2 & -1 & -1 & -2 \\ 0 & 1 & 0 & 0 & -1 & 1 & 1 & 2 \\ 0 & 0 & 1 & 0 & -2 & 1 & 2 & 3 \\ 0 & 0 & 0 & 1 & -1 & 1 & 1 & 1 \end{array}\right]; \quad \begin{bmatrix} 1 & 1 & 0 & 0 \\ 0 & 1 & -1 & 1 \\ 1 & -1 & 1 & 1 \\ 0 & 1 & 0 & -1 \end{bmatrix}^{-1} = \begin{bmatrix} 2 & -1 & -1 & -2 \\ -1 & 1 & 1 & 2 \\ -2 & 1 & 2 & 3 \\ -1 & 1 & 1 & 1 \end{bmatrix}$$

21.

$$\left[\begin{array}{cc|cc} 4 & 6 & 1 & 0 \\ 2 & 3 & 0 & 1 \end{array}\right] \to \left[\begin{array}{cc|cc} 4 & 6 & 1 & 0 \\ 0 & 0 & -\frac{1}{2} & 0 \end{array}\right]$$

The 0's in row 2 indicate that I_2 cannot be obtained on the left side of the augmented matrix.

23.

$$\left[\begin{array}{cc|cc} -8 & 4 & 1 & 0 \\ -4 & 2 & 0 & 1 \end{array}\right] \to \left[\begin{array}{cc|cc} -8 & 4 & 1 & 0 \\ 0 & 0 & -\frac{1}{2} & 0 \end{array}\right]$$

25.

$$\left[\begin{array}{ccc|ccc} 1 & 1 & 1 & 1 & 0 & 0 \\ 3 & -4 & 2 & 0 & 1 & 0 \\ 0 & 0 & 0 & 0 & 0 & 1 \end{array}\right]$$

27.

$$\begin{bmatrix} 1 & 1 \\ 1 & 2 \end{bmatrix}\begin{bmatrix} a & b \\ c & d \end{bmatrix} = \begin{bmatrix} a+c & b+d \\ a+2c & b+2d \end{bmatrix} = \begin{bmatrix} 1 & 0 \\ 0 & 1 \end{bmatrix};$$ solve for a, b, c, d:

$$\left.\begin{array}{l} a+c=1 \\ a+2c=0 \end{array}\right\} \begin{array}{l} a=2 \\ c=-1 \end{array} \qquad \left.\begin{array}{l} b+d=0 \\ b+2d=1 \end{array}\right\} \begin{array}{l} b=-1 \\ d=1 \end{array}$$

$$\begin{bmatrix} 1 & 1 \\ 1 & 2 \end{bmatrix}^{-1} = \begin{bmatrix} a & b \\ c & d \end{bmatrix} = \begin{bmatrix} 2 & -1 \\ -1 & 1 \end{bmatrix}$$

29.

$$\begin{bmatrix} 3 & -2 \\ 0 & 2 \end{bmatrix}\begin{bmatrix} a & b \\ c & d \end{bmatrix} = \begin{bmatrix} 3a-2c & 3b-2d \\ 2c & 2d \end{bmatrix} = \begin{bmatrix} 1 & 0 \\ 0 & 1 \end{bmatrix}$$

$$\left.\begin{array}{r} 3a-2c=1 \\ 2c=0 \end{array}\right\} \begin{array}{l} a=\frac{1}{3} \\ c=0 \end{array} \qquad \left.\begin{array}{r} 3b-2d=0 \\ 2d=1 \end{array}\right\} \begin{array}{l} b=\frac{1}{3} \\ d=\frac{1}{2} \end{array}$$

Hence $\begin{bmatrix} \frac{1}{3} & \frac{1}{3} \\ 0 & \frac{1}{2} \end{bmatrix}$, is the inverse of $\begin{bmatrix} 3 & -2 \\ 0 & 2 \end{bmatrix}$

31.

$$\begin{bmatrix} 3 & 2 \\ 6 & 4 \end{bmatrix}\begin{bmatrix} a & b \\ c & d \end{bmatrix} = \begin{bmatrix} 3a+2c & 3b+2d \\ 6a+4c & 6b+4d \end{bmatrix} = \begin{bmatrix} 1 & 0 \\ 0 & 1 \end{bmatrix}$$

$$\begin{array}{lcl} 3a+2c = 1 & & a = -\frac{2}{3}c+\frac{1}{3} \\ & \Rightarrow & \\ 6a+4c = 0 & & a = -\frac{2}{3}c \end{array}$$

No solution; hence, no inverse.

33.

$$\begin{bmatrix} x \\ y \end{bmatrix} = \begin{bmatrix} 1 & 1 \\ 2 & -1 \end{bmatrix}^{-1}\begin{bmatrix} 6 \\ 0 \end{bmatrix} = \begin{bmatrix} \frac{1}{3} & \frac{1}{3} \\ \frac{2}{3} & -\frac{1}{3} \end{bmatrix}\begin{bmatrix} 6 \\ 0 \end{bmatrix} = \begin{bmatrix} 2 \\ 4 \end{bmatrix}; \quad x = 2,\ y = 4$$

35.

$$\begin{bmatrix} x \\ y \end{bmatrix} = \begin{bmatrix} 2 & 3 \\ 3 & -1 \end{bmatrix}^{-1}\begin{bmatrix} 7 \\ 5 \end{bmatrix} = \begin{bmatrix} \frac{1}{11} & \frac{3}{11} \\ \frac{3}{11} & -\frac{2}{11} \end{bmatrix}\begin{bmatrix} 7 \\ 5 \end{bmatrix} = \begin{bmatrix} 2 \\ 1 \end{bmatrix}; \quad x = 2, y = 1$$

37.

$$\begin{bmatrix} 2 & -3 \\ 4 & 9 \end{bmatrix}^{-1}\begin{bmatrix} 0 \\ 5 \end{bmatrix} = \begin{bmatrix} \frac{3}{10} & \frac{1}{10} \\ -\frac{2}{15} & \frac{1}{15} \end{bmatrix}\begin{bmatrix} 0 \\ 5 \end{bmatrix} = \begin{bmatrix} \frac{1}{2} \\ \frac{1}{3} \end{bmatrix}; \quad x = \frac{1}{2},\ y = \frac{1}{3}$$

39.

$$\begin{bmatrix} \frac{1}{2} & \frac{1}{3} \\ 1 & 1 \end{bmatrix}^{-1}\begin{bmatrix} 2 \\ 5 \end{bmatrix} = \begin{bmatrix} 6 & -2 \\ -6 & 3 \end{bmatrix}\begin{bmatrix} 2 \\ 5 \end{bmatrix} = \begin{bmatrix} 2 \\ 3 \end{bmatrix}; \quad x = 2, y = 3$$

41.

$$\begin{bmatrix} 2 & 1 & 1 \\ 1 & -1 & -1 \\ 3 & 1 & 2 \end{bmatrix}^{-1}\begin{bmatrix} 6 \\ -3 \\ 7 \end{bmatrix} = \begin{bmatrix} \frac{1}{3} & \frac{1}{3} & 0 \\ \frac{5}{3} & -\frac{1}{3} & -1 \\ -\frac{4}{3} & -\frac{1}{3} & 1 \end{bmatrix}\begin{bmatrix} 6 \\ -3 \\ 7 \end{bmatrix} = \begin{bmatrix} 1 \\ 4 \\ 0 \end{bmatrix}; \quad x = 1, y = 4, z = 0$$

43.

$$\begin{bmatrix} 2 & 1 & -1 \\ 1 & 3 & 2 \\ 1 & 1 & 1 \end{bmatrix}^{-1}\begin{bmatrix} 2 \\ 1 \\ 2 \end{bmatrix} = \begin{bmatrix} 0.2 & -0.4 & 1 \\ 0.2 & 0.6 & -1 \\ -0.4 & -0.2 & 1 \end{bmatrix}\begin{bmatrix} 2 \\ 1 \\ 2 \end{bmatrix} = \begin{bmatrix} 2 \\ -1 \\ 1 \end{bmatrix}; \quad x = 2, y = -1, z = 1$$

45.

$$\begin{bmatrix} 3 & 1 & -1 \\ 2 & -1 & 1 \\ 4 & 2 & 0 \end{bmatrix}^{-1}\begin{bmatrix} \frac{2}{3} \\ 1 \\ \frac{8}{3} \end{bmatrix} = \begin{bmatrix} 0.2 & -0.2 & 0 \\ -0.4 & -0.4 & 0.5 \\ -0.8 & 0.2 & 0.5 \end{bmatrix}\begin{bmatrix} \frac{2}{3} \\ 1 \\ \frac{8}{3} \end{bmatrix} = \begin{bmatrix} \frac{1}{3} \\ \frac{2}{3} \\ 1 \end{bmatrix}; \quad x = \frac{1}{3}, \; y = \frac{2}{3}, \; z = 1$$

47.

$$A^{-1} = \begin{bmatrix} 5 & -7 \\ -2 & 3 \end{bmatrix}; \begin{bmatrix} 5 & -7 \\ -2 & 3 \end{bmatrix}\begin{bmatrix} 10 \\ 7 \end{bmatrix} = \begin{bmatrix} 1 \\ 1 \end{bmatrix}; \quad x = 1, y = 1$$

49.

$$\begin{bmatrix} 5 & -7 \\ -2 & 3 \end{bmatrix}\begin{bmatrix} 13 \\ 9 \end{bmatrix} = \begin{bmatrix} 2 \\ 1 \end{bmatrix}; \quad x = 2, y = 1$$

51.

$$\begin{bmatrix} a & b \\ c & d \end{bmatrix}\begin{bmatrix} d & -b \\ -c & a \end{bmatrix} = \begin{bmatrix} ad - bc & 0 \\ 0 & -bc + ad \end{bmatrix} = \begin{bmatrix} \Delta & 0 \\ 0 & \Delta \end{bmatrix}; \text{ thus, } \begin{bmatrix} a & b \\ c & d \end{bmatrix}\begin{bmatrix} \frac{d}{\Delta} & \frac{-b}{\Delta} \\ \frac{-c}{\Delta} & \frac{a}{\Delta} \end{bmatrix} = \begin{bmatrix} 1 & 0 \\ 0 & 1 \end{bmatrix}$$

Exercise 2.6A (page 97)

1. $A = \frac{1}{2}A + \frac{1}{3}B + \frac{1}{4}C \qquad -\frac{1}{2}A + \frac{1}{3}B + \frac{1}{4}C = 0$

   $B = \frac{1}{4}A + \frac{1}{3}B + \frac{1}{4}C \qquad \frac{1}{4}A - \frac{2}{3}B + \frac{1}{4}C = 0$

   $C = \frac{1}{4}A + \frac{1}{3}B + \frac{1}{2}C \qquad \frac{1}{4}A + \frac{1}{3}B - \frac{1}{2}C = 0$

   The coefficient matrix for the homogeneous system is

$$\begin{bmatrix} -\frac{1}{2} & \frac{1}{3} & \frac{1}{4} \\ \frac{1}{4} & -\frac{2}{3} & \frac{1}{4} \\ \frac{1}{4} & \frac{1}{3} & -\frac{1}{2} \end{bmatrix} \rightarrow \begin{bmatrix} 1 & 0 & -1 \\ 0 & 1 & -\frac{3}{4} \\ 0 & 0 & 0 \end{bmatrix}; \quad A = C = \$10{,}000, \; B = \frac{3}{4}C = \$7500$$

3. $A = 0.2A + 0.3B + 0.1C$ $\qquad -0.8A + 0.3B + 0.1C = 0$

$B = 0.6A + 0.4B + 0.2C$ $\qquad 0.6A - 0.6B + 0.2C = 0$

$C = 0.2A + 0.3B + 0.7C$ $\qquad 0.2A + 0.3B - 0.3C = 0$

The coefficient matrix is

$$\begin{bmatrix} -0.8 & 0.3 & 0.1 \\ 0.6 & -0.6 & 0.2 \\ 0.2 & 0.3 & -0.3 \end{bmatrix} \rightarrow \begin{bmatrix} 1 & 0 & -\frac{6}{15} \\ 0 & 1 & -\frac{11}{15} \\ 0 & 0 & 0 \end{bmatrix}; \ A = \frac{6}{15}C, \ \ B = \frac{11}{15}C, \ \text{ where } C = \$\,10{,}000$$

5.

$$X = (I - A)^{-1} D_2 = \begin{bmatrix} 1.6048 & 0.3568 & 0.7131 \\ 0.2946 & 1.3363 & 0.3857 \\ 0.3660 & 0.2721 & 1.4013 \end{bmatrix} \begin{bmatrix} 80 \\ 90 \\ 60 \end{bmatrix} = \begin{bmatrix} 203.282 \\ 166.977 \\ 137.847 \end{bmatrix}$$

7. Where x_1 = Farmer's income, x_2 = Builder's income, x_3 = Tailor's income, x_4 = Rancher's income, the system of equations is

$x_1 = 0.3x_1 + 0.3x_2 + 0.3x_3 + 0.2x_4$

$x_2 = 0.2x_1 + 0.3x_2 + 0.3x_3 + 0.2x_4$

$x_3 = 0.2x_1 + 0.1x_2 + 0.1x_3 + 0.2x_4$

$x_4 = 0.3x_1 + 0.3x_2 + 0.3x_3 + 0.4x_4$

which we may write as

$$\begin{aligned} -0.7x_1 + 0.3x_2 + 0.3x_3 + 0.2x_4 &= 0 \\ 0.2x_1 + (-0.7)x_2 + 0.3x_3 + 0.2x_4 &= 0 \\ 0.2x_1 + 0.1x_2 + (-0.9)x_3 + 0.2x_4 &= 0 \\ 0.3x_1 + 0.3x_2 + 0.3x_3 + (-0.6)x_4 &= 0 \end{aligned}$$

The coefficient matrix is

$$\begin{bmatrix} -0.7 & 0.3 & 0.3 & 0.2 \\ 0.2 & -0.7 & 0.3 & 0.2 \\ 0.2 & 0.1 & -0.9 & 0.2 \\ 0.3 & 0.3 & 0.3 & -0.6 \end{bmatrix} \rightarrow \begin{bmatrix} 1 & 0 & 0 & -0.8 \\ 0 & 1 & 0 & -0.72 \\ 0 & 0 & 1 & -0.48 \\ 0 & 0 & 0 & 0 \end{bmatrix}$$

$x_1 = 0.8x_4 = 8000$, $x_2 = 0.72x_4 = 7200$, $x_3 = 0.48x_4 = 4800$, $x_4 = \$10{,}000$

9.

$$A = \begin{bmatrix} \frac{3}{13} & \frac{4}{7} \\ \frac{2}{13} & \frac{1}{7} \end{bmatrix}; \ (I - A)^{-1} = \begin{bmatrix} \frac{3}{2} & 1 \\ \frac{7}{26} & \frac{35}{26} \end{bmatrix}; \qquad X = \begin{bmatrix} \frac{3}{2} & 1 \\ \frac{7}{26} & \frac{35}{26} \end{bmatrix} \begin{bmatrix} 80 \\ 40 \end{bmatrix} = \begin{bmatrix} 160. \\ 75.38 \end{bmatrix}$$

Exercise 2.6B (page 101)

1. (a) (i) 41 23 70 45 41 23 62 41 64 36 19 11 59 39 7 4 94 60
   (ii) 13 69 -21 20 98 -35 1 123 18 8 4 -13 1 32 0 1 141 24
   (b) (i) 85 50 71 43 90 54 99 61 43 24 59 32 45 24 69 41 67 43
   (ii) 20 140 -27 15 153 -12 15 138 -16 5 62 -5 18 132 -21 13 139 07
   (c) (i) 64 36 49 31 75 47 65 37 72 43 75 47 57 35 77 46 95 57 24 13 39 22
   (ii) 20 93 -35 13 143 07 19 141 -23 14 164 -9 9 120 -2 15 159 -11 9 89 -6 5 170 16

3.

$$A^{-1} = \begin{bmatrix} 1 & 0 & 0 \\ -13 & 1 & -5 \\ 2 & 0 & 1 \end{bmatrix}; \quad A^{-1}\begin{bmatrix} 25 \\ 195 \\ -29 \end{bmatrix} = \begin{bmatrix} 25 \\ 15 \\ 21 \end{bmatrix} = \begin{bmatrix} Y \\ O \\ U \end{bmatrix}; \quad A^{-1}\begin{bmatrix} 6 \\ 135 \\ 9 \end{bmatrix} = \begin{bmatrix} 6 \\ 12 \\ 21 \end{bmatrix} = \begin{bmatrix} F \\ L \\ U \end{bmatrix};$$

$$A^{-1}\begin{bmatrix} 14 \\ 183 \\ -2 \end{bmatrix} = \begin{bmatrix} 14 \\ 11 \\ 26 \end{bmatrix} = \begin{bmatrix} N \\ K \\ Z \end{bmatrix}; \quad \text{YOU FLUNK}$$

EXERCISE 2.6C (page 106)

1.

$$A^T = \begin{bmatrix} 4 & 3 \\ 1 & 1 \\ 2 & 0 \end{bmatrix}$$

3.

$$A^T = \begin{bmatrix} 1 & 0 & 1 \\ 11 & 12 & 4 \end{bmatrix}$$

5.

$$A^T = [8\ 6\ 3]$$

7.

(a)
$$\begin{bmatrix} 3 & 5 & 6 & 7 \\ 1 & 1 & 1 & 1 \end{bmatrix}\begin{bmatrix} 3 & 1 \\ 5 & 1 \\ 6 & 1 \\ 7 & 1 \end{bmatrix}\begin{bmatrix} a \\ b \end{bmatrix} = \begin{bmatrix} 3 & 5 & 6 & 7 \\ 1 & 1 & 1 & 1 \end{bmatrix}\begin{bmatrix} 10 \\ 13 \\ 15 \\ 16 \end{bmatrix}$$

$$\begin{bmatrix} 119 & 21 \\ 21 & 4 \end{bmatrix}\begin{bmatrix} a \\ b \end{bmatrix} = \begin{bmatrix} 297 \\ 54 \end{bmatrix}$$

$$\left.\begin{aligned} 119a + 21b &= 297 \\ 21a + 4b &= 54 \end{aligned}\right\} a = \frac{54}{35}, \quad b = \frac{27}{5}$$

$$y = \frac{54}{35}x + \frac{27}{5}$$

(b) $y = \frac{54}{35}(8) + \frac{27}{5} = 17.74$

9.

$$\begin{bmatrix} 10 & 17 & 11 & 18 & 21 \\ 1 & 1 & 1 & 1 & 1 \end{bmatrix}\begin{bmatrix} 10 & 1 \\ 17 & 1 \\ 11 & 1 \\ 18 & 1 \\ 21 & 1 \end{bmatrix}\begin{bmatrix} a \\ b \end{bmatrix} = \begin{bmatrix} 10 & 17 & 11 & 18 & 21 \\ 1 & 1 & 1 & 1 & 1 \end{bmatrix}\begin{bmatrix} 50 \\ 61 \\ 55 \\ 60 \\ 70 \end{bmatrix}$$

$$\begin{bmatrix} 1275 & 75 \\ 77 & 5 \end{bmatrix}\begin{bmatrix} a \\ b \end{bmatrix} = \begin{bmatrix} 4692 \\ 296 \end{bmatrix}$$

$$\left.\begin{aligned} 1275a + 77b &= 4692 \\ 77a + 5b &= 296 \end{aligned}\right\} a = \frac{334}{223},\ b = \frac{8058}{223}$$

$$y = \frac{334}{223}x + \frac{8058}{223}$$

11.

(1) $A^T = \begin{bmatrix} 1 & 1 & 3 \\ 1 & 0 & 2 \\ 2 & 1 & 3 \end{bmatrix} \neq A$ Not symmetric

(2) $A^T = \begin{bmatrix} 0 & 1 & 3 \\ 1 & 4 & 7 \\ 3 & 7 & 5 \end{bmatrix} = A$ Is symmetric

(3) $A^T = \begin{bmatrix} 1 & 2 & 3 \\ 2 & 4 & 5 \\ 3 & 5 & 1 \\ 0 & 0 & 0 \end{bmatrix} \neq A$ Not symmetric

Yes. A symmetric matrix must be square.

CHAPTER REVIEW

Review Exercises (page 112)

1. $\begin{bmatrix} -1 & 3 & 16 \\ 3 & 15 & 8 \\ 5 & 10 & 29 \end{bmatrix}$

3. $\begin{bmatrix} -3 & 9 & 48 \\ 9 & 45 & 24 \\ 15 & 30 & 87 \end{bmatrix}$

5. $\begin{bmatrix} -9 & -9 & -6 \\ -3 & 3 & -6 \\ -3 & -6 & 39 \end{bmatrix}$

7. $\begin{bmatrix} -20 & 0 & 70 \\ 10 & 80 & 30 \\ 20 & 40 & 210 \end{bmatrix}$

9.

$$\begin{bmatrix} -\frac{7}{2} & -\frac{3}{2} & \frac{25}{2} \\ 3 & \frac{9}{2} & \frac{11}{2} \\ -\frac{37}{2} & -10 & 19 \end{bmatrix}$$

11.

$$\begin{bmatrix} 19 & 36 & 38 \\ 26 & 77 & 73 \\ 73 & 160 & 206 \end{bmatrix}$$

13.

$$\begin{bmatrix} 3 & 3 & 2 \\ 1 & -1 & 2 \\ 1 & 2 & -13 \end{bmatrix}\begin{bmatrix} 0 & 1 & 2 \\ 0 & 5 & 1 \\ 8 & 7 & 9 \end{bmatrix} = \begin{bmatrix} 16 & 32 & 27 \\ 16 & 10 & 19 \\ -104 & -80 & -113 \end{bmatrix}$$

15.

$$\left[\begin{array}{cc|cc} 3 & 0 & 1 & 0 \\ -2 & 1 & 0 & 1 \end{array}\right] \to \left[\begin{array}{cc|cc} 1 & 0 & \frac{1}{3} & 0 \\ -2 & 1 & 0 & 1 \end{array}\right] \to \left[\begin{array}{cc|cc} 1 & 0 & \frac{1}{3} & 0 \\ 0 & 1 & \frac{2}{3} & 1 \end{array}\right]; \quad \begin{bmatrix} 3 & 0 \\ -2 & 1 \end{bmatrix}^{-1} = \begin{bmatrix} \frac{1}{3} & 0 \\ \frac{2}{3} & 1 \end{bmatrix}$$

17.

$$\left[\begin{array}{ccc|ccc} 1 & 2 & 3 & 1 & 0 & 0 \\ 2 & 4 & 5 & 0 & 1 & 0 \\ 3 & 5 & 6 & 0 & 0 & 1 \end{array}\right] \to \left[\begin{array}{ccc|ccc} 1 & 2 & 3 & 1 & 0 & 0 \\ 0 & 0 & -1 & -2 & 1 & 0 \\ 0 & -1 & -3 & -3 & 0 & 1 \end{array}\right]$$

$$\to \left[\begin{array}{ccc|ccc} 1 & 2 & 3 & 1 & 0 & 0 \\ 0 & 1 & 3 & 3 & 0 & -1 \\ 0 & 0 & -1 & -2 & 1 & 0 \end{array}\right] \to \left[\begin{array}{ccc|ccc} 1 & 0 & -3 & -5 & 0 & 2 \\ 0 & 1 & 3 & 3 & 0 & -1 \\ 0 & 0 & 1 & 2 & -1 & 0 \end{array}\right]$$

$$\to \left[\begin{array}{ccc|ccc} 1 & 0 & 0 & 1 & -3 & 2 \\ 0 & 1 & 0 & -3 & 3 & -1 \\ 0 & 0 & 1 & 2 & -1 & 0 \end{array}\right]; \quad \begin{bmatrix} 1 & 2 & 3 \\ 2 & 4 & 5 \\ 3 & 5 & 6 \end{bmatrix}^{-1} = \begin{bmatrix} 1 & -3 & 2 \\ -3 & 3 & -1 \\ 2 & -1 & 0 \end{bmatrix}$$

19.

$$\left[\begin{array}{ccc|ccc} 4 & 3 & -1 & 1 & 0 & 0 \\ 0 & 2 & 2 & 0 & 1 & 0 \\ 3 & -1 & 0 & 0 & 0 & 1 \end{array}\right] \to \left[\begin{array}{ccc|ccc} 1 & \frac{3}{4} & -\frac{1}{4} & \frac{1}{4} & 0 & 0 \\ 0 & 2 & 2 & 0 & 1 & 0 \\ 3 & -1 & 0 & 0 & 0 & 1 \end{array}\right]$$

$$\to \left[\begin{array}{ccc|ccc} 1 & \frac{3}{4} & -\frac{1}{4} & \frac{1}{4} & 0 & 0 \\ 0 & 2 & 2 & 0 & 1 & 0 \\ 0 & -\frac{13}{4} & \frac{3}{4} & -\frac{3}{4} & 0 & 1 \end{array}\right] \to \left[\begin{array}{ccc|ccc} 1 & \frac{3}{4} & -\frac{1}{4} & \frac{1}{4} & 0 & 0 \\ 0 & 1 & 1 & 0 & \frac{1}{2} & 0 \\ 0 & -\frac{13}{4} & \frac{3}{4} & -\frac{3}{4} & 0 & 1 \end{array}\right]$$

$$\rightarrow\left[\begin{array}{ccc|ccc} 1 & 0 & -1 & \frac{1}{4} & -\frac{3}{8} & 0 \\ 0 & 1 & 1 & 0 & \frac{1}{2} & 0 \\ 0 & 0 & 4 & -\frac{3}{4} & \frac{13}{8} & 1 \end{array}\right]\rightarrow\left[\begin{array}{ccc|ccc} 1 & 0 & -1 & \frac{1}{4} & -\frac{3}{8} & 0 \\ 0 & 1 & 1 & 0 & \frac{1}{2} & 0 \\ 0 & 0 & 1 & -\frac{3}{16} & \frac{13}{32} & \frac{1}{4} \end{array}\right]$$

$$\rightarrow\left[\begin{array}{ccc|ccc} 1 & 0 & 0 & \frac{1}{16} & \frac{1}{32} & \frac{1}{4} \\ 0 & 1 & 0 & \frac{3}{16} & \frac{3}{32} & -\frac{1}{4} \\ 0 & 0 & 1 & -\frac{3}{16} & \frac{13}{32} & \frac{1}{4} \end{array}\right];\begin{bmatrix} 4 & 3 & -1 \\ 0 & 2 & 2 \\ 3 & -1 & 0 \end{bmatrix}^{-1}\begin{bmatrix} \frac{1}{16} & \frac{1}{32} & \frac{1}{4} \\ \frac{3}{16} & \frac{3}{32} & -\frac{1}{4} \\ -\frac{3}{16} & \frac{13}{32} & \frac{1}{4} \end{bmatrix}$$

21.

$$\left[\begin{array}{ccc|ccc} 1 & 2 & -3 & 1 & 0 & 0 \\ 4 & 6 & 2 & 0 & 1 & 0 \\ -3 & -6 & 9 & 0 & 0 & 1 \end{array}\right]\rightarrow\left[\begin{array}{ccc|ccc} 1 & 2 & -3 & 1 & 0 & 0 \\ 0 & -2 & 14 & -4 & 1 & 0 \\ 0 & 0 & 0 & 3 & 0 & 1 \end{array}\right]$$

The matrix has no inverse.

23.

$$\left[\begin{array}{ccc|c} 2 & -1 & 1 & 1 \\ 1 & 1 & -1 & 2 \\ 3 & -1 & 1 & 0 \end{array}\right]\rightarrow\left[\begin{array}{ccc|c} 1 & 1 & -1 & 2 \\ 2 & -1 & 1 & 1 \\ 3 & -1 & 1 & 0 \end{array}\right]\rightarrow\left[\begin{array}{ccc|c} 1 & 1 & -1 & 2 \\ 0 & -3 & 3 & -3 \\ 0 & -4 & 4 & -6 \end{array}\right]\left[\begin{array}{ccc|c} 1 & 1 & -1 & 2 \\ 0 & 1 & -1 & 1 \\ 0 & 1 & -1 & \frac{3}{2} \end{array}\right]\rightarrow$$

$$\left[\begin{array}{ccc|c} 1 & 1 & -1 & 2 \\ 0 & 1 & -1 & 1 \\ 0 & 0 & 0 & \frac{1}{2} \end{array}\right]$$

There is no solution.

25.

$$\left[\begin{array}{ccc|c} 1 & -2 & 0 & 6 \\ 3 & 2 & -1 & 2 \\ 4 & 0 & 3 & -1 \end{array}\right]\rightarrow\left[\begin{array}{ccc|c} 1 & -2 & 0 & 6 \\ 0 & 8 & -1 & -16 \\ 0 & 8 & 3 & -25 \end{array}\right]\rightarrow\left[\begin{array}{ccc|c} 1 & -2 & 0 & 6 \\ 0 & 1 & -\frac{1}{8} & -2 \\ 0 & 8 & 3 & -25 \end{array}\right]$$

$$\rightarrow\left[\begin{array}{ccc|c} 1 & 0 & -\frac{1}{4} & 2 \\ 0 & 1 & -\frac{1}{8} & -2 \\ 0 & 0 & 4 & -9 \end{array}\right]\rightarrow\left[\begin{array}{ccc|c} 1 & 0 & -\frac{1}{4} & 2 \\ 0 & 1 & -\frac{1}{8} & -2 \\ 0 & 0 & 1 & -\frac{9}{4} \end{array}\right]\rightarrow\left[\begin{array}{ccc|c} 1 & 0 & 0 & \frac{23}{16} \\ 0 & 1 & 0 & -\frac{73}{32} \\ 0 & 0 & 1 & -\frac{9}{4} \end{array}\right]$$

$x_1 = \frac{23}{16}$, $x_2 = -\frac{73}{32}$, $x_3 - \frac{9}{4}$

27.

$$\left[\begin{array}{ccc|c} 1 & -3 & 0 & 5 \\ 0 & 3 & 1 & 0 \\ 2 & -1 & 2 & 2 \end{array}\right] \to \left[\begin{array}{ccc|c} 1 & -3 & 0 & 5 \\ 0 & 3 & 1 & 0 \\ 0 & 5 & 2 & -8 \end{array}\right] \to \left[\begin{array}{ccc|c} 1 & -3 & 0 & 5 \\ 0 & 1 & \frac{1}{3} & 0 \\ 0 & 5 & 2 & -8 \end{array}\right]$$

$$\to \left[\begin{array}{ccc|c} 1 & 0 & 1 & 5 \\ 0 & 1 & \frac{1}{3} & 0 \\ 0 & 0 & \frac{1}{3} & -8 \end{array}\right] \to \left[\begin{array}{ccc|c} 1 & 0 & 1 & 5 \\ 0 & 1 & \frac{1}{3} & 0 \\ 0 & 0 & 1 & -24 \end{array}\right] \to \left[\begin{array}{ccc|c} 1 & 0 & 0 & 29 \\ 0 & 1 & 0 & 8 \\ 0 & 0 & 1 & -24 \end{array}\right];$$

$x_1 = 29, \; x_2 = 8, \; x_3 = -24$

29.

$$\left[\begin{array}{ccc|c} 3 & 1 & -2 & 3 \\ 1 & -2 & 1 & 4 \end{array}\right] \to \left[\begin{array}{ccc|c} 1 & -2 & 1 & 4 \\ 3 & 1 & -2 & 3 \end{array}\right] \to \left[\begin{array}{ccc|c} 1 & -2 & 1 & 4 \\ 0 & 7 & -5 & -9 \end{array}\right]$$

$$\to \left[\begin{array}{ccc|c} 1 & -2 & 1 & 4 \\ 0 & 1 & -\frac{5}{7} & -\frac{9}{7} \end{array}\right] \to \left[\begin{array}{ccc|c} 1 & 0 & -\frac{3}{7} & \frac{10}{7} \\ 0 & 1 & -\frac{5}{7} & -\frac{9}{7} \end{array}\right]$$

$x_1 = \frac{10}{7} + \frac{3}{7}x_3, \; x_2 = -\frac{9}{7} + \frac{5}{7}x_3$

$x_1 = \frac{10}{7}, \; x_2 = -\frac{9}{7}, \; x_3 = 0; \; x_1 = \frac{13}{7}, \; x_2 = -\frac{4}{7}, \; x_3 = 1;$

$x_1 = \frac{16}{7}, \; x_2 = \frac{1}{7}, \; x_3 = 2$

31.

$$\left[\begin{array}{ccc|c} 1 & 2 & -1 & 5 \\ 2 & -1 & 2 & 0 \end{array}\right] \to \left[\begin{array}{ccc|c} 1 & 2 & -1 & 5 \\ 0 & -5 & 4 & -10 \end{array}\right] \to \left[\begin{array}{ccc|c} 1 & 2 & -1 & 5 \\ 0 & 1 & -\frac{4}{5} & 2 \end{array}\right]$$

$$\to \left[\begin{array}{ccc|c} 1 & 0 & \frac{3}{5} & 1 \\ 0 & 1 & -\frac{4}{5} & 2 \end{array}\right]; \; x_1 = 1 - \frac{3}{5}x_3, \; x_2 = 2 + \frac{4}{5}x_3$$

$x_1 = 1, \; x_2 = 2, \; x_3 = 0; \; x_1 = \frac{2}{5}, \; x_2 = \frac{14}{5}, \; x_3 = 1; \; x_1 = -\frac{1}{5}, \; x_2 = \frac{18}{5}, \; x_3 = 2$

33.

$$\begin{bmatrix} 2 & -1 & | & 6 \\ 1 & -2 & | & 0 \\ 3 & -1 & | & 6 \end{bmatrix} \rightarrow \begin{bmatrix} 1 & -2 & | & 0 \\ 2 & -1 & | & 6 \\ 3 & -1 & | & 6 \end{bmatrix} \rightarrow \begin{bmatrix} 1 & -2 & | & 0 \\ 0 & 3 & | & 6 \\ 0 & 5 & | & 6 \end{bmatrix} \rightarrow \begin{bmatrix} 1 & -2 & | & 0 \\ 0 & 1 & | & \frac{1}{2} \\ 0 & 5 & | & 6 \end{bmatrix} \rightarrow \begin{bmatrix} 1 & 0 & | & 1 \\ 0 & 1 & | & \frac{1}{2} \\ 0 & 0 & | & \frac{7}{2} \end{bmatrix}$$

There is no solution.

35.

$$\begin{bmatrix} x & y \\ z & w \end{bmatrix}\begin{bmatrix} 1 & 1 \\ -1 & 1 \end{bmatrix} = \begin{bmatrix} 1 & 1 \\ -1 & 1 \end{bmatrix}\begin{bmatrix} x & y \\ z & w \end{bmatrix}; \quad \begin{bmatrix} x-y & x+y \\ z-w & z+w \end{bmatrix} = \begin{bmatrix} x+z & y+w \\ -x+z & -y+w \end{bmatrix};$$

$y = -z, \ x = w$

37.

$$\begin{bmatrix} 2 & -3 \\ -1 & 2 \end{bmatrix}\begin{bmatrix} 11 \\ 7 \end{bmatrix} = \begin{bmatrix} 1 \\ 3 \end{bmatrix} = \begin{bmatrix} A \\ C \end{bmatrix}; \begin{bmatrix} 2 & -3 \\ -1 & 2 \end{bmatrix}\begin{bmatrix} 84 \\ 51 \end{bmatrix} = \begin{bmatrix} 15 \\ 18 \end{bmatrix} = \begin{bmatrix} O \\ R \end{bmatrix}; \begin{bmatrix} 2 & -3 \\ -1 & 2 \end{bmatrix}\begin{bmatrix} 51 \\ 28 \end{bmatrix} = \begin{bmatrix} 18 \\ 5 \end{bmatrix} = \begin{bmatrix} R \\ E \end{bmatrix};$$

$$\begin{bmatrix} 2 & -3 \\ -1 & 2 \end{bmatrix}\begin{bmatrix} 66 \\ 43 \end{bmatrix} = \begin{bmatrix} 3 \\ 20 \end{bmatrix} = \begin{bmatrix} C \\ T \end{bmatrix}; \begin{bmatrix} 2 & -3 \\ -1 & 2 \end{bmatrix}\begin{bmatrix} 44 \\ 29 \end{bmatrix} = \begin{bmatrix} 1 \\ 14 \end{bmatrix} = \begin{bmatrix} A \\ N \end{bmatrix}; \begin{bmatrix} 2 & -3 \\ -1 & 2 \end{bmatrix}\begin{bmatrix} 107 \\ 65 \end{bmatrix} = \begin{bmatrix} 19 \\ 23 \end{bmatrix} = \begin{bmatrix} S \\ W \end{bmatrix};$$

$$\begin{bmatrix} 2 & -3 \\ -1 & 2 \end{bmatrix}\begin{bmatrix} 64 \\ 41 \end{bmatrix} = \begin{bmatrix} 5 \\ 18 \end{bmatrix} = \begin{bmatrix} E \\ R \end{bmatrix};$$ A CORRECT ANSWER

CHAPTER 3

Exercise 3.2 (page 124)

1. $x \geq 0$

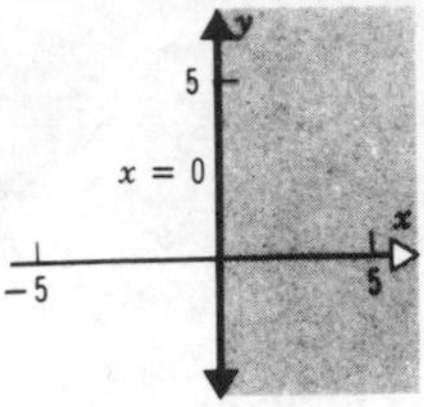

3. $x \geq 0,\ y \geq 0$

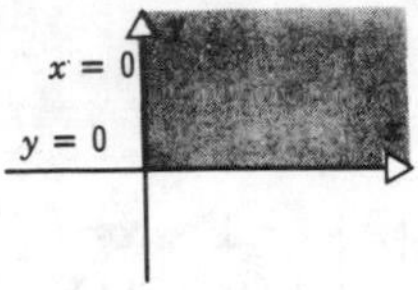

5. $2x - 3y \leq 6$

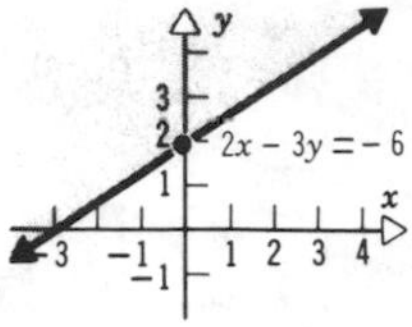

7. $5x + y \leq -10$

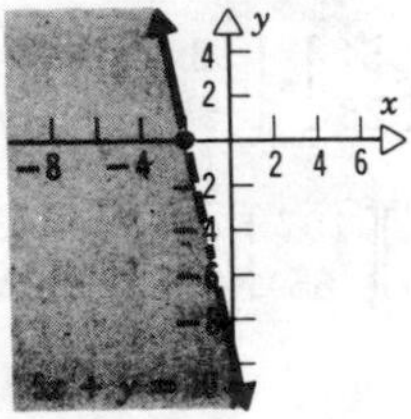

9. $x \geq 5$

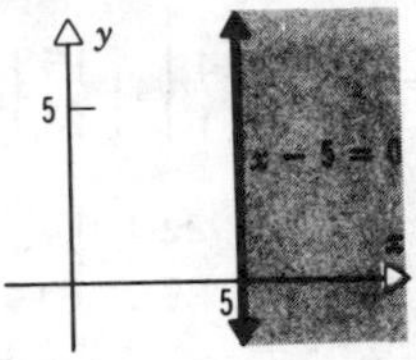

11. $x \geq 0,\ y \geq 0$
$x + y \leq 2$
Bounded,
Vertices: (0,0),(0,2), (2,0)

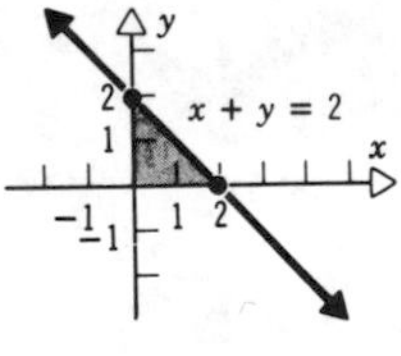

13. $x \geq 0,\ y \geq 0$
$x + y \geq 2$
$2x + 3y \leq 6$
Bounded,
Vertices: (0,2), (2,0), (3,0)

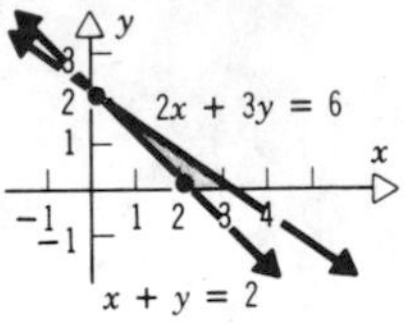

15. $x \geq 0,\ y \geq 0$
$2 \leq x + y,\ x + y \leq 8$
$2x + y \leq 10$
Bounded,
Vertices: (0,2), (0,8), (2,6), (5,0), (2,0)

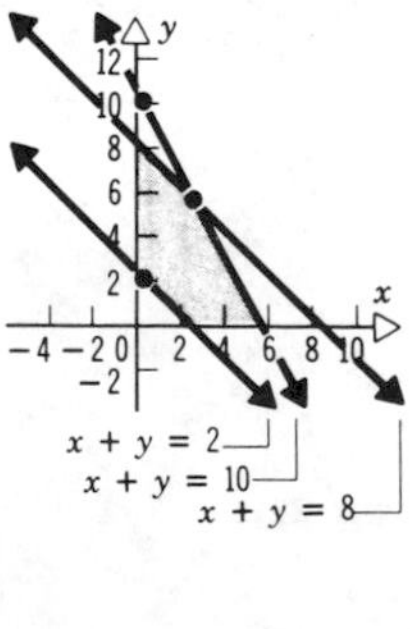

17. $x \geq 0,\ y \geq 0$
$x + y \geq 2,\ 2x + 3y \leq 12$
$3x + y \leq 12$
Bounded,
Vertices: $(0, 2), (0, 4), \left(\frac{24}{7}, \frac{12}{7}\right), (4, 0), (2, 0)$

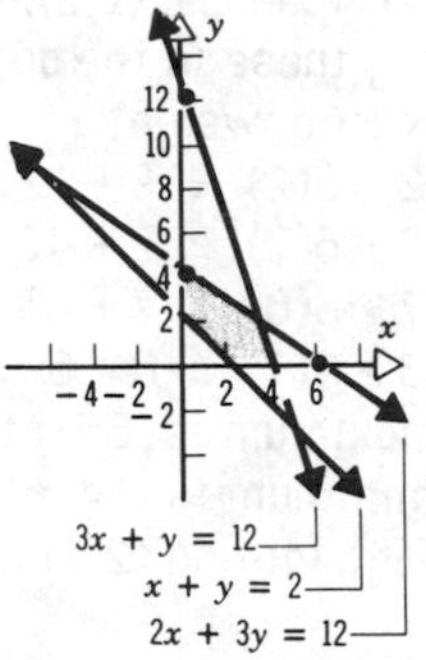

19. $x \geq 0,\ y \geq 0$
$1 \leq x + 2y,\ x + 2y \leq 10$
Bounded,
Vertices: $(0,1), (0,5), (10,0), (1,0)$

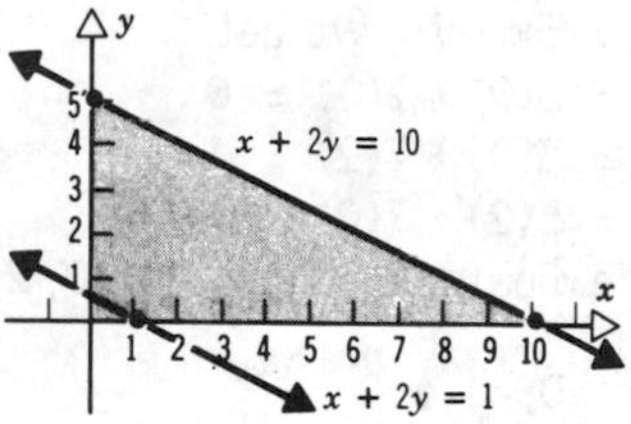

Exercise 3.3 (page 136)

1. The vertices are $(2, 2), (2, 7), (7, 8), (8, 1)$. Testing these in the objective equation $z = 2x + 3y$, we get:
$z = 2(2) + 3(2) = 4 + 6 = 10$
$z = 2(2) + 3(7) = 4 + 21 = 25$
$z = 2(7) + 3(8) = 14 + 24 = 38$
$z = 2(8) + 3(1) = 16 + 3 = 19$
The maximum is 38 at $(7,8)$. The minimum is 10 at $(2, 2)$.

3. The vertices are $(2, 2), (2, 7), (7,8), (8, 1)$.
Testing these in the objective equation
$z = x + 8y$, we get:
$z = 2 + 8(2) = 2 + 16 = 18$
$z = 2 + 8(7) = 2 + 56 = 58$
$z = 7 + 8(8) = 7 = 64 = 71$
$z = 8 + 8(1) = 8 + 8 = 16$
The maximum is 71 at $(7, 8)$.
The minimum is 16 at $(8, 1)$.

5. The vertices are (2,2), (2,7),(7,8),(8,1).
Testing these in the objective equation
$z = x + 6y$, we get:
$z = 2 + 6(2) = 2 + 12 = 14$
$z = 2 + 6(7) = 2 + 42 = 44$
$z = 7 + 6(8) = 7 + 48 = 55$
$z = 8 + 6(1) = 8 + 6 = 14$
The maximum is 55 at (7,8).
The minimum is 14 at points on the line segment joining (2,2) and (8,1).

7. The vertices are (0, 0), (0, 2), (2, 0).
Testing theese in the objective equation
$z = 5x + 7y$, we get:
$z = 5(0) + 7(0) = 0$
$z = 5(0) + 7(2) = 14$
$z = 5(2) + 7(0) = 10$
The maximum is 14 at (0, 2).

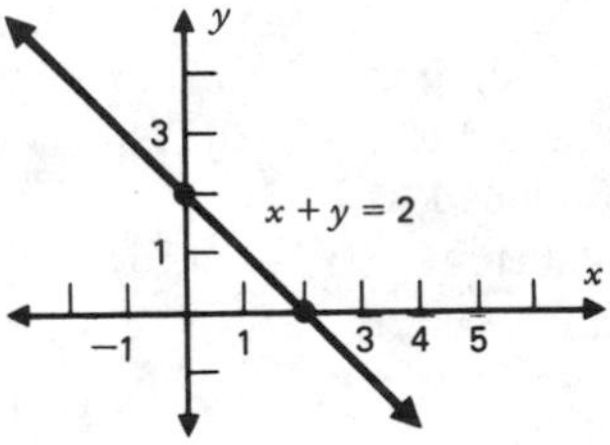

9. $x \geq 0,\ y \geq 0$
1 $x + y \geq 2$
2 $2x + 3y \leq 6$
The boundary lines for **1** and **2** intersect when

$$\left.\begin{aligned} x + y &= 2 \\ 2x + 3y &= 6 \end{aligned}\right\} \qquad \left.\begin{aligned} y &= 2 - x \\ 2x + 3(2 - x) &= 6 \end{aligned}\right\} \qquad x = 0,\ y = 2$$

The vertices are (0,2), (2,0), (3,0).
Testing these in the objective equation
$z = 5x + 7y$, we get:
$z = 5(0) + 7(2) = 14$
$z = 5(2) + 7(0) = 10$
$z = 5(3) + 7(0) = 15$
The maximum is 15 at (3,0).

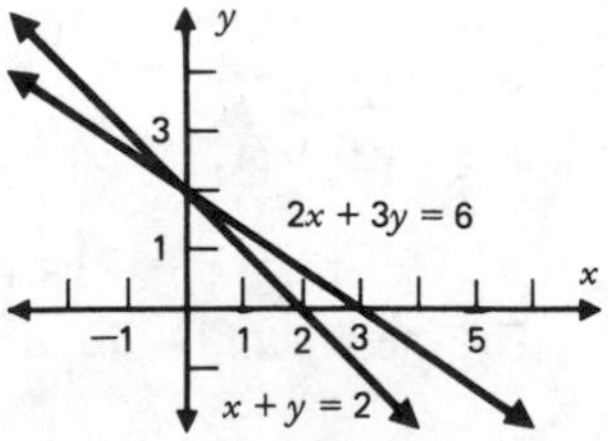

11. $x \geq 0,\ y \geq 0$
1 $x + y \leq 8$ **3** $x + y \geq 2$
2 $2x + y \leq 10$
The boundary lines for **1** and **2** cross the axes at (8,0), (0,8), (5,0), and (0,10). Of these, (0,8) and (5,0) are feasible [(8,0) does not obey **2** and (0,10) does not obey **1**]. The boundary lines for **1** and **2** intersect when

$$\begin{aligned} x + y &= 8 \\ \underline{2x + y} &\underline{= 10} \\ -x &= -2 \end{aligned} \qquad x = 2,\ y = 6$$

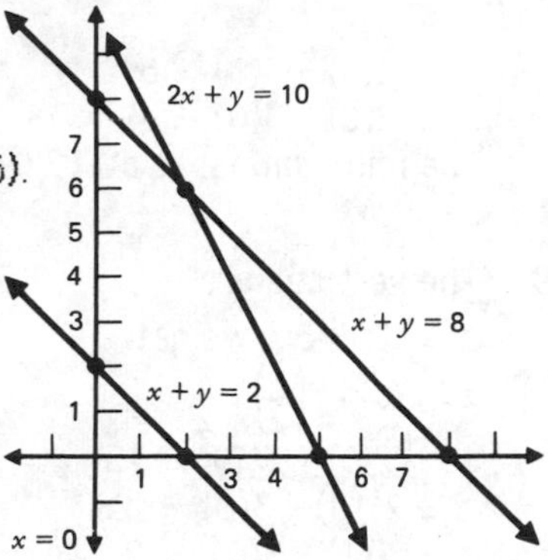

The boundary line for **3** crosses the axes at (2,0) and (0,2)
The vertices are (0,2), (0,8), (2,0), (5,0), (2,6).
Testing these in the objective equation
$z = 5x + 7y$, we get:
$z = 5(0) + 7(2) = 14$
$z = 5(0) + 7(8) = 56$
$z = 5(2) + 7(0) = 10$
$z = 5(5) + 7(0) = 25$
$z = 5(2) + 7(6) = 52$
The maximum is 56 at (0,8).

13. $z = 5x + 7y$ has no maximum under these conditions.

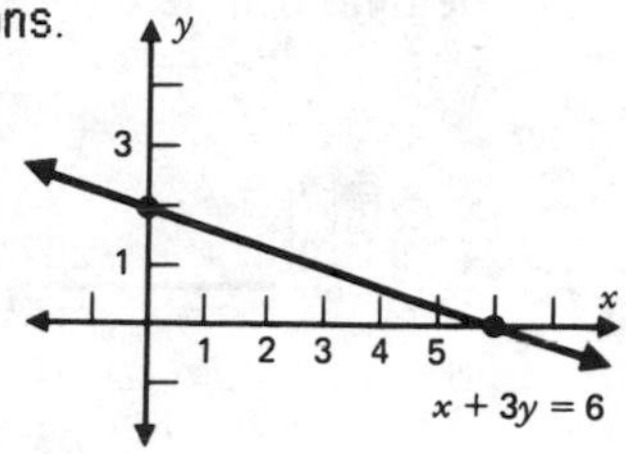

15. The vertices are (0,2), (2,0). Testing these in the objective equation
$z = 2x + 3y$, we get:
$z = 2(0) + 3(2) = 6$
$z = 2(2) + 3(0) = 4$
The minimum is 4 at (2,0).

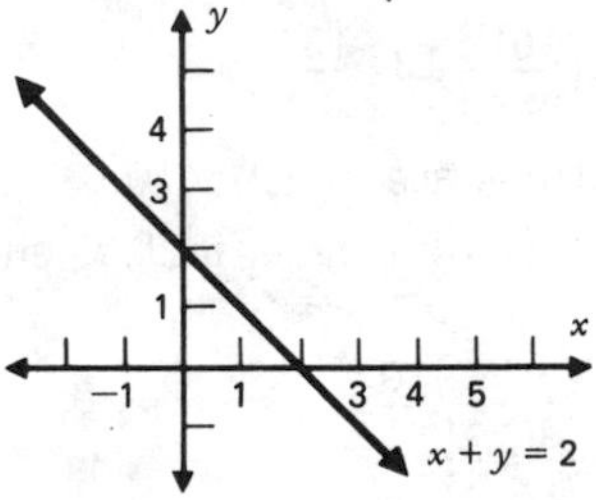

17. Four of the vertices lie on the axes.
The other is found by solving the two equations

$$\begin{array}{r|l} 2x+3y=12 & 2x+3y=12 \\ 3x+y=12 & \underline{9x+3y=36} \end{array}$$

$$7x = 24$$

$$x = \frac{24}{7}$$

$$y = -3\left(\frac{24}{7}\right) + 12 = \frac{12}{7}$$

The vertices are (0,2), (0,4), $\left(\frac{24}{7}, \frac{12}{7}\right)$, (4,0), (2,0).
Testing these in the objective equation $z = 2x + 3y$, we get:
$z = 2(0) + 3(2) = 6$
$z = 2(0) + 3(4) = 12$
$z = 2\left(\frac{24}{7}\right) + 3\left(\frac{12}{7}\right) = \frac{84}{7} = 12$

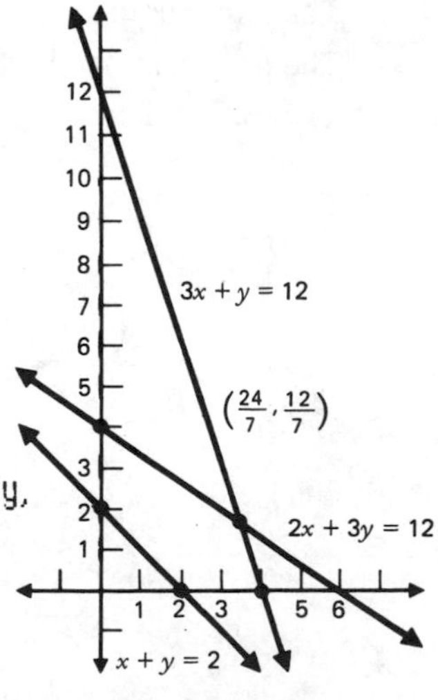

$z = 2(4) + 3(0) = 8$
$z = 2(2) + 3(0) = 4$
The minimum is 4 at (2,0).

19. The vertices are $\left(0, \frac{1}{2}\right)$, (0,5), (10,0), (1,0). Testing these in the objective equation $z = 2x + 3y$, we get:

$z = 2(0) + 3\left(\frac{1}{2}\right) = \frac{3}{2}$
$z = 2(0) + 3(5) = 15$
$z = 2(10) + 3(0) = 20$
$z = 2(1) + 3(0) = 2$
The minimum is $\frac{3}{2}$ at $\left(0, \frac{1}{2}\right)$.

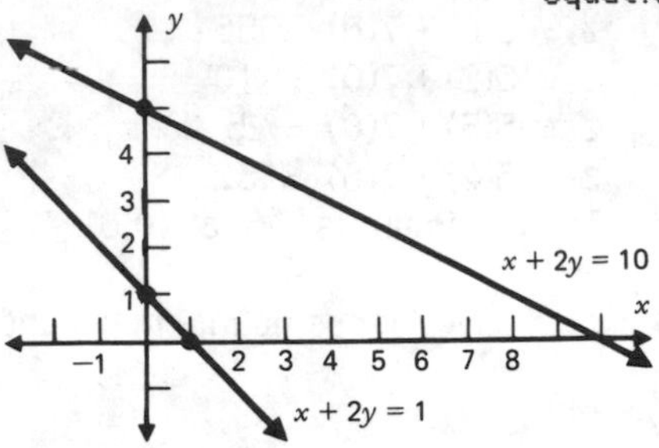

21.

$$\begin{array}{l|l} x + 2y = 10 & x + 2y = 10 \\ 2x + y = 10 & \underline{4x + 2y = 20} \\ & 3x = 10 \\ & x = \frac{10}{3} \end{array}$$

$y = -2\left(\frac{10}{3}\right) + 10 = \frac{10}{3}$

The vertices are (0,10), (10,0), $\left(\frac{10}{3}, \frac{10}{3}\right)$.
Testing these in the objective equation $z = x + y$, we get:
$z = 0 + 10 = 10$
$z = 10 + 0 = 10$
$z = \frac{10}{3} + \frac{10}{3} = \frac{20}{3}$
The minimum is $\frac{20}{3}$ at $\left(\frac{10}{3}, \frac{10}{3}\right)$.
The maximum is 10 at any point on the line segment between (0,10) and (10,0).

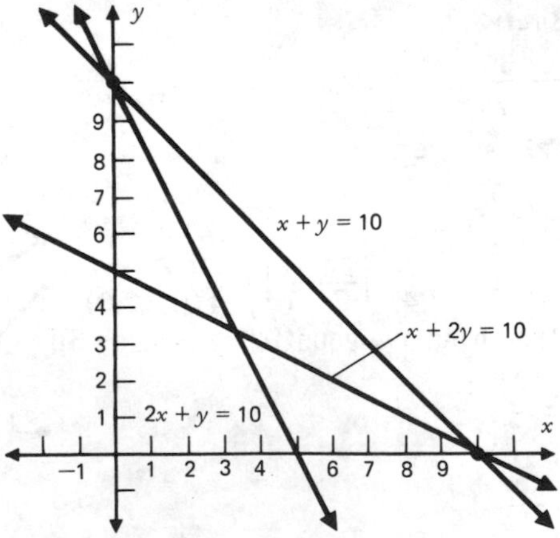

23. (see solution to Problem 21.)

$z = 5x + 2y$

$z = 0 + 2(10) = 20$

$z = 50 + 2(0) = 50$

$z = \frac{50}{3} + \frac{20}{3} = \frac{70}{3}$

The minimum is 20 at (0,10); the maximum is 50 at (10,0).

25. (See solution to Problem 21.)

$z = 3x + 4y$

$z = 3(0) + 4(10) = 40$

$z = 3(10) + 4(0) = 30$

$z = 3\left(\frac{10}{3}\right) + 4\left(\frac{10}{3}\right) = \frac{70}{3}$

The minimum is $\frac{70}{3}$ at $\left(\frac{10}{3}, \frac{10}{3}\right)$;

27. $P = (\$0.30)x + (\$0.40)y$

$P_1 = 0.3(0) + 0.4(0) = 0$

$P_2 = 0.3(0) + 0.4(150) = \$60.00$

$P_3 = 0.3(160) + 0.4(0) = \$48.00$

$P_4 = 0.3(90) + 0.4(105) = \$69.00$

90 packages of the low-grade mixture and 105 packages of the high-grade mixture.

29. $P = \$4x + \$3y$

$P_1 = 4(0) + 3(0) = 0$

$P_2 = 4(0) + 3(30) = 90$

$P_3 = 4(40) + 3(0) = 160$

$P_4 = 4(20) + 3(20) = 140$

40 standard models and no deluxe models should be manufactured.

31. x = Number of units of first product

y = Number of units of second product

Maximize: $P = 40x + 60y$

Subject to: $x \geq 0, y \geq 0$

1 $2x + y \leq 70$

2 $x + y \leq 40$

3 $x + 3y \leq 90$

The boundary lines for **1** and **2** intersect at $(x,y) = (30,10)$.

The boundary lines for **1** and **3** intersect at $(x,y) = (24,22)$, but this is not a feasible point (**1** is not satisfied).

The boundary lines for **2** and **3** intersect at (x,y) = (15,25).
The vertices are (0,30), (35,0), (30,10), (15,25).
Testing each of these in the equation P = 40x + 60y, we get:
P = 40(0) + 60(30) = 1800
P = 40(35) + 60(0) = 1400
P = 40(30) + 60(10) = 1800
P = 40(15) + 60(25) = 2100
Thus, 15 units of the first product and 25 units of the second maximizes profit at $2100.

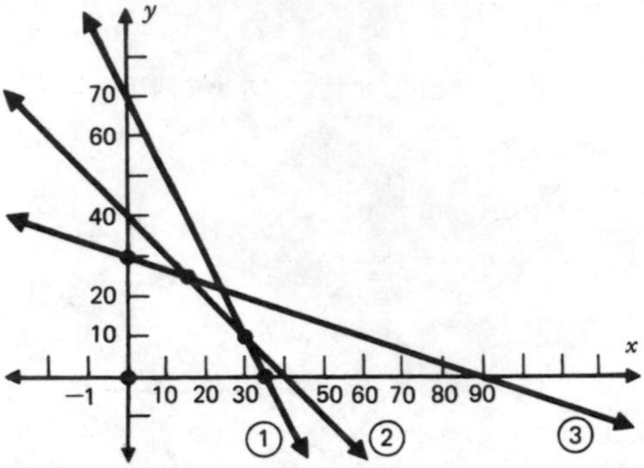

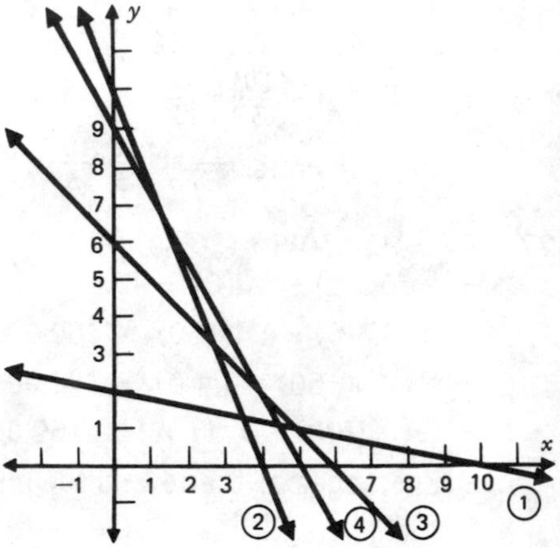

33. x = Ounces of Supplement I
y = Ounces of Supplement II
The problem is to minimuze C = (\$0.03)x + (\$0.04y)
subject to $x \geq 0$, $y \geq 0$,
1 $5x + 25y \geq 50$ or $x + 5y \geq 10$
2 $25x + 10y \geq 100$ or $5x + 2y \geq 20$
3 $10x + 10y \geq 60$ or $x + y \geq 6$
4 $35x + 20y \geq 180$ or $7x + 4y \geq 36$
The vertices are (0,10), (10,0), (5,1), (4,2), $\left(\frac{4}{3}, \frac{20}{3}\right)$.
$C_1 = 0.03(0) + 0.04(10) = \$0.40$
$C_2 = 0.03(10) + 0.04(0) = \$0.30$
$C_3 = 0.03(5) + 0.04(1) = \$0.19$
$C_4 = 0.03(4) + 0.04(2) = \$0.20$
$C_5 = 0.03\left(\frac{4}{3}\right) + 0.04\left(\frac{20}{3}\right) = \$0.307$
He should add 5 ounces of Supplement I and 1 ounce of Supplement II to each 100 ounces of feed.

35. Let P = Pounds of pork ground into hamburger and picnic patties
CS = Pounds of chuck steak ground into hamburger and picnic patties
RS = Pounds of round steak ground into hamburger and picnic patties
x = Pounds of hamburger patties made
y = Pounds of picnic patties made

We wish to maximize S, the amount of meat used to make the patties, namely,

$$S = P + CS + RS$$

where $P = 0.3y$, $CS = 0.6x + 0.5y$, $RS = 0.2x$

Thus, the problem is to maximize $S = 0.8x + 0.8y$ subject to $x \geq 0$, $y \geq 0$,

1	$0.3y \leq 150$	or	$y \leq 500$
2	$0.6x + 0.5y \leq 300$	or	$6x + 5y \leq 3000$
3	$0.2x \leq 80$	or	$x \leq 400$

The vertices are (0,0), (0,500), $\left(83\frac{1}{3}, 500\right)$, (400,120), (400,0).

$S_1 = 0.8(0) + 0.8(0) = 0$

$S_2 = 0.8(0) + 0.8(500) = 400$

$S_3 = 0.8\left(83\frac{1}{3}\right) + 0.8(500) = 466.67$

$S_4 = 0.8(400) + 0.8(120) = 416$

$S_5 = 0.8(400) + 0.8(0) = 320$

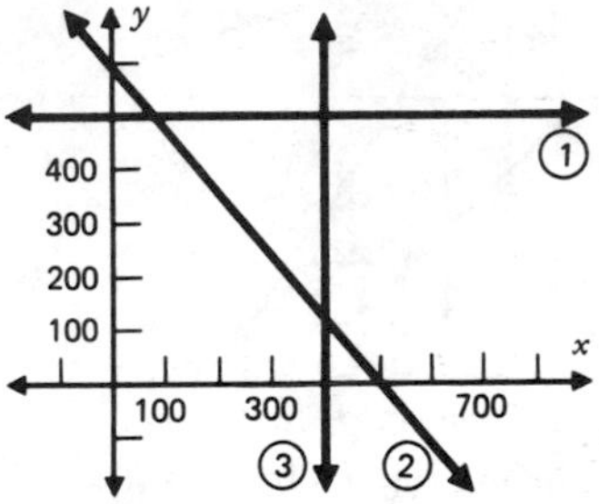

500 pounds of picnic patties and $88\frac{1}{3}$ pounds of hamburger should be made.

37. Let x = Number of rolls of high-grade carpet
y = Number of rolls of low-grade carpet
p = Selling price of high-grade carpet

Revenue $= px + 300y$

Income $I = (p - 420)x + 100y$

The vertices of the set of feasible solutions are (0,0), (0,25), (15,10), and (20,0); but (15,10) is the only vertex for which some of each type of carpet is produced. For the vertex (15,10) to be the one that maximizes I requires that the slope of the objective equation I lie between -1 and -2. Thus, $(p - 420)/(-100)$ must lie between -1 and -2. That is,

$$-2 \leq \frac{p - 420}{-100} \leq -1 \quad \text{or} \quad 100 \leq p - 420 \leq 200$$

The price of the high-grade carpet should be between \$520 and \$620 per roll.

CHAPTER REVIEW

Review Exercises (page 140)

1. $x - 3y < 0$

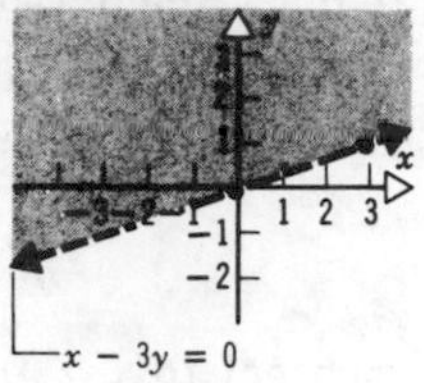

3. $5x + y \ge 10$

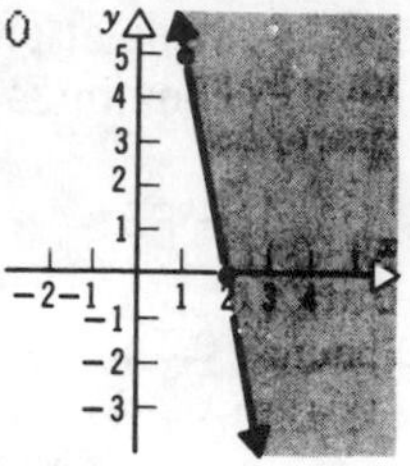

5. $x \ge 0, y \ge 0,$
$3x + 2y \le 12,$
$x + y \ge 1$

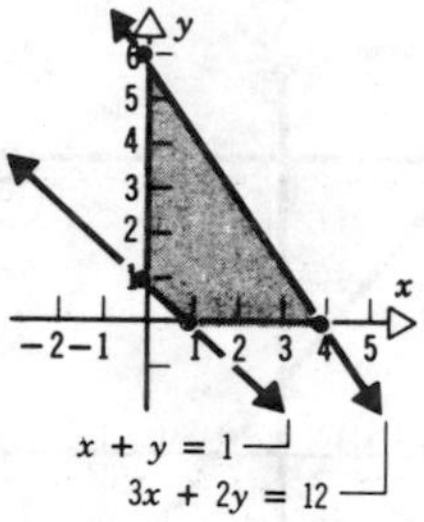

Bounded; vertices (0,1), (0,6), (4,0), (1,0)

7. $x \ge 0, y \ge 0$
$x + 2y \ge 4,$
$3x + y \ge 6$

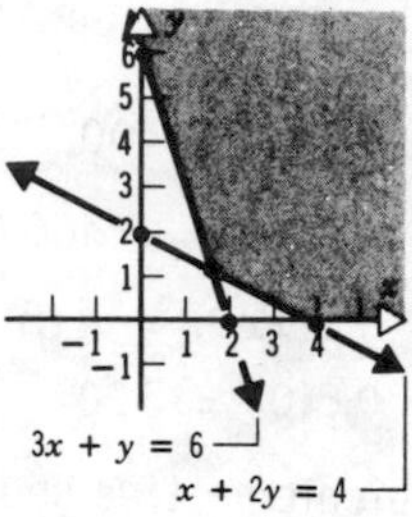

Unbounded; vertices (0,2), (0,6), $\left(\frac{8}{5}, \frac{6}{5}\right)$, (4,0), (2,0)

9. $x \geq 0,\ y \geq 0,$
$3x + 2y \geq 6,$
$3x + 2y \leq 12,$
$x + 2y \leq 8$

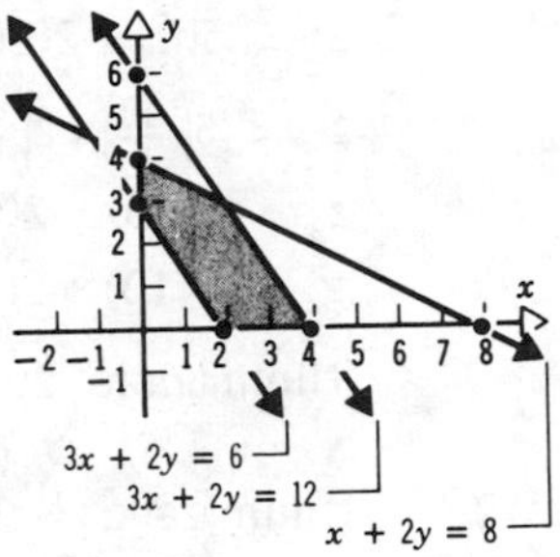

Bounded, Vertices (0,3),
(2,3), (4,0),(2,0)

Problems 11 – 18 use the following:

$x \geq 0,\ y \geq 0$
$x + 2y \leq 40,$
$2x + y \leq 40,$
$x + y \geq 10$

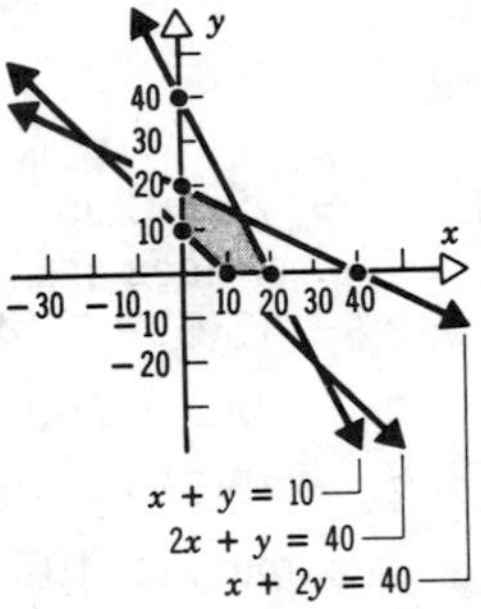

The vertices are at (0,10), (0,20), $\left(\frac{40}{3}, \frac{40}{3}\right)$, (20, 0), (10, 0)

11. Maximize $z = x + y$

$z_1 = 0 + 10 = 10$

$z_2 = 0 + 20 = 20$

$z_3 = \frac{40}{3} + \frac{40}{3} = \frac{80}{3}$

$z_4 = 20 + 0 = 20$

$z_5 = 10 + 0 = 10$

Maximum is $\frac{80}{3}$ at $\left(\frac{40}{3}, \frac{40}{3}\right)$

13. Minimize $z = 5x + 2y$

$z_1 = 5(0) + 2(10) = 20$

$z_2 = 5(0) + 2(20) = 40$

$z_3 = 5\left(\frac{40}{3}\right) + 2\left(\frac{40}{3}\right) = \frac{280}{3}$

$z_4 = 5(20) + 2(0) = 100$

$z_5 = 5(10) + 2(0) = 50$

Minimum is 20 at (0,10)

15. Maximize $z = 2x + y$

$z_1 = 2(0) + 10 = 10$

$z_2 = 2(0) + 20 = 20$

$z_3 = 2\left(\frac{40}{3}\right) + \frac{40}{3} = 40$

$z_4 = 2(20) + 0 = 40$

$z_5 = 2(10) + 0 = 20$

Maximum is 40 at any point on the line segment between $\left(\frac{40}{3}, \frac{40}{3}\right)$ and (20, 0)

17. Minimize $z + 2x + 5y$

$z_1 = 2(0) + 5(10) = 50$

$z_2 = 2(0) + 5(20) = 200$

$z_3 = 2\left(\frac{40}{3}\right) + 5\frac{40}{3} = \frac{280}{3}$

$z_4 = 2(20) + 5(0) = 40$

$z_5 = 2(10) + 5(0) = 20$

Minimum is 20 at (10,0)

19. $z = 15x + 20y$

The vertices are (0,3), (0,8), (5,8), (5,0), (4,0)

$z_1 = 15(0) + 20(3) = 60$

$z_2 = 15(0) + 20(8) = 160$

$z_3 = 15(5) + 20(8) = 235$

$z_4 = 15(5) + 20(0) = 75$

$z_5 = 15(4) + 20(0) = 60$

Minimum is 60 at any point on the line segment between (0,3) and (4,0)

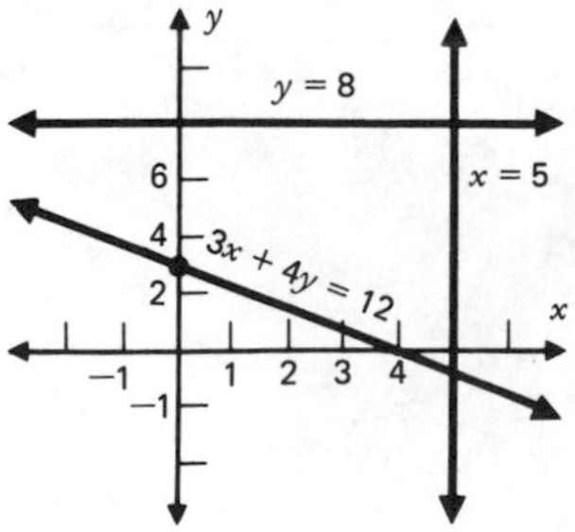

21. $z = 15x + 20y$

The vertices are (5,4), (2,6), (5,6)

$z_1 = 15(5) + 20(4) = 155$

$z_2 = 15(2) + 20(6) = 150$

$z_3 = 15(5) + 20(6) = 1915$

Maximum is 195 at (5,6)

Minimum is 150 at (2,6)

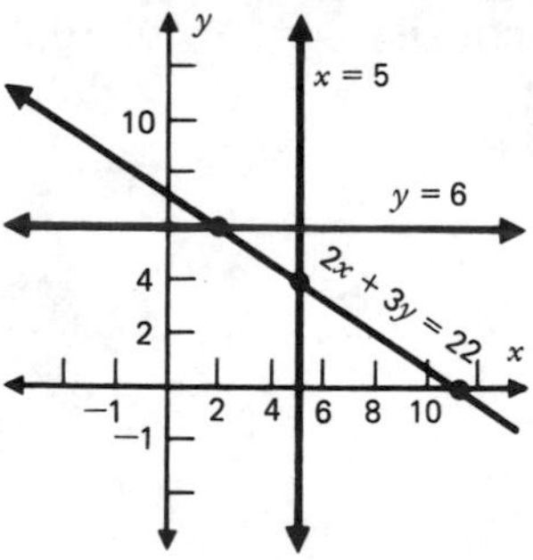

23. x = Pounds of Food A
y = Pounds of Food B
C = Cost of the foods per month
The problem is to minimize
C = \$1.30x + \$0.80y subject
to $x \geq 0$, $y \geq 0$,
1 $5x + 2y \geq 60$
2 $3x + 2y \geq 45$
3 $4x + y \geq 30$

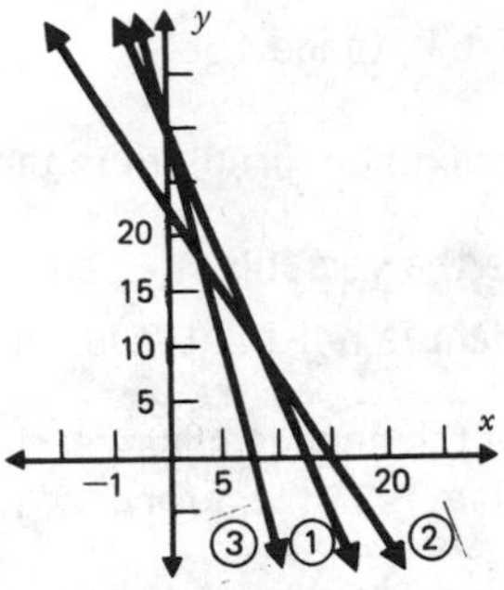

The vertices are $(0,30)$, $\left(\frac{15}{2}, \frac{45}{4}\right)$, $(15, 0)$.

$C_1 = 1.3(0) + 0.8(30) = \$24$

$C_2 = 1.3\left(\frac{15}{2}\right) + 0.8\left(\frac{45}{4}\right) = \$\,18.75$

$C_3 = 1.3(15) + 0.8(0) = \$19.50$

She should buy 7.5 pounds of A and 11.25 pounds of B.

25. x = Number of downhill skis
y = Number of cross-country skis
Maximize $P = 70x + 50y$ subject to $x \geq 0$, $y \geq 0$, $2x + y \leq 40$, $x + y \leq 32$

Vertex	Profit
(0,0)	P = 0
(20,0)	P = \$1400
(0,32)	P = \$1600
(8,24)	P = \$1760

Maximum profit of \$1760 with 8 downhill skis and 24 cross-country skies.

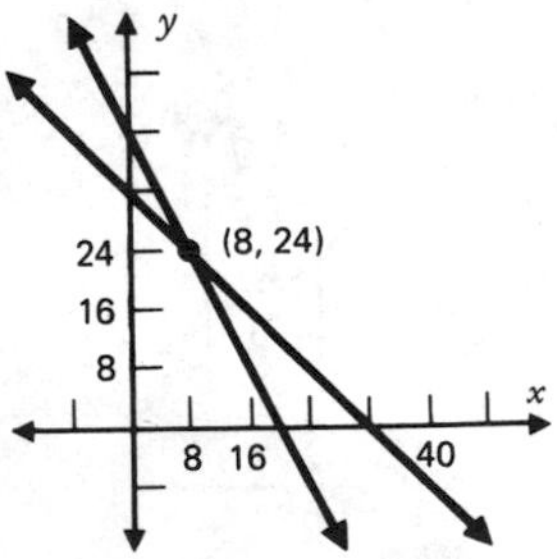

CHAPTER 4

Exercise 4.1 (page 156)

1. The maximum problem is in standard form.

3. Since the variables x_2 and x_3 are not given as nonnegative, the maximum problem is not in standard form.

5. Since the second constraint is not $\le$ a positive constant, the maximum problem is not in standard form.

7. Since the first constraint is not $\le$ a positive constant, the maximum problem is not in standard form.

9. The maximum problem is in standard form.

11. The maximum problem cannot be modified so as to be in standard form.

13. The maximum problem cannot be modified so as to be in standard form.

15. The maximum problem can be modified so as to be in standard form by multiplying both sides of the first and second constraint by -1. The modified version is

Maximize

$$P = 2x_1 + x_2 + 3x_3$$

Subject to the constraints

$$x_1 - x_2 - x_3 \le 6 \qquad x_1 \ge 0,\ x_2 \ge 0,$$
$$-2x_1 + 3x_2 \le 12 \qquad x_3 \ge 0$$

17.

$$5x_1 + 2x_2 + x_3 + s_1 = 20$$
$$6x_1 + x_2 + 4x_3 + s_2 = 24$$
$$x_1 + x_2 + 4x_3 + s_3 = 16$$

$$x_1 \ge 0,\ x_2 \ge 0,\ x_3 \ge 0$$
$$s_1 \ge 0,\ s_2 \ge 0,\ s_3 \ge 0$$

$$\begin{array}{ccccccc|c} x_1 & x_2 & x_3 & s_1 & s_2 & s_3 & P & \\ \hline 5 & 2 & 1 & 1 & 0 & 0 & 0 & 20 \\ 6 & 1 & 4 & 0 & 1 & 0 & 0 & 24 \\ \underline{1} & \underline{1} & \underline{4} & \underline{0} & \underline{0} & \underline{1} & \underline{0} & \underline{16} \\ 1 & 1 & 4 & 0 & 0 & 1 & 0 & 0 \end{array}$$

19.

$$2.2x_1 - 1.8x_2 + s_1 = 5$$
$$0.8x_1 + 1.2x_2 + s_2 = 2.5$$
$$x_1 + x_2 + s_3 = 0.1$$

$x_1 \geq 0,\ x_2 \geq 0,\ s_1 \geq 0,\ s_2 \geq 0,\ s_3 \geq 0$

$$\begin{array}{cccccc|c} x_1 & x_2 & s_1 & s_2 & s_3 & P & \\ 2.2 & -1.8 & 1 & 0 & 0 & 0 & 5 \\ 0.8 & 1.2 & 0 & 1 & 0 & 0 & 2.5 \\ 1 & 1 & 0 & 0 & 1 & 0 & 0.1 \\ -3 & -5 & 0 & 0 & 0 & 1 & 0 \end{array}$$

21.

$$x_1 + x_2 + x_3 + s_1 = 50$$
$$3x_1 + 2x_2 + x_3 + s_2 = 10$$

$x_1 \geq 0,\ x_2 \geq 0,\ x_3 \geq 0$
$s_1 \geq 0,\ s_2 \geq 0$

$$\begin{array}{cccccc|c} x_1 & x_2 & x_3 & s_1 & s_2 & P & \\ 1 & 1 & 1 & 1 & 0 & 0 & 50 \\ 3 & 2 & 1 & 0 & 1 & 0 & 10 \\ -2 & -3 & -1 & 0 & 0 & 1 & 0 \end{array}$$

23.

$$3x_1 + x_2 + 4x_3 + s_1 = 5$$
$$x_1 + x_2 + s_2 = 5$$
$$2x_1 - x_2 + x_3 + s_3 = 6$$

$x_1 \geq 0,\ x_2 \geq 0,\ x_3 \geq 0$
$s_1 \geq 0,\ s_2 \geq 0,\ s_3 \geq 0$

$$\begin{array}{ccccccc|c} x_1 & x_2 & x_3 & s_1 & s_2 & s_3 & P & \\ 3 & 1 & 4 & 1 & 0 & 0 & 0 & 5 \\ 1 & 1 & 0 & 0 & 1 & 0 & 0 & 5 \\ 2 & -1 & 1 & 0 & 0 & 1 & 0 & 6 \\ -3 & -4 & -2 & 0 & 0 & 0 & 1 & 0 \end{array}$$

25.

$$\begin{array}{ccccc|c|l} x_1 & x_2 & s_1 & s_2 & P & & \\ 1 & \underline{2} & 1 & 0 & 0 & 300 & s_1 \\ 3 & 2 & 0 & 1 & 0 & 480 & s_2 \\ -1 & -2 & 0 & 0 & 1 & 0 & P \end{array}$$

$$s_1 = 300 - x_1 - 2x_2$$
$$s_2 = 480 - 3x_1 - 2x_2$$
$$P = x_1 + x_2$$

$$\left[\begin{array}{ccccc|c} \frac{1}{2} & 1 & \frac{1}{2} & 0 & 0 & 150 \\ 3 & 2 & 0 & 1 & 0 & 480 \\ -1 & -2 & 0 & 0 & 1 & 0 \end{array}\right]$$

$$\left[\begin{array}{ccccc|c} \frac{1}{2} & 1 & \frac{1}{2} & 0 & 0 & 150 \\ 2 & 0 & -1 & 1 & 0 & 180 \\ 0 & 0 & 1 & 0 & 1 & 300 \end{array}\right] \begin{array}{l} x_2 \\ s_2 \\ P \end{array}$$

$$x_2 = 150 - \tfrac{1}{2}x_1 - \tfrac{1}{2}s_1$$
$$s_2 = 180 - 2x_1 + s_1$$
$$P = 300 - s_1$$

27.

$$\begin{array}{c} \begin{array}{ccccccc} x_1 & x_2 & x_3 & s_1 & s_2 & s_3 & P \end{array} \\ \left[\begin{array}{ccccccc|c} 1 & 2 & 4 & 1 & 0 & 0 & 0 & 24 \\ 2 & -1 & 1 & 0 & 1 & 0 & 0 & 32 \\ 3 & 2 & 4 & 0 & 0 & 1 & 0 & 18 \\ -1 & -2 & -3 & 0 & 0 & 0 & 1 & 0 \end{array}\right] \begin{array}{c} s_1 \\ s_2 \\ s_3 \\ P \end{array} \end{array}$$

$s_1 = 24 - x_1 - 2x_2 - 4x_3$

$s_2 = 32 - 2x_1 + x_2 - x_3$

$s_3 = 18 - 3x_1 - 2x_2 - 4x_3$

$P = x_1 + 2x_2 + 3x_3$

$$\left[\begin{array}{ccccccc|c} 1 & 2 & 4 & 1 & 0 & 0 & 0 & 24 \\ 2 & -1 & 1 & 0 & 1 & 0 & 0 & 32 \\ \frac{3}{2} & 1 & 2 & 0 & 0 & \frac{1}{2} & 0 & 9 \\ -1 & -2 & -3 & 0 & 0 & 0 & 1 & 0 \end{array}\right]$$

$$\left[\begin{array}{ccccccc|c} -2 & 0 & 0 & 1 & 0 & -1 & 0 & 6 \\ \frac{7}{2} & 0 & 3 & 0 & 1 & \frac{1}{2} & 0 & 41 \\ \frac{3}{2} & 1 & 2 & 0 & 0 & \frac{1}{2} & 0 & 9 \\ 2 & 0 & 1 & 0 & 0 & 1 & 1 & 18 \end{array}\right] \begin{array}{c} s_1 \\ s_2 \\ x_2 \\ P \end{array}$$

$s_1 = 6 + 2x_1 + s_3$

$s_2 = 41 - \frac{7}{2}x_1 - 3x_3 - \frac{1}{2}s_3$

$x_2 = 9 - \frac{3}{2}x_1 - 2x_3 - \frac{1}{2}s_3$

$P = 18 - 2x_1 - x_3 - s_3$

29.

$$\begin{array}{c} \begin{array}{ccccccccc} x_1 & x_2 & x_3 & x_4 & s_1 & s_2 & s_3 & s_4 & P \end{array} \\ \left[\begin{array}{ccccccccc|c} -3 & 0 & 1 & 0 & 1 & 0 & 0 & 0 & 0 & 20 \\ 2 & 0 & 0 & 1 & 0 & 1 & 0 & 0 & 0 & 24 \\ 0 & 3 & 1 & 0 & 0 & 0 & 1 & 0 & 0 & 28 \\ 0 & -3 & 0 & 1 & 0 & 0 & 0 & 1 & 0 & 24 \\ -1 & -2 & -3 & -4 & 0 & 0 & 0 & 0 & 1 & 0 \end{array}\right] \begin{array}{c} s_1 \\ s_2 \\ s_3 \\ s_4 \\ P \end{array} \end{array}$$

$s_1 = 20 + 3x_1 - x_3$

$s_2 = 24 - 2x_1 - x_4$

$s_3 = 28 + 3x_2 - x_3$

$s_4 = 24 + 3x_2 - x_4$

$P = x_1 + 2x_2 + 3x_3 + 4x_4$

$$\left[\begin{array}{ccccccccc|c} -3 & 0 & 1 & 0 & 1 & 0 & 0 & 0 & 0 & 20 \\ 1 & 0 & 0 & \frac{1}{2} & 0 & \frac{1}{2} & 0 & 0 & 0 & 12 \\ 0 & -3 & 1 & 0 & 0 & 0 & 1 & 0 & 0 & 28 \\ 0 & -3 & 0 & 1 & 0 & 0 & 0 & 1 & 0 & 24 \\ -1 & -2 & -3 & -4 & 0 & 0 & 0 & 0 & 1 & 0 \end{array}\right]$$

$$\left[\begin{array}{ccccccccc|c} 0 & 0 & 1 & \frac{3}{2} & 1 & \frac{3}{2} & 0 & 0 & 0 & 56 \\ 1 & 0 & 0 & \frac{1}{2} & 0 & \frac{1}{2} & 0 & 0 & 0 & 12 \\ 0 & -3 & 1 & 0 & 0 & 0 & 1 & 0 & 0 & 28 \\ 0 & -3 & 0 & 1 & 0 & 0 & 0 & 1 & 0 & 24 \\ 0 & -2 & -3 & -\frac{7}{2} & 0 & \frac{1}{2} & 0 & 0 & 1 & 12 \end{array}\right] \begin{array}{c} s_1 \\ x_1 \\ s_3 \\ s_4 \\ P \end{array}$$

$s_1 = 56 - x_3 - \frac{3}{2}x_4 - \frac{3}{2}s_2$ $\qquad s_4 = 24 + 3x_2 - x_4$

$x_1 = 12 = \frac{1}{2}x_4 - \frac{1}{2}s_2$ $\qquad P = 12 + 2x_2 + 3x_3 + \frac{7}{2}x_4 - \frac{1}{2}$

$s_3 = 28 + 3x_2 - x_3$

Exercise 4.2 (page 170)

1. (b) Requires additional pivoting; the pivot element is in row 1, column 1.
3. (a) Final tableau; $P = \frac{256}{7}$; $x_1 = \frac{32}{7}$, $x_2 = 0$
5. (c) No solution; all the entries in the pivot column are negative.

7.

$$\begin{array}{c} \begin{array}{cccc} x_1 & x_2 & s_1 & s_2 \end{array} \\ \left[\begin{array}{cccc|c} 2 & \underline{3} & 1 & 0 & 12 \\ 3 & 1 & 0 & 1 & 12 \\ -5 & -7 & 0 & 0 & 0 \end{array}\right] \begin{array}{c} s_1 \\ s_2 \\ \ \end{array} \end{array}$$

$$\left[\begin{array}{cccc|c} \frac{2}{3} & 1 & \frac{1}{3} & 0 & 4 \\ \underline{\frac{7}{3}} & 0 & -\frac{1}{3} & 1 & 8 \\ -\frac{1}{3} & 0 & \frac{7}{3} & 0 & 28 \end{array}\right] \begin{array}{c} x_2 \\ s_2 \\ \ \end{array}$$

$\downarrow$

$$\begin{array}{c} \begin{array}{cccc} x_1 & x_2 & s_1 & s_2 \end{array} \\ \left[\begin{array}{cccc|c} 0 & 1 & \frac{3}{7} & -\frac{2}{7} & \frac{12}{7} \\ 1 & 0 & -\frac{1}{7} & \frac{3}{7} & \frac{24}{7} \\ 0 & 0 & \frac{16}{7} & \frac{1}{7} & \frac{204}{7} \end{array}\right] \begin{array}{c} x_2 \\ x_1 \\ \ \end{array} \end{array}$$

$P = \frac{204}{7}$, $x_1 = \frac{24}{7}$, $x_2 = \frac{12}{7}$

9.

$$\begin{array}{c} \begin{array}{cccc} x_1 & x_2 & s_1 & s_2 \end{array} \\ \left[\begin{array}{cccc|c} 1 & \underline{2} & 1 & 0 & 2 \\ 2 & 1 & 0 & 1 & 2 \\ -5 & -7 & 0 & 0 & 0 \end{array}\right] \begin{array}{c} s_1 \\ s_2 \\ \ \end{array} \end{array}$$

$$\left[\begin{array}{cccc|c} \frac{1}{2} & 1 & \frac{1}{2} & 0 & 1 \\ \underline{\frac{3}{2}} & 0 & -\frac{1}{2} & 1 & 1 \\ -\frac{3}{2} & 0 & \frac{7}{2} & 0 & 7 \end{array}\right] \begin{array}{c} x_2 \\ s_2 \\ \ \end{array}$$

$\downarrow$

$$\begin{array}{c} \begin{array}{cccc} x_1 & x_2 & s_1 & s_2 \end{array} \\ \left[\begin{array}{cccc|c} 0 & 1 & \frac{2}{3} & -\frac{1}{3} & \frac{2}{3} \\ 1 & 0 & -\frac{1}{3} & \frac{2}{3} & \frac{2}{3} \\ 0 & 0 & 3 & 1 & 8 \end{array}\right] \begin{array}{c} x_2 \\ x_1 \\ \ \end{array} \end{array}$$

$P = 8$, $x_1 = \frac{2}{3}$, $x_2 = \frac{2}{3}$

11.

$$\begin{array}{ccccc} x_1 & x_2 & s_1 & s_2 & s_3 \end{array}$$

$$\left[\begin{array}{ccccc|c} 1 & 1 & 1 & 0 & 0 & 2 \\ 2 & 3 & 0 & 1 & 0 & 12 \\ 3 & 1 & 0 & 0 & 1 & 12 \\ -3 & -1 & 0 & 0 & 0 & 0 \end{array}\right] \begin{array}{c} s_1 \\ s_2 \\ s_3 \\ \end{array}$$

$$\left[\begin{array}{ccccc|c} 1 & 1 & 1 & 0 & 0 & 2 \\ 0 & 1 & -2 & 1 & 0 & 8 \\ 0 & -2 & -3 & 0 & 1 & 6 \\ 0 & 2 & 3 & 0 & 0 & 6 \end{array}\right] \begin{array}{c} x_1 \\ s_2 \\ s_3 \\ \end{array}$$

$P = 6,\ x_1 = 2, x_2 = 0, x_3 = 0$

13.

$$\begin{array}{ccccc} x_1 & x_2 & x_3 & s_1 & s_2 \end{array}$$

$$\left[\begin{array}{ccccc|c} -2 & 1 & -2 & 1 & 0 & 4 \\ \underline{1} & -2 & 1 & 0 & 1 & 2 \\ -2 & -1 & -1 & 0 & 0 & 0 \end{array}\right] \begin{array}{c} s_1 \\ s_2 \\ \\ \end{array}$$

$$\left[\begin{array}{ccccc|c} 0 & -3 & 0 & 1 & 2 & 8 \\ 1 & -2 & 1 & 0 & 1 & 2 \\ 0 & -5 & 1 & 0 & 2 & 4 \end{array}\right] \begin{array}{c} s_1 \\ x_1 \\ \\ \end{array}$$

No solution, since all the ratios for column 2 are negative.

15.

$$\begin{array}{ccccc} x_1 & x_2 & x_3 & s_1 & s_2 \end{array}$$

$$\left[\begin{array}{ccccc|c} 1 & 2 & 1 & 1 & 0 & 25 \\ 3 & 2 & \underline{3} & 0 & 1 & 30 \\ -2 & -1 & -3 & 0 & 0 & 0 \end{array}\right] \begin{array}{c} s_1 \\ s_2 \\ \\ \end{array}$$

$$\left[\begin{array}{ccccc|c} 0 & \frac{4}{3} & 0 & 1 & -\frac{1}{3} & 15 \\ 1 & \frac{2}{3} & 1 & 0 & \frac{1}{3} & 10 \\ 1 & 1 & 0 & 0 & 1 & 30 \end{array}\right] \begin{array}{c} s_1 \\ x_3 \\ \\ \end{array}$$

$P = 30,\ \ x_1 = 0,\ \ x_2 = 0,\ \ x_3 = 10$

17.

$$\begin{array}{ccccccc} x_1 & x_2 & x_3 & x_4 & s_1 & s_2 & s_3 \end{array}$$

$$\left[\begin{array}{ccccccc|c} 2 & 1 & 2 & 3 & 1 & 0 & 0 & 12 \\ 0 & \underline{2} & 1 & 2 & 0 & 1 & 0 & 20 \\ 2 & 1 & 4 & 0 & 0 & 0 & 1 & 16 \\ -2 & -4 & -1 & -1 & 0 & 0 & 0 & 0 \end{array}\right]$$

$$\left[\begin{array}{ccccccc|c} \underline{2} & 0 & \frac{3}{2} & 2 & 1 & -\frac{1}{2} & 0 & 2 \\ 0 & 1 & \frac{1}{2} & 1 & 0 & \frac{1}{2} & 0 & 10 \\ 2 & 0 & \frac{7}{2} & -1 & 0 & -\frac{1}{2} & 1 & 6 \\ -2 & 0 & 1 & 3 & 0 & 2 & 0 & 40 \end{array}\right] \begin{array}{c} s_1 \\ x_2 \\ s_3 \\ \\ \end{array}$$

$$\left[\begin{array}{ccccccc|c} 1 & 0 & \frac{3}{4} & 1 & \frac{1}{2} & -\frac{1}{4} & 0 & 1 \\ 0 & 1 & \frac{1}{2} & 1 & 0 & \frac{1}{2} & 0 & 10 \\ 0 & 0 & 2 & -3 & -1 & 0 & 1 & 4 \\ 0 & 0 & \frac{5}{2} & 5 & 1 & \frac{3}{2} & 0 & 42 \end{array}\right] \begin{array}{c} x_1 \\ x_2 \\ s_3 \\ \end{array}$$

$P = 42,\ x_1 = 1,\ x_2 = 10,\ x_3 = 0,\ x_4 = 0$

19.

$$\begin{array}{cccccc} x_1 & x_2 & x_3 & s_1 & s_2 & s_3 \end{array}$$

$$\left[\begin{array}{cccccc|c} 1 & 2 & 4 & 1 & 0 & 0 & 20 \\ 2 & 4 & 4 & 0 & 1 & 0 & 60 \\ 3 & 4 & 1 & 0 & 0 & 1 & 90 \\ -2 & -1 & -1 & 0 & 0 & 0 & 0 \end{array}\right] \begin{array}{c} s_1 \\ s_2 \\ s_3 \\ \end{array}$$

$$\downarrow$$

$$\left[\begin{array}{cccccc|c} 1 & 2 & 4 & 1 & 0 & 0 & 20 \\ 0 & 0 & -4 & -2 & 1 & 0 & 20 \\ 0 & -2 & -11 & -3 & 0 & 1 & 30 \\ 0 & 3 & 7 & 2 & 0 & 1 & 40 \end{array}\right] \begin{array}{c} x_1 \\ s_2 \\ s_3 \\ \end{array}$$

$P = 40,\ x_1 = 20,\ x_2 = 0,\ x_3 = 0$

21.

$$\begin{array}{cccccc} x_1 & x_2 & x_3 & x_4 & s_1 & s_2 \end{array}$$

$$\left[\begin{array}{cccccc|c} 5 & 0 & \underline{4} & 6 & 1 & 0 & 20 \\ 4 & 2 & 2 & 8 & 0 & 1 & 40 \\ -1 & -2 & -4 & -1 & 0 & 0 & 0 \end{array}\right] \begin{array}{c} s_1 \\ s_2 \\ \end{array}$$

$$\downarrow$$

$$\left[\begin{array}{cccccc|c} \frac{5}{4} & 0 & 1 & \frac{3}{2} & \frac{1}{4} & 0 & 5 \\ -\frac{3}{2} & \underline{2} & 0 & 5 & -\frac{1}{2} & 1 & 30 \\ 4 & -2 & 0 & 5 & 1 & 0 & 20 \end{array}\right] \begin{array}{c} x_3 \\ s_2 \\ \end{array}$$

$$\downarrow$$

$$\left[\begin{array}{cccccc|c} \frac{5}{4} & 0 & 1 & \frac{3}{2} & \frac{1}{4} & 0 & 5 \\ -\frac{3}{4} & 1 & 0 & \frac{5}{2} & -\frac{1}{4} & \frac{1}{4} & 15 \\ \frac{5}{2} & 0 & 0 & 10 & \frac{1}{2} & \frac{1}{2} & 50 \end{array}\right]\begin{array}{c} x_3 \\ s_2 \\ \end{array}$$

$P = 50,\ x_1 = 0,\ x_2 = 15,\ x_3 = 5,\ x_4 = 0$

23. Let x_1 = number of cans of Can I, x_2 = number of cans of Can II, x_3 = number of cans of Can III

Maximize $P = 8x_1 + 7x_2 + 5x_3$ subject to $3x_1 + 4x_2 + 5x_3 \leq 500$, $x_1 + \frac{1}{2}x_2 \leq 100$, $x_1 + \frac{1}{2}x_2 \leq 50$, $x_1 \geq 0$, $x_2 \geq 0$, $x_3 \geq 0$

$$\begin{array}{cccccc} x_1 & x_2 & x_3 & s_1 & s_2 & s_3 \end{array}$$

$$\left[\begin{array}{cccccc|c} 3 & 4 & 5 & 1 & 0 & 0 & 500 \\ 1 & \frac{1}{2} & 0 & 0 & 1 & 0 & 100 \\ 1 & \frac{1}{2} & 0 & 0 & 0 & 1 & 50 \\ -8 & -7 & -5 & 0 & 0 & 0 & 0 \end{array}\right]$$

$$\downarrow$$

$$\left[\begin{array}{cccccc|c} 0 & \frac{5}{2} & 5 & 1 & 0 & -3 & 350 \\ 0 & 0 & 0 & 0 & 1 & -1 & 50 \\ 1 & \frac{1}{2} & 0 & 0 & 0 & 1 & 50 \\ 0 & -3 & -5 & 0 & 0 & 8 & 400 \end{array}\right]$$

$$\left[\begin{array}{cccccc|c} 0 & \frac{1}{2} & 1 & \frac{1}{5} & 0 & -\frac{3}{5} & 70 \\ 0 & 0 & 0 & 0 & 1 & -1 & 50 \\ 1 & \frac{1}{2} & 0 & 0 & 0 & 1 & 50 \\ 0 & -\frac{1}{2} & 0 & 1 & 0 & 5 & 750 \end{array}\right]$$

$$\left[\begin{array}{cccccc|c} -1 & 0 & 1 & \frac{1}{5} & 0 & -\frac{8}{5} & 20 \\ 0 & 0 & 0 & 0 & 1 & -1 & 50 \\ 2 & 1 & 0 & 0 & 0 & 2 & 100 \\ 1 & 0 & 0 & 1 & 0 & 6 & 800 \end{array}\right]$$

$P = 800,\ x_1 = 0,\ x_2 = 100,\ x_3 = 20$

25. Let x_1 = Number of television console cabinets, x_2 = Number of stereo system cabinets, x_3 = Number of radio cabinets.
Maximize $P = 10x_1 + 25x_2 + 3x_3$ subject to $3x_1 + 10x_2 + x_3 \le 30{,}000$, $5x_1 + 8x_2 + x_3 \le 40{,}000$, $0.1x_1 + 0.6x_2 + 0.1x_3 \le 120$.

$$\begin{array}{c} \\ \\ \\ \\ \\ \end{array}\begin{array}{cccccc|c} x_1 & x_2 & x_3 & s_1 & s_2 & s_3 & \end{array}$$

$$\left[\begin{array}{cccccc|c} 3 & 10 & 1 & 1 & 0 & 0 & 30{,}000 \\ 5 & 8 & 1 & 0 & 1 & 0 & 40{,}000 \\ 0.1 & \underline{0.6} & 0.1 & 0 & 0 & 1 & 120 \\ -10 & -25 & -3 & 0 & 0 & 0 & 0 \end{array}\right]\begin{array}{l} s_1 \\ s_2 \\ s_3 \\ \\ \end{array}$$

$$\left[\begin{array}{cccccc|c} \frac{4}{3} & 0 & -\frac{2}{3} & 1 & 0 & -\frac{50}{3} & 28{,}000 \\ \frac{11}{3} & 0 & -\frac{1}{3} & 0 & 1 & -\frac{40}{3} & 38{,}400 \\ \underline{\frac{1}{6}} & 1 & \frac{1}{6} & 0 & 0 & \frac{5}{3} & 200 \\ -\frac{35}{6} & 0 & \frac{7}{6} & 0 & 0 & \frac{125}{3} & 5{,}000 \end{array}\right]\begin{array}{l} s_1 \\ s_2 \\ x_2 \\ \\ \end{array}$$

$$\left[\begin{array}{cccccc|c} 0 & -8 & -2 & 1 & 0 & -30 & 26{,}400 \\ 0 & -22 & -4 & 0 & 1 & -50 & 34{,}000 \\ 1 & 6 & 1 & 0 & 0 & 10 & 1{,}200 \\ 0 & 35 & 7 & 0 & 0 & 100 & 12{,}000 \end{array}\right]\begin{array}{l} s_1 \\ s_2 \\ x_1 \\ \\ \end{array}$$

$P = \$12{,}000$, $x_1 = 1200$, $x_2 = 0$, $x_3 = 0$

27. Let x_1 = number of TVs made in Chicago,
x_2 = number of TVs made in New York,
x_3 = number of TVs made in Denver.
Maximize $P = 50x_1 + 80x_2 + 40x_3$ subject to $x_1 + x_2 + x_3 \le 400$, $20x_1 + 20x_2 + 40x_3 \le 10{,}000$, $6x_1 + 8x_2 + 4x_3 \le 3000$, $x_1 \ge 0$, $x_2 \ge 0$, $x_3 \ge 0$

$$\begin{array}{cccccc|c} x_1 & x_2 & x_3 & s_1 & s_2 & s_3 & \end{array}$$

$$\left[\begin{array}{cccccc|c} 1 & 1 & 1 & 1 & 0 & 0 & 400 \\ 20 & 20 & 40 & 0 & 1 & 0 & 10{,}000 \\ 6 & \underline{8} & 4 & 0 & 0 & 1 & 3{,}000 \\ -50 & -80 & -40 & 0 & 0 & 0 & 0 \end{array}\right]\begin{array}{l} s_1 \\ s_2 \\ s_3 \\ \\ \end{array}$$

$$\left[\begin{array}{cccccc|c} -\frac{1}{2} & 0 & \frac{1}{2} & 1 & 0 & -\frac{1}{8} & 25 \\ -10 & 0 & 30 & 0 & 1 & \frac{5}{2} & 2{,}500 \\ \frac{3}{2} & 1 & \frac{1}{2} & 0 & 0 & \frac{1}{8} & 375 \\ 70 & 0 & 0 & 0 & 0 & 10 & 30{,}000 \end{array}\right]\begin{array}{l} s_1 \\ s_2 \\ x_2 \\ \end{array}$$

$P = \$30{,}000 \quad x_1 = 0, \; x_2 = 375, \; x_3 = 0$

Exercise 4.3 (page 184)

1. The minimum problem is in standard form.
3. Since the coefficient of x_2 in the objective function is negative, the minimum problem is not in standard form.
5. Since the first constraint is not written with a $\geq$ sign, the minimum problem is not in standard form.

7.

$$\left[\begin{array}{cc|c} 1 & 1 & 2 \\ 2 & 3 & 6 \\ 2 & 3 & 0 \end{array}\right]\left[\begin{array}{cc|c} 1 & 2 & 2 \\ 1 & 3 & 3 \\ 2 & 6 & 0 \end{array}\right]$$

Dual problem:
Maximize $P = 2y_1 + 6y_2$ subject to $y_1 + 2y_2 \leq 2$, $y_1 + 3y_2 \leq 3$, $y_1 \geq 0$, $y_2 \geq 0$.

9.

$$\left[\begin{array}{ccc|c} 1 & 1 & 1 & 5 \\ 2 & 1 & 0 & 4 \\ 3 & 1 & 1 & 0 \end{array}\right]; \left[\begin{array}{cc|c} 1 & 2 & 3 \\ 1 & 1 & 1 \\ 1 & 0 & 1 \\ 5 & 4 & 0 \end{array}\right]$$

Dual problem;
Maximize $P = 5y_1 + 4y_2$ subject to
$y_1 + 2y_2 \leq 3$, $y_1 + y_2 \leq 1$, $y_1 \leq 1$, $y_1 \geq 0$, $y_2 \geq 0$.

11.

$$\left[\begin{array}{cc|c} 1 & 1 & 2 \\ 2 & 6 & 6 \\ 6 & 3 & 0 \end{array}\right]; \left[\begin{array}{cc|c} 1 & 2 & 6 \\ 1 & 6 & 3 \\ 2 & 6 & 0 \end{array}\right]$$

Dual problem:
Maximize $P = 2y_1 + 6y_2$ subject to
$y_1 + 2y_2 \leq 6$, $y_1 + 6y_2 \leq 3$, $y_1 \geq 0$, $y_2 \geq 0$.

$$\begin{array}{c} \\ \\ \\ \end{array}\begin{array}{cc|cc|c} y_1 & y_2 & s_1 & s_2 & \end{array}$$

$$\left[\begin{array}{cc|cc|c} 1 & 2 & 1 & 0 & 6 \\ 1 & \underline{6} & 0 & 1 & 3 \\ -2 & -6 & 0 & 0 & 0 \end{array}\right]\begin{array}{c} s_1 \\ s_2 \\ \\ \end{array}$$

$$\left[\begin{array}{cc|cc|c} \frac{2}{3} & 0 & 1 & -\frac{1}{3} & 5 \\ \underline{\frac{1}{6}} & 1 & 0 & \frac{1}{6} & \frac{1}{2} \\ -1 & 0 & 0 & 1 & 3 \end{array}\right]\begin{array}{c} s_1 \\ y_2 \\ \\ \end{array}$$

$$\left[\begin{array}{cc|cc|c} 0 & -4 & 1 & -1 & 3 \\ 1 & 6 & 0 & 1 & 3 \\ 0 & 6 & 0 & 2 & 6 \end{array}\right]\begin{array}{c} s_1 \\ y_1 \\ \\ \end{array}$$

$C = 6,\ x_1 = 0,\ x_2 = 2$

13.

$$\left[\begin{array}{cc|c} 1 & 1 & 4 \\ 3 & 4 & 12 \\ 6 & 3 & 0 \end{array}\right];\ \left[\begin{array}{cc|c} 1 & 3 & 6 \\ 1 & 4 & 3 \\ 4 & 12 & 0 \end{array}\right]$$

Dual problem:
Maximize $P = 4y_1 + 12y_2$ subject to
$y_1 + 3y_2 \le 6,\ y_1 + 4y_2 \le 3,\ y_1 \ge 0,\ y_2 \ge 0.$

$$\begin{array}{cc|cc|c} y_1 & y_2 & s_1 & s_2 & \end{array}$$

$$\left[\begin{array}{cc|cc|c} 1 & 3 & 1 & 0 & 6 \\ 1 & \underline{4} & 0 & 1 & 3 \\ -4 & -12 & 0 & 0 & 0 \end{array}\right]\begin{array}{c} s_1 \\ s_2 \\ \\ \end{array}$$

$$\left[\begin{array}{cc|cc|c} \frac{1}{4} & 0 & 1 & -\frac{3}{4} & \frac{15}{4} \\ \underline{\frac{1}{4}} & 1 & 0 & \frac{1}{4} & \frac{3}{4} \\ -1 & 0 & 0 & 3 & 9 \end{array}\right]\begin{array}{c} s_1 \\ y_2 \\ \\ \end{array}$$

$$\left[\begin{array}{cc|cc|c} 0 & -1 & 1 & -1 & 3 \\ 1 & 4 & 0 & 1 & 3 \\ 0 & 4 & 0 & 4 & 12 \end{array}\right]\begin{array}{c} s_1 \\ y_1 \\ \\ \end{array}$$

$C = 12,\ x_1 = 0,\ x_2 = 4$

15.

$$\left[\begin{array}{ccc|c} 1 & -3 & 4 & 12 \\ 3 & 1 & 2 & 10 \\ 1 & -1 & -1 & -8 \\ 1 & 2 & 1 & 0 \end{array}\right]; \left[\begin{array}{ccc|c} 1 & 3 & 1 & 1 \\ -3 & 1 & -1 & 2 \\ 4 & 2 & -1 & 1 \\ 12 & 10 & -8 & 0 \end{array}\right]$$

Dual problem:
Maximize $P = 12y_1 + 10y_2 - 8y_3$
subject to $y_1 + 3y_2 + y_3 \leq 1$, $-3y_1 + y_2 - y_3 \leq 2$, $4y_1 + 2y_2 - y_3 \leq 1$, $y_1 \geq 0$, $y_2 \geq 0$, $y_3 \geq 0$.

$$\begin{array}{c} \\ s_1 \\ s_2 \\ s_3 \\ \\ \end{array} \begin{array}{c} \begin{array}{cccccc} y_1 & y_2 & y_3 & s_1 & s_2 & s_3 \end{array} \\ \left[\begin{array}{ccc|ccc|c} 1 & 3 & 1 & 1 & 0 & 0 & 1 \\ -3 & 1 & -1 & 0 & 1 & 0 & 2 \\ \underline{4} & 2 & -1 & 0 & 0 & 1 & 1 \\ -12 & -10 & 8 & 0 & 0 & 0 & 0 \end{array}\right] \end{array}$$

$$\begin{array}{cccccc} y_1 & y_2 & y_3 & s_1 & s_2 & s_3 \end{array}$$
$$\left[\begin{array}{ccc|ccc|c} 0 & \underline{\frac{5}{2}} & \frac{5}{4} & 1 & 0 & -\frac{1}{4} & \frac{3}{4} \\ 0 & \frac{5}{2} & -\frac{7}{4} & 0 & 1 & \frac{3}{4} & \frac{11}{4} \\ 1 & \frac{1}{2} & -\frac{1}{4} & 0 & 0 & \frac{1}{4} & \frac{1}{4} \\ 0 & -4 & 5 & 0 & 0 & 3 & 3 \end{array}\right] \begin{array}{c} s_1 \\ s_2 \\ y_1 \\ \\ \end{array}$$

$$\left[\begin{array}{ccc|ccc|c} 0 & 1 & \frac{1}{2} & \frac{2}{5} & 0 & -\frac{1}{10} & \frac{3}{10} \\ 0 & 0 & -3 & -1 & 1 & 1 & 2 \\ 1 & 0 & -\frac{1}{2} & -\frac{1}{5} & 0 & \frac{3}{10} & \frac{1}{10} \\ 0 & 0 & 7 & \frac{8}{5} & 0 & \frac{13}{5} & \frac{21}{5} \end{array}\right] \begin{array}{c} y_2 \\ s_2 \\ y_1 \\ \\ \end{array}$$

$C = \frac{21}{5}$, $x_1 = \frac{8}{5}$, $x_2 = 0$, $x_3 = \frac{13}{5}$

17. Let x_1 = Amount of Food I, x_2 = Amount of Food II, x_3 = Amount of Food III. Minimize $C = 2x_1 + x_2 + 3x_3$ subject to $2x_1 + 3x_2 + 4x_3 \geq 20$, $4x_1 + 2x_2 + 2x_3 \geq 15$, $x_1 \geq 0$, $x_2 \geq 0$, $x_3 \geq 0$.

$$\begin{array}{ccc} x_1 & x_2 & x_3 \end{array}$$

$$\left[\begin{array}{ccc|c} 2 & 3 & 4 & 20 \\ 4 & 2 & 2 & 15 \\ 2 & 1 & 3 & 0 \end{array}\right]; \quad \left[\begin{array}{cc|c} 2 & 4 & 2 \\ 3 & 2 & 1 \\ 4 & 2 & 3 \\ 20 & 15 & 0 \end{array}\right]$$

Dual problem:
Maximize $P = 20y_1 + 15y_2$ subject to
$2y_1 + 4y_2 \le 2$, $3y_1 + 2y_2 \le 1$, $4y_1 + 2y_2 \le 3$,
$y_1 \ge 0$, $y_2 \ge 0$.

$$\begin{array}{ccccc} y_1 & y_2 & s_1 & s_2 & s_3 \end{array}$$

$$\left[\begin{array}{cc|ccc|c} 2 & 4 & 1 & 0 & 0 & 2 \\ \underline{3} & 2 & 0 & 1 & 0 & 1 \\ 4 & 2 & 0 & 0 & 1 & 3 \\ -20 & -15 & 0 & 0 & 0 & 0 \end{array}\right] \begin{array}{c} s_1 \\ s_2 \\ s_3 \\ \end{array}$$

$$\left[\begin{array}{cc|ccc|c} 0 & \frac{8}{3} & 1 & -\frac{2}{3} & 0 & \frac{4}{3} \\ 1 & \underline{\frac{2}{3}} & 0 & \frac{1}{3} & 0 & \frac{1}{3} \\ 0 & -\frac{2}{3} & 0 & -\frac{4}{3} & 1 & \frac{5}{3} \\ 0 & -\frac{5}{3} & 0 & \frac{20}{3} & 0 & \frac{20}{3} \end{array}\right] \begin{array}{c} s_1 \\ y_1 \\ s_3 \\ \end{array}$$

$$\left[\begin{array}{cc|ccc|c} -4 & 0 & 1 & -2 & 0 & 0 \\ \frac{3}{2} & 1 & 0 & \frac{1}{2} & 0 & \frac{1}{2} \\ 1 & 0 & 0 & -1 & 1 & 2 \\ \frac{5}{2} & 0 & 0 & \frac{15}{2} & 0 & \frac{15}{2} \end{array}\right] \begin{array}{c} s_1 \\ y_2 \\ s_3 \\ \end{array}$$

$C = \$7.50$, $x_1 = 0$, $x_2 = 7.5$, $x_3 = 0$

Exercise 4.4 (page 200)

1.

$$\begin{array}{ccccc} x_1 & x_2 & s_1 & s_2 & s_3 \end{array}$$

$$\left[\begin{array}{ccccc|c} 1 & 1 & 1 & 0 & 0 & 12 \\ \underline{-5} & -2 & 0 & 1 & 0 & -36 \\ -7 & -4 & 0 & 0 & 1 & -14 \\ -3 & -4 & 0 & 0 & 0 & 0 \end{array}\right] \begin{array}{c} s_1 \\ s_2 \\ s_3 \\ \end{array}$$

$$\left[\begin{array}{ccccc|c} 0 & \frac{3}{5} & 1 & \frac{1}{5} & 0 & \frac{24}{5} \\ 1 & \frac{2}{5} & 0 & -\frac{1}{5} & 0 & \frac{36}{5} \\ 0 & -\frac{6}{5} & 0 & -\frac{7}{5} & 1 & \frac{182}{5} \\ 0 & -\frac{14}{5} & 0 & -\frac{3}{5} & 0 & \frac{108}{5} \end{array}\right] \begin{array}{l} s_1 \\ x_1 \\ s_3 \\ \end{array}$$

$$\left[\begin{array}{ccccc|c} 0 & 1 & \frac{5}{3} & \frac{1}{3} & 0 & 8 \\ 1 & 0 & -\frac{2}{3} & -\frac{1}{3} & 0 & 4 \\ 0 & 0 & 2 & -1 & 1 & 46 \\ 0 & 0 & \frac{14}{3} & \frac{1}{3} & 0 & 44 \end{array}\right] \begin{array}{l} x_2 \\ x_1 \\ s_3 \\ \end{array}$$

$P = 44,\ x_1 = 4,\ x_2 = 8$

3.

$$\begin{array}{cccccc} x_1 & x_2 & x_3 & s_1 & s_2 & s_3 \end{array}$$

$$\left[\begin{array}{cccccc|c} 1 & 3 & 1 & 1 & 0 & 0 & 9 \\ -2 & -3 & 1 & 0 & 1 & 0 & -2 \\ \underline{-3} & 2 & -1 & 0 & 0 & 1 & -5 \\ -3 & -2 & 1 & 0 & 0 & 0 & 0 \end{array}\right] \begin{array}{l} s_1 \\ s_2 \\ s_3 \\ \end{array}$$

$$\downarrow$$

$$\left[\begin{array}{cccccc|c} 0 & \underline{\frac{11}{3}} & \frac{2}{3} & 1 & 0 & \frac{1}{3} & \frac{22}{3} \\ 0 & -\frac{13}{3} & \frac{5}{3} & 0 & 1 & -\frac{2}{3} & \frac{4}{3} \\ 1 & -\frac{2}{3} & \frac{1}{3} & 0 & 0 & -\frac{1}{3} & \frac{5}{3} \\ 0 & -4 & 2 & 0 & 0 & -1 & 5 \end{array}\right] \begin{array}{l} s_1 \\ s_2 \\ x_1 \\ \end{array}$$

$$\downarrow$$

$$\left[\begin{array}{cccccc|c} 0 & 1 & \frac{2}{11} & \frac{3}{11} & 0 & \frac{1}{11} & 2 \\ 0 & 0 & \frac{27}{11} & \frac{13}{11} & 1 & -\frac{3}{11} & 10 \\ 1 & 0 & \frac{15}{33} & \frac{2}{11} & 0 & -\frac{3}{11} & 3 \\ 0 & 0 & \frac{30}{11} & \frac{12}{11} & 0 & -\frac{7}{11} & 13 \end{array}\right] \begin{array}{l} x_2 \\ s_2 \\ x_1 \\ \end{array}$$

$$\left[\begin{array}{cccccc|c} 0 & 11 & 2 & 3 & 0 & 1 & 22 \\ 0 & 3 & 3 & 2 & 1 & 0 & 16 \\ 1 & 3 & 1 & 1 & 0 & 0 & 9 \\ 0 & 7 & 4 & 3 & 0 & 0 & 27 \end{array}\right] \begin{array}{c} s_3 \\ s_2 \\ x_1 \\ \end{array}$$

$P = 27,\ x_1 = 9,\ x_2 = 0,\ x_3 = 0$

5.

$$\begin{array}{ccccccc} x_1 & x_2 & x_3 & s_1 & s_2 & s_3 & s_4 \end{array}$$

$$\left[\begin{array}{ccccccc|c} -3 & -5 & -3 & 1 & 0 & 0 & 0 & -20 \\ -1 & -3 & -2 & 0 & 1 & 0 & 0 & -9 \\ \underline{-6} & -2 & -5 & 0 & 0 & 1 & 0 & -30 \\ 1 & 1 & 1 & 0 & 0 & 0 & 1 & 10 \\ 6 & 8 & 1 & 0 & 0 & 0 & 0 & 0 \end{array}\right] \begin{array}{c} s_1 \\ s_2 \\ s_3 \\ s_4 \\ \end{array}$$

$$\downarrow$$

$$\left[\begin{array}{ccccccc|c} 0 & \underline{-4} & -\frac{1}{2} & 1 & 0 & -\frac{1}{2} & 0 & -5 \\ 0 & -\frac{8}{3} & -\frac{7}{6} & 0 & 1 & -\frac{1}{6} & 0 & -4 \\ 1 & \frac{1}{3} & \frac{5}{6} & 0 & 0 & -\frac{1}{6} & 0 & 5 \\ 0 & \frac{2}{3} & \frac{1}{6} & 0 & 0 & \frac{1}{6} & 1 & 5 \\ 0 & 6 & -4 & 0 & 0 & 1 & 0 & -30 \end{array}\right] \begin{array}{c} s_1 \\ s_2 \\ x_1 \\ s_4 \\ \end{array}$$

$$\left[\begin{array}{ccccccc|c} 0 & 1 & \frac{1}{8} & -\frac{1}{4} & 0 & \frac{1}{8} & 0 & \frac{5}{4} \\ 0 & 0 & \underline{-\frac{5}{6}} & -\frac{2}{3} & 1 & \frac{1}{6} & 0 & -\frac{2}{3} \\ 1 & 0 & \frac{19}{24} & \frac{1}{12} & 0 & -\frac{5}{24} & 0 & \frac{55}{12} \\ 0 & 0 & \frac{1}{12} & \frac{1}{6} & 0 & \frac{1}{12} & 1 & \frac{25}{6} \\ 0 & 0 & -\frac{19}{4} & \frac{3}{2} & 0 & \frac{1}{4} & 0 & -\frac{75}{2} \end{array}\right] \begin{array}{c} x_2 \\ s_2 \\ x_1 \\ s_4 \\ \end{array}$$

$$\downarrow$$

$$\left[\begin{array}{ccccccc|c} 0 & 1 & 0 & -\frac{7}{20} & \frac{3}{20} & \frac{3}{20} & 0 & \frac{23}{20} \\ 0 & 0 & \underline{1} & \frac{4}{5} & -\frac{6}{5} & -\frac{1}{5} & 0 & \frac{4}{5} \\ 1 & 0 & 0 & -\frac{11}{20} & \underline{\frac{19}{20}} & -\frac{1}{20} & 0 & \frac{79}{20} \\ 0 & 0 & 0 & \frac{1}{10} & \frac{1}{10} & \frac{1}{10} & 1 & \frac{41}{10} \\ 0 & 0 & 0 & \frac{53}{10} & -\frac{57}{10} & -\frac{7}{10} & 1 & -\frac{337}{10} \end{array}\right]$$

$$\downarrow$$

$$\left[\begin{array}{ccccccc|c} -\frac{3}{19} & 1 & 0 & -\frac{5}{19} & 0 & \underline{-\frac{3}{19}} & 0 & \frac{10}{19} \\ \frac{24}{19} & 0 & \underline{1} & \frac{2}{19} & 0 & -\frac{5}{19} & 0 & \frac{110}{19} \\ \frac{20}{19} & 0 & 0 & -\frac{11}{19} & \underline{1} & -\frac{1}{19} & 0 & \frac{79}{19} \\ -\frac{2}{19} & 0 & 0 & \frac{3}{19} & 0 & \frac{2}{19} & 1 & \frac{70}{19} \\ 6 & 0 & 0 & 2 & 0 & -1 & 1 & -10 \end{array}\right]$$

$$\left[\begin{array}{ccccccc|c} -1 & \frac{19}{3} & 0 & -\frac{5}{3} & 0 & \underline{1} & 0 & \frac{10}{3} \\ 1 & \frac{5}{3} & \underline{1} & -\frac{1}{3} & 0 & 0 & 0 & \frac{20}{3} \\ 1 & \frac{1}{3} & 0 & -\frac{2}{3} & \underline{1} & 0 & 0 & \frac{13}{3} \\ 0 & -\frac{2}{3} & 0 & \frac{1}{3} & 0 & 0 & 1 & \frac{10}{3} \\ 5 & \frac{19}{3} & 0 & \frac{1}{3} & 0 & 0 & 1 & -\frac{20}{3} \end{array}\right] \begin{array}{l} s_3 \\ x_3 \\ s_2 \\ s_4 \\ \\ \end{array}$$

$C = \frac{20}{3}$, $x_1 = 0$, $x_2 = 0$, $x_3 = \frac{20}{3}$

7.
$$\begin{array}{l} 2x_1 + x_2 \le 4 \\ x_1 + x_2 \le 3 \\ x_1 + x_2 \ge 3 \end{array} \quad \Rightarrow \quad \begin{array}{l} 2x_1 + x_2 + s_1 = 4 \\ x_1 + x_2 + s_2 = 3 \\ -x_1 - x_2 + s_3 = -3 \end{array}$$

$$\begin{array}{c} \begin{array}{ccccc} x_1 & x_2 & s_1 & s_2 & s_3 \end{array} \\ \left[\begin{array}{ccccc|c} 2 & 1 & 1 & 0 & 0 & 4 \\ 1 & 1 & 0 & 1 & 0 & 3 \\ \underline{-1} & -1 & 0 & 0 & 1 & -3 \\ -3 & -2 & 0 & 0 & 0 & 1 \end{array}\right] \begin{array}{l} s_1 \\ s_2 \\ s_3 \end{array} \end{array}$$

$$\left[\begin{array}{ccccc|c} 0 & \underline{-1} & 1 & 0 & 2 & -2 \\ 0 & 0 & 0 & 1 & 1 & 0 \\ \underline{1} & 1 & 0 & 0 & -1 & 3 \\ 0 & 1 & 0 & 0 & -3 & 9 \end{array}\right]\begin{array}{l} s_1 \\ s_2 \\ x_1 \\ \end{array}$$

$$\left[\begin{array}{ccccc|c} 0 & 1 & -1 & 0 & -2 & 2 \\ 0 & 0 & 0 & 1 & 1 & 0 \\ \underline{1} & 0 & 1 & 0 & \underline{1} & 1 \\ 0 & 0 & 1 & 0 & -1 & 7 \end{array}\right]\begin{array}{l} x_2 \\ s_2 \\ x_1 \\ \end{array}$$

$$\left[\begin{array}{ccccc|c} 2 & 1 & 1 & 0 & 0 & 4 \\ -1 & 0 & -1 & 1 & 0 & -1 \\ \underline{1} & 0 & 1 & 0 & \underline{1} & 1 \\ 1 & 0 & 2 & 0 & 0 & 8 \end{array}\right]\begin{array}{l} x_2 \\ s_2 \\ s_3 \\ \end{array}$$

$P = 8,\ x_1 = 0,\ x_2 = 4$

9. x_1 = number of units shipped from M_1 to A_1,
x_2 = number of units shipped from M_1 to A_2,
x_3 = number of units shipped from M_2 to A_1,
x_4 = number of units shipped from M_2 to A_2.

Minimize

$C = 400x_1 + 100x_2 + 200x_3 + 300x_4$ subject to the constraints

$$x_1 + x_2 \le 600$$
$$x_3 + x_4 \le 400$$
$$x_1 + x_3 \ge 500$$
$$x_2 + x_4 \ge 300$$

Maximize

$z = -C = -400x_1 - 100x_2 - 200x_3 - 300x_4$

$$x_1 + x_2 + s_1 = 600$$
$$x_3 + x_4 + s_2 = 40$$
$$-x_1 - x_3 + s_3 = -500$$
$$-x_2 - x_4 + s_4 = -300$$

$$\begin{array}{c} \\ s_1 \\ s_2 \\ s_3 \\ s_4 \end{array}\;
\begin{array}{cccccccc|c} x_1 & x_2 & x_3 & x_4 & s_1 & s_2 & s_3 & s_4 & \\ 1 & 1 & 0 & 0 & 1 & 0 & 0 & 0 & 600 \\ 0 & 0 & 1 & 1 & 0 & 1 & 0 & 0 & 400 \\ \underline{-1} & 0 & -1 & 0 & 0 & 0 & 1 & 0 & -500 \\ 0 & -1 & 0 & -1 & 0 & 0 & 0 & 1 & -300 \\ 400 & 100 & 200 & 300 & 0 & 0 & 0 & 0 & 0 \end{array}$$

$$\left[\begin{array}{cccccccc|c} 0 & 1 & -1 & 0 & 1 & 0 & 1 & 0 & 100 \\ 0 & 0 & 1 & 1 & 0 & 1 & 0 & 0 & 400 \\ 1 & 0 & 1 & 0 & 0 & 0 & -1 & 0 & 500 \\ 0 & \underline{-1} & 0 & -1 & 0 & 0 & 0 & 1 & -300 \\ 400 & 100 & 200 & 300 & 0 & 0 & 0 & 0 & 0 \end{array}\right]$$

$$\left[\begin{array}{cccccccc|c} 0 & 0 & \underline{-1} & -1 & 1 & 0 & 1 & 1 & -200 \\ 0 & 0 & 1 & 1 & 0 & 1 & 0 & 0 & 400 \\ 1 & 0 & 1 & 0 & 0 & 0 & -1 & 0 & 500 \\ 0 & 1 & 0 & 1 & 0 & 0 & 0 & -1 & 300 \\ 400 & 0 & 200 & 200 & 0 & 0 & 0 & 100 & -30{,}000 \end{array}\right]$$

$$\left[\begin{array}{cccccccc|c} 0 & 0 & 1 & 1 & -1 & 0 & -1 & -1 & 200 \\ 0 & 0 & 0 & 0 & 1 & 1 & 1 & 1 & 200 \\ 1 & 0 & 0 & -1 & 1 & 0 & 0 & 1 & 300 \\ 0 & 1 & 0 & 1 & 0 & 0 & 0 & -1 & 300 \\ 400 & 0 & 0 & 0 & 200 & 0 & 200 & 300 & -70{,}000 \end{array}\right]$$

$C = \$70{,}000$, $x_1 = 0$, $x_2 = 300$, $x_3 = 200$, $x_4 = 0$

Chapter Review

Review Exercises (page 202)

1.

$$\begin{array}{c} \\ s_1 \\ s_2 \\ s_3 \\ \end{array}\;
\begin{array}{cccccc|c} x & y & z & s_1 & s_2 & s_3 & \\ 5 & 5 & 10 & 1 & 0 & 0 & 1000 \\ 10 & 8 & 5 & 0 & 1 & 0 & 2000 \\ 10 & \underline{5} & 0 & 0 & 0 & 1 & 500 \\ -100 & -200 & -50 & 0 & 0 & 0 & 0 \end{array}$$

$$\left[\begin{array}{cccccc|c} -5 & 0 & \underline{10} & 1 & 0 & -1 & 500 \\ -6 & 0 & 5 & 0 & 1 & -\frac{8}{5} & 1200 \\ 2 & 1 & 0 & 0 & 0 & \frac{1}{5} & 100 \\ 300 & 0 & -50 & 0 & 0 & 40 & 20{,}000 \end{array}\right]$$

$$\left[\begin{array}{cccccc|c} -\frac{1}{2} & 0 & 1 & \frac{1}{10} & 0 & -\frac{1}{10} & 50 \\ -\frac{7}{2} & 0 & 0 & -\frac{1}{2} & 1 & -\frac{11}{10} & 950 \\ 2 & 1 & 0 & 0 & 0 & \frac{1}{5} & 100 \\ 325 & 0 & 0 & 5 & 0 & 30 & 22{,}500 \end{array}\right]$$

$P = 22{,}500$, $x = 0$, $y = 100$, $z = 50$

3.

$$\begin{array}{ccccc} x_1 & x_2 & x_3 & s_1 & s_2 \end{array}$$

$$\left[\begin{array}{ccccc|c} 2 & \underline{2} & 1 & 1 & 0 & 8 \\ 1 & -4 & 3 & 0 & 1 & 12 \\ -40 & -60 & -50 & 0 & 0 & 0 \end{array}\right]\begin{array}{c} s_1 \\ s_2 \\ \end{array}$$

$$\left[\begin{array}{ccccc|c} 1 & 1 & \frac{1}{2} & \frac{1}{2} & 0 & 4 \\ 5 & 0 & \underline{5} & 2 & 1 & 28 \\ 20 & 0 & -20 & 30 & 0 & 240 \end{array}\right]\begin{array}{c} x_2 \\ s_2 \\ \end{array}$$

$$\left[\begin{array}{ccccc|c} \frac{1}{2} & 1 & 0 & \frac{3}{10} & -\frac{1}{10} & \frac{6}{5} \\ 5 & 0 & 1 & \frac{2}{5} & \frac{1}{5} & \frac{28}{5} \\ 40 & 0 & 0 & 38 & 4 & 352 \end{array}\right]\begin{array}{c} x_2 \\ x_3 \\ \end{array}$$

$P = 352$, $x_1 = 0$, $x_2 = \frac{6}{5}$, $x_3 = \frac{28}{5}$

5.

$$\left[\begin{array}{cc|c} 2 & 2 & 8 \\ 1 & -1 & 2 \\ 2 & 1 & 0 \end{array}\right]; \quad \left[\begin{array}{cc|c} 2 & 1 & 2 \\ 2 & -1 & 1 \\ 8 & 2 & 0 \end{array}\right]$$

Dual problem:
Maximize $P = 8y_1 + 2y_2$
subject to $2y_1 + y_2 \le 2$,
$2y_1 - y_2 \le 1$, $y_1 \ge 0$, $y_2 \ge 0$

$$\begin{array}{cccc} y_1 & y_2 & s_1 & s_2 \end{array}$$

$$\left[\begin{array}{cccc|c} 2 & 1 & 1 & 0 & 2 \\ \underline{2} & -1 & 0 & 1 & 1 \\ -8 & -2 & 0 & 0 & 0 \end{array}\right]$$

$$\left[\begin{array}{cccc|c} 0 & 2 & 1 & -1 & 1 \\ 1 & -\frac{1}{2} & 0 & \frac{1}{2} & \frac{1}{2} \\ 0 & -6 & 0 & 4 & 4 \end{array}\right]$$

$$\left[\begin{array}{cccc|c} 0 & 1 & \frac{1}{2} & -\frac{1}{2} & \frac{1}{2} \\ 1 & 0 & \frac{1}{4} & \frac{1}{4} & \frac{3}{4} \\ 0 & 0 & 3 & 1 & 7 \end{array}\right]$$

$C = 7,\ x_1 = 3,\ x_2 = 1$

7.

$$\left[\begin{array}{ccc|c} 1 & 1 & 1 & 100 \\ 2 & 1 & 0 & 50 \\ 5 & 4 & 3 & 0 \end{array}\right]; \left[\begin{array}{cc|c} 1 & 2 & 5 \\ 1 & 1 & 4 \\ 1 & 0 & 3 \\ 100 & 50 & 0 \end{array}\right]$$

Dual problem:
Maximize $P = 10y_1 + 50y_2$
subject to $y_1 + 2y_2 \le 5,\ y_1 + y_2 \le 4, y_1 \le 3,$
$y_1 \ge 0,\ y_2 \ge 0.$

$$\begin{array}{cc|ccc|c} y_1 & y_2 & s_1 & s_2 & s_3 & \\ 1 & 2 & 1 & 0 & 0 & 5 \\ 1 & 1 & 0 & 1 & 0 & 4 \\ 1 & 0 & 0 & 0 & 1 & 3 \\ -100 & -50 & 0 & 0 & 0 & 0 \end{array}$$

$$\left[\begin{array}{cc|ccc|c} 0 & 2 & 1 & 0 & -1 & 2 \\ 0 & 1 & 0 & 1 & -1 & 1 \\ 1 & 0 & 0 & 0 & 1 & 3 \\ 0 & -50 & 0 & 0 & 100 & 300 \end{array}\right]$$

$$\left[\begin{array}{cc|ccc|c} 0 & 0 & 1 & -2 & 1 & 0 \\ 0 & 1 & 0 & 1 & -1 & 1 \\ 1 & 0 & 0 & 0 & 1 & 3 \\ 0 & 0 & 0 & 50 & 50 & 350 \end{array}\right]$$

$C = 350,\ x_1 = 0,\ x_2 = 50,\ x_3 = 50$

CHAPTER 5

Exercise 5.1 (page 210)

1. $(\$1000)(0.10)\left(\frac{1}{4}\right) = \$25$ 3. $(\$500)(0.12)\left(\frac{9}{12}\right) = \$45$

5. $(\$1000)(0.10)(1.5) = \$150$ 7. $\$50 = (\$1000)(r)\frac{1}{2}$; $r = 0.10 = 10\%$

9. $\$100 = (\$300)(r)1$; $r = \frac{1}{3} = 33\frac{1}{3}\%$ 11. $\$100 = (\$900)(r)\frac{10}{12}$; $r = \frac{1200}{9000} = 13\frac{1}{3}\%$

13. $P = \$1200 - (1200)(.10)\left(\frac{1}{2}\right) = \$1160$

15. $P = \$2000 - (2000)(.08)(2) = \$1680$

17. $\$1200 = A\left(1 - (.10)\left(\frac{1}{2}\right)\right)$; $A = \$1263.16$

19. $\$2000 = A(1 - (.08)(2))$; $A = \$1428.57$

21. $A = P/\left(1 - (.09)\left(\frac{1}{2}\right)\right) \approx 1.047P$

    $A = P\left(1 + (.10)\left(\frac{1}{2}\right)\right) = 1.05P$;

    Simple discount rate of 9% better

Exercise 5.2 (page 216)

1. $\$1000\left(1+\frac{.10}{12}\right)^{36} \approx \$1348.18$ 3. $\$500(1 + .09) = \$545$

5. $\$800\left(1+\frac{.12}{365}\right)^{200} \approx \$854.36$ 7. $\$100\left(1+\frac{.10}{12}\right)^{-6} \approx \$95.14$

9. $\$500\left(1+\frac{.09}{365}\right)^{-365} \approx \$456.97$ 11. $33\frac{1}{3}\%$ simple interest

13. Between 11 and 12 years

15. On the simple interest loan, the interest is 24% of \$240. On the compound interest loan (10%, compounded monthly, 24 months), the interest is

    $\$1000(1.22039) - \$1000 = \$220.39$

    The 10% compounded loan (b) results in less interest due.

17. $P_1 = 1000(1 + .09)^{-1} \approx \$917.43$;

    $P_2 = 1000(1 + .09)^{-2} \approx \$841.68$;

    $P = P_1 + P_2 \approx \$1759.11$

19. $\left(1+\frac{.0525}{4}\right)^4 - 1 \approx .0535; 5.35\%$

21. $\left(1+\frac{i}{4}\right)^4 - 1 = .07;\ i = 4\left((1.07)^{\frac{1}{4}} - 1\right) \approx\ .0682;\ 6.82\%$

23. $\left(1+\frac{.06}{4}\right)^4 \approx 1.0614$ Effective rate 6.14%; $6\frac{1}{4}\%$ compounded annually better

25. $\left(1+\frac{.09}{12}\right)^{12} - 1 \approx\ .0938$, Eff. rate 9.38% ; $\left(1+\frac{.088}{365}\right)^{365} - 1 \approx .0920$,
Eff. rate 9.20%; 9% compounded monthly better

27. $\$90,000(1.05)^4 = \$109.395.56$

Exercise 5.3 (page 221)

1. $A = \$100\ A(10, .10) = 100(15.93742) = \$1593.74$

3. $A = \$400\ A(12, .01) = 400(12.68250) = \$5073.00$
5. $A = \$200\ A\left(36, \frac{.10}{12}\right) = 200(41.78182) = \$8356.36$
7. $P = \$100,000\left[\frac{1}{A(4, .08)}\right] = 100,000(.221920804) = \$22,192.08$

9. As in Example 8,

$$0.14p + p\left[\frac{1}{A(30, 0.10)}\right] = 30,000$$
$$0.14p + 0.0060792p = 30,000$$
$$p = \frac{30,000}{0.1460792} \approx \$\ 205.368$$

Exercise 5.4 (page 226)

1. $V = \$500\ P(36, \frac{.10}{12}) = (500)(30.9912356) = \$\ 15495.62$
3. $V = \$100\ P(9, .01) = (100)(8.566017576) = \$856.60$

5. $V = \$10,000\ P(20, .1) = 10,000(8.51356372) = \$85135.64$

7. $V = \$4,000\ P(20, .1) = 4000(8.51356372) = \$34,054.26$

9. $P = 10,000\left[\frac{1}{P(24, .01)}\right] = 10,00(.047073472) = \$\ 470.73$

11. 5 years (20 years remaining):
Equity = \$70,000 - (\$461.56)(111.14495) = \$18,699.94
10 years (15 years remaining):
Equity = \$70,000 - (\$561.56)(98.5934) = \$24,493.23

13. $P = \$15{,}000 \left[\frac{1}{P(20, .12)}\right] = (15000)(.13387878) = \$2008.18$

15. $A = \$250P\left(240, \frac{0.10}{12}\right) = \$250(103.625) = \$25,906$

17. The principal of either loan is \$95,000(= \$120,000 - \$25,000)

	Monthly Payment
8%, 240 months	(\$95,000)(0.008364) = \$794.58
9%, 300 months	(\$95,000)(0.008392) = \$797.24

The 9% loan requires the larger monthly payment. Since the payments are larger and there are more of them, the total amount of the payments, and therefore the total interest to be paid, is also larger.

	Equity after 10 years
8%, 120 months remaining	\$120,000 - (\$794.58)(82.42148) = \$54,509.54
9%, 180 months remaining	\$120,000 - (\$797.24)(98.5934) = \$41,397.40

After 10 years, the equity from the 8%, 20 year loan is larger.

19. $V = \$300\,P\left(360, \frac{.09}{12}\right) = (300)(124.2818657) = \$37,284.56$

$P = \$37{,}284.56 \left|\frac{1}{P(240}, \frac{.09}{12}\right| = (37,284.56)(.008997259) = \$335.46$

Exercise 5.5 (page 230)

1. The present value of an annuity of \$2000 for 5 years at 10% is (\$2000)(3.79079) = \$7581.58. The corporation should lease the machine.

3. The present value of the annual cost savings of Machine A is (\$2000)P(8, 0.10) = (\$2000)(5.33493) = \$10,669.86. Since the machine costs \$10,000, the effective amount saved by its purchase is \$669.86. Similarly, the present value of the cost savings of Machine B is

($1800)P(6, 0.10) = $7839.47. Thus, Machine B costs $160.53 more than it will save in labor costs, so Machine A is preferable.

5. The semiannual interest payment is $\frac{1}{2}(0.09)(\$1000) = \$45$. The present value of these payments is:

$(\$45)P\left(30, \frac{0.08}{2}\right) = (\$45)(17.292) = \$778.14$

The present value of the amount payable at maturity is:

$$\$1000(1 + 0.04)^{-30} = \$308.32$$

Thus, the price of the bond should be $778.14 + $308.32 = $1086.46.

CHAPTER REVIEW

Review Exercises

1. $I = Prt = \$400\left(\frac{3}{4}\right)(.12) = \$36.00$; $A = P + I = 400 + 36 = \$436$

3. $A = P(1 + i)^n = (\$100)\left(1 + \frac{10}{12}\right)^{27} = 100(1.25115569) = \$125.12$

5. (a) $I = Prt = (3000)(.12)(3) = \$1080$

   (b) $A = P(1 + i)^n = (3000)\left(1 + \frac{10}{12}\right)^{36} = \$4044.55$; $I = A - P = 4044.55 - 3000 = \$1044.55$

   The compound interest loan costs less

7. $P = \$75\left(1 + \frac{10}{12}\right)^{-6} = (\$75)(.951426523) = \$71.36$

9. $P = \$10{,}000\left[\frac{1}{A(n,i)}\right] = (\$10{,}000)(0.037812) = \$378.12$

11. $P = \$60{,}000\left[\frac{1}{P(n,i)}\right] = (\$60{,}000)(0.0090870) = \$545.22$ monthly payment

    Total interest = (300)($545.22) - $60,000 = $103,566

    Equity after 5 years (n - 240 months remaining):
    $80,000 - ($545.22)P(n, i) = $80,000 - ($545.22)(103.625) = $23,502.

13. $P = \$125{,}000\left[\frac{1}{P(n,i)}\right] = (\$125{,}000)(0.008392) = \$1049$

    $125,000 - ($1049)(98.5934) = $21,575.52

15. $0.15p + p\left[\frac{1}{A(n, i)}\right] = \$20,000$ (n = 20, i = 10%)

$0.15p + (0.0174596245)p = \$20,000$

$(0.1674596)p = \$20,000$

$p = \$119,432$

17. $0.20p + p\left[\frac{1}{A(n, i)}\right] = \$25,000$ (n = 15, i = 10%)

$(0.20 + 0.03147378)p = \$25,000$

$p = \$108.004$

CHAPTER 6

Exercise 6.1 (page 247)

1. None of these 3. None of these 5. $\subset, \subseteq$ 7. $\subset, \subseteq$ 9. $\subset, \subseteq$

11. $A \subseteq C$. this is called the transitive law.

13. {a, b, c, d}, {a, b, c}, {a, b, d}, {a, c, d}, {b, c, d}, {a, b}, {a, c}, {a, d}, {b, c}, {b, d}, {c, d}, {a}, {b}, {c}, {d}, $\emptyset$

15. $A \cap B = \{13\}$ 17. $A \cup C = \{1, 2, 3, 5, 7\}$

19. $(A \cup B) \cap C = \{1, 2, 3, 4, 5, 6\} \cap \{3, 5, 7\} = \{3, 5\}$

21. $A \cup (B \cup C) = A \cup \{3, 4, 5, 6, 7\} = \{1, 2, 3, 4, 5, 6, 7\}$

23. (a) $A \cup B = \{0, 1, 2, 3, 5, 7, 8\}$
    (b) $B \cap C = \{5\}$
    (c) $A \cap B = \{5\}$
    (d) $\overline{A \cap B} = \overline{\{5\}} = \{0, 1, 2, 3, 4, 6, 7, 8, 9\}$
    (e) $\bar{A} \cap \bar{B} = \{2, 3, 4, 6, 8, 9\} \cap \{0, 1, 4, 6, 7, 9\} = \{4, 6, 9\}$
    (f) $A \cup (B \cap A) = A = \{0, 1, 5, 7\}$
    (g) $(C \cap A) \cap \bar{A} = \{5\} \cap \{2, 3, 4, 6, 8, 9\} = \emptyset$
    (h) $(A \cap B) \cup (B \cap C) = \{5\} \cup \{5\} = \{5\}$

25. (a) $A \cup B = \{b, c, d, e, f, g\}$
    (b) $A \cap B = \{c\}$
    (c) $\bar{A} \cap \bar{B} = \overline{A \cup B} = \{a, h, i, j, \ldots, z\}$
    (d) $\bar{A} \cup \bar{B} = \overline{A \cap B} = \{a, b, d, e, f, \ldots, z\}$

27.

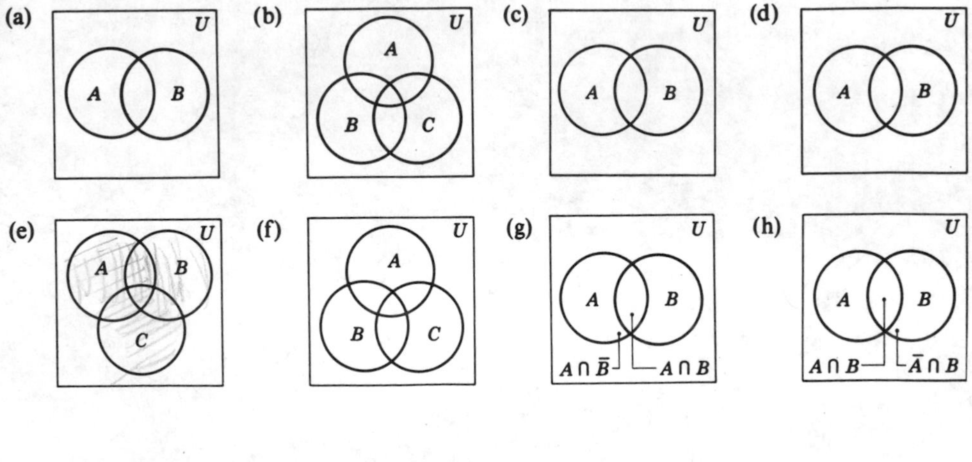

29. $A \cap E$ = {x | x is a customer of IBM and is a member of the Board of Directors of IBM}

31. $A \cup D$ = {x | x is a customer of IBM or is a stockholder of IBM}

33. $M \cap S$ = {All male college students who smoke}

35. $\overline{M} \cap \overline{S}$ = {All female college students who do not smoke}

37. $c(\{1,3,5,7\}) = 4$ **39.** $c(\{0,1,2,3,4,5,6,7,8,9\}) = 10$ **41.** $c(A) = 4$

43. $c(A \cap B) = c(\emptyset) = 0$ **45.** $c[(A \cap B) \cup A] = c(A) = 4$

47. $c[A \cup (B \cap C)] = c(\{1, 3, 6, 8\}) = 4$ **49.** $c[A \cap (B \cap C)] = c(\{8\}) = 1$

51. $c(A \cup B) = 4 + 3 - 2 = 5$ **53.** $7 = 5 + 4 - c(A \cap B)$; $c(A \cap B) = 2$

55. $14 = c(A) + 8 - 4$; $c(A) = 10$ **57.** $325 + 216 - 89 = 452$

59. $c(A) = 20 + 4 + 3 + 9 = 36$ **61.** $c(A \cup B) = 20 + 4 + 3 + 9 + 2 + 8 = 46$

63. $c(A \cap \overline{B}) = 20 + 4 = 24$ **65.** $c(A \cap B \cap C) = 3$ **67.** $c(A \cap B \cap C) = 3$

69. 109 = Number of male seniors who are not on the dean's list
97 = Number of female seniors who are not on the dean's list
369 = Number of female students who are not seniors and not on the dean's list
24 = Number of female seniors on the dean's list
73 = Number of female students on the dean's list who are not seniors
89 = Number of male students on the dean's list who are not seniors
347 = Number of male students who are not seniors and not on the dean's list
0 = Number of male seniors on the dean's list

71. (a) 42
(b) 9
(c) 5
(d) 2
(e) 44
(f) 31

73. Total for English, according to the diagram, is at least 303 whereas the staff member indicated that the total taking English was 281.

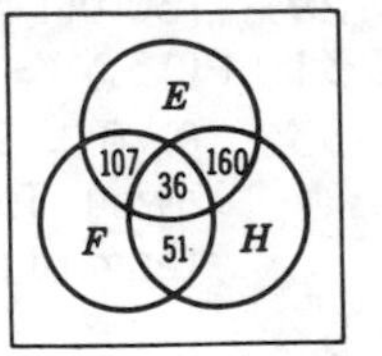

75. $143 - 30 - 45 = 68$

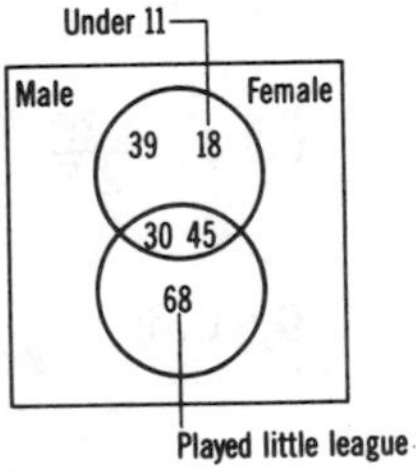

Exercise 6.2 (page 255)

1. $(2)(4) = 8$ **3.** $(3)(2)(4) = 24$ **5.** $(3)(8)(4)(9) = 864$

7. $(12)(3) = 36$ **9.** $(12)(11)(10) = 1320$ **11.** $(6)(5)(10)(4) = 1200$

13. $(6)(5)(4)(3)(2)(1) = 720$, $(8)(7)(6)(5)(4)(3)(2)(1) = 40320$

15. $(6)(5)(4)(3) = 360$, $(6)(6)(6)(6) = 1296$ **17.** $2^4 = 16$

19. $(7)(6)(5)(4)(3)(2)(1) = 5040$

21. $4^{10}2^{15} = 2^{20}2^{15} = 2^{35} \simeq 3 \cdot 436 \times 10^{10}$

23. (a) (26)(26)(10)(10)(10)(10) = 6,760,000

(b) (26)(26)(10)(9)(8)(7)(= 3,407,040

(c) (26)(25)(10)(9)(8)(7) = 3,276,000

25. (6)(5)(4) = 120

27. # MODEL A or B + # MODEL C = (2)(3)(2) + (1)(2)(2) = 16

Exercise 6.3 (page 261)

1. $\frac{5!}{2!} = 5 \cdot 4 \cdot 3 = 60$ **3.** $\frac{6!}{3!} = 6 \cdot 5 \cdot 4 = 120$ **5.** $\frac{10!}{8!} = 10 \cdot 9 = 90$

7. $\frac{9!}{8!} = 9$ **9.** $\frac{8!}{2!\,6!} = \frac{8 \cdot 7 \cdot 6!}{2 \cdot 6!} = 4 \cdot 7 = 28$ **11.** $P(7, 2) = 7 \cdot 6 = 42$

13. P(8, 1) = 8 **15.** P(5,0) = 1 **17.** $\frac{8!}{5!\,3!} = \frac{(8)(7)(6)(5!)}{5!(3)(2)(1)} = (8)(7) = 56$

19. $\frac{6!}{(6-6)!\,6!} = \frac{6!}{0!\,6!} = \frac{6!}{6!} = 1$ **21.** (a) 6! = 720, (b) 5! = 120, (c) 4! = 24

23. (10)(9)(8)(7) = 5040 **25.** (9)(8)(7)(6)(5) = 15120

27. P(12, 8) = (12)(11)(10)(9)(8)(7)(6)(5) = 19,958,400

29. (1500)(1499)(1498) = 3,368,253,000

31. P(15, 4) = (15)(14)(13)(12) = 32,760

33. $10 \cdot 9 = 90$ (Suppose each of the 10 teams plays one game at home and one away. There are 10 choices for the home team and 9 teams for the home team to play against.)

Exercise 6.4 (page 265)

1. $C(6, 4) = \frac{6!}{4!\,2!} = \frac{6 \cdot 5}{2} = 15$ **3.** $C(7, 2) = \frac{7!}{2!\,5!} = \frac{7 \cdot 6}{2} = 21$

5. $\binom{5}{1} = 5$ **7.** $\binom{8}{6} = \frac{8!}{6!\,2!} = \frac{8 \cdot 7}{2} = 28$ **9.** $C(8, 3) = \frac{8 \cdot 7 \cdot 6}{1 \cdot 2 \cdot 3} = 56$

11. $C(17, 4) = \frac{17 \cdot 16 \cdot 15 \cdot 14}{1 \cdot 2 \cdot 3 \cdot 4} = 2380$

13. If the 3 officers are of equal rank, the answer is C(25, 3) = 2300. If there are 3 distinct offices (e.g., president, vice-president, secretary), the answer is P(25, 3) = 13,800.

15. $\binom{6}{2} = 15$ **17.** $3 \cdot 2 \cdot \binom{5}{2} = 3 \cdot 2 \cdot 10 = 60$

19. $\binom{3}{1}\binom{8}{2}\binom{4}{1}\binom{20}{7} = 3 \cdot 28 \cdot 4 \cdot (77{,}520) = 26{,}046{,}720$ (Order is not important if we assume that specific positions will be assigned to the 7 linemen after the team is formed.)

21. $\binom{5}{3} = 10$ (The possible sums are 16¢, 31¢, 36¢, 40¢, 56¢, 61¢, 65¢, 76¢, 80¢, and 85¢.)

23. $\binom{100}{6} = \frac{100!}{6!\,94!} = \frac{(100)(99)(98)(97)(96)(95)}{(6)(5)(4)(3)(2)} = 1{,}192{,}052{,}400$

25. $\binom{100}{5} = \frac{100!}{5!\,95!} = \frac{(100)(99)(98)(97)(96)}{(5)(4)(3)(2)(1)} = 75{,}287{,}520$

27. $\binom{6}{2}\binom{8}{2} + \binom{6}{1}\binom{8}{3} + \binom{6}{0}\binom{8}{4} = \frac{6!}{2!\,4!} \cdot \frac{8!}{2!\,6!} + \frac{6!}{1!\,5!} \cdot \frac{8!}{3!\,5!} + \frac{6!}{0!\,6!} \cdot \frac{8!}{4!\,4!} = 826$

29 $\binom{8}{0} + \binom{8}{2} + \binom{8}{4} + \binom{8}{6} + \binom{8}{8} = 1 + 28 + 70 + 28 + 1 = 128,\ 2^8 - 128 = 128$

31. $\binom{55}{8} = \frac{55!}{8!\,47!} = 1{,}217{,}566{,}350$

33. $(5)(4)(3) = 60$ **35.** $\binom{24}{4} = 10{,}626$ **37.** $P(50, 15) = \frac{50!}{35!}$

Review Exercises (page 268)

1. None of these **3.** None of these **5.** None of these **7.** $\in$

9. $\subset$ **11.** None of these **13.** $\subset, \subseteq$ **15.** None of these

17. (a) $(A \cap B) \cup C = \{3, 6\} \cup \{6, 8, 9\} = \{3, 6, 8, 9\}$

(b) $(A \cap B) \cap C = \{3, 6\} \cap \{6, 8, 9\} = \{6\}$

(c) $(A \cup B) \cap B = \{1, 2, 3, 5, 6, 7, 8\} \cap \{2, 3, 6, 7\} = \{2, 3, 6, 7\}$

19. $c(A \cap B) = 24 + 12 - 33 = 3$

21.

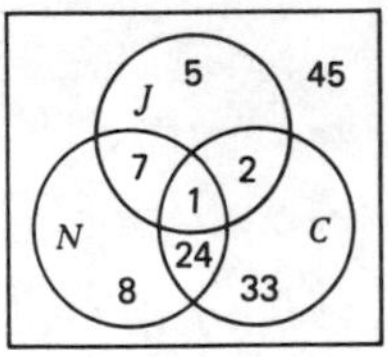

(a) 45 (c) 50

(b) 33

23. $P(6,3) = 6 \cdot 5 \cdot 4 = 120$ **25.** $C(5,3) = \frac{5!}{3!\,2!} = 10$ **27.** $3! = 6$

29. $3 \cdot 4 \cdot 6 = 72$ **31.** Maximum: $P(4,2) = 12$; $C(4,2) = 6$

33. $\binom{16}{4}\binom{10}{3} = (1820)(120) = 218{,}400$

35. (a) $\binom{7}{3}\binom{6}{4} = (35)(15) = 525$

(b) $\binom{7}{1}\binom{6}{6} + \binom{7}{2}\binom{6}{5} + \binom{7}{3}\binom{6}{4} + \binom{7}{4}\binom{6}{3} + \binom{7}{5}\binom{6}{2} + \binom{7}{6}\binom{6}{1} = 7 + 126 + 525 + 700 + 315 + 42$
$= 1715$

37. $(3 \cdot 2 \cdot 1)4!5!6! = 3!4!5!6! = 12{,}441{,}600$

39. One path from A to B is RRRRRRUUUUUU. All paths from A to B are exactly 12 moves, of which exactly 6 are to the right (R). Thus, in all, there are $\binom{12}{6} = 924$ paths from A to B.

41. $5 \cdot 6 \cdot 8 = 240$ **43.** $\binom{3}{1}\binom{5}{3} = 3 \cdot 10 = 30$

45. Let AB = X. We have X, C, D, E to order: $4! = 24$.

CHAPTER 7

Exercise 7.2 (page 283)

1. (a) {H, T} (b) {0, 1, 2} (c) {M, D}
3. {HHH, HHT, HTH, HTT, THH, THT, TTH, TTT}
5. {HH1, HH2, HH3, HH4, HH5, HH6, HT1, HT2, HT3, HT4, HT5, HT6, TH1, TH2, TH3, TH4, TH5, TH6, TT1, TT2, TT3, TT4, TT5, TT6}
7. {RA, RB, RC, GA, GB, GC} **9.** {RR, RG, GR, GG}
11. { AA1, AA2, AA3, AA4, AB1, AB2, AB3, AB4, AC1, AC2, AC3, AC4, BA1, BA2, BA3, BA4, BB1, BB2, BB3, BB4, BC1, BC2, BC3, BC4, CA1, CA2, CA3, CA4, CB1, CB2, CB3, CB4, CC1, CC2, CC3, CC4}
13. {RA2, RA2, RA3, RA4, RB1, RB2, RB3, RB4, RC1, RC2, RC3, RC4, GA1, GA2, GA3, GA4, GB1, GB2, GB3, GB4, GC1, GC2, GC3, GC4}
15. $2^4 = 16$ **17.** $6^3 = 216$ **19.** $\binom{52}{2} = 1326$
21. 1, 2, 3, and 6 **23.** 2 **25.** $P(HH) = P(HT) = P(TH) = P(TT) = \frac{1}{4}$
27. $P(1H) = P(1T) = P(2H) = P(2T) = P(3H) = P(3T) = P(4H) = P(4T) = P(5H) = P(5T) = P(6H) = P(6T) = \frac{1}{12}$
29. {HHHH, HHHT, HHTH, HHTT, HTHH, HTHT, HTTH, HTTT, THHH, THHT, THTH, THTT, TTHH, TTHT, TTTH, TTTT}; assign $\frac{1}{16}$ to each simple event.
31. {HTTT, TTTT}
33. {HHHT, HHTH, HHTT, HTHH, HTHT, HTTH, THHH, THHT, THTH, TTHH}
35. $P(A) = \frac{2}{36} = \frac{1}{18}$ **37.** $P(C) = \frac{4}{36} = \frac{1}{9}$ **39.** $P(E) = \frac{6}{36} = \frac{1}{6}$ **41.** $P(A) = \frac{1}{2}$
43. $P(C) = \frac{5}{6}$ **45.** $P(E) = \frac{1}{2}$
47. (i) $P(E) = \frac{3}{4}$, (ii) $P(E) = \frac{5}{9}$; (i) $P(F) = \frac{1}{2}$, (ii) $P(F) = \frac{4}{9}$; (i) $P(G) = \frac{1}{4}$, (ii) $P(G) = \frac{4}{9}$
49. {RRR, RRL, RLR, RLL, LRR, LRL, LLR, LLL}. Probability of each simple event is $\frac{1}{8}$. (We assume that the rat does not know left from right.)
    (a) $P(E) = \frac{3}{8}$ (b) $P(F) = \frac{1}{8}$ (c) $P(G) = \frac{1}{2}$ (d) $P(H) = \frac{1}{2}$
51. (a) The number on the red die is three times the number on the green die.
    (b) The number on the red die is 1 larger than the number on the green die.
    (c) The number on the red die is smaller than or equal to the number on the green die.
    (d) The sum of the numbers on the two dice is 8.
    (e) The number on the green die is the square of the number on the red die.
    (f) The numbers on the two dice are the same.

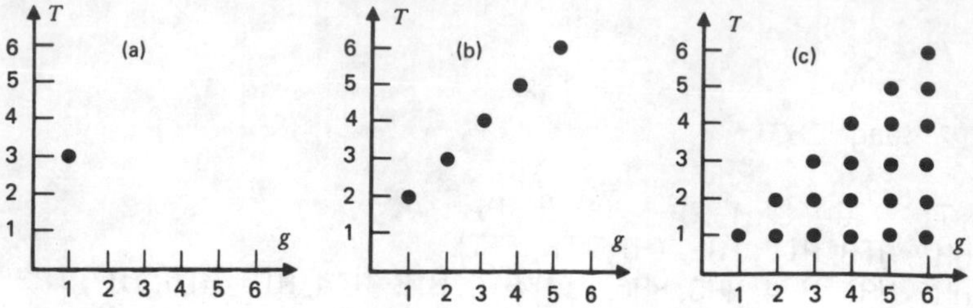

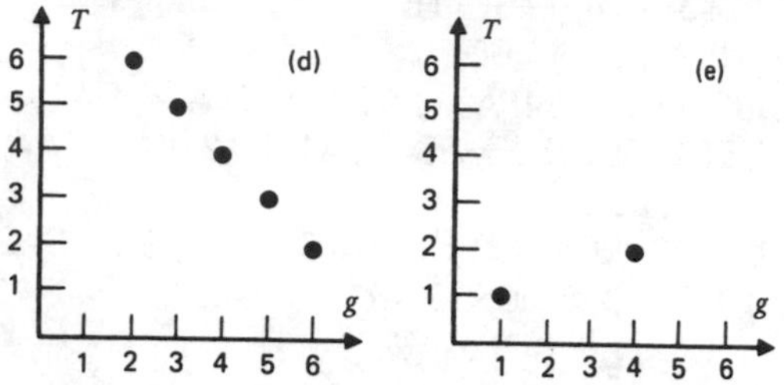

(f) r = g

53. $1 = P(C_1) + P(C_2) + P(C_3) = p + 2p + p = 4p$, so $p = \frac{1}{4}$; then $P(C_1) = \frac{1}{4}$; $P(C_2) = \frac{2}{4} = \frac{1}{2}$; $P(C_3) = \frac{1}{4}$; $P(C_1 \cup C_2) = \frac{3}{4}$; $P(C_1 \cup C_3) = \frac{1}{2}$

Exercise 7.3 (page 292)

1. $P(\bar{A}) = .8$ **3.** $P(A \cup B) = .5$ **5.** $P(A \cup B) = .5 - .15 = .35$

7. The events "Sum is 2" and "Sum is 12" are mutually exclusive. The probability of obtaining a 2 or a 12 is $\frac{1}{36} + \frac{1}{36} = \frac{1}{18}$.

9. P(Losing) = .35

11. $P(E \cap M) = P(E) + P(M) - P(E \cup M) = .4 + .6 - .8 = .2$

13. (a) $P(E \cup B) = .5 + .3 - .1 = .7$

(b) $P(A \cap \bar{B}) = .4$

(c) $P(B \cap \bar{A}) = .2$

(d) $P(\overline{A \cup B}) = 3$

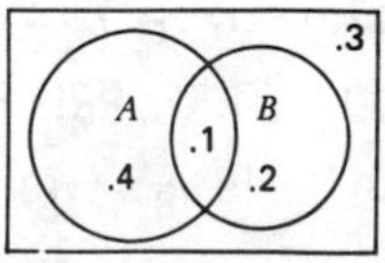

15. Let T = Car needs a tuneup, B = Car needs a brake job.

(a) $P(T \cup B) = P(T) + P(B) - P(T \cap B)$

$= .6 + .1 - .02 = .68$

(b) $P(T \cap \bar{B}) = .58$

(c) $P(\overline{T \cup B}) = .32$

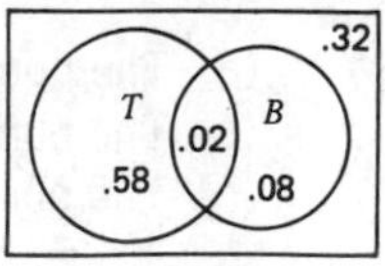

17. (a) $.24 + .33 = .57$ (b) $1 - .05 = .95$ (c) $1 - .17 = .83$

(d) $.21 + .17 = .38$ (e) $.05 + .24 = .29$ (f) $.05$

(g) $.24 + .33 + .21 = .78$ (h) $1 - .29 = .71$

19. $P(E) = \frac{3}{3+1} = \frac{3}{4}$ **21.** $P(E) = \frac{5}{5+7} = \frac{5}{12}$ **23.** $P(E) = \frac{1}{2}$

25. $\frac{.7}{1-.7} = \frac{.7}{.3} = \frac{7}{3}$ The odds for E are 7 to 3; the odds against E are 3 to 7.

27. $\frac{4}{5} = \frac{4}{4+1}$ The odds for F are 4 to 1; the odds against F are 1 to 4.

29. $P(7) = \frac{1}{6}$; 1 to 5; $P(11) = \frac{1}{18}$; 1 to 17; $P(7 \text{ or } 11) = \frac{1}{6} + \frac{1}{18} = \frac{2}{9}$, 2 to 7

31. $P(A \text{ or } B) = \frac{1}{3} + \frac{2}{5} = \frac{11}{15}$ The odds are 1 to 4.

33.

$$P(A \cup B \cup C) = P(A \cup B) + P(C) - P[(A \cup B) \cap C]$$
$$= P(A) + P(B) - P(A \cap B) + P(C) - P[(A \cap C) \cup (B \cap C)]$$
$$= P(A) + P(B) + P(C) - P(A \cap B) - (P(A \cap C) + P(B \cap C) - P[(A \cap C) \cap (B \cap C)])$$
$$= P(A) + P(B) + P(C) - P(A \cap B) - (P(A \cap C) - P(B \cap C) + P(A \cap B \cap C)$$

Exercise 7.4 (page 299)

1. $\frac{1}{52}$ **3.** $\frac{13}{52} = \frac{1}{4}$ **5.** $\frac{12}{52} = \frac{3}{13}$ **7.** $\frac{20}{52} = \frac{5}{13}$ **9.** $\frac{48}{52} = \frac{12}{13}$

11. $\frac{3}{23}$ **13.** $\frac{7}{23}$ **15.** $\frac{8}{23}$ **17.** $\frac{11}{23}$

19. $P\{(1,2),(2,1),(2,4),(4,2),(3,6),(6,3)\} = \frac{6}{36} = \frac{1}{6}$

21. Let A = Single, B = College.

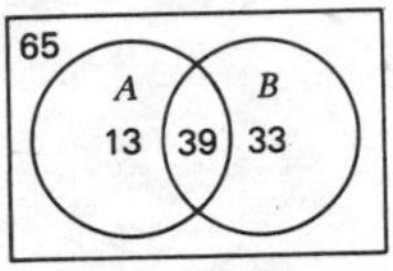

$P(A \cup B) = \frac{85}{150} \approx .567$

$P(\overline{A \cup B}) = \frac{65}{150} \approx .433$

23. P(At least 2 in same month) = 1 - P(All different months)

$$= 1 - \frac{(12)(11)(10)}{(12)(12)(12)} = .236$$

25. P(At least 2 have the same number) = 1 - P(All the numbers are different)

$$= 1 - \frac{(100)(99)(98)}{(100)(100)(100)} = .0298$$

27. Probability is greater than .99999.

29. Probability that all 5 are defective:

$$\frac{\binom{6}{5}}{\binom{50}{5}} = \frac{6}{\frac{50 \cdot 49 \cdot 48 \cdot 47 \cdot 46}{1 \cdot 2 \cdot 3 \cdot 4 \cdot 5}} = \frac{6 \cdot 5 \cdot 4 \cdot 3 \cdot 2 \cdot 1}{50 \cdot 49 \cdot 48 \cdot 47 \cdot 46} \approx .0000028$$

Probability that at least 2 are defective:

$$\frac{\binom{44}{3}\binom{6}{2}}{\binom{50}{5}} + \frac{\binom{44}{2}\binom{6}{3}}{\binom{50}{5}} + \frac{\binom{44}{1}\binom{6}{4}}{\binom{50}{5}} + \frac{\binom{6}{5}}{\binom{50}{5}} = \frac{218{,}246}{2{,}118{,}760} \approx .103$$

31. (a) $\dfrac{\binom{13}{5}}{\binom{52}{5}} = \dfrac{1287}{2{,}598{,}960}$ (b) $\dfrac{\binom{13}{4}\binom{39}{1}}{\binom{52}{5}} \approx 0.0107$ (c) $\dfrac{13 \cdot 48}{\binom{52}{5}} \approx .00024$

(d) $\dfrac{13\binom{4}{3}12\binom{4}{2}}{\binom{52}{5}} \approx .0014$ (e) .0076

Exercise 7.5 (page 308)

1. $P(C) = P(A \cap C) + P(B \cap C) = (.7)(.9) + (.3)(.2) = .69$ **3.** $P(C|D) = \dfrac{P(C \cap D)}{P(D)} = 0$

7. .40 **9.** .24 **11.** .10 **13.** .08 **15.** $\dfrac{P(E \cap H)}{P(H)} = \dfrac{.10}{.24} = \dfrac{5}{12}$

17. $\dfrac{P(G \cap H)}{P(H)} = \dfrac{.08}{.24} = \dfrac{1}{3}$ **19.** $P(E|F) = \dfrac{P(E \cap F)}{P(F)} = \dfrac{.1}{.2} = \dfrac{1}{2}$; $P(F|E) = \dfrac{P(E \cap F)}{P(E)} = \dfrac{.1}{.4} = \dfrac{1}{4}$

21. $P(E|F) = \dfrac{P(E \cap F)}{P(F)}$, so $.2 = \dfrac{.1}{P(F)}$, $P(F) = \dfrac{1}{2}$

23. (a) $\dfrac{2}{52} = \dfrac{1}{26}$

(b) $\dfrac{1}{2}$

(c) $\dfrac{1}{13}$

25.

(a) $P(F|I) = \dfrac{25}{55} = \dfrac{5}{11}$

(b) $P(R|F) = \dfrac{30}{115} = \dfrac{6}{23}$

(c) $P(M|D) = \dfrac{50}{110} = \dfrac{5}{11}$

(d) $P(D|M) = \dfrac{50}{120} = \dfrac{5}{12}$

(e) $P(M|R \cup I) = \dfrac{70}{125} = \dfrac{14}{25}$

(f) $P(I|M) = \dfrac{30}{120} = \dfrac{1}{4}$

27. P(2 girls | 1st girl) = $\dfrac{1}{2}$

29. P(4 heads) = $\dfrac{1}{16}$; P(4 heads | 2nd toss head) = $\dfrac{\frac{1}{16}}{\frac{1}{2}} = \dfrac{1}{8}$

31. P(More than 2 | At least 1) $= \frac{.32}{.75} = \frac{32}{75}$ **33.** $\left(\frac{13}{52}\right)\left(\frac{25}{51}\right) = \frac{25}{204}$

35. $\frac{1}{13}$

37. Let W = Woman, M = Man, t = Under 160. Assume 1000 people.

Then $P(W \mid E) = \frac{P(W \cap E)}{P(E)} = \frac{350}{525} = .67$

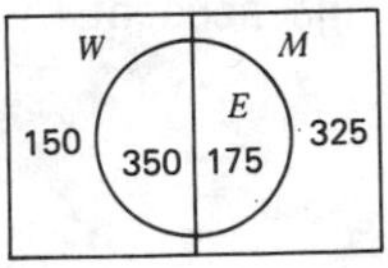

39. Let A = Private, B = Public, E = A average. Assume 100 people for convenience. Then:

$P(A \mid E) = \frac{P(A \cap E)}{P(E)} = \frac{12}{24} = .5$

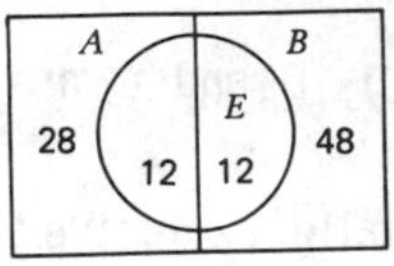

41. $P(F) \cdot P(E \mid F) = P(E \cap F) = P(E) \cdot P(F \mid E)$

43. Since $F = (E \cap F) \cup (\bar{E} \cap F)$ and $(E \cap F) \cap (\bar{E} \cap F) = \emptyset$,

$\frac{P(E \cap F)}{P(F)} + \frac{P(\bar{E} \cap F)}{P(F)} = \frac{P(E \cap F) + (\bar{E} \cap F)}{P(F)} = \frac{P(F)}{P(F)} = 1$

Exercise 7.6 (page 314)

1. $P(E \cap F) = P(E)P(F) = (.3)(.5) = .15$

3. $P(E \cup F) = P(E) + P(F) - P(E \cap F) = P(E) + P(F) - P(E)P(F)$, so $.3 = .2 + P(F) - .2P(F)$

$.1 = .8P(F)$

$P(F) = \frac{1}{8}$

5. $P(E \mid F) = \frac{P(E \cap F)}{P(F)} = \frac{P(E) + P(F) - P(E \cup F)}{P(F)} = \frac{.3 + .2 - .4}{.2} = \frac{1}{2}$; E and F are not independent

7. $P(E) = \frac{1}{2}$

$P(F) = \frac{1}{2}$

$P(E \cap F) = \frac{1}{6}$

E and F are not independent

9. $P(E) = \frac{4}{8} = \frac{1}{2}$

$P(F) = \frac{3}{4}$

$P(E \cap F) = \frac{3}{8} = \frac{3}{4} \cdot \frac{1}{2}$

E and F are independent

11. (a) $\frac{1}{4}$

(b) $\frac{13}{52} = \frac{1}{4}$

(c) P(1st club and 2nd heart) = $\frac{1}{4} \cdot \frac{1}{4} = \frac{1}{16}$

13. E = {RRR, RRL, LRR}

$P(E) = \frac{3}{8}$

$P(F) = \frac{1}{8}$

$P(E \cap F) = P(\emptyset) = 0 \neq P(E)P(F)$

E and F are not independent

15. $P(A) = \frac{1}{4} + \frac{1}{4} = \frac{1}{2}$

$P(B) = \frac{1}{4} + \frac{1}{4} = \frac{1}{2}$

$P(C) = \frac{1}{4} + \frac{1}{4} = \frac{1}{2}$

$P(A \cap B) = P(2) = \frac{1}{4} = P(A)P(B)$; A and B are independent

$P(A \cap C) = P(1) = \frac{1}{4} = P(A)P(C)$; A and C are independent

$P(B \cap C) = P(3) = \frac{1}{4} = P(B)P(C)$; B and C are independent

17. Consider Problem 15.

(a) A and B are not mutually exclusive but they are independent.

(b) Let D = {4}. Then: $P(D) = \frac{1}{12}$; $A \cap D = \emptyset$. Hence, they are mutually exclusive, but since $P(A \cap D) = P(\emptyset) = 0 \neq \frac{1}{12} \cdot \frac{1}{2}$, they are not independent.

(c) Let E = {1, 4}. Then: $A \cap E = \frac{1}{4} + \frac{1}{12} = \frac{1}{3}$; $P(A \cap E) = P(1) = \frac{1}{4} \neq \frac{1}{2} \cdot \frac{1}{3}$.

Thus, A and E are not independent and are not mutually exclusive.

19. $P(F) = 0$

$E \cap F \subset F$; hence, $P(E \cap F) \leq P(F) = 0$

Thus, $P(E \cap F) = 0$. But $P(E)P(F) = P(E) \cdot 0 = 0$

Hence, E and F are independent.

21. If $E \cap F = \emptyset$, then $P(E \cap F) = P(\emptyset) = 0$.

But, by independence, $P(E \cap F) = P(E)P(F)$.

Hence, $P(E)P(F) = 0$, which implies that

$P(E) = 0$ or $P(F) = 0$–a contradiction.

Thus, we have $E \cap F \neq \emptyset$.

23. (a) Let E = At least one ace, F = No ace.

$P(E) = 1 - P(F) = 1 - .4823 = .5177$

(b) Let G = At least one pair of aces, H = No pair of aces.

$P(G) = 1 - P(H) = 1 - .509 = .491$

Exercise 7.7 (page 324)

1. $$P(A|E) = \frac{P(A \cap E)}{P(E)} = \frac{(.3)(.4)}{(.3)(.4) + (.6)(.2) + (.1)(.7)} = \frac{.12}{.31} = \frac{12}{31}$$

3. $P(C|E) = \frac{P(C \cap E)}{P(E)} = \frac{(.1)(.7)}{.31} = \frac{7}{31}$

5. $P(B|E) = \frac{P(B \cap E)}{P(E)} = \frac{.12}{.31} = \frac{12}{31}$

7. $P(E) = P(A_1)P(E|A_1) + P(A_2)P(E|A_2) = (.3)(.01) + (.7)(.02) = .017$

9. $P(E) = P(A_1)P(E|A_1) + P(A_2)P(E|A_2) + P(A_3)P(E|A_3) =$
$(.5)(.01) + (.3)(.03) + (.2)(.02) = .018$

11. $P(A_1|E) = \frac{P(E|A_1)P(A_1)}{P(E)} = \frac{(.01)(.3)}{.017} = \frac{.003}{.017} = \frac{3}{17} \approx .176$

$P(A_2|E) = \frac{P(E|A_2)P(A_2)}{P(E)} = \frac{(.02)(.7)}{.017} = \frac{.014}{.017} = \frac{14}{17} \approx .824$

13. $P(A_1|E) = \frac{P(E|A_1)P(A_1)}{P(E)} = \frac{(.01)(.5)}{.018} = \frac{.005}{.018} = \frac{5}{18} \approx .278$

$P(A_2|E) = \frac{P(E|A_2)P(A_2)}{P(E)} = \frac{(.03)(.3)}{.018} = \frac{.009}{.018} = \frac{9}{18} \approx .500$

$P(A_3|E) = \frac{P(E|A_3)P(A_3)}{P(E)} = \frac{(.02)(.2)}{.018} = \frac{.004}{.018} = \frac{4}{18} \approx .222$

15. Let E = Item is defective, A_1 = Item is from Machine I, A_2 = Item is from Machine II,
A_3 = Item is from Machine III.

$P(A_1|E) = \frac{(.02)(.4)}{(.02)(.4)+(.04)(.5)+(.01)(.1)} = \frac{8}{29} \approx .276$

$P(A_2|E) = \frac{(.04)(.5)}{(.02)(.4)+(.04)(.5)+(.01)(.1)} = \frac{20}{29} \approx .690$

$P(A_3|E) = \frac{(.01)(.1)}{(.02)(.4)+(.04)(.5)+(.01)(.1)} = \frac{1}{29} \approx .034$

17. $P(A_2|E) = 0$; $P(A_3|E) = .065$; $P(A_4|E) = 0$; $P(A_5|E) = .065$

19. $P(U_I|E) = \frac{\left(\frac{5}{16}\right)\left(\frac{1}{3}\right)}{\left(\frac{5}{16}\right)\left(\frac{1}{3}\right)+\left(\frac{3}{16}\right)\left(\frac{1}{3}\right)+\left(\frac{7}{16}\right)\left(\frac{1}{3}\right)} = \frac{\frac{5}{16}}{\frac{15}{16}} = \frac{1}{3} \approx .333$

$P(U_{II}|E) = .20$

$P(U_{III}|E) = .467$

21. $P(I) = .67$; $P(II) = .33$; $P(D|I) = .02$; $P(D|II) = .01$;

$$P(I|D) = \frac{P(D|I)P(I)}{P(D|I)P(I) + P(D|II)P(II)} = \frac{(.02)(.67)}{(.02)(.67) + (.33)(.01)} = .80$$

23. Let R = Soil is rock, C = Soil is clay, S = Soil is sand, A = Test is positive. Then:
$P(R) = .53$; $P(C) = .21$; $P(S) = .2$; $P(A|R) = .35$; $P(A|C) = .48$; $P(A|S) = .75$;

$$P(R|A) = \frac{P(R)P(A|R)}{P(R)P(A|R) + P(C)P(A|C) + P(S)P(A|S)} = \frac{(.53)(.35)}{(.53)(.35) + (.21)(.48) + (.26)(.75)} \approx .39$$

$$P(C|A) = \frac{P(C)P(A|C)}{P(A)} = \frac{.1008}{.4813} \approx .21$$

$$P(S|A) = \frac{P(S)P(A|S)}{P(A)} = \frac{.1950}{.4813} \approx .41$$

25. Let R = Republican.
$P(R) = P(R|N)P(N) + P(R|S)P(S) + P(R|M)P(M) + P(R|W)P(W)$
$= (.4)(.4) + (.560(.1) + (.48)(.25) + (.52)(.25) = .466$

$$P(N|R) = \frac{P(R|N)P(N)}{P(R)} = \frac{(.4)(.4)}{.466} \approx .343$$

Review Exercises (page 327)

1. $S = \{BB, BG, GB, GG\}$

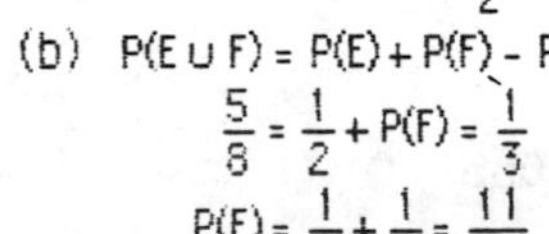

3. (a) $\dfrac{\binom{5}{2}}{\binom{14}{2}} = \dfrac{10}{91}$ (b) $\dfrac{\binom{5}{1}\binom{9}{1}}{\binom{14}{2}} = \dfrac{45}{91}$

(c) $\dfrac{10}{91} + \dfrac{45}{91} = \dfrac{55}{91}$

5. $b(4,3;\ .5) = .2500$

7. (a) $P(\bar{E}) = 1 - P(E) = 1 - \frac{1}{2} = \frac{1}{2}$

(b) $P(E \cup F) = P(E) + P(F) - P(E \cap F)$

$\frac{5}{8} = \frac{1}{2} + P(F) = \frac{1}{3}$

$P(F) = \frac{1}{8} + \frac{1}{3} = \frac{11}{24}$

(c) $P(\bar{F}) = 1 - P(F) = \frac{13}{24}$

9. There are $3! = 6$ ways of putting the letters in the envelopes. There are only 2 ways to have each letter in the wrong envelope. Hence, the probability that at least one person receives the correct letter is $\frac{4}{6} = \frac{2}{3}$.

11. $\frac{7}{7+6} = \frac{7}{13}$

13. Let M = Failed Math, P = Failed Physics. Then: $P(M) = .38$, $P(P) = .27$, $P(M \cap P) = .09$.

(a) $P(M|P) = \frac{P(M \cap P)}{P(P)} = \frac{.09}{.27} = \frac{1}{3}$

(b) $P(P|M) = \frac{P(M \cap P)}{P(M)} = \frac{.09}{.38} = \frac{9}{38}$

(c) $P(M \cup P) = P(M) + P(P) - P(M \cap P) = .38 + .27 - .09 = .56$

15. Let A = Blue-eyed, B = Brown-eyed, L = Left-handed. Then: $P(A) = .25$, $P(B) = .75$, $P(L|A) = .10$, $P(L|B) = .05$.

(a) $P(A \cap L) = P(L|A)P(A) = (.10)(.25) = .0250$

(b) $P(L) = P(A)P(L \mid A) + P(B)P(L|B) = (.10)(.25) + (.05)(.75) = .0625$

(c) $P(A|L) = \frac{P(L|A)P(A)}{P(L)} = \frac{.025}{.0625} = .4$

17. Let C = Have cancer, D = Test detects cancer. Then: $P(C) = .018$, $P(\bar{C}) = .982$, $P(D|C) = .85$, $P(D|\bar{C}) = .08$.

$$P(C|D) = \frac{P(D|C)P(C)}{P(D|C)P(C) + P(D|\bar{C})P(\bar{C})} = \frac{(.85)(.018)}{(.85)(.018) + (.08)(.982)} = .163$$

CHAPTER 8

Exercise 8.1 (page 339)

1. (a) $2^{10} = 1024$ (b) $\binom{10}{4} = 210$ (c) $\binom{10}{0} + \binom{10}{1} + \binom{10}{2} = 1 + 10 + 45 = 56$
(d) $1024 - 56 = 968$

3. (a) $c(10, 3) = 120$ (b) $\binom{7}{2}\binom{3}{1} = 21 \cdot 3 = 63$ (c) $\binom{7}{3} = 35$
(d) $\binom{3}{3} = 1$

5. $\frac{8!}{4!\,4!} = 70$ (This is equal to the number of sequences of 8 letters in which A and N each appear 4 times. Consider AAAANNNN to be equivalent to AAAA, NAAAANNN TO NAAAA, etc.)

7. $\frac{9!}{4!\,3!\,2!}$ 1260 9. $\frac{11!}{2!2!2!} = 4{,}989{,}600$

11. $\left(\frac{10!}{3!3!4!}\right) \div 2 = 2100$

13. (a) $\binom{5}{1}\binom{8}{3} = 280$ (b) $\binom{8}{2}\binom{5}{2} = 280$
(c) $\binom{5}{1}\binom{8}{3} + \binom{5}{2}\binom{8}{2} + \binom{5}{3}\binom{8}{1} = 640$

15. $\frac{30!}{(6!)^5} \simeq 1.37 \times 10^{18}$ 17. $\binom{8}{5} + \binom{8}{6} + \binom{8}{7} + \binom{8}{8} = 56 + 28 + 8 + 1 = 93$

19. $\frac{\binom{10}{6}}{2^{10}} = \frac{210}{1024} = \frac{105}{512}$ 21. $1 - \frac{\binom{21}{5}}{\binom{26}{5}} = 1 - \frac{20349}{65780} \simeq .6907$

23. $\frac{10}{\binom{20}{2}} = \frac{10}{190} = \frac{1}{19}$ 25. $\frac{1}{5!} = \frac{1}{120}$ 27. $\frac{1}{2}$

Exercise 8.2 (page 346)

1. $(x + y)^5 = x^5 + 5x^4y + 10x^3y^2 + 10x^2y^3 + 5xy^4 + y^5$

3. $(x + 3y)^3 = x^3 + 3x^2(3y) + 3x(3y)^2 + (3y)^3 = x^3 + 9x^2y + 27xy^2 + 27y^3$

5. $(2x - y)^4 = (2x)^4 + 4(2x)^3(-y) + 6(2x)^2(-y)^2 + 4(2x)(-y)^3 + (-y)^4$
$= 16x^4 - 32x^3y + 24x^2y^2 - 8xy^3 + y^4$

7. $\binom{5}{2} = 10$ 9. $\binom{10}{8} \cdot 3^2 = 405$ 11. $2^5 = 32$ 13. $2^{10} - 1 = 1023$

15. $512 = \binom{10}{1} + \binom{10}{3} + \binom{10}{5} + \binom{10}{7} + \binom{10}{9}$

17. $\binom{10}{7} = \binom{9}{7} + \binom{9}{6} = \binom{8}{7} + \binom{8}{6} + \binom{9}{6} = \binom{7}{7} + \binom{7}{6} + \binom{8}{6} + \binom{9}{6} = \binom{6}{6} + \binom{7}{6} + \binom{8}{6} + \binom{9}{6}$

19. $\binom{12}{6}$ by Example 5 page 344.

Exercise 8.3 (page 354)

1. b(7, 5; .30) = .0250 **3.** b(15, 8; .70) = .0811 **5.** $b\left(15, 10; \frac{1}{2}\right) = .0916$

7. b(15, 3; .3) + b(15, 2; .3) + b(15, 1; .3) + b(15, 0; .3)
= .1700 + .0916 + .0305 + .0047 = .2968

9. $b\left(3, 2; \frac{1}{3}\right) = \binom{3}{2}\left(\frac{1}{3}\right)^2\left(\frac{2}{3}\right) = 3 \cdot \frac{1}{9} \cdot \frac{2}{3} = \frac{2}{9} = .22\ldots$

11. $b\left(3, 0; \frac{1}{6}\right) = \left(\frac{5}{6}\right)^3 = \frac{125}{216} \approx .5787$

13. $b\left(5, 3; \frac{2}{3}\right) = \binom{5}{3}\left(\frac{2}{3}\right)^3\left(\frac{1}{3}\right)^2 = 10 \cdot \frac{8}{27} \cdot \frac{1}{9} = \frac{80}{243} \approx .3292$

15. b(10, 6; .3) = .0368 **17.** b(12, 9; .8) = b(12, 3; .2) = .2362

19. b(8, 5; .25) + b(8, 6; .25) + b(8, 7; .25) + b(8, 8; .25)
= .0231 + .0038 + .0004 + .0000 = .0273

21. $b\left(8, 1; \frac{1}{2}\right) = .03125$

23. $b\left(8, 5; \frac{1}{2}\right) = b\left(8, 6; \frac{1}{2}\right) + b\left(8, 7; \frac{1}{2}\right) + b\left(8, 8; \frac{1}{2}\right) = .2188 + .1094 + .0313 + .0039 = .3634$

25. Let A = 2 heads, B = At least 1 head. Then: $P(A) = b\left(8, 2; \frac{1}{2}\right) = .1094$
and $P(B) = 1 - P(\bar{B}) = 1 - .0039 = .9961$, so

$$P(A|B) = \frac{P(A \cap B)}{P(B)} = \frac{P(A)}{P(B)}$$

$$P(A|B) = \frac{.1094}{.9961} \approx .1098$$

27. b(8,8; .4) = .00065536

29. $b\left(5, 2; \frac{1}{6}\right) = \binom{5}{2}\left(\frac{1}{6}\right)^2\left(\frac{5}{6}\right)^3 = (10)\left(\frac{1}{36}\right)\left(\frac{125}{216}\right) = \frac{625}{3888} \approx .1608$

31. P(k items are defective) = b(8, k; .05)
(a) b(8, 1; .05) = .2792
(b) b(8, 2; .05) = .0515
(c) 1 - b(8, 0; .05) = 1 - .6634 = .3366
(d) b(8, 0; .05) + b(8, 1; .05) + b(8, 2; .05) = .6634 + .2793 + .0515 = .9942

33. b(6, 3; .5) = .3125

35. (a)

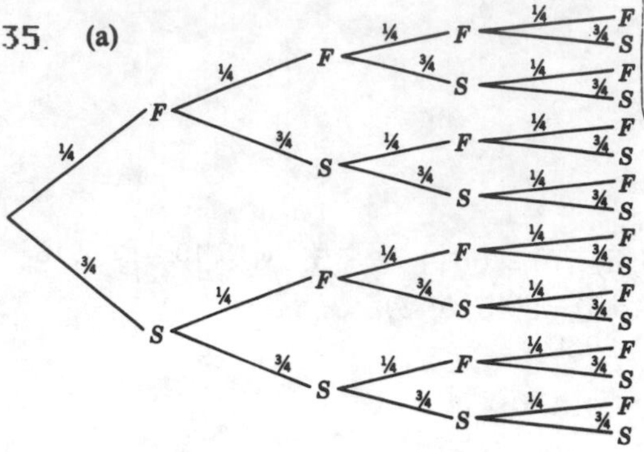

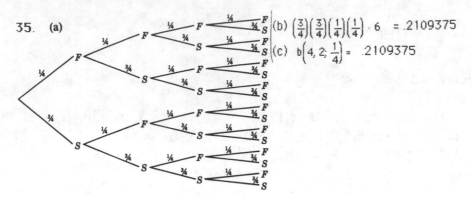

(b) $\left(\frac{3}{4}\right)\left(\frac{3}{4}\right)\left(\frac{1}{4}\right)\left(\frac{1}{4}\right) \cdot 6 = .2109375$

(c) $b\left(4, 2; \frac{1}{4}\right) = .2109375$

37. 1 - P(Hitting 0 or 1 time) = 1 - [(b(10, 0; .2) + b(10, 1; .2)]
= 1 - (.1074 + .2684) = .6242

39. Probability that student gets at least 10 correct answers:
b(15, 10; .5) + b(15, 11; .5) + b(15, 12; .5) + b(15, 13; .5) + b(15, 14; .5) + b(15, 15; .5) = .0916 + .0417 + .0139 + .0032 + .0005 + .0000 = .1509

41. Probability that student gets at least 12 correct answers: .6481

(a) $b\left(6, 5; \frac{1}{2}\right) + b\left(6, 6; \frac{1}{2}\right) = .1094$

(b) 1 - [b(6, 5; .75) + b(6, 6; .75)] = 1 - (.3560 + .1780) = .4660

43. $b(15, 15; .98) + b(15, 14; .98) = (.98)^{15} + 15(.98)^{14}(.02) = .7386 + .2260 = .9647$

45. P(k birthdays in January and 6 - k in February) = $\dfrac{\binom{6}{k}}{12^6}$ if $1 \le k \le 5$. Thus, the solution is $\binom{12}{2}\left[\binom{6}{1}+\binom{6}{2}+\binom{6}{3}+\binom{6}{4}+\binom{6}{5}\right]\frac{1}{12^6} = \frac{341}{12^5}$

47. Investigate the binomial probabilities for n = 5, 6, 7; k = 1, 2 3; and $p = \frac{1}{3}$. When n = 5, there is a dual maximum for 1 or 2 successes. When n = 7, there is a single maximum at 2 successes. We are looking for the smallest n that has a single maximum at 2 successes. Thus, n = 6.

Exercise 8.4 (page 363)

1. (.4)(2) + (.2)(3) + (.1)(-2) + (.3)(0) = 1.2
3. Expected attendance is (.08)(35,000) + (.42)(40,000) + (.42)(48,000) + (.08)(60,000) = 44,560
5. Her expected value is $8\left(\frac{1}{10}\right) + (0)\left(\frac{9}{10}\right) = .8$. She should pay $0.80 for a fair game.

7. His expected value is $\left(\frac{1}{6}\right)(10) + \left(\frac{5}{6}\right)(0) = \frac{5}{3}$. He should pay $1.67 for a fair game.

9. Expected value: (.001)(100) + (.003)(50) + (.996)0 = $0.25. IF a ticket sells for 60¢, its cost exceeds the expected value by 35¢.

11. (a) $\left(\frac{1}{8}\right)(3) + \left(\frac{3}{8}\right)(2) + \left(\frac{3}{8}\right)(0) + \left(\frac{1}{8}\right)(-3) =$ $0.75 (b) No (c) Lose $2

13. Your expected value is $\left(\frac{9}{14}\right)(-4) + \left(\frac{5}{14}\right)(6) = -\frac{6}{14}$. It is not a fair bet.

15. The outcomes are

e_1 = Heart not an ace, $p_1 = \frac{12}{52} = \frac{3}{13}$, $m_1 = .25$

e_2 = Ace not ace of hearts, $p_2 = \frac{3}{52}$, $m_2 = .35$

e_3 = Ace of hearts, $p_3 = \frac{1}{52}$

e_4 = Neither an ace nor a heart, $p_4 = \frac{36}{52} = \frac{9}{13}$, $m_4 = -.15$

Her expected value is

$$\left(\frac{3}{13}\right)(.25) + \left(\frac{3}{52}\right)(.35) + \left(\frac{1}{52}\right)(.75) + \left(\frac{9}{13}\right)(-.15) = -.012$$

No, she should not play the game.

17. $7

19. The expected profit from the first site is $\left(\frac{1}{2}\right)(15{,}000) + \left(\frac{1}{2}\right)(-3000) =$ $6000.

The expectd profit from the second site is $\left(\frac{1}{2}\right)(20{,}000) + \left(\frac{1}{2}\right)(-6000) =$ $7000.

The second site has a higher expected profit.

21. The sample space is equivalent to a Bernoulli process of 2000 trials where S = Face 5 occurs and F = Any face other than 5 occurs. Then: $p = \frac{1}{6}$ and

$E = np = 2000\left(\frac{1}{6}\right) \approx 333.3.$

23. $np = (500)(.02) = 10$

25. $np = (500)(.002) = 1$

27. $S = \{H, TH, TTH, TTTH, TTTT\}$

$P(H) = \frac{1}{4}$

$P(TH) = \frac{3}{4} \cdot \frac{1}{4} = \frac{3}{16}$

$P(TTH) = \frac{3}{4} \cdot \frac{3}{4} \cdot \frac{1}{4} = \frac{9}{64}$

$P(TTTH) = \frac{3}{4} \cdot \frac{3}{4} \cdot \frac{3}{4} \cdot \frac{1}{4} = \frac{27}{256}$

$P(TTTT) = \frac{3}{4} \cdot \frac{3}{4} \cdot \frac{3}{4} \cdot \frac{3}{4} = \frac{81}{256}$

$E = 1 \cdot \frac{1}{4} + 2 \cdot \frac{3}{16} + 3 \cdot \frac{9}{64} + 4 \cdot \frac{27}{256} + 4 \cdot \frac{81}{256} = \frac{175}{64} \approx 2.73$ tosses

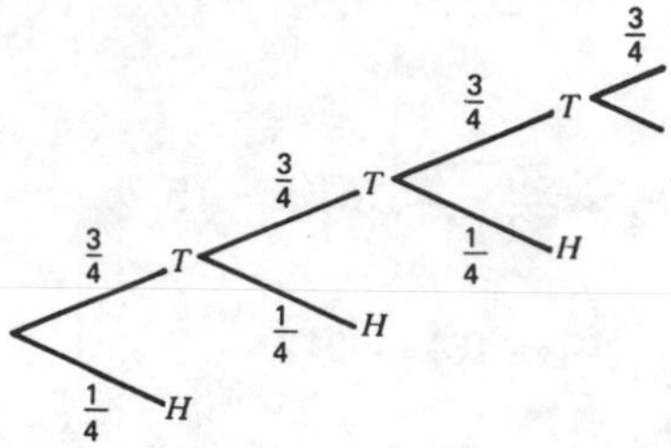

29. $E_1 = m_1p_1 + m_2p_2 + \ldots + m_np_n$. Multiplying each value by k we get

$E_2 = km_1p_1 + km_2p_2 + \ldots + km_np_n = k[m_1p_1 + m_2p_2 + \ldots + m_np_n] = k \cdot E_1$

Thus, we can see that the expected value of the new experiment, E_2, is k times the original expected value E_1. Add to each outcome used in figuring E_1 the constand k. The new expected value is:

$E_3 = (m_1 + k)p_1 + (m_2 + k)p_2 + \ldots + (m_n + k)p_n = m_1p_1 + kp_1 + m_2p_2 + kp_2 + \ldots + m_np_n + kp_n = m_1p_1 + m_2p_2 + \ldots + m_np_n + kp_1 + kp_2 + \ldots + kp_n$

$= E_1 + k(p_1 + p_2 + \ldots + p_n)$ Since $p_1 + p_2 + \ldots + p_n = 1$, we get $E_3 = E_1 + k$. Thus, we see that the expected value of the new experiment, E_3, is the expected value of the original experiment, E_1, plus k.

Exercise 8.5 (page 371)

1. The expected number of customers is (.10)(7) + (.20)(8) + (.40)(9) + (.20)(10) + (.10)(11) = 9. The optimal number of cars is 9. The expected daily profit is (.10)(7)(14) + (.20)(8)(14) + (.70)(9)(14) - (9)(8) = \$48.40.

3.

Group size	$p^n - \frac{1}{n}$
2	$(.95)^2 - .5 = .4025$
3	$(.95)^3 - .333 = .524$
4	$(.95)^4 - .25 = .565$
5	$(.95)^5 - .2 = .574$
6	$(.95)^6 - .167 = .568$

5. (a) $E(x) = 75,000 - 75,000(.05)^x - 500x$. (b) Two divers should be used.

7. (792)(.27) + (726)(.46) + (664)(.27) = 727.08; (980)(.27) + (881)(.46) + (789)(.27) = 882.89;
(1228)(.27)(.45) + (1193)(.27)(.30) + (1162)(.27)(.25 + (1093)(.46)(.36) + (1060)(.46)(.31) + (1029)(.46)(.33) + (908)(.27)(.24) + 936(.27)(.48) + 907(.27)(.28) = 1061.34

Review Exercises (page 373)

1. (a) $\binom{20}{4} = 4845$ (b) $\binom{20}{3}\binom{5}{1} = 5700$

   (c) $\binom{25}{4} - \binom{20}{4} = 12650 - 4845 = 7805$

3. b(5,0; .2) = .3277; b(5,1; .2) = .4096; b(5,2; .2) = .2048; b(5,3; .2) = .0512; b(5,4; .2) = .0064; b(5,5; .2) = .0003

5. (a) $\left(\frac{1}{2}\right)^{12} = \frac{1}{4096}$ (b) b(12,7; .5) + b(12,8; .5) + b(12,9; .5) +b(12,10; .5) + b(12,11; .5) + b(12,12; .5) = .1934 + .1208 + .0537 + .0161 + .0029 + .0002 = .3871

   (c) $\frac{.3871}{.6129} \approx .6316$ or .3871 to .6129

7. Expected cost for a fair game is $\left(\frac{1}{7}\right)(89.99) + \frac{1}{3}(49.99) = 29.52$.

9. Let e_1 = Lose all 3 prizes, $p_1 = \frac{(995)(994)(993)}{(1000)(999)(998)}$, $m_1 = 0$

   e_2 = Win just \$30, $p_2 = \frac{(995)(994)(5)}{(1000)(999)(998)}$, $m_2 = 30$

   e_3 = Win just \$50, $p_3 = \frac{(995)(994)(5)}{(1000)(999)(998)}$, $m_3 = 50$

   e_4 = Win just \$100, $p_4 = \frac{(995)(994)(5)}{(1000)(999)(998)}$, $m_4 = 100$

   e_5 = Win just \$50 and \$30, $p_5 = \frac{(995)(5)(4)}{(1000)(999)(998)}$, $m_5 = 80$

   e_6 = Win just \$100 and \$30, $p_6 = \frac{(995)(5)(4)}{(1000)(999)(998)}$, $m_6 = 130$

e_7 = Win just \$100 and \$50, $p_7 = \frac{(995)(5)(4)}{(1000)(999)(998)}$, $m_7 = 150$

e_8 = Win all three, $p_8 = \frac{(5)(4)(3)}{(1000)(999)(998)}$, $m_8 = 180$

11. (a) Expected value for five tickets is \$0.90. (b) She paid \$0.35 extra.

$S = \{(I, 10), (I, 5), (I, 8), (I, 70), (I, 80), (II, 1), (II, 5)\}$

$P(I, 10) = P(I, 70) = P(I, 80) = \frac{1}{21}$

$P(I, 5) = P(I, 8) = \frac{2}{21}$

$P(II, 1) = P(II, 5) = \frac{2}{6}$

$E = \left(\frac{1}{21}\right)(10) + \left(\frac{1}{21}\right)(70) + \left(\frac{1}{21}\right)(80) + \left(\frac{2}{21}\right)(5) + \left(\frac{2}{21}\right)(8) + \left(\frac{2}{6}\right)(5) = \frac{76}{7}$

13. The expected value of the game is $(1)\left(\frac{18}{37}\right) + (-1)\left(\frac{19}{37}\right) = -\frac{1}{37}$. Game is not fair.

15. $(0)\left(\frac{1}{8}\right) + (1)\left(\frac{3}{8}\right) + 2\left(\frac{3}{8}\right) + 3\left(\frac{1}{8}\right) = 1\frac{1}{2}$

CHAPTER 9

Exercise 9.1 (page 380)

1. A study of the opinions of people about a certain television program: A poll should be taken either door-to-door or by means of the telephone.
3. A study of the opinions of people toward Medicare: A poll should be taken door-to-door in which people are asked to fill out a questionnaire.
5. A study of the number of savings accounts per family in the United States: The data should be gathered from all different kinds of banks.
7. (a) Asking a group of children if they like candy to determine what percentage of people like candy.
   (b) Asking a group of people over 65 their opinion toward Medicare to determine the opinion of people in general about Medicare.
9. By taking a poll downtown, you would question mostly people who are either shopping or working downtown. For instance, you would question few students.

Exercise 9.2 (page 386)

1. (a) The lower limit of the 5th class is 250.
   (b) The upper limit of the 4th class is 249.
   (c) The midpoint of the 5th class is 275.
   (d) The size of the 5th interval is 50.
   (e) The frequency of the 3rd class is 33.
   (f) The class interval having the largest frequency is the 5th.
   (g) The number of precincts with less than 600 votes is 752.
   (h) Histogram
   (i) Frequency polygon

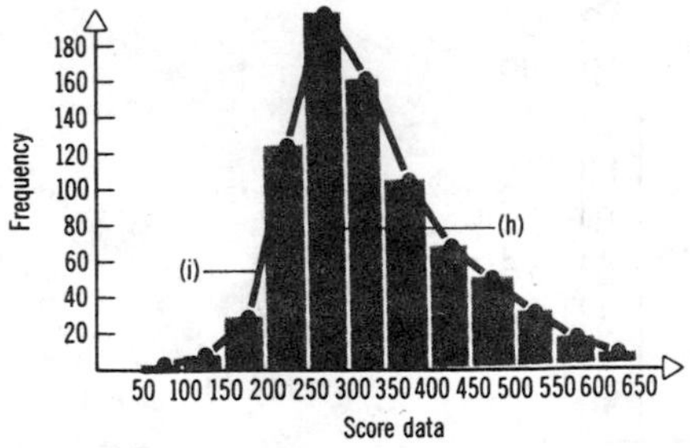

3. (a)

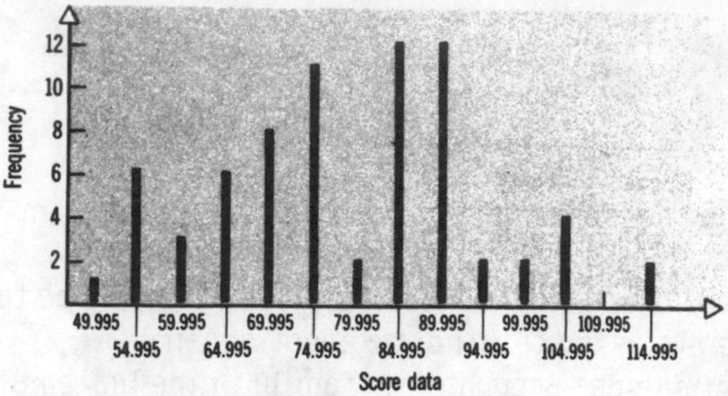

(b) Histogram (c) Frequency polygon

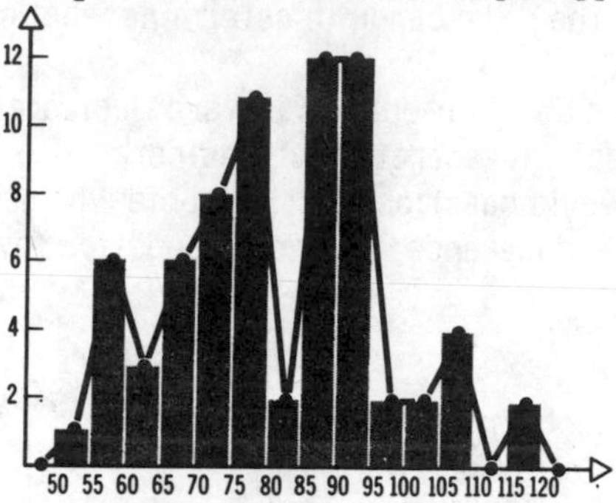

(d) Cumulative frequency

Class Interval	Tally	f	cf
114.995-119.995	||	2	71
109.995-114.995		0	69
104.995-109.995	||||	4	69
99.995-104.995	||	2	65
94.995- 99.995	||	2	63
89.995-994.995	||||| ||||| ||	12	61
84.995- 89.995	||||| ||||| ||	12	49
79.995-84.995	||	2	37
74.995-79.995	||||| ||||| |	11	35
69.995-74.995	||||| |||	8	24
64.995-69.995	||||| |	6	16
59.995-64.995	|||	3	10
54.995-59.995	||||| |	6	7
49.995-54.995	|	1	1

(e) Cumulative frequency distribution

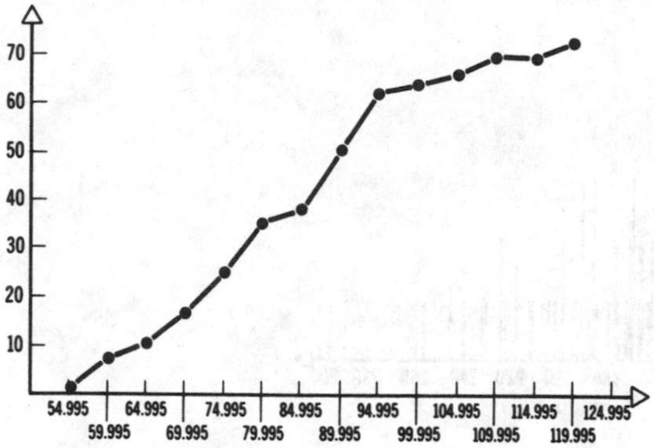

5. (a) Range = 296 - 78 = 218

Score	Tally	f	Score	Tally	f	Score	Tally	f
296	|	1	175	|	1	137	||	2
289	|	1	172	|	1	136	||	2
256	|	1	171	||	2	134	|	1
245	||	2	169	|||	3	132	||	2
240	|	1	166	||	2	131	||||	4
232	|	1	165	||	2	130	|	1
230	|	1	162	|	1	129	|||	3
224	||	2	161	||	2	128	||	2
222	|	1	158	|	1	127	|||	3
218	||	2	157	|	1	126	|	1
212	|	1	156	||	2	123	||	2
211	|	1	155	|	1	122	|	1
207	|	1	154	||	2	119	||	2
204	|	1	153	|||	3	116	|||	3
202	|	1	152	|	1	115	|	1
198	||	2	149	|	1	113	|	1
194	|	1	148	|	1	112	|	1
192	|	1	146	||	2	111	|	1
190	|||	3	145	||	2	110	|	1
188	|	1	144	||	2	108	|	1
185	|||	3	142	|	1	105	|	1
184	|	1	141	|	1	100	|	1
178	|	1	140	|	1	95	|	1
176	||	2	138	|	1	91	|	1

(b) Line chart

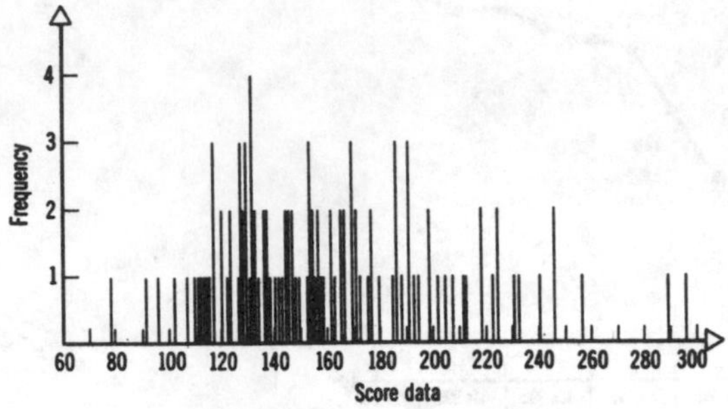

(c) Histogram (d) Frequency polygon

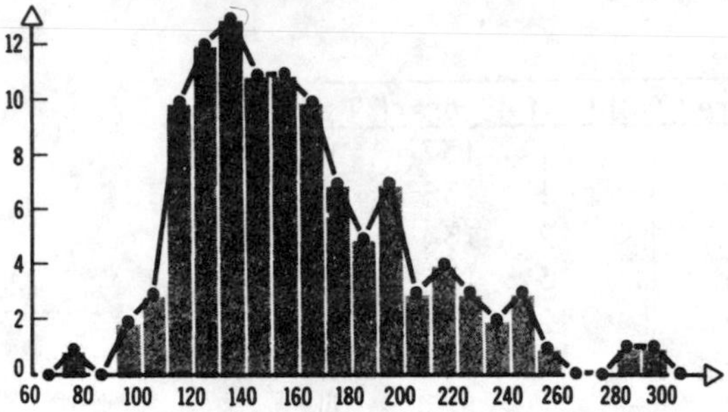

(e) Cumulative (less than) frequency

Class Interval	Tally	f	cf	Class Interval	Tally	f	cf
290.5-300.5	I	1	110	170.5-180.5	IIIII II	7	80
280.5-290.5	I	1	109	160.5-170.5	IIIII IIIII	10	73
270.5-280.5		0	108	150.5-160.5	IIIII IIIII I	11	63
260.5-270.5		0	108	140.5-150.5	IIIII IIIII	10	52
250.5-260.5	I	1	108	130.5-140.5	IIIII IIIII III	13	42
240.5-250.5	II	2	107	120.5-130.5	IIIII IIIII IIII	14	29
230.5-240.5	II	2	105	110.5-120.5	IIIII IIII	9	15
220.5-230.5	IIII	4	103	100.5-110.5	III	3	6
210.5-220.5	IIII	4	99	90.5-100.5	II	2	3
200.5-210.5	III	3	95	80.5-90.5		0	1
190.5-200.5	IIII	4	92	70.5-80.5	I	1	1
180.5-190.5	IIIII III	8	88				

(f)

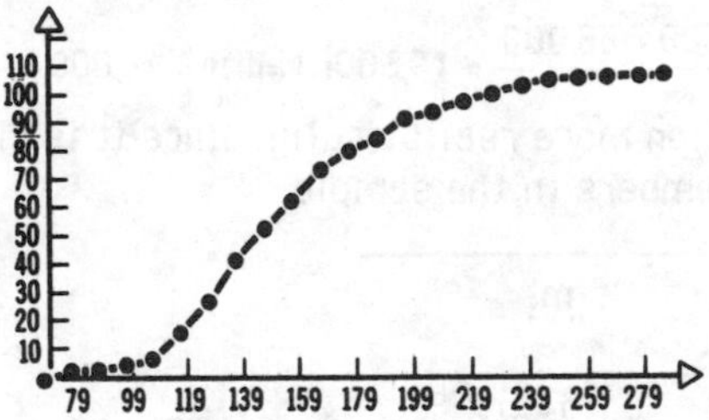

(g) Cumulative (more than) frequency

<table>
<tr><th>Class Interval</th><th>Tally</th><th>f</th><th>cf</th><th>Class Interval</th><th>Tally</th><th>f</th><th>cf</th></tr>
<tr><td>70.5-80.5</td><td>|</td><td>1</td><td>110</td><td>180.5-190.5</td><td>||||| |||</td><td>8</td><td>30</td></tr>
<tr><td>80.5-90.5</td><td></td><td>0</td><td>109</td><td>190.5-20.5</td><td>||||</td><td>4</td><td>22</td></tr>
<tr><td>90.5-100.5</td><td>||</td><td>2</td><td>109</td><td>200.5-210.5</td><td>|||</td><td>3</td><td>18</td></tr>
<tr><td>100.5-110.5</td><td>|||</td><td>3</td><td>107</td><td>210.5-220.5</td><td>||||</td><td>4</td><td>15</td></tr>
<tr><td>110.5-120.5</td><td>||||| ||||</td><td>9</td><td>104</td><td>220.5-230.5</td><td>||||</td><td>4</td><td>11</td></tr>
<tr><td>120.5-130.5</td><td>||||| ||||| ||||</td><td>14</td><td>95</td><td>230.5-240.5</td><td>||</td><td>2</td><td>7</td></tr>
<tr><td>130.5-140.5</td><td>||||| ||||| |||</td><td>13</td><td>81</td><td>240.5-250.5</td><td>||</td><td>2</td><td>5</td></tr>
<tr><td>140.5-150.5</td><td>||||| |||||</td><td>10</td><td>68</td><td>250.5-260.5</td><td>|</td><td>1</td><td>3</td></tr>
<tr><td>150.5-160.5</td><td>||||| ||||| |</td><td>11</td><td>58</td><td>260.5-270.5</td><td></td><td>0</td><td>2</td></tr>
<tr><td>160.5-170.5</td><td>||||| |||||</td><td>10</td><td>47</td><td>270.5-280.5</td><td></td><td>0</td><td>2</td></tr>
<tr><td>170.5-180.5</td><td>||||| ||</td><td>7</td><td>37</td><td>280.5-290.5</td><td>|</td><td>1</td><td>2</td></tr>
<tr><td></td><td></td><td></td><td></td><td>290.5-300.5</td><td>|</td><td>1</td><td>1</td></tr>
</table>

(h)

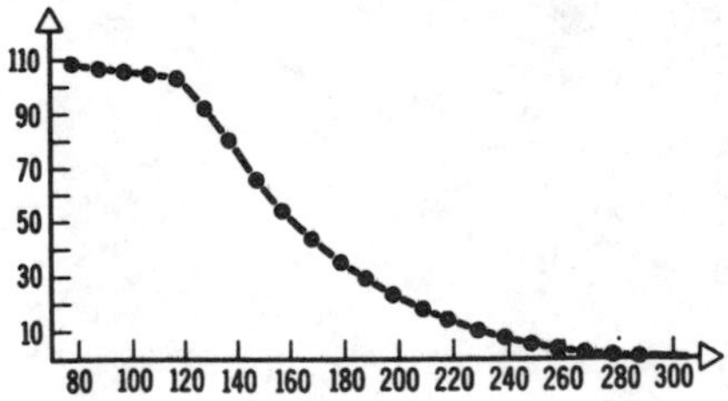

Exercise 9.3 (page 392)

1. Mean = $\bar{X} = \dfrac{21+25+43+36}{4} = \dfrac{125}{4} = 31.25$; Median = $\dfrac{25+36}{2} = 30.5$; no mode

3. Mean = 70.4; Median = 70; Mode = 55.

5. Mean = 76.2; Median = 75; no mode

7. Mean = $\bar{X}$ = 3.51; Median = 3.45

9. $\bar{X} = \dfrac{(50)(155)+(90)(190)+(120)(210)+(75)(255)}{50+90+120+75} = 206.49$

11. $\bar{X} = \frac{14{,}000 + 15{,}000 + 16{,}000 + 16{,}500 + 35{,}000}{5} = 19{,}300$; Median = 16,000

The median describes the situation more realistically, since it is closer to the salary of most of the faculty members in the sample.

13.

	f_i	m_i	$f_i m_i$
Under \$100	25	87.50	2,187.50
\$100 - \$125	55	112.50	6,187.50
\$125 - \$150	325	137.50	44,687.50
\$150 - \$175	410	162.50	66,625.00
\$175 - \$200	215	187.50	40,312.50
\$200 - \$225	75	212.50	15,937.50
Over \$225	50	237.50	11,875.00
	1,155		187,812.50

Mean = \$162.61

Median = \$160.52

15. For Table 5, $C_{75} \approx 91.77$, $C_{40} \approx 77.0$. For Table 6, $C_{75} \approx 93.03$, $C_{40} \approx 76.52$.

17. Let 325 be the assumed mean.

	f	x'	fx'
600-649	1	6	6
550-599	9	5	45
500-549	26	4	104
450-499	48	3	144
400-449	67	2	134
350-399	104	1	104
300-349	150	0	0
250-299	190	-1	-190
200-249	120	-2	-240
150-199	33	-3	-99
100-149	4	-4	-16
50-99	1	-5	-5

$n = 753$

$\Sigma fx' = -13$

$\bar{X} = 325 + \left(\frac{-13}{753}\right)(50) \approx 324.1$

Exercise 9.4 (page 399)

1. (b)

3. $\bar{X} = \dfrac{4+5+9+9+10+14+25}{7} \approx 10.86$

x	$x - \bar{x}$	$(x - \bar{x})^2$
4	-6.86	47.0596
5	-5.86	34.3396
9	-1.86	3.4596
9	-1.86	3.4596
10	-.86	.7596
14	3.14	9.8596
25	14.14	199.9396
		298.9572

$\sigma = \sqrt{\dfrac{298.8572}{7}} \approx 6.53$

5. $\bar{X} = \dfrac{58+62+70+70}{4} = \dfrac{260}{4} = 65$

x	$x - \bar{x}$	$(x - \bar{x})$
58	-7	49
62	-3	9
70	5	25
70	5	25
		108

$\sigma = \sqrt{\dfrac{108}{4}} \approx 5.196$

7. $\bar{X} = \dfrac{62+75+78+85+100}{5} = 80$

x	$x - \bar{x}$	$(x - \bar{x})^2$
62	-18	324
75	-5	25
78	-2	4
85	5	25
100	20	400
		778

$\sigma = \sqrt{\dfrac{778}{5}} \approx 12.47$

9. $\bar{X} = \dfrac{769+815+845+893+922+968}{6} \approx 868.67$

x	$x - \bar{x}$	$(x - \bar{x})^2$
769	-99.67	9,934.1089
815	-53.67	2,880.4689
845	-23.67	560.2689
893	24.33	591.9489
922	53.33	2,844.0889
968	99.33	9,866.4489
		26,677.3334

$\sigma = \sqrt{\dfrac{26{,}677.3334}{6}} \approx 66.68$

11. $\bar{X} = 324.14$

Class Midpoint	f_i	$x - \bar{X}_i$	$(x - \bar{X})^2$	$(x - \bar{X})^2 \cdot f_i$
625	1	300.86	90,516.7396	90,516.7396
575	9	250.86	62,930.7396	566,376.6564
525	26	200.86	40,344.7396	1,048,963.2296
475	48	150.86	22,758.7396	1,092,419.5008
425	67	100.86	10,172.7396	1,092,419.5008
375	104	50.86	2,586.7396	269,020.9184
325	150	.86	.7396	110.9400
275	190	-49.14	2,414.7396	458,800.5240
225	120	-99.14	9,828.7396	1,179,448.7520
175	33	-149.14	22,242.7396	734,010.4068
125	4	-199.14	39,656.7396	158,626.9584
75	1	-249.14	62,070.7396	62,070.7396
				6,341,938.9188

$$\sigma = \sqrt{\frac{6{,}341{,}938.9188}{753}} \approx 91.77$$

13. (a) $k = 6,\ 1 = \frac{3^2}{6^2} = .75,\ 75\%$ (b) $k = 5,\ 64\%$

(c) $k = 9,\ 88\frac{8}{9}\%$ (d) $1 = .75 = .25,\ 25\%$

(e) $11\frac{1}{9}\%$

Exercise 9.5 (page 407)

1. $\bar{X} = 8;\ \sigma = 1$ **3.** $\bar{X} = 18;\ \sigma = 1$

5. $Z = \frac{7 - 13.1}{9.3} \approx -.6559$, $Z = \frac{9 - 13.1}{9.3} \approx -.4409$, $Z = \frac{13 - 13.1}{9.3} \approx -.0108$,

$Z = \frac{15 - 13.1}{9.3} \approx .2043$, $Z = \frac{29 - 13.1}{9.3} \approx 1.7097$, $Z = \frac{37 - 13.1}{9.3} \approx 2.5699$,

$Z = \frac{41 - 13.1}{9.3} = 3.0000$

7. $P(Z \le -0.5) = \frac{1}{2} - P(-0.5 \le Z \le 0) = \frac{1}{2} - P(0 \le Z \le 0.5) = \frac{1}{2} - 0.1915 = 0.3085.$

9. $P(Z \ge 1.5) = \frac{1}{2}$ $P(0 \le Z \le 1.5) = \frac{1}{2} - 0.4332 = 0.0668$

11. (a) 0.3133 (b) 0.3642 (c) 0.4938 (d) 0.4987
(e) 0.2734 (f) 0.4896 (g) 0.2881 (h) 0.4988

13. $Z = \frac{x - \bar{X}}{\sigma}$, $\bar{X} = 64$, $\sigma = 2$

(a) When $x = 66$, $Z = 1$; when $x = 62$, $Z = -1$;
$P(-1 \le Z \le 1) = 2P(0 \le Z \le 1) = 0.6826$
This means 68.26% of the women are between 62 and 66 inches tall;
$(0.6826)(2000) = 1365.2 \approx 1365$ women

(b) $P(-2 \le Z \le 2) = 2(0.4772) = 0.9544$; $(0.9544)(2000) = 1908.8 \approx 1909$ women

(c) $(0.9974)(2000) = 1994.8 \approx 1995$ women

15. (a) $\frac{142 - 130}{5.2} = 2.31$; $P(Z \ge 2.31) = \frac{1}{2} - P(0 \le Z \le 2.31) = 0.5 - 0.4896 = 0.01404$
$= 1.04\%$

(b) According to the table, Z must be close to 1.04 if the proportional area is 35% (≈ 0.3508).
$(1.04)\sigma = (1.04)(5.2) \approx 5.4$ pounds
Thus, we expect 70% of the students to be within 5.4 pounds of the mean, or between 134.6 and 135.4 pounds.

17. The Z-score for 1 is $Z = (1 - 2.2)/1.7 = -0.71$; the area under the normal curve between -0.71 and 0 is 0.2611; the area under the normal curve for scores less than -0.71 is $0.5000 - 0.2611 = 0.2389$. The number of shoes he should expect to replace out of 1000 is 239.

19. Caryl: $Z = (76 - 82)/7 = -0.86$; Mary: $Z = (89 - 93)/2 = -2$,
Kathleen: $Z = (21 - 24)/9 = -0.33$; Kathleen has the highest relative standing.

21 b(15,0; .3) ≈ .0047
b(15,1; .3) ≈ .0305
b(15,2; .3) ≈ .0916
b(15,3; .3) ≈ .1700
b(15,4; .3) ≈ .2186
b(15,5; .3) ≈ .2061
b(15,6; .3) ≈ .1472
b(15,7; .3) ≈ .0811
b(15,8; .3) ≈ .0348
b(15,9; .3) ≈ .0116
b(15,10; .3) ≈ .0030
b(15,11; .3) ≈ .0006
b(15,12; .3) ≈ .0001
b(15,13; .3) ≈ .0000
b(15,14; .3) ≈ .0000
b(15,15; .3) ≈ .0000

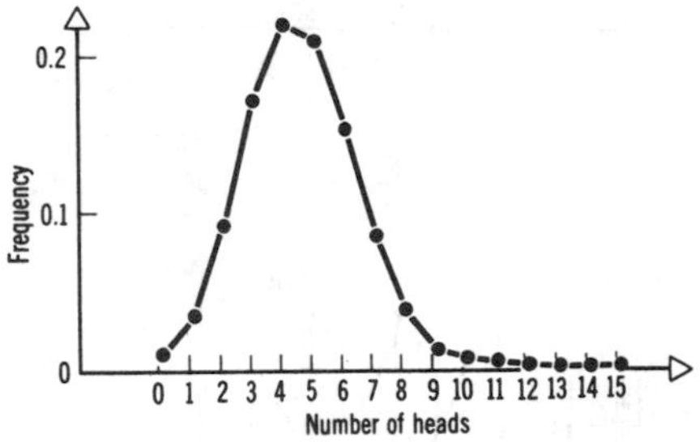

23. $Z(285) = \dfrac{285 - 300}{13} \approx -1.2$

$Z(3150 = \dfrac{315 - 300}{13} \approx 1.2$

$P(-1.2 \le Z \le 1.2) \approx (2)(0.3849) = 0.7698$

25. $P(Z \ge 0) = 0.5$

27. $Z(325) = \dfrac{325 - 300}{13} \approx 1.9$

$P(Z \ge 1.9) \approx 0.5 - 0.4713 = 0.0287$

Review Exercises (page 410)

1. (a)

Score	Tally	Frequency	Score	Tally	Frequency
100	||	2	66	||	2
99	|	1	63	||	2
95	|	1	60	|	1
92	|	1	55	|	1
90	|	1	62	||	2
89	|	1	48	|	1
87	||	2	44	|	1
85	||	2	42	|	1
83	|	1	33	|	1
82	|	1	30	|	1
80	|||	3	26	|	1
78	||	2	21	|	1
77	|	1	20	|	1
75	|	1	19	|	1
74	|	1	17	|	1
73	||	2	14	||	2
72	||	2	12	|	1
70	|	1	10	|	1
69	|	1	8	|	1

Range = 100 - 8 = 92

(b)

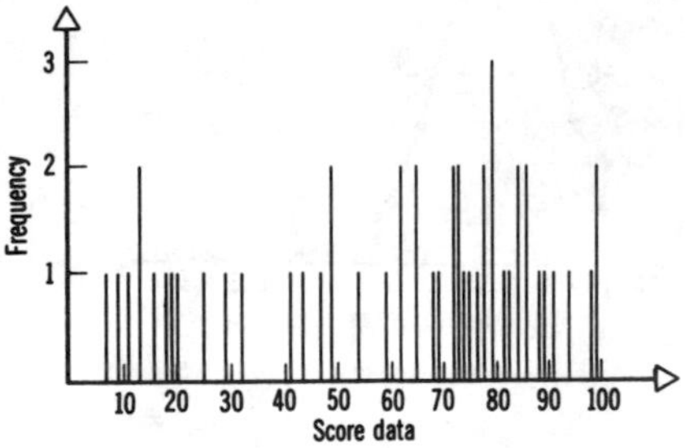

(c) Histogram

(d) Frequency polygon

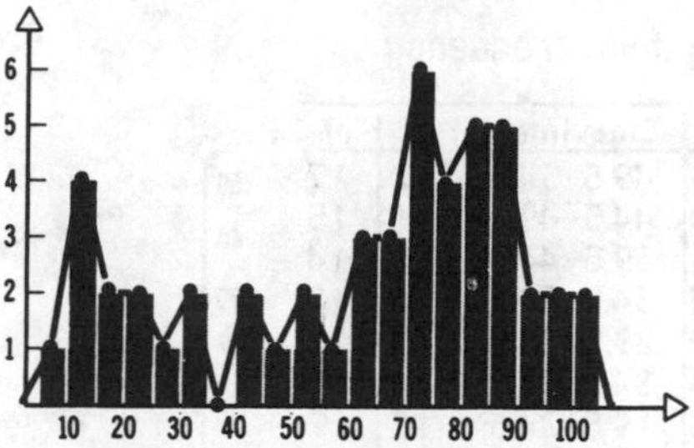

(e) Cumulative (more than)frequency

<table>
<tr><th>Class Interval</th><th>Tally</th><th>f</th><th>cf</th><th>Class Interval</th><th>Tally</th><th>f</th><th>cf</th></tr>
<tr><td>99.5-104.5</td><td>||</td><td>2</td><td>2</td><td>49.5-54.5</td><td>||</td><td>2</td><td>35</td></tr>
<tr><td>94.5-99.5</td><td>||</td><td>2</td><td>4</td><td>44.5-49.5</td><td>|</td><td>1</td><td>36</td></tr>
<tr><td>89.5-94.5</td><td>||</td><td>2</td><td>6</td><td>39.5-44.5</td><td>||</td><td>2</td><td>38</td></tr>
<tr><td>84.5-89.5</td><td>|||||</td><td>5</td><td>11</td><td>34.5-39.5</td><td></td><td>0</td><td>38</td></tr>
<tr><td>79.5-84.5</td><td>|||||</td><td>5</td><td>16</td><td>29.5-34.5</td><td>||</td><td>2</td><td>40</td></tr>
<tr><td>74.5-79.5</td><td>||||</td><td>4</td><td>20</td><td>24.5-29.5</td><td>|</td><td>1</td><td>41</td></tr>
<tr><td>69.5-74.5</td><td>||||||</td><td>6</td><td>26</td><td>19.5-24.5</td><td>||</td><td>2</td><td>43</td></tr>
<tr><td>64.5-69.5</td><td>|||</td><td>3</td><td>29</td><td>14.5-19.5</td><td>||</td><td>2</td><td>45</td></tr>
<tr><td>59.5-64.5</td><td>|||</td><td>3</td><td>32</td><td>9.5-14.5</td><td>||||</td><td>4</td><td>49</td></tr>
<tr><td>54.5-59.5</td><td>|</td><td>1</td><td>33</td><td>4.5- 9.5</td><td>|</td><td>1</td><td>50</td></tr>
</table>

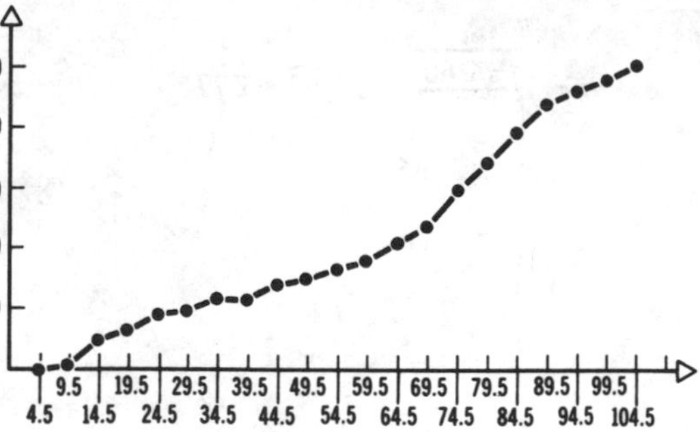

(f) Cumulative (less than) frequency

Class interval	f	cf	Class Interval	f	cf
99.5-104.5	2	50	49.5-54.5	2	17
94.5-99.5	2	48	44.5-49.5	1	15
89.5-94.5	2	46	39.5-44.5	2	14
84.5-89.5	5	44	34.5-39.5	0	12
79.5-84.5	5	39	29.5-34.5	2	12
74.5-79.5	4	34	24.5-29.5	1	10
69.5-74.5	6	30	19.5-24.5	2	9
64.5-69.5	3	24	14.5-19.5	2	7
59.5-64.5	3	21	9.5-14.5	4	5
54.5-59.5	1	18	4.5-9.5	1	1

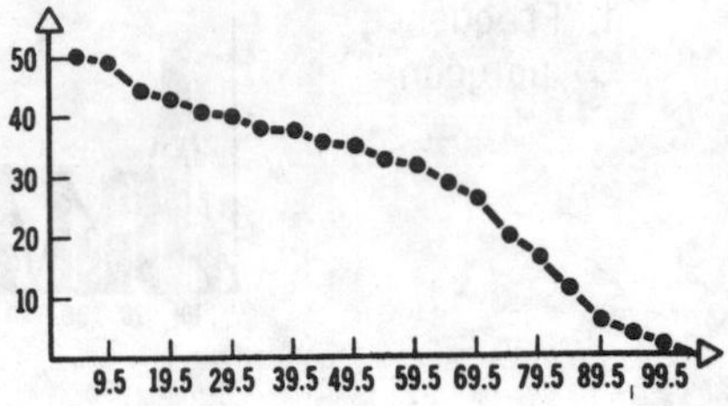

3. The mean is a poor measure in (b) because it gives too much importance to the extreme value 195.

5. A = {20, 15, 5, 0}; B = {12, 11, 10, 9, 8}: Both sets have a mean of 10. The standard diviation for the first set is $\sigma_1 = \sqrt{250/5} \approx 7.07$. The standard deviation for the second set is $\sigma_2 = \sqrt{10/5} \approx 1.41$.

7.

	$x - \bar{x}$	$(x - \bar{x})^2$
81	5.43	29.48
77	1.43	2.04
76	.43	.18
76	.43	.18
74	-1.57	2.46
73	-2.57	6.60
72	-3.57	12.74
		53.68

Mean = 75.57

$$\sigma = \sqrt{\frac{53.68}{7}} \approx \sqrt{7.67} \approx 2.77$$

9. (a) (0.6827)(600) = 409.62
(b) [(0.4987) - (0.3413)](600) = 94.44
(c) (0.4972)(600) = 298.32

11. (a) (0.4970) - (0.4115) = 0.0855
(b) ().4599) - (0.3849) = 0.0750

13. at least .75

CHAPTER 10

Exercise 10.1 (page 417)

1. Let the entries denote Tami's winnings in cents. Laura chooses columns and Tami chooses rows:

		Laura I	Laura II
Tami	I	-10	10
	II	10	-10

3. The entries denote Tami's winnings in cents.

		Laura 1	Laura 4	Laura 7
Tami	1	-20	50	-80
	4	50	-80	110
	7	-80	110	-140

5. Strictly determined; value is -1.
7. Strictly determined; value is 2.
9. Not strictly determined.
11. Strictly determined; value is 2.
13. Not strictly determined.
15. $0 \le a \le 3$ (There is no saddle point in row 1, unless $a \le 3$; in row 2, unless $a \le -9$; in row 3, unless $a \le -5$; in column 1, unless $a \ge 0$; in column 2, unless $a \ge 8$; in column 3, unless $a \ge 5$. Thus, there is no saddle point unless $0 \le a \le 3$. But if $0 \le a \le 3$, then there is a saddle point in row 1, column 1.)
17. $a \le 0 \le b$ or $b \le 0 \le a$ (The matrix $\begin{bmatrix} a & 0 \\ 0 & b \end{bmatrix}$ is strictly determined if and only if there is a saddle point; a is a saddle point if and only if $a = 0$; b is a saddle point if and only if $b = 0$. The 0 in row 1, column 2 is a saddle point if and only if $0 \le a$ and $0 \ge b$. The 0 in row 2, column 1 is a saddle point if and only if $0 \le b$ and $0 \ge a$.)

Exercise 10.2 (page 420)

1. $P = [.3 \ \ .7]$, $Q = \begin{bmatrix} .4 \\ .6 \end{bmatrix}$, $E = [.3 \ \ .7]\begin{bmatrix} 6 & 0 \\ -2 & 3 \end{bmatrix}\begin{bmatrix} .4 \\ .6 \end{bmatrix} = .16 + 1.26 = 1.42$

3. $E = \begin{bmatrix} \frac{1}{2} & \frac{1}{2} \end{bmatrix}\begin{bmatrix} 4 & 0 \\ 2 & 3 \end{bmatrix}\begin{bmatrix} \frac{1}{2} \\ \frac{1}{2} \end{bmatrix} = \frac{3}{2} + \frac{3}{4} = \frac{9}{4}$

5. $E = \begin{bmatrix} \frac{1}{4} & \frac{3}{4} \end{bmatrix}\begin{bmatrix} 4 & 0 \\ 2 & 3 \end{bmatrix}\begin{bmatrix} \frac{1}{2} \\ \frac{1}{2} \end{bmatrix} = \frac{19}{8}$

7. $E = \begin{bmatrix} \frac{2}{3} & \frac{1}{3} \end{bmatrix} \begin{bmatrix} 4 & 0 \\ -3 & 6 \end{bmatrix} \begin{bmatrix} \frac{1}{3} \\ \frac{2}{3} \end{bmatrix} = \frac{5}{9} + \frac{4}{3} = \frac{17}{9}$

9. $E = \begin{bmatrix} \frac{1}{3} & \frac{1}{3} & \frac{1}{3} \end{bmatrix} \begin{bmatrix} 1 & 0 & 0 \\ 0 & 1 & 0 \\ 0 & 0 & 1 \end{bmatrix} \begin{bmatrix} \frac{1}{3} \\ \frac{1}{3} \\ \frac{1}{3} \end{bmatrix} = \frac{1}{3}$

11. The nonstrictly determined games are those without saddle points. If $a_{11} = a_{12}$ or $a_{21} = a_{22}$, then the game is strictly determined. (See Problem 16 in Exercise 1.)

(a) If $a_{11} > a_{12}$, then $a_{12} < a_{22}$ to prevent a_{12} from being a saddle point. This means that $a_{21} < a_{22}$ to prevent a_{22} from being a saddle point. Also, $a_{11} > a_{21}$ to prevent a_{21} from being a saddle point.

(b) If $a_{11} < a_{12}$, then $a_{21} > a_{11}$ to prevent a_{11} from being a saddle point. This means that $a_{22} < a_{21}$ to prevent a_{21} from being a saddle point. Also, $a_{12} > a_{22}$ to prevent a_{22} from being a saddle point.

Exercise 10.3 (page 427)

1. $E_I = p + 4(1 - p) = 4 - 3p$

$E_I = 2p + (1 - p) = p + 1$

The optimal strategy for Player I is [.75 .25].

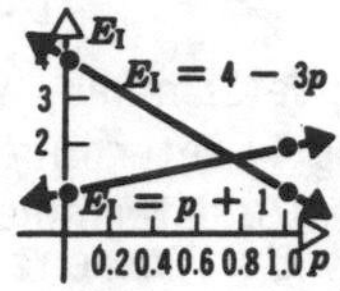

$E_{II} = q + 2(1 - q) = 2 - q$

$E_{II} = 4q + (1 - q) = 1 + 3q$

The optimal strategy for Player II is [.25 .75].

$E = PAQ = [.75 \;\; .25] \begin{bmatrix} 1 & 2 \\ 4 & 1 \end{bmatrix} \begin{bmatrix} .25 \\ .75 \end{bmatrix} = 1.75$

3. $E_I = -3p + (1 - p) = 1 - 4p$

$E_I = 2p - 0(1 - p) = 2p$

The optimum strategy for Player I is $\begin{bmatrix} \frac{1}{6} & \frac{5}{6} \end{bmatrix}$.

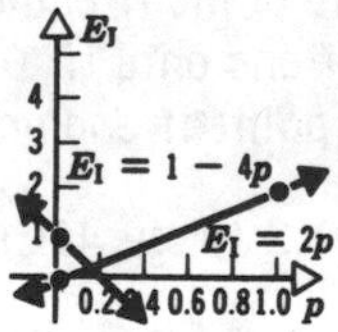

$E_{II} = -3q + 2(1 - q) = 2 - 5q$

$E_{II} = q + 0(1 - q) = q$

The optimum strategy for Player II is $\begin{bmatrix} \frac{1}{3} & \frac{2}{3} \end{bmatrix}$.

The value of the game is

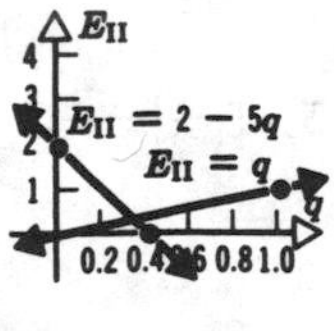

$E = PAQ = \begin{bmatrix} \frac{1}{6} & \frac{5}{6} \end{bmatrix} \begin{bmatrix} -3 & 2 \\ 1 & 0 \end{bmatrix} \begin{bmatrix} \frac{1}{3} \\ \frac{2}{3} \end{bmatrix} = \frac{1}{3}$

5. $E_I = 2p - (1 - p) = 3p - 1$

$E_I = -p + 4(1 - p) = 4 - 5p$

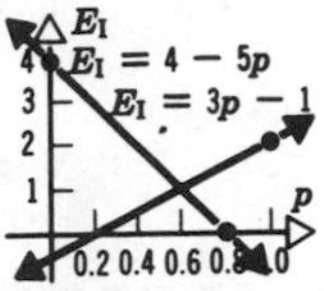

The optimum strategy for Player I is $\begin{bmatrix} \frac{5}{8} & \frac{3}{8} \end{bmatrix}$.

$E_{II} = 2q - (1 - q) = 3q - 1$

$E_{II} = -q + 4(1 - q) = 4 - 5q$

The optimum strategy for Player II is $\begin{bmatrix} \frac{5}{8} & \frac{3}{8} \end{bmatrix}$.

The value of the game is

$$E = PAQ = \begin{bmatrix} \frac{5}{8} & \frac{3}{8} \end{bmatrix} \begin{bmatrix} 2 & -1 \\ -1 & 4 \end{bmatrix} \begin{bmatrix} \frac{5}{8} \\ \frac{3}{8} \end{bmatrix} = \frac{7}{8}$$

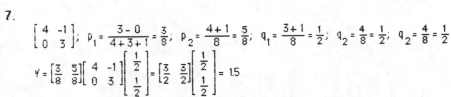

7.

$$\begin{bmatrix} 4 & -1 \\ 0 & 3 \end{bmatrix}; \quad p_1 = \frac{3 - 0}{4 + 3 + 1} = \frac{3}{8}; \quad p_2 = \frac{4 + 1}{8} = \frac{5}{8}; \quad q_1 = \frac{3 + 1}{8} = \frac{1}{2}; \quad q_2 = \frac{4}{8} = \frac{1}{2}; \quad q_2 = \frac{4}{8} = \frac{1}{2}$$

$$V = \begin{bmatrix} \frac{3}{8} & \frac{5}{8} \end{bmatrix} \begin{bmatrix} 4 & -1 \\ 0 & 3 \end{bmatrix} \begin{bmatrix} \frac{1}{2} \\ \frac{1}{2} \end{bmatrix} = \begin{bmatrix} \frac{3}{2} & \frac{3}{2} \end{bmatrix} \begin{bmatrix} \frac{1}{2} \\ \frac{1}{2} \end{bmatrix} = 1.5$$

The game favors the Democrat.

9.

		Opponent: Deserted	Opponent: Busy
Spy	Deserted	-100	30
	Busy	10	-2

$$p_1 = \frac{-12}{-142} = \frac{6}{71}; \quad p_2 = \frac{65}{71}; \quad q_1 = \frac{-32}{-142} = \frac{16}{71}; \quad q_2 = \frac{55}{71}$$

The value is $\begin{bmatrix} \frac{6}{71} & \frac{65}{71} \end{bmatrix} \begin{bmatrix} -100 & 30 \\ 10 & -2 \end{bmatrix} \begin{bmatrix} \frac{16}{71} \\ \frac{55}{71} \end{bmatrix} = \frac{50}{71}$.

11. If $a_{11} + a_{22} - a_{12} - a_{21} = 0$, then the game is strictly determined. Otherwise, from Problem 11 in Exercise 2, we must have either:

(a) $a_{11} - a_{12} > 0$ and $a_{22} - a_{21} > 0$; hence, $a_{11} + a_{22} - a_{21} > 0$, or

(b) $a_{11} - a_{12} < 0$ and $a_{22} - a_{21} < 0$; hence, $a_{11} + a_{22} - a_{21} < 0$.

Exercise 10.4 (page 437)

1.

$$\begin{bmatrix} 8 & 3 & 8 \\ 6 & 5 & 4 \\ -2 & 4 & 1 \end{bmatrix}$$

Row 2 dominates row 3; the reduced matrix is $\begin{bmatrix} 8 & 3 & 8 \\ 6 & 5 & 4 \end{bmatrix}$.

Column 2 dominates column 1; the reduced matrix is $\begin{bmatrix} 3 & 8 \\ 5 & 4 \end{bmatrix}$.

$$p_1 = \frac{4 - 5}{3 + 4 - 8 - 5} = \frac{-1}{-6} = \frac{1}{6} \qquad q_1 = \frac{4 - 8}{-6} = \frac{-4}{-6} = \frac{2}{3}$$

$$p_2 = \frac{3-8}{-6} = \frac{-5}{-6} = \frac{5}{6} \qquad q_2 = \frac{3-5}{-6} = \frac{-2}{-6} = \frac{1}{3}$$

$$v = \begin{bmatrix} \frac{1}{6} & \frac{5}{6} \end{bmatrix} \begin{bmatrix} 3 & 8 \\ 5 & 4 \end{bmatrix} \begin{bmatrix} \frac{2}{3} \\ \frac{1}{3} \end{bmatrix} = \begin{bmatrix} \frac{14}{3} & \frac{14}{3} \end{bmatrix} \begin{bmatrix} \frac{2}{3} \\ \frac{1}{3} \end{bmatrix} = \frac{14}{3}$$

3.

$\begin{bmatrix} 2 & 1 & 0 & 6 \\ 3 & -2 & 1 & 2 \end{bmatrix}$ Column 3 dominates columns 1 and 4; the reduced matrix is $\begin{bmatrix} 1 & 0 \\ -2 & 1 \end{bmatrix}$

$$p_1 = \frac{1+2}{1+1+2} = \frac{3}{4} \qquad q_1 = \frac{1}{4}$$

$$p_2 = \frac{1}{4} \qquad q_2 = \frac{1+2}{4} = \frac{3}{4}$$

$$v = \begin{bmatrix} \frac{3}{4} & \frac{1}{4} \end{bmatrix} \begin{bmatrix} 1 & 0 \\ -2 & 1 \end{bmatrix} \begin{bmatrix} \frac{1}{4} \\ \frac{3}{4} \end{bmatrix} = \begin{bmatrix} \frac{1}{4} & \frac{1}{4} \end{bmatrix} \begin{bmatrix} \frac{1}{4} \\ \frac{3}{4} \end{bmatrix} = \frac{1}{4}$$

5.

$\begin{bmatrix} 6 & -4 & 2 & -3 \\ -4 & 6 & -5 & 7 \end{bmatrix}$ Column 3 dominates column 1; column 2 dominates column 4; the reduced matrix is $\begin{bmatrix} -4 & 2 \\ 6 & -5 \end{bmatrix}$.

$$p_1 = \frac{-5-6}{-4-5-2-6} = \frac{11}{17} \qquad q_1 = \frac{-5-2}{-17} = \frac{7}{17}$$

$$p_2 = \frac{6}{17} \qquad q_2 = \frac{10}{17}$$

$$v = \begin{bmatrix} \frac{11}{7} & \frac{6}{17} \end{bmatrix} \begin{bmatrix} -4 & 2 \\ 6 & -5 \end{bmatrix} \begin{bmatrix} \frac{7}{17} \\ \frac{10}{17} \end{bmatrix} = \begin{bmatrix} -\frac{8}{17} & -\frac{8}{17} \end{bmatrix} \begin{bmatrix} \frac{7}{17} \\ \frac{10}{17} \end{bmatrix} = -\frac{8}{17}$$

7.

$\begin{bmatrix} 4 & -5 & 5 \\ -6 & 3 & 3 \\ 2 & -6 & 3 \end{bmatrix}$ Row 1 dominates row 3; the reduced matrix is $\begin{bmatrix} 4 & -5 & 5 \\ -6 & 3 & 3 \end{bmatrix}$.

Column 2 dominates column 3; the reduced matrix is $\begin{bmatrix} 4 & -5 \\ -6 & 3 \end{bmatrix}$

$$p_1 = \frac{3+6}{4+3+5+6} = \frac{9}{18} = \frac{1}{2} \qquad q_1 = \frac{3+5}{18} = \frac{8}{18} = \frac{4}{9}$$

$$p_2 = \frac{4+5}{18} = \frac{9}{18} = \frac{1}{2} \qquad q_2 = \frac{4+6}{18} = \frac{10}{18} = \frac{5}{9}$$

$$v = \begin{bmatrix} \frac{1}{2} & \frac{1}{2} \end{bmatrix} \begin{bmatrix} 4 & -5 \\ -6 & 3 \end{bmatrix} \begin{bmatrix} \frac{4}{9} \\ \frac{5}{9} \end{bmatrix} = \begin{bmatrix} -1 & -1 \end{bmatrix} \begin{bmatrix} \frac{4}{9} \\ \frac{5}{9} \end{bmatrix} = -1$$

9.

$\begin{bmatrix} 1 & 3 & 0 \\ 0 & -3 & 1 \\ 0 & 4 & 1 \\ -2 & 1 & 1 \end{bmatrix}$ Row 3 dominates rows 2 and 4; the reduced matrix is

$\begin{bmatrix} 1 & 3 & 0 \\ 0 & 4 & 1 \end{bmatrix}$. Column 1 dominates column 2; the reduced matrix is $\begin{bmatrix} 1 & 0 \\ 0 & 1 \end{bmatrix}$.

$$p_1 = \frac{1-0}{1+1-0-0} = \frac{1}{2} \qquad q_1 = \frac{1-0}{2} = \frac{1}{2}$$

$$p_2 = \frac{1-0}{2} = \frac{1}{2} \qquad q_2 = \frac{1-0}{2} = \frac{1}{2}$$

$$v = \begin{bmatrix} \frac{1}{2} & \frac{1}{2} \end{bmatrix} \begin{bmatrix} 1 & 0 \\ 0 & 1 \end{bmatrix} \begin{bmatrix} \frac{1}{2} \\ \frac{1}{2} \end{bmatrix} = \begin{bmatrix} \frac{1}{2} & \frac{1}{2} \end{bmatrix} \begin{bmatrix} \frac{1}{2} \\ \frac{1}{2} \end{bmatrix} = \frac{1}{2}$$

11.

$\begin{bmatrix} 4 & 3 & -1 \\ 1 & 1 & 4 \\ 1 & 0 & 2 \end{bmatrix}$ Row 2 dominates row 3; the reduced matrix is $\begin{bmatrix} 4 & 3 & -1 \\ 1 & 1 & 4 \end{bmatrix}$.

Column 2 dominates column 1; the reduced matrix is $\begin{bmatrix} 3 & -1 \\ 1 & 4 \end{bmatrix}$.

$$p_1 = \frac{4-1}{3+4-1-(-1)} = \frac{3}{7} \qquad q_1 = \frac{4+1}{7} = \frac{5}{7}$$

$$p_2 = \frac{3+1}{7} = \frac{4}{7} \qquad q_2 = \frac{3-1}{7} = \frac{2}{7}$$

$$v = \begin{bmatrix} \frac{3}{7} & \frac{4}{7} \end{bmatrix} \begin{bmatrix} 3 & -1 \\ 1 & 4 \end{bmatrix} \begin{bmatrix} \frac{5}{7} \\ \frac{2}{7} \end{bmatrix} = \begin{bmatrix} \frac{13}{7} & \frac{13}{7} \end{bmatrix} \begin{bmatrix} \frac{5}{7} \\ \frac{2}{7} \end{bmatrix} = \frac{13}{7}$$

13. Let the thief be in area A with probability q_1. He is then in area B with probability $(1 - q_1)$. The detectives have six choices. The expected values for the probabilities for the detectives to find and arrest a thief for each of the six choices are:

1 $E_I = -.24q_1 + .75$
2 $E_I = .28q_1 + .36$
3 $E_I = -.72q_1 + .91$
4 $E_I = -.02q_1 + .60$
5 $E_I = -.48q_1 + .85$
6 $E_I = -.20q_1 + .76$

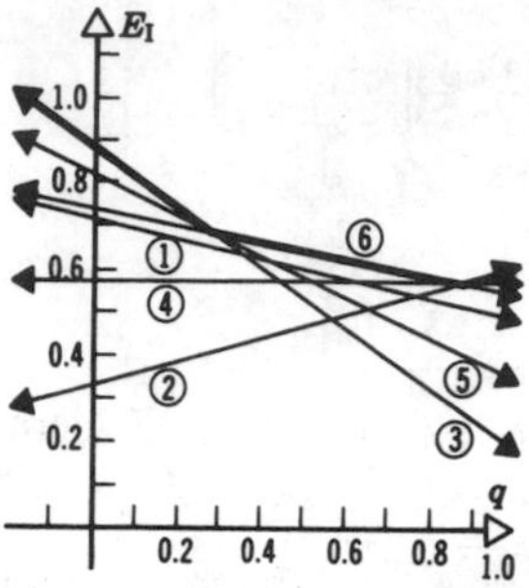

The intersection of lines 2 and 6 gives the optimum strategy of the thief.

$q_1 = \frac{5}{6}$ $\qquad q_2 = 1 - q_1 = \frac{1}{6}$

Eliminating rows 1, 3, 4, and 5, we get:

$p_1 = \frac{5}{12}$ $\qquad p_2 = \frac{7}{12}$ $\qquad V = .5933...$

Review Exercises (page 441)

1. (a) Not strictly determined.
   (b) Strictly determined; value is 15.
   (c) Strictly determined; value is 50.
   (d) Strictly determined; value is 9.
   (e) Strictly determined; value is 12.

3. Let's first examine the 2 X 2 matrix $\begin{bmatrix} a & b \\ c & d \end{bmatrix}$.

Let a be the saddle point. We know that $a \le b$ and $a \ge c$. If $d \le c$, then $b \ge d$ and row 1 dominates row 2. If $d \ge c$, then column 1 dominates column 2. Similar reasoning would have shown the desired result if we had chosen a saddle point other than a.

Now consider the matrix $\begin{bmatrix} a & b & c \\ d & e & f \end{bmatrix}$.

Let a be the saddle point. We know that $a \le b$, $a \le c$, and $a \ge d$. If $d \le e$, then column 1 dominates column 2. If $d \le f$, then column 1 dominates column 3. If $d \ge e$ and $d \ge f$, then row 1 dominates row 2. Similar reasoning would have been shown the desired result if we had chosen a saddle point other than a.

5.

(a) $\begin{bmatrix} 4 & 6 & 3 \\ 1 & 2 & 5 \end{bmatrix}$ Column 1 dominates column 2; the reduced matrix is $\begin{bmatrix} 4 & 3 \\ 1 & 5 \end{bmatrix}$.

$p_1 = \frac{5-1}{4+5-3-1} = \frac{4}{5}$ $\qquad q_1 = \frac{5-3}{5} = \frac{2}{5}$

$p_2 = \frac{4-3}{5} = \frac{1}{5}$ $\qquad$ $q_2 = \frac{4-1}{5} = \frac{3}{5}$

$$V = \begin{bmatrix} \frac{4}{5} & \frac{1}{5} \end{bmatrix} \begin{bmatrix} 4 & 3 \\ 1 & 5 \end{bmatrix} \begin{bmatrix} \frac{2}{5} \\ \frac{3}{5} \end{bmatrix} = \begin{bmatrix} \frac{17}{5} & \frac{17}{5} \end{bmatrix} \begin{bmatrix} \frac{2}{5} \\ \frac{3}{5} \end{bmatrix} = \frac{17}{5}$$

(b) $\begin{bmatrix} 1 & 6 \\ 5 & 2 \\ 7 & 4 \end{bmatrix}$ Row 3 dominates row 2; the reduced matrix is $\begin{bmatrix} 1 & 6 \\ 7 & 4 \end{bmatrix}$.

$p_1 = \frac{4-7}{1+4-7-6} = \frac{3}{8}$ $\qquad$ $q_1 = \frac{4-6}{-8} = \frac{1}{4}$

$p_2 = \frac{5}{8}$ $\qquad$ $q_2 = \frac{3}{4}$

$$V = \begin{bmatrix} \frac{3}{8} & \frac{5}{8} \end{bmatrix} \begin{bmatrix} 1 & 6 \\ 7 & 4 \end{bmatrix} \begin{bmatrix} \frac{1}{4} \\ \frac{3}{4} \end{bmatrix} = \frac{19}{4}$$

(c) $\begin{bmatrix} 2 & 1 \\ 4 & 0 \\ 3 & 4 \end{bmatrix}$ Row 3 dominates row 1; the reduced matrix is $\begin{bmatrix} 4 & 0 \\ 3 & 4 \end{bmatrix}$.

$p_1 = \frac{4-3}{4+4-3} = \frac{1}{5}$ $\qquad$ $q_1 = \frac{4-0}{5} = \frac{4}{5}$

$p_2 = \frac{4}{5}$ $\qquad$ $q_2 = \frac{1}{5}$

$$V = \begin{bmatrix} \frac{1}{5} & \frac{4}{5} \end{bmatrix} \begin{bmatrix} 4 & 0 \\ 3 & 4 \end{bmatrix} \begin{bmatrix} \frac{4}{5} \\ \frac{1}{5} \end{bmatrix} = \frac{16}{5}$$

(d) $\begin{bmatrix} 0 & 3 & 2 \\ 4 & 2 & 3 \end{bmatrix}$

Let Player I play row 1 with probability p. He then plays row 2 with probability (1 - p). Player II has 3 choices. The expected earnings for Player I for each of the 3 choices are:

1 $E_I = 0p + 4(1-p) = 4 - 4p$

2 $E_I = 3p + 2(1-p) = 2 + p$

3 $E_I = 2p + 3(1-p) = 3 - p$

By examining the graphs of these equations, we see that the intersection of lines 1 and 2 gives the optimum strategy for Player I: $p = \frac{2}{5}$, $1 - p = \frac{3}{5}$.

Eliminating column 3, we get $\begin{bmatrix} 0 & 3 \\ 4 & 2 \end{bmatrix}$.

$q_1 = \frac{2-3}{2-4-3} = \frac{1}{5}$ $\qquad$ $q_2 = \frac{4}{5}$

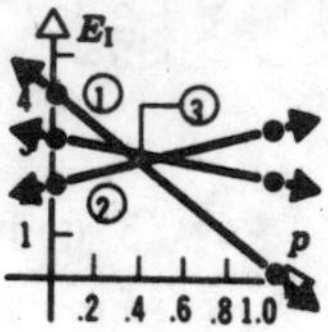

Player I should select row 1 with probability $\frac{2}{5}$ and row 2 with probability $\frac{3}{5}$. Player II should select column 1 with probability $\frac{1}{5}$, column 2 with probability $\frac{4}{5}$, and never select column 3.

$V = \frac{12}{5}$

CHAPTER 11

Exercise 11.1 (page 450)

1. The sum of the entries in row 3 is not equal to 1; there is a negative entry in row 3, column 2.

3. (a) The probability of a change from state 1 to state 2 is $\frac{2}{3}$.

   (b) $\begin{bmatrix} \frac{1}{3} & \frac{2}{3} \end{bmatrix}$ (c) $\begin{bmatrix} \frac{1}{4} & \frac{3}{4} \end{bmatrix}$

   (d) $A^{(0)} = [0 \quad 1]$

   $$p_{21}^{(2)} = \frac{1}{4} \cdot \frac{1}{3} + \frac{3}{4} \cdot \frac{1}{4} = \frac{13}{38}$$

   $$p_{22}^{(2)} = \frac{1}{4} \cdot \frac{2}{3} + \frac{3}{4} \cdot \frac{3}{4} = \frac{35}{48}$$

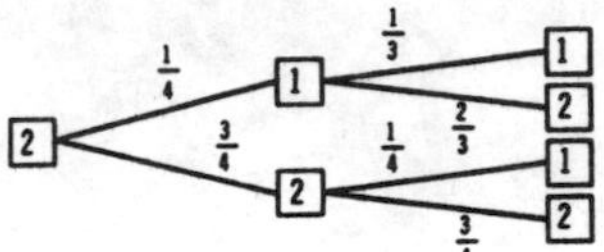

5. $[25 \quad .75]\begin{bmatrix} .3 & .7 \\ .4 & .6 \end{bmatrix}^2 = [.375 \quad .625]\begin{bmatrix} .3 & .7 \\ .4 & .6 \end{bmatrix} = [.3625 \quad .6375]$

7. $2 + a + .4 = 1 \qquad a = .4$
   $b + .6 + .2 = 1 \qquad b = .2$
   $c = 1 \qquad c = 1$

9. $A^{(5)} = A^{(0)}P^5 = [.7 \quad .3]\begin{bmatrix} .7017 & .2983 \\ .0429 & .9574 \end{bmatrix} = [.5040 \quad .4960]$

11. (a) The probability that a Democratic candidate is elected depends only on whether the previous mayor was a Democrat or a Republican (and similarly for a Republican candidate).

    (b) $\begin{array}{c} \\ D \\ R \end{array}\begin{array}{c} \begin{array}{cc} D & R \end{array} \\ \begin{bmatrix} .6 & .4 \\ .3 & .7 \end{bmatrix} \end{array}$ (c) $\begin{bmatrix} .48 & .52 \\ .39 & .61 \end{bmatrix}; \begin{bmatrix} .444 & .556 \\ .417 & .583 \end{bmatrix}$

13. $A^{(2)} = A^{(0)}P^2$, where $P = \begin{array}{c} \text{Brand X} \\ \text{Other} \end{array}\begin{bmatrix} .75 & .25 \\ .35 & .65 \end{bmatrix}$; $p2 = \begin{bmatrix} .65 & .35 \\ .49 & .51 \end{bmatrix}$

    $[5 \quad .5]\begin{bmatrix} .65 & .35 \\ .49 & .51 \end{bmatrix} = [.57 \quad .43]$ 57% will drink brand X after 2 months.

15.

$$\begin{array}{c} T \\ G \\ Other \end{array}\begin{array}{c} \begin{array}{ccc} T & G & Other \end{array} \\ \begin{bmatrix} .92 & .08 & 0 \\ .04 & .90 & .06 \\ .10 & .08 & .82 \end{bmatrix} \end{array} = P;\ [.45\ \ .30\ \ .25] = A^{(0)}$$

(a) $A^{(1)} = A^{(0)}P = [.451\ \ .326\ \ .223]$; $.451 + .326 = .777 = 77.7\%$
(Check: $1 - .223 = .777$)

(b) $A^{(2)} = A^{(1)}P = [.45026\ \ .34732\ \ .20242]$; $.40526 + .34732 = .79758 =$ 79.758% (Check: $1 - .20242 = .79758$)

17.

$$uA = [u_1a_{11} + u_2a_{21}\quad u_1a_{12} + u_2a_{22}]$$

$$(uA)_1 + (uA)_2 = (u_1a_{11} + u_2a_{21}) + (u_1a_{12} + u_2a_{22})$$

$$= u_1(a_{11} + a_{12}) + u_2(a_{21} + a_{22})$$

$$= u_1 + u_2 = 1$$

Exercise 11.2 (page 461)

1.

$$\begin{bmatrix} \frac{1}{2} & \frac{1}{2} \\ 1 & 0 \end{bmatrix}^2 = \begin{bmatrix} \frac{3}{4} & \frac{1}{4} \\ \frac{1}{2} & \frac{1}{2} \end{bmatrix}$$; P is regular. If $[t_1 t_2]\begin{bmatrix} \frac{1}{2} & \frac{1}{2} \\ 1 & 0 \end{bmatrix} = [t_1 t_2]$, then

$[\frac{1}{2}t_1 + t_2\quad \frac{1}{2}t_1] = [t_1\quad t_2]$ or $\frac{1}{2}t_1 = t_2$, $t_1 + t_2 = 1$, $t_1 = \frac{2}{3}$, $t_2 = \frac{1}{3}$ and $[\frac{2}{3}\quad \frac{1}{3}]$

is the fixed vector.

3.

$$P^2 = \begin{bmatrix} \frac{1}{4} & \frac{3}{4} \\ \frac{3}{16} & \frac{13}{16} \end{bmatrix}$$; P is regular. $[t_1\quad t_2] = [\frac{1}{5}\quad \frac{4}{5}]$

5.

$$P^2 = \begin{bmatrix} 1 & 0 & 0 \\ \frac{3}{8} & \frac{1}{2} & \frac{1}{8} \\ \frac{1}{4} & \frac{1}{2} & \frac{1}{4} \end{bmatrix}$$

Every power of P will have two 0's in row 1, so the matrix is not regular.

7. If $[t_1 t_2]\begin{bmatrix} 1-p & p \\ p & 1-p \end{bmatrix} = [t_1 t_2]$, then:

$$\left.\begin{aligned}(1-p)t_1 + pt_2 &= t_1\\ pt_1 + (1-p)t_2 &= t_2\end{aligned}\right\} t_1 = t_2,\ t_1 + t_2 = 1,\ t_1 = \frac{1}{2},\ t_2 = \frac{1}{2}$$

9.

$$P = \begin{array}{c} \\ A \\ B \\ C \end{array}\begin{array}{c} \begin{array}{ccc} A & B & C \end{array} \\ \begin{bmatrix} .7 & .15 & .15 \\ .1 & .8 & .1 \\ .2 & .2 & .6 \end{bmatrix}\end{array} \quad \text{If } [t_1\ \ t_2\ \ t_3]P = [t_1\ \ t_2\ \ t_3], \text{ then}$$

$[t_1\ \ t_2\ \ t_3] = [.3077\ \ .4615\ \ .2308]$. Thus, he stocks Brand A 30.77% of the time, Brand B 46.15% of the time, Brand C 23.08% of the time.

11. The transition matrix is

	Conservative	Labor	Socialist
Conservative	.70	.30	.00
Labor	.40	.50	.10
Socialist	.20	.40	.40

The probability that the grandson of a Laborite will vote Socialist is .09.
The fixed probability vector is $[t_1\ \ t_2\ \ t_3] = [.5532\ \ \ .3830\ \ \ .0638]$.

13. Let B, U, R denote Blond, Brunette, and Redhead, respectively.

$$P = \begin{array}{c} \\ B \\ U \\ R \end{array}\begin{array}{c} \begin{array}{ccc} B & U & R \end{array} \\ \begin{bmatrix} .6 & .2 & .2 \\ .1 & .7 & .2 \\ .4 & .2 & .4 \end{bmatrix}\end{array} \qquad P^2 = \begin{bmatrix} .46 & .30 & .24 \\ .21 & .55 & .24 \\ .42 & .30 & .28 \end{bmatrix} 30\%\text{(row 1, column 2 of } P^2)$$

(a) $[.5\ \ \ .3\ \ \ .2]\begin{bmatrix} .46 & .30 & .24 \\ .21 & .55 & .24 \\ .42 & .30 & .28 \end{bmatrix} = [.377\ \ .375\ \ .248]$

(b) $[t_1\ \ \ t_2\ \ \ t_3]\begin{bmatrix} .6 & .2 & .2 \\ .1 & .7 & .2 \\ .4 & .2 & .4 \end{bmatrix} = [t_1\ \ \ t_2\ \ \ t_3]$

$$\begin{aligned} .6t_1 + .1t_2 + .4t_3 &= t_1 \\ .2t_1 + .7t_2 + .2t_3 &= t_2 \\ .2t_1 + .2t_2 + .4t_3 &= t_3 \\ t_1 + t_2 + t_3 &= 1 \end{aligned}$$

$[t_1\ \ t_2\ \ t_3] = [.35\ \ .40\ \ .25]$

Exercise 11.3 (page 470)

1. Non-absorbing (no absorbing states) 3. Absorbing

5. Non-absorbing (absorbing state 3 is not accessible to states 1 and 2).

7.

$$\begin{array}{c} \\ 1 \\ 3 \\ 2 \end{array}\begin{array}{c} \begin{array}{ccc} 1 & 3 & 2 \end{array} \\ \left[\begin{array}{cc|c} 1 & 0 & 0 \\ \underline{0} & \underline{1} & \underline{0} \\ \frac{1}{8} & \frac{2}{8} & \frac{5}{8} \end{array}\right] \end{array} \quad Q = \left[\frac{5}{8}\right]; \; S = \left[\frac{1}{8} \;\; \frac{2}{8}\right]; \; T = \left[1 - \frac{5}{8}\right]^{-1} = \frac{8}{3}; \; T \cdot S = \left[\frac{1}{3} \;\; \frac{2}{3}\right]$$

9. (a) $T_{13} = .8$; $T_{23} = .6$ (b) $.3 + 1.8 + 2.1 = 4.2$

11.

$$\begin{array}{c} \\ 0 \\ 3 \\ 1 \\ 2 \end{array}\begin{array}{c} \begin{array}{cccc} 0 & 3 & 1 & 2 \end{array} \\ \left[\begin{array}{cc|cc} 1 & 0 & 0 & 0 \\ \underline{0} & \underline{1} & \underline{0} & \underline{0} \\ .6 & 0 & 0 & .4 \\ 0 & .4 & .6 & 0 \end{array}\right] \end{array} = P;$$

$$Q = \begin{bmatrix} 0 & .4 \\ .6 & 0 \end{bmatrix}; \; S = \begin{bmatrix} .6 & 0 \\ 0 & .4 \end{bmatrix}; \; T = [I_2 - Q]^{-1} = \begin{bmatrix} 1 & -.4 \\ -.6 & 1 \end{bmatrix}^{-1} = \begin{bmatrix} \frac{25}{19} & \frac{10}{19} \\ \frac{15}{19} & \frac{25}{19} \end{bmatrix};$$

$$T \cdot S = \begin{array}{c} \begin{array}{cc} 0 & 3 \end{array} \\ \begin{bmatrix} \frac{15}{19} & \frac{4}{19} \\ \frac{9}{19} & \frac{10}{19} \end{bmatrix} \end{array}\begin{array}{c} \\ 1 \\ 2 \end{array}$$

With a stake of \$1, the probability is $\frac{4}{19}$. With \$2, the probability is $\frac{10}{19}$.

13.

$$\begin{array}{c} \\ 0 \\ 1 \\ 2 \\ 4 \end{array}\begin{array}{c} \begin{array}{cccc} 0 & 1 & 2 & 4 \end{array} \\ \begin{bmatrix} 1 & 0 & 0 & 0 \\ .6 & 0 & .4 & 0 \\ .6 & 0 & 0 & .4 \\ 0 & 0 & 0 & 1 \end{bmatrix} \end{array} \qquad \begin{array}{c} \\ 0 \\ 4 \\ 1 \\ 2 \end{array}\begin{array}{c} \begin{array}{cccc} 0 & 4 & 1 & 2 \end{array} \\ \left[\begin{array}{cc|cc} 1 & 0 & 0 & 0 \\ \underline{0} & \underline{1} & \underline{0} & \underline{0} \\ .6 & 0 & 0 & .4 \\ .6 & .4 & 0 & 0 \end{array}\right] \end{array}$$

$$S = \begin{bmatrix} .6 & 0 \\ .6 & .4 \end{bmatrix}; \; Q = \begin{bmatrix} 0 & .4 \\ 0 & 0 \end{bmatrix}; \; T = (I - Q)^{-1} = \begin{bmatrix} 1 & -.4 \\ 0 & 1 \end{bmatrix}^{-1} = \begin{bmatrix} 1 & .4 \\ 0 & 1 \end{bmatrix}$$

(a) Expected number of wagers is 1.4.

(b) $T \cdot S = \begin{bmatrix} 1 & .4 \\ 0 & 1 \end{bmatrix}\begin{bmatrix} .6 & 0 \\ .6 & .4 \end{bmatrix} = \begin{bmatrix} .84 & .16 \\ .6 & .4 \end{bmatrix}$ The probability that she is wiped out is .84.

(c) The probability that she wins is .16.

Exercise 11.4 (page 475)

1.

$$\begin{bmatrix}\frac{1}{4} & \frac{1}{2} & \frac{1}{4}\end{bmatrix}\begin{bmatrix}\frac{1}{2} & \frac{1}{2} & 0 \\ \frac{1}{4} & \frac{1}{2} & \frac{1}{4} \\ 0 & \frac{1}{2} & \frac{1}{2}\end{bmatrix} = \begin{bmatrix}\frac{1}{4} & \frac{1}{2} & \frac{1}{4}\end{bmatrix}$$

3.

(a)

$$P = \begin{array}{c} \\ D \\ H \\ R \end{array}\begin{array}{c} \begin{array}{ccc} D & H & R \end{array} \\ \begin{bmatrix} 0 & 1 & 0 \\ 0 & \frac{1}{2} & \frac{1}{2} \\ 0 & 0 & 1 \end{bmatrix}\end{array}$$

(b) P is not regular, but a fixed probability vector does exist. It is [0 0 1]. This indicates that in the long run the unknown genotype will be R

(c)

$$\begin{array}{c} \text{RHD} \\ \begin{array}{c} R \\ H \\ D \end{array}\left[\begin{array}{c|c|cc} 1 & 0 & 0 \\ \frac{1}{2} & \frac{1}{2} & 0 \\ 0 & 1 & 0 \end{array}\right]\end{array} \qquad T = \begin{array}{c} \\ H \\ D \end{array}\begin{array}{c} \begin{array}{cc} H & D \end{array} \\ \begin{bmatrix} 2 & 0 \\ 2 & 1 \end{bmatrix}\end{array}$$

(d) If the unknown is D to start, three stages are required.
If the unknown is H to start, two stages are required.

Review Exercises (page 476)

1. (a)

$$\begin{bmatrix} t_1 & t_2 \end{bmatrix}\begin{bmatrix}\frac{1}{4} & \frac{3}{4} \\ \frac{1}{2} & \frac{1}{2}\end{bmatrix} = \begin{bmatrix}\frac{1}{4}t_1 + \frac{1}{2}t_2 & \frac{3}{4}t_1 + \frac{1}{2}t_2\end{bmatrix} = \begin{bmatrix} t_1 & t_2 \end{bmatrix}$$

$$t_1 = \frac{1}{4}t_1 + \frac{1}{2}t_2$$

$$t_2 = \frac{3}{4}t_1 + \frac{1}{2}t_2$$

$$t_1 = \frac{2}{3}t_2$$

$$t_1 + t_2 = 1$$

$$t_1 = \frac{2}{5},\ t_2 = \frac{3}{5}$$

$\begin{bmatrix}\frac{2}{5} & \frac{3}{5}\end{bmatrix}$ is the fixed vector

(b)

$$\begin{bmatrix} t_1 & t_2 \end{bmatrix} \begin{bmatrix} \frac{1}{3} & \frac{2}{3} \\ \frac{2}{3} & \frac{1}{3} \end{bmatrix} = \begin{bmatrix} t_1 & t_2 \end{bmatrix}$$

$\frac{1}{3}t_1 + \frac{2}{3}t_2 = t_1$ $\qquad$ $t_1 = t_2$

$\frac{2}{3}t_1 + \frac{1}{3}t_2 = t_2$ $\qquad$ $\begin{bmatrix} t_1 & t_2 \end{bmatrix} = \begin{bmatrix} \frac{1}{2} & \frac{1}{2} \end{bmatrix}$ is the fixed vector

3.

$$P = \begin{array}{c} \\ A \\ B \\ C \end{array} \begin{array}{c} \begin{array}{ccc} A & B & C \end{array} \\ \begin{bmatrix} .5 & .2 & .3 \\ .4 & .4 & .2 \\ .5 & .25 & .25 \end{bmatrix} \end{array} \qquad P^2 = \begin{bmatrix} .48 & .255 & .265 \\ .46 & .29 & .25 \\ .475 & .2625 & .2625 \end{bmatrix}$$

$$\begin{bmatrix} \frac{1}{3} & \frac{1}{3} & \frac{1}{3} \end{bmatrix} P^2 = [.4717 \quad .2692 \quad .2592]$$

The fixed vector of P is $\begin{bmatrix} \frac{80}{169} & \frac{45}{169} & \frac{44}{169} \end{bmatrix}$; hence, in the long run, A's share is $\frac{80}{169}$, B's share is $\frac{45}{169}$, and C's share is $\frac{44}{169}$.

5. The transition matrix is

$$\begin{array}{c} \\ U_1 \\ U_2 \\ U_3 \end{array} \begin{array}{c} \begin{array}{ccc} U_1 & U_2 & U_3 \end{array} \\ \begin{bmatrix} 0 & 1 & 0 \\ \frac{3}{4} & 0 & \frac{1}{4} \\ \frac{3}{4} & \frac{1}{4} & 0 \end{bmatrix} \end{array}$$

The fixed vector is $\begin{bmatrix} \frac{15}{35} & \frac{16}{35} & \frac{4}{35} \end{bmatrix}$.

In the long run, she sells $\frac{11}{31}$ of the time at U_1, $\frac{16}{31}$ of the time at U_2, and $\frac{4}{31}$ of the time at U_3.

7. Transition matrix:

$$\begin{array}{c|cccccc} & 0 & 1 & 2 & 3 & 4 & 5 \\ \hline 0 & 1 & 0 & 0 & 0 & 0 & 0 \\ 1 & .55 & 0 & .45 & 0 & 0 & 0 \\ 2 & 0 & .55 & 0 & .45 & 0 & 0 \\ 3 & 0 & 0 & .55 & 0 & .45 & 0 \\ 4 & 0 & 0 & 0 & .55 & 0 & .45 \\ 5 & 0 & 0 & 0 & 0 & 0 & 1 \end{array}$$

or

$$\begin{array}{c|cc|cccc} & 0 & 5 & 1 & 2 & 3 & 4 \\ \hline 0 & 1 & 0 & 0 & 0 & 0 & 0 \\ 5 & \underline{0} & 1 & \underline{0} & \underline{0} & \underline{0} & \underline{0} \\ 1 & .55 & 0 & 0 & .45 & 0 & 0 \\ 2 & 0 & 0 & .55 & 0 & .45 & 0 \\ 3 & 0 & 0 & 0 & .55 & 0 & .45 \\ 4 & 0 & .45 & 0 & 0 & .55 & 0 \end{array}$$

The expected length of the game is 1.298405 + 2.360736 + 1.411736 + .635281 = 5.706158.

$$T \cdot S = \begin{bmatrix} .87135510 & .12864420 \\ .71412275 & .28587645 \\ .52194450 & .47804895 \\ .28706760 & .71292645 \end{bmatrix}$$

The probability that he is wiped out is .7142275.

CHAPTER 12

Exercise 12.1 (page 484)

1. Proposition **3.** Not a proposition **5.** Proposition **7.** Proposition
9. A fox is not an animal. **11.** I am not buying stocks and bonds.
13. Someone wants to buy my house. **15.** Every person has a car.
17. John is an economics major or a sociology major.
19. John is an economics major and a sociology major.
21. John is not an economics major or he is not a sociology major.
23. John is not an economics major or he is a sociology major.

Exercise 12.2 (page 492)

1.

p	q	$\sim q$	$p \vee \sim q$
T	T	F	T
T	F	T	T
F	T	F	F
F	F	T	T

3.

p	q	$\sim p$	$\sim q$	$\sim \wedge \sim q$
T	T	F	F	F
T	F	F	T	F
F	T	T	F	F
F	F	T	T	T

5.

p	q	$\sim p$	$\sim p \wedge q$	$\sim(\sim p \wedge q)$
T	T	F	F	T
T	F	F	F	T
F	T	T	T	F
F	F	T	F	T

7.

p	q	$\sim p$	$\sim q$	$\sim p \vee \sim q$	$\sim(\sim p \vee \sim q)$
T	T	F	F	F	T
T	F	F	T	T	F
F	T	T	F	T	F
F	F	T	T	T	F

9.

p	q	$\sim q$	$p \vee \sim q$	$(p \vee \sim q) \wedge p$
T	T	F	T	T
T	F	T	T	T
F	T	F	F	F
F	F	T	T	F

11.

p	q	$\sim q$	$p \underline{\vee} q$	$p \wedge \sim q$	$(p \underline{\vee} q) \wedge (p \wedge \sim q)$
T	T	F	F	F	F
T	F	T	T	T	T
F	T	F	T	F	F
F	F	T	F	F	F

13.

p	q	$\sim p$	$\sim q$	$p \wedge q$	$\sim p \wedge \sim q$	$(p \wedge q) \vee (\sim p \wedge \sim q)$
T	T	F	F	T	F	T
T	F	F	T	F	F	F
F	T	T	F	F	F	F
F	F	T	T	F	T	T

15.

p	q	r	~q	p ∧ ~q	(p ∧ ~q) ⊻ r
T	T	T	F	F	F
T	T	F	F	F	F
T	F	T	T	T	F
T	F	F	T	T	T
F	T	T	F	F	T
F	T	F	F	F	F
F	F	T	T	F	T
F	F	F	T	F	F

17.

p	p ∧ p	p ∨ p
T	T	T
F	F	F

Since each column is the same, p ≡ p ∧ p ≡ p ∨ p

19.

p	q	r	p ∧ q	q ∧ r	(p ∧ q) ∧ r	p ∧ (q ∧ r)
T	T	T	T	T	T	T
T	T	F	T	F	F	F
T	F	T	F	F	F	F
T	F	F	F	F	F	F
F	T	T	F	T	F	F
F	T	F	F	F	F	F
F	F	T	F	F	F	F
F	F	F	F	F	F	F

The last two columns are the same, so (p ∧ q) ∧ r ≡ p ∧ (q ∧ r)

p	q	r	p ∨ q	q ∨ r	(p ∨ q) ∨ r	p ∨ (q ∨ r)
T	T	T	T	T	T	T
T	T	F	T	T	T	T
T	F	T	T	T	T	T
T	F	F	T	F	T	T
F	T	T	T	T	T	T
F	T	F	T	T	T	T
F	F	T	F	T	T	T
F	F	F	F	F	F	F

The last two columns are the same, so (p ∨ q) ∨ r ≡ p ∨ (q ∨ r)

21.

1 p	2 q	3 p ∨ q	4 p ∧ q	5 p ∧ (p ∨ q)	6 p ∨ (p ∧ q)
T	T	T	T	T	T
T	F	T	F	T	T
F	T	T	F	F	F
F	F	F	F	F	F

Since columns 1 and 5 are the same, p ≡ p ∧ (p ∨ q).
Since columns 1 and 6 are the same, p ≡ p ∨ (p ∧ q).

23.

1	2	3	4	5
p	q	$\sim q$	$\sim q \vee q$	$p \wedge (\sim q \vee q)$
T	T	F	T	T
T	F	T	T	T
F	T	F	T	F
F	F	T	T	F

Since columns 1 and 5 are the same, $p \equiv p \wedge (\sim q \vee q)$.

25.

1	2	3
p	$\sim p$	$\sim (\sim p$
T	F	T
F	T	F

Since columns 1 and 3 are the same $p \equiv \sim (\sim p)$

27.

p	q	$\sim p$	$q \wedge (\sim p)$	$p \wedge (q \wedge \sim p)$
T	T	F	F	F
T	F	F	F	F
F	T	T	T	F
F	F	T	F	F

29.

p	q	$\sim p$	$\sim q$	$p \wedge q$	$\sim p \wedge \sim q$	$(p \wedge q) \vee (\sim p \wedge \sim q)$	$[(p \wedge q) \vee (\sim p \wedge \sim q) \wedge p$
T	T	F	F	T	F	T	T
T	F	F	T	F	F	F	F
F	T	T	F	F	F	F	F
F	F	T	T	F	T	T	F

31. Smith is an exconvict and he is an exconvict. ≡ Smith is an exconvict or he is an exconvict. ≡ Smith is an exconvict.

33. "It is not true that Smith is an exconvict or rehabilitated" means the same as the statement "Smith is not an exconvict and he is not rehabilitated." "It is not true that Smith is an exconvict and he is rehabilitated" means the same as "Smith is not an exconvict or he is not rehabilitated."

35. $(p \wedge q) \vee r \equiv r \vee (p \wedge q) \equiv (r \vee p) \wedge (r \vee q) \equiv (p \vee r) \wedge (r \vee q) \equiv (p \vee r) \wedge (q \vee r)$.

37. Let $p \equiv$ Michael will sell his car
$q \equiv$ Michael will buy a bicycle
$r \equiv$ Michael will rent a truck.
Then $a \equiv p \wedge (q \vee r) \equiv (p \wedge q) \vee (p \wedge r)$, $b \equiv (p \wedge q) \vee r$
Use a truth table to show that b is true and a is false if Michael rents a truck and does not sell his car.

39. Katy is not a good volley ball player or she is conceited.

Exercise 12.3 (page 500)

1. $\sim p \Rightarrow q$; Converse: $q \Rightarrow \sim p$; Contrapositive: $\sim q \Rightarrow p$; Inverse: $p \Rightarrow \sim q$
3. $\sim q \Rightarrow \sim p$; Converse: $\sim p \Rightarrow \sim q$; Contrapositive: $p \Rightarrow q$: $q \Rightarrow p$
5. If it is raining, the grass is wet.
   Converse: If the grass is wet, it is raining.
   Contrapositive: If the grass is not wet, it is not raining.
   Inverse: If it is not raining, the grass is not wet.
7. "It is raining or it is cloudy" is equivalent to "If it is not raining, it is cloudy,"
   Converse: If it is cloudy, it is not raining.
   Contrapositive: If it is not cloudy, it is raining.
   Inverse: If it is raining, it is not cloudy.
9. If it is raining, it is cloudy.
   Converse: If it is cloudy, it is raining.
   Contrapositive: If it is not cloudy, it is not raining.
   Inverse: If it is not raining, it is not cloudy.
11. (a) If Jack studies psychology, then Mary studies sociology.
    (b) If Mary studies sociology, then Jack studies psychology.
    (c) If Jack does not study psychology, then Mary studies sociology.

13. (a)

p	q	r	$q \vee r$	$p \Rightarrow (q \vee r)$	$p \wedge \sim q$	$(p \wedge \sim q) \Rightarrow r$
T	T	T	T	T	F	T
T	T	F	T	T	F	T
T	F	T	T	T	T	T
T	F	F	F	F	T	F
F	T	T	T	T	F	T
F	T	F	T	T	F	T
F	F	T	T	T	F	T
F	F	F	F	T	F	T

T ——— ≡ ——— T

(b) $p \Rightarrow (q \vee r) \equiv \sim p \vee (q \vee r)$;

$$(p \wedge \sim q) \Rightarrow r \equiv \sim (p \wedge \sim q) \vee r$$
$$\equiv (\sim p \vee \sim(\sim q)) \vee r$$
$$\equiv (\sim p \vee q) \vee r$$

15.

p	q	$\sim p$	$p \wedge q$	$\sim p \vee (p \wedge q)$
T	T	F	T	T
T	F	F	F	F
F	T	T	F	T
F	F	T	F	T

17.

p	q	$\sim p$	$\sim p \wedge q$	$p \vee (\sim p \wedge q)$
T	T	F	F	T
T	F	F	F	T
F	T	T	T	T
F	F	T	F	F

19.

p	q	~ p	~ p ⇒ q
T	T	F	T
T	F	F	T
F	T	T	T
F	F	T	F

21.

p	~ p	~ p v p
T	F	T
F	T	T

23.

p	q	p ⇒ q	p ^ p ⇒ q
T	T	T	T
T	F	F	F
F	T	T	F
F	F	T	F

25.

p	q	r	q ^ r	p ^ (q ^ r)	p ^ q	(p ^ q) ^ r	p ^ (q ^ r) ⇔ (q ^ r) ^ r
T	T	T	T	T	T	T	T
T	T	F	F	F	T	F	T
T	F	T	F	F	F	F	T
T	F	F	F	F	F	F	T
F	T	T	T	F	F	F	T
F	T	F	F	F	F	F	T
F	F	T	F	F	F	F	T
F	F	F	F	F	F	F	T

27.

p	q	p v q	p ^ (p v q)	p ^ (p v q) ⇔ p
T	T	T	T	T
T	F	T	T	T
F	T	T	F	T
F	F	F	F	T

29. p ⇒ q

31. ~ p ^ q

33. q ⇒ p

Exercise 12.4 (page 507)

1. Let p and q be the statements, p: It is raining, q: John is going to school. Assume that p ⇒ ~ q and q are true statements.

Prove: ~p is true.

Direct: p ⇒ ~ q is ture.

Also, its contrapositive q ⇒ ~ p is true and q is true.

Thus, ~ p is true by the law of detachment.

Indirect: Assume ~ p is false.

Then p is true; p ⇒ ~ q is true.

Thus, ~ q is true by the law of detachment.

But q is true, and we have a contradiction.

The assumption is false and ~ p is true.

3. Let p, q, and r be the statements, p: Smith is elected president; q: Kuntz is elected secretary; r: Brown is elected treasurer. Assume that $p \Rightarrow q$, $q \Rightarrow \sim r$, and p are true statements.

Prove: $\sim r$ is true.

Direct: $p \Rightarrow q$ and $q \Rightarrow \sim r$ are true.
So $p \Rightarrow \sim r$ is true by the law of syllogism, and p is true.
Thus, $\sim r$ is true by the law of detachment.

Indirect: Assume $\sim r$ is false.
Then r is true, $p \Rightarrow q$ is true; $q \Rightarrow \sim r$ is true.
So, $q \Rightarrow \sim r$ is true by the law of syllogism.
$r \Rightarrow \sim p$, its contrapositive, is true.
Thus, $\sim p$ is true by the law of detachment.
But p is true, and we have a contradiction.
The assumption is false and $\sim r$ is true.

5. Not valid   **7.** Valid

Exercise 12.5 (page 510)

1.

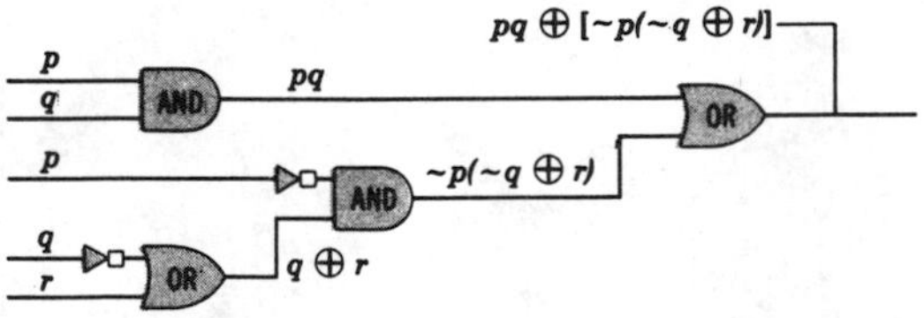

The output $pq \oplus [\sim p(\sim q \oplus r)]$ is 1 when

1. $p = q = 1$
2. $p = 0$ and $q = 0$
3. $p = 0$ and $r = 1$

3. The output is $(\sim q \oplus [p(\sim p \oplus q)])\, q = (\sim q)\, q \oplus p(\sim p \oplus q)\, q = p(\sim p \oplus q)\, q = [p(\sim p) \oplus pq]\, q = pqq = pq$, which is 1 if and only if p and q are both 1.

5.

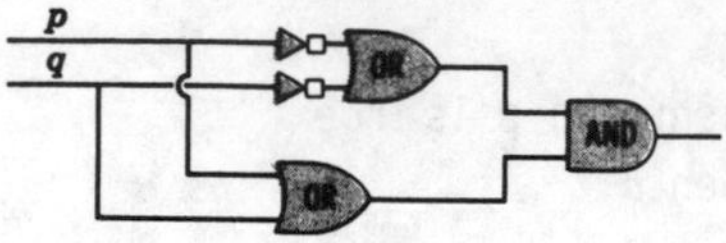

7.

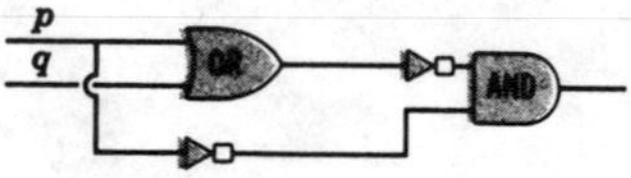

9. (For Problem 3):

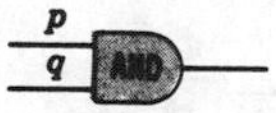

(For Problem 5):

p	q	~p ⊕ ~q	p ⊕ q	(~p ⊕ ~q)(p ⊕ q)
1	1	0	1	0
1	0	1	1	1
0	1	1	1	1
0	0	1	0	0

$(\sim p \oplus \sim q)(p \oplus q) = [\sim(pq)](p \oplus q)$

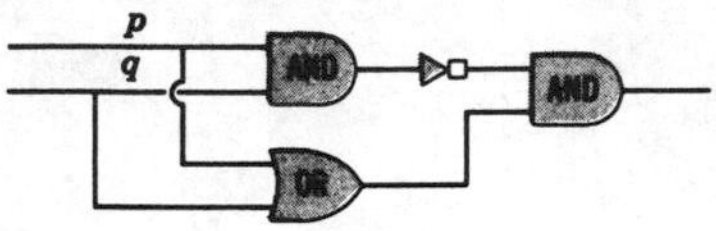

(For Problem 7): $\sim(p \oplus q)\sim p = [(p \oplus q) \oplus p] = \sim[p \oplus q]$

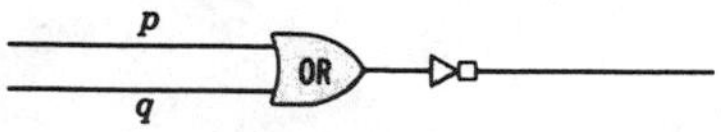

11. The truth table for this circuit is either

p	q	
1	1	1
1	0	0
0	1	0
0	0	1

or

p	q	
1	1	0
1	0	1
0	1	1
0	0	0

Thus, two possible circuits are

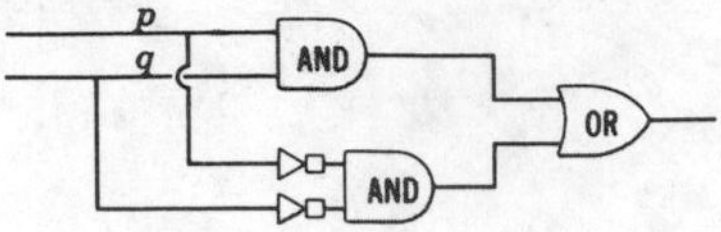

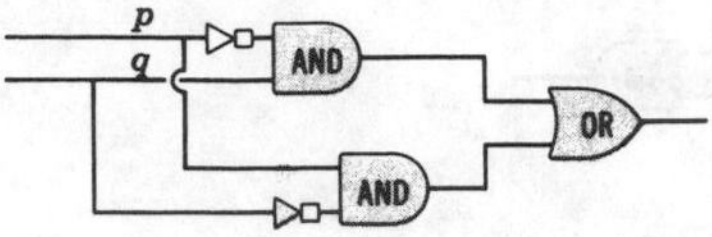

13.

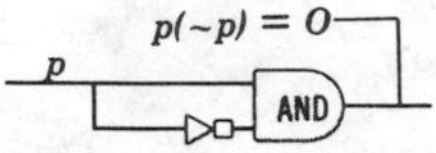

15. $p \vee q \equiv \sim(\sim p \sim q)$

(a)

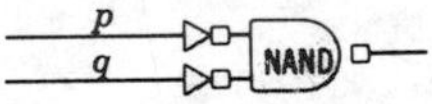

(b)

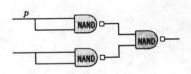

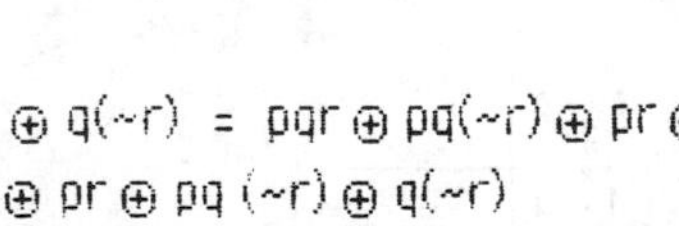

17. $pq \oplus pr \oplus q(\sim r) = pqr \oplus pq(\sim r) \oplus pr \oplus q(\sim r)$

$= pqr \oplus pr \oplus pq(\sim r) \oplus q(\sim r)$

$= pr(q \oplus 1) \oplus (p \oplus 1)[q(\sim r)] = pr(1) \oplus 1[q(\sim r)]$

$= pr \oplus q(\sim r)$

Review Exercises (page 513)

1. (c) **3.** (a) **5.** Nobody is rich **7.** Danny is tall or Mary is not short.

9.

p	q	$\sim p$	$p \wedge q$	$(p \wedge q) \vee \sim p$
T	T	F	T	T
T	F	F	F	F
F	T	T	F	T
F	F	T	F	T

11.

p	q	$\sim p$	$\sim q$	$p \vee \sim q$	$\sim p \vee (p \vee \sim q)$
T	T	F	F	T	T
T	F	F	T	T	T
F	T	T	F	F	T
F	F	T	T	T	T

13. $q \Rightarrow p$ **15.** $p \Leftrightarrow q$

17. Let p be the statement "I paint the house" and let q be the statement "I go bowling". Assume $\sim p \Rightarrow q$ and $\sim q$ are true.
Prove: p is true.
Since $\sim p \Rightarrow q$ is true, its contrapositive $\sim q \Rightarrow p$ is true. We have $\sim q$ is true and hence, by the law of detachment, p is true.

19.

p	q	$\sim p$	$\sim p \vee q$	$p \Rightarrow q$
T	T	F	T	T
T	F	F	F	F
F	T	T	T	T
F	F	T	T	T

$\sim p \vee q \equiv p \Rightarrow q$

21.

p	q	$(p \oplus q)[\sim(pq)]$	$p \underline{\vee} q$
1	1	0	0
1	0	1	1
0	1	1	1
0	0	0	0

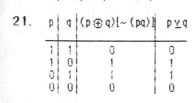

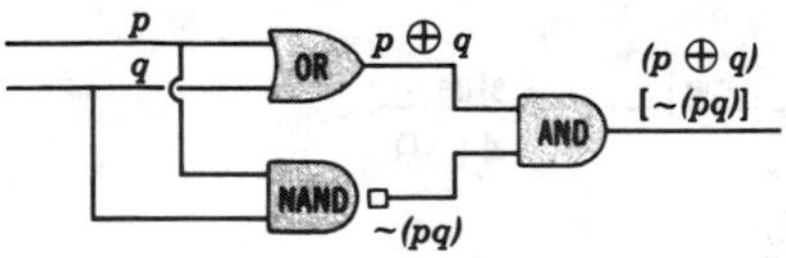

CHAPTER 13

Exercise 13.1 (page 520)

1. True, false, true, false, true, false, false, false, false
3. {(2, 2), (2, 4), (2, 6), (2, 10), (3, 6), (5, 10)}
5. 1, 4, 9, 16, 25, 2, 5
7. (a) {(1, 2), (1, 4), (1, 7), (2, 2), (2, 4), (2, 7), (5, 2), (5, 4), (5, 7)}
   (b) {(1, 2), (1, 4), (1, 7), (2, 4), (2, 7), (5, 7)}
   (c) R is a subset of A x B.
9. (a) {aa, ab, ba, bb}
   (b) {(aa, ab), (ab, aa), (ba, bb), (bb, ba)}
11. 50, 97, 64, 80, 116, 110, 125
13. {(1, 2), (1, 4), (1, 6), (1, 8), (2, 2), (2, 4), (2, 6), (2, 8), (3, 6)}
15. {(1, 1), (2, 2), (3, 3), (4, 4), (5, 5), (6, 6), (7, 7), (8, 8), (9, 9), (10, 10), (1, 3), (3, 1), (1, 5), (5, 1), (1, 7), (7, 1), (1, 8), (8, 1), (1, 9), (9, 1), (1, 10), (10, 1), (2, 4), (4, 2), (2, 6), (6, 2), (2, 8), (8, 2), (2, 10), (10, 2), (3, 5), (5, 3), (3, 7), (7, 3), (3, 9), (9, 3), (4, 6), (6, 4), (4, 8), (8, 4), (4, 10), (10, 4), (5, 7), (7, 5), (5, 9), (9, 5), (6, 8), (8, 6), (6, 10), (10, 6), (7, 9), (9, 7), (8, 10), (10, 8)}
17. {(0, 0), (0, 00), (00, 0), (0, 000), (000, 0), (1, 1), (1, 01), (01, 1), (1, 10), (10, 1), (1, 001), (001, 1), (1, 010), (010, 1), (1, 100), (100, 1), (00, 00), (00, 000), (000, 00), (01, 01), (10, 10), (01, 10), (10, 01), (01, 001), (001, 01), (01, 010), (010, 01), (01, 100), (100, 01), (11, 11), (11, 011), (011, 11), (11, 101), (101, 11), (11, 110), (110, 11), (000, 000), (001, 001), (001, 010), (010, 001), (001, 100), (100, 001), (010, 010), (010, 100), (100, 010), (100, 100), (011, 011), (011, 101), (101, 011), (011, 110), (110, 011), (101, 101), (101, 110), (110, 110), (111, 111)}
19. {(0, 0), (0, 1), (0, 2), (0, 3), (1, 1), (1, 2), (1, 3), (2, 2), (2, 3), (3, 3)}
21. {(0, 0), (1, 1), (2, 4), (3, 9), (4, 16)}
23. {(1, 1), (2, 1), (5, 2), (7, 3)}
25. {(42, *), (72, H), (47, 1), (88, X)}
27.

Variable Name	Value
PI	3.14159
RADIUS	10
RSQR	100
AREA	314.159
CIRCUM	628.318

29. Reflexive, symmetric, and transitive.
31. Reflexive, symmetric, and transitive.
33. Reflexive, symmetric, and transitive.

35. Reflexive. Not symmetric because (A, C) ∈ R but (C, A) ∉ R. Not transitive because (C, B) ∈ R and (B, A) ∈ R but (C, A) ∉.
37. Reflexive, symmetric, and transitive.
39. Since we cannot find a and b in A such that aRb, then R is symmetric. Similarly, since we cannot find a, b, and c in A such that aRb and bRc, then R is transitive. And since (t, t) ∉ R etc. then R is not reflexive.

Exercise 13.2 (page 527)

1. 1, 4, 2. Domain = {a, b, c}, range = 1, 2, 4}
3. 5, 0, 10, -5, 15. Domain = ℝ, range = ℝ.
5. Does not define a function, because f assigns two difdferent values (1 and 3) to x.
7. Yes, f defines a function.
9. Yes, f is a function.
11. No, f is not a function. Domain ≠ A.
13. C, 9, ´, (, =
15. 0, 100, 0, -2
17. x1 = 12675.2; x2 = 12675; ABSX = 126.75
19. Yes.
21. Yes.
23. One - one, not onto, therefore, not bijective.
25. Neither one-to-one nor onto, therefore, not bijective.
27. For example, TRUNC (1.0) = 1 = TRUNC (1.1) And ROUND (2.7) = 3 = ROUND (3.1). Thus, TRUNC and ROUND are not one-to-one.
29. For example H(10, 10) = 0 = H(01, 01). Thus, H is not one-to-one.
31. No. Odd integers in the range are not associated with any integers in the domain.
33. 3, 2, 1
35. g of (1) = g[f(1)] = g(b) = z
    g of (2) = g[f(2)] = g(a) = x
    g of (3) = g[f(3)] = g(c) = y

Exercise 13.3 (page 532)

1. $-1, \frac{1}{2}, -\frac{1}{3}, \frac{1}{4}, \frac{1}{100}$
3. (a) $0, \frac{1}{2}, \frac{2}{3}, \frac{3}{4}, \frac{4}{5}, \frac{5}{6}$

(b) $n = 0, \quad b_1 - b_0 = \frac{1}{2} - 0 = \frac{1}{2}$

$n = 1, \quad b_2 - b_1 = \frac{2}{3} - \frac{1}{2} = \frac{1}{6}$

5. 1, 2, 4, 8, 16, 32, 64, 128
7. 1, 1, 2, 6, 24, 120, 720
9. 1, 1, 1, 1, . . ., 1.
11. $M_0 = \begin{bmatrix} 1 & 1 & 0 \\ 1 & 0 & -1 \\ 0 & -1 & 1 \end{bmatrix}$

$M_1 = \begin{bmatrix} 1 & 0 & 0 \\ 0 & 1 & 0 \\ 0 & 0 & 2 \end{bmatrix}$

$M_2 = \begin{bmatrix} 1 & -1 & 0 \\ -1 & 2 & 1 \\ 0 & 1 & 3 \end{bmatrix}$

$M_3 = \begin{bmatrix} 1 & -2 & 0 \\ -2 & 3 & 2 \\ 0 & 2 & 4 \end{bmatrix}$

13. $(-1)^n, n = 0, 1, 2, \ldots$
15. $2n + 1, \; n = 0, 1, 2, \ldots$
17. $\frac{1}{n+1}, \; n = 0, 1, 2, \ldots$
19. 0, 1, 3, 7, 15, 31, 63, 127
21. 1, 1, 2, 3, 5, 8, 13, 21, 34

Exercise 13.4 (page 537)

1. 10
3. Algorithm AVRG

```
Sum := 0
x : = 1
Do While (x ≤ M)
   Input N(x)
   Sum : = Sum + N(x)
   x : = x + 1
End of While
Average : = Sum/M
End of AVRG
```

5. Algorithm PRODUCT
```
     Prod : = 1
     x : = 1
     Do While (x ≤ M)
       Input N(x)
       Prod : = Prod * N(x)
       x : = x + 1
     End of While
   End of PRODUCT
```

7. Algorithm SCHOLARSHIP
```
     J : = 1
     Do While (J ≤ 20)
       Input Name (J), GPA (J)
       If (GPA (J)> 3.5)
         Then output Name (J), GPA (J)
       J : = J + 1
     End of While
   End of SCHOLARSHIP
```

9. Algorithm GRADE
```
     Input name, score
     If (score ≤ 59)
       Then output name, 'Grade is F'
     Else if ((score > 59) and (score ≤ 69))
       Then output name, 'Grade is D'
     Else if ((score > 69) and (score ≤ 79))
       Then output name, 'Grade is C'
     Else if ((score > 79) and (score ≤ 89))
       Then output name, 'Grade is B'
     Else output name, 'Grade is A'
   End of GRADE
```

11. Algorithm NUMBER
```
     Input N
     If (N < 0)
       Then output 'Number is negative'
     Else output 'Number is positive or zero'
   End of NUMBER
```

13. Algorithm PRICE

```
    Input age
    If (age > 65)
      Then costs is discounted
    Else cost is regular
    Output cost
End of PRICE
```

Exercise 13.5 (page 544)

1. (a) $a < 2$. Yes.

(b) $2 < 2^2$. Yes.

(c) $k < 2^k$.

(d) $(k + 1) < 2^{k+1}$.

3. (a) $1^2 = \frac{1(1+1)(2+1)}{6}$. Yes.

(b) $1^2 + 2^2 + 3^2 + 4^2 + 5^2 = \frac{5(5+1)(10+1)}{6}$. Yes.

(c) $1^2 + 2^2 + 3^2 + \ldots + k^2 = \frac{k(k+1)(2k+1)}{6}$

(d) $$1^2 + 2^2 + 3^2 + \ldots + k^2 + (k+1)^2 = \frac{(k+1)[(k+1)+1][2(k+1)+1}{6}$$
$$= \frac{(k+1)(k+2)(2k+3)}{6}$$

5. (a) $1 + 2 = 2^2 - 1$. Yes.

(b) $1 + 2 + 2^2 + 2^3 + 2^4 + 2^5 = 2^{5+1} - 1$. Yes.

(c) $1 + 2 + 2^2 + \ldots + 2^k = 2^{k+1} - 1$.

(d) $1 + 2 + 2^2 + \ldots + 2^k + 2^{k+1} = 2^{(k+1)+1} - 1$

7. Since $1 \cdot 2 = \frac{1(1+1)(1+2)}{3}$ then s(1) is true and condition I is true. Assume that s(k) is true. Show s(k + 1) is true. s(k + 1) states:

$$1 \cdot 2 + 2 \cdot 3 + 3 \cdot 4 + \ldots + k \cdot (k+1) + (k+1)[(k+1)+1] = \frac{(k+1)[(k+1)+1][(k+1)+2]}{3} \quad (1)$$

Using our assumption that s(k) is true the left hand side of

$$(1) = \frac{k(k+1)(k+2)}{3} + (k+1)[(k+1)+1]$$
$$= \frac{k(k+1)(k+2) + 3(k+1)(k+2)}{3}$$

$$= \frac{(k+1)(k+2)(k+3}{3} = \frac{(k+1)[(k+1)+1][(k+1)+2]}{3}$$

which shows that $s(k + 1)$ is true and thus condition II is true.

9. Since $\frac{1}{1\cdot 2} = \frac{1}{1+1}$, then $s(1)$ is true and thus condition I is satisfied. Assume $s(k)$ is true. Show that $s(k + 1)$ is also true. $s(k + 1)$ states:

(1) $$\frac{1}{1\cdot 2} + \frac{1}{2\cdot 3} + \frac{1}{3\cdot 4} + \ldots + \frac{1}{(k+1)[(k+1)+1]} = \frac{k+1}{(k+1)+1}$$

Since by assumption $s(k)$ is true then the left hand side of (1) gives

$$\frac{k}{k+1} + \frac{1}{(k+1)[(k+1)+1]} = \frac{k[(k+1)+1]+1}{(k+1)[(k+1)+1]}$$

$$= \frac{k(k+2)+1}{(k+1)[(k+1)+1]} = \frac{k^2+2k+1}{(k+1)[(k+1)+1]} = \frac{(k+1)(k+1}{(k+1)[(k+1)+1]} = \frac{k+1}{[(k+1)+1]}$$

which is the right hand side of (1). Thus $s(k + 1)$ is true and so condition II is satisfied.

11. Since $2 = \frac{1(3+1)}{2}$, then $s(1)$ is true and thus condition I is satisfied. Assume $s(k)$ is true show $s(k + 1)$ is also true. $s(k + 1)$ states:

(1) $$2 + 5 + 8 + \ldots + [3(k+1) - 1] = \frac{(k+1)[3(k+1)+1]}{2}$$

By our assumption that $s(k)$ is true the left hand side of (1) is then

$$\frac{k(3k+1)}{2} + 3(k+1) - 1 = \frac{k(3k+1)+6(k+1)-2}{2}$$

$$= \frac{3k^2+7k+4}{2} = \frac{(k+1)(3k+4)}{2}$$

$$= \frac{(k+1)(3k+3+1)}{2}$$

$$= \frac{(k+1)[3(k+1)+1]}{2}$$ which

is the right hand side of (1). Thus s(k+1) is true and so condition II is satisfied.

13. $100 + 99 + \ldots + 2 + 1 = 100\ \frac{(100+1)}{2} = 5050$

15. $2 + 2 + 2 + 4 + 2 + 6 + \ldots + 2 + 2000 = 2000 + 2 + 4 + 6 + \ldots + 2000$
$= 2000 + 1000(1001) = 100{,}300.$

17. $1 \cdot 2 + 2 \cdot 3 + \ldots + 1000 \cdot 1001 = \frac{1000(1001)(1002)}{3} = 334{,}334{,}000$

Exercise 13.6 (page 550)

1. 1, 2, 4, 8, 16, 32
3. 1, 0, −1, −4, −17, −86
5. 2, 4, 12, 48, 240, 1440
7. 1, 1, 3, 7, 16, 33
9. 1, 2, 2, 4, 8, 32
11. 1, 2, 2, 5, 9, 16
13. 1, −1, −1, −5, −20, −104
15. 89, 144, 233, 277, 610
17. (a) The word that contains no bits is of length 0 that does not contain the bit pattern 00.
The words 0 and 1 are of length 1 that do not contain the pattern 00.
The words 01,10,11 are of length 2 that do not contain the pattern 00.
The words 010, 101, 011, 110, 111 are of length 3 that do not contain the bit pattern 00.
The words 1010, 1101, 1110, 1111, 0101, 1011, 0111, 0110 are of length 4 that do not contain the bit pattern 00.
(b) Recurrence relation $s_n = s_{n-1} + 2_{n-2}$ with $s_0 = 1$ $s_1 = 2$ as initial conditions.
19. (a) \$1000, \$1100, \$1210, \$1331, \$1464.1
(b) $A_n = A_{n-1} + 0.1\ A_{n-1}$ (recurrence relations)
$A_0 = 1{,}000$ (initial condition)
21. (a) 2, 4, 7, 11
(b) $P_n = P_{n-1} + n$ (recurrence relation)
$P_1 = 2$ (initial condition)

REVIEW EXERCISES (Page 552)

1. {(1, 1), (8, 2), (27, 3)}
3. (a) and (b)

5. (a) 1, 0, 3, 2, 5, 4, 7, 6, 9, 8
   (b) 0, -1, 2, -3, 4, -5, 6, -7, 8, -9

7.

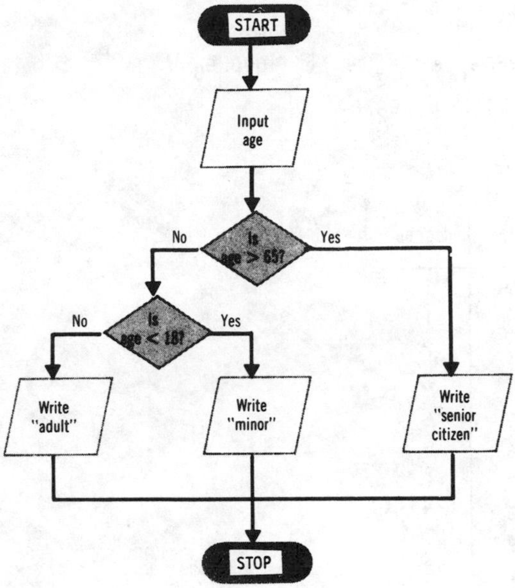

9. 1,000,000

11. 2, 2, 1, 4, 12, 60, 960

CHAPTER 14

Exercise 14.1 (page 560)

1. vertices: v_1, v_2, v_3, v_4. Edges: e_1, e_2, e_3, e_4, e_5. loop: e_5.
   Isolated vertex: v_4. Parallel edges: e_1, e_2, e_3.

3.

5.

Vertex	degree
v_1	3
v_2	4
v_3	3
v_4	0

Vertex	degree
v_1	1
v_2	1
v_3	2
v_4	2
v_5	2
v_6	4
v_7	2
v_8	4
v_9	2
v_{10}	2

7. 9 as following Figure shows

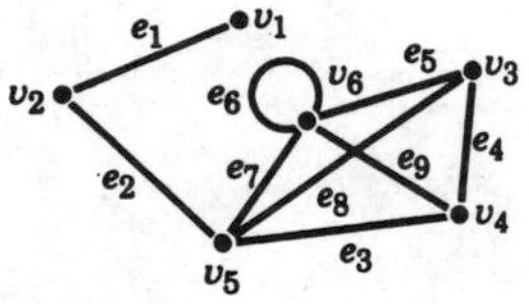

9. No, for $\deg(v_4) = 4$ there must be a loop.

11. (a)

(b)

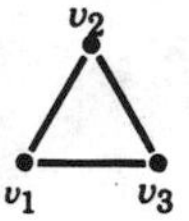

13. 15

15.

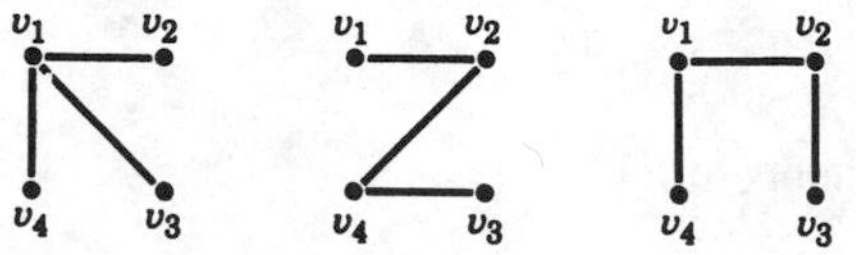

17.

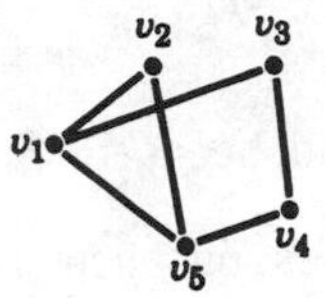

Exercise 14.2 (page 563)

1. (a) and (b) Path, but neither a simple path nor a circuit. (c) Simple path, but not a circuit. (d) Circuit but not a simple circuit. (e) Simple circuit.
3. (a), (b) and (c) Simple circuit. (d) Path, but neither a simple path nor a circuit.
5. (a) $v_1e_1v_2$
   $v_5e_5v_6e_9v_3$
   $v_1e_6v_6e_5v_5e_4v_4$
   $v_2e_2v_3e_3v_4e_4v_5$

   (b) $v_1e_1v_2e_7v_6e_5v_5e_{10}v_3e_9v_6e_6v_1$
   $v_1e_1v_2e_8v_5e_5v_6e_9v_3e_2v_2e_7v_6e_6v_1$
   $v_1e_1v_2e_7v_6e_9v_3e_{10}v_5e_5v_6e_6v_1$
   $v_2e_8v_5e_{10}v_3e_3v_4e_4v_5e_5v_6e_9v_3e_2v_2$

   (c) $v_1e_1v_2e_7v_6e_6v_1$
   $v_3e_{10}v_5e_4v_4e_3v_3$
   $v_2e_8v_5e_{10}v_3e_9v_6e_7v_2$
   $v_6e_5v_5e_4v_4e_3v_3e_2v_2e_1v_1e_6v_6$

7. $v_1e_1v_2e_2v_3e_9v_5e_4v_4e_3v_3e_8v_6e_6v_1$

9. (a)

(b)

11. (a) e_1, e_2, e_3, e_4 (b) e_4 (c) e_2, e_4, e_5

13.

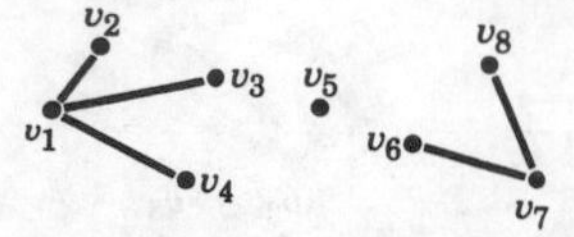

15. (a) No, because $1 > \binom{5}{2} = 10$ (Theorem II).

(b) Yes, because $10 \not> \binom{5}{2} = 10$ (Theorem III).

Exercise 14.3 (page 570)

1. (a) Every vertex is of even degree. By Theorem I, there is an Eulerian circuit. $v_1e_1v_2e_2v_3e_4v_4e_5v_5e_6v_3e_3v_2e_9v_1$ is an Eulerian circuit.
   (b) Graph is not connected. Therefore, no Eulerian circuit.
   (c) Degree of $v_1 = 3$, not even. Therefore, no Eulerian circuit.
   (d) Every vertex is of even degree. Therefore graph contains an Eulerian circuit. The circuit $v_1e_1v_2e_2v_3e_3v_1e_5v_4e_4v_2e_6v_5e_7v_1$ is Eulerian.
   (e) Every vetex is of even degree. Therefore graph contains an Eulerian circuit. The circuit
   $v_1e_1v_2e_{10}v_3e_{11}v_5e_{12}v_1e_{13}v_6e_5v_5e_4v_4e_3v_3e_2v_2e_{14}v_4e_{15}v_6e_9v_2e_8v_7e_7v_6e_6v_1$
   is Eulerian.
   (f) Degree of $v_1 = 3$, not even. Therefore, graph does not contain an Eulerain circuit.
3. Yes, each vertex is of even degree.
5.

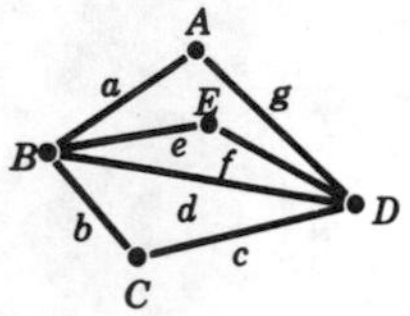

Yes. Let A and C in the figure be the land masses, B, E, and D be the three islands and a, b, c, d, e, f, and g be the seven bridges. Note that each vertex has even degree. Therefore, the graph contains an Eulerian circuit. the following circuit is the desired round trip:

AaBbCcDdBeEfDgA.

7. No, the corresponding graph has vertex B (vertex representing room B) of degree 3 which is not even.

9. (a) $v_1e_1v_2e_9v_7e_{10}v_8e_3v_3e_4v_4e_5v_5e_6v_6e_7v_1$
   (b) $v_1e_1v_7e_2v_2e_4v_8e_5v_3e_6v_4e_7v_5e_8v_6e_9v_1$
   (c) $v_1e_1v_2e_2v_3e_3v_4e_{11}v_7e_{10}v_6e_{13}v_5e_5v_1$
   (d) $v_4e_3v_3e_9v_8e_{12}v_7e_{11}v_6e_7v_2e_1v_1e_5v_5e_4v_4$

11. Use Theorem 2,
   (a) $\deg(v_1) + \deg(v_5) = 4 < 6$, number of vertices.
   (b) $\deg(v_2) + \deg(v_7) = 4 < 8$, number of vertices.
   (c) $\deg(v_1) + \deg(v_6) = 4 < 7$, number of vertices.
   (d) $\deg(v_5) + \deg(v_{10}) = 4 < 10$, number of vertices.

13.

15.

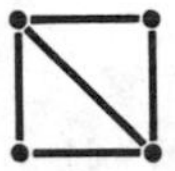

Exercise 14.4 (page 579)

1.

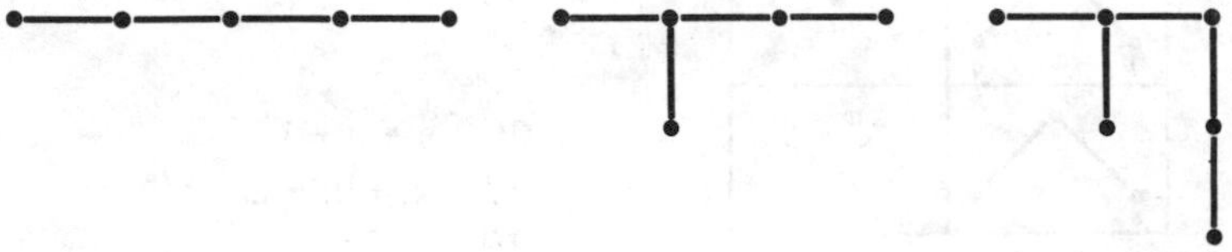

3.

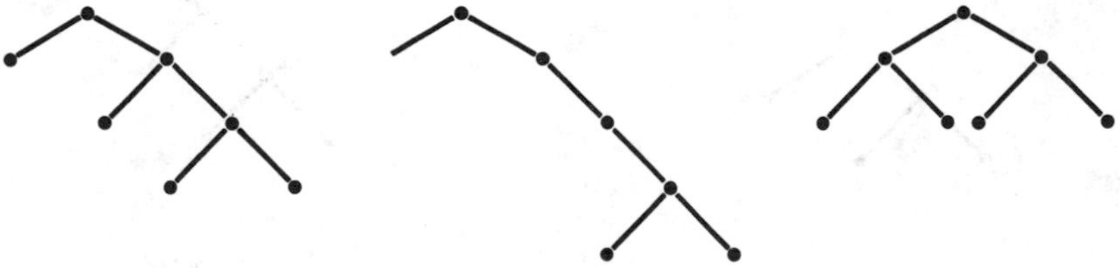

5. By Theorem 1, such a tree cannot exist.
7. Cannot exist. A graph with the given specifications must contain a circuit.
9. Cannot exist. Such a graph must contain a circuit.
11. Cannot exist. Such a graph <u>must</u> be a tree.
13. Yes. Use Theorem 1.

15.

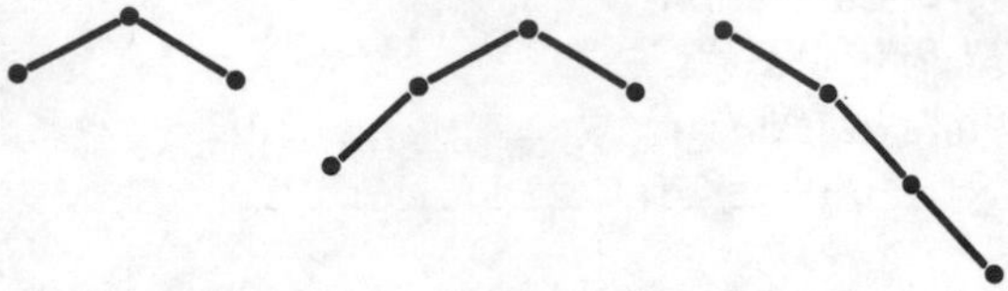

17. Leaves: $v_1, v_3, v_4, v_5, v_6, v_7$.
Internal vertices: $v_2, v_9, v_8, v_{10}, v_{11}, v_{12}$.

19. No. By definition a leaf is connected to the rest of a tree by only one edge.

21.

23. (a) r, p, q, u are the descendants of x.
u, s, t, w, a, b c are the descendants of y.

(b)

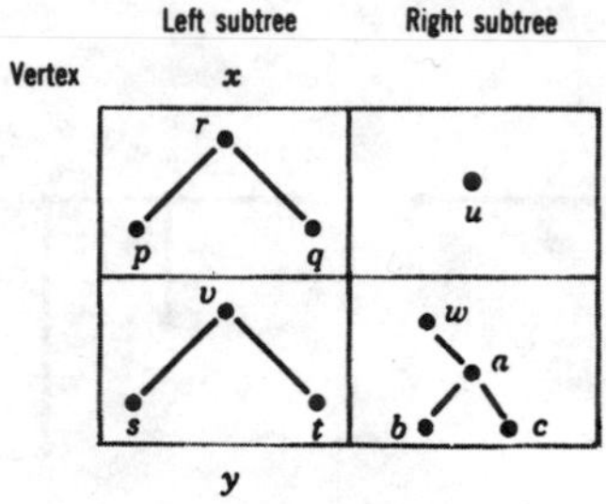

(c)

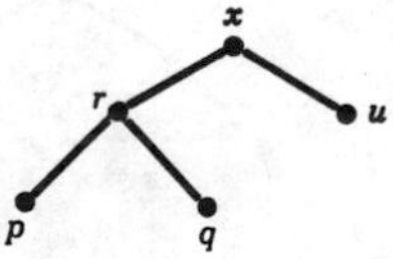

25. a * b + 1

27. (x + y) * z - a/b

29.

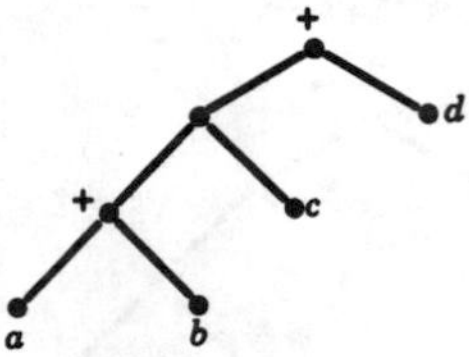

31.

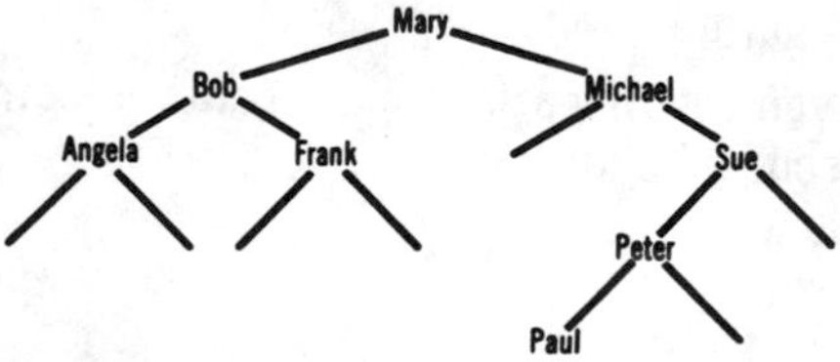

33. (a) Yes.
(b) Yes.

Exercise 14.5 (page 587)

1. (a)

Arc	initial point	terminal point
e_1	a	a
e_2	a	b
e_3	a	c
e_4	b	c
e_5	d	c
e_6	c	e
e_7	d	e
e_8	d	h
e_9	f	c
e_{10}	c	f
e_{11}	f	g
e_{12}	f	h
e_{13}	g	h

(b)

Vertex	Indegree	Outdegree
a	1	3
b	1	1
c	4	2
d	0	3
e	2	0
f	1	3
g	2	0
h	2	1

3.

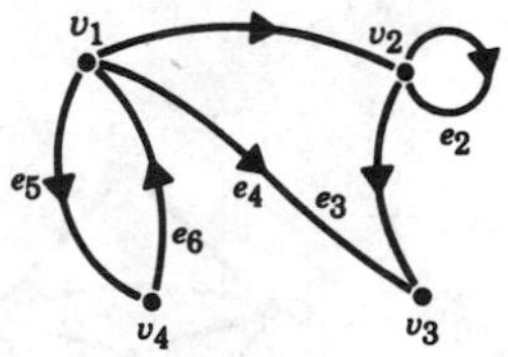

5.

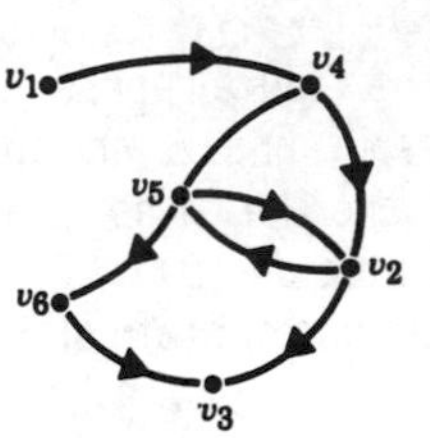

7.

9. (a) Yes. $v_1e_1v_2e_8v_7e_{10}v_5$ is a directed path from v_1 to v_5
   (b) No. No arcs go into v_1 i.e. indeg(v_1) = 0.
11. $v_1e_1v_2e_8v_7e_{10}v_5\,e_5v_6$; $v_1e_6v_6$; $v_1e_1v_2e_8v_7e_{11}v_4e_{12}v_6$
13. No. v_1 cannot send messages to v_5 because indeg(v_5) = 0.
15.

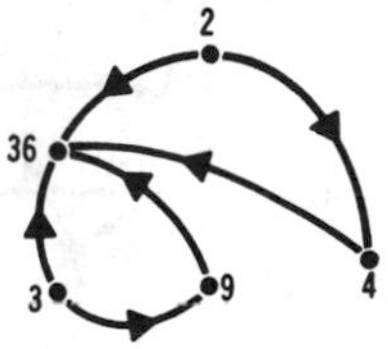

17. Graph is connected and contains no bridges. Thus it is orientable. The graph in the figure is the desired strongly connected digraph.

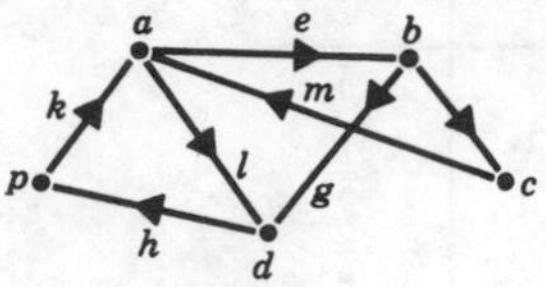

19. Graph contains a bridge that connects the vertices v and z. Therefore, the graph is not orientable.

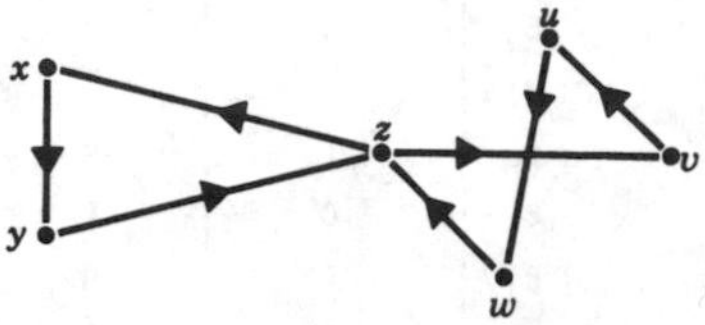

CHAPTER REVIEW (page 590)

1. No. Such a simple graph must at most have 6 edges.
3. (a) $v_1e_9v_5e_5v_7e_4v_6e_{12}v_3$
   (b) $v_1e_9v_5e_5v_7e_4v_6e_{12}v_3e_3v_5e_9v_1$
   (c) $v_1e_9v_5e_5v_7e_4v_6e_{11}v_2e_1v_1$
5. No. The graph in the figure represents the city where the vertices A and B are the two banks,C, D, and E are the three islands and the edges are the bridges. Since deg(B) = 3 which is odd, then the graph does not contain an Eulerian circuit.

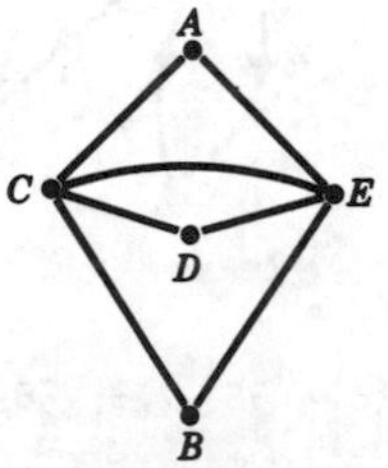

7. $v_1e_1v_2e_2v_3e_8v_5e_6v_2e_7v_4e_9v_1e_{10}v_3e_3v_4e_4v_5e_5v_1$ is an Eulerian circuit.
9.

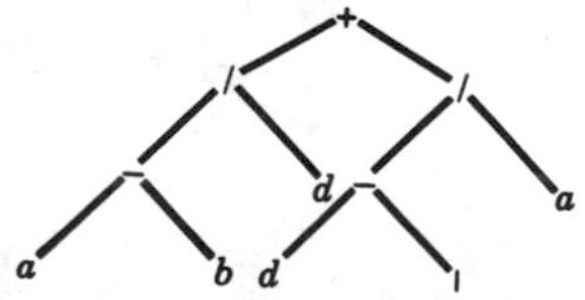

11.

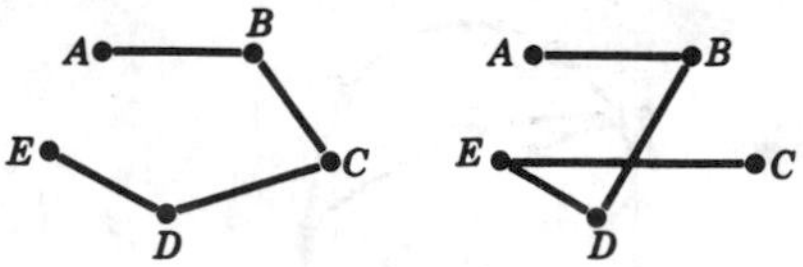

13. Yes. Every vertex is reachable from the others.

Solutions to Even-Numbered Problems

CHAPTER 1

Exercise 1.1 (page 11)

2. 0.75

4. 1.875

6. 1.666...

8. 0.833...

10. 85%

12. 125%

14. 7%

16. 0.15%

18. 0.0725

20. 3.00

22. 0.043

24. 0.92

26. 5/9

28. 1/3

30. 100

32. 5

34. $x = 2 - 6$
$x = -4$

36. $x = -6$

38. $x + 1 = 2$
$x = 2 - 1$
$x = 1$

40. $5x - 2x = 8 + 1$
$3x = 9$
$x = 3$

42.
$$\frac{2x}{5} + \frac{x}{5} = 9$$
$$\frac{3x}{5} = 9$$
$$x = \frac{5}{3} \cdot 9$$
$$x = 15$$

44.
$$\frac{2x+1}{x-1} = 3$$
$$2x + 1 = 3(x - 1)$$
$$2x + 1 = 3x - 3$$
$$x = 4$$

46. $x(x + 7) = 0$
$x = 0, x = -7$

48. $(x - 3)(x + 2) = 0$
$x = 3, x = -2$

50. $(x - 3)(x - 3) = 0$
$x = 3$

52. $x = 8$

54. $x = \frac{1}{3^2}$

56. $x = 9$

58. $x = -2$

60. $3^x = 3^4$
$x = 4$

62. $x = 10$

64. $1/4 = 0.25$

66. $\pi < 22/7$

68. $14x - 21x + 16 \le 3x - 2$
$-7x + 16 \le 3x - 2$
$-10x \le -18$
$x \ge 1.8$

70. $4 - 5x \ge 3$
$-5x \ge 3 - 4$
$x \le 1/5$

72. $8 - 2x \le 5x - 6$
$-7x \le -14$
$x \ge 2$

74. $-3x \le 2x + 5$
$-5x \ge 5$
$x \le -1$

76. $1 + 2 < 3x - 2x$
$3 < x$

78. $3x - 2x \ge 1 + 5$
$x \ge 6$

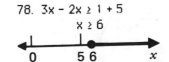

Exercise 1.2 (page 15)

2

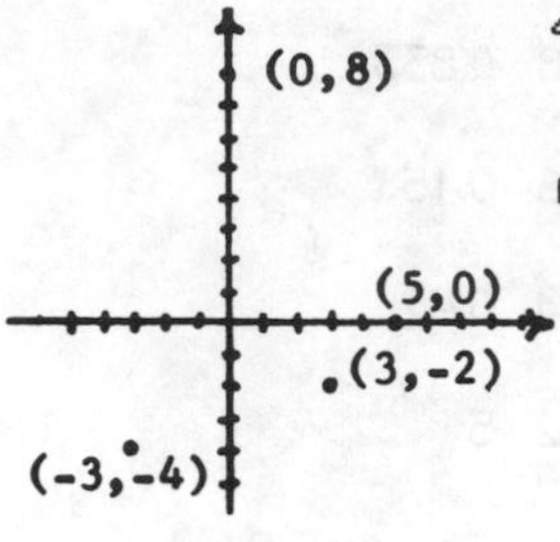

4. $\dfrac{-2-3}{3-5} = \dfrac{-5}{-2} = \dfrac{5}{2}$

6. $\dfrac{2-2}{4-6} = \dfrac{0}{-2} = 0$

8. $y = -3x + 3$

x	0	1	2	-2	4	-4
y	3	0	-3	9	-9	15

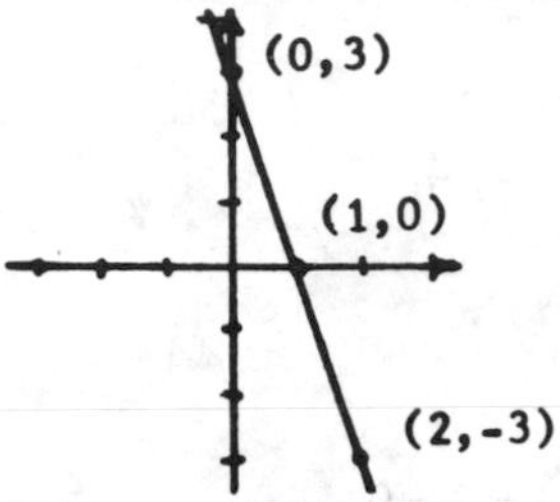

10. $x + 3y = 9$

x	0	9	2	-2	4	-4
y	3	0	7/3	11/3	5/3	13/3

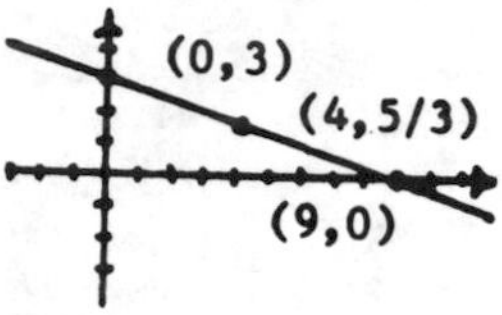

12.

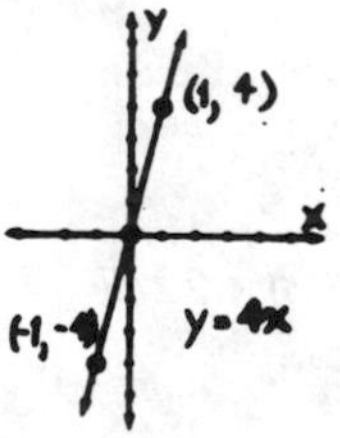

14.

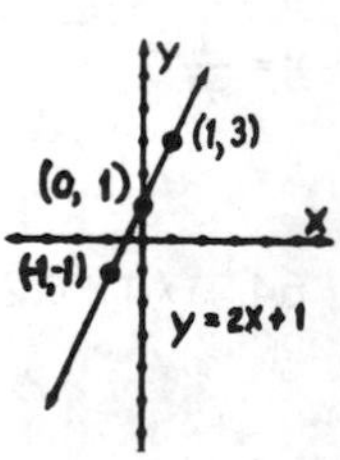

16.

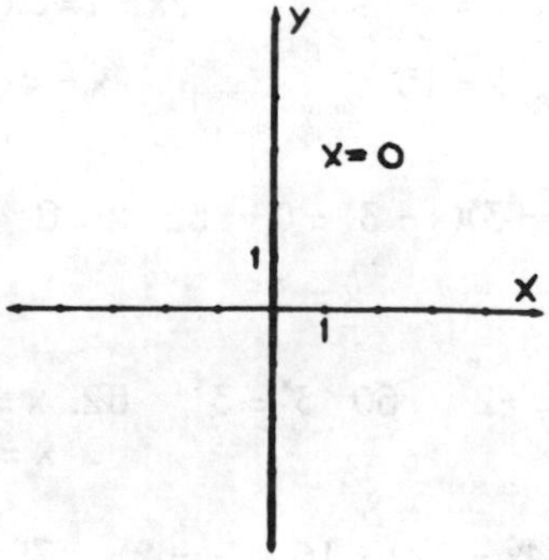

18.

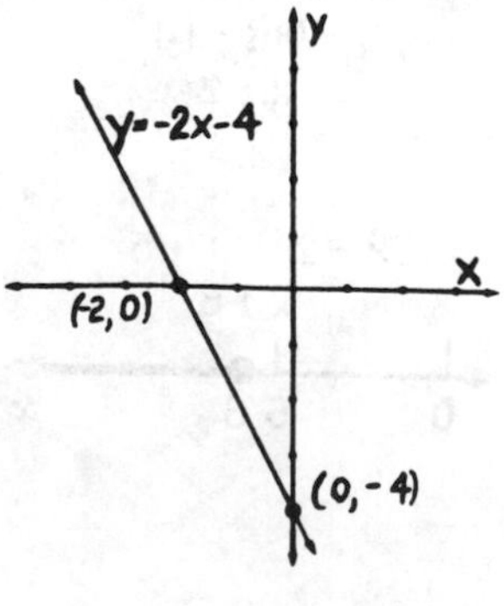

20

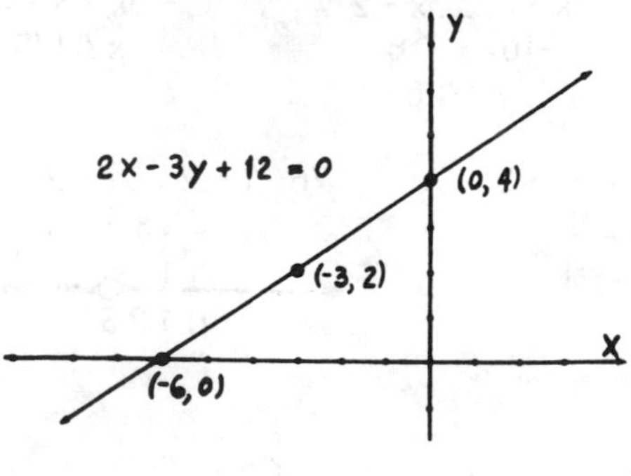

Exercise 1.3 (page 23)

2. $\frac{-6-1}{5-1} = -\frac{7}{4}$

4. $\frac{0-(-3)}{0-4} = -\frac{3}{4}$

6. $\frac{-2-(-2)}{6-(-3)} = \frac{0}{9} = 0$

8. $y - (-3) = 3(x-4)$

$y + 3 = 3x - 12$

$y = 3x - 15$

10. $y - 1 = \frac{1}{2}(x-3)$

$y = \frac{1}{2}x - \frac{1}{2}$

12. $m = \frac{5-4}{2-(-3)} = \frac{1}{5}$

$y - 4 = \frac{1}{5}[x - (-3)]$

$y = \frac{1}{5}x + \frac{23}{5}$

14. $y = -2x - 2$

16. $m = \frac{4-0}{0-(-4)} = 1$

$y = x + 4$

18. $x = 2$

20. slope = -4, y-intercept = 2

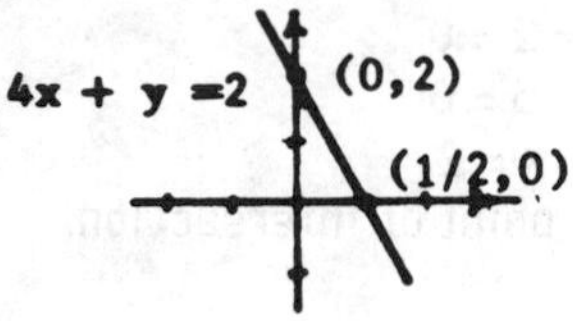

22. slope = -1, y-intercept = -4

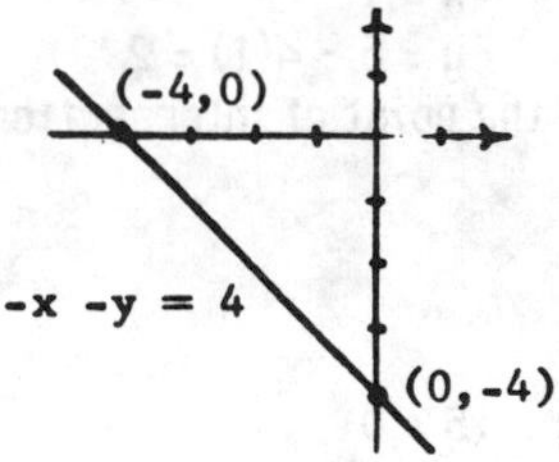

24. slope = 0, y-intercept = 3

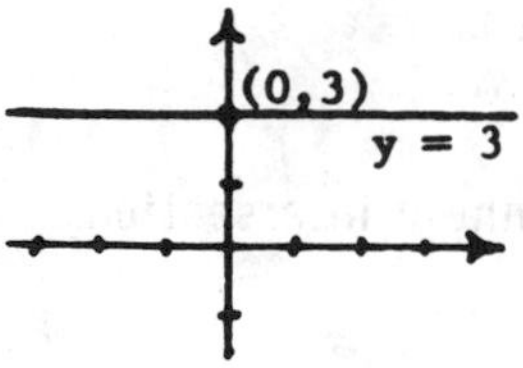

26. $y = -x/2$

28. $m = \frac{2-1}{2-(-1)} = \frac{1}{3}$

$y - 2 = \frac{1}{3}(x-2)$

Exercise 1.4 (page 30)

2. $y = x - 5$
   $y = x + 7/2$
   slope = 1

4. $y = 2x + 7/2$
   $y = 2x - 2$
   slope = 2

6.
$$y = 7 - 2x$$
$$x - (7 - 2x) + 4 = 0$$
$$x - 7 + 2x + 4 = 0$$
$$3x - 3 = 0$$
$$3x = 3$$
$$x = 1$$
$$y = 7 - 2(1) = 5$$
(1,5) is the point of intersection

8.
$$y = 2x + 1$$
$$4x + 3(2x + 1) = 2$$
$$4x + 6x + 3 = 2$$
$$10x = -1$$
$$x = -\frac{1}{10}$$
$$y = 2\left(-\frac{1}{10}\right) + 1 = \frac{4}{5}$$
$\left(-\frac{1}{10}, \frac{4}{5}\right)$ is the intersection

10.
$$y = 6 - 4x$$
$$4x - 2(6 - 4x) = 0$$
$$4x - 12 + 8x = 0$$
$$12x - 12 = 0$$
$$x = 1$$
$$y = 6 - 4(1) = 2$$
(1,2) is the point of intersection.

12.
$$3x - 4y - 2 = 0$$
$$2x + 5y - 9 = 0$$
$$6x - 8y - 4 = 0$$
$$6x + 15y - 27 = 0$$
$$23y - 23 = 0$$
$$y = 1$$
$$3x - 4(1) - 2 = 0$$
$$3x - 6 = 0$$
$$x = 2$$
(2,1) is the point of intersection.

14.
$$5x + 2y - 15 = 0$$
$$2x - 3y - 6 = 0$$
$$15x + 6y - 45 = 0$$
$$4x - 6y - 12 = 0$$
$$19x - 57 = 0$$
$$x=3$$
$$2(3) - 3y - 6 = 0$$
$$y = 0$$
(3,0) is the point of intersection.

16.
$$-3x + 4y - 10 = 0$$
$$2x - 3y + 7 = 0$$
$$-6x + 8y - 20 = 0$$
$$6x - 9y + 21 = 0$$
$$-y + 1 = 0$$
$$y = 1$$
$$2x - 3(1) + 7 = 0$$
$$x = -2$$
(-2,1) is the point of intersection.

18.
$$4x + 3y + 1 = 0$$
$$2x + 5y - 3 = 0$$
$$-4x - 10y + 6 = 0$$
$$-7y + 7 = 0$$
$$7y = 7$$
$$y = 1$$
$$4x + 3(1) + 1 = 0$$
$$4x + 4 = 0$$
$$4x = -4$$
$$x = -1$$
(-1,1) is the point of intersection.

20. L: $4x - y + 2 = 0$
M: $3x + 2y = 0$

$$8x - 2y + 4 = 0$$
$$11x = -4$$
$$x = -\frac{4}{11}$$
$$3\left(-\frac{4}{11}\right) + 2y = 0$$
$$2y = \frac{12}{11}$$
$$y = \frac{6}{11}$$

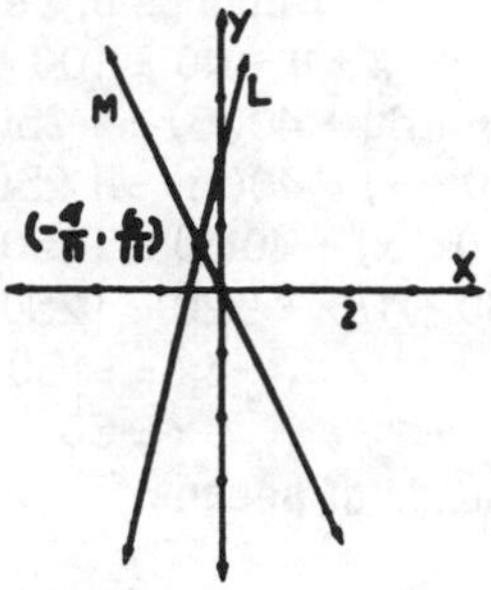

22. L: $2x + 3y - 5 = 0$
M: $5x - 6y + 1 = 0$

$$4x + 6y - 10 = 0$$
$$9x - 9 = 0$$
$$x = 1$$
$$2(1) + 3y - 5 = 0$$
$$y = 1$$

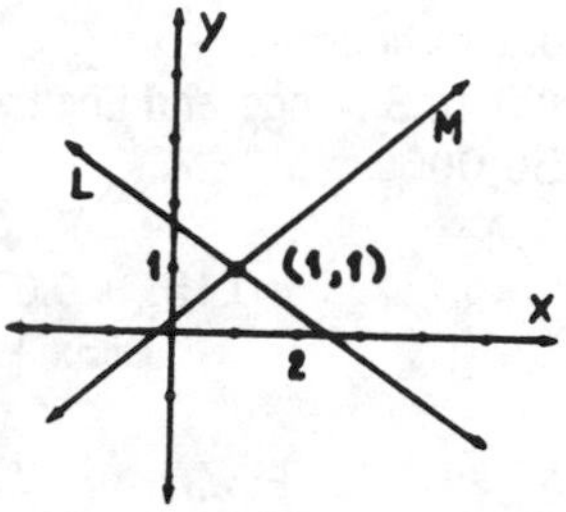

24. L: $2x - 5y - 1 = 0$
M: $x - 2y - 1 = 0$

$$2x - 4y - 2 = 0$$
$$y - 1 = 0$$
$$y = 1$$
$$x - 2(1) - 1 = 0$$
$$x = 3$$

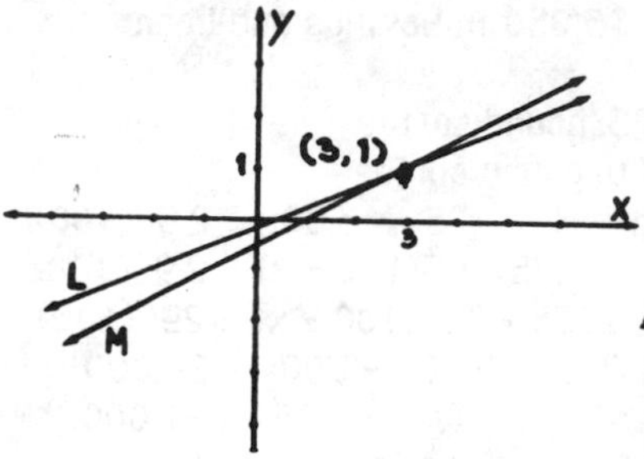

26. L: $8x - 2y + 4 = 0$
M: $-4x + y - 2 = 0$

$$-8x + 2y - 4 = 0$$
$$0 = 0$$

Thus, L = M

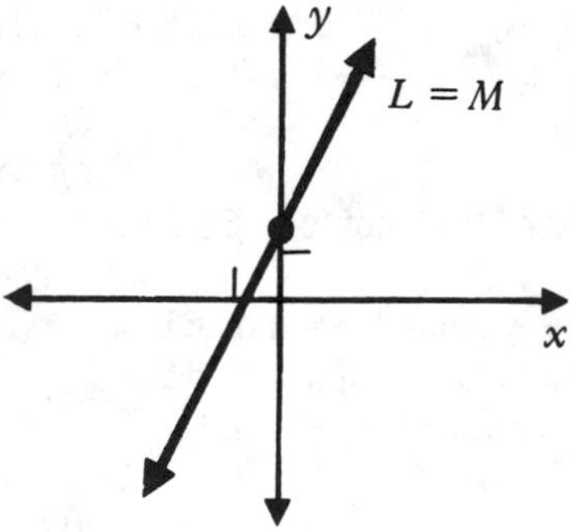

28. $y = -x + 4$; the slope of any parallel line is -1. For a line of slope -1 passing through $(-1,3)$,

$$y - 3 = -1[x - (-1)] \text{ or } y = -x + 2$$

30. x = pounds of cashews 40 = pounds of peanuts

y = pounds of pecans $x + y + 40 = 100$

$y = 60 - x$ and $1.5x + 1.8y + 40(.8) = 1.25(100)$

$$1.5x + 1.8(60 - x) + 40(.8) = 1.25(100)$$
$$15x + 18(60 - x) + 40(8) = 1250$$
$$15x + 1080 - 18x + 320 = 1250$$
$$-3x = -150$$
$$x = 50$$

50 pounds of cashews; 10 pounds of pecans

32. x = amount in bonds

y = amount in Savings and Loan

$x + y = \$50{,}000$

$$0.15x + 0.07y = 7000$$
$$0.15x + 0.07(50{,}000 - x) = 7000$$
$$0.15x + 3500 - 0.07x = 7000$$
$$0.08x = 35{,}000$$
$$x = 43{,}750$$

\$43,750 in bonds, \$6,250 in Savings and Loan

34. x = amount of \$2.75/pound coffee

y = amount of \$3.00/pound coffee

$y = 100 - x$ and $2.75x + 3.00y = 2.90(100)$

$$2.75x + 3(100 - x) = 2.90(100)$$
$$275x + 300(100 - x) = 290(100)$$
$$275x + 30{,}000 - 300x = 29{,}000$$
$$-25x = -1{,}000$$
$$x = 40$$

40% \$2.75 coffee; 60% \$3.00 coffee

36. x = amount loaned at 8%

y = amount loaned at 18%

$y = 10{,}000 - x$ and $0.08x + 0.18y = 1{,}000$

$$0.08x + 0.18(10{,}000 - x) = 1{,}000$$
$$8x + 18(10{,}000 - x) = 100{,}000$$
$$8x + 180{,}000 - 18x = 100{,}000$$
$$80{,}000 = 10x$$
$$8{,}000 = x$$

\$8,000 at 8%; \$2,000 at 18%

38. x = total distance
y = speed
x = 3y

$$\frac{x}{2} + 18 = 2y$$
$$\frac{3y}{2} + 18 = 2y$$
$$3y + 36 = 4y$$
$$36 = y$$

Speed = 36 mph; distance = 108 miles; time = 3 hours.

Exercise 1.5 (page 38)

2. (a) $\$4000(1 + 0.14t) = \$4000 + \$560t$ (b) $4000 + 560(1/2) = \$4280$
(c) $4000 + 560 = \$4560$ (d) $5120

4. $5x + 200 = 8x$
$$200 = 3x$$
$$x = 66\frac{2}{3} \quad \text{or} \quad 67$$

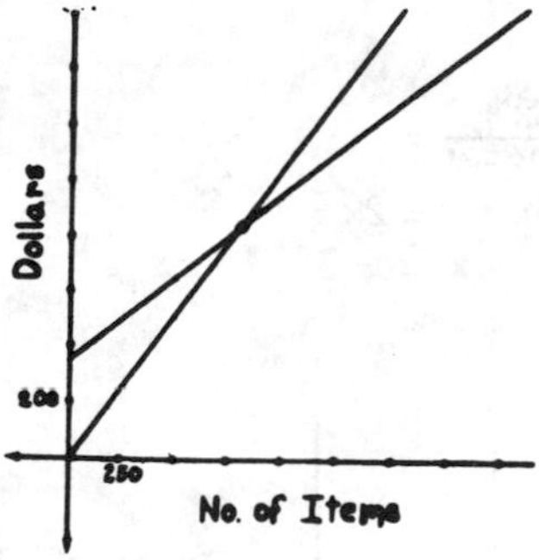

6. $1800x + 3000 = 2500x$
$$3000 = 700x$$
$$x = \frac{30}{7} = 4\frac{2}{7}$$

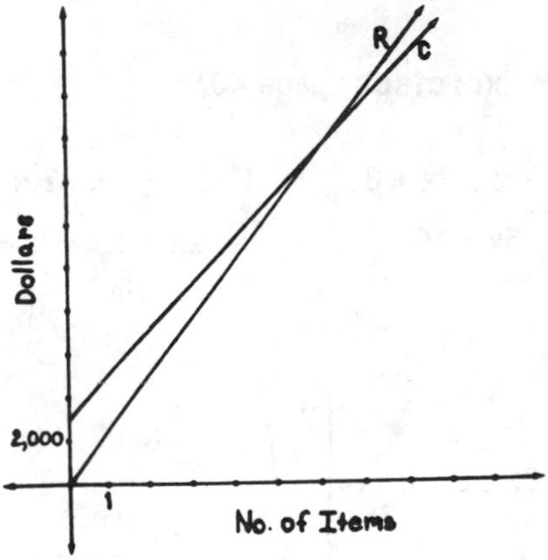

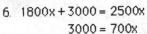

8. C = $.65x + $350
R = $1.00x
$$.65x + 350 = x$$
$$65x + 35{,}000 = 100x$$
$$35{,}000 = 35x$$
$$1{,}000 = x$$
Yes; it takes fewer items to break even.

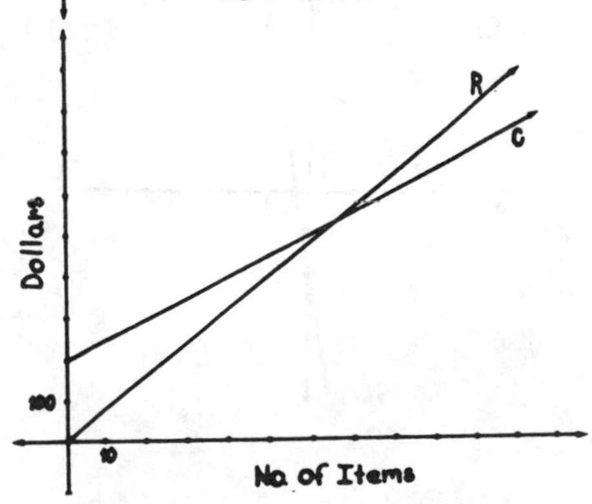

10. (a) $S = \$60,000$
(b) $S = \$3000 \times 3 + \$60,000 = \$69,000$
(c) $S = \$3000 \times 5 + \$60,000 = \$75,000$
(d) $S = \$3000 \times 8 + \$60,000 = \$84,000$

12. $S = 2p + 3$
$D = 6 - p$
$2p + 3 = 6 - p$
$3p = 3$
$p = 1$

14. $S = 40p + 300$
$D = 1000 - 30p$
$40p + 300 = 1000 - 30p$
$70p = 700$
$p = 10$

$D(5) = 14,000$
$D(19) = 0$

16. $S(5) = 14,000$
$S(1) = 0$

Thus $S = \frac{14,000}{5-1}(p-1) = 3500p - 3500$

$D = \frac{14,000}{5-19}(p-19) = 19,000 - 1000p$

Review Exercises (page 40)

2. $-3x - 2 = 2x + 8$
$-5x = 10$
$x = -2$

4. $2x - 3 = -2(x + 2)$
$2x - 3 = -2x - 4$
$4x = -1$
$x = -\frac{1}{4}$

6. $\frac{3x+2}{2x-1} = 1$
$3x + 2 = 2x - 1$
$x = -3$

8. $8x + 1 \geq 9$
$8x \geq 8$
$x \geq 1$

12. $y = 6x - 2$

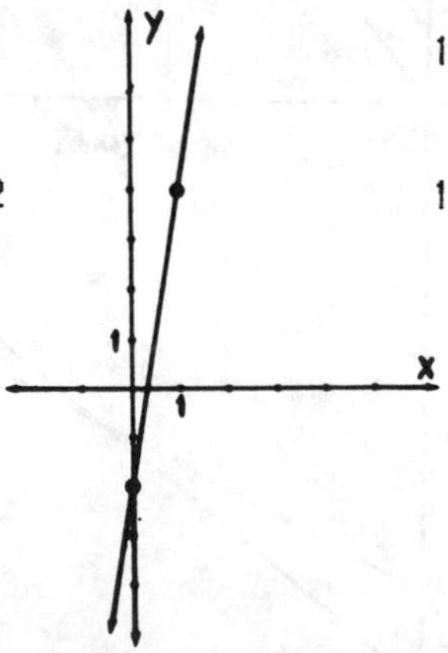

10. $-3x + 4 \leq 2x - 1$
$-5x \leq -5$
$x \geq 1$

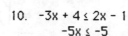

14. $3y = 2x + 6$

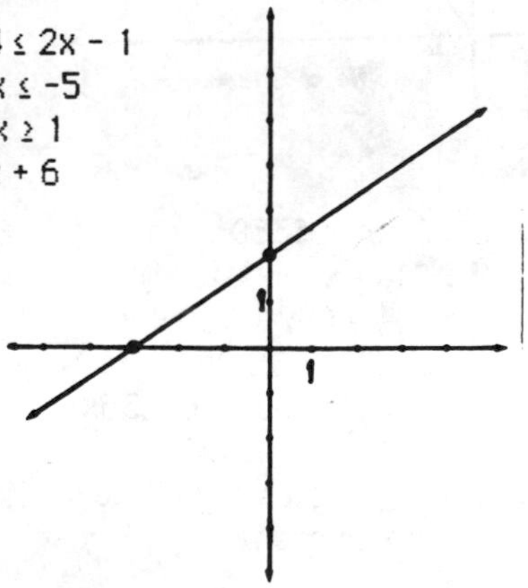

16. $\text{slope} = \dfrac{3-1}{-1-1} = -\dfrac{2}{2} = -1$

$y - 3 = -1[x - (-1)]$

$y - 3 = -x - 1$

$y + x - 2 = 0$

18. $\text{slope} = \dfrac{3-0}{-2-0} = -\dfrac{3}{2}$

$y = -\dfrac{3}{2}x$

$2y + 3x = 0$

20. $y = -x + 1$

22. $y + 1 = -2(x - 2)$

$y = -2x + 3$

24. $-4x - 5y + 20 = 0$

$-5y = 4x - 20$

$y = -\dfrac{4}{5}x + 4$

$\text{slope} = -\dfrac{4}{5}$

$y\text{-intercept} = 4$

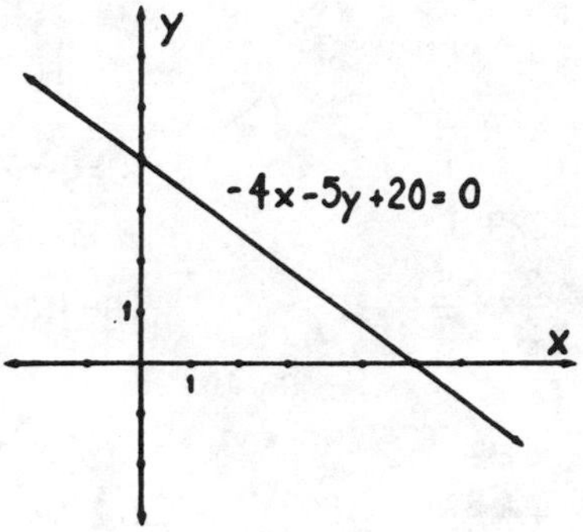

26. $3x + 2y - 8 = 0$

$2y = -3x + 8$

$y = -\dfrac{3}{2}x + 4$

$\text{slope} = -\dfrac{3}{2}$

$y\text{-intercept} = 4$

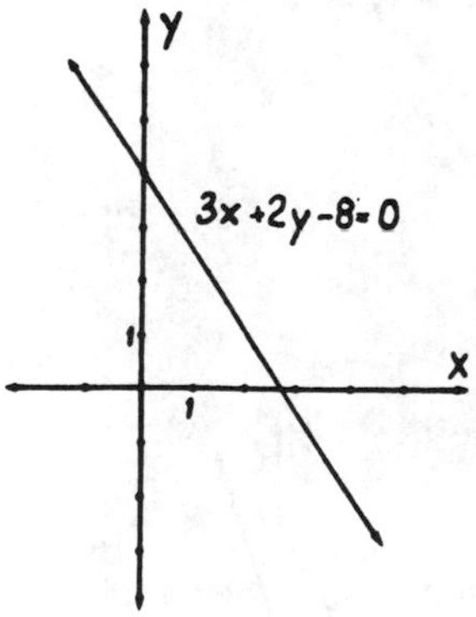

28. $2x + 3y + 5 = 0$

$$3y = -2x - 5$$

$$y = -\frac{2}{3}x - \frac{5}{3}$$

They are the same line.

$4x + 6y + 10 = 0$

$$6y = -4x + 10$$

$$y = -\frac{2}{3}x - \frac{5}{3}$$

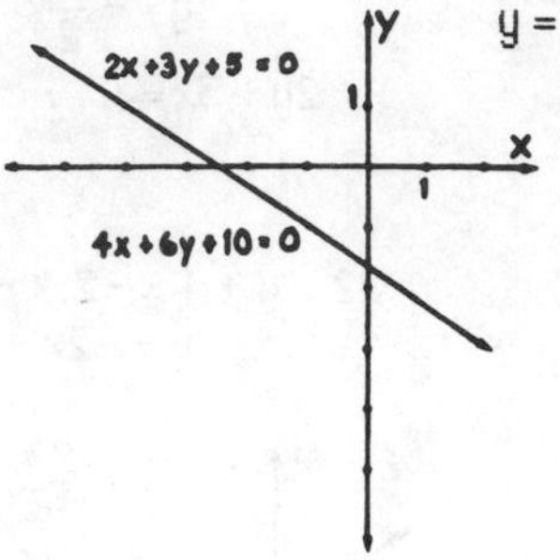

30. $2x + 3y - 5 = 0$

$$3y = -2x + 5$$

$$y = -\frac{2}{3}x + \frac{5}{3}$$

$x + y - 2 = 0$

$$y = -x + 2$$

The lines intersect.

$$-\frac{2}{3}x + \frac{5}{3} = -x + 2$$

$$-2x + 5 = -3 + 6$$

$$x = 1$$

$$y = 1$$

The lines intersect at (1, 1).

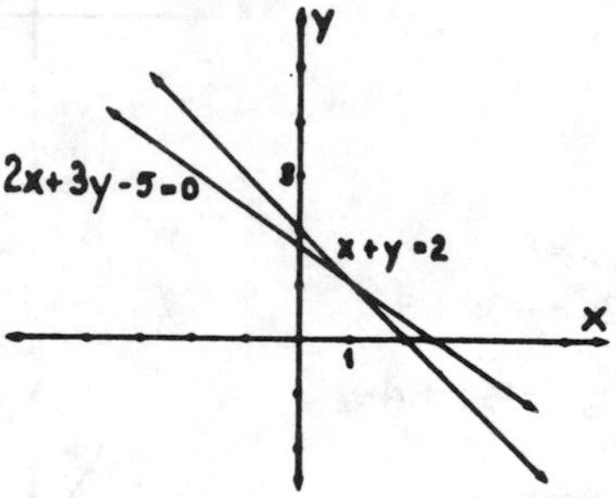

32. $3x - y = 0$

$$y = 3x$$

$6x - 2y + 5 = 0$

$$2y = 6x + 5$$

$$y = 3x + \frac{5}{2}$$

The lines are parallel.

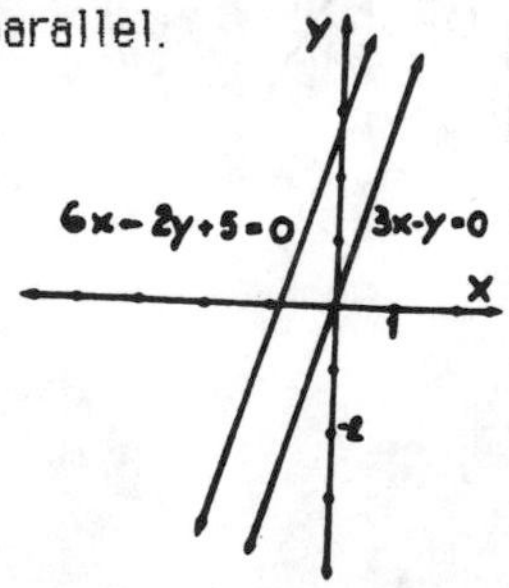

34. Let x = amount of 20% solution

y = amount of 12% solution

$$x + y = 100$$
$$.20x + .12y = 15$$
$$.20x + .12(100 - x) = 15$$
$$.20x - .12x + 12 = 15$$
$$.08x = 3$$

$x = 37.5$ cc of 20% solution

$y = 62.5$ cc of 12% solution

36. Let x = number attending

$$C = 2x + 500 + 100 = 2x + 600$$
$$R = 5x$$
$$P = R - C = 3x - 600$$

(a) In order to break even, $3x - 600 = 0$ or $x = 200$ people.

(b) If $P = 900$, $3x = 1500$ or $x = 500$.

(c) $P = 6x - (2x + 600) = 4x - 600$

150 people to break even, 375 to make a profit of $900.

CHAPTER 2

Exercise 2.1 (page 54)

2. $\left[\begin{array}{cc|c} 4 & 1 & 5 \\ 2 & 1 & 5 \end{array}\right]$ **4.** $\left[\begin{array}{cc|c} 1 & -1 & -3 \\ 4 & -1 & -2 \end{array}\right]$ **6.** $\left[\begin{array}{ccc|c} 1 & 1 & 1 & 3 \\ 2 & 0 & 1 & 0 \\ 3 & -1 & -1 & 1 \end{array}\right]$

8. $\left[\begin{array}{cccc|c} 5 & -3 & 0 & 6 & -1 \\ -1 & -1 & 1 & 0 & 1 \\ 2 & 3 & 0 & 0 & -5 \end{array}\right]$ **10.** $\left[\begin{array}{ccc|c} 3 & 0 & 0 & 5 \\ 1 & -1 & 1 & 6 \\ 0 & 2 & 1 & -4 \end{array}\right]$ **12.** $R_1 = -r_2 + r_1$

14. $R_2 = 2r_2$ **16.** $\begin{bmatrix} 1 & 2 & 3 \\ 0 & 1 & 4 \\ 1 & 0 & 2 \end{bmatrix}$ **18.** $\begin{bmatrix} 3 & 7 & 13 \\ 0 & 1 & 4 \\ 1 & 0 & 2 \end{bmatrix}$

20. $\begin{bmatrix} 3 & 6 & 9 \\ 0 & 1 & 4 \\ 0 & -2 & -1 \end{bmatrix}$

22. $\left[\begin{array}{cc|c} 1 & -1 & 2 \\ 2 & 1 & 1 \end{array}\right] \rightarrow \left[\begin{array}{cc|c} 1 & -1 & 2 \\ 0 & 3 & -3 \end{array}\right] \rightarrow \left[\begin{array}{cc|c} 1 & -1 & 2 \\ 0 & 1 & -1 \end{array}\right] \rightarrow$
$\left[\begin{array}{cc|c} 1 & 0 & 1 \\ 0 & 1 & -1 \end{array}\right]$ $x = 1, y = -1$

24. $\left[\begin{array}{cc|c} 3 & 2 & 7 \\ 1 & 1 & 3 \end{array}\right] \rightarrow \left[\begin{array}{cc|c} 1 & 1 & 3 \\ 3 & 2 & 7 \end{array}\right] \rightarrow \left[\begin{array}{cc|c} 1 & 1 & 3 \\ 0 & -1 & -2 \end{array}\right] \rightarrow$
$R_1 = r_1, R_2 = r_1 \quad R_2 = -3r_1 + r_2 \quad R_2 = -r_2$

$\left[\begin{array}{cc|c} 1 & 1 & 3 \\ 0 & 1 & 2 \end{array}\right] \rightarrow \left[\begin{array}{cc|c} 1 & 0 & 1 \\ 0 & 1 & 2 \end{array}\right]$ $x = 1, y = 2$
$R_1 = -r_2 + r_1$

26. $\left[\begin{array}{cc|c} 2 & -3 & 5 \\ 3 & 1 & 2 \end{array}\right] \rightarrow \left[\begin{array}{cc|c} 2 & -3 & 5 \\ 1 & 4 & -3 \end{array}\right] \rightarrow \left[\begin{array}{cc|c} 1 & 4 & -3 \\ 2 & -3 & 5 \end{array}\right] \rightarrow$
$R_2 = -r_1 + r_2 \quad R_1 = r_2, R_2 = r_1 \quad R_2 = -r_1 + r_2$
$\left[\begin{array}{cc|c} 1 & 4 & -3 \\ 0 & -11 & 11 \end{array}\right] \rightarrow \left[\begin{array}{cc|c} 1 & 4 & -3 \\ 0 & 1 & -1 \end{array}\right] \rightarrow \left[\begin{array}{cc|c} 1 & 0 & 1 \\ 0 & 1 & -1 \end{array}\right]$ $x = 1, y = -1$
$R_2 = (-1/11)r_2 \quad R_1 = -4r_2 + r_1$

28.

$$\left[\begin{array}{rr|r} 2 & 8 & 17 \\ 3 & -1 & 1 \end{array}\right] \underset{R_2=-r_1+r_2}{\rightarrow} \left[\begin{array}{rr|r} 2 & 8 & 17 \\ 1 & -9 & -16 \end{array}\right] \underset{R_2=r_1, R_1=r_2}{\rightarrow} \left[\begin{array}{rr|r} 1 & -9 & -16 \\ 2 & 8 & 17 \end{array}\right] \underset{R_2=-2r_1+r_2}{\rightarrow}$$

$$\left[\begin{array}{rr|r} 1 & -9 & -16 \\ 0 & 26 & 49 \end{array}\right] \underset{R_2=(1/26)r_2}{\rightarrow} \left[\begin{array}{rr|r} 1 & -9 & -16 \\ 0 & 1 & 49/26 \end{array}\right] \underset{R_1=9r_2+r_1}{\rightarrow} \left[\begin{array}{rr|r} 1 & 0 & 25/26 \\ 0 & 1 & 49/26 \end{array}\right] \quad x=\frac{25}{26}, y=\frac{49}{26}$$

30.

$$\left[\begin{array}{rr|r} 3 & -4 & 3 \\ 6 & 2 & 1 \end{array}\right] \underset{R_1=(1/3)r_1}{\rightarrow} \left[\begin{array}{rr|r} 1 & -4/3 & 1 \\ 6 & 2 & 1 \end{array}\right] \underset{R_2=-6r_1+r_2}{\rightarrow} \left[\begin{array}{rr|r} 1 & -4/3 & 1 \\ 0 & 10 & -5 \end{array}\right] \underset{R_2=(1/10)r_2}{\rightarrow}$$

$$\left[\begin{array}{rr|r} 1 & -4/3 & 1 \\ 0 & 1 & -1/2 \end{array}\right] \underset{R_1=(4/3)r_2+r_1}{\rightarrow} \left[\begin{array}{rr|r} 1 & 0 & 1/3 \\ 0 & 1 & -1/2 \end{array}\right] \quad x=\frac{1}{3}, y=-\frac{1}{2}$$

32.

$$\left[\begin{array}{rr|r} 3 & -5 & 3 \\ 6 & 10 & 10 \end{array}\right] \underset{R_1=(1/3)r_1}{\rightarrow} \left[\begin{array}{rr|r} 1 & -5/3 & 1 \\ 6 & 10 & 10 \end{array}\right] \underset{R_2=-6r_1+r_2}{\rightarrow} \left[\begin{array}{rr|r} 1 & -5/3 & 1 \\ 0 & 20 & 4 \end{array}\right] \underset{R_2=(1/20)r_2}{\rightarrow}$$

$$\left[\begin{array}{rr|r} 1 & -5/3 & 1 \\ 0 & 1 & 1/5 \end{array}\right] \underset{R_1=(5/3)r_2+r_1}{\rightarrow} \left[\begin{array}{rr|r} 1 & 0 & 4/3 \\ 0 & 1 & 1/5 \end{array}\right] \quad x=\frac{4}{3}, y=\frac{1}{5}$$

34.

$$\left[\begin{array}{rr|r} 4 & -1 & 0 \\ 1 & 1 & 5 \end{array}\right] \underset{R_1=(1/4)r_1}{\rightarrow} \left[\begin{array}{rr|r} 1 & 5/4 & 0 \\ 1/2 & 1/2 & 5/2 \end{array}\right] \underset{R_2=(-1/2)r_1+r_2}{\rightarrow} \left[\begin{array}{rr|r} 1 & -1/4 & 0 \\ 0 & 5/8 & 5/2 \end{array}\right] \underset{R_2=(8/5)r_2}{\rightarrow}$$

$$\left[\begin{array}{rr|r} 1 & -1/4 & 0 \\ 0 & 1 & 4 \end{array}\right] \underset{R_1=(1/4)r_2+r_1}{\rightarrow} \left[\begin{array}{rr|r} 1 & 0 & 1 \\ 0 & 1 & 4 \end{array}\right] \quad x=1, y=4$$

36.

$$\left[\begin{array}{cc|c} 4 & -1 & 2.75 \\ 3 & 1 & 2.50 \end{array}\right] \to \left[\begin{array}{cc|c} 1 & -2 & 1/4 \\ 3 & 1 & 5/2 \end{array}\right] \to \left[\begin{array}{cc|c} 1 & -2 & 1/4 \\ 0 & 7 & 7/4 \end{array}\right] \to$$

$R_1 = -r_2 + r_1 \quad R_2 = -3r_1 + r_2 \quad R_2 = (1/7)r_2$

$$\left[\begin{array}{cc|c} 1 & -2 & 1/4 \\ 0 & 1 & 1/4 \end{array}\right] \to \left[\begin{array}{cc|c} 1 & 0 & 3/4 \\ 0 & 1 & 1/4 \end{array}\right] \quad x = \frac{3}{4},\ y = \frac{1}{4}$$

$R_1 = 2r_2 + r_1$

38.

$$\left[\begin{array}{ccc|c} 1 & 1 & 1 & 5 \\ 2 & -1 & 1 & 2 \\ 1 & 2 & -1 & 3 \end{array}\right] \to \left[\begin{array}{ccc|c} 1 & 1 & 1 & 5 \\ 0 & -3 & -1 & -8 \\ 0 & 1 & -2 & -2 \end{array}\right] \to \left[\begin{array}{ccc|c} 1 & 1 & 1 & 5 \\ 0 & 1 & -2 & -2 \\ 0 & -3 & -1 & -8 \end{array}\right] \to$$

$R_2 = -2r_1 + r_2 \quad R_2 \leftrightarrow R_3 \quad R_3 = 3r_2 + r_3$

$R_3 = -r_1 + r_3 \quad R_1 = -r_2 + r_1$

$$\left[\begin{array}{ccc|c} 1 & 0 & 3 & 7 \\ 0 & 1 & -2 & -2 \\ 0 & 0 & -7 & -14 \end{array}\right] \to \left[\begin{array}{ccc|c} 1 & 0 & 3 & 7 \\ 0 & 1 & -2 & -2 \\ 0 & 0 & 1 & 2 \end{array}\right] \to \left[\begin{array}{ccc|c} 1 & 0 & 0 & 1 \\ 0 & 1 & 0 & 2 \\ 0 & 0 & 1 & 2 \end{array}\right] \quad x = 1,\ y = 2,\ z = 2$$

$R_3 = (-1/7)r_3 \quad R_1 = -3r_3 + r_1,\ R_2 = 2r_3 + r_2$

40.

$$\left[\begin{array}{ccc|c} 2 & -1 & -1 & -5 \\ 1 & 1 & 1 & 2 \\ 1 & 2 & 2 & 5 \end{array}\right] \to \left[\begin{array}{ccc|c} 1 & 1 & 1 & 2 \\ 2 & -1 & -1 & -5 \\ 1 & 2 & 2 & 5 \end{array}\right] \to \left[\begin{array}{ccc|c} 1 & 1 & 1 & 2 \\ 0 & -3 & -3 & -9 \\ 0 & 1 & 1 & 3 \end{array}\right] \to$$

$R_1 \leftrightarrow R_2 \quad R_2 = -2r_1 + r_2 \quad R_2 \leftrightarrow R_3$

$R_3 = -r_1 + r_3$

$$\left[\begin{array}{ccc|c} 1 & 1 & 1 & 2 \\ 0 & 1 & 1 & 3 \\ 0 & -3 & -3 & -9 \end{array}\right] \to \left[\begin{array}{ccc|c} 1 & 0 & 0 & -1 \\ 0 & 1 & 1 & 3 \\ 0 & 0 & 0 & 0 \end{array}\right] \quad x = -1 \quad y = 3 - z$$

$R_1 = -r_2 + r_1,\ R_3 = 3r_2 + r_3$

$$\left[\begin{array}{ccc|c} 2-1 & 2-1 & 1-2 & 6 \\ 1 & -1 & -1 & -2 \\ 11 & -2 & -2 & -5 \end{array}\right] \rightarrow \left[\begin{array}{ccc|c} 1 & -1 & -1 & 2 \\ 2 & 2 & 1 & 6 \\ 1 & -2 & -2 & -5 \end{array}\right] \rightarrow \left[\begin{array}{ccc|c} 1 & -1 & -1 & -2 \\ 0 & 4 & 3 & 10 \\ 0 & -1 & -1 & -3 \end{array}\right] \rightarrow$$

$R_1 \Leftrightarrow R_2$ $\qquad$ $R_2 = -2r_1 + r_2$, $R_3 = -r_1 + r_3$ $\qquad$ $R_1 = r_2 + r_1$, $R_3 = r_2 + r_3$

42.

$$\left[\begin{array}{ccc|c} 1 & 0 & -1/4 & 1/2 \\ 0 & 1 & 3/4 & 5/2 \\ 0 & 0 & -1/4 & -1/2 \end{array}\right] \rightarrow \left[\begin{array}{ccc|c} 1 & 0 & -1/4 & 1/2 \\ 0 & 1 & 3/4 & 5/2 \\ 0 & 0 & 1 & 2 \end{array}\right] \rightarrow \left[\begin{array}{ccc|c} 1 & 0 & 0 & 1 \\ 0 & 1 & 0 & 1 \\ 0 & 0 & 1 & 2 \end{array}\right] \rightarrow \left[\begin{array}{c} x = 1 \\ y = 1 \\ z = 2 \end{array}\right]$$

$R_3 = -4r_3$ $\qquad$ $R_1 = (1/4)r_3 + r_1, R_2 = (-3/4)r_3 + r_2$

$$\left[\begin{array}{ccc|c} 1 & 1 & -1 & 0 \\ 4 & 2 & -4 & 0 \\ 1 & 2 & 1 & 0 \end{array}\right] \rightarrow \left[\begin{array}{ccc|c} 1 & 1 & -1 & 0 \\ 0 & -2 & 0 & 0 \\ 0 & 1 & 2 & 0 \end{array}\right] \rightarrow \left[\begin{array}{ccc|c} 1 & 1 & -1 & 0 \\ 0 & 1 & 0 & 0 \\ 0 & 1 & 2 & 0 \end{array}\right] \rightarrow$$

$R_2 = -4r_1 + r_2$, $R_3 = -r_1 + r_3$ $\qquad$ $R_2 = (-1/2)r_2$ $\qquad$ $R_1 = -r_2 + r_1$, $R_3 = -r_2 + r_3$

44.

$$\left[\begin{array}{ccc|c} 1 & 0 & -1 & 0 \\ 0 & 1 & 0 & 0 \\ 0 & 0 & 2 & 0 \end{array}\right] \rightarrow \left[\begin{array}{ccc|c} 1 & 0 & -1 & 0 \\ 0 & 1 & 0 & 0 \\ 0 & 0 & 1 & 0 \end{array}\right] \rightarrow \left[\begin{array}{ccc|c} 1 & 0 & 0 & 0 \\ 0 & 1 & 0 & 0 \\ 0 & 0 & 1 & 0 \end{array}\right] \rightarrow \left[\begin{array}{c} x = 0 \\ y = 0 \\ z = 0 \end{array}\right]$$

$R_3 = (1/2)r_3$ $\qquad$ $R_1 = -r_3 + r_1$

$$\left[\begin{array}{ccc|c} 1 & 1 & 0 & 1 \\ 2 & -1 & 1 & 1 \\ 1 & 2 & 1 & 8/3 \end{array}\right] \rightarrow \left[\begin{array}{ccc|c} 1 & 1 & 0 & 1 \\ 0 & -3 & 1 & -1 \\ 0 & 1 & 1 & 5/3 \end{array}\right] \rightarrow \left[\begin{array}{ccc|c} 1 & 1 & 0 & 1 \\ 0 & 1 & 1 & 5/3 \\ 0 & -3 & 1 & -1 \end{array}\right] \rightarrow$$

$R_2 = -2r_1 + r_2$, $R_3 = -r_1 + r_3$ $\qquad$ $R_2 \Leftrightarrow R_3$ $\qquad$ $R_1 = -r_2 + r_1$, $R_3 = 3r_2 + r_3$

46.

$$\left[\begin{array}{ccc|c} 1 & 0 & -1 & -2/3 \\ 0 & 1 & 1 & 5/3 \\ 0 & 0 & 4 & 4 \end{array}\right] \rightarrow \left[\begin{array}{ccc|c} 1 & 0 & -1 & -2/3 \\ 0 & 1 & 1 & 5/3 \\ 0 & 0 & 1 & 1 \end{array}\right] \rightarrow \left[\begin{array}{ccc|c} 1 & 0 & 0 & 1/3 \\ 0 & 1 & 0 & 2/3 \\ 0 & 0 & 1 & 1 \end{array}\right] \rightarrow \left[\begin{array}{c} x = 1/3 \\ y = 2/3 \\ z = 1 \end{array}\right]$$

$R_3 = (1/4)r_3$ $\qquad$ $R_1 = r_3 + r_1, R_2 = -r_3 + r_2$

$$\left[\begin{array}{cccc|c} 1 & 1 & 1 & 1 & 4 \\ -1 & 2 & 1 & 0 & 0 \\ 2 & 3 & 1 & 1 & 6 \\ -2 & 1 & -2 & 2 & -1 \end{array}\right] \to \left[\begin{array}{cccc|c} 1 & 1 & 1 & 1 & 4 \\ 0 & 3 & 2 & 1 & 4 \\ 0 & 1 & -1 & -3 & -2 \\ 0 & 3 & 0 & 4 & 7 \end{array}\right] \to \left[\begin{array}{cccc|c} 1 & 1 & 1 & 1 & 4 \\ 0 & 1 & -1 & -3 & -2 \\ 0 & 3 & 2 & 1 & 4 \\ 0 & 3 & 0 & 4 & 7 \end{array}\right] \to$$

$R_2 = r_1 + r_2$, $R_3 = -2r_1 + r_3$ $\quad$ $R_2 \Leftrightarrow R_3$ $\quad$ $R_3 = -3r_2 + r_3$

$R_4 = 2r_1 + r_4$ $\quad$ $R_4 = -3r_2 + r_4$

$$\left[\begin{array}{cccc|c} 1 & 0 & 2 & 4 & 6 \\ 0 & 1 & -1 & -3 & -2 \\ 0 & 0 & 5 & 10 & 10 \\ 0 & 0 & 3 & 13 & 13 \end{array}\right] \to \left[\begin{array}{cccc|c} 1 & 0 & 2 & 4 & 6 \\ 0 & 1 & -1 & -3 & -2 \\ 0 & 0 & 1 & 2 & 2 \\ 0 & 0 & 3 & 13 & 13 \end{array}\right] \to \left[\begin{array}{cccc|c} 1 & 0 & 2 & 4 & 6 \\ 0 & 1 & -1 & -3 & -2 \\ 0 & 0 & 1 & 2 & 2 \\ 0 & 0 & 0 & 7 & 7 \end{array}\right] \to$$

$R_3 = (1/5)r_3$ $\quad$ $R_4 = -3r_3 + r_4$ $\quad$ $R_4 = (1/7)r_4$

48.

$$\left[\begin{array}{cccc|c} 1 & 0 & 2 & 4 & 6 \\ 0 & 1 & -1 & -3 & -2 \\ 0 & 0 & 1 & 2 & 2 \\ 0 & 0 & 0 & 1 & 1 \end{array}\right] \to \left[\begin{array}{cccc|c} 1 & 0 & 2 & 0 & 2 \\ 0 & 1 & -1 & 0 & 1 \\ 0 & 0 & 1 & 0 & 0 \\ 0 & 0 & 0 & 1 & 1 \end{array}\right] \to \left[\begin{array}{cccc|c} 1 & 0 & 0 & 0 & 2 \\ 0 & 1 & 0 & 0 & 1 \\ 0 & 0 & 1 & 0 & 0 \\ 0 & 0 & 0 & 1 & 1 \end{array}\right] \to \left[\begin{array}{c} x = 2 \\ y = 1 \\ z = 0 \\ w = 1 \end{array}\right]$$

$R_1 = -4r_4 + r_1$, $R_2 = 3r_4 + r_2$ $\quad$ $R_1 = -2r_3 + r_1$

$R_3 = -2r_4 + r_3$ $\quad$ $R_2 = r_3 + r_2$

50. $\left[\begin{array}{cc|c} 4 & 1 & 5 \\ 8 & 2 & 10 \end{array}\right] \to \left[\begin{array}{cc|c} 4 & 1 & 5 \\ 0 & 0 & 0 \end{array}\right] \to$ infinitely many solutions.

52. $\left[\begin{array}{cc|c} 2 & -3 & 6 \\ 4 & -6 & 8 \end{array}\right] \to \left[\begin{array}{cc|c} 2 & -3 & 6 \\ 0 & 0 & -4 \end{array}\right] \to$ No solution.

54. $\left[\begin{array}{cc|c} 3 & 4 & 7 \\ 1 & -1 & 2 \end{array}\right] \to \left[\begin{array}{cc|c} 1 & -1 & 2 \\ 3 & 4 & 7 \end{array}\right] \to \left[\begin{array}{cc|c} 1 & -1 & 2 \\ 0 & 7 & 1 \end{array}\right] \to$ Unique solution.

56. $\left[\begin{array}{cc|c} 2 & -1 & 0 \\ 4 & -2 & 0 \end{array}\right] \to \left[\begin{array}{cc|c} 2 & -1 & 0 \\ 0 & 0 & 0 \end{array}\right] \to$ Infinitely many solutions.

58. $\left[\begin{array}{ccc|c} 1 & 1 & 1 & 3 \\ 2 & 1 & 1 & 0 \\ 3 & 1 & 1 & 1 \end{array}\right] \to \left[\begin{array}{ccc|c} 1 & 1 & 1 & 3 \\ 0 & -1 & -1 & -6 \\ 0 & -2 & -2 & -8 \end{array}\right] \to \left[\begin{array}{ccc|c} 1 & 1 & 1 & 3 \\ 0 & 1 & 1 & 6 \\ 0 & -2 & -2 & -8 \end{array}\right] \to \left[\begin{array}{ccc|c} 1 & 0 & 0 & -3 \\ 0 & 1 & 1 & 6 \\ 0 & 0 & 0 & 4 \end{array}\right] \to$ No solution.

60. $\begin{bmatrix} 1 & -1 & 1 & | & 2 \\ 2 & -3 & 1 & | & 0 \\ 3 & -3 & 3 & | & 6 \end{bmatrix} \rightarrow \begin{bmatrix} 1 & -1 & 1 & | & 2 \\ 0 & -1 & -1 & | & -4 \\ 0 & 0 & 0 & | & 0 \end{bmatrix} \rightarrow \begin{bmatrix} 1 & -1 & 1 & | & 2 \\ 0 & 1 & 1 & | & 4 \\ 0 & 0 & 0 & | & 0 \end{bmatrix} \rightarrow$

$\begin{bmatrix} 1 & 0 & 2 & | & 6 \\ 0 & 1 & 1 & | & 4 \\ 0 & 0 & 0 & | & 0 \end{bmatrix} \rightarrow$ Infinitely many solutions.

62. x_1 = amount at 6% $\quad x_1 + x_2 + x_3 = 6500$

x_2 = amount at 8% $\quad .06x_1 + .08x_2 + .09x_3 = 480$

x_3 = amount at 9% $\quad .08x_2 + .09x_3 = -60$

A|B=

$$\begin{bmatrix} 1 & 1 & 1 & | & 6500 \\ .06 & .08 & .09 & | & 480 \\ 0 & .08 & -.09 & | & -60 \end{bmatrix} \rightarrow \begin{bmatrix} 1 & 1 & 1 & | & 6500 \\ 6 & 8 & 9 & | & 48000 \\ 0 & 8 & -9 & | & -6000 \end{bmatrix} \rightarrow \begin{bmatrix} 1 & 1 & 1 & | & 6500 \\ 0 & 2 & 3 & | & 9000 \\ 0 & 8 & -9 & | & -6000 \end{bmatrix} \rightarrow$$

$$\begin{bmatrix} 1 & 1 & 1 & | & 6500 \\ 0 & 1 & \frac{3}{2} & | & 4500 \\ 0 & 8 & -9 & | & -6000 \end{bmatrix} \rightarrow \begin{bmatrix} 1 & 0 & -\frac{1}{2} & | & 6500 \\ 0 & 1 & \frac{3}{2} & | & 4500 \\ 0 & 8 & -9 & | & -6000 \end{bmatrix} \rightarrow \begin{bmatrix} 1 & 0 & -\frac{1}{2} & | & 2000 \\ 0 & 1 & \frac{3}{2} & | & 4500 \\ 0 & 0 & 1 & | & 2000 \end{bmatrix} \rightarrow$$

$$\begin{bmatrix} 1 & 0 & 0 & | & 3000 \\ 0 & 1 & 0 & | & 1500 \\ 0 & 0 & 1 & | & 2000 \end{bmatrix} \rightarrow \begin{bmatrix} x_1 = \$3000 \\ x_2 = \$1500 \\ x_3 = \$2000 \end{bmatrix}$$

Exercise 2.2 (page 64)

2. Yes. **4.** Yes. **6.** Yes. **8.** Yes. **10.** No. **12.** No solution.

14. Infinitely many solutions. **16.** No solution. **18.** Unique solution.

20. Unique solution. **22.** $\begin{bmatrix} 1 & -1 & | & 5 \\ 2 & 3 & | & 15 \end{bmatrix} \rightarrow \begin{bmatrix} 1 & -1 & | & 5 \\ 0 & 5 & | & 5 \end{bmatrix} \rightarrow \begin{bmatrix} 1 & -1 & | & 5 \\ 0 & 1 & | & 1 \end{bmatrix} \rightarrow \begin{bmatrix} 1 & 0 & | & 6 \\ 0 & 1 & | & 1 \end{bmatrix} \rightarrow \begin{bmatrix} x = 6 \\ y = 1 \end{bmatrix}$

24.

$$\begin{bmatrix} 6 & 1 & | & 8 \\ 1 & -3 & | & -5 \end{bmatrix} \rightarrow \begin{bmatrix} 1 & -3 & | & -5 \\ 6 & 1 & | & 8 \end{bmatrix} \rightarrow \begin{bmatrix} 1 & -3 & | & -5 \\ 0 & 19 & | & 38 \end{bmatrix} \rightarrow \begin{bmatrix} 1 & -3 & | & -5 \\ 0 & 1 & | & 2 \end{bmatrix} \rightarrow \begin{bmatrix} 1 & 0 & | & 1 \\ 0 & 1 & | & 2 \end{bmatrix} \rightarrow \begin{bmatrix} x = 1 \\ y = 2 \end{bmatrix}$$

26. $$\left[\begin{array}{cc|c} 2.0 & 3.0 & 8.0 \\ 2.0 & -1.0 & 12.0 \end{array}\right] \rightarrow \left[\begin{array}{cc|c} 2.0 & 3.0 & 8.0 \\ 0.0 & -4.0 & 4.0 \end{array}\right] \rightarrow$$

$$\left[\begin{array}{cc|c} 1.0 & 1.5 & 4.0 \\ 0.0 & 1.0 & -1.0 \end{array}\right] \rightarrow \left[\begin{array}{cc|c} 1.0 & 0.0 & 5.5 \\ 0.0 & 1.0 & -1.0 \end{array}\right] \rightarrow \left[\begin{array}{l} x_1 = 5.5 \\ x_2 = -1 \end{array}\right]$$

28. $$\left[\begin{array}{cc|c} 3 & -4 & 7 \\ 5 & 2 & 3 \end{array}\right] \rightarrow \left[\begin{array}{cc|c} 3 & -4 & 7 \\ 2 & 6 & -4 \end{array}\right] \rightarrow \left[\begin{array}{cc|c} 3 & -4 & 7 \\ 1 & 3 & -2 \end{array}\right] \rightarrow \left[\begin{array}{cc|c} 1 & 3 & -2 \\ 3 & -4 & 7 \end{array}\right] \rightarrow$$

$R_2 = -r_1 + r_2$ $R_2 = (1/2)r_2$

$$\left[\begin{array}{cc|c} 1 & 3 & -2 \\ 0 & -13 & 13 \end{array}\right] \rightarrow \left[\begin{array}{cc|c} 1 & 3 & -2 \\ 0 & 1 & -1 \end{array}\right] \rightarrow \left[\begin{array}{cc|c} 1 & 0 & 1 \\ 0 & 1 & -1 \end{array}\right] \rightarrow \left[\begin{array}{l} x_1 = 1 \\ x_2 = -1 \end{array}\right]$$

30. $$\left[\begin{array}{ccc|c} 2 & -1 & 3 & 0 \\ 1 & 2 & -1 & 5 \\ 2 & 0 & 1 & 1 \end{array}\right] \rightarrow \left[\begin{array}{ccc|c} 1 & 2 & -1 & 5 \\ 2 & -1 & 3 & 0 \\ 2 & 0 & 1 & 1 \end{array}\right] \rightarrow \left[\begin{array}{ccc|c} 1 & 2 & -1 & 5 \\ 0 & -5 & 5 & -10 \\ 0 & -4 & 3 & -9 \end{array}\right] \rightarrow$$

$$\left[\begin{array}{ccc|c} 1 & 2 & -1 & 5 \\ 0 & 1 & -1 & 2 \\ 0 & -4 & 3 & -9 \end{array}\right] \rightarrow \left[\begin{array}{ccc|c} 1 & 0 & 1 & 1 \\ 0 & 1 & -1 & 2 \\ 0 & 0 & -1 & -1 \end{array}\right] \rightarrow \left[\begin{array}{ccc|c} 1 & 0 & 1 & 1 \\ 0 & 1 & -1 & 2 \\ 0 & 0 & 1 & 1 \end{array}\right] \rightarrow$$

$$\left[\begin{array}{ccc|c} 1 & 0 & 1 & 1 \\ 0 & 1 & 0 & 3 \\ 0 & 0 & 1 & 1 \end{array}\right] \rightarrow \left[\begin{array}{l} x_1 = 0 \\ x_2 = 3 \\ x_3 = 1 \end{array}\right]$$

32. $$\left[\begin{array}{cccc|c} 1 & 1 & 1 & 1 & 0 \\ 2 & -1 & -1 & 1 & 0 \\ 1 & -1 & -1 & 1 & 0 \\ 1 & 1 & -1 & -1 & 0 \end{array}\right] \rightarrow \left[\begin{array}{cccc|c} 1 & 1 & 1 & 1 & 0 \\ 0 & -3 & -3 & -1 & 0 \\ 0 & -2 & -2 & 0 & 0 \\ 0 & 0 & -2 & -2 & 0 \end{array}\right] \rightarrow \left[\begin{array}{cccc|c} 1 & 1 & 1 & 1 & 0 \\ 0 & 1 & 1 & 0 & 0 \\ 0 & -3 & -3 & -1 & 0 \\ 0 & 0 & -2 & -2 & 0 \end{array}\right] \rightarrow$$

$$\left[\begin{array}{cccc|c} 1 & 0 & 0 & 1 & 0 \\ 0 & 1 & 1 & 0 & 0 \\ 0 & 0 & 0 & -1 & 0 \\ 0 & 0 & -2 & -2 & 0 \end{array}\right] \rightarrow \left[\begin{array}{cccc|c} 1 & 0 & 0 & 1 & 0 \\ 0 & 1 & 1 & 0 & 0 \\ 0 & 0 & 1 & 1 & 0 \\ 0 & 0 & 0 & -1 & 0 \end{array}\right] \rightarrow \left[\begin{array}{cccc|c} 1 & 0 & 0 & 1 & 0 \\ 0 & 1 & 0 & -1 & 0 \\ 0 & 0 & 1 & 1 & 0 \\ 0 & 0 & 0 & -1 & 0 \end{array}\right] \rightarrow$$

$$\left[\begin{array}{cccc|c} 1 & 0 & 0 & 0 & 0 \\ 0 & 1 & 0 & 0 & 0 \\ 0 & 0 & 1 & 0 & 0 \\ 0 & 0 & 0 & 1 & 0 \end{array}\right] \rightarrow \left[\begin{array}{l} x_1 = 0 \\ x_2 = 0 \\ x_3 = 0 \end{array}\right]$$

34. $\left[\begin{array}{ccc|c} 2 & -3 & 4 & 7 \\ 1 & -2 & 3 & 2 \end{array}\right] \rightarrow \left[\begin{array}{ccc|c} 1 & -2 & 3 & 2 \\ 2 & -3 & 4 & 7 \end{array}\right] \rightarrow \left[\begin{array}{ccc|c} 1 & -2 & 3 & 2 \\ 0 & 1 & -2 & 3 \end{array}\right] \rightarrow \left[\begin{array}{ccc|c} 1 & 0 & -1 & 8 \\ 0 & 1 & -2 & 3 \end{array}\right] \rightarrow \left[\begin{array}{l} x_1 = 8 + x_3 \\ x_2 = 3 + 2x_3 \end{array}\right]$

36.

$$\left[\begin{array}{ccc|c} 1 & 1 & 1 & 3 \\ 1 & -1 & 1 & 7 \\ 1 & -1 & -1 & 1 \end{array}\right] \rightarrow \left[\begin{array}{ccc|c} 1 & 1 & 1 & 3 \\ 0 & -2 & 0 & 4 \\ 0 & -2 & -2 & -2 \end{array}\right] \rightarrow \left[\begin{array}{ccc|c} 1 & 1 & 1 & 3 \\ 0 & 1 & 0 & -2 \\ 0 & -2 & -2 & -2 \end{array}\right] \rightarrow$$

$$\left[\begin{array}{ccc|c} 1 & 0 & 1 & 5 \\ 0 & 1 & 0 & -2 \\ 0 & 0 & -2 & -6 \end{array}\right] \rightarrow \left[\begin{array}{ccc|c} 1 & 0 & 1 & 5 \\ 0 & 1 & 0 & -2 \\ 0 & 0 & 1 & 3 \end{array}\right] \rightarrow \left[\begin{array}{ccc|c} 1 & 0 & 1 & 2 \\ 0 & 1 & 0 & -2 \\ 0 & 0 & 1 & 3 \end{array}\right] \rightarrow \left[\begin{array}{l} x_1 = 2 \\ x_2 = -2 \\ x_3 = 3 \end{array}\right]$$

38.

$$\left[\begin{array}{ccc|c} 1 & 1 & -1 & 12 \\ 3 & -1 & 0 & 1 \\ 2 & -3 & 4 & 3 \end{array}\right] \rightarrow \left[\begin{array}{ccc|c} 1 & 1 & -1 & 12 \\ 0 & -4 & 3 & -35 \\ 0 & -5 & 6 & -21 \end{array}\right] \rightarrow \left[\begin{array}{ccc|c} 1 & 1 & -1 & 12 \\ 0 & 1 & -\frac{3}{4} & \frac{35}{4} \\ 0 & -5 & 6 & -21 \end{array}\right] \rightarrow$$

$$\left[\begin{array}{ccc|c} 1 & 0 & -\frac{3}{4} & \frac{15}{4} \\ 0 & 1 & -\frac{3}{4} & \frac{35}{4} \\ 0 & 0 & \frac{9}{4} & \frac{91}{4} \end{array}\right] \rightarrow \left[\begin{array}{ccc|c} 1 & 0 & -\frac{1}{4} & \frac{15}{4} \\ 0 & 1 & -\frac{3}{4} & \frac{35}{4} \\ 0 & 0 & 1 & \frac{91}{4} \end{array}\right] \rightarrow \left[\begin{array}{ccc|c} 1 & 0 & 0 & \frac{52}{9} \\ 0 & 1 & 0 & \frac{49}{3} \\ 0 & 0 & 1 & \frac{91}{9} \end{array}\right] \rightarrow \left[\begin{array}{l} x_1 = \frac{52}{9} \\ x_2 = \frac{49}{3} \\ x_3 = \frac{91}{9} \end{array}\right]$$

40. Let $x_1, x_2, x_3 \rightarrow$ 10%, 30%, 50%. $x_1 \geq 0, x_2 \geq 0, x_3 \geq 0$.
Also $x_1 + x_2 + x_3 = 100$, and $0.1x_1 + 0.3x_2 + 0.5x_3 = 40$.
Then by matrix techniques we obtain the solution :
$x_1 = x_3 - 50$, $x_2 = 150 - 2x_3$. By the nonnegative constraints $50 \leq x_3 \leq 75$.

No. of liters 10%	No. of liters of 30%	No. of liters of 50%
0	50	50
5	40	55
10	30	60
15	20	65
20	10	70
25	0	75

Exercise 2.3 (page 73)

2. 2 x 2 **4.** 3 x 2 **6.** 1 x 3 **8.** 1 x 1 **10.** False. $4 \neq 0$.

12. False.The matrix is 2 x 3.**14.**False.One matrix is 2 x 2, the other is 1 x 2

16. True. **18.** If corresponding entries are equal, then

$$\begin{aligned} x + y &= 6 \\ \underline{x - y} &\underline{= 2} \\ 2x &= 8 \\ x &= 4 \\ y &= 6 - x = 2 \\ z &= 0 \end{aligned}$$

20. (1) $x - 2 = y$ (2) $z = 3$
(3) $2z = 6$ (4) $6y = 18z$
(5) $x = y + 2$ (6) $2y = 6z$
From (2) and (4), $z = 3$ and $y = 3z = 9$.
From (5), $x = 9 + 2 = 11$. (Check to see that (1), (3), and (6) are also satisfied.)
Both matrices are equal to :

$$\begin{bmatrix} 9 & 3 & 6 \\ 54 & 11 & 18 \end{bmatrix}$$

22. $B + C = \begin{bmatrix} 1 & -2 & 0 \\ 5 & 1 & 2 \end{bmatrix} + \begin{bmatrix} -3 & 0 & 5 \\ 2 & 1 & 3 \end{bmatrix} = \begin{bmatrix} -2 & -2 & 5 \\ 7 & 2 & 5 \end{bmatrix}$

24. $3C - 4B = \begin{bmatrix} -9 & 0 & 15 \\ 6 & 3 & 9 \end{bmatrix} - \begin{bmatrix} 4 & -8 & 0 \\ 20 & 4 & 8 \end{bmatrix} = \begin{bmatrix} -13 & 8 & 15 \\ -14 & -1 & 1 \end{bmatrix}$

26. $4C + (A - B) = \begin{bmatrix} -12 & 0 & 20 \\ 8 & 4 & 12 \end{bmatrix} + \begin{bmatrix} 1 & -1 & 4 \\ -5 & 1 & -1 \end{bmatrix} = \begin{bmatrix} -11 & -1 & 24 \\ 3 & 5 & 11 \end{bmatrix}$

28. $(A + B) + 3C = \begin{bmatrix} 3 & -5 & 4 \\ 5 & 3 & 3 \end{bmatrix} + \begin{bmatrix} -9 & 0 & 15 \\ 6 & 3 & 9 \end{bmatrix} = \begin{bmatrix} -6 & -5 & 19 \\ 11 & 6 & 12 \end{bmatrix}$

30. $2A - 5(B + C) = \begin{bmatrix} 4 & -6 & 8 \\ 0 & 4 & 2 \end{bmatrix} - 5\left(\begin{bmatrix} 1 & -2 & 0 \\ 5 & 1 & 2 \end{bmatrix} + \begin{bmatrix} -3 & 0 & 5 \\ 2 & 1 & 3 \end{bmatrix}\right) =$

$$\begin{bmatrix} 4 & -6 & 8 \\ 0 & 4 & 2 \end{bmatrix} - 5\begin{bmatrix} -2 & -2 & 5 \\ 7 & 2 & 5 \end{bmatrix} = \begin{bmatrix} 14 & 4 & -17 \\ -35 & -16 & -23 \end{bmatrix}$$

32. $\begin{bmatrix} 3+x-y & 0 & 0 \\ 5 & x & 5 \end{bmatrix} = \begin{bmatrix} 6 & 0 & 0 \\ 5 & 2x+y & 5 \end{bmatrix}$

$3 + x - y = 6 \qquad x = 2x + y$

$\underline{x + y = 0} \qquad y = -x$

$3 + 2x = 6 \qquad y = -3/2$

$2x = 3$

$x = 3/2$

34. $2 + a_1 = 2 \quad a_1 = 0$

$1 + a_2 = -1 \quad a_2 = -2$

$0 + a_3 = 3 \quad a_3 = 3$

36.

	Gum	Ice Cream Cones	Jelly Beans	Candy Bars
Katy	5	2	10	0
Mike	2	0	15	2
Danny	1	1	0	4

38. (a)

	Compact	Intermediate	Full-size	
A	100	50	40	June
B	120	40	35	

A	80	30	10	July
B	70	40	20	

A	300	120	65	June-August
B	250	100	80	

(b) $\begin{bmatrix} 100 & 50 & 40 \\ 120 & 40 & 35 \end{bmatrix} + \begin{bmatrix} 80 & 30 & 10 \\ 70 & 40 & 20 \end{bmatrix} = \begin{bmatrix} 180 & 80 & 50 \\ 190 & 80 & 55 \end{bmatrix}$

(c) $\begin{bmatrix} 300 & 120 & 65 \\ 250 & 100 & 80 \end{bmatrix} - \begin{bmatrix} 180 & 80 & 50 \\ 190 & 80 & 55 \end{bmatrix} = \begin{bmatrix} 120 & 40 & 15 \\ 60 & 20 & 25 \end{bmatrix}$

Exercise 2.4 (page 80)

2. CD : (2 x 3) (3 x 2),Dimension is 2 x 2.

4. DC : (3 x 2) (2 x 3),Dimension is 3 x 3.

6. A(CD): (3 x 4)(2 x 2) is not defined.

8. CD + BA: (2 x 2)(3 x 4) is not defined.

10. CB: (2 x 3)(3 x 3) is dimension 2 x 3 and since A is of dimension 3 x 4, CB − A is not defined.

12. $DC = \begin{bmatrix} 1 & 0 & 4 \\ 0 & 1 & 2 \\ 0 & -1 & 1 \end{bmatrix}\begin{bmatrix} 3 & 1 \\ 4 & -1 \\ 0 & 2 \end{bmatrix} = \begin{bmatrix} 3 & 9 \\ 4 & 3 \\ -4 & 3 \end{bmatrix}$

14. $AA = \begin{bmatrix} 1 & 2 \\ 0 & 4 \end{bmatrix}\begin{bmatrix} 1 & 2 \\ 0 & 4 \end{bmatrix} = \begin{bmatrix} 1 & 10 \\ 0 & 16 \end{bmatrix}$

16. $DC + C = \begin{bmatrix} 3 & 9 \\ 4 & 3 \\ -4 & 3 \end{bmatrix} + \begin{bmatrix} 3 & 1 \\ 4 & -1 \\ 0 & 2 \end{bmatrix} = \begin{bmatrix} 6 & 10 \\ 8 & 2 \\ -4 & 5 \end{bmatrix}$

18. $D(CB) = D\begin{bmatrix} 3 & 1 \\ 4 & -1 \\ 0 & 2 \end{bmatrix}\begin{bmatrix} 1 & 2 & 3 \\ -1 & 4 & -2 \end{bmatrix} = \begin{bmatrix} 1 & 0 & 4 \\ 0 & 1 & 2 \\ 0 & -1 & 1 \end{bmatrix}\begin{bmatrix} 2 & 10 & 7 \\ 5 & 4 & 14 \\ -2 & 8 & -4 \end{bmatrix} = \begin{bmatrix} -6 & 42 & -9 \\ 1 & 20 & 6 \\ -7 & 4 & -18 \end{bmatrix}$

or $D(CB) = (DC)B = \begin{bmatrix} 3 & 9 \\ 4 & 3 \\ -4 & 3 \end{bmatrix}\begin{bmatrix} 1 & 2 & 3 \\ -1 & 4 & -2 \end{bmatrix} = \begin{bmatrix} -6 & 42 & -9 \\ 1 & 20 & 6 \\ -7 & 4 & -18 \end{bmatrix}$

20. $I_3D = \begin{bmatrix} 1 & 0 & 0 \\ 0 & 1 & 0 \\ 0 & 0 & 1 \end{bmatrix}\begin{bmatrix} 1 & 0 & 4 \\ 0 & 1 & 2 \\ 0 & -1 & 1 \end{bmatrix} = \begin{bmatrix} 1 & 0 & 4 \\ 0 & 1 & 2 \\ 0 & -1 & 1 \end{bmatrix} = D$

22. $E(2B) = \begin{bmatrix} 2 & -1 \\ 4 & 2 \end{bmatrix}\left(2\begin{bmatrix} 1 & 2 & 3 \\ -1 & 4 & -2 \end{bmatrix}\right) = \begin{bmatrix} 2 & -1 \\ 4 & 2 \end{bmatrix}\begin{bmatrix} 2 & 4 & 6 \\ -2 & 8 & -4 \end{bmatrix} = \begin{bmatrix} 4 & 40 & 16 \\ 4 & 32 & 16 \end{bmatrix}$

24. $3A + 2E = 3\begin{bmatrix} 1 & 2 \\ 0 & 4 \end{bmatrix} + 2\begin{bmatrix} 2 & -1 \\ 4 & 2 \end{bmatrix} = \begin{bmatrix} 3 & 6 \\ 0 & 12 \end{bmatrix} + \begin{bmatrix} 4 & -2 \\ 8 & 4 \end{bmatrix} = \begin{bmatrix} 7 & 4 \\ 8 & 16 \end{bmatrix}$

26. $2EA - 3BC = 2\begin{bmatrix} 3 & -1 \\ 4 & 2 \end{bmatrix}\begin{bmatrix} 1 & 2 \\ 0 & 4 \end{bmatrix} - 3\begin{bmatrix} 1 & 2 & 3 \\ -1 & 4 & -2 \end{bmatrix}\begin{bmatrix} 3 & 1 \\ 4 & -1 \\ 0 & 2 \end{bmatrix} = 2\begin{bmatrix} 3 & 2 \\ 4 & 16 \end{bmatrix} - 3\begin{bmatrix} 11 & 5 \\ 13 & -9 \end{bmatrix}$

$$= \begin{bmatrix} 6 & 4 \\ 8 & 32 \end{bmatrix} - \begin{bmatrix} 33 & 15 \\ 39 & -27 \end{bmatrix} = \begin{bmatrix} -27 & -11 \\ -31 & 59 \end{bmatrix}$$

28. $A = \begin{bmatrix} a & b \\ -b & a \end{bmatrix}$ $B = \begin{bmatrix} c & d \\ -d & c \end{bmatrix}$ To show $AB = BA$:

$$AB = \begin{bmatrix} a & b \\ -b & a \end{bmatrix}\begin{bmatrix} c & d \\ -d & c \end{bmatrix} = \begin{bmatrix} ac - bd & ad + bc \\ -bc - ad & -bd + ac \end{bmatrix}$$

$$BA = \begin{bmatrix} c & d \\ -d & c \end{bmatrix}\begin{bmatrix} a & b \\ -b & a \end{bmatrix} = \begin{bmatrix} ac - bd & ad + bc \\ -bc - ad & -bd + ac \end{bmatrix}$$

30. $[x\ 4\ 1]\begin{bmatrix} 2 & 1 & 0 \\ 1 & 0 & 2 \\ 0 & 2 & 4 \end{bmatrix}\begin{bmatrix} x \\ -7 \\ 5/4 \end{bmatrix} = 0 \rightarrow [2x+4\quad x+2\quad 12]\begin{bmatrix} x \\ -7 \\ 5/4 \end{bmatrix} = 0$

$$2x^2 + 4x - 7x - 14 + 15 = 0$$
$$2x^2 - 3x + 1 = 0$$
$$(2x - 1)(x - 1) = 0$$
$$2x = 1 \text{ or } x - 1 = 0$$
$$x = 1/2 \text{ or } x = 1$$

32. $AB = \begin{bmatrix} a & b \\ c & d \end{bmatrix}\begin{bmatrix} 1 & 1 \\ -1 & 1 \end{bmatrix} = \begin{bmatrix} a-b & a+b \\ c-d & c+d \end{bmatrix}$ $BA = \begin{bmatrix} 1 & 1 \\ -1 & 1 \end{bmatrix}\begin{bmatrix} a & b \\ c & d \end{bmatrix} = \begin{bmatrix} a+c & b+d \\ -a+c & -b+d \end{bmatrix}$

$AB = BA$ if and only if each of the following equations is true:

$a - b = a + c$	$a + b = b + d$
$-b = c$	$a = d$
$c - d = -a + c$	$c + d = -b + d$
$d = a$	$c = -b$

or:

$$\begin{bmatrix} a & b \\ c & d \end{bmatrix} = \begin{bmatrix} a & b \\ -b & a \end{bmatrix}$$

34. $A^2 = \begin{bmatrix} a & 1-a \\ 1+a & -a \end{bmatrix}\begin{bmatrix} a & 1-a \\ 1+a & -a \end{bmatrix} = \begin{bmatrix} a^2+1-a^2 & a-a^2-a+a^2 \\ a+a^2-a-a^2 & 1-a^2+a^2 \end{bmatrix} = \begin{bmatrix} 1 & 0 \\ 0 & 1 \end{bmatrix}$

36.

$$\begin{array}{l} \\ \text{Mike} \\ \text{Dan} \end{array} \begin{array}{c} \begin{array}{ccc} \text{Pants} & \text{Shirts} & \text{Jackets} \end{array} \\ \begin{bmatrix} 6 & 8 & 2 \\ 2 & 5 & 3 \end{bmatrix} \end{array} \begin{vmatrix} 5 \\ 3 \\ 9 \end{vmatrix} = \begin{vmatrix} 72 \\ \\ 52 \end{vmatrix}$$

;$72 for Mike, $52 for Dan.

38. (a) $A^2 = A \cdot A = \begin{bmatrix} 1 & 0 \\ 3 & 2 \end{bmatrix}\begin{bmatrix} 1 & 0 \\ 3 & 2 \end{bmatrix} = \begin{bmatrix} 1 & 0 \\ 9 & 4 \end{bmatrix}$ $A^3 = A \cdot A^2 = \begin{bmatrix} 1 & 0 \\ 3 & 2 \end{bmatrix}\begin{bmatrix} 1 & 0 \\ 9 & 4 \end{bmatrix} = \begin{bmatrix} 1 & 0 \\ 21 & 8 \end{bmatrix}$

$A^4 = A \cdot A^3 = \begin{bmatrix} 1 & 0 \\ 3 & 2 \end{bmatrix}\begin{bmatrix} 1 & 0 \\ 21 & 8 \end{bmatrix} = \begin{bmatrix} 1 & 0 \\ 45 & 16 \end{bmatrix}$

(b) $A^2 = A \cdot A = \begin{bmatrix} 3 & 1 \\ -2 & -1 \end{bmatrix}\begin{bmatrix} 3 & 1 \\ -2 & -1 \end{bmatrix} = \begin{bmatrix} 7 & 2 \\ -4 & -1 \end{bmatrix}$ $A^3 = A \cdot A^2 = \begin{bmatrix} 3 & 1 \\ -2 & -1 \end{bmatrix}\begin{bmatrix} 7 & 2 \\ -4 & -1 \end{bmatrix} = \begin{bmatrix} 17 & 5 \\ -10 & -3 \end{bmatrix}$

$A^4 = A \cdot A^3 = \begin{bmatrix} 3 & 1 \\ -2 & -1 \end{bmatrix}\begin{bmatrix} 17 & 5 \\ -10 & -3 \end{bmatrix} = \begin{bmatrix} 41 & 12 \\ -24 & -7 \end{bmatrix}$

(c) $A^2 = A \cdot A = \begin{bmatrix} 0 & 1 & 1 \\ 0 & -1 & 2 \\ 6 & 3 & -2 \end{bmatrix}\begin{bmatrix} 0 & 1 & 1 \\ 0 & -1 & 2 \\ 6 & 3 & -2 \end{bmatrix} = \begin{bmatrix} 6 & 2 & 0 \\ 12 & 7 & -6 \\ -12 & -3 & 16 \end{bmatrix}$

$A^3 = A \cdot A^2 = \begin{bmatrix} 0 & 1 & 1 \\ 0 & -1 & 2 \\ 6 & 3 & -2 \end{bmatrix}\begin{bmatrix} 6 & 2 & 0 \\ 12 & 7 & -6 \\ -12 & -3 & 16 \end{bmatrix} = \begin{bmatrix} 0 & 4 & 10 \\ -36 & -13 & 38 \\ 96 & 39 & -50 \end{bmatrix}$

$A^4 = A \cdot A^3 = \begin{bmatrix} 0 & 1 & 1 \\ 0 & -1 & 2 \\ 6 & 3 & -2 \end{bmatrix}\begin{bmatrix} 0 & 4 & 10 \\ -36 & -13 & 38 \\ 96 & 39 & -50 \end{bmatrix} = \begin{bmatrix} 60 & 26 & -12 \\ 228 & 91 & -138 \\ -300 & -93 & 274 \end{bmatrix}$

(d) $A^2 = A \cdot A = \begin{bmatrix} 1 & 0 \\ 0 & 1 \end{bmatrix}\begin{bmatrix} 1 & 0 \\ 0 & 1 \end{bmatrix} = \begin{bmatrix} 1 & 0 \\ 0 & 1 \end{bmatrix}$ $A^3 = A \cdot A^2 = \begin{bmatrix} 1 & 0 \\ 0 & 1 \end{bmatrix}\begin{bmatrix} 1 & 0 \\ 0 & 1 \end{bmatrix} = \begin{bmatrix} 1 & 0 \\ 0 & 1 \end{bmatrix}$

$A^4 = \begin{bmatrix} 1 & 0 \\ 0 & 1 \end{bmatrix}$ $A^n = \begin{bmatrix} 1 & 0 \\ 0 & 1 \end{bmatrix}$ for all n.

(e) $A^2 = A \cdot A = \begin{bmatrix} \frac{1}{2} & \frac{1}{2} \\ \frac{1}{4} & \frac{3}{4} \end{bmatrix}\begin{bmatrix} \frac{1}{2} & \frac{1}{2} \\ \frac{1}{4} & \frac{3}{4} \end{bmatrix} = \begin{bmatrix} \frac{3}{8} & \frac{5}{8} \\ \frac{5}{16} & \frac{11}{16} \end{bmatrix}$

$A^3 = A \cdot A^2 = \begin{bmatrix} \frac{1}{2} & \frac{1}{2} \\ \frac{1}{4} & \frac{3}{4} \end{bmatrix}\begin{bmatrix} \frac{3}{8} & \frac{5}{8} \\ \frac{5}{16} & \frac{11}{16} \end{bmatrix} = \begin{bmatrix} \frac{11}{32} & \frac{21}{32} \\ \frac{21}{64} & \frac{43}{64} \end{bmatrix}$

$A^4 = A \cdot A^3 = \begin{bmatrix} \frac{1}{2} & \frac{1}{2} \\ \frac{1}{4} & \frac{3}{4} \end{bmatrix}\begin{bmatrix} \frac{11}{32} & \frac{21}{32} \\ \frac{21}{64} & \frac{43}{64} \end{bmatrix} = \begin{bmatrix} \frac{43}{128} & \frac{85}{128} \\ \frac{85}{256} & \frac{171}{256} \end{bmatrix}$

$$A^n = \begin{bmatrix} (1+2/4^n)/3 & 2(1-1/4^n)/3 \\ (1-1/4^n)/3 & (2+1/4^n)/3 \end{bmatrix}$$

Exercise 2.5 (page 90)

2. $\begin{bmatrix} 1 & 5 \\ 2 & 0 \end{bmatrix}\begin{bmatrix} 0 & \frac{1}{2} \\ \frac{1}{5} & -\frac{1}{10} \end{bmatrix} = \begin{bmatrix} 1 & 0 \\ 0 & 1 \end{bmatrix} \quad \begin{bmatrix} 0 & \frac{1}{2} \\ \frac{1}{5} & -\frac{1}{10} \end{bmatrix}\begin{bmatrix} 1 & 5 \\ 2 & 0 \end{bmatrix} = \begin{bmatrix} 1 & 0 \\ 0 & 1 \end{bmatrix}$

4. $\begin{bmatrix} 1 & 3 \\ 2 & -1 \end{bmatrix}\begin{bmatrix} \frac{1}{7} & \frac{3}{7} \\ \frac{2}{7} & -\frac{1}{7} \end{bmatrix} = \begin{bmatrix} 1 & 0 \\ 0 & 1 \end{bmatrix} \quad \begin{bmatrix} \frac{1}{7} & \frac{3}{7} \\ \frac{2}{7} & -\frac{1}{7} \end{bmatrix}\begin{bmatrix} 1 & 3 \\ 2 & -1 \end{bmatrix} = \begin{bmatrix} 1 & 0 \\ 0 & 1 \end{bmatrix}$

6. $\begin{bmatrix} 1 & 3 & 3 \\ 1 & 4 & 3 \\ 1 & 3 & 4 \end{bmatrix}\begin{bmatrix} 7 & -3 & -3 \\ -1 & 1 & 0 \\ -1 & 0 & 1 \end{bmatrix} = \begin{bmatrix} 1 & 0 & 0 \\ 0 & 1 & 0 \\ 0 & 0 & 1 \end{bmatrix} \quad \begin{bmatrix} 7 & -3 & -3 \\ -1 & 1 & 0 \\ -1 & 0 & 1 \end{bmatrix}\begin{bmatrix} 1 & 3 & 3 \\ 1 & 4 & 3 \\ 1 & 3 & 4 \end{bmatrix} = \begin{bmatrix} 1 & 0 & 0 \\ 0 & 1 & 0 \\ 0 & 0 & 1 \end{bmatrix}$

8. $\left[\begin{array}{cc|cc} 4 & 1 & 1 & 0 \\ 3 & 1 & 0 & 1 \end{array}\right] \to \left[\begin{array}{cc|cc} 1 & 0 & 1 & -1 \\ 3 & 1 & 0 & 1 \end{array}\right] \to \left[\begin{array}{cc|cc} 1 & 0 & 1 & -1 \\ 0 & 1 & -3 & 4 \end{array}\right] \to A^{-1} = \begin{bmatrix} 1 & -1 \\ -3 & 4 \end{bmatrix}$

10.

$\left[\begin{array}{cc|cc} 5 & 3 & 1 & 0 \\ 3 & 2 & 0 & 1 \end{array}\right] \to \left[\begin{array}{cc|cc} -1 & -1 & 1 & -2 \\ 3 & 2 & 0 & 1 \end{array}\right] \to \left[\begin{array}{cc|cc} 1 & 1 & -1 & 2 \\ 3 & 2 & 0 & 1 \end{array}\right] \to$

$R_1 = -2r_2 + r_1 \quad R_1 = -r_1 \quad R_2 = -3r_1 + r_2$

$\left[\begin{array}{cc|cc} 1 & 1 & -1 & 2 \\ 0 & -1 & 3 & -5 \end{array}\right] \to \left[\begin{array}{cc|cc} 1 & 1 & -1 & 2 \\ 0 & 1 & -3 & 5 \end{array}\right] \to \left[\begin{array}{cc|cc} 1 & 0 & 2 & -3 \\ 0 & 1 & -3 & 5 \end{array}\right] \to A^{-1} = \begin{bmatrix} 2 & -3 \\ -3 & 5 \end{bmatrix}$

$R_2 = -r_2 \quad R_1 = -r_2 + r_1$

12. $\left[\begin{array}{cc|cc} 2 & 3 & 1 & 0 \\ 2 & -1 & 0 & 1 \end{array}\right] \rightarrow \left[\begin{array}{cc|cc} 2 & 3 & 1 & 0 \\ 0 & -4 & -1 & 1 \end{array}\right] \rightarrow \left[\begin{array}{cc|cc} 1 & 1.5 & 0.50 & 0 \\ 0 & 1 & 0.25 & -0.25 \end{array}\right] \rightarrow$

$R_2 = -r_1 + r_2 \quad R_1 = \frac{1}{2}r_1, R_2 = -\frac{1}{4}r_2 \quad R_1 = -\frac{3}{2}r_2 + r_1$

$\left[\begin{array}{cc|cc} 1 & 0 & 0.125 & 0.375 \\ 0 & 1 & 0.25 & -0.250 \end{array}\right] \rightarrow A^{-1} = \begin{bmatrix} \frac{1}{8} & \frac{3}{8} \\ \frac{1}{4} & -\frac{1}{4} \end{bmatrix}$

14. $\left[\begin{array}{ccc|ccc} -1 & 1 & 0 & 1 & 0 & 0 \\ 1 & 0 & 2 & 0 & 1 & 0 \\ 3 & 1 & 0 & 0 & 0 & 1 \end{array}\right] \rightarrow \left[\begin{array}{ccc|ccc} 1 & -1 & 0 & -1 & 0 & 0 \\ 1 & 0 & 2 & 0 & 1 & 0 \\ 3 & 1 & 0 & 0 & 0 & 1 \end{array}\right] \rightarrow \left[\begin{array}{ccc|ccc} 1 & -1 & 0 & -1 & 0 & 0 \\ 0 & 1 & 2 & 1 & 1 & 0 \\ 0 & 4 & 0 & 3 & 0 & 1 \end{array}\right] \rightarrow$

$R_1 = -r_1 \quad R_2 = -r_1 + r_2, R_3 = -3r_1 + r_3 \quad R_1 = r_2 + r_1, R_3 = -4r_2 + r_3$

$\left[\begin{array}{ccc|ccc} 1 & 0 & 2 & 0 & 1 & 0 \\ 0 & 1 & 2 & 1 & 1 & 0 \\ 0 & 0 & -8 & -1 & -4 & 1 \end{array}\right] \rightarrow \left[\begin{array}{ccc|ccc} 1 & 0 & 0 & -\frac{1}{4} & 0 & \frac{1}{4} \\ 0 & 1 & 0 & \frac{3}{4} & 0 & \frac{1}{4} \\ 0 & 0 & 1 & \frac{1}{8} & \frac{1}{2} & -\frac{1}{8} \end{array}\right] \rightarrow A^{-1} = \begin{bmatrix} -\frac{1}{4} & 0 & \frac{1}{4} \\ \frac{3}{4} & 0 & \frac{1}{4} \\ \frac{1}{8} & \frac{1}{2} & -\frac{1}{8} \end{bmatrix}$

$R_3 = -\frac{1}{8}r_3, R_1 = -2r_3 + r_1, R_2 = -2r_3 + r_2$

16. $\left[\begin{array}{ccc|ccc} 1 & 1 & 1 & 1 & 0 & 0 \\ 2 & 1 & 1 & 0 & 1 & 0 \\ 1 & 1 & 2 & 0 & 0 & 1 \end{array}\right] \rightarrow \left[\begin{array}{ccc|ccc} 1 & 1 & 1 & 1 & 0 & 0 \\ 0 & -1 & -1 & -2 & 1 & 0 \\ 0 & 0 & 1 & -1 & 0 & 1 \end{array}\right] \rightarrow \left[\begin{array}{ccc|ccc} 1 & 1 & 1 & 1 & 0 & 0 \\ 0 & 1 & 1 & 2 & -1 & 0 \\ 0 & 0 & 1 & -1 & 0 & 1 \end{array}\right] \rightarrow$

$R_2 = -2r_1 + r_2, R_3 = -r_1 + r_3 \quad R_2 = -r_2 \quad R_1 = -r_2 + r_1$

$\left[\begin{array}{ccc|ccc} 1 & 0 & 0 & -1 & 1 & 0 \\ 0 & 1 & 1 & 2 & -1 & 0 \\ 0 & 0 & 1 & -1 & 0 & 1 \end{array}\right] \rightarrow \left[\begin{array}{ccc|ccc} 1 & 0 & 0 & -1 & 1 & 0 \\ 0 & 1 & 0 & 3 & -1 & -1 \\ 0 & 0 & 1 & -1 & 0 & 1 \end{array}\right] \rightarrow A^{-1} = \begin{bmatrix} -1 & 1 & 0 \\ 3 & -1 & -1 \\ -1 & 0 & 1 \end{bmatrix}$

$R_2 = -r_3 + r_2$

18. $\left[\begin{array}{ccc|ccc} 2 & 3 & -1 & 1 & 0 & 0 \\ 1 & 1 & 1 & 0 & 1 & 0 \\ 0 & 2 & -1 & 0 & 0 & 1 \end{array}\right] \rightarrow \left[\begin{array}{ccc|ccc} 1 & 1 & 1 & 0 & 1 & 0 \\ 2 & 3 & -1 & 1 & 0 & 0 \\ 0 & 2 & -1 & 0 & 0 & 1 \end{array}\right] \rightarrow \left[\begin{array}{ccc|ccc} 1 & 1 & 1 & 0 & 1 & 0 \\ 0 & 1 & -3 & 1 & -2 & 0 \\ 0 & 2 & -1 & 0 & 0 & 1 \end{array}\right] \rightarrow$

$R_1 \leftrightarrow R_2 \quad R_2 = -2r_1 + r_2 \quad R_3 = -2r_2 + r_3, R_1 = -r_2 + r_1, R_3 = \frac{1}{5}r_3$

$\left[\begin{array}{ccc|ccc} 1 & 0 & 4 & -1 & 3 & 0 \\ 0 & 1 & -3 & 1 & -2 & 0 \\ 0 & 0 & 5 & -2 & 4 & 1 \end{array}\right] \rightarrow \left[\begin{array}{ccc|ccc} 1 & 0 & 4 & -1 & 3 & 0 \\ 0 & 1 & -3 & 1 & -2 & 0 \\ 0 & 0 & 1 & -\frac{2}{5} & \frac{4}{5} & \frac{1}{5} \end{array}\right] \rightarrow \left[\begin{array}{ccc|ccc} 1 & 0 & 0 & \frac{3}{5} & -\frac{1}{5} & -\frac{4}{5} \\ 0 & 1 & 0 & -\frac{1}{5} & \frac{2}{5} & \frac{3}{5} \\ 0 & 0 & 1 & -\frac{2}{5} & \frac{4}{5} & \frac{1}{5} \end{array}\right] \rightarrow A^{-1} = \left[\begin{array}{cc} \frac{3}{5} & -\frac{1}{5} \\ -\frac{1}{5} & \frac{2}{5} \\ -\frac{2}{5} & \frac{4}{5} \end{array}\right.$

$R_1 = -4r_3 + r_1, R_2 = 3r_3 + r_2$

20. $$\left[\begin{array}{cccc|cccc} 1 & 2 & -3 & -2 & 1 & 0 & 0 & 0 \\ 0 & 1 & 4 & -2 & 0 & 1 & 0 & 0 \\ 3 & -1 & 4 & 0 & 0 & 0 & 1 & 0 \\ 2 & 1 & 0 & 3 & 0 & 0 & 0 & 1 \end{array}\right] \rightarrow \left[\begin{array}{cccc|cccc} 1 & 2 & -3 & -2 & 1 & 0 & 0 & 0 \\ 0 & 1 & 4 & -2 & 0 & 1 & 0 & 0 \\ 0 & -7 & 13 & 6 & -3 & 0 & 1 & 0 \\ 0 & -3 & 6 & 7 & -2 & 0 & 0 & 1 \end{array}\right] \rightarrow$$

$R_3 = -3r_1 + r_3, R_4 = -2r_1 + r_4$ $\quad$ $R_1 = -2r_2 + r_1, R_3 = 7r_2 + r_1, R_4 = 3r_2 + r_4$

$$\left[\begin{array}{cccc|cccc} 1 & 0 & -11 & 2 & 1 & -2 & 0 & 0 \\ 0 & 1 & 4 & -2 & 0 & 1 & 0 & 0 \\ 0 & 0 & 41 & -8 & -3 & 7 & 1 & 0 \\ 0 & 0 & 18 & 1 & -2 & 3 & 0 & 1 \end{array}\right] \rightarrow \left[\begin{array}{cccc|cccc} 1 & 0 & -11 & 2 & 1 & -2 & 0 & 0 \\ 0 & 1 & 4 & -2 & 0 & 1 & 0 & 0 \\ 0 & 0 & 5 & -10 & 1 & 1 & 1 & -2 \\ 0 & 0 & 18 & 1 & -2 & 3 & 0 & 1 \end{array}\right] \rightarrow$$

$R_3 = -2r_4 + r_3$ $\quad$ $R_3 = \frac{1}{5}r_3$

$$\left[\begin{array}{cccc|cccc} 1 & 0 & -11 & 2 & 1 & -2 & 0 & 0 \\ 0 & 1 & 4 & -2 & 0 & 1 & 0 & 0 \\ 0 & 0 & 1 & -2 & \frac{1}{5} & \frac{1}{5} & \frac{1}{5} & -\frac{2}{5} \\ 0 & 0 & 18 & 1 & -2 & 3 & 0 & 1 \end{array}\right] \rightarrow \left[\begin{array}{cccc|cccc} 1 & 0 & 0 & -20 & 3.2 & -0.2 & 2.2 & -4.4 \\ 0 & 1 & 0 & 6 & -0.8 & 0.2 & -0.8 & 1.6 \\ 0 & 0 & 1 & -2 & 0.2 & 0.2 & 0.2 & -0.4 \\ 0 & 0 & 0 & 37 & -5.6 & -0.6 & -3.6 & 8.2 \end{array}\right] \rightarrow$$

$R_4 = -18r_3 + r_4$ $\quad$ $R_4 = (1/37)r_4$

$$\left[\begin{array}{cccc|cccc} 1 & 0 & 0 & -20 & 3.2 & -0.2 & 2.2 & -4.4 \\ 0 & 1 & 0 & 6 & -0.8 & 0.2 & -0.8 & 1.6 \\ 0 & 0 & 1 & -2 & 0.2 & 0.2 & 0.2 & -0.4 \\ 0 & 0 & 0 & 1 & -0.151 & -0.016 & -0.097 & 0.222 \end{array}\right] \rightarrow \left[\begin{array}{cccc|cccc} 1 & 0 & 0 & 0 & \frac{32}{185} & -\frac{25}{185} & \frac{47}{185} & \frac{6}{185} \\ 0 & 1 & 0 & 0 & \frac{4}{37} & \frac{11}{37} & -\frac{8}{37} & \frac{10}{37} \\ 0 & 0 & 1 & 0 & -\frac{19}{185} & \frac{31}{185} & \frac{1}{185} & \frac{8}{185} \\ 0 & 0 & 0 & 1 & -\frac{28}{185} & -\frac{3}{185} & -\frac{18}{185} & \frac{41}{185} \end{array}\right] \rightarrow$$

$R_1 = 20r_4 + r_1, R_2 = -6r_4 + r_2, R_3 = 2r_4 + r_3$

$$A^{-1} = \begin{bmatrix} \frac{32}{185} & -\frac{25}{185} & \frac{47}{185} & \frac{6}{185} \\ \frac{4}{37} & \frac{11}{37} & -\frac{8}{37} & \frac{10}{37} \\ -\frac{19}{185} & \frac{31}{185} & \frac{1}{185} & \frac{8}{185} \\ -\frac{28}{185} & -\frac{3}{185} & -\frac{18}{185} & \frac{41}{185} \end{bmatrix}$$

22. $$\left[\begin{array}{cc|cc} -1 & 2 & 1 & 0 \\ 3 & -6 & 0 & 1 \end{array}\right] \rightarrow \left[\begin{array}{cc|cc} 1 & -2 & -1 & 0 \\ 3 & -6 & 0 & 1 \end{array}\right] \rightarrow \left[\begin{array}{cc|cc} 1 & -2 & -1 & 0 \\ 0 & 0 & 3 & 1 \end{array}\right]$$

$R_1 = -r_1$ $\quad$ $R_2 = -3r_1 + r_2$

The zeros in row 2 indicate that no inverse exists.

24. $$\left[\begin{array}{cc|cc} 2 & 10 & 1 & 0 \\ 1 & 5 & 0 & 1 \end{array}\right] \rightarrow \left[\begin{array}{cc|cc} 1 & 5 & \frac{1}{2} & 0 \\ 1 & 5 & 0 & 1 \end{array}\right] \rightarrow \left[\begin{array}{cc|cc} 1 & 5 & \frac{1}{2} & 0 \\ 0 & 0 & -\frac{1}{2} & 1 \end{array}\right]$$ No inverse.

26. $\left[\begin{array}{ccc|ccc} -1 & 2 & 3 & 1 & 0 & 0 \\ 5 & 2 & 0 & 0 & 1 & 0 \\ 2 & -4 & -6 & 0 & 0 & 1 \end{array}\right] \to \left[\begin{array}{ccc|ccc} 1 & -2 & -3 & -1 & 0 & 0 \\ 5 & 2 & 0 & 0 & 1 & 0 \\ 2 & -4 & -6 & 0 & 0 & 1 \end{array}\right] \to \left[\begin{array}{ccc|ccc} 1 & -2 & -3 & -1 & 0 & 0 \\ 0 & 12 & 15 & 5 & 1 & 0 \\ 0 & 0 & 0 & 2 & 0 & 1 \end{array}\right] \to$ No inverse.

28. $\left[\begin{array}{cc|cc} 2 & 1 & 1 & 0 \\ 1 & 1 & 0 & 1 \end{array}\right] \to \left[\begin{array}{cc|cc} 1 & 1 & 0 & 1 \\ 2 & 1 & 1 & 0 \end{array}\right] \to \left[\begin{array}{cc|cc} 1 & 1 & 0 & 1 \\ 0 & -1 & 1 & -2 \end{array}\right] \to$

$\left[\begin{array}{cc|cc} 1 & 0 & 1 & -1 \\ 0 & -1 & 1 & -2 \end{array}\right] \to \left[\begin{array}{cc|cc} 1 & 0 & 1 & -1 \\ 0 & 1 & -1 & 2 \end{array}\right] \to A^{-1} = \begin{bmatrix} 1 & -1 \\ -1 & 2 \end{bmatrix}$

30. $\left[\begin{array}{cc|cc} 4 & -1 & 1 & 0 \\ -1 & 0 & 0 & 1 \end{array}\right] \to \left[\begin{array}{cc|cc} -1 & 0 & 0 & 1 \\ 4 & -1 & 1 & 0 \end{array}\right] \to \left[\begin{array}{cc|cc} -1 & 0 & 0 & 1 \\ 0 & -1 & 1 & 4 \end{array}\right] \to \left[\begin{array}{cc|cc} 1 & 0 & 0 & -1 \\ 0 & 1 & -1 & -4 \end{array}\right] \to A^{-1} = \begin{bmatrix} 0 & -1 \\ -1 & -4 \end{bmatrix}$

32. $\left[\begin{array}{cc|cc} 4 & 2 & 1 & 0 \\ 2 & 1 & 0 & 1 \end{array}\right] \to \left[\begin{array}{cc|cc} 2 & 1 & 0 & 1 \\ 4 & 2 & 1 & 0 \end{array}\right] \to \left[\begin{array}{cc|cc} 2 & 1 & 0 & 1 \\ 0 & 0 & 1 & -2 \end{array}\right] \to$ No solution.

34. $\left[\begin{array}{cc|cc} 1 & -1 & 1 & 0 \\ 2 & 1 & 0 & 1 \end{array}\right] \to \left[\begin{array}{cc|cc} 1 & 0 & \frac{1}{3} & \frac{1}{3} \\ 0 & 1 & -\frac{2}{3} & -\frac{2}{3} \end{array}\right]$

$\begin{bmatrix} x \\ y \end{bmatrix} = \begin{bmatrix} \frac{1}{3} & \frac{1}{3} \\ -\frac{2}{3} & -\frac{2}{3} \end{bmatrix} \begin{bmatrix} 2 \\ 1 \end{bmatrix} = \begin{bmatrix} 1 \\ -1 \end{bmatrix}$

36. $\left[\begin{array}{cc|cc} 2 & -3 & 1 & 0 \\ 3 & 1 & 0 & 1 \end{array}\right] \to \left[\begin{array}{cc|cc} 1 & 0 & \frac{1}{11} & \frac{3}{11} \\ 0 & 1 & -\frac{3}{11} & \frac{2}{11} \end{array}\right]$

$\begin{bmatrix} x \\ y \end{bmatrix} = \begin{bmatrix} \frac{1}{11} & \frac{3}{11} \\ -\frac{3}{11} & \frac{2}{11} \end{bmatrix} \begin{bmatrix} 5 \\ 2 \end{bmatrix} = \begin{bmatrix} 1 \\ -1 \end{bmatrix}$

38. $\left[\begin{array}{cc|cc} 3 & -4 & 1 & 0 \\ 6 & 2 & 0 & 1 \end{array}\right] \to \left[\begin{array}{cc|cc} 1 & 0 & \frac{1}{15} & \frac{2}{15} \\ 0 & 1 & -\frac{1}{5} & \frac{1}{10} \end{array}\right] \quad \begin{bmatrix} x \\ y \end{bmatrix} = \begin{bmatrix} \frac{1}{15} & \frac{2}{15} \\ -\frac{1}{5} & \frac{1}{10} \end{bmatrix} \begin{bmatrix} 3 \\ 1 \end{bmatrix} = \begin{bmatrix} \frac{1}{3} \\ \frac{1}{2} \end{bmatrix}$

40. $$\left[\begin{array}{cc|cc} 1 & -0.25 & 1 & 0 \\ 0.5 & 0.5 & 0 & 1 \end{array}\right] \rightarrow \left[\begin{array}{cc|cc} 1 & 0 & 0.8 & 0.4 \\ 0 & 1 & -0.8 & 1.6 \end{array}\right] \quad \begin{bmatrix} x \\ y \end{bmatrix} = \begin{bmatrix} 0.8 & 0.4 \\ -0.8 & 1.6 \end{bmatrix} \begin{bmatrix} 0 \\ 2.5 \end{bmatrix} = \begin{bmatrix} 1 \\ 4 \end{bmatrix}$$

42. $$\left[\begin{array}{ccc|ccc} 1 & 1 & 1 & 1 & 0 & 0 \\ 2 & -1 & 1 & 0 & 1 & 0 \\ 1 & 2 & -1 & 0 & 0 & 1 \end{array}\right] \rightarrow \left[\begin{array}{ccc|ccc} 1 & 0 & 0 & -\frac{1}{7} & \frac{3}{7} & \frac{2}{7} \\ 0 & 1 & 0 & \frac{3}{7} & -\frac{2}{7} & \frac{1}{7} \\ 0 & 0 & 1 & \frac{5}{7} & -\frac{1}{7} & -\frac{3}{7} \end{array}\right]$$

$$\begin{bmatrix} x \\ y \\ z \end{bmatrix} = \begin{bmatrix} -\frac{1}{7} & \frac{3}{7} & \frac{2}{7} \\ \frac{3}{7} & -\frac{2}{7} & \frac{1}{7} \\ \frac{5}{7} & -\frac{1}{7} & -\frac{3}{7} \end{bmatrix} \begin{bmatrix} 5 \\ 2 \\ 3 \end{bmatrix} = \begin{bmatrix} 1 \\ 2 \\ 2 \end{bmatrix}$$

44. $$\left[\begin{array}{ccc|ccc} 2 & 2 & 1 & 1 & 0 & 0 \\ 1 & -1 & -1 & 0 & 1 & 0 \\ 1 & -2 & -2 & 0 & 0 & 1 \end{array}\right] \rightarrow \left[\begin{array}{ccc|ccc} 1 & 0 & 0 & 0 & 2 & -1 \\ 0 & 1 & 0 & 1 & -5 & 3 \\ 0 & 0 & 1 & -1 & 6 & -4 \end{array}\right]$$

$$\begin{bmatrix} x \\ y \\ z \end{bmatrix} = \begin{bmatrix} 0 & 2 & -1 \\ 1 & -5 & 3 \\ -1 & 6 & -4 \end{bmatrix} \begin{bmatrix} 6 \\ -2 \\ -5 \end{bmatrix} = \begin{bmatrix} 1 \\ 1 \\ 2 \end{bmatrix}$$

46. $$\left[\begin{array}{ccc|ccc} 1 & 1 & 0 & 1 & 0 & 0 \\ 2 & -1 & 1 & 0 & 1 & 0 \\ 1 & 2 & 1 & 0 & 0 & 1 \end{array}\right] \rightarrow \left[\begin{array}{ccc|ccc} 1 & 0 & 0 & \frac{3}{4} & \frac{1}{4} & -\frac{1}{4} \\ 0 & 1 & 0 & \frac{1}{4} & -\frac{1}{4} & \frac{1}{4} \\ 0 & 0 & 1 & -\frac{5}{4} & \frac{1}{4} & \frac{3}{4} \end{array}\right]$$

$$\begin{bmatrix} x \\ y \\ z \end{bmatrix} = \begin{bmatrix} \frac{3}{4} & \frac{1}{4} & -\frac{1}{4} \\ \frac{1}{4} & -\frac{1}{4} & \frac{1}{4} \\ -\frac{5}{4} & \frac{1}{4} & \frac{3}{4} \end{bmatrix} \begin{bmatrix} 1 \\ 1 \\ \frac{8}{3} \end{bmatrix} = \begin{bmatrix} \frac{1}{3} \\ \frac{2}{3} \\ 1 \end{bmatrix}$$

48. $$\left[\begin{array}{cc|cc} 3 & 7 & 1 & 0 \\ 2 & 5 & 0 & 1 \end{array}\right] \rightarrow \left[\begin{array}{cc|cc} 1 & 2 & 1 & -1 \\ 2 & 5 & 0 & 1 \end{array}\right] \rightarrow \left[\begin{array}{cc|cc} 1 & 2 & 1 & -1 \\ 0 & 1 & -2 & 3 \end{array}\right] \rightarrow \left[\begin{array}{cc|cc} 1 & 0 & 5 & -7 \\ 0 & 1 & -2 & 3 \end{array}\right]$$

$$\begin{bmatrix} x \\ y \end{bmatrix} = \begin{bmatrix} 5 & -7 \\ -2 & 3 \end{bmatrix} \begin{bmatrix} -4 \\ -3 \end{bmatrix} = \begin{bmatrix} 1 \\ -1 \end{bmatrix}$$

50. $$\begin{bmatrix} x \\ y \end{bmatrix} = \begin{bmatrix} 5 & -7 \\ -2 & 3 \end{bmatrix} \begin{bmatrix} 20 \\ 14 \end{bmatrix} = \begin{bmatrix} 2 \\ 2 \end{bmatrix}$$

Exercise 2.6A (page 97)

2. A = (1/4)A + (2/3)B + (1/2)C
B = (1/2)A + (1/6)B + (1/4)C
C = (1/4)A + (1/6)B + (1/4)C

(-3/4)A + (2/3)B + (1/2)C = 0
(1/2)A - (5/6)B + (1/4)C = 0
(1/4)A + (1/6)B - (3/4)C = 0

$$\begin{bmatrix} -\frac{3}{4} & \frac{2}{3} & \frac{1}{2} \\ \frac{1}{2} & -\frac{5}{6} & \frac{1}{4} \\ \frac{1}{4} & \frac{1}{6} & -\frac{3}{4} \end{bmatrix} \to \begin{bmatrix} 1 & 0 & -2 \\ 0 & 1 & -\frac{3}{2} \\ 0 & 0 & 0 \end{bmatrix} \quad \begin{bmatrix} X_1 = 2X_3 = \$20,000 \\ X_2 = \frac{3}{2}X_3 = \$15,000 \\ X_3 = \$10,000 \end{bmatrix}$$

4. A = 0.4A + 0.3B + 0.2C
B = 0.2A + 0.3B + 0.3C
C = 0.4A + 0.4B + 0.5C

-0.6A + 0.3B + 0.2C = 0
0.2A - 0.7B + 0.3C = 0
0.4A + 0.4B - 0.5C = 0

$$\begin{bmatrix} -\frac{6}{10} & \frac{3}{10} & \frac{2}{10} \\ \frac{2}{10} & -\frac{7}{10} & \frac{3}{10} \\ \frac{4}{10} & \frac{4}{10} & \frac{5}{10} \end{bmatrix} \to \begin{bmatrix} 1 & 0 & -\frac{25}{26} \\ 0 & 1 & -\frac{11}{18} \\ 0 & 0 & 0 \end{bmatrix} \to \begin{bmatrix} X_1 = \frac{25}{26}X_3 = \$6,388.89 \\ X_2 = \frac{11}{18}X_3 = \$6,111.11 \\ X_3 = \$10,000 \end{bmatrix}$$

6. $$x = (I - A)^{-1}D = \begin{bmatrix} 1.6048 & 0.3568 & 0.7131 \\ 0.2946 & 1.3363 & 0.3857 \\ 0.3660 & 0.2721 & 1.4013 \end{bmatrix} \begin{bmatrix} 100 \\ 80 \\ 60 \end{bmatrix} = \begin{bmatrix} 231.81 \\ 159.506 \\ 142.446 \end{bmatrix}$$

8. See solution to problem 7 in text; with the appropriate changes in column 4, the coefficient matrix is :

$$\begin{bmatrix} -.7 & .3 & .3 & .25 \\ .2 & -.7 & .3 & .25 \\ .2 & .1 & -.9 & .25 \\ .3 & .3 & .3 & -.75 \end{bmatrix} \to \begin{bmatrix} 1 & 0 & 0 & -1 \\ 0 & 1 & 0 & -.9 \\ 0 & 0 & 1 & -.6 \\ 0 & 0 & 0 & 0 \end{bmatrix} \to \begin{bmatrix} x_1 = x_4 = \$10,000 \\ x_2 = .9x_4 = \$9,000 \\ x_3 = .6x_4 = \$6,000 \\ x_4 = \$10,000 \end{bmatrix}$$

Exercise 2.6B (page 101)

2. $A = \begin{bmatrix} 2 & 3 \\ 1 & 2 \end{bmatrix} \qquad A^{-1} = \begin{bmatrix} 2 & -3 \\ -1 & 2 \end{bmatrix}$

(a) $\begin{bmatrix} 2 & -3 \\ -1 & 2 \end{bmatrix}\begin{bmatrix} 51 & 27 & 75 & 19 & 48 \\ 30 & 16 & 47 & 10 & 26 \end{bmatrix} = \begin{bmatrix} 12 & 6 & 9 & 8 & 18 \\ 9 & 5 & 19 & 1 & 4 \end{bmatrix}$

12 9 6 5   9 19   8 1 18 4
L I F E   I S   H A R D

(b) $\begin{bmatrix} 2 & -3 \\ -1 & 2 \end{bmatrix}\begin{bmatrix} 70 & 103 & 58 & 102 & 88 \\ 45 & 62 & 38 & 61 & 57 \end{bmatrix} = \begin{bmatrix} 5 & 20 & 2 & 21 & 5 \\ 20 & 21 & 18 & 20 & 26 \end{bmatrix}$

5 20   20 21   2 18 21 20 21 26
E T   T U   B R U T U S

Exercise 2.6C (page 106)

2. $A^T = \begin{bmatrix} 5 & 1 & 1 \\ 2 & 3 & -1 \\ -1 & 6 & 2 \end{bmatrix}$ 4. $A^T = \begin{bmatrix} -1 \\ 6 \\ 4 \end{bmatrix}$ 6. $A^T = \begin{bmatrix} 5 & 3 \\ 3 & 7 \end{bmatrix}$

8. (a) $\begin{bmatrix} 0 & 2 & 4 & 6 & 8 \\ 1 & 1 & 1 & 1 & 1 \end{bmatrix}\begin{bmatrix} 0 & 1 \\ 2 & 1 \\ 4 & 1 \\ 6 & 1 \\ 8 & 1 \end{bmatrix}\begin{bmatrix} a \\ b \end{bmatrix} = \begin{bmatrix} 0 & 2 & 4 & 6 & 8 \\ 1 & 1 & 1 & 1 & 1 \end{bmatrix}\begin{bmatrix} 50 \\ 74 \\ 85 \\ 90 \\ 92 \end{bmatrix}$

$\begin{bmatrix} 120 & 20 \\ 20 & 5 \end{bmatrix}\begin{bmatrix} a \\ b \end{bmatrix} = \begin{bmatrix} 1764 \\ 391 \end{bmatrix} \qquad \begin{bmatrix} a \\ b \end{bmatrix} = \begin{bmatrix} 5 \\ 58 \end{bmatrix} \qquad y = 5x + 58$

(b) $y = 5(9) + 58 = 103$

10. (a) $\begin{bmatrix} 2 & 4 & 6 & 8 \\ 1 & 1 & 1 & 1 \end{bmatrix}\begin{bmatrix} 2 & 1 \\ 4 & 1 \\ 6 & 1 \\ 8 & 1 \end{bmatrix} = \begin{bmatrix} a \\ b \end{bmatrix}\begin{bmatrix} 2 & 4 & 6 & 8 \\ 1 & 1 & 1 & 1 \end{bmatrix}\begin{bmatrix} 2.1 \\ 1.6 \\ 1.4 \\ 1.0 \end{bmatrix}$

$\begin{bmatrix} 120 & 20 \\ 20 & 4 \end{bmatrix}\begin{bmatrix} a \\ b \end{bmatrix} = \begin{bmatrix} 27 \\ 6.1 \end{bmatrix} \qquad \begin{bmatrix} a \\ b \end{bmatrix} = \begin{bmatrix} -.175 \\ 2.4 \end{bmatrix} \qquad y = -.175x + 2.4$

(b) $y = -.175(5) + 2.4 = 1.525$

12. $(A^TA)^T = A^T(A^T)^T = A^TA$

Exercise 2.6D (page 111)

2. With $C = \begin{bmatrix} 0.20 & 0.10 & 0.10 \\ 0.40 & 0.15 & 0.30 \\ 0.10 & 0.05 & 0.30 \end{bmatrix}$ and $D = \begin{bmatrix} 500 \\ 1000 \\ 500 \end{bmatrix}$,

the system of equations (I-C)X = D does not have a meaningful solution:

$$\begin{array}{ccc|c} x_1 & x_2 & x_3 & \\ 0.80 & -0.10 & -0.10 & 500 \\ -0.40 & 0.85 & -0.30 & 1000 \\ -0.10 & -0.05 & 0.70 & 500 \end{array} \rightarrow \left[\begin{array}{ccc|c} 1 & 0 & 0 & 471 \\ 0 & 1 & 0 & 713 \\ 0 & 0 & 1 & -1943 \end{array}\right]$$

In any realistic application, x_3 could not be negative.

Review Exercises (page 112)

2. B + A = A + B; see solution to problem 1 in text.

4. 3A + 3B = 3(A + B); see solution to problem 3.

6. $B - C = \begin{bmatrix} 1-0 & 3-1 & 9-2 \\ 2-0 & 7-5 & 5-1 \\ 3-8 & 6-7 & 8-9 \end{bmatrix} = \begin{bmatrix} 1 & 2 & 7 \\ 2 & 2 & 4 \\ -5 & -1 & -1 \end{bmatrix}$

8. $\frac{3}{2}A = \begin{bmatrix} -3 & 0 & \frac{21}{2} \\ \frac{3}{2} & 12 & \frac{9}{2} \\ 3 & 6 & \frac{45}{2} \end{bmatrix}$

10. $\begin{bmatrix} -2-2+0 & 0-6+3 & 7-18+6 \\ 1-4+0 & 8-14+15 & 3-10+3 \\ 2-6+24 & 4-12+21 & 21-16+27 \end{bmatrix} = \begin{bmatrix} -4 & -3 & -5 \\ -3 & 9 & -4 \\ 20 & 13 & 32 \end{bmatrix}$

12. $\begin{bmatrix} 1 & 3 & 9 \\ 2 & 7 & 5 \\ 3 & 6 & 8 \end{bmatrix} \begin{bmatrix} -2 & 0 & 7 \\ 1 & 8 & 3 \\ 2 & 4 & 21 \end{bmatrix} = \begin{bmatrix} 19 & 60 & 205 \\ 13 & 76 & 140 \\ 16 & 80 & 207 \end{bmatrix}$

14. BC - AC = (B - A)C; see solution to problem 13.

16. $\left[\begin{array}{cc|cc} 4 & 1 & 1 & 0 \\ 3 & 1 & 0 & 1 \end{array}\right] \rightarrow \left[\begin{array}{cc|cc} 1 & \frac{1}{4} & \frac{1}{4} & 0 \\ 3 & 1 & 0 & 1 \end{array}\right] \rightarrow \left[\begin{array}{cc|cc} 1 & \frac{1}{4} & \frac{1}{4} & 0 \\ 0 & \frac{1}{4} & -\frac{3}{4} & 1 \end{array}\right] \rightarrow \left[\begin{array}{cc|cc} 1 & 0 & 1 & -1 \\ 0 & 1 & -3 & 4 \end{array}\right] \rightarrow A^{-1} = \begin{bmatrix} 1 & -1 \\ -3 & 4 \end{bmatrix}$

18. $\left[\begin{array}{ccc|ccc} -1 & 2 & 0 & 1 & 0 & 0 \\ 3 & 2 & -1 & 0 & 1 & 0 \\ 4 & 0 & 3 & 0 & 0 & 1 \end{array}\right] \rightarrow \left[\begin{array}{ccc|ccc} 1 & -2 & 0 & -1 & 0 & 0 \\ 0 & 8 & -1 & 3 & 1 & 0 \\ 0 & 8 & 3 & 4 & 0 & 1 \end{array}\right] \rightarrow \left[\begin{array}{ccc|ccc} 1 & -2 & 0 & -1 & 0 & 0 \\ 0 & 1 & -\frac{1}{8} & \frac{3}{8} & \frac{1}{8} & 0 \\ 0 & 0 & 4 & 1 & -1 & 1 \end{array}\right] \rightarrow$

$\left[\begin{array}{ccc|ccc} 1 & 0 & -\frac{1}{4} & -\frac{1}{4} & \frac{1}{4} & 0 \\ 0 & 1 & 0 & \frac{15}{32} & \frac{11}{32} & \frac{1}{32} \\ 0 & 0 & 1 & \frac{1}{4} & -\frac{1}{4} & \frac{1}{4} \end{array}\right] \rightarrow \left[\begin{array}{ccc|ccc} 1 & 0 & 0 & -\frac{3}{16} & \frac{3}{16} & \frac{1}{16} \\ 0 & 1 & 0 & \frac{15}{32} & \frac{11}{32} & \frac{1}{32} \\ 0 & 0 & 1 & \frac{1}{4} & -\frac{1}{4} & \frac{1}{4} \end{array}\right] \rightarrow A^{-1} = \begin{bmatrix} -\frac{3}{16} & \frac{3}{16} & \frac{1}{16} \\ \frac{15}{32} & \frac{11}{32} & \frac{1}{32} \\ \frac{1}{4} & -\frac{1}{4} & \frac{1}{4} \end{bmatrix}$

20. $\left[\begin{array}{ccc|ccc} -6 & 6 & 2 & 1 & 0 & 0 \\ 13 & 3 & 1 & 0 & 1 & 0 \\ 8 & -8 & 8 & 0 & 0 & 1 \end{array}\right] \rightarrow \left[\begin{array}{ccc|ccc} 1 & -1 & -\frac{1}{3} & \frac{1}{6} & 0 & 0 \\ 0 & 16 & -\frac{10}{3} & -\frac{15}{6} & 1 & 0 \\ 0 & 0 & \frac{32}{3} & -\frac{4}{3} & 0 & 1 \end{array}\right] \rightarrow \left[\begin{array}{ccc|ccc} 1 & -1 & -\frac{1}{3} & \frac{1}{6} & 0 & 0 \\ 0 & 1 & -\frac{5}{24} & -\frac{15}{96} & \frac{1}{16} & 0 \\ 0 & 0 & 1 & -\frac{1}{8} & 0 & \frac{3}{32} \end{array}\right] \rightarrow$

$\left[\begin{array}{ccc|ccc} 1 & 0 & -\frac{15}{24} & \frac{1}{32} & \frac{1}{16} & 0 \\ 0 & 1 & 0 & -\frac{109}{192} & \frac{1}{16} & \frac{5}{256} \\ 0 & 0 & 1 & -\frac{1}{8} & 0 & \frac{3}{32} \end{array}\right] \rightarrow \left[\begin{array}{ccc|ccc} 1 & 0 & 0 & -\frac{7}{192} & \frac{1}{16} & \frac{15}{256} \\ 0 & 1 & 0 & -\frac{109}{192} & \frac{1}{16} & \frac{5}{256} \\ 0 & 0 & 1 & -\frac{1}{8} & 0 & \frac{3}{32} \end{array}\right] \rightarrow A^{-1} = \begin{bmatrix} -\frac{7}{192} & \frac{1}{16} & \frac{15}{256} \\ -\frac{109}{192} & \frac{1}{16} & \frac{5}{256} \\ -\frac{1}{8} & 0 & \frac{3}{32} \end{bmatrix}$

22. $\left[\begin{array}{ccc|ccc} 9 & 6 & -3 & 1 & 0 & 0 \\ 2 & -6 & 4 & 0 & 1 & 0 \\ -3 & 2 & 1 & 0 & 0 & 1 \end{array}\right] \rightarrow \left[\begin{array}{ccc|ccc} 0 & 12 & 0 & 1 & 0 & 3 \\ 1 & -3 & 2 & 0 & \frac{1}{2} & 0 \\ -3 & 2 & 1 & 0 & 0 & 1 \end{array}\right] \rightarrow \left[\begin{array}{ccc|ccc} 1 & -3 & 2 & 0 & \frac{1}{2} & 0 \\ 0 & 12 & 0 & 1 & 0 & 3 \\ 0 & -7 & 7 & 0 & \frac{3}{2} & 1 \end{array}\right] \rightarrow$

$\left[\begin{array}{ccc|ccc} 1 & -3 & 2 & 0 & \frac{1}{2} & 0 \\ 0 & 1 & 0 & \frac{1}{12} & 0 & \frac{1}{4} \\ 0 & -1 & 1 & 0 & \frac{3}{14} & \frac{1}{7} \end{array}\right] \rightarrow \left[\begin{array}{ccc|ccc} 1 & 0 & 2 & \frac{1}{4} & \frac{1}{2} & \frac{3}{4} \\ 0 & 1 & 0 & \frac{1}{12} & 0 & \frac{1}{4} \\ 0 & 0 & 1 & \frac{1}{12} & \frac{3}{14} & \frac{11}{28} \end{array}\right] \rightarrow \left[\begin{array}{ccc|ccc} 1 & 0 & 0 & \frac{1}{12} & \frac{1}{14} & -\frac{1}{28} \\ 0 & 1 & 0 & \frac{1}{12} & 0 & \frac{1}{4} \\ 0 & 0 & 1 & \frac{1}{12} & \frac{3}{14} & \frac{11}{28} \end{array}\right] \rightarrow$

$A^{-1} = \begin{bmatrix} \frac{1}{12} & \frac{1}{14} & -\frac{1}{28} \\ \frac{1}{12} & 0 & \frac{1}{4} \\ \frac{1}{12} & \frac{3}{14} & \frac{11}{28} \end{bmatrix}$

24. $\left[\begin{array}{ccc|c} 2 & 3 & -1 & 5 \\ 1 & -1 & 1 & 1 \\ 3 & -3 & 3 & 3 \end{array}\right] \rightarrow \left[\begin{array}{ccc|c} 1 & -1 & 1 & 1 \\ 2 & 3 & -1 & 5 \\ 3 & -3 & 3 & 3 \end{array}\right] \rightarrow \left[\begin{array}{ccc|c} 1 & -1 & 1 & 1 \\ 0 & 5 & -3 & 3 \\ 0 & 0 & 0 & 0 \end{array}\right] \rightarrow \left[\begin{array}{ccc|c} 1 & -1 & 1 & 1 \\ 0 & 1 & -\frac{3}{5} & \frac{3}{5} \\ 0 & 0 & 0 & 0 \end{array}\right] \rightarrow$

$\left[\begin{array}{ccc|c} 1 & 0 & \frac{2}{5} & \frac{8}{5} \\ 0 & 1 & -\frac{3}{5} & \frac{3}{5} \\ 0 & 0 & 0 & 0 \end{array}\right] \rightarrow \left[\begin{array}{c} x_1 = 1.6 - 0.4x_3 \\ x_2 = 0.6 + 0.6x_3 \\ \text{Infinitely many solutions.} \end{array}\right] \left[\begin{array}{lll} \text{If } x_3 = -1 \rightarrow & x_1 = 2.0 & x_2 = 0 \\ \text{If } x_3 = 0 \rightarrow & x_1 = 1.6 & x_2 = 0.6 \\ \text{If } x_3 = 1 \rightarrow & x_1 = 1.2 & x_2 = 1.2 \end{array}\right]$

26. $\left[\begin{array}{ccc|c} 2 & -1 & 3 & 5 \\ 1 & 0 & 2 & 0 \\ 3 & 2 & 1 & -3 \end{array}\right] \rightarrow \left[\begin{array}{ccc|c} 1 & 0 & 2 & 0 \\ 2 & -1 & 3 & 5 \\ 3 & 2 & 1 & -3 \end{array}\right] \rightarrow \left[\begin{array}{ccc|c} 1 & 0 & 2 & 0 \\ 0 & -1 & -1 & 5 \\ 0 & 2 & -5 & -3 \end{array}\right] \rightarrow$

$\left[\begin{array}{ccc|c} 1 & 0 & 2 & 0 \\ 0 & 1 & 1 & -5 \\ 0 & 0 & -7 & 7 \end{array}\right] \rightarrow \left[\begin{array}{ccc|c} 1 & 0 & 2 & 0 \\ 0 & 1 & 1 & -5 \\ 0 & 0 & 1 & -1 \end{array}\right] \rightarrow \left[\begin{array}{ccc|c} 1 & 0 & 0 & 2 \\ 0 & 1 & 0 & -4 \\ 0 & 0 & 1 & -1 \end{array}\right] \rightarrow \left[\begin{array}{c} x_1 = 2 \\ x_2 = -4 \\ x_3 = -1 \end{array}\right]$

28. $\left[\begin{array}{ccc|c} 1 & 0 & -1 & 2 \\ 2 & -1 & 0 & 4 \\ 1 & 1 & 1 & 6 \end{array}\right] \rightarrow \left[\begin{array}{ccc|c} 1 & 0 & -1 & 2 \\ 0 & -1 & 2 & 0 \\ 0 & 1 & 0 & 4 \end{array}\right] \rightarrow \left[\begin{array}{ccc|c} 1 & 0 & -1 & 2 \\ 0 & 1 & -2 & 0 \\ 0 & 0 & 4 & 4 \end{array}\right] \rightarrow \left[\begin{array}{ccc|c} 1 & 0 & 0 & 3 \\ 0 & 1 & 0 & 2 \\ 0 & 0 & 1 & 1 \end{array}\right] \rightarrow \left[\begin{array}{c} x_1 = 3 \\ x_2 = 2 \\ x_3 = 1 \end{array}\right]$

30. $\left[\begin{array}{ccc|c} 2 & -1 & -3 & 0 \\ 1 & -2 & 1 & 4 \end{array}\right] \rightarrow \left[\begin{array}{ccc|c} 1 & -2 & 1 & 4 \\ 0 & 3 & -5 & -8 \end{array}\right] \rightarrow \left[\begin{array}{ccc|c} 1 & 0 & -\frac{7}{3} & -\frac{4}{3} \\ 0 & 1 & -\frac{5}{3} & -\frac{8}{3} \end{array}\right] \rightarrow$

$\left[\begin{array}{c} x_1 = -\frac{4}{3} + \frac{7}{3}x_3 \\ x_2 = -\frac{8}{3} + \frac{5}{3}x_3 \\ \text{Infinitely many solutions} \end{array}\right] \left[\begin{array}{lll} \text{If } x_3 = -1 \text{, then;} & x_1 = -\frac{11}{3}, & x_2 = -\frac{13}{3}. \\ \text{If } x_3 = 0 \text{, then;} & x_1 = -\frac{4}{3}, & x_2 = -\frac{8}{3}. \\ \text{If } x_3 = 1 \text{, then;} & x_1 = 1, & x_2 = -1. \end{array}\right]$

32. $\left[\begin{array}{ccc|c} 1 & -1 & 2 & 6 \\ 2 & 2 & -1 & -1 \end{array}\right] \rightarrow \left[\begin{array}{ccc|c} 1 & -1 & 2 & 6 \\ 0 & 4 & -5 & -13 \end{array}\right] \rightarrow \left[\begin{array}{ccc|c} 1 & -1 & 2 & 6 \\ 0 & 1 & -\frac{5}{4} & -\frac{13}{4} \end{array}\right] \rightarrow \left[\begin{array}{ccc|c} 1 & 0 & \frac{3}{4} & \frac{11}{4} \\ 0 & 1 & -\frac{5}{4} & -\frac{13}{4} \end{array}\right] \rightarrow$

$\left[\begin{array}{c} x_1 = \frac{11}{4} - \frac{3}{4}x_3 \\ x_2 = -\frac{13}{4} + \frac{5}{4}x_3 \\ \text{Infinitely many solutions.} \end{array}\right] \left[\begin{array}{lll} \text{If } x_3 = -1 \text{, then;} & x_1 = \frac{7}{2}, & x_2 = -\frac{9}{2}. \\ \text{If } x_3 = 0 \text{, then;} & x_1 = \frac{11}{4}, & x_2 = -\frac{13}{4}. \\ \text{If } x_3 = 1 \text{, then;} & x_1 = 2, & x_2 = -2. \end{array}\right]$

Chapter 2 - p.35

34. $\left[\begin{array}{rr|r} 1 & -2 & 0 \\ 2 & 1 & 5 \\ 1 & -3 & -3 \end{array}\right] \rightarrow \left[\begin{array}{rr|r} 1 & -2 & 0 \\ 0 & 5 & 5 \\ 0 & -1 & -3 \end{array}\right] \rightarrow \left[\begin{array}{rr|r} 1 & 0 & 6 \\ 0 & 1 & 1 \\ 0 & 1 & 3 \end{array}\right] \rightarrow \left[\begin{array}{rr|r} 1 & 0 & 6 \\ 0 & 1 & 1 \\ 0 & 0 & 2 \end{array}\right] \rightarrow$ No solution.

36. $[t_1 \;\; t_2]\begin{bmatrix} \frac{1}{4} & \frac{3}{4} \\ \frac{2}{3} & \frac{1}{3} \end{bmatrix} = [t_1 \;\; t_2]; \; t_1 + t_2 = 1$

$\frac{1}{4}t_1 + \frac{2}{3}t_2 = t_1$

$\frac{3}{4}t_1 + \frac{1}{3}t_2 = t_2$

$\frac{3}{4}t_1 = \frac{2}{3}t_2$

$9t_1 = 8t_2$

$t_2 = 1 - t_1$

$t_1 = \frac{8}{17}, \; t_2 = \frac{9}{17}$

38. I T S O V E R Z
9 20 19 15 22 5 18 26

$$\begin{bmatrix} 1 & 0 & 0 \\ 3 & 1 & 5 \\ -2 & 0 & 1 \end{bmatrix}\begin{bmatrix} 9 & 15 & 18 \\ 20 & 22 & 26 \\ 19 & 5 & 26 \end{bmatrix} = \begin{bmatrix} 9 & 15 & 18 \\ 142 & 92 & 210 \\ 1 & -25 & -10 \end{bmatrix}$$

The coded message is: 9 142 1 15 92 -25 18 210 -10

CHAPTER 3

Exercise 3.2 (page 124)

2.

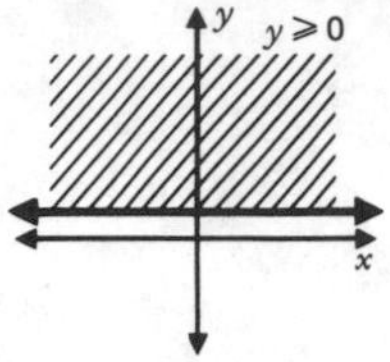

4.

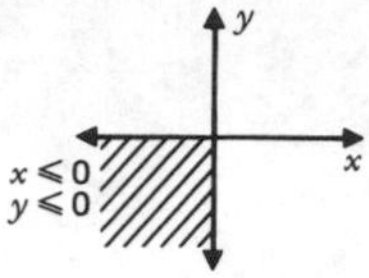

6.

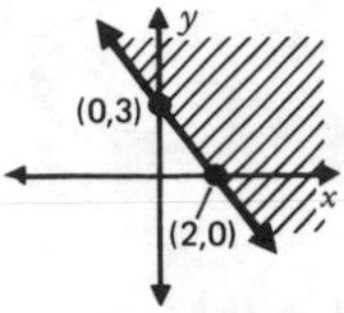

8

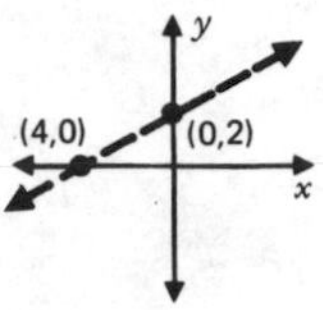

10.

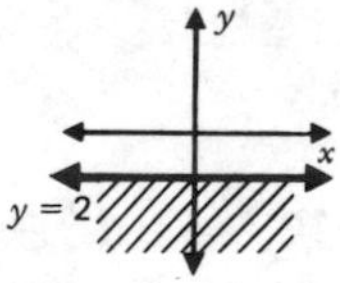

12.

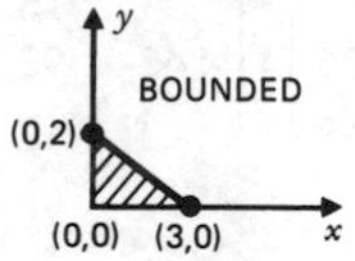

14.

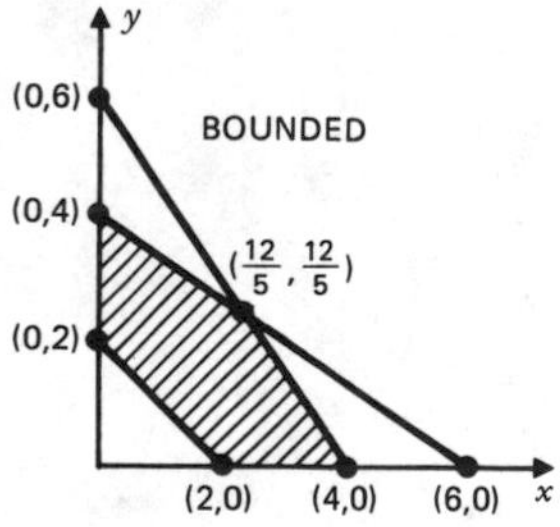

16.

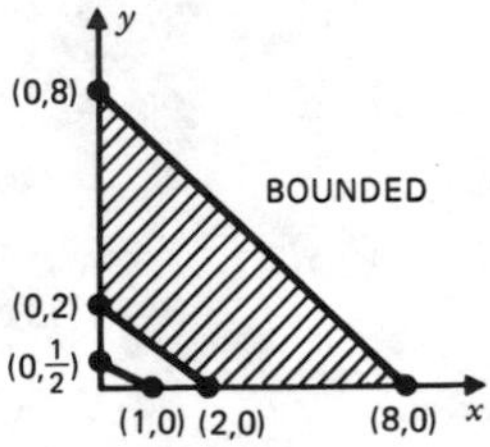

18.

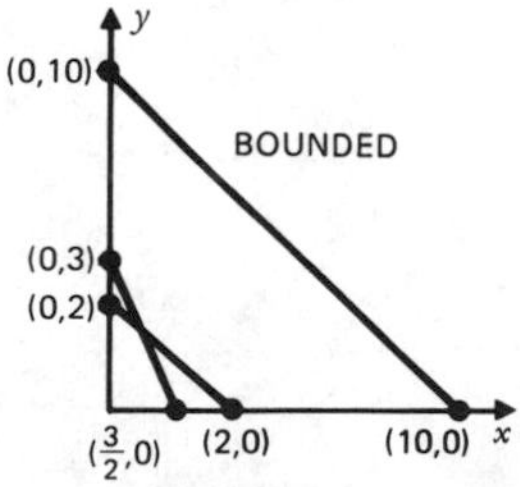

20.

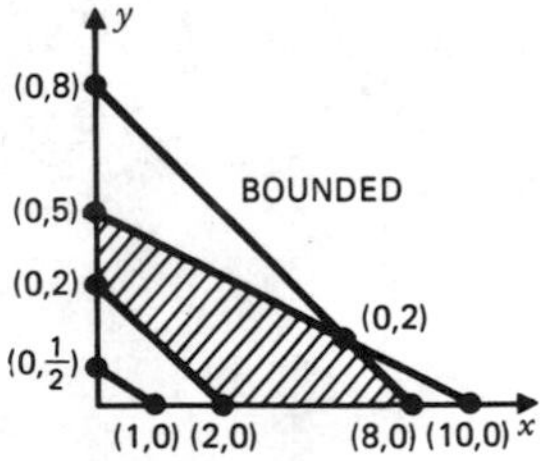

22.

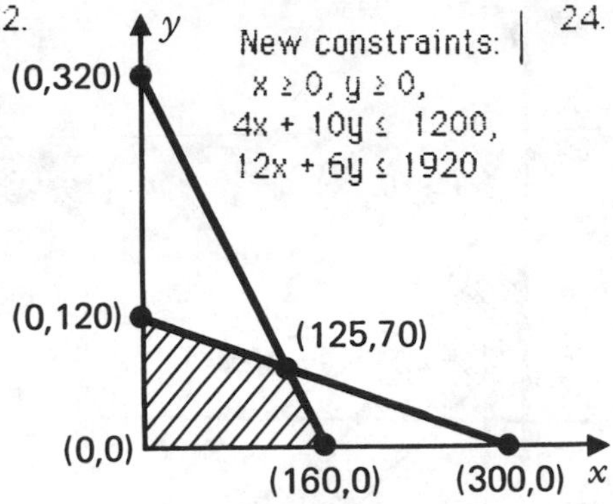

New constraints:
$x \geq 0,\ y \geq 0,$
$4x + 10y \leq 1200,$
$12x + 6y \leq 1920$

24.

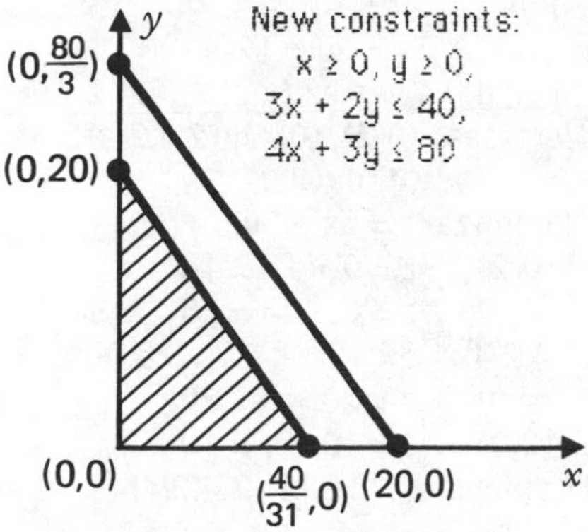

New constraints:
$x \geq 0,\ y \geq 0,$
$3x + 2y \leq 40,$
$4x + 3y \leq 80$

Exercise 3.3 (page 136)

2. Vertices: (2,2), (2,7), (7,8), (8,1)
Objective function: $z = 3x + 27y$
At (2,2), $z = 6 + 54 = 60$
At (2,7), $z = 6 + 189 = 195$
At (7,8), $z = 21 + 216 = 237$
At (8,1), $z = 24 + 27 = 51$
The maximum value is 237 at (7,8).
The minimum value is 51 at (8,1).

4. $z = 3x + y$
(2,2): $z = 6 + 2 = 8$
(2,7): $z = 6 + 7 = 15$
(7,8): $z = 21 + 8 = 29$
(8,1): $z = 24 + 1 = 25$
Maximum: 29 at (7,8)
Minimum: 8 at (2,2)

6. $z = x + 5y$
(2,2): $z = 2 + 10 = 12$
(2,7): $z = 2 + 35 = 37$
(7,8): $z = 7 + 40 = 47$
(8,1): $z = 8 + 5 = 13$
Maximum: 47 at (7,8)
Minimum: 12 at (2,2)

8. Vertices: (0,0), (0,2), (3,0)
Maximize $z = 5x + 7y$
(0,0): $z = 0 + 0 = 0$
(0,2): $z = 0 + 14 = 14$
(3,0): $z = 15 + 0 = 15$
Maximum: 15 at (3,0)

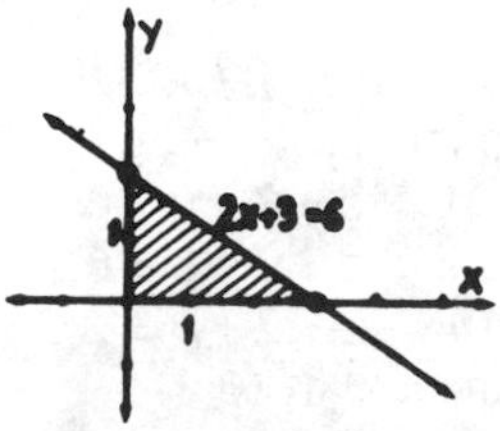

10. Solve $2x + 3y = 12$
$3x + 2y = 12$
to find the vertex $(x,y) = (2.4,2.4)$
Vertices: (0,2), (0,4), (2.4,2.4), (4,0), (2,0)
Maximize $z = 5x + 7y$
(0,2): $z = 0 + 14 = 14$
(0,4): $z = 0 + 28 = 28$
(2.4,2.4): $z = 12 + 16.8 = 28.8$
(4,0): $z = 20 + 0 = 20$
(2,0): $z = 10 + 0 = 10$
Maximum: 28.8 at (2.4,2.4)

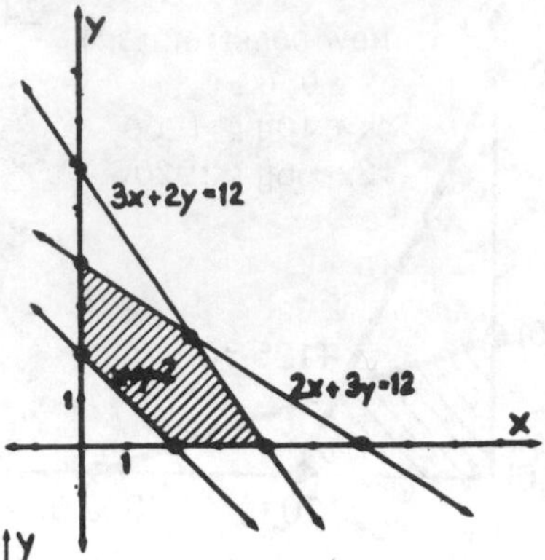

12. Solve $x + y = 8$
$x + 2y = 10$
to find the vertex $(x,y) = (6,2)$
Vertices: (0,2), (0,5), (6,2), (8,0), (2,0)
Maximize $z = 5x + 7y$
(0,2): $z = 0 + 14 = 14$
(0,5): $z = 0 + 35 = 35$
(6,2): $z = 30 + 14 = 44$
(8,0): $z = 40 + 0 = 40$
(2,0): $z = 10 + 0 = 10$
Maximum: 44 at (6,2)

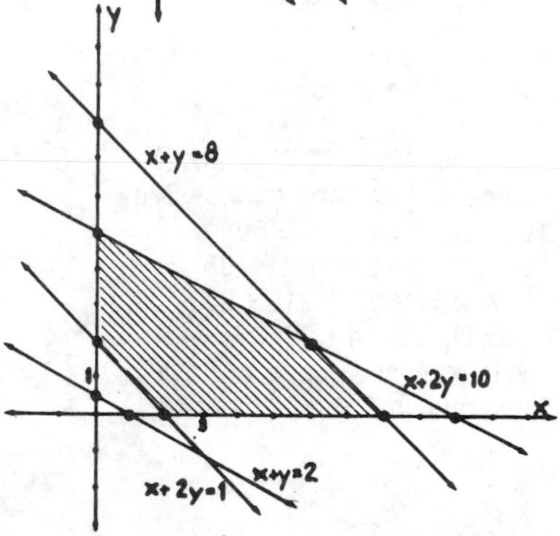

14. $z = 5x + 7y$ has no maximum under these conditions.

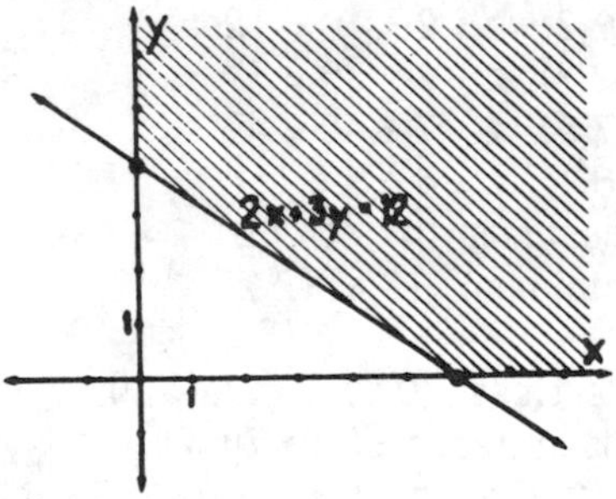

16. Vertices: (0,0), (0,2), (1,0)
Minimize $z = 2x + 3y$
(0,0): $z = 0 + 0 = 0$
(0,2): $z = 0 + 6 = 6$
(1,0): $z = 2 + 0 = 2$
Minimum 0 at (0,0)

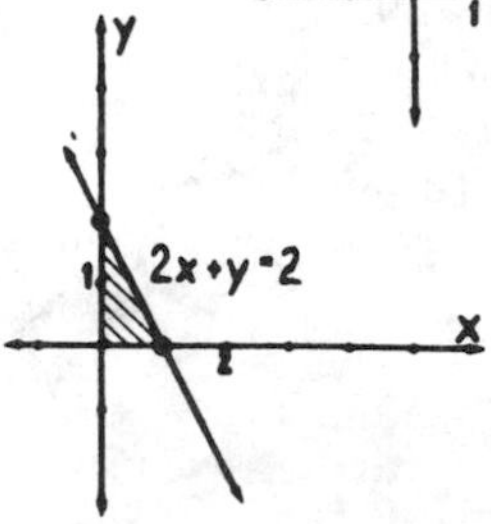

18. Vertices: (0,2), (0,10), (10,0), (3,0)

Minimize $z = 2x + 3y$

(0,2): $z = 0 + 6 = 6$

(0,10): $z = 0 + 30 = 30$

(10,0): $z = 20 + 0 = 20$

(3,0): $z = 6 + 0 = 6$

The minimum value is 6, on the line segment between (0,2) and (3,0).

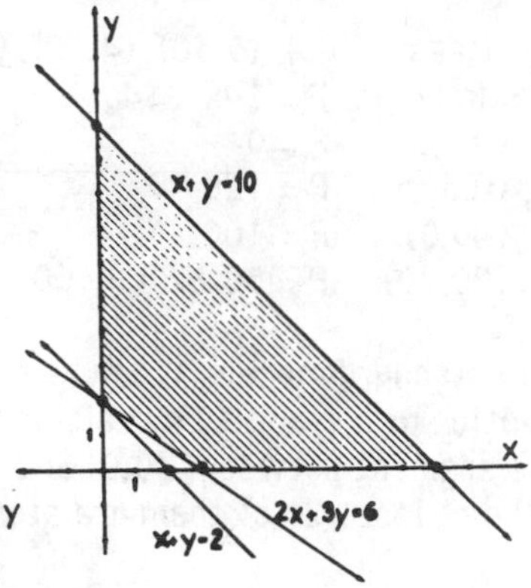

20. Solve $x + 2y = 10$
$x + y = 8$

to find the vertex (x,y) = (2,6)

Vertices: (0,2), (0,5), (8,0), (3,0), (6,2)

Minimize $z = 2x + 3y$

(0,2): $z = 0 + 6 = 6$

(0,5): $z = 0 + 15 = 15$

(8,0): $z = 16 + 0 = 16$

(3,0): $z = 6 + 0 = 6$

(6,2): $z = 12 + 6 = 18$

The minimum value is 6, on the line segment between (0,2) and (3,0).

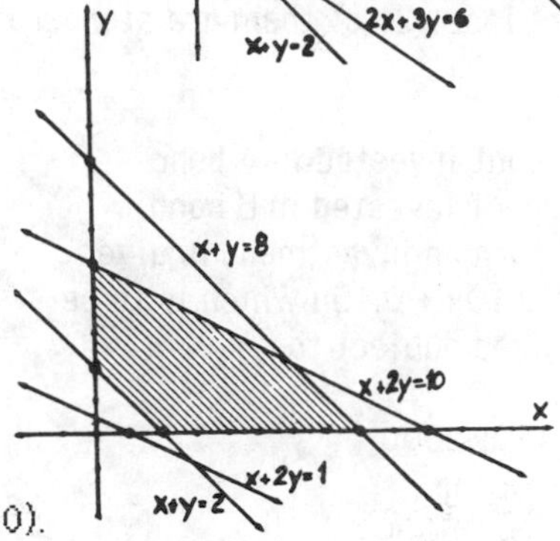

22. Solve $x + 2y = 10$
$2x + y = 10$

to find the vertex (x,y) = (10/3,10/3)

Vertices: (10/3,10/3), (0,10), (10,0)

$z = 2x + 3y$

(10/3,10/3): $z = 20/3 + 10 = 50/3$

(0,10): $z = 0 + 30 = 30$

(10,0): $z = 20 + 0 = 20$

Minimum: 50/3 at (10/3,10/3)

Maximum: 30 at (0,10)

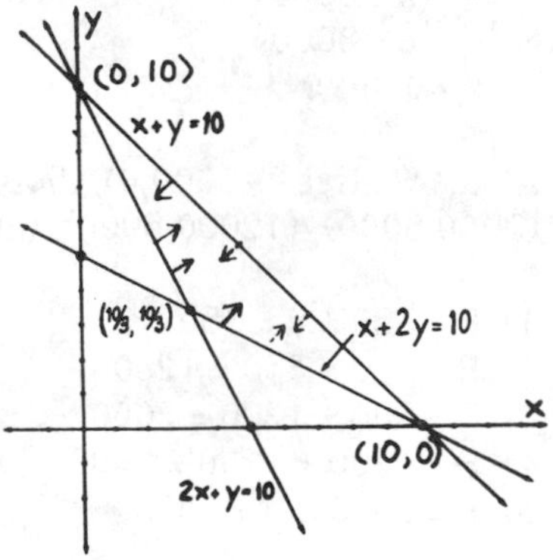

24. (Same vertices as problem 22)

$z = x + 2y$

(10/3,10/3): $z = 10/3 + 20/3 = 10$

(0,10): $z = 0 + 20 = 20$

(10,0): $z = 10 + 0 = 10$

Minimum: 10, on the line segment between (0,10) and (10/3,10/3).

Maximum: 20 at (0,10).

26. (Same vertices as problem 22)

$z = 3x + 6y$

(10/3,10/3): $z = 10 + 20 = 30$

(0,10): $z = 0 + 60 = 60$

(10,0): $z = 30 + 0 = 30$

Minimum: 30, on the line segment between (0,10) and (10/3,10/3).

Maximum: 60 at (0,10).

28. Vertices: (0,0), (0,30), (40,0), (20,20)
Maximize $P = \$4x + \$4y$
(0,0): $P = 0$
(0,30): $P = 120$
(40,0): $P = 160$
(20,20): $P = 80 + 80 = 160$

40 standard models, 0 deluxe models; or 20 of each; or any combination of x standard models and y deluxe models such that (x,y) lies on the line segment between (40,0) and (20,20). (That is, the number of trucks is 40 and at least 20 of them are standard models.)

30. x = amount invested in A bond
y = amount invested in B bond
The return on investment is given by $P = 0.10x + 0.15y$ which is to be minimized subject to

$$x + y \leq 2000$$
$$x \geq y$$
$$x \geq 5000$$
$$y \leq 8000$$
$$x \geq 0,\ y \geq 0$$

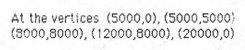

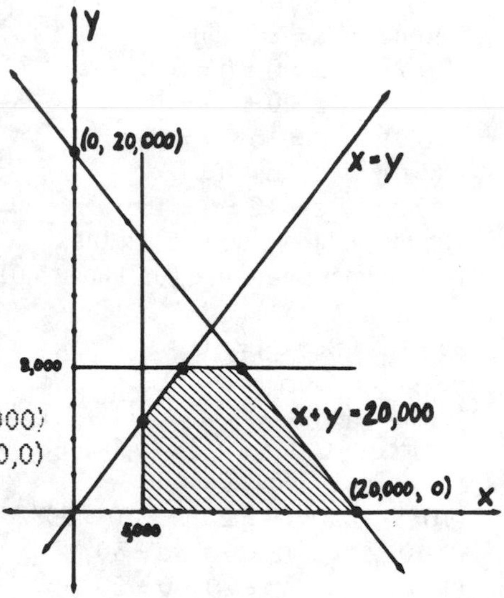

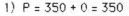

At the vertices (5000,0), (5000,5000) (8000,8000), (12000,8000), (20000,0)

1) $P = 350 + 0 = 350$
2) $P = 500 + 750 = 1250$
3) $P = 800 + 1200 = 2000$
4) $P = 1200 + 1200 = 2400$
5) $P = 2000 + 0 = 2000$

The maximum income is \$2400, obtained by investing \$12,000 in the type A bond and \$8,000 in type B.

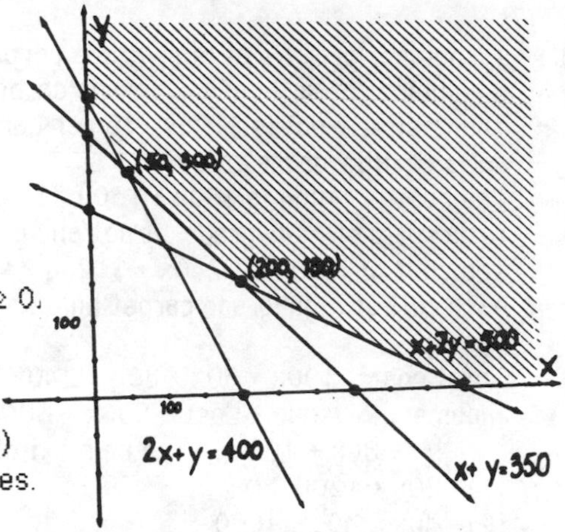

32. x = units of F_1, y = units of F_2

vitamins $2x + y \geq 400$
minerals $x + 2y \geq 500$
calories $4x + 4y \geq 1400$
Solve $2x + y = 400$
$4x + 4y = 1400$ $x \geq 0, y \geq 0.$
to find the vertex $(x,y) = (50,300)$
Solve $x + 2y = 500$
$4x + 4y = 1400$
to find the vertex $(x,y) = (200,150)$
(500,0) and (0,400) are also vertices.
Minimize $C = 0.05x + 0.03y$
1) $C = (0.05)(50) + (0.03)(300) = 11.50$
2) $C = (0.05)(200) + (0.03)(150) = 14.50$
3) $C = (0.05)(500) + 0 = 25.00$
4) $C = 0 + (0.03)(400) = 12.00$
The minimum cost is \$11.50, using 50 units of F_1 and 300 units of F_2.

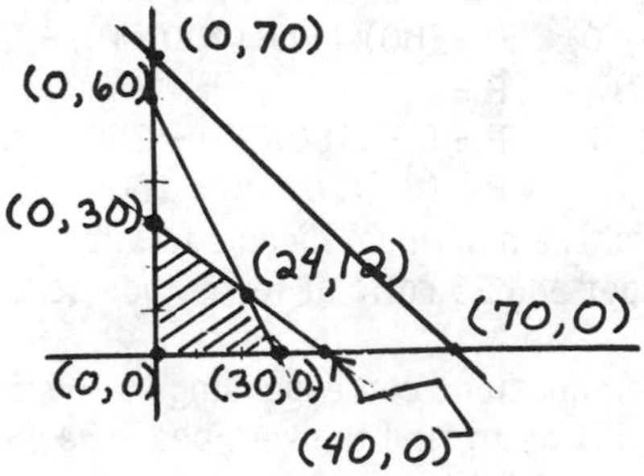

34. x = acres of soybeans
y = acres of corn
$P = \$300x + \$150y$
$x + y \leq 70$
$60x + 30y \leq 1800$
$3x + 4y \leq 120$
$x \geq 0, y \geq 0$
Solve $60x + 30y = 1800$
$3x + 4y = 120$
to find the vertex $(x,y) = (24,12)$
The other vertices are (0,0), (30,0), and (0,30).
Maximize $P = 300x + 150y$
1) $P = (300)(24) + (150)(12) = 9000$
2) $P = 0 + 0 = 0$
3) $P = (300)(30) + 0 = 9000$
4) $P = 0 + (150)(30) = 4500$

The maximum profit is \$9,000 , obtained by planting x acres of soybeans and y acres of corn, where (x,y) is any point on the line segment between (30,0) and (24,12).

36. x = number of rolls of high-grade carpet
y = number of rolls of low-grade carpet
The cost of wool is \$100x (\$5 per yard times 20 yards per roll, for x rolls of high-grade carpet)
The cost of nylon is \$80x + \$80y (\$2 per yard times 40 yards per roll, for x rolls of high-grade carpet and y rolls of low-grade carpet)
The cost of labor is \$240x + \$120y (\$6 per hour times 40 hours for each roll of high-grade carpet and 20 hours for each roll of low-grade carpet)
Total cost: $100x + 80x + 80y + 240x + 120y = 420x + 200y$
Income = Revenue - Cost = $500x + 300y - (420x + 200y)$
$= 80x + 100y = P$ to be maximized, subject to the constraints:
(1) $20x \le 1200$
(2) $40x + 40y \le 1000$
(3) $40x + 20y \le 800$
$x \ge 0,\ y \ge 0.$

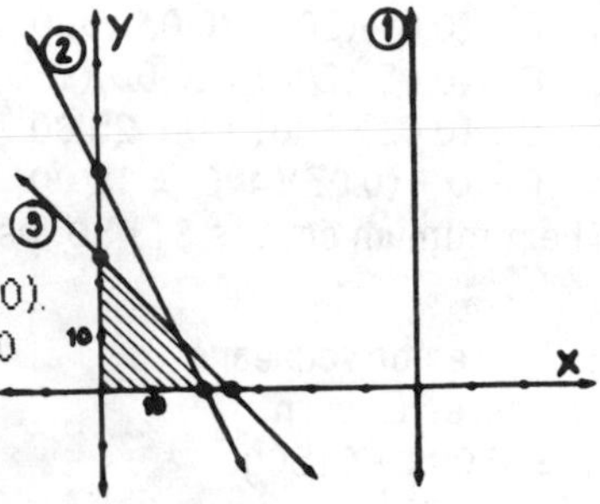

Solve the equations $40x + 40y = 1000$
$40x + 20y = 800$
to find the vertex (15,10).
The other vertices are (0,0), (0,25), (20,0).
(15,10): $P = (80)(15) + (100)(10) = 2200$
(0,0): $P = 0$
(0,25): $P = 0 + (100)(25) = 2500$
(20,0): $P = (80)(20) + 0 = 1600$
Thus, the maximum income is \$2500, from 0 rolls of high-grade carpet and 25 rolls of low-grade carpet.

38. Write equations corresponding to the 5 constraints and solve them 3 at a time to find the vertices. (Be careful, however, to avoid non-feasible solutions.)

(1) $x + 2y + z = 25$
(2) $3x + 2y + 3z = 30$
(3) $x = 0$
(4) $y = 0$
(5) $z = 0$

(1), (2), (3):
$x = 0$
$2y + z = 25$
$2y + 3z = 30$
$2z = 5$
$z = 2.5,\ y = 11.25,\ x = 0$

(1), (2), (4):
$y = 0$
$x + z = 25$
$3x + 3z = 30$
No solution

(1), (2), (5):
$z = 0$
$x + 2y = 25$
$3x + 2y = 30$
$2x = 5$
$x = 2.5,\ y = 11.25,\ z = 0$

(1), (3), (4): $x = y = 0$, $z = 25$ (Not feasible - the constraint
$3x + 2y + 3z \leq 30$ is not satisfied.)
(1), (3), (5): $x = z = 0$, $y = 12.5$
(1), (4), (5): $x = z = 0$, $y = 25$ (Not feasible.)
(2), (3), (4); $x = y = 0$, $z = 10$
(2), (3), (5): $x = z = 0$, $y = 15$ (Not feasible - the constraint
$x + 2y + z \leq 25$ is not satisfied.)
(2), (4), (5): $y = z = 0$, $x = 10$
(3), (4), (5): $x = y = z = 0$
The vertices are (0,11.25,2.5), (2.5,11.25,0), (0,12.5,0), (0,0,10), (10,0,0), and (0,0,0). Testing the objective function ($P = 2x + y + 3z$) at each:

$P = 0 + 11.25 + 3(2.5) = 18.75$
$P = 2(2.5) + 11.25 + 0 = 16.25$
$P = 0 + 12.5 + 0 = 12.5$
$P = 0 + 0 + 3(10) = 30$
$P = 2(10) + 0 + 0 = 20$
$P = 0 + 0 + 0 = 0$

We see that the maximum value is 30, when $x = y = 0$ and $z = 10$.

Review Exercises (page 140)

2.

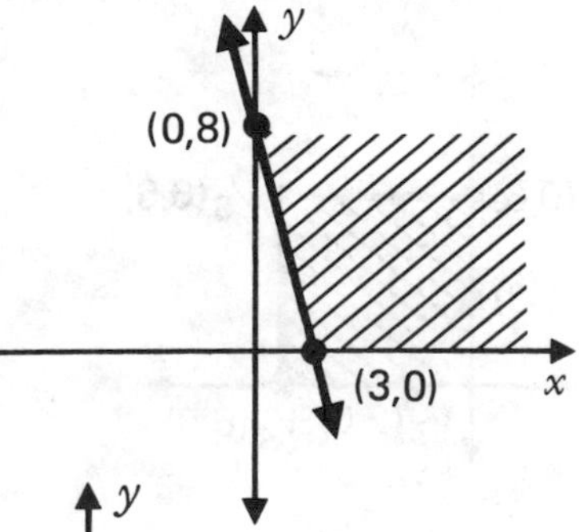

4.

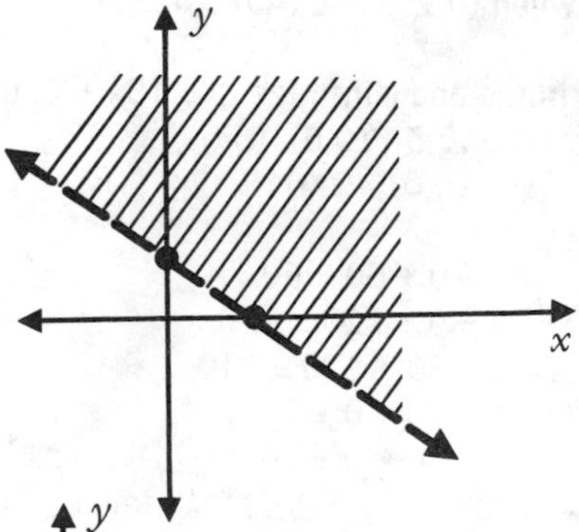

6.

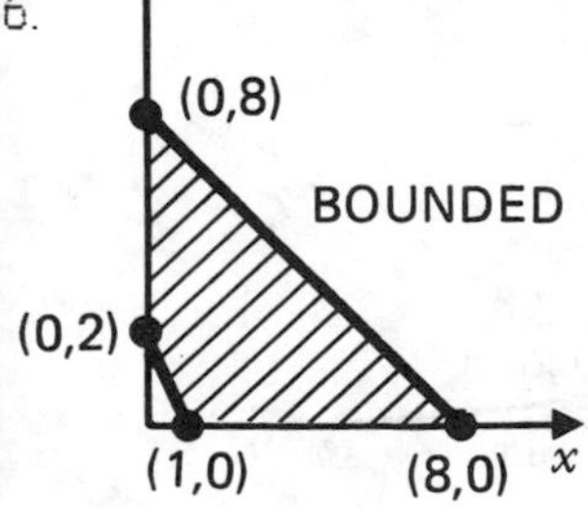

8.

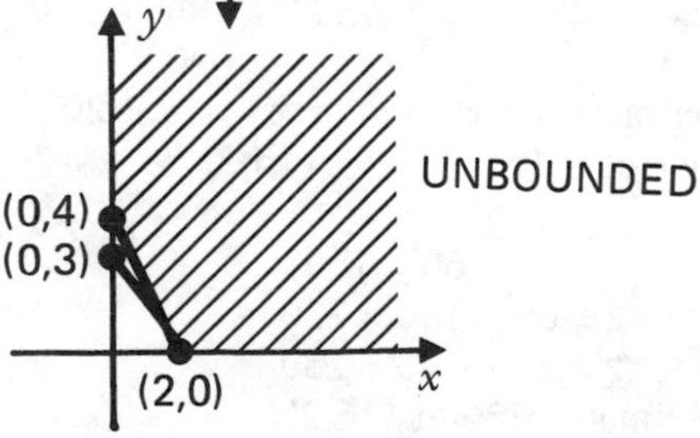

10.

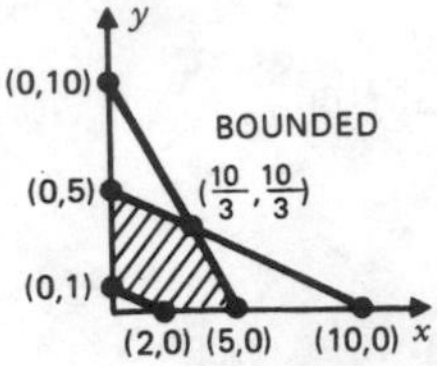

(12-18) Vertices: (0,10), (0,20), (40/3,40/3)
(20,0), (10,0)

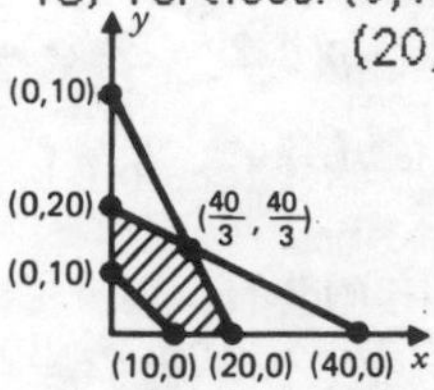

12. Maximize $z = x + y$
1) $z = 0 + 10 = 10$
2) $z = 0 + 20 = 20$
3) $z = 40/3 + 40/3 = 80/3$
4) $z = 20 + 0 = 20$
5) $z = 10 + 0 = 10$
Maximum: 80/3 at (40/3,40/3)

14. Minimize $z = 3x + 2y$
1) $z = 20 + 0 = 20$
2) $z = 0 + 40 = 40$
3) $z = 40 + 80/3 = 200/3$
4) $z = 60 + 0 = 60$
5) $z = 30 + 0 = 30$
Minimum: 20 at (0,10)

16. Maximize $z = x + 2y$
1) $z = 0 + 20 = 20$
2) $z = 0 + 40 = 40$
3) $z = 40/3 + 80/3 = 40$
4) $z = 20 + 0 = 20$
5) $z = 30 + 0 = 30$
Maximum: 40 on line segment between (0,20) and (40/3,40/3).

18. Minimize $z = x + y$
1) $z = 0 + 10 = 10$
2) $z = 0 + 20 = 20$
3) $z = 40/3 + 40/3 = 80/3$
4) $z = 20 + 0 = 20$
5) $z = 10 + 0 = 10$
Minimum: 10 on line segment between (0,10) and (10,0).

20. Maximize and Minimize $z = 15x + 20y$
Vetices: (0,3), (0,6), (6,6),
(6,0), (2,0)

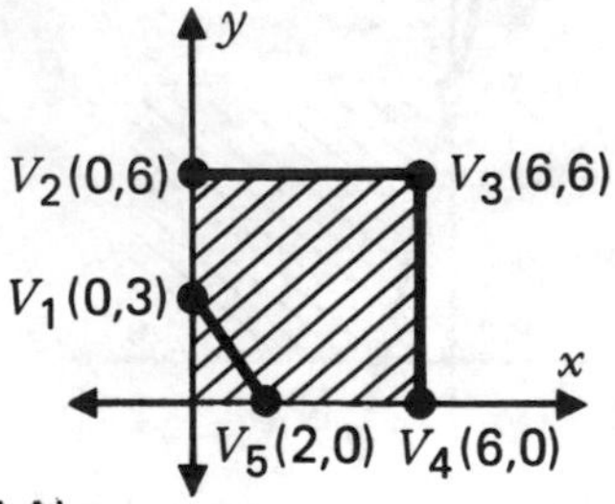

1) $z = 0 + 60 = 60$
2) $z = 0 + 120 = 120$
3) $z = 90 + 120 = 210$
4) $z = 90 + 0 = 90$
5) $z = 30 + 0 = 30$
Maximum: 210 at (6,6); Minimum: 30 at (2,0).

22. Maximize and Minimize $z = 15x + 20y$
Vertices: (6,3), (4,8), (16,2)

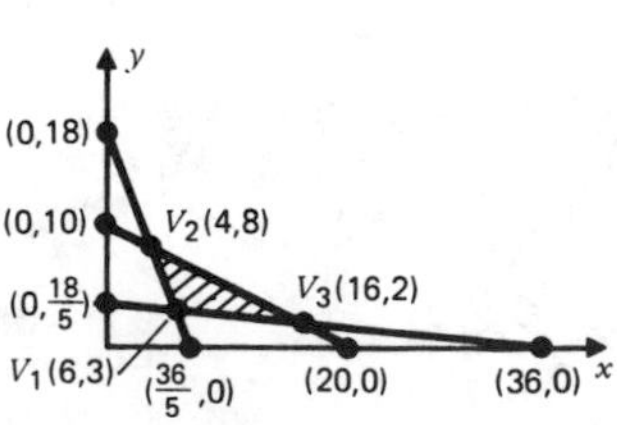

1) $z = 90 + 60 = 150$
2) $z = 60 + 160 = 220$
3) $z = 240 + 40 = 280$
Maximum: 280 at (16,2)
Minimum: 150 at (6,3)

24. Let x = number of # of beef
y = number of # of pork

Assume x + y = 100 to minimize the cost per hundredweight of the meatloaf mixture. Since beef is 25% fat, pork is 40% fat, and the mixture must be no more than 30% fat, we have:

$$.25x + .40y \le .30(x + y) = 30$$

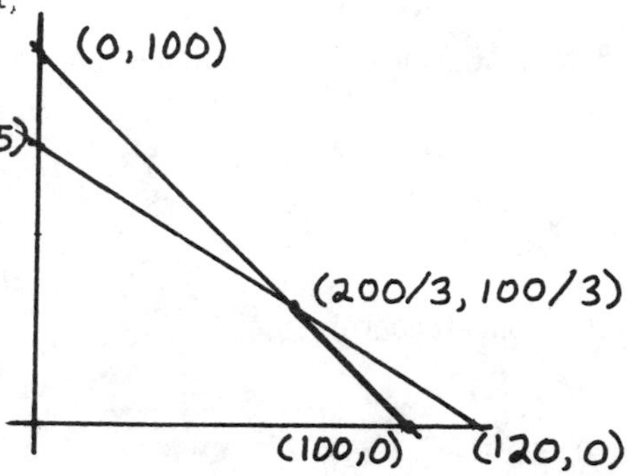

Therefore, minimize C = .70x + .50y subject to

$$x + y = 100$$
$$.25x + .40y \le 30$$
$$x \ge 0, y \ge 0$$

Vertices: (200/3,100/3) and (100,0)

$$C = (.70)(200/3) + (.50)(100/3) = 63.33$$
$$C = (.70)(100) + 0 = 70$$

Thus, the minimum cost of $63.33 per hundredweight is obtained by mixing two parts beef to one part pork.

26. Maximize P = 70x + 50y subject to

$$2x + y \le 48$$
$$x + y \le 32$$
$$x \ge 0, y \ge 0$$

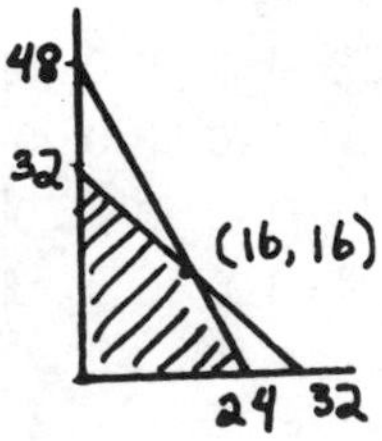

Vertices: (0,32), (16,16), (24,0)

1) P = 0 + 59(32) = 1600
2) P = 70(16) + 50(16) = 1920
3) P = 70(24) + 0 = 1680

The maximum profit of $1920 is obtained with 16 of each type of ski. (Fortunately, 16 is an even number.)

CHAPTER 4

Exercise 4.1 (page 156)

2. Standard.

4. Non-standard (must state $x_1 \geq 0$, $x_3 \geq 0$)

6. Non-standard

8. Non-standard

10. Non-standard

12. $4x_1 - 2x_2 \leq 8 \quad x_1 \geq 0$
    $x_1 - x_2 \leq 6 \quad x_2 \geq 0$

14. Non-standardizable.

16. Non-standardizable.

18.
$$\begin{aligned} 3x_1 + 2x_2 - x_3 + x_4 \qquad\qquad &= 10 \\ x_1 - x_2 + 3x_3 \qquad + x_5 \qquad &= 12 \\ 2x_1 + x_2 + x_3 \qquad\qquad + x_6 &= 6 \\ -3x_1 - 2x_2 - x_3 \qquad\qquad + P &= 0 \end{aligned}$$
$x_1 \geq 0, x_2 \geq 0, x_3 \geq 0, x_4 \geq 0, x_5 \geq 0, x_6 \geq 0$

$$\begin{array}{c} \begin{matrix} x_1 & x_2 & x_3 & x_4 & x_5 & x_6 & P & \end{matrix} \\ \left[\begin{array}{rrrrrrr|r} 3 & 2 & -1 & 1 & 0 & 0 & 0 & 10 \\ 1 & -1 & 3 & 0 & 1 & 0 & 0 & 12 \\ 2 & 1 & 1 & 0 & 0 & 1 & 0 & 6 \\ -3 & -2 & -1 & 0 & 0 & 0 & 1 & 0 \end{array}\right] \end{array}$$

20. $$\begin{aligned} 1.2x_1 - 2.1x_2 + x_3 \qquad\qquad &= 0.5 \\ 0.3x_1 + 0.4x_2 \qquad + x_4 \qquad &= 1.5 \\ x_1 + x_2 \qquad\qquad + x_5 &= 0.7 \\ -2x_1 - 3x_2 \qquad\qquad + P &= 0 \end{aligned}$$

$$x_1 \geq 0,\ x_2 \geq 0,\ x_3 \geq 0,\ x_4 \geq 0,\ x_5 \geq 0$$

$$\begin{array}{cccccc} x_1 & x_2 & x_3 & x_4 & x_5 & P \end{array}$$
$$\left[\begin{array}{cccccc|c} 1.2 & -2.1 & 1 & 0 & 0 & 0 & 0.5 \\ 0.3 & 0.4 & 0 & 1 & 0 & 0 & 1.5 \\ 1 & 1 & 0 & 0 & 1 & 0 & 0.7 \\ -2 & -3 & 0 & 0 & 0 & 1 & 0.0 \end{array}\right]$$

22. $$\begin{aligned} 3x_1 + x_2 + x_3 + x_4 \qquad &= 10 \\ x_1 + x_2 + 3x_3 \qquad + x_5 &= 5 \\ -x_1 - 4x_2 - 2x_3 \qquad + P &= 0 \end{aligned}$$

$$x_1 \geq 0,\ x_2 \geq 0, x_3 \geq 0, x_4 \geq 0, x_5 \geq 0$$

$$\begin{array}{cccccc} x_1 & x_2 & x_3 & x_4 & x_5 & P \end{array}$$
$$\left[\begin{array}{cccccc|c} 0 & 1 & 1 & 1 & 0 & 0 & 10 \\ 1 & 1 & 3 & 0 & 1 & 0 & 5 \\ -1 & -4 & -2 & 0 & 0 & 1 & 0 \end{array}\right]$$

24. $$\begin{aligned} 2x_1 + x_2 + x_3 + x_4 \qquad &= 2 \\ x_1 - x_2 \qquad + x_5 \qquad &= 4 \\ 2x_1 + x_2 - x_3 \qquad + x_6 &= 2 \\ -2x_1 - x_2 - 3x_3 \qquad + P &= 0 \end{aligned}$$

$$x_1 \geq 0,\ x_2 \geq 0,\ x_3 \geq 0,\ x_4 \geq 0,\ x_5 \geq 0,\ x_6 \geq 0$$

$$\begin{array}{ccccccc} x_1 & x_2 & x_3 & x_4 & x_5 & x_6 & P \end{array}$$
$$\left[\begin{array}{ccccccc|c} 2 & 1 & 1 & 1 & 0 & 0 & 0 & 2 \\ 1 & -1 & 0 & 0 & 1 & 0 & 0 & 4 \\ 2 & 1 & -1 & 0 & 0 & 1 & 0 & 5 \\ -2 & -1 & -3 & 0 & 0 & 0 & 1 & 0 \end{array}\right]$$

26. $\quad x_1\ x_2\ x_3\ x_4$

$$\left[\begin{array}{cccc|c} 1 & 4 & 1 & 0 & 100 \\ 2 & \underline{5} & 0 & 1 & 50 \end{array}\right]\left[\begin{array}{c} x_3 \\ x_4 \end{array}\right] \qquad \left[\begin{array}{c} x_1 + 4x_2 + x_3 = 100 \\ 2x_1 + 5x_2 + x_4 = 50 \end{array}\right]$$

$$\left[\begin{array}{cccc|c} 1 & 4 & 1 & 0 & 100 \\ \frac{2}{5} & 1 & 0 & \frac{1}{5} & 10 \end{array}\right]\left[\begin{array}{c} x_3 \\ x_2 \end{array}\right]$$

$$\left[\begin{array}{cccc|c} -\frac{3}{5} & 0 & 1 & -\frac{4}{5} & 60 \\ \frac{2}{5} & 1 & 0 & \frac{1}{5} & 10 \end{array}\right]\left[\begin{array}{c} x_3 \\ x_2 \end{array}\right] \qquad \left[\begin{array}{c} x_3 = 60 + \frac{3}{5}x_1 + \frac{4}{5}x_4 \\ x_2 = 10 - \frac{2}{5}x_1 - \frac{1}{5}x_4 \end{array}\right]$$

28. $\quad x_1\ \ x_2\ x_3\ x_4\ x_5\ x_6$

$$\left[\begin{array}{cccccc|c} 1 & \underline{2} & 1 & 1 & 0 & 0 & 6 \\ 2 & 3 & 1 & 0 & 1 & 0 & 12 \\ 1 & -2 & 3 & 0 & 0 & 1 & 0 \end{array}\right]\left[\begin{array}{c} x_4 \\ x_5 \\ x_6 \end{array}\right] \qquad \left[\begin{array}{c} x_1 + 2x_2 + x_3 + x_4 = 6 \\ 2x_1 + 3x_2 + x_3 + x_5 = 12 \\ x_1 - 2x_2 + 3x_3 + x_6 = 0 \end{array}\right]$$

$$\begin{array}{cccccc} x_1 & x_2 & x_3 & x_4 & x_5 & x_6 \end{array}$$
$$\left[\begin{array}{cccccc|c} 0.5 & 1.0 & 0.5 & 0.5 & 0.0 & 0.0 & 3.0 \\ 2.0 & 3.0 & 1.0 & 0.0 & 1.0 & 0.0 & 12.0 \\ 1.0 & -2.0 & 3.0 & 0.0 & 0.0 & 1.0 & 0.0 \end{array}\right]$$

$$\left[\begin{array}{cccccc|c} 0.5 & 1.0 & 0.5 & 0.5 & 0.0 & 0.0 & 3.0 \\ 0.5 & 0.0 & -0.5 & -1.5 & 1.0 & 0.0 & 3.0 \\ 2.0 & 0.0 & 4.0 & 1.0 & 0.0 & 1.0 & 6.0 \end{array}\right]\left[\begin{array}{c} x_2 \\ x_5 \\ x_6 \end{array}\right] \qquad \left[\begin{array}{r} 0.5x_1 + x_2 + 0.5x_3 + 0.5x_4 = 3 \\ 0.5x_1 - 0.5x_3 - 0.5x_4 + x_5 = 3 \\ 2x_1 + 4x_3 + x_4 + x_6 = 6 \end{array}\right.$$

Exercise 4.2 (page 170)

2. (a) Final tableau. $P = 140$, $x_1 = 20$, $x_2 = 30$.

4. (b) Additional pivoting. Use the 3 in row 2, column 2.

6. (b) Additional pivoting. Use the 3 in row 1, column 2.

Chapter 4 - p.49

8. $x_1 \; x_2 \; x_3 \; x_4$

$$\left[\begin{array}{cccc|c} 2 & 1 & 1 & 0 & 10 \\ 1 & 2 & 0 & 1 & 10 \\ -1 & -5 & 0 & 0 & 0 \end{array}\right]\left[\begin{array}{c} x_3 \\ x_4 \\ \ \end{array}\right] \rightarrow \left[\begin{array}{cccc|c} \frac{3}{2} & 0 & 1 & -\frac{1}{2} & 5 \\ \frac{1}{2} & 1 & 0 & \frac{1}{2} & 5 \\ \frac{3}{2} & 0 & 0 & \frac{5}{2} & 25 \end{array}\right]\left[\begin{array}{c} x_3 \\ x_2 \\ \ \end{array}\right]$$

$P = 25, x_1 = 0, x_2 = 5$

10. $x_1 \; x_2 \; x_3 \; x_4$

$$\left[\begin{array}{cccc|c} 1 & 1 & 1 & 0 & 2 \\ 2 & 3 & 0 & 1 & 6 \\ -5 & -4 & 0 & 0 & 0 \end{array}\right]\left[\begin{array}{c} x_3 \\ x_4 \\ \ \end{array}\right] \rightarrow \left[\begin{array}{cccc|c} 1 & 1 & 1 & 0 & 2 \\ 0 & 1 & -2 & 1 & 2 \\ 0 & 1 & 5 & 0 & 10 \end{array}\right]\left[\begin{array}{c} x_1 \\ x_4 \\ \ \end{array}\right]$$

$P = 10, x_1 = 2, x_2 = 0$

12. $x_1 \; x_2 \; x_3 \; x_4$

$$\left[\begin{array}{cccc|c} 2 & 1 & 1 & 0 & 4 \\ 1 & 2 & 0 & 1 & 6 \\ -3 & -5 & 0 & 0 & 0 \end{array}\right]\left[\begin{array}{c} x_3 \\ x_4 \\ \ \end{array}\right] \rightarrow \left[\begin{array}{cccc|c} \frac{3}{2} & 0 & 1 & -\frac{1}{2} & 1 \\ \frac{1}{2} & 1 & 0 & \frac{1}{2} & 3 \\ -\frac{1}{2} & 0 & 0 & \frac{5}{2} & 15 \end{array}\right]\left[\begin{array}{c} x_3 \\ x_2 \\ \ \end{array}\right] \rightarrow \left[\begin{array}{cccc|c} 1 & 0 & \frac{2}{3} & -\frac{1}{3} & \frac{2}{3} \\ 0 & 1 & -\frac{1}{3} & \frac{2}{3} & \frac{8}{3} \\ 0 & 0 & \frac{1}{3} & \frac{7}{3} & \frac{46}{3} \end{array}\right]\left[\begin{array}{c} x_1 \\ x_2 \\ \ \end{array}\right]$$

$P = 46/3, x_1 = 2/3, x_2 = 8/3$

14. $x_1 \; x_2 \; x_3 \; x_4 \; x_5$

$$\left[\begin{array}{ccccc|c} 1 & 3 & 2 & 1 & 0 & 30 \\ 2 & 1 & 3 & 0 & 1 & 12 \\ -4 & -2 & -5 & 0 & 0 & 0 \end{array}\right]\left[\begin{array}{c} x_4 \\ x_5 \\ \ \end{array}\right] \rightarrow \left[\begin{array}{ccccc|c} -\frac{1}{3} & \frac{7}{3} & 0 & 1 & -\frac{2}{3} & 22 \\ \frac{2}{3} & \frac{1}{3} & 1 & 0 & \frac{1}{3} & 4 \\ -\frac{2}{3} & -\frac{1}{3} & 0 & 0 & \frac{5}{3} & 20 \end{array}\right]\left[\begin{array}{c} x_4 \\ x_3 \\ \ \end{array}\right] \rightarrow \left[\begin{array}{ccccc|c} 0 & \frac{5}{2} & \frac{1}{2} & 1 & -\frac{1}{2} & 25 \\ 1 & \frac{1}{2} & \frac{3}{2} & 0 & \frac{1}{2} & 6 \\ 0 & 0 & 1 & 0 & 2 & 24 \end{array}\right]\left[\begin{array}{c} x_4 \\ x_1 \\ \ \end{array}\right]$$

$P = 24, x_1 = 5, x_2 = 0, x_3 = 0$

16. $x_1 \; x_2 \; x_3 \; x_4 \; x_5$

$$\left[\begin{array}{ccccc|c} 2 & 2 & 3 & 1 & 0 & 30 \\ 2 & 2 & 1 & 0 & 1 & 12 \\ -6 & -3 & -2 & 0 & 0 & 0 \end{array}\right]\left[\begin{array}{c} x_4 \\ x_5 \\ \ \end{array}\right] \rightarrow \left[\begin{array}{ccccc|c} 0 & 1 & 2 & 1 & -1 & 18 \\ 1 & 1 & \frac{1}{2} & 0 & \frac{1}{2} & 6 \\ 0 & 3 & 1 & 0 & 3 & 36 \end{array}\right]\left[\begin{array}{c} x_4 \\ x_1 \\ \ \end{array}\right]$$

$P = 36, x_1 = 6, x_2 = 0, x_3 = 0$

18.

$$\begin{array}{c} \\ \\ \\ \\ \end{array}\begin{matrix} x_1 & x_2 & x_3 & x_4 & x_5 & x_6 & \end{matrix}$$

$$\left[\begin{array}{cccccc|c} -1 & 2 & 3 & 1 & 0 & 0 & 6 \\ -1 & \underline{4} & 5 & 0 & 1 & 0 & 5 \\ -1 & 5 & 7 & 0 & 0 & 1 & 7 \\ -2 & -4 & -1 & 0 & 0 & 0 & 0 \end{array}\right]\left[\begin{array}{c} x_4 \\ x_5 \\ x_6 \\ \\ \end{array}\right] \rightarrow \left[\begin{array}{cccccc|c} -\frac{1}{2} & 0 & \frac{1}{2} & 1 & -\frac{1}{2} & 0 & \frac{7}{2} \\ -\frac{1}{4} & 1 & \frac{5}{4} & 0 & \frac{1}{4} & 0 & \frac{5}{4} \\ \underline{\frac{1}{4}} & 0 & \frac{3}{4} & 0 & -\frac{5}{4} & 1 & \frac{3}{4} \\ -3 & 0 & 4 & 0 & 1 & 0 & 5 \end{array}\right]\left[\begin{array}{c} x_4 \\ x_2 \\ x_6 \\ \\ \end{array}\right] \rightarrow$$

$$\left[\begin{array}{cccccc|c} 0 & 0 & 2 & 1 & -3 & 2 & 5 \\ 0 & 1 & 2 & 0 & -1 & 1 & 2 \\ 1 & 0 & 3 & 0 & -5 & 4 & 3 \\ 0 & 0 & 13 & 0 & -14 & 12 & 14 \end{array}\right]\left[\begin{array}{c} x_4 \\ x_2 \\ x_1 \\ \\ \end{array}\right]$$

$P = 14, x_1 = 3, x_2 = 2, x_3 = 0 ; x_4 = 5, x_5 = x_6 = 0$

20.

$$\begin{matrix} x_1 & x_2 & x_3 & x_4 & x_5 & x_6 \end{matrix}$$

$$\left[\begin{array}{cccccc|c} 8 & 5 & -4 & 1 & 0 & 0 & 30 \\ -2 & 6 & \underline{1} & 0 & 1 & 0 & 5 \\ -2 & 2 & 1 & 0 & 0 & 1 & 15 \\ -1 & -2 & -4 & 0 & 0 & 0 & 0 \end{array}\right]\left[\begin{array}{c} x_4 \\ x_5 \\ x_6 \\ \\ \end{array}\right] \rightarrow \left[\begin{array}{cccccc|c} 0 & 29 & 0 & 1 & 4 & 0 & 50 \\ -2 & 6 & 1 & 0 & 1 & 0 & 5 \\ 0 & -4 & 0 & 0 & -1 & 1 & 10 \\ -9 & 22 & 0 & 0 & 4 & 0 & 20 \end{array}\right]\left[\begin{array}{c} x_4 \\ x_3 \\ x_6 \\ \\ \end{array}\right]$$

$P = 20, x_1 = 0, x_2 = 0, x_3 = 0 ; x_4 = 50, x_5 = 0, x_6 = 10$

22.

$$\begin{matrix} x_1 & x_2 & x_3 & x_4 & x_5 & x_6 \end{matrix}$$

$$\left[\begin{array}{cccccc|c} 2 & 4 & 5 & 6 & 1 & 0 & 24 \\ 4 & 4 & 2 & \underline{2} & 0 & 1 & 4 \\ -1 & -2 & 1 & -3 & 0 & 0 & 0 \end{array}\right]\left[\begin{array}{c} x_5 \\ x_6 \\ \\ \end{array}\right] \rightarrow \left[\begin{array}{cccccc|c} -10 & -8 & -1 & 0 & 1 & -3 & 12 \\ 2 & 2 & 1 & 1 & 0 & \frac{1}{2} & 2 \\ 5 & 4 & 4 & 0 & 0 & \frac{3}{2} & 6 \end{array}\right]\left[\begin{array}{c} x_5 \\ x_4 \\ \\ \end{array}\right]$$

$P = 6, x_1 = x_2 = x_3 = 0 ; x_4 = 2, x_5 = 12, x_6 = 0$

24. Let x_1 = units of copper
x_2 = units of lead
x_3 = units of zinc

Maximize $P = 45x_1 + 30x_2 + 35x_3$
subject to
(oiling) $2x_1 + 2x_2 + x_3 \le 10$
(mixing) $2x_1 + 3x_2 + x_3 \le 11$
(seperation) $x_1 + x_2 + 3x_3 \le 10$
$x_1 \ge 0, x_2 \ge 0, x_3 \ge 0$

$$\begin{array}{c} \begin{array}{cccccc} x_1 & x_2 & x_3 & x_4 & x_5 & x_6 \end{array} \\ \left[\begin{array}{cccccc|c} \underline{2} & 2 & 1 & 1 & 0 & 0 & 10 \\ 2 & 3 & 1 & 0 & 1 & 0 & 11 \\ 1 & 1 & 3 & 0 & 0 & 1 & 10 \\ -45 & -30 & -35 & 0 & 0 & 0 & 0 \end{array}\right] \end{array} \begin{bmatrix} x_4 \\ x_5 \\ x_6 \\ \\ \end{bmatrix} \rightarrow \left[\begin{array}{cccccc|c} 1 & 1 & \frac{1}{2} & \frac{1}{2} & 0 & 0 & 5 \\ 0 & 1 & 0 & -1 & 1 & 0 & 1 \\ 0 & 0 & \frac{5}{2} & -\frac{1}{2} & 0 & 1 & 5 \\ 0 & 15 & -\frac{25}{2} & \frac{45}{2} & 0 & 0 & 225 \end{array}\right] \begin{bmatrix} x_1 \\ x_4 \\ x_6 \\ \\ \end{bmatrix} \rightarrow$$

$$\left[\begin{array}{cccccc|c} 1 & 1 & 0 & \frac{2}{5} & 0 & -\frac{1}{5} & 4 \\ 0 & 1 & 0 & -1 & 1 & 0 & 1 \\ 0 & 0 & 1 & -\frac{1}{5} & 0 & \frac{2}{5} & 2 \\ 0 & 15 & 0 & 20 & 0 & 5 & 250 \end{array}\right] \begin{bmatrix} x_1 \\ x_5 \\ x_3 \\ \\ \end{bmatrix}$$

$P = 250, x_1 = 4, x_2 = 0, x_3 = 2$

26.

$$\begin{array}{c} \begin{array}{ccccc} ET & CT & x_1 & x_2 & x_3 \end{array} \\ \left[\begin{array}{ccccc|c} 8 & 4 & 1 & 0 & 0 & 6 \\ 10 & 4 & 0 & 1 & 0 & 6 \\ 4 & \underline{8} & 0 & 0 & 1 & 6 \\ -15 & -20 & 0 & 0 & 0 & 0 \end{array}\right] \end{array} \begin{bmatrix} x_1 \\ x_2 \\ x_3 \\ \\ \end{bmatrix} \rightarrow \left[\begin{array}{ccccc|c} 6 & 0 & 1 & 0 & -\frac{1}{2} & 3 \\ \underline{8} & 0 & 0 & 1 & -\frac{1}{2} & 3 \\ \frac{1}{2} & 1 & 0 & 0 & \frac{1}{8} & \frac{3}{4} \\ -5 & 0 & 0 & 0 & \frac{20}{8} & 15 \end{array}\right] \begin{bmatrix} x_1 \\ x_2 \\ CT \\ \\ \end{bmatrix} \rightarrow$$

$$\left[\begin{array}{ccccc|c} 0 & 0 & 1 & -\frac{3}{4} & -\frac{1}{8} & \frac{3}{4} \\ 1 & 0 & 0 & \frac{1}{8} & -\frac{1}{16} & \frac{3}{8} \\ 0 & 1 & 0 & -\frac{1}{16} & \frac{3}{32} & \frac{9}{16} \\ 0 & 0 & 0 & \frac{3}{8} & \frac{35}{16} & \frac{135}{8} \end{array}\right] \begin{bmatrix} x_1 \\ ET \\ CT \\ \\ \end{bmatrix}$$

$P = 16\frac{7}{8}$, $ET = \frac{3}{8}$, $CT = \frac{9}{16}$

Exercise 4.3 (page 184)

2. Standard 4. Non-standard 6. Standard

8. The matrix form is:

$$\begin{bmatrix} 2 & 1 & | & 2 \\ 2 & 1 & | & 6 \\ 1 & 4 & | & 0 \end{bmatrix}$$

The transpose is:

$$\begin{bmatrix} 2 & 2 & | & 1 \\ 1 & 1 & | & 4 \\ 2 & 6 & | & 0 \end{bmatrix}$$

Dual problem: Maximize $P = 2y_1 + 6y_2$

subject to
$$2y_1 + 2y_2 \le 3$$
$$y_1 + y_2 \le 4$$
$$y_1 \ge 0, y_2 \ge 0$$

10. The matrix form is:

$$\begin{bmatrix} 2 & 1 & 1 & | & 4 \\ 1 & 2 & 1 & | & 6 \\ 2 & 1 & 1 & | & 0 \end{bmatrix}$$

The transpose is:

$$\begin{bmatrix} 2 & 1 & | & 2 \\ 1 & 2 & | & 1 \\ 1 & 1 & | & 1 \\ 4 & 6 & | & 0 \end{bmatrix}$$

Dual problem: Maximize $P = 4y_1 + 6y_2$

subject to
$$2y_1 + 2y_2 \le 2$$
$$y_1 + 2y_2 \le 1$$
$$y_1 + y_2 \le 1$$
$$y_1 \ge 0, y_2 \ge 0$$

12. The matrix form is:

$$\begin{bmatrix} 1 & 1 & | & 3 \\ 2 & 1 & | & 4 \\ 3 & 4 & | & 0 \end{bmatrix}$$

The transpose is:

$$\begin{bmatrix} 1 & 2 & | & 3 \\ 1 & 1 & | & 4 \\ 3 & 4 & | & 0 \end{bmatrix}$$

Dual problem: Maximize $P = 3y_1 + 4y_2$

subject to
$$y_1 + 2y_2 \le 2$$
$$y_1 + y_2 \le 4$$
$$y_1 \ge 0, y_2 \ge 0$$

$$
\begin{array}{c}
\quad y_1 \quad\; y_2 \quad u_1 u_2 \\
\left[\begin{array}{rrrr|r} 1 & 2 & 1 & 0 & 3 \\ 1 & 1 & 0 & 1 & 4 \\ -3 & -4 & 0 & 0 & 0 \end{array}\right]
\end{array}
\rightarrow
\left[\begin{array}{rrrr|r} \underline{\tfrac{1}{2}} & 1 & \tfrac{1}{2} & 0 & \tfrac{3}{2} \\ \tfrac{1}{2} & 0 & -\tfrac{1}{2} & 1 & \tfrac{5}{2} \\ -1 & 0 & 2 & 0 & 6 \end{array}\right]
\rightarrow
\left[\begin{array}{rrrr|r} 1 & 2 & 1 & 0 & 3 \\ 0 & -1 & -1 & 1 & 1 \\ 0 & 2 & 3 & 0 & 9 \end{array}\right]
$$

$C = 9,\ x_1 = 3,\ x_2 = 0$

14. The matrix form is:

$$
\left[\begin{array}{rrr|r} 1 & -2 & -3 & -2 \\ 1 & 1 & 1 & 2 \\ 2 & 0 & 1 & 3 \\ 2 & 3 & 4 & 0 \end{array}\right]
$$

The transpose is:

$$
\left[\begin{array}{rrr|r} 1 & 1 & 2 & 2 \\ -2 & 1 & 0 & 3 \\ -3 & 1 & 1 & 4 \\ -2 & 2 & 3 & 0 \end{array}\right]
$$

Dual problem: Maximize $P = -2y_1 + 2y_2 + 3y_3$

subject to

$$
\begin{aligned}
y_1 + y_2 + 2y_3 &\le 2 \\
-2y_1 + y_2 &\le 3 \\
-3y_1 + y_2 + y_3 &\le 4 \\
y_1 \ge 0,\ y_2 \ge 0,\ y_3 &\ge 0
\end{aligned}
$$

$$
\begin{array}{c}
\quad y_1 \quad y_2 \quad y_3 \; u_1 \; u_2 \; u_3 \\
\left[\begin{array}{rrrrrr|r} 1 & 1 & \underline{2} & 1 & 0 & 0 & 2 \\ -2 & 1 & 0 & 0 & 1 & 0 & 3 \\ -3 & 1 & 1 & 0 & 0 & 1 & 4 \\ 2 & -2 & -3 & 0 & 0 & 0 & 0 \end{array}\right]
\end{array}
\rightarrow
\left[\begin{array}{rrrrrr|r} \tfrac{1}{2} & \underline{\tfrac{1}{2}} & 1 & \tfrac{1}{2} & 0 & 0 & 1 \\ -2 & 1 & 0 & 0 & 1 & 0 & 3 \\ -\tfrac{7}{2} & \tfrac{1}{2} & 0 & -\tfrac{1}{2} & 0 & 1 & 3 \\ \tfrac{7}{2} & -\tfrac{1}{2} & 0 & \tfrac{3}{2} & 0 & 0 & 3 \end{array}\right]
\rightarrow
\left[\begin{array}{rrrrrr|r} 1 & 1 & 2 & 1 & 0 & 0 & 2 \\ -3 & 0 & -2 & -1 & 1 & 0 & 1 \\ -4 & 0 & -1 & -1 & 0 & 1 & 2 \\ 4 & 0 & 1 & 2 & 0 & 0 & 4 \end{array}\right]
$$

$C = 4,\ x_1 = 2,\ x_2 = 0,\ x_3 = 0$

16. (Note all inequality signs are inadvertently reversed.)

The matrix form is:

$$
\left[\begin{array}{rrr|r} 1 & -1 & 3 & 4 \\ 2 & 2 & -3 & 6 \\ -1 & 2 & 3 & 2 \\ 1 & 2 & 4 & 0 \end{array}\right]
$$

The transpose is:

$$
\left[\begin{array}{rrr|r} 1 & 2 & -1 & 1 \\ -1 & 2 & 2 & 2 \\ 3 & -3 & 3 & 4 \\ 4 & 6 & 2 & 0 \end{array}\right]
$$

Dual problem: Maximize $P = 4y_1 + 6y_2 + 2y_3$

subject to

$$
\begin{aligned}
y_1 + 2y_2 - y_3 &\le 1 \\
-y_1 + 2y_2 + 2y_3 &\le 2 \\
-3y_1 - 3y_2 + 3y_3 &\le 4 \\
y_1 \ge 0,\ y_2 \ge 0,\ y_3 &\ge 0
\end{aligned}
$$

$$
\begin{array}{cccccc|c}
y_1 & y_2 & y_3 & u_1 & u_2 & u_3 & \\
\end{array}
$$

$$
\left[\begin{array}{cccccc|c}
1 & \underline{2} & -1 & 1 & 0 & 0 & 1 \\
-1 & 2 & 2 & 0 & 1 & 0 & 2 \\
3 & -3 & 3 & 0 & 0 & 1 & 4 \\
-4 & -6 & -2 & 0 & 0 & 0 & 0
\end{array}\right]
\rightarrow
\left[\begin{array}{cccccc|c}
\frac{1}{2} & 1 & -\frac{1}{2} & \frac{1}{2} & 0 & 0 & \frac{1}{2} \\
-2 & 0 & \underline{3} & -1 & 1 & 0 & 1 \\
\frac{9}{2} & 0 & \frac{3}{2} & \frac{3}{2} & 0 & 1 & \frac{11}{2} \\
-1 & 0 & -5 & 3 & 0 & 0 & 3
\end{array}\right]
\rightarrow
$$

$$
\left[\begin{array}{cccccc|c}
\frac{1}{6} & 1 & 0 & \frac{1}{3} & \frac{1}{6} & 0 & \frac{2}{3} \\
-\frac{2}{3} & 0 & 1 & -\frac{1}{3} & \frac{1}{3} & 0 & \frac{1}{3} \\
\frac{11}{2} & 0 & 0 & 2 & -\frac{1}{2} & 1 & 5 \\
-\frac{15}{3} & 0 & 0 & \frac{4}{3} & \frac{5}{3} & 0 & \frac{14}{3}
\end{array}\right]
\rightarrow
\left[\begin{array}{cccccc|c}
0 & 1 & 0 & \frac{3}{11} & \frac{2}{11} & -\frac{1}{35} & \frac{17}{35} \\
0 & 0 & 1 & -\frac{1}{11} & \frac{3}{11} & \frac{4}{35} & \frac{31}{35} \\
1 & 0 & 0 & \frac{4}{11} & -\frac{1}{11} & \frac{2}{11} & \frac{10}{11} \\
0 & 0 & 0 & \frac{32}{11} & \frac{14}{11} & \frac{26}{35} & \frac{284}{35}
\end{array}\right]
$$

$C = 8\frac{28}{35}$, $x_1 = 2\frac{10}{11}$, $x_2 = 1\frac{3}{11}$, $x_3 = \frac{26}{35}$

18. N - Newspaper ads R - Radio ads $C = N + R$

$50N + 70R \ge 100{,}000$

$40N + 20R \ge 120{,}000$

The matrix form is:

$$
\left[\begin{array}{cc|c}
50 & 70 & 100{,}000 \\
40 & 20 & 120{,}000 \\
1 & 1 & 0
\end{array}\right]
$$

The transpose is:

$$
\left[\begin{array}{cc|c}
50 & 40 & 1 \\
70 & 20 & 1 \\
100{,}000 & 120{,}000 & 0
\end{array}\right]
$$

Dual problem: Maximize $P = 100{,}000y_1 + 120{,}000y_2$

subject to

$$
\begin{aligned}
50y_1 + 40y_2 &\le 1 \\
70y_1 + 20y_2 &\le 1 \\
y_1 \ge 0,\ y_2 &\ge 0
\end{aligned}
$$

Chapter 4 - p.55

$$\begin{array}{c} \\ \left[\begin{array}{cccc|c} 50 & \underline{40} & 1 & 0 & 1 \\ 70 & 20 & 0 & 1 & 1 \\ -100,000 & -120,000 & 0 & 0 & 0 \end{array}\right] \end{array} \begin{array}{c} \\ \rightarrow \left[\begin{array}{cccc|c} \frac{5}{4} & 1 & \frac{1}{40} & 0 & \frac{1}{40} \\ 45 & 0 & -\frac{1}{2} & 1 & \frac{1}{2} \\ 50,000 & 0 & 3,000 & 0 & 3,000 \end{array}\right] \end{array}$$

(column labels: N, R)

P = 3,000, N = 3,000, R = 0

Exercise 4.4 (page 200)

2. $x_1 \quad x_2 \quad s_1 \quad s_2 \quad s_3$

$$\left[\begin{array}{ccccc|c} -1 & -1 & 1 & 0 & 0 & -11 \\ -2 & \underline{-3} & 0 & 1 & 0 & -24 \\ 1 & 3 & 0 & 0 & 1 & 18 \\ -5 & -2 & 0 & 0 & 0 & 0 \end{array}\right] \rightarrow \left[\begin{array}{ccccc|c} -\frac{1}{3} & 0 & 1 & -\frac{1}{3} & 0 & -3 \\ \frac{2}{3} & 1 & 0 & -\frac{1}{3} & 0 & 8 \\ \underline{-1} & 0 & 0 & 1 & 1 & -6 \\ -\frac{11}{3} & 0 & 0 & -\frac{2}{3} & 0 & 16 \end{array}\right] \rightarrow \left[\begin{array}{ccccc|c} 0 & 0 & 1 & \underline{-\frac{2}{3}} & -\frac{1}{3} & -1 \\ 0 & 1 & 0 & \frac{1}{3} & \frac{2}{3} & 4 \\ 1 & 0 & 0 & -1 & -1 & 6 \\ 0 & 0 & 0 & -\frac{15}{3} & -\frac{11}{3} & 38 \end{array}\right] \rightarrow$$

$$\left[\begin{array}{ccccc|c} 0 & 0 & -\frac{3}{2} & 1 & \frac{1}{2} & \frac{3}{2} \\ 0 & 1 & \frac{1}{2} & 0 & \frac{1}{2} & \frac{7}{2} \\ 1 & 0 & -\frac{3}{2} & 0 & -\frac{1}{2} & \frac{15}{2} \\ 0 & 0 & -\frac{15}{2} & 0 & -\frac{3}{2} & \frac{89}{2} \end{array}\right] \rightarrow \left[\begin{array}{ccccc|c} 0 & 3 & 0 & 1 & 2 & 12 \\ 0 & 2 & 1 & 0 & 1 & 7 \\ 1 & 3 & 0 & 0 & 1 & 18 \\ 0 & 13 & 0 & 0 & 5 & 90 \end{array}\right]$$

$P = 90,\ x_1 = 18,\ x_2 = 0$

4.

$$\left[\begin{array}{cccccc|c} 2 & -1 & -1 & 1 & 0 & 0 & 2 \\ -1 & -2 & -1 & 0 & 1 & 0 & -2 \\ 1 & \underline{-3} & -2 & 0 & 0 & 1 & -5 \\ -3 & -2 & 1 & 0 & 0 & 0 & 0 \end{array}\right] \rightarrow \left[\begin{array}{cccccc|c} \frac{5}{3} & 0 & -\frac{1}{3} & 1 & 0 & -\frac{1}{3} & \frac{11}{3} \\ -\frac{5}{3} & 0 & \frac{1}{3} & 0 & 1 & -\frac{2}{3} & \frac{4}{3} \\ -\frac{1}{3} & 1 & \frac{2}{3} & 0 & 0 & -\frac{1}{3} & \frac{5}{3} \\ -\frac{11}{3} & 0 & \frac{7}{3} & 0 & 0 & -\frac{2}{3} & \frac{10}{3} \end{array}\right] \rightarrow$$

$$\left[\begin{array}{cccccc|c} 1 & 0 & -\frac{1}{5} & \frac{3}{5} & 0 & -\frac{1}{5} & \frac{11}{5} \\ 0 & 0 & 0 & 1 & 1 & -1 & 5 \\ 0 & 1 & \frac{3}{5} & \frac{1}{5} & 0 & -\frac{2}{5} & \frac{12}{5} \\ 0 & 0 & \frac{8}{5} & \frac{11}{5} & 0 & -\frac{7}{5} & \frac{57}{5} \end{array}\right]$$

No solution.

6.

$$\begin{array}{cccccc} x_1 & x_2 & x_3 & s_1 & s_2 & s_3 \end{array}$$

$$\left[\begin{array}{cccccc|c} 3 & -1 & \underline{-4} & 1 & 0 & 0 & -12 \\ -1 & -3 & -2 & 0 & 1 & 0 & -10 \\ 1 & -1 & 1 & 0 & 0 & 1 & 8 \\ 2 & 1 & 1 & 0 & 0 & 0 & 0 \end{array}\right] \rightarrow \left[\begin{array}{cccccc|c} -\frac{3}{4} & \frac{1}{4} & 1 & -\frac{1}{4} & 0 & 0 & 3 \\ \underline{-\frac{5}{2}} & -\frac{5}{2} & 0 & -\frac{1}{2} & 1 & 0 & -4 \\ \frac{7}{4} & -\frac{5}{4} & 0 & \frac{1}{4} & 0 & 1 & 5 \\ \frac{11}{4} & \frac{3}{4} & 0 & \frac{1}{4} & 0 & 0 & -3 \end{array}\right] \rightarrow$$

$$\left[\begin{array}{cccccc|c} 0 & 1 & 1 & -\frac{1}{10} & -\frac{3}{10} & 0 & \frac{21}{5} \\ 1 & \underline{1} & 0 & \frac{1}{5} & -\frac{2}{5} & 0 & \frac{8}{5} \\ 0 & -3 & 0 & -\frac{1}{10} & \frac{7}{10} & 1 & \frac{11}{5} \\ 0 & -2 & 0 & -\frac{3}{10} & \frac{11}{10} & 0 & -\frac{37}{5} \end{array}\right] \rightarrow \left[\begin{array}{cccccc|c} -1 & 0 & 1 & -\frac{3}{10} & \frac{1}{10} & 0 & \frac{13}{5} \\ 1 & 1 & 0 & \frac{1}{5} & -\frac{2}{5} & 0 & \frac{8}{5} \\ 3 & 0 & 0 & \frac{1}{2} & -\frac{1}{2} & 1 & 7 \\ 2 & 0 & 0 & \frac{1}{10} & \frac{3}{10} & 0 & -\frac{21}{5} \end{array}\right]$$

Maximum of $-C = -21/5$; therefore, Minimum of $C = 21/5$

$x_1 = 0$, $x_2 = 8/5$, $x_3 = 13/5$

8.

$$\begin{array}{cccccccc} x_1 & x_2 & x_3 & x_4 & s_1 & s_2 & s_3 & s_4 \end{array}$$

$$\left[\begin{array}{cccccccc|c} 5 & 1 & 1 & 8 & 1 & 0 & 0 & 0 & 30 \\ -5 & -1 & -1 & \underline{-8} & 0 & 1 & 0 & 0 & -30 \\ 2 & 4 & 3 & 2 & 0 & 0 & 1 & 0 & 30 \\ -2 & -4 & -3 & -2 & 0 & 0 & 0 & 1 & -30 \\ -45 & -27 & -18 & -36 & 0 & 0 & 0 & 0 & 0 \end{array}\right] \rightarrow \left[\begin{array}{cccccccc|c} 0 & 0 & 0 & 0 & 1 & 1 & 0 & 0 & 0 \\ \frac{5}{8} & \frac{1}{8} & \frac{1}{8} & 1 & 0 & \frac{1}{8} & 0 & 0 & \frac{15}{4} \\ \frac{3}{4} & \frac{15}{4} & \frac{11}{4} & 0 & 0 & -\frac{1}{4} & 1 & 0 & \frac{45}{2} \\ -\frac{3}{4} & \underline{-\frac{15}{4}} & -\frac{11}{4} & 0 & 0 & \frac{1}{4} & 0 & 1 & -\frac{45}{2} \\ -\frac{45}{2} & -\frac{45}{2} & -\frac{27}{2} & 0 & 0 & \frac{9}{2} & 0 & 0 & 135 \end{array}\right]$$

$$\left[\begin{array}{cccccccc|c} 0 & 0 & 0 & 0 & 1 & 1 & 0 & 0 & 0 \\ \underline{\frac{3}{5}} & 0 & \frac{1}{30} & 1 & 0 & \frac{2}{15} & 0 & \frac{1}{30} & 3 \\ 0 & 0 & 0 & 0 & 0 & 0 & 1 & 1 & 0 \\ \frac{1}{5} & 1 & \frac{11}{15} & 0 & 0 & -\frac{1}{15} & 0 & -\frac{4}{15} & 6 \\ -18 & 0 & 3 & 0 & 0 & 3 & 0 & -6 & 270 \end{array}\right] \rightarrow \left[\begin{array}{cccccccc|c} 0 & 0 & 0 & 0 & 1 & 1 & 0 & 0 & 0 \\ 1 & 0 & \frac{1}{18} & \frac{5}{3} & 0 & \frac{2}{9} & 0 & \frac{1}{18} & 5 \\ 0 & 0 & 0 & 0 & 0 & 0 & 1 & 1 & 0 \\ 0 & 1 & \frac{15}{18} & -\frac{1}{3} & 0 & -\frac{1}{9} & 0 & -\frac{5}{18} & 5 \\ 0 & 0 & 4 & 30 & 0 & 7 & 0 & -5 & 360 \end{array}\right]$$

$P = 360$, $x_1 = 5$, $x_2 = 5$, $x_3 = x_4 = 0$

10. Minimize $B = 9T_1 + 9T_2 + 3T_3$ $\quad$ $T_1 + T_2 + 2T_3 \leq 8$

$2T_1 + T_2 + 2T_3 \geq 6$

Maximize $-B = -9T_1 - 9T_2 - 3T_3$ $\quad$ $T_1 + T_2 + 2T_3 \leq 8$

$-2T_1 - T_2 - 2T_3 \leq -6$

$$\left[\begin{array}{ccccc|c} 1 & 1 & 2 & 1 & 0 & 8 \\ \underline{-2} & -1 & -1 & 0 & 1 & -6 \\ 9 & 9 & 3 & 0 & 0 & 0 \end{array}\right] \rightarrow \left[\begin{array}{ccccc|c} 0 & \frac{1}{2} & \frac{3}{2} & 1 & \frac{1}{2} & 5 \\ 1 & \frac{1}{2} & \frac{1}{2} & 0 & -\frac{1}{2} & 3 \\ 0 & \frac{9}{2} & -\frac{3}{2} & 0 & \frac{9}{2} & -27 \end{array}\right] \rightarrow$$

$$\left[\begin{array}{ccccc|c} 0 & \frac{1}{3} & 1 & \frac{2}{3} & \frac{1}{3} & \frac{10}{3} \\ 1 & \frac{1}{3} & 0 & -\frac{1}{3} & -\frac{2}{3} & \frac{4}{3} \\ 0 & 5 & 0 & 1 & 5 & -22 \end{array}\right]$$

Maximum $-B = -22$, thus Minimum $B = 22$ at $T_1 = 4/3$, $T_2 = 0$, $T_3 = 10/3$.

Review Exercises (page 202)

2. $\quad x \quad y \quad z \quad s_1 \quad s_2$

$$\left[\begin{array}{ccccc|c} 3 & 1 & 1 & 1 & 0 & 3 \\ 1 & -10 & -4 & 0 & 1 & 20 \\ -1 & -2 & -1 & 0 & 0 & 0 \end{array}\right] \rightarrow \left[\begin{array}{ccccc|c} 3 & 1 & 1 & 1 & 0 & 3 \\ 31 & 0 & 6 & 10 & 1 & 50 \\ 5 & 0 & 1 & 2 & 0 & 6 \end{array}\right]$$

$P = 6$, $x = 0$, $y = 3$, $z = 0$.

4. $\quad x_1 \quad x_2 \quad x_3 \quad x_4 \quad x_5 \quad x_6$

$$\left[\begin{array}{cccccc|c} 1 & 2 & 1 & 1 & 1 & 0 & 50 \\ 3 & 1 & 2 & 1 & 0 & 1 & 100 \\ -2 & -8 & -10 & -1 & 0 & 0 & 0 \end{array}\right] \rightarrow \left[\begin{array}{cccccc|c} 1 & 2 & 1 & 1 & 1 & 0 & 50 \\ 1 & -3 & 0 & -1 & -2 & 1 & 0 \\ 8 & 12 & 0 & 9 & 10 & 0 & 500 \end{array}\right]$$

$P = 250$, $x_1 = 4$, $x_2 = 0$, $x_3 = 2$

6. The matrix form is: The transpose is:

$$\left[\begin{array}{cc|c} -1 & -2 & -4 \\ -1 & -4 & -6 \\ 4 & 2 & 0 \end{array}\right] \qquad \left[\begin{array}{cc|c} -1 & -1 & 4 \\ -2 & -4 & 2 \\ -4 & -6 & 0 \end{array}\right]$$

Dual Maximize $P = -4y_1 - 6y_2$

subject to $-y_1 - y_2 \le 4$

$-2y_1 - 4y_2 \le 2$

$$\left[\begin{array}{cccc|c} -1 & -1 & 1 & 0 & 4 \\ -2 & -4 & 0 & 1 & 2 \\ 4 & 6 & 0 & 0 & 0 \end{array}\right]$$

Minimum $z = 0$, $x_1 = x_2 = 0$

8. Maximize $-Z = -2x_1 - x_2 - 3x_3 - x_4$

$$\left[\begin{array}{cccccc|c} -1 & -1 & -1 & -1 & 1 & 0 & -50 \\ \underline{-3} & -1 & -2 & -1 & 0 & 1 & -100 \\ 2 & 1 & 3 & 1 & 0 & 0 & 0 \end{array}\right] \to \left[\begin{array}{cccccc|c} 0 & \underline{-\frac{2}{3}} & -\frac{1}{3} & -\frac{2}{3} & 1 & -\frac{1}{3} & -\frac{50}{3} \\ 1 & \frac{1}{3} & \frac{2}{3} & \frac{1}{3} & 0 & -\frac{1}{3} & \frac{100}{3} \\ 0 & \frac{1}{3} & \frac{5}{3} & \frac{1}{3} & 0 & -\frac{2}{3} & -\frac{200}{3} \end{array}\right] \to$$

$$\left[\begin{array}{cccccc|c} 0 & 1 & \frac{1}{2} & 1 & -\frac{3}{2} & \underline{\frac{1}{2}} & 25 \\ 1 & 0 & \frac{1}{2} & 0 & \frac{1}{2} & -\frac{1}{2} & \frac{75}{3} \\ 0 & 0 & \frac{3}{2} & 0 & \frac{1}{2} & -\frac{5}{6} & -75 \end{array}\right] \to \left[\begin{array}{cccccc|c} 0 & 2 & 1 & 2 & -3 & 1 & 50 \\ 1 & 1 & 1 & 1 & -1 & 0 & 50 \\ 0 & \frac{5}{3} & \frac{7}{3} & \frac{5}{3} & -2 & 0 & -\frac{100}{3} \end{array}\right]$$

No solution.

CHAPTER 5

Exercise 5.1 (page 210)

2. $I = Pnr = \$100(6/12)(0.08) = \$4.00$

4. $I = Pnr = \$800(8/12)(0.12) = \$64.00$

6. $I = Pnr = \$100(24/12)(0.12) = \$24.00$

8. $I = A-P;\ r = I/(Pn)$

   $I = 600 - 500 = \$100$

   $r = 100/(500 \cdot 8/12) = 0.3 = 30\%$

10. $I = 660 - 600 = \$60$

    $r = 60/(600 \cdot 9/12) \approx 0.133 = 13\frac{1}{3}\%$

12. $I = 900 - 800 = \$100$

    $r = 100/(800 \cdot 3/12) \approx 0.5 = 50\%$

14. $P = A(1 - rt) = 500[1 - (0.09)(2/3)] = \$470$

16. $P = A(1 - rt) = 1500[1 - (0.10)(3/2)] = \$1275$

18. $A = \dfrac{P}{1-rt} = \dfrac{500}{1-(0.09)(\frac{2}{3})} = \$531.91$

20. $A = \dfrac{P}{1-rt} = \dfrac{1500}{1-(0.10)(\frac{3}{2})} = \$1764.71$

22. Simple discount: $I = A - P = \dfrac{P}{1-rt} - P = P\left(\dfrac{1}{1-.08(\frac{3}{4})} - 1\right) = .0638\,P$

    Simple interest: $I = Prt = P(.085)(\frac{3}{4}) = .06375\,P$

    Thus, less interest paid on a simple interest rate of $8\frac{1}{2}\%$.

Exercise 5.2 (page 216)

2. $A = P(1+r)^n = 100(1+0.14/12)^{36} = 100(1.518266) = \$151.83$

(from compound interest table)

4. $A = P(1+r)^n = 200(1+0.1)^{10} = 200(2.59374) = \$518.75$

6. $A = P(1+r)^n = 400(1+0.18/.365)^{180} = 400(1.0928) = \$437.12$

8. $P = A(1+r)^{-n} = 500(1+0.12)^{-1} = \$446.43$

10. $P = A(1+r)^{-n} = 800(1+0.1/12)^{-24} = \$655.53$

12. $2P = P(1+r)^{10}$

$2 = (1+r)^{10}$

$\sqrt[10]{2} = 1+r$

$r = 1 - \sqrt[10]{2} \approx 0.07177 \approx 7.18\%$

14. $3P = P(1+.09)^n$

$\ln 3 = n \ln 1.09$

$n = \frac{\ln 3}{\ln 1.09} \approx 12.75$ years

16. (a) $I = Pnr = 1000(2)(0.15) = \$300.00$

(b) $I = A - P = P(1+r)^n - P$

$= 1000(1+0.14/365)^{730} - 1000$

$= 1000(1.32302) - 1000 = \$323.02$

Thus, 15% simple interest is better for the borrower.

18. $P = A(1+r)^{-n} = 1000(1+.09/365)^{-365} = \$913.94;$

$P = A(1+r)^{-n} = 1000(1+.09/365)^{-730} = \$835.29$

20. Effective interest: $I = A_n - P = P(1+.06/4)^4 - P = .0614P \rightarrow r = .0614$

22. $.07 = (1+r/4)^4 - 1 \rightarrow r = .068 = 6.8\%$

24. $A_1 = 10,000(1+.09/4)^4 = \$10,930.83$ vs.

$A_2 = 10,000(1+.0925) = \$10,925.00$

Thus, 9% compounded quarterly yields a greater return.

26. $A_1 = 10,000(1+.08/2)^2 = \$10,816.00$ vs.

$A_2 = 10,000(1+.079/365)^{365} = \$10,821.95$

Thus, 7.9% compounded daily yields a greater return.

Exercise 5.3 (page 221)

2. $A = PA(nr) = 200A(12,.08) = 200(12.4499260) = \$2489.99$

4. $A = PA(nr) = 1000A(5,.10) = 1000(6.105100) = \$6105.10$

6. $A = PA(nr) = 2000A(20,.10) = 2000(57.2750003) = \$114,550.01$

8. $P = 5,000,000[1/A(20,.10)] = 5,000,000(0.0174596245) = \$87,298.12$

10. $1,000,000 = 10,000\left[\frac{(1+.08)^n - 1}{.08}\right]$

$100(.08) + 1 = 1.08^n$

$\ln 9 = n \ln 1.08$

$n = \frac{\ln 9}{\ln 1.08} \approx 28.5$ years

Exercise 5.4 (page 226)

2. $V = P \cdot P(n, r) = 1000P(3, 0.08) = 1000(2.57709699) = \$2577.10$

4. $V = P \cdot P(n, r) = 400P(18, 0.10/12) = 400(16.650826) = \$6660.33$

6. $V = P \cdot P(n, r) = 2000P(36, 0.12/12) = 2000(30.1075050) = \$60,215.01$

8. $V = P \cdot P(n, r) = 4000P(20, 0.08) = 4000(9.81814741) = \$39,272.59$

10. $P = V/[P(n, r)] = 500/[P(24, 0.12/12)] = 500(0.04707347) = \$23.54$

12. $P = 55,000/[P(180, 0.12/12)] = 55,000(0.01200168) = \$660.09$

14. $P = 30,000/[P(120, 0.10/12)] = 30,000(0.01321507) = \$396.45$;
$P = 30,000/[P(240, 0.10/12)] = 30,000(0.00965022) = \$289.51$

16. $V = P \cdot P(n, r) = 300P(300, 0.10/12) = 300(110.047) = \$33,014.10$

18. $P = 80,000 / [P(300, 0.08/12)] = 80,000(0.007718)$
$= \$617.44$ (monthly payment)

$(617.44)(300) = \$185,232$

$\$185,232 - 80,000 = \$105,232$ total interest

At 5 years, the present value of the loan is:

$(617.44)(119.55429) = \$73,817.60$

Thus the equity after 5 years is:

$100,000 - 73,817.60 = \$26,182.40$

After 20 years, the present value of the loan is:

$(617.44)(49.3184) = \$30,451.15$

Thus the equity after 20 years is:

$100,000 - 30,451.15 = \$69,548.85$

20. $V = 300,000P(20, 0.08) = 300,000(9.81814741) = \$2,945,444.22$

Exercise 5.5 (page 230)

2. The present value of an annuity of $2000 for 5 years at 14% is:

$2000(6.61010421) = \$13,220.21$

The company should purchase the machine.

4. Machine A costs $10,000 and has a useful life of 8 years. The equivalent annual cost of the machine at 14% interest is:

$10,000/P(8,0.14) = 10,000(0.21557) = \$2155.70$

The machine will generate savings of $2000 a year, thus a net loss of $155.70.

Machine B has a life of 6 years. Its equivalent annual cost is:

$8000/P(6,0.14) = 8000(0.257158) = \$2057.26$

Machine B will generate savings of \$1800 a year, thus a net loss of \$257.26.

Thus, machine A is a better investment, but it should be realized that each machine is more expensive than the labor it replaces.

6. $(1/2)(0.09)(1000) = \$45.00$ (semiannual payment)
$45P(30,0.05) = 45(14.90972) = \$870.94$ present value of payments
$1000(1.05)^{-30} = 1000(0.231377) = \$231.38$ present value

Price of bone = $\$870.94 + 231.38 = \$\ 1102.32$

Review Exercises (page 231)

2. $I = Pnr = (500)(14/12)(0.09) = \$52.50$
$A = P + I = 500 + 52.50 = \$552.50$

4. $A = 200(1 + 0.10/12)^{9} = \$215.51$

6. $P = 100(1 + 0.09/12)^{-24} = 100(0.8358) = \$83.58$

8. $P = 500/A(12, 0.14/12) = 500(0.07182) = \$39.06$

10. $V = 50P(18, 0.12/12) = 50(16.398) = \$819.91$

12. $P = 25{,}000/P(5, 0.10) = 25{,}000(0.263798) = \$6594.95$

14. $P = 8{,}000{,}000/A(25, 0.10) = 8{,}000{,}000(0.010168072) = \$81{,}344.58$

16. $V = 300P(180, 0.12/12) = 300(83.3216640) = \$24{,}996.50$

18. $A = P \cdot A(n,i) = 100A(300, 0.09/12) = 100(1121.1219) = \$112{,}112.19$

$$P = V/P(n,i) = \frac{112{,}112.19}{P(420, 0.09/12)} = \frac{112{,}112.19}{127.55} = \$878.95$$

CHAPTER 6

Exercise 6.1 (page 247)

2. $\subset, \subseteq$

4. None of these.

6. None of these.

8. None of these.

10. $=, \subseteq$

12. $\varnothing, \{b\}, \{c\}, \{a, b\}, \{a, c\}, \{b, c\}, \{a, b, c\}$

14. $C \subset A, C \subset B, C \subseteq A, C \subseteq B$, etc.

16. $A \cap C = \{3\}$

18. $B \cup C = \{3, 4, 5, 6, 7\}$

20. $(A \cap B) \cap C = \{3\} \cap \{3, 5, 7\} = \{3\}$

22. $(A \cap B) \cup C = \{3\} \cup \{3, 5, 7\} = \{3, 5, 7\}$

24. (a) $\bar{A} \cap \bar{C} = \{1, 2, 4\} \cap \{1, 5\} = \{1\}$
(b) $(A \cup B) \cap C = \{1, 2, 3, 5\} \cap \{2, 3, 4\} = \{2, 3\}$
(c) $A \cup (B \cap C) = \{3, 5\} \cup \{2, 3\} = \{2, 3, 5\}$
(d) $(A \cup B) \cap (A \cup C) = \{1, 2, 3, 5\} \cap \{2, 3, 4, 5\} = \{2, 3, 5\}$
(e) $\overline{A \cap C} = \overline{\{3\}} = \{1, 2, 4, 5\}$
(f) $\overline{A \cup B} = \overline{\{1, 2, 3, 5\}} = \{4\}$
(g) $\bar{A} \cap \bar{B} = \{1, 2, 4\} \cap \{4, 5\} = \{4\}$
(h) $(A \cap B) \cup C = \{3\} \cup \{2, 3, 4\} = \{2, 3, 4\}$

26. (a) $A \cup B = \{b, c, d, e\}$
(b) $A \cup B = \{c\}$
(c) $\bar{A} = \{a, d, e, f\}$
(d) $\bar{B} = \{a, b, f\}$
(e) $\overline{A \cap B} = \overline{\{c\}} = \{a, b, d, e, f\}$

28. (a) $A \cap (B \cup C)$

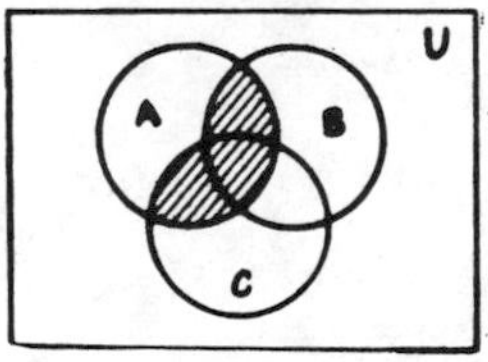

$(A \cap B) \cup (A \cap C)$

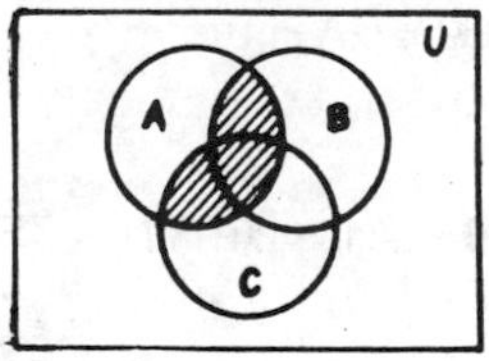

(b) $A \cap (A \cup B) = A$

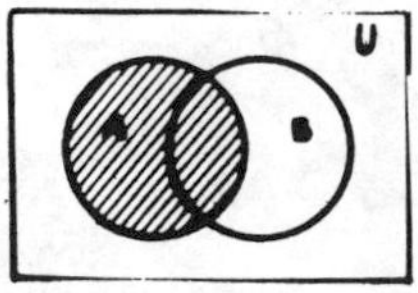

(c) $\overline{A \cap B}$

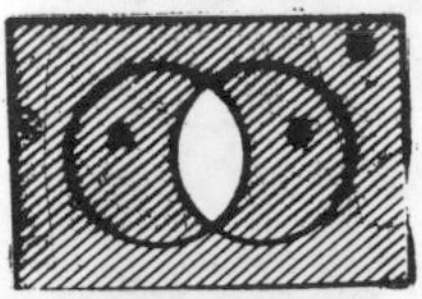

$\bar{A} \cup \bar{B}$

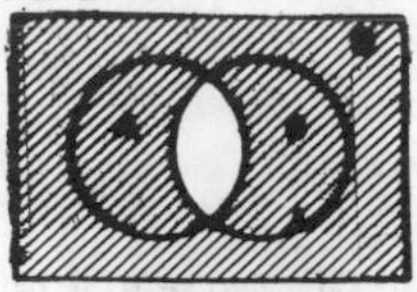

(d) $(A \cup B) \cup C$

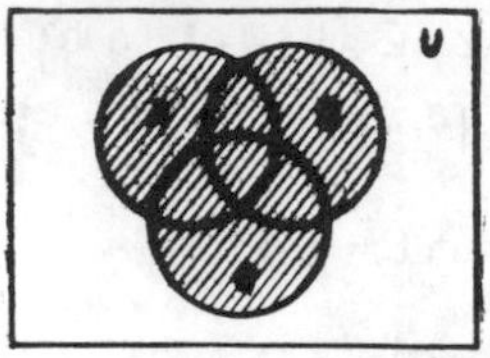

$A \cup (B \cup C)$

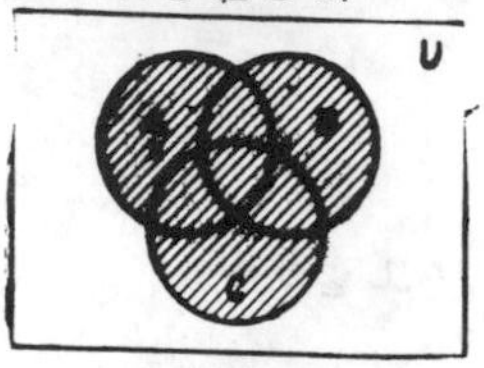

30. $B \cap D = \{x|$ x is a secretary employed by IBM and a stockholder of IBM$\}$

32. $C \cap D = \{x|$ x is a computer operator at IBM and a member of the Board Directors of IBM.$\}$

34. $\bar{M} = \{$All female college students.$\}$

36. $M \cup S = \{$All college students who are male or who smoke$\}$

38. $c(\{0,1,2\}) = 3$

40. $c(\{2,4\}) = 2$

42. $c(B) = 3$

44. $c(A \cup B) = c(\{1, 2, 3, 4, 5, 6, 8\}) = 7$

46. $c(A \cap B) \cup B = c(B) = 3$

48. $c(A \cup (B \cup C)) = c(\{1, 3, 6, 8, 10\}) = 5$

50. $c((A \cap B) \cup C) = c(\{8, 10\}) = 2$

52. $c(A \cup B) = 14 + 11 - 6 = 19$

54. $c(A \cup B) = c(A) + c(B) - c(A \cap B)$
$16 = 8 + 9 - c(A \cap B)$
$c(A \cap B) = 1$

56. $c(B) = c(A \cup B) - [c(A) - c(A \cap B)] = 24$

58. $c(H \cup M) = c(H) + c(M) - c(H \cap M) = 350 + 300 - 270 = 380$

60. $9 + 8 + 3 + 2 = 22$

62. $22 + (4 + 17) = 43$

64. $9 + 8 = 17$

66. 5

68. (a) $(82+152+111)+(27+33+7)+(44+47+43)=546$
(b) $(111+15+7+33)+(33+47)+(27+44)=317$
(c) $(42+44)+(15+33)=134$

70. (a) $96+87+45+31=259$

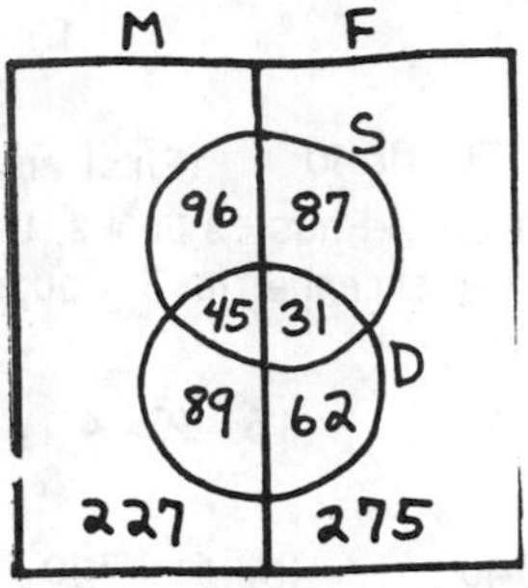

(b) $87+31+62+275=455$

(c) $45+31+89+62=227$

(d) $45+31=76$

(e) $87+31=118$

(f) $31+62=93$

(g) $96+87+45+31+89+62+227+275=912$

72. (a) $35+5=40$

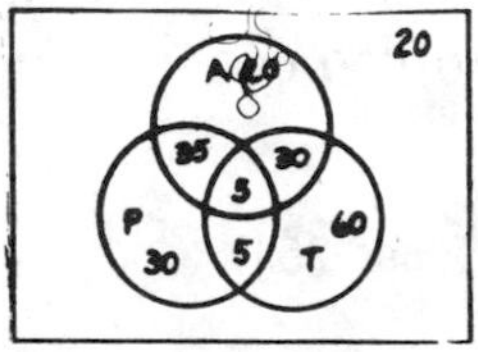

(b) $30+5=35$

(c) $20+20=40$

(d) $20+35+5+30+30+5+60+20=205$

(e) $205-20-30=155$

74. There are 8 blood types:

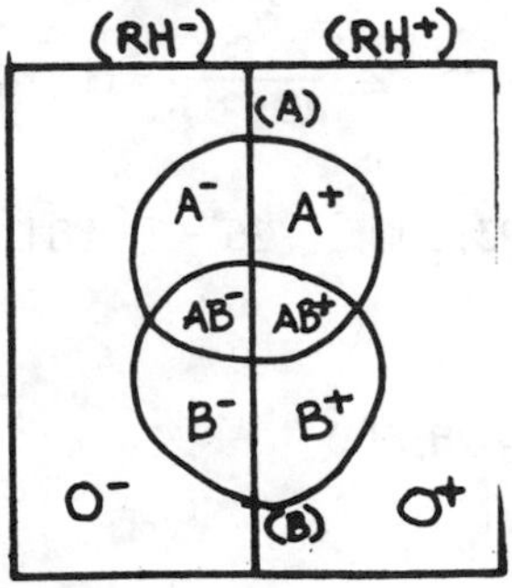

Exercise 6.2 (page 255)

2. $4 \cdot 5 = 20$ 4. $3 \cdot 6 = 18$ 6. $14 \cdot 13 = 182$

8. $4 \cdot 3 = 12$ 10. $26 \cdot 26 \cdot 10 \cdot 10 = 67,600$

12. $(5! \cdot 3! \cdot 2!) \cdot 3! = 8640$ (First arrange the 5 Math books in order, then the 3 Physics books, then the 2 Computer Science books, finally, arrange the 3 groups.)

14. $5! = 120$ 16. $2^2 = 4$ 18. $\frac{1}{2} \cdot 2^4 = 8$

20. (a) $7! = 5040$ (b) $6! = 720$ (c) $5! = 120$

22. $4 \cdot 4 \cdot 4 \cdot 4 = 256$ 24. $2^7 = 128$

26. (a) $10 \cdot 9 \cdot 8 \cdot 7 \cdot 6 \cdot 5 \cdot 4 = 604,800$
(b) $9 \cdot 9 \cdot 8 \cdot 7 \cdot 6 \cdot 5 \cdot 4 = 544,320$
(c) $10^7 = 10,000,000$

Exercise 6.3 (page 261)

2. $\frac{8!}{2!} = 8 \cdot 7 \cdot 6 \cdot 5 \cdot 4 \cdot 3 = 20,160$ 4. $\frac{9!}{3!} = 9 \cdot 8 \cdot 7 \cdot 6 \cdot 5 \cdot 4 = 60,480$

6. $\frac{11}{9!} = 11 \cdot 10 = 110$ 8. $\frac{10!}{9!} = 10$ 10. $\frac{9!}{3!\,6!} = \frac{9 \cdot 8 \cdot 7 \cdot 6!}{3 \cdot 2 \cdot 6!} = 84$

12. $P(5,1) = 5$ 14. $P(6,6) = 6! = 720$ 16. $P(6,4) = 360$

18. $\frac{6 \cdot 7 \cdot 8 \cdot 9}{2 \cdot 3 \cdot 4} = 126$ 20. $\frac{7!}{7!} = 1$ 22. $\frac{8!}{(8-8)!} = 8! = 40,320$

24. $\frac{26!}{(26-5)!} = 26 \cdot 25 \cdot 24 \cdot 23 \cdot 22 = 7,893,600;$ $26^5 = 11,881,376$

26. (a) $(5!\,5!) \cdot 2! = 28,800$
(b) $(5 \cdot 5 \cdot 4 \cdot 4 \cdot 3 \cdot 3 \cdot 2 \cdot 2 \cdot 1 \cdot 1) \cdot 2 = 28,800$

28. $\dfrac{8!}{(8-4)!} = 8 \cdot 7 \cdot 6 \cdot 5 = 1680$

30. $\dfrac{10!}{(10-7)!} = 10 \cdot 9 \cdot 8 \cdot 7 \cdot 6 \cdot 5 \cdot 4 = 604,800$

32. $\dfrac{15!}{(15-2)!} = 15 \cdot 14 = 210$

Exercise 6.4 (page 265)

2. $c(5,4) = 5$

4. $c(8,7) = 8$

6. $c(8,1) = 8$

8. $c(8,4) = \dfrac{8 \cdot 7 \cdot 6 \cdot 5}{1 \cdot 2 \cdot 3 \cdot 4} = 70$

10. $c(9,4) = \dfrac{9 \cdot 8 \cdot 7 \cdot 6}{1 \cdot 2 \cdot 3 \cdot 4} = 126$

12. $c(52,13) = 635,013,558,500$

14. $c(10,4) = 210$

16. $c(2,1)c(3,2)c(7,2) = (2)(3)(21) = 126$

18. $c(1352, 641)c(711, 234)c(477, 477) = \dfrac{1352!}{641!\,711!\,234!\,477!}$

20. $c(3,1)c(12,8) = (3)(495) = 1485$

22. (a) $\dfrac{8!}{2!\,6!} = \dfrac{8 \cdot 7}{2} = 28$ (b) $\dfrac{8!}{3!\,5!} = \dfrac{8 \cdot 7 \cdot 6}{3 \cdot 2} = 56$

24. $\dfrac{13!}{5!\,8!} = \dfrac{13 \cdot 12 \cdot 11 \cdot 10 \cdot 9}{5!} = 1287$

26. $\dfrac{5!}{2!\,3!} \cdot \dfrac{4!}{2!\,2!} \cdot \dfrac{6!}{3!\,3!} = 1200$

28. $\binom{4}{1} + \binom{4}{2} + \binom{4}{3} + \binom{4}{4} = 4 + 6 + 4 + 1 = 15$

30. $\dfrac{12!}{6!\,6!} \cdot \dfrac{6!}{4!\,2!} \cdot \dfrac{2!}{0!\,2!} = 13,860$

32. $\dfrac{8!}{4!\,4!} \cdot \dfrac{6!}{4!\,2!} = 1050$

34. $\dfrac{100!}{95!\,5!} \cdot \dfrac{435!}{431!\,4!} = 1.1 \times 10^{17}$

36. $\dfrac{12!}{11!\,1!} \cdot \dfrac{4!}{3!\,1!} = 48$

38. $\dfrac{8!}{3!\,5!} = 56$

Review Exercises (page 268)

2. $\subset, \subseteq$
4. None of these.
6. None of these.
8. $\subset, \subseteq$
10. None of these.
12. None of these.
14. None of these.
16. None of these.

18. (a) $\overline{A \cap B} = \overline{\{3, 6\}} = \{1, 2, 4, 5, 7\}$
(b) $(B \cap C) \cap A = \{6, 7\} \cap \{1, 3, 5, 6\} = \{6\}$
(c) $\bar{B} \cup \bar{A} = \{1, 4, 5\} \cup \{2, 4, 7\} = \{1, 2, 4, 5, 7\}$

20. (a) $75 + 10 + 30 + 40 + 10 = 165$

(b) $95 - (30 + 20 + 5) = 40$
$50 - 20 = 30$
$60 - 20 = 40$
$75 - (20 + 40 + 10) = 5$
$100 - (30 + 20 + 40) = 10$

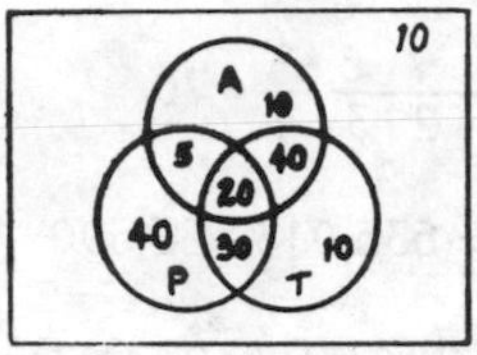

22. $A = \{1\}$, $A = \{1,2\}$, $A = \{1,2,3\}$

24. $\dfrac{6 \cdot 5}{2} = 15$

26. $4! = 24$
28. $P(4, 3) = 24$
30. $2^{10} = 1024$

32. (a) $P(6, 3) = 120$
(b) $c(6, 3) = 20$

34. (a) $13! = 6,227,020,800$
(b) $7!\,6! = 3,628,800$

36. (a) $31^2 = 961$
(b) $P(31, 2) = 930$
(c) $c(31, 2) = 465$

38. Suppose the 5 are A, B, C, D, E and A cannot be next to B. If we let X = (A,B) and Y = (B,A) then there are 4! ways to arrange X, C, D, E and 4! ways to arrange Y, C, D, E; thus, $2 \cdot 4! = 48$ "wrong" ways to arrange A, B, C, D, E. There are altogether $5! = 120$ arrangements, thus the number of "right" ways is $120 - 48 = 72$.

40. Each route from A to B requires one to go north 2 blocks and east 8 blocks, thus there are c(10,2) possible routes. Similarly, there are c(6,2) possible routes from B to C. $c(10,2)c(6,2) = 45 \cdot 15 = 675$.

42. We assume that a child may be given two or more identical names like Gonzalez Gonzalez, Ford Madox Ford, or Major Major Major.

$100 + 100^2 + 100^3 = 1,010,100$

44. A precedes B in exactly half of the possible arrangements: $5!/2 = 60$.

46. There are 27 possibilities for the first symbol (blank or one of the 26 letters), 26 possibilities for the second symbol, 9 possibilities (1,...,9) for the third symbol, and 10 possibilities (0,...,9) for each of the last three symbols.

$$27 \cdot 26 \cdot 9 \cdot 10^3 = 6,318,000$$

CHAPTER 7

Exercise 7.2 (page 283)

2. {R,B}

4. {HHH, HHT, HTH, HTT, THH, THT, TTH, TTT}

6. {H1, H2, H3, H4, H5, H6, T1, T2, T3, T4, T5, T6}

8. {1R, 1G, 2R, 2G, 3R, 3G, 4R, 4G}

10. {11, 12, 13, 14, 21, 22, 23, 24, 31, 32, 33, 34, 41, 42, 43, 44}

12. {1AA, 1AB, 1AC, 1BA, 1BB, 1BC, 1CA, 1CB, 1CC, 2AA, 2AB, 2AC, 2BA, 2BB, 2BC, 2CA, 2CB, 2CC, 3AA, 3AB, 3AC, 3BA, 3BB, 3BC, 3CA, 3CB, 3CC, 4AA, 4AB, 4AC, 4BA, 4BB, 4BC, 4CA, 4CB, 4CC}

14. {1AR, 1AG, 1BR, 1BG, 1CR, 1CG, 2AR, 2AB, 2BR, 2BG, 2CR, 2CG, 3AR, 3AG, 3BR, 3BG, 3CR, 3CG, 4AR, 4AG, 4BR, 4BG, 4CR, 4CG}

16. $2^5 = 32$ 18. $6^2 \cdot 2 = 72$ 20. $C(52, 5) = 2,598,960$

22. Assignment #1 24. Assignment #6

26. The probability of each simple event is 1/8.

28. The probability of each simple event is 1/24.

30. HHHH, HHHT, HHTH, HHTT 32. HTTT, THTT, TTHT, TTTH

34. HHTT 36. P(B) = 5/36 38. P(D) = 6/36 = 1/6 40. P(F) = 1/36

42. P(B) = P(1H) + P(1T) = (1/12) + (1/12) = 1/6

44. $P(D) = P(5H) + P(5T) + P(6H) + P(6T) = \frac{1}{12} + \frac{1}{12} + \frac{1}{12} + \frac{1}{12} = \frac{1}{3}$

46. P(F) = P(1H) + P(2H) + P(3H) = 1/4

48. (a) The probability that common stocks are a good buy or corporate

bonds are a good buy.

(b) The probability that common stocks are not a good buy.

(c) The probability that common stocks are not a good buy and corporate bonds are not a good buy.

(d) The probability that common stocks are a good buy or that corporate bonds are not a good buy.

(e) The probability that common stocks are not a good buy or that corporate bonds are a good buy.

(f) The probability that common stocks are not a good buy and corporate bonds are a good buy.

50. S = {[G, Habcd], [Ga,Hbd], [Gb, Hacd], [Ga, Habd], [Gd, Habc], [Gab, Hcd], [Gac, Hbd], [Gad, Hbc], [Gbc, Had], [Gbd, Hac], [Gcd, Hab], [Gabc, Hd], [Gabd, Hc], [Gacd, Hb], [Gbcd, Ha], [Gabcd, H]}
Free competition = {[Gab, Hcd], [Gac, Hbd], [Gad, Hbc], [Gbc, Had], [Gbd, Hac], [Gad, Hab]}

52. (a) Let $x = P(e_1)$

$P(e_2) = x, \quad P(e_3) = \frac{x}{2}, \quad P(e_4) = \frac{x}{4},$

$P(e_5) = \frac{x}{4}, \quad P(e_6) = x, \quad P(e_7) = \frac{x}{2}$

$P(e_1) + P(e_2) + \ldots + P(e_7) = 1$

$x + x + \frac{x}{2} + \frac{x}{4} + \frac{x}{4} + x + \frac{x}{2} = 1; \qquad \frac{9x}{2} = 1; \qquad x = \frac{2}{9}$

$P(e_1) = P(e_2) = P(e_6) = \frac{2}{9} \qquad P(e_3) = P(e_7) = \frac{1}{9} \qquad P(e_4) = P(e_5) = \frac{1}{18}$

(b) $P(A) = \frac{2}{9} + \frac{2}{9} = \frac{4}{9}$ $\qquad P(A \cup B) = P(e_1, e_2, e_3, e_4) = \frac{11}{18}$

$P(B) = \frac{2}{9} + \frac{1}{9} + \frac{1}{18} = \frac{7}{18}$ $\qquad P(A \cap D) = P(e_1) = \frac{2}{9}$

$P(C) = \frac{2}{9} + \frac{1}{9} + \frac{1}{18} = \frac{7}{18}$ $\qquad P(B \cap D) = P(\emptyset) = 0$

$P(D) = \frac{2}{9} + \frac{2}{9} + \frac{1}{18} = \frac{1}{2}$ $\qquad P(A \cap \bar{B}) = P(e_1) = \frac{2}{9}$

54. (a) $S = \{1, 2, 3, 4, 5, 6\}$

(b) Let $x = P(1)$

$P(1) + \ldots + P(6) = 1$

$x + 2x + 3x + 4x + 5x + 6x = 1$

$21x = 1; \quad x = \frac{1}{21}$

$P(1) = \frac{1}{21}$ $\qquad$ $P(4) = \frac{4}{21}$

$P(2) = \frac{2}{21}$ $\qquad$ $P(5) = \frac{5}{21}$

$P(3) = \frac{3}{21}$ $\qquad$ $P(6) = \frac{6}{21}$

(c) $P(A) = \frac{2}{21} + \frac{4}{21} + \frac{6}{21} = \frac{12}{21} = \frac{4}{7}$

$P(B) = 1 - P(A) = \frac{3}{7}$

$P(C) = \frac{2}{21} + \frac{3}{21} + \frac{5}{21} = \frac{10}{21}$

$P(A \cup B) = 1$

$P(A \cup \bar{C}) = P(1) + P(2) + P(4) + P(6) = \frac{13}{21}$

Exercise 7.3 (page 292)

2. $P(\bar{B}) = .7$ $\qquad$ 4. $P(A \cap B) = 0$ $\qquad$ 6. $P(A \cap B) = .2 + .3 - .4 = .1$

8. The two events are mutually exclusive, thus P("6" or "8") = $\frac{5}{36} + \frac{5}{36} = \frac{5}{18}$

10. P(win or lose) = .6 + .25 = .85; P(tie) = 1 - .85 = .15

12. $P(M \cup E) = P(M) + P(E) - P(M \cap E)$

$.8 = .7 + P(E) - .1$

$.2 = P(E)$

She should drop English.

14. (a) $P(A \cup B) = .85$ (b) $P(\overline{A \cup B}) = .15$
(c) $P(\bar{B}) = 1 - .5 = .5$ (d) $P(\bar{A}) = .65$
(e) $P(A \cap B) = 0$

16. P(Shortage of E $\cup$ Shortage of F) $= .06 + .04 - .02 = .08$

18. (a) P(at most 2) = P(0) + P(1) + P(2) = .20 + .15 + .10 = .45
(b) P(at least 2) = P(2) + P(3) + P(4 or more) = .75
(c) P(at least 1) = 1 − P(0) = .9

20. $P(\bar{E}) = \frac{4}{4+1} = \frac{4}{5}$; $P(E) = 1 - \frac{4}{5} = \frac{1}{5}$

22. $P(E) = \frac{2}{9+2} = \frac{2}{11}$

24. $P(E) = \frac{50}{51}$

26. $P(H) = \frac{1}{3}$; $P(\bar{H}) = \frac{2}{3}$

The odds for H are $\frac{1}{3}$ to $\frac{2}{3}$ or 1 to 2.

The odds against H are 2 to 1.

28. $P(G) = .01$; $P(\bar{G}) = .99$

The odds for G are .01 to .99 or 1 to 99.

The odds against G are .99 to 1.

30. $P(A)\frac{1}{6}$, $P(B) = \frac{1}{4}$, $P(A \cap B) = 0$

Thus $P(A \cup B) = \frac{1}{6} + \frac{1}{4} = \frac{5}{12}$, and the odds for $A \cup B$ are 5 to 7.

32. If $P(E) = .70 = \frac{1}{70}$ then the odds for E are 7 to 3; these are the odds that should be given for a friendly bet.

Exercise 7.4 (page 299)

2. 4/52 = 1/13 4. 26/52 = 1/2 6. 40/52 = 10/13

8. There are 20 cards with values of 10 or higher (10, Jack, Queen, King, Ace in all four suits).

P(E) = 20/52 = 5/13

10. 8/52 = 2/13 12. 3 + 5 + 8 + 7 = 23; P(Blue) = 8/23

14. 5/23 16. (7 + 8)/23 = 15/23 18. 16/23

20. P({(1,5), (2,5), (3,5), (4,5), (5,1), (5,2), (5,3), (5,4)}) = 8/36 = 2/9

22. (a) 360/850 = 36/85

(b) 270/850 = 27/85

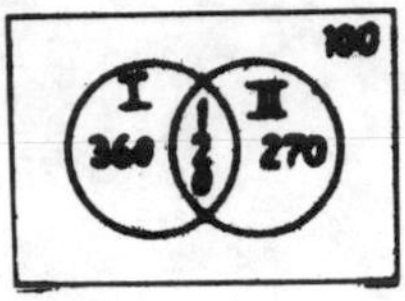

24. $P(2 \text{ in same month}) = 1 - P(2 \text{ different months}) = 1 - \frac{12 \cdot 11}{12 \cdot 12} = \frac{1}{12}$

26. P(at least two numbers are the same) = 1 − P(all 10 slips are different)

$$= 1 - \frac{(100)(99)\ldots(91)}{100^{10}}$$

28. In any group of more than 365 people, it is certain that at least 2 will have the same birthday, thus P(E) = 1.

30. $\frac{C(40,30)}{C(50,30)} = \frac{40!\,20!}{10!\,50!} \approx 0.000018$

32. $\frac{\binom{13}{5}\binom{13}{4}\binom{13}{3}\binom{13}{1}}{\binom{52}{13}} \approx 0.00539$

34. $\frac{P(8,5)}{8^5} = \frac{8 \cdot 7 \cdot 6 \cdot 5 \cdot 4}{8^5} = \frac{840}{8^4} = \frac{840}{4096} \approx 0.205$

Exercise 7.5 (page 308)

2. $P(B) = (.7)(.1) + (.3)(.8) = .31$ 4. $P(D|A) = .1$ 6. $P(D|C) = 0$

8. $P(G) = .40$ 10. $P(I) = .76$ 12. $P(E \cap I) = .30$

14. $P(G \cap I) = .32$ 16. $P(E|I) = \frac{.30}{.76} \approx .39$ 18. $P(G|I) = \frac{.32}{.76} \approx .42$

20. (a) $P(E|F) = \frac{P(E \cap F)}{P(F)} = \frac{.3}{.5} = .6$ (b) $P(F|E) = \frac{P(E \cap F)}{P(E)} = \frac{.3}{.6} = .5$

22. $P(E|F) = \frac{P(E \cap F)}{P(F)}$, $.5 = \frac{.2}{P(F)}$, $P(F) = .4$

24. (a) 2/52 = 1/26 (b) P(black jack | jack) =2/4 = 1/2
(c) P(black jack | black) = 2/26 = 1/13

26. (a) The probability that a person is an executive given that he earns over $25,000.

(b) The probability that a person earns over $25,000 given that he is an executive.

(c) The probability that a person is not an executive given that he does not earn over $25,000.

(d) The probability that a person is not an executive given that he earns over $25,000.

28. $P(\text{One girl}|\text{First child is a boy}) = \frac{\frac{1}{4}}{\frac{1}{2}} = \frac{1}{2}$

30. $P(r + g = 7 | r = g \text{ or } g = 2) = \frac{P(2,5) + P(5,2)}{P(r = 2 \text{ or } g = 2)} = \frac{\frac{2}{36}}{\frac{11}{36}} = \frac{2}{11}$

32. (1/2)(26/51) = 13/51

34. $P(W, Y) = \frac{3}{6} \cdot \frac{1}{5} + \frac{1}{6} \cdot \frac{3}{5} = \frac{1}{5}$

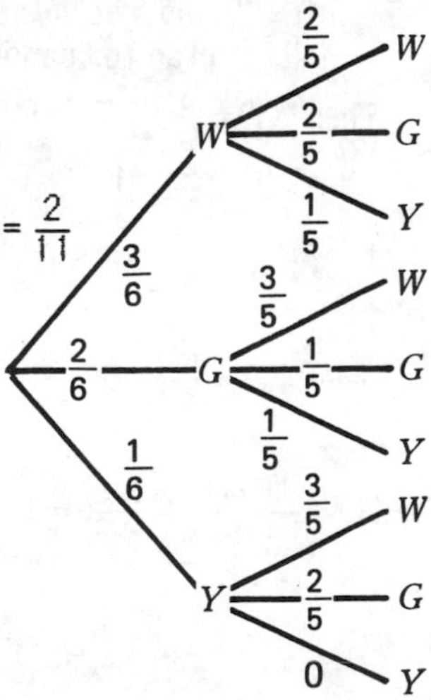

36. $P(S) = (.7)(.85) + (.3)(.4) = .715 = 71.5\%$

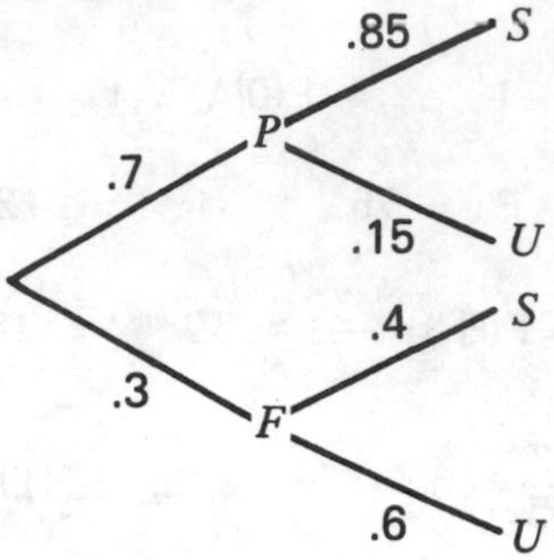

38.(a) P(husband & wife vote)= P(husband votes)P(wife votes | husband votes)
$= (.5)(.9) = .45$

(b) $P(\text{husband votes} \mid \text{husband or wife votes}) = \dfrac{P(\text{husband votes})}{P(\text{husband or wife votes})}$

$$= \frac{P(\text{husband votes})}{P(\text{husband votes}) + P(\text{wife votes}) - P(\text{husband and wife vote})}$$

$$= \frac{.5}{.5 + .6 - .45} = \frac{10}{13}$$

40. (a) $P(\text{Republican}) = 3/(3+1) = 3/4$

(b) Let R = {Republican voter}
D = {Democrat voter}
V = {Voted for candidate}

Then $P(V) = \frac{5}{9} = P(D) + P(R \cap V)$

$$\frac{5}{9} = \frac{1}{4} + x$$

$$x = \frac{5}{9} - \frac{1}{4} = \frac{11}{36}$$

$$P(R \mid V) = \frac{\frac{11}{36}}{\frac{5}{9}} = .55$$

42. $P(E \mid E) = \dfrac{P(E \cap E)}{P(E)} = \dfrac{P(E)}{P(E)} = 1$

Exercise 7.6 (page 314)

2. $P(E \cap F) = P(E)P(F)$

$.3 = .6P(F)$

$P(F) = .5$

4. $P(E \cup F) = P(E) + P(F) - P(E \cap F)$

$P(E \cup F) = P(E) + P(F) - P(E)P(F)$

$.6 = P(E) + .3 - .3P(E)$

$.3 = .7P(E)$

$P(E) = \frac{3}{7}$

6. $P(E \mid F) = \frac{P(E \cap F)}{P(F)} = \frac{P(E) + P(F) - P(E \cup F)}{P(F)} = \frac{.4 + .6 - .7}{.6} = \frac{1}{2} \neq .4$

E and F are not independent.

8. $P(E) = \frac{1}{8} + \frac{1}{8} + \frac{1}{4} = \frac{1}{2}$

$P(F) = \frac{1}{4} + \frac{1}{8} + \frac{1}{8} = \frac{1}{2}$

$P(E \cap F) = P(3) = \frac{1}{4} = P(E)P(F)$

E and F are independent.

10. $P(E) = \frac{3}{4}$

$P(F) = \frac{1}{2}$

$P(E \cap F) = \frac{1}{2} \neq \frac{3}{4} \cdot \frac{1}{2}$

E and F are not independent.

12. (a) $\frac{4}{52} = \frac{1}{13}$

(b) $P(K_2 A_1) = P(K_2) = \frac{1}{13}$

(c) $P(A_1 \cap K_2) = P(A_1)P(K_2) = \frac{1}{13} \cdot \frac{1}{13} = \frac{1}{169}$

14. $P(E) = \frac{1}{2}$, $P(F) = \frac{1}{2}$; $P(E \cap F) = \frac{1}{4} = P(E)P(F)$

16. $P(E) = .7$, $P(F) = .6$

(a) $P(E \cap F) = .52 \neq (.7)(.6)$ — E and F are not independent.

(b) $P(\bar{E} \cap \bar{F}) = .22 \neq (.3)(.4)$ — $\bar{E}$ and $\bar{F}$ are not independent.

(c) $P(E \cap \bar{F}) = .18 \neq (.7)(.4)$ — E and $\bar{F}$ are not independent.

18. If $P(E \cap F) = P(E)P(F)$ and $P(E \cap F) = 0$, then $P(E) = 0$ or $P(F) = 0$

20. $P(\bar{E} \cap \bar{F}) = P(\overline{E \cup F}) = 1 - P(E \cup F) = 1 - [P(E) + P(F) - P(E)P(F)]$

$= 1 - P(E) - P(F) + P(E)P(F)$

$= [1 - P(E)][1 - P(F)] = P(\bar{E})P(\bar{F})$

22. $P(E) = P(F) = P(G) = \frac{1}{6}$

$P(E \cap F) = P(E \cap G) = P(F \cap G) = \frac{1}{36}$

E and F are independent, E and G are independent, and F and G are independent. However,

$$P(E \cap F \cap G) = 0 \neq P(E)P(F)P(G)$$

thus, E, F, and G are not independent.

24. $\frac{9}{10} \cdot \frac{8}{9} \cdot \frac{7}{8} \cdot \frac{6}{7} \cdot \frac{1}{6} = \frac{1}{10}$

Exercise 7.7 (page 324)

2. $P(B \mid \bar{E}) = \dfrac{P(B)P(\bar{E} \mid B)}{P(A)P(\bar{E} \mid A) + P(B)P(\bar{E} \mid B) + P(C)P(\bar{E} \mid C)}$

$= \dfrac{(.6)(.8)}{(.3)(.6) + (.6)(.8) + (.1)(.3)} = \dfrac{.48}{.69} = 0.70$

4. $P(A \mid \bar{E}) = \dfrac{.18}{.69} = 0.26$

6. $P(C \mid \bar{E}) = \dfrac{.03}{69} = 0.043$

8. $P(E) = P(E \cap A_1) + P(E \cap A_2) = P(E \mid A_1)P(A_1) = P(E \mid A_2)P(A_2)$

$= (.03)(.4) + (.01)(.6) = 0.018$

10. $P(E) = P(E \mid A_1)P(A_1) + P(E \mid A_2)P(A_2) + P(E \mid A_3)P(A_3)$

$= (.01)(.3) + (.02)(.3) + (.02)(.4) = 0.017$

12. $P(A_1 \mid E) = \dfrac{P(E \mid A_1)P(A_1)}{P(E \mid A_1)P(A_1) + P(E \mid A_2)P(A_2)} = \dfrac{(.03)(.4)}{.018} = \dfrac{2}{3}$

$P(A_2 \mid E) = \dfrac{P(E \mid A_2)P(A_2)}{P(E)} = \dfrac{(.01)(.6)}{.018} = \dfrac{1}{3}$

14. $P(A_1 \mid E) = \dfrac{P(E \mid A_1)P(A_1)}{P(E)} = \dfrac{(.01)(.3)}{.017} = \dfrac{3}{17}$

$P(A_2 \mid E) = \dfrac{P(E \mid A_2)P(A_2)}{P(E)} = \dfrac{(.02)(.3)}{.017} = \dfrac{6}{17}$

$P(A_3 \mid E) = \dfrac{P(E \mid A_3)P(A_3)}{P(E)} = \dfrac{(.02)(.4)}{.017} = \dfrac{8}{17}$

16. $P(A_2 \mid E) = \dfrac{P(E \mid A_2)}{P(E \mid A_1) + P(E \mid A_2) + P(E \mid A_3)} = \dfrac{.018}{.010 + .018 + .020} = .375$

$P(A_3 \mid E) = \dfrac{.020}{.048} \approx .417$

18. $P(A_1 \mid E) = \dfrac{(.05)(.98)}{(.05)(.98) + (.95)(.15)} = \dfrac{.049}{.1915} \approx .256$

20. Let A = the event that the person has tuberculosis
B = the test is positive

$$P(A \mid B) = \frac{P(B \mid A)P(A)}{P(B \mid A)P(A) + P(B \mid \bar{A})P(\bar{A})} = \frac{(.90)(.11)}{(.90)(.11) + (.3)(.89)} = .27$$

If the test indicates that a person has tuberculosis, you can be 27% certain that this is the case; therefore, 73% of those diagnosed as having tuberculosis by this test actually do not have it.

22. Let A = the event that the nurse forgot the pill
2D = Mr. Brown died

$$P(A \mid D) = \frac{P(D \mid A)P(A)}{P(D \mid A)P(A) + P(D \mid \bar{A})P(\bar{A})} = \frac{(\frac{3}{4})(\frac{2}{3})}{(\frac{3}{4})(\frac{2}{3}) + (\frac{1}{3})(\frac{1}{3})} = \frac{9}{11}$$

24. P = positive result A = oil present B = oil not present

$$P(A \mid P) = \frac{P(P \mid A)P(A)}{P(P \mid A)P(A) + P(P \mid B)P(B)} = \frac{(.95)(.01)}{(.95)(.01) + (.02)(.99)} = \frac{.095}{.293} = .32$$

26. $P(A_j \mid E) = \dfrac{P(A_j \cap E)}{P(E)}$

$P(A_j \cap E) = P(A_j)P(E \mid A_j)$

$P(E) = P(A_1 \cap E) + \ldots + P(A_n \cap E)$

$= P(A_1)P(E \mid A_1) + \ldots + P(A_n)P(E \mid A_n)$

Review Exercises (page 327)

2. (a) S = {HHH, HHT, HTH, HTT, THH, THT, TTH, TTT}.
The probability of each simple event is 1/8.

(b) (i) 1/2 (ii) 1/2
(iii) 1 - P(HHT, HTT) = 3/4 (iv) 1 - P(TTT) = 7/8
(v) 1/2 (vi) 1/8

4. (a) $P(A \cup B) = P(A) + P(B) - P(A \cup B) = .3 + .5 - .2 = .6$
(b) $P(\bar{A}) = 1 - P(A) = 1 - .3 = .7$
(c) $P(\overline{A \cup B}) = 1 - P(A \cup B) = 1 - .6 = .4$
(d) $P(\bar{A} \cup \bar{B}) = P(\overline{A \cap B}) = 1 - .2 = .8$

6. (a) No; e.g., P(0,0,0) = 1/8, P(1,1,1) = 1/512
(b) (0,0,0) (c) P(F) = 3!(1/2)(1/8)(3/8) = 9/64

8. (a) $P(\bar{E}) = 1 - P(E) = .7$ (b) $P(\bar{F}) = 1 - P(F) = .55$
(c) $P(E \cap F) = P(\varnothing) = 0$ (d) $P(E \cup F) = P(E) + P(F) = .75$
(e) $P(\overline{E \cap F}) = 1 - 0 = 1$ (f) $P(\overline{E \cup F}) = 1 - .75 = .25$
(g) $P(\bar{E} \cup \bar{F}) = P(\overline{E \cap F}) = 1$ (h) $P(\bar{E} \cap \bar{F}) = P(\overline{E \cup F}) = .25$

10. P(5) = 4/36 thus the odds are 4/36 to 32/36 or 1 to 8.

12. $P(E) = \frac{1}{4}$, $P(F) = \frac{3}{4}$, $P(E \cap F) = \frac{3}{16} = \frac{1}{4} \cdot \frac{1}{4} = P(E)P(F)$

14. (a) 9/13 (b) 12/23 (c) 22/69 (d) 11/69

(e) 3/13 (f) 2/7 (g) 17/42 (h) 13/42

16. Let A = output from A_1, B = output from A_2,
C = output from A_3, D = defective output

$P(A) = .55, \quad P(B) = .30, \quad P(C) = .15$

$P(D \mid A) = .01, \quad P(D \mid B) = .02, \quad P(D \mid C) = .03$

$$P(A \mid D) = \frac{P(A \cap D)}{P(D)} = \frac{P(D \mid A) \cdot P(A)}{P(D \mid A) \cdot P(A) + P(D \mid B) \cdot P(B) + P(D \mid C) \cdot P(C)}$$

$$= \frac{(.55)(.01)}{(.55)(.01) + (.30)(.02) + (.15)(.03)} = \frac{11}{32} = .34375$$

$$P(B \mid D) = \frac{P(D \mid B) \cdot P(B)}{P(D)} = \frac{(.30)(.02)}{.0160} = \frac{6}{16} = .375$$

$$P(C \mid D) = \frac{P(D \mid C) \cdot P(C)}{P(D)} = \frac{(.15)(.03)}{.0160} = \frac{9}{32} = .28125$$

18. Each toss is independent of the others.
Let A = even sum on first toss
B = sum less than 6 on second toss
C = 7 on third toss

$P(A)P(B)P(C) = (1/2)(10/36)(1/6) = 5/216$

CHAPTER 8

Exercise 8.1 (page 339)

2. (a) 2^6 (b) $C(6,3) = 20$
   (c) $C(6,2)+C(6,3)+C(6,4)+C(6,5)+C(6,6) = 15+20+15+6+1 = 57$
   (d) $C(6,4)+C(6,5) = 15+6 = 21$

4. (a) $C(25,5) = 53{,}130$ (b) $C(15,5) = 3{,}003$
   (c) $C(15,3)\cdot C(10,2) = 455\cdot 45 = 20{,}475$
   (d) $C(15,4)\cdot C(10,1)+C(15,5)\cdot C(10,0) = 13{,}650+3{,}003 = 16{,}653$

6. $\dfrac{12!}{3!\,4!\,5!} = 27{,}720$

8. $\dfrac{9!}{2!\,2!} = 90{,}720$ (There are 9 letters, including 2 C's and 2 O's.)

10. $\dfrac{100!}{22!\,13!\,10!\,5!\,16!\,17!\,17!}$

12. (a) $C(9,4)C(9,3)C(9,2) = 381{,}024$ (b) $C(9,4)C(5,3) = 1260$

14. (a) $\dfrac{7!}{2!\,2!\,3!} = 210$ (b) $\dfrac{6!}{2!\,2!\,2!} = 90$

16. $\dfrac{1}{2}\cdot\dfrac{7!}{2!\,1\,3!\,1!} = 210$

18. (a) $8\cdot C(6,1) = 48$
    (b) $2\cdot C(8,3) = 112$

20. (a) $\dfrac{\binom{8}{4}}{2^8} = .2734$ (b) $\dfrac{\binom{8}{3}+\binom{8}{4}+\binom{8}{5}}{2^8} = .7109$
    (c) $\dfrac{\binom{8}{0}+\binom{8}{1}+\binom{8}{2}+\binom{8}{3}}{2^8} = .3633$

22. (a) $\dfrac{P(10,5)}{10^5} = .3024$ (b) $1-.3024 = .6976$ (c) $1-\left(\dfrac{9}{10}\right)^5 = .4095$

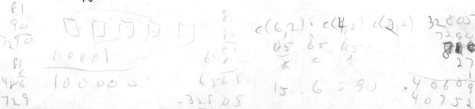

24. $1-\left(\frac{5}{13}\cdot\frac{4}{12}+\frac{8}{13}\cdot\frac{7}{12}\right)=.5128$

26. .5

28. $\dfrac{\binom{10}{1}+\binom{10}{3}+\binom{10}{5}+\binom{10}{7}+\binom{10}{9}}{2^{10}}=.5$

Exercise 8.2 (page 346)

2. $(x+y)^4=x^4+4x^3y+6x^2y^2+4xy^3+y^4$

4. $(2x+y)^3=8x^3+12x^2y+6xy^2+y^3$

6. $(x-y)^4=x^4-4x^3y+6x^2y^2-4xy^3+y^4$

8. $C(8,2)x^2=28x^2$

10. $C(5,3)2^2=10\cdot 4=40$

12. 2^{30}

14. $\binom{10}{0}+\binom{10}{2}+\binom{10}{4}+\binom{10}{6}+\binom{10}{8}+\binom{10}{10}=512$

16. $\binom{8}{5}=\binom{7}{5}+\binom{7}{4}=\binom{6}{5}+\binom{6}{4}+\binom{7}{4}=\binom{5}{5}+\binom{5}{4}+\binom{6}{4}+\binom{7}{4}=\binom{4}{4}+\binom{5}{4}+\binom{6}{4}+\binom{7}{4}$

18. $\binom{7}{1}+\binom{7}{3}+\binom{7}{5}+\binom{7}{7}=\binom{6}{1}+\binom{6}{0}+\binom{6}{3}+\binom{6}{2}+\binom{6}{5}+\binom{6}{4}+\binom{6}{6}=2^6$

20. $\binom{8}{8}+\binom{9}{8}+\binom{10}{8}=\left[\binom{9}{9}+\binom{9}{8}\right]+\binom{10}{8}=\binom{10}{9}+\binom{10}{8}=\binom{11}{8}$

Exercise 8.3 (page 354)

2. $b(8,6;.4)=.0413$

4. $b(8,5;.6)=b(8,3;.4)=.2787$

6. $b(12,6;.9)=b(12,6;.1)=.0005$

8. $b(8,6;.4)+b(8,7;.4)+b(8,8;.4)=.0413+.0079+.0007=.0499$

10. $b\left(3,1;\frac{1}{3}\right)=3\left(\frac{1}{3}\right)\left(\frac{2}{3}\right)^2=.444\ldots$

12. $b\left(3,3;\frac{1}{6}\right)=\left(\frac{1}{6}\right)^3=.004\overline{629}$

14. $b\left(5,0;\frac{2}{3}\right)=\left(\frac{1}{3}\right)^5\approx.0041152$

16. $b(9,5;.2)=.0165$

18. b(15, 8; .75) = b(15, 7; .25) = .0393

20. b(7, 0; .15) + b(7, 1; .15) + b(7, 2; .15) + b(7, 3; .15) =
.3206 + .3960 + .2097 + .0617 = .9880

22. b(8, 2; .5) = .1094

24. b(8, 2; .5) + b(8, 1; .5) + b(8, 0; .5) = .1094 + .0312 + .0039 = .1445

26. (a) b(10, 3; .25) = .2503 (b) b(10, 0; .25) = .0563
(c) b(10, 8; .25) + b(10, 9; .25) + b(10, 10; .25) = .0004
(d) 1 - .0004 = .9996

28. (a) b(8, 2; .4) = .2090
(b) 1 - [b(8, 0; .4) + b(8, 1; .4)] = 1 - .1064 = .8936
(c) b(8, 0; .4) = .0168
(d) b(8, 0; .4) + b(8, 1; .4) + b(8, 2; .4) + b(8, 3; .4) = .5941

30. P(" 11" on one roll) = $\frac{1}{18}$

P(" 11" 3 times in 7 rolls) = $b\left(7,3;\frac{1}{8}\right)=\binom{7}{3}\left(\frac{1}{18}\right)^3\left(\frac{17}{18}\right)^4\approx.00477$

32. b(8, 0; .6) + b(8, 1; .6) +b(8, 2, .6) +b(8, 3; .6)
= b(8, 8; .4) +b(8, 7; .4) +b(8, 6; .4) +b(8, 5; .4)
= .0007 + .0079 + .0413 + .1239 = .1738

34. (a) b(7, 4; .5) = .2734
(b) 1 - [b(7, 0; .5) +b(7, 1; .5)] = 1 - (.0078 + .0574) = .9348
(c) b(7, 2; .5) +b(7, 3; .5) +b(7, 4; .5) = .1641 + .2734 + .2734 = .7109

36. (a) b(4, 2; .25) + b(4, 3; .25) +b(4, 4; .25)= .2109 + .0469 + .0039 = .2617
(b) b(4, 1; .25) =.4219; .4219 + .2617 = .6836

38. (a) b(15, 0; .05) = .4633
(b) 1 - [b(15, 0; .05) + b(15, 1; .05)] = 1 - (.4633 + .3658) = .1709

40. Let A = exactly 3 tails

B = at least one tail

$$P(A \mid B) = \frac{P(A \cap B)}{P(B)} = \frac{P(A)}{P(B)}$$

$P(A) = b(8, 3; .5) = .2188$

$P(B) = 1 - P(\bar{B})$ $\quad$ $P(\bar{B}) = b(8, 0; .5) = .0039$

$= .9961$ $\quad$ $P(A \mid B) = \frac{.2188}{.9961} = .2198$

42. b(7, 4; .35) + b(7, 5; .35) + b(7, 6; .35) + b(7, 7; .35)
= .1442 + .0466 + .0084 + .0006 = .1998

44. b(23, 23; .98) + b(23, 22; .98) + b(23, 21; .98) + b(23, 20; .98) = .9990

46. Assume that each error is equally likely to occur on any of the 500 pages, independently of the location of the other errors; then

P(at least 3 errors on p.1) = 1 - P(less than 3 errors)
= 1 - [P(500, 0; .002) + P(500, 1; .002) + P(500, 2; .002)]
≈ 0.076

48. We want to find n so that $1 - b(n, 0; .5) \geq .98$, or $b(n, 0; .5) \leq .02$. From the table we find that the smallest such n is 6; therefore flip the coin 6 times.

Exercise 8.4 (page 363)

2. (1)(1/3) + 0(1/6) + (4)(1/4) + (-2)(1/4) = 5/6

4. The least a player should expect to pay is the expected value:

(1)(1/6) + (2)(1/6) + (3)(1/6) + . . . + (6)(1/6) = $3.50

6. A fair price is the expected value, which is (1/13)(1) + (12/13)(0) = .077

8. The expected value is (1/4)(2) + (1/2)(1) + (1/4)(0) = 1
Since $1 was paid to play this game, this is a fair game.

10. The expected value is (.001)(100) + (.002)(50) + (.005)(10) = .25
    The price of a ticket exceeds this value by 35¢

12. (a) Expected value is (.01)(75) + (.99)(-1) = -.24 This game is unfair.
    (b) She expects to lose 24¢

14. (a) Expectation is (11/43)(41) + (32/43)(9) = 17.19
    (b) Expected profit is 13 - 17.19 = -4.19, that is a loss of $4.19 per box

16. The expected number is (.102)(0) + (.159)(1) + (.318)(2) + (.421)(3)=2.058

18. Her expected value each time is (1/38)(35) + (37/38)(-1) = -.053
    Her expected value for 200 times is (200)(-.053) = -10.53

20. $E_1 = \frac{2}{3}(15,000) - \frac{1}{3}(3000) = 9000$

    $E_2 = \frac{1}{3}(20,000) - \frac{2}{3}(6000) = 2666.67$

    Choose location 1.

22. np = (1/2)(582) = 291

24. np = (.1)(20) = 2

26. np = (30)(1/2) = 15 right answers. The students expected score is 0.

28. $$E = 1 \cdot \frac{\binom{3}{1} \cdot \binom{9}{4}}{\binom{12}{5}} + 2 \cdot \frac{\binom{3}{2} \cdot \binom{9}{3}}{\binom{12}{5}} + 3 \cdot \frac{\binom{3}{3} \cdot \binom{9}{2}}{\binom{12}{5}} = 1.25$$

30. $$k\binom{n}{k} = k \cdot \frac{n!}{k!(n-k)!} = \frac{n!}{(k-1)!(n-k)!} = n \cdot \frac{(n-1)!}{(k-1)![n-1-(k-1)]!} = n\binom{n-1}{k-1}$$

Exercise 8.5 (page 371)

2.

Group Size	$p^n - 1/n$ (Tests Saved)
2	$(.8)^2 - 0.50 = 0.64 - 0.50 = 0.14$
3	$(.8)^3 - 0.333 = 0.512 - 0.33 = 0.179$
4	$(.8)^4 - 0.25 = 0.410 - 0.25 = 0.16$
5	$(.8)^5 - 0.20 = 0.328 - 0.20 = 0.128$

4.

Group Size	$p^n - 1/n$ (Tests Saved)
10	$(.99)^{10} - 0.100 = 0.803$
11	$(.99)^{11} - 0.091 = 0.804$
12	$(.99)^{12} - 0.083 = 0.803$

6. $A = .2(150 \cdot 180) + .3(180 \cdot 180) + .5(200 \cdot 180) - 6000 = \$27,120$

$B = 2(150 \cdot 170) + .3(180 \cdot 170) + .2(200 \cdot 170) + .2(250 \cdot 170)$
$\quad + .1(300 \cdot 170) - 8000 = \$26,680$

Therefore, the airline should schedule aircraft A.

8.

	5 years	6 years	7 years
3 year ARM	\$792	\$980	\$1228
5 year ARM	695	901	1107

Thus, 3 year ARM better for 5,6, or 7 years.

Review Exercises (page 373)

2. (a) $2^{10} = 1024$ (b) $\binom{10}{10} + \binom{10}{9} + \binom{10}{8} = 56$ 4. $1 - b(5, 0; .05) = .2262$

6. (a) $b(20, 20; .5) = 9.537 \times 10^{-7}$

   (b) $b(20, 12; .5) + b(20, 13; .5) + b(20, 14; .5) + b(20, 15; .5) + b(20, 16; .5)$
   $+ b(20, 17; .5) + b(20, 18; .5) + b(20, 19; .5) + b(20, 20; .5) = .2517$

   (c) $\frac{.2517}{1 - .2517} = .3364$

8. $P(0 \text{ red balls}) = \frac{\binom{4}{2}}{\binom{6}{2}} = \frac{6}{15}$ $P(1 \text{ red ball}) = \frac{\binom{2}{1} \cdot \binom{4}{1}}{\binom{6}{2}} = \frac{8}{15}$

   $P(2 \text{ red balls}) = \frac{\binom{2}{2}}{\binom{6}{2}} = \frac{1}{15}$

   His expected value is $\frac{6}{15}(-.70) + \frac{8}{15}(1 - .70) + \frac{1}{15}(2 - .70) = -.033$

   He overpaid by $3\frac{1}{3}$¢.

10. The expected value of the spin is $\frac{1}{3}(.30) + \frac{1}{6}(.80) + \frac{1}{2}(.10) = .283$
    The game is not fair at 30¢ per spin.

12. The expected number is $np = (200)(1/4) = 50$

14. (a) $1 - q^{30}$, where $q = 1 - p$

    (b) Expected number of tests is $(1)(q^{30}) + (31)(1 - q^{30}) = 31 - 30q^{30}$

16. $b\left(5, 3; \frac{1}{18}\right) + b\left(5, 4; \frac{1}{18}\right) + b\left(5, 5; \frac{1}{18}\right) = 1.575 \times 10^{-3}$

CHAPTER 9

Exercise 9.1 (page 380)

2. Hand-pick resistors from a production line at random time intervals during a typical workweek.

4. Randomly choose names and addresses of registered voters from representative precincts. (Consult professional polling organizations for methods of choosing representative precincts.)

6. Program a computer to utilize a random-number generator to randomly select four-person families from IRS or U.S.Census Bureau records.

8. The sample neglects families who have no savins accounts, who keep their savings in one large account in preference to several small accounts, or who have so much money that it is not efficient for them to keep it in small accounts.

10. Apparently, voters who did not have cars or telephones were more likely to vote for the winning candidate than those who did; i.e., the sample was biased against low-income voters.

Exercise 9.2 (page 386)

2. (a)

Score	Tally	Frequency f	Score	Tally	Frquency f
25	|	1	41	|||||	5
26	|	1	42	|||	3
28	|	1	43	|	1
29	|	1	44	||	2
30	|||	3	45	|	1
31	||	2	46	||	2
32	|	1	47	|	1
33	||	2	48	|||	3
34	||	2	49	|	1
35	|	1	50	|	1
36	||	2	51	|	1
37	||||	4	52	|||	3
38	|	1	53	||	2
39	|	1	54	||	2
40	|	1	55	|	1

range = 55 − 25 = 30

(b)

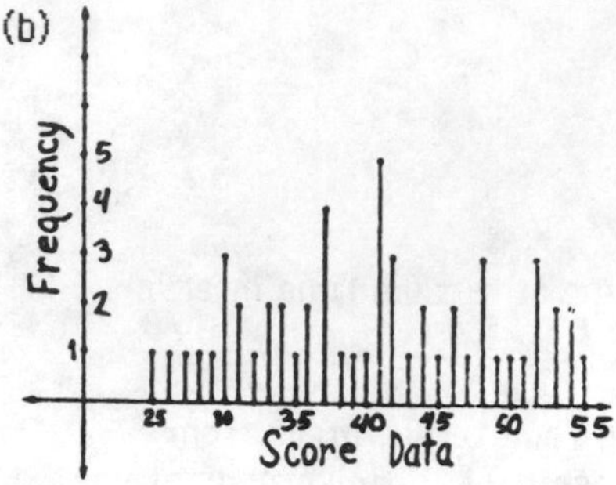

(c)

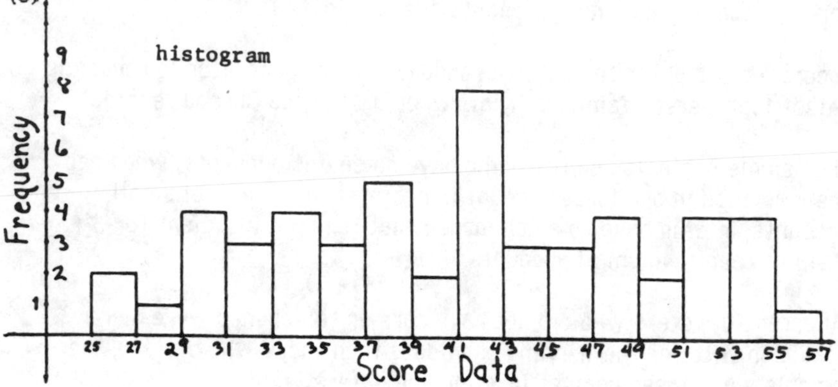

(d)

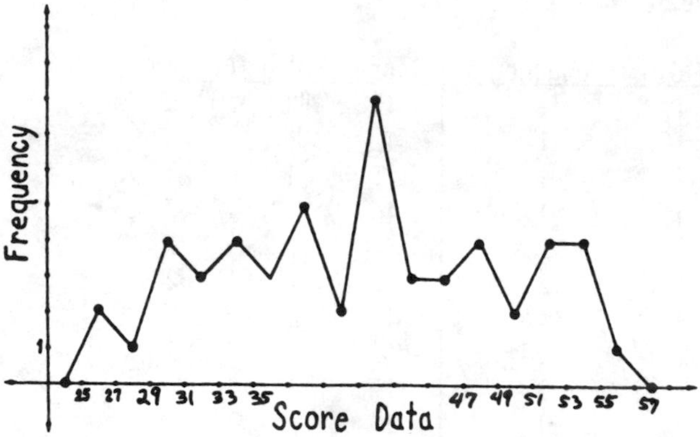

frequency polygon

(e) and (g) : Cumulative frequencies

Interval	f	c.f. (less than)	c.f. (greater than)
24.5 - 26.5	2	2	53
26.5 - 28.5	1	3	51
28.5 - 30.5	4	7	50
30.5 - 32.5	3	10	46
32.5 - 34.5	4	14	43
34.5 - 36.5	3	17	39
36.5 - 38.5	5	22	36
38.5 - 40.5	2	24	31
40.5 - 42.5	8	32	29
42.5 - 44.5	3	35	21
44.5 - 46.5	3	38	18
46.5 - 48.5	4	42	15
48.5 - 50.5	2	44	11
50.5 - 52.5	4	48	9
52.5 - 54.5	4	52	5
54.5 - 56.5	1	53	1

(f) Cumulative less than frequency

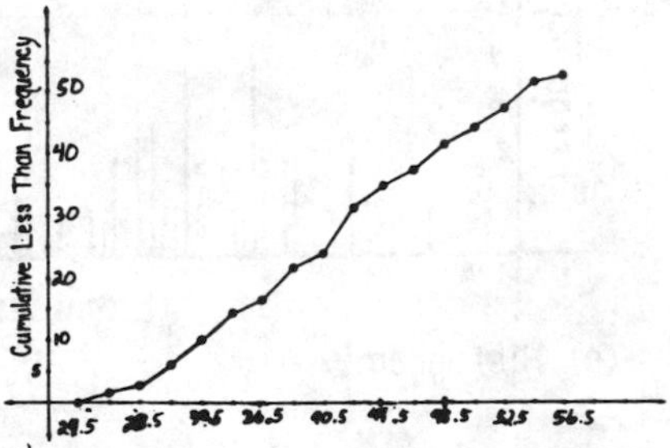

(h) Cumulative greater than **frequency**

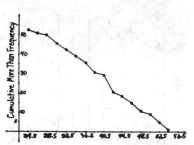

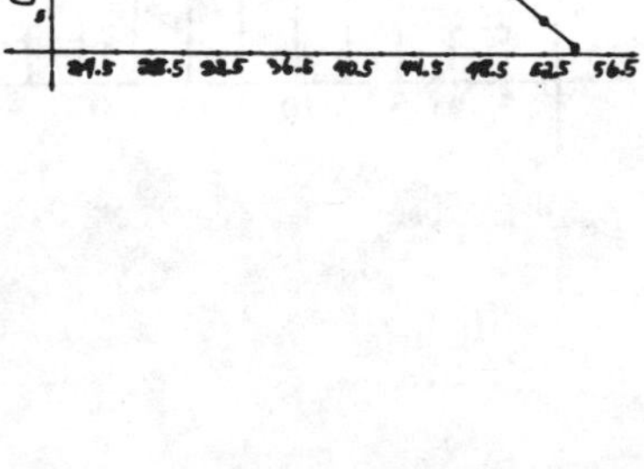

4. (a)

Earnings	Tally	Frequency f	Earnings	Tally	Frequency f
8.4	|	1	11.8	|	1
9.2	||	2	12.2	|	1
9.8	||	2	12.3	||	2
9.9	||	2	12.5	|	1
10.1	||	2	12.6	||	2
10.2	||||	4	12.8	||	2
10.3	|	1	12.9	|	1
10.4	|	1	13.0	|	1
10.9	|||||	5	13.1	|	1
11.0	|	1	13.2	|	1
11.1	|	1	13.4	|	1
11.2	|||	3	13.6	|	1
11.4	|||	3	14.4	|	1
11.5	|	1	14.6	|	1
11.6	||	2	16.0	|	1
11.7	|	1			

range = 16.0 - 8.4 = 7.6

(b)

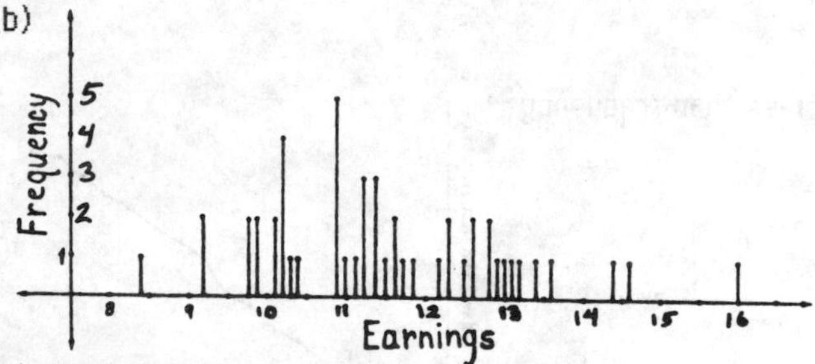

(c) Histogram

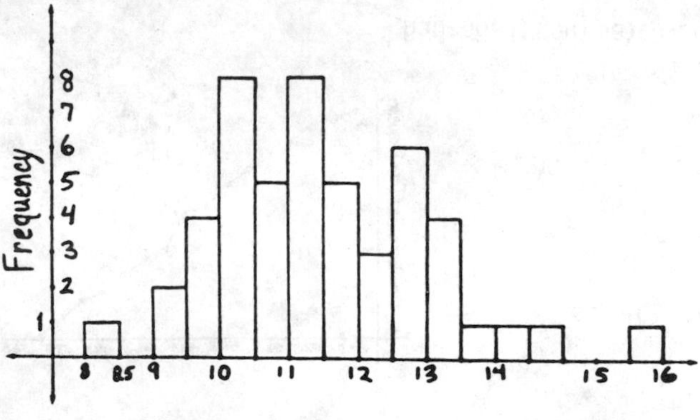

(d)

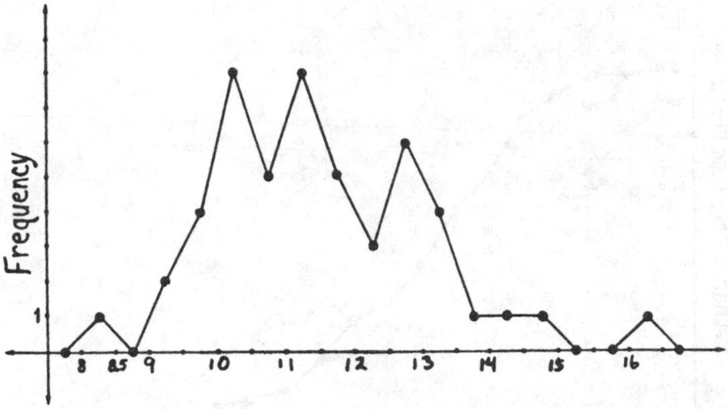

(e) and (g) : Cumulative Frequencies

Interval	f	c.f. (less than)	c.f. (greater than)
7.95 - 8.45	1	1	50
8.45 - 8.95	0	1	49
8.95 - 9.45	2	3	49
9.45 - 9.95	4	7	47
9.95 -10.45	8	15	43
10.45 -10.95	5	20	35
10.95 -11.45	8	28	30
11.45 -11.95	5	33	22
11.95 -12.45	3	36	17
12.45 -12.95	6	42	14
12.95 -13.45	4	46	8
13.45 -13.95	1	47	4
13.95 -14.45	1	48	3
14.45 -14.95	1	49	2
14.95 -15.45	0	49	1
15.45 -15.95	0	49	1
15.95 -16.45	1	50	1

(f)

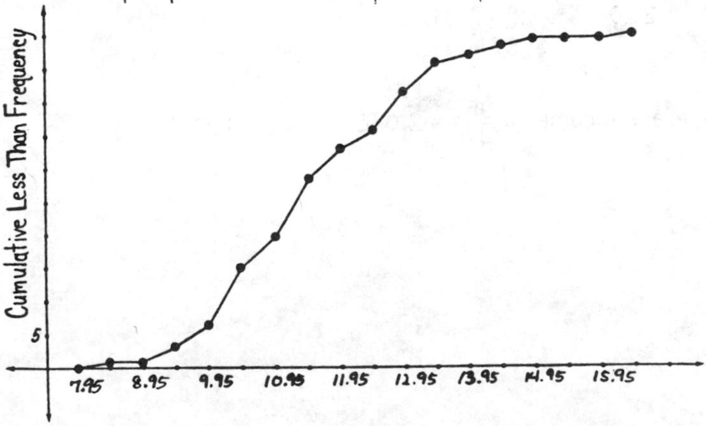

(h)

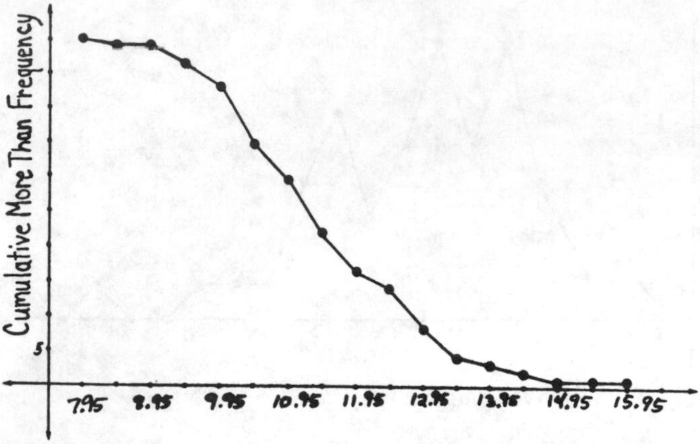

Exercise 9.3 (page 392)

2. $\bar{x} = \dfrac{16+18+24+30}{4} = 22$, median $= \dfrac{18+24}{2} = 21$, no mode

4. $\bar{x} = \dfrac{65+82+82+95+70}{5} = \dfrac{394}{5} = 78.8$, median = 82, mode = 82

6. $\bar{x} = \dfrac{48+65+80+92+80}{5} = 73$, median = 80, mode = 80

8. mean $= \dfrac{55+58+62+64+68+74+72}{7} = 64.7$, median = 64

10.

f	Cost	Total Income
120	$2.00	$240
80	2.10	168
150	1.90	285
120	2.20	264
470		$957

Average Income $= \dfrac{957}{470} \approx 2.03617 \approx \$2.04$ per bushel

12. median = class 7 (79.995 - 84.995)
mode = classes 8 and 9 (84.995 - 89.995 and 89.995 - 94.995)

i	f_i	m_i	$f_i m_i$
1	2	117.5	235
2	0	112.5	0
3	4	107.5	430
4	2	102.5	205
5	2	97.5	195
6	12	92.5	1110
7	12	87.5	1050
8	2	82.5	165
9	11	77.5	852.5
10	8	72.5	580
11	6	67.5	405
12	3	62.5	187.5
13	6	57.5	345
14	1	52.5	52.5
			5812.5

$$\text{mean} = \frac{5812}{71} \approx 81.87$$

14. From problem 2, Exercise 9.2:
mode = 41, median = 41, mean = 2163/53 ≈ 40.81
From problem 4, Exercise 9.2:
mode = 10.9, median = 11.3, mean = 574.8/50 ≈ 11.5
From problem 5, Exercise 9.2:
mode = 131, median = 153, mean = 17595/110 ≈ 159.95

16. Labor would tend to use the median in order to demonstrate how low their wages are. The mode might be even better for this purpose, in a collective-bargaining situation in which there are a large number of laborers who are all paid according to the same wage scale. Management would tend to use the mean for the opposite purpose.

18. $$\bar{x} = \frac{x_1 \cdot f_1 + x_2 \cdot f_2 + \ldots + x_n \cdot f_n}{f_1 + f_2 + \ldots + f_n}$$

Since the numerator of this fraction is the total of all individual scores and the denominator is the total number of scores.

Exercise 9.4 (page 399)

2. c has the largest variance.

4.

x	$x-\bar{X}$	$(x-\bar{X})^2$
6	-4.714	22.22
8	-2.714	7.37
10	-0.714	.51
10	-0.714	.51
11	.286	.08
12	1.286	1.65
18	7.286	53.08
75		85.42

$$\bar{X} = \frac{75}{7} \approx 10.71$$

$$\sigma = \sqrt{\frac{85.42}{7}} \approx \sqrt{12.20} \approx 3.49$$

6.

x	$x-\bar{X}$	$(x-\bar{X})^2$
55	-19	361
65	- 9	81
80	6	36
80	6	36
90	16	256
370		770

$$\bar{X} = \frac{370}{5} = 74$$

$$\sigma = \sqrt{\frac{770}{5}} \approx \sqrt{154} \approx 12.41$$

8.

x	$x-\bar{X}$	$(x-\bar{X})^2$
75	-6.2	38.44
75	-6.2	38.44
82	.8	.64
82	.8	.64
92	10.8	116.64
406		194.8

$$\bar{X} = \frac{406}{5} = 81.2$$

$$\sigma = \sqrt{\frac{194.8}{5}} \approx \sqrt{38.96} \approx 6.24$$

10. mean $\approx$ 521.84, $\sigma = \sqrt{\dfrac{96,889.346}{25}} \approx \sqrt{3,875.5738} \approx 62.25$

12. mean ≈ 81.87, $\sigma = \sqrt{\dfrac{15,946.48}{71}} \approx 14.99$

14. $\bar{x} = 6$, $\sigma = 2$ Expected number of boxes having between 0 and 12 defects $(\bar{x} - 6, \bar{x} + 6)$ will be at least $1000\left(1 - \dfrac{\sigma^2}{k^2}\right) = 1000\left(1 - \dfrac{4}{36}\right) \approx 889$.

Exercise 9.5 (page 407)

2. $\bar{X} = 100$, $\sigma = 10$

4. $\bar{X} = 2.0$, $\sigma = 0.1$

6. $z = \dfrac{x - \bar{X}}{\sigma} = \dfrac{x - 15.2}{5.1}$

x	z
8	-1.412
9	-1.216
15	-0.039
16	0.157
22	1.333
23	1.529
25	1.922

8. $z(2) - z(1) = 0.4772 - 0.3413 = 0.1359$

10. $1 - (2)(0.1915) = 0.6170$

12. $P(z > 1.6) = .5 - .4452 = .0548$; 5.48% get A's
$P(16 > z > .6) = .4452 - .2257 = .2195$; 21.95% get B's
$P(.6 > z > -.3) = .1179 + .2257 = .3436$; 34.36% get C's
$P(-.3 > z > -1.4) = .4192 - .1179 = .3013$; 30.13% get D's
$P(z < -1.4) = .5 - .4192 = .0808$; 8.08% get F's

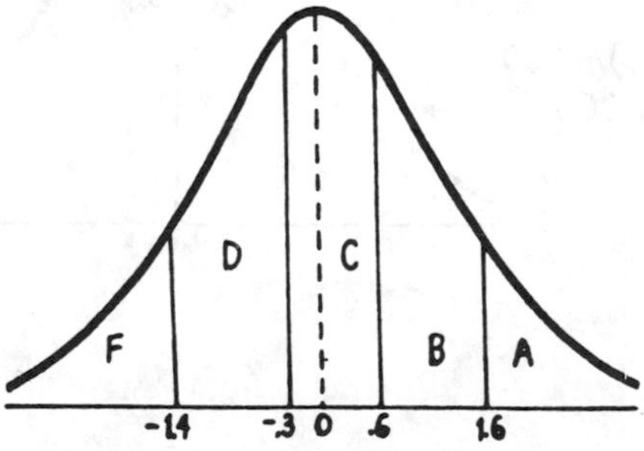

14. $z = (x - 16)/0.1$

(a) $P(15.9 \le x \le 16.1) = P(-1 \le z \le 1) = 0.6826$
$(600{,}000)(0.6826) = 409{,}560$ boxes

(b) $P(15.8 \le x \le 16.2) = P(-2 \le z \le 2) = 0.9544$
$(600{,}000)(0.9544) = 572{,}640$ boxes

(c) $P(15.7 \le x \le 16.3) = P(-3 \le z \le 3) = 0.9974$
$(600{,}000)(0.9974) = 598{,}440$ boxes

(d) $600{,}000 - 598{,}440 = 1560$

(e) $P(x < 15.7) = P(z < -.3) = .5 - .4987 = 0.0013$
$(600{,}000)(0.0013) = 780$ boxes

16. $z = \dfrac{42 - 40}{7} = 0.29$

$z = \dfrac{28 - 40}{7} = -1.71$

$P(-1.71 < z < 0.29) = 0.4564 + .1141$
$= .5705$

Approximately 57% of the clothing can be expected to last from 28 months to 42 months.

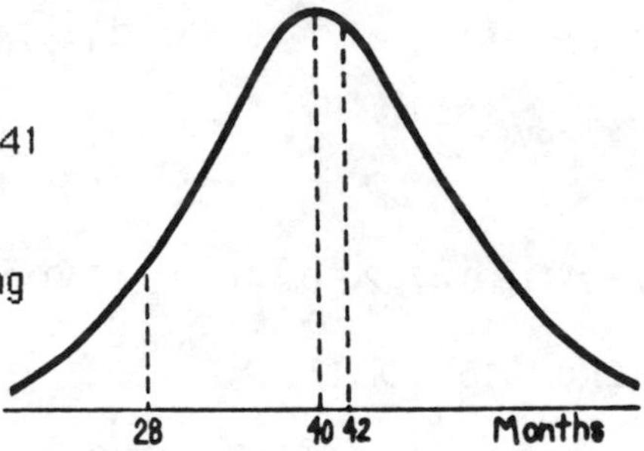

18. (a) $z = (x - 10{,}000)/1000$
Find b so that $P(z \le b) \approx .70$ or $P(0 \le z \le b) \approx 0.20$. The nearest entry in Table 2 is 0.1985, for $b = 0.52$
$z = b = 0.52 = (x - 10{,}000)/1000$
$x = 10{,}520$ in the lowest 20%

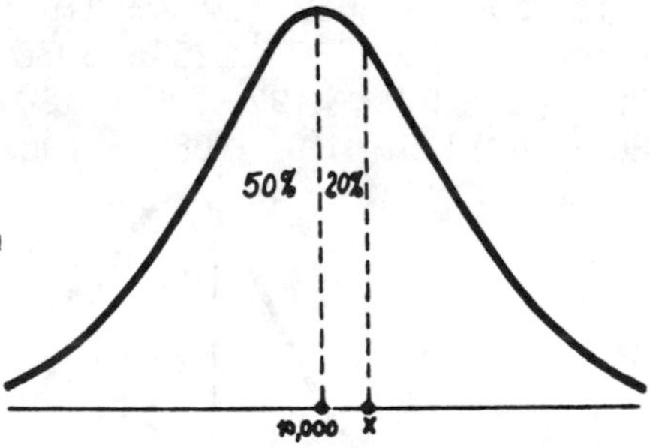

(b) $z \geq \frac{11,000 - 10,000}{1,000} = 1$

$z \leq \frac{8,500 - 10,000}{1,000} = -1.5$

$P(-1.5 < z < 1) = .4332 + .3413$
$= .7745$

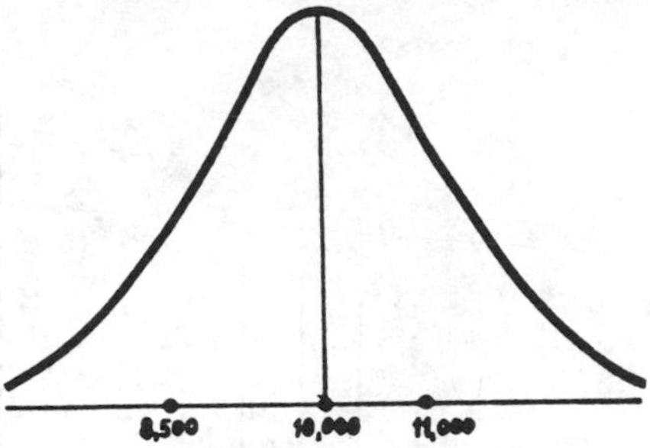

Approximately 77.45% of the attendence figures fall between 8,500 and 11,000 persons.

(c) Since $1500 = 1.5\sigma$,

$P(x \leq \bar{X} - 1500) + P(x \geq \bar{X} + 1500)$
$= P(z \leq -1.5) + P(z \geq 1.5)$
$= (.5 - .4332) + (.5 - .4332)$
$= 0.1336$ = approximately 13% of the attendence figures.

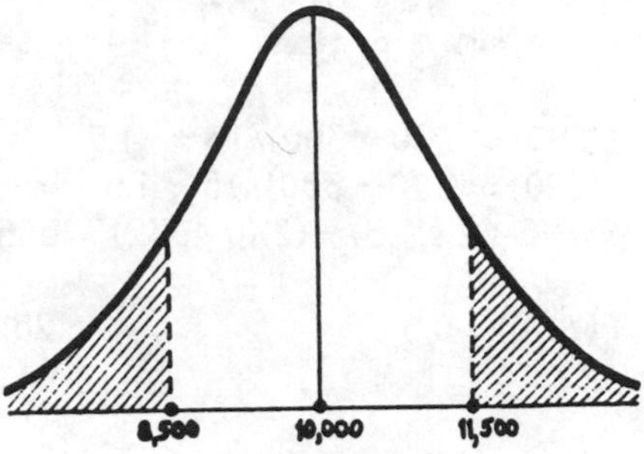

20. $z \geq \frac{68 - 75}{10} = -.7$

$z \leq \frac{82 - 75}{10} = .7$

$P(-.7 \leq z \leq .7) = .2580 + .2580 = .516$

15 scores represent 51.6% of the class.

$.516x = 15$

$x = 29$ students in the class

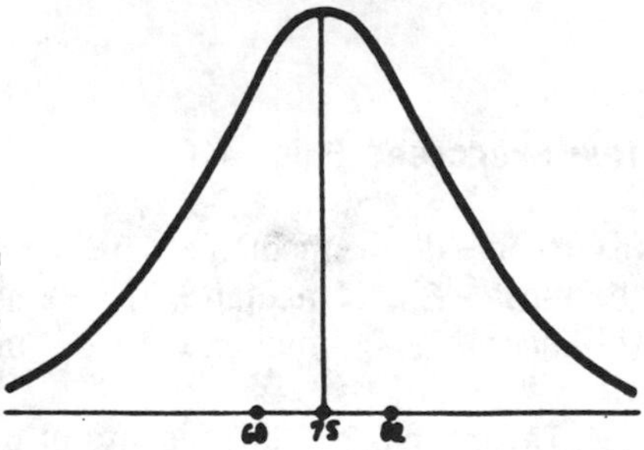

22. b(8, k; .75) = b(8, 8-k; .25)
b(8, 0; .75) = b(8, 8; .25) = .0000
b(8, 1; .75) = b(8, 7; .25) = .0004
b(8, 2; .75) = b(8, 6; .25) = .0038
b(8, 3; .75) = b(8, 5; .25) = .0231
b(8, 4; .75) = b(8, 4; .25) = .0865
b(8, 5; .75) = b(8, 3; .25) = .2076
b(8, 6; .75) = b(8, 2; .25) = .3115
b(8, 7; .75) = b(8, 1; .25) = .2670
b(8, 8; .75) = b(8, 0; .25) = .1001

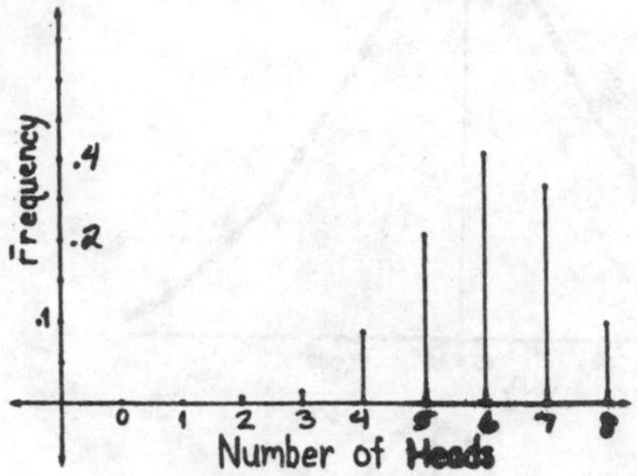

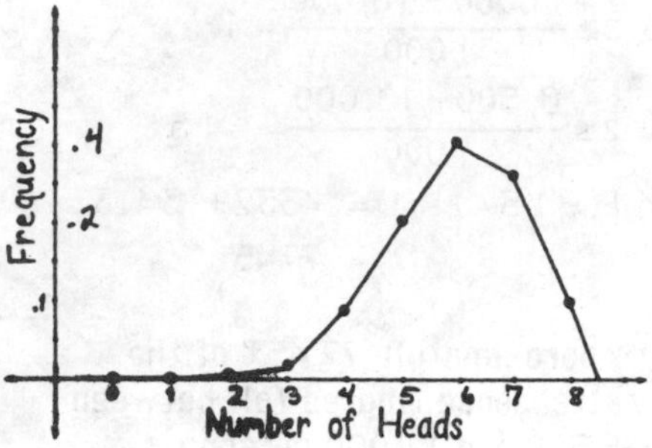

24. $z(280) = (280 - 300)/13 \approx -1.5$
    $z(320) = (320 - 300)/13 \approx 1.5$
    $P(-1.5 \le z \le 1.5) = (2)(0.4332) = .8664$

26. $P(z \le 0) = 0.5$

28. $z(275) = (275 - 300)/13 \approx -1.9$
    $P(z \le -1.9) = 0.5 - 0.4713 = 0.0287$

Review Exercises (page 410)

2. (a) mode = 4, median = 4.5, mean = 67/12 ≈ 5.58
   (b) mode = 2, median = 2, mean = 26.125
   (c) mode = 7, median = 7, mean = 62/9 ≈ 6.89

4. (a) The mean G.P.A. of students at a college.
   (b) The mode of family sizes for a group of families would identify the most typical family size.
   (c) The median income for a particular occupation or profession in a particular geographical area.

6. In any normally distributed set of data, the standard deviation is used to compute degrees of deviation from the mean (z-scores). The variance is significant to such an application only in that it is the square of the standard deviation.

Chapter 9 - p.103

8. (a) $\sigma = 5, \quad \bar{X} = 25$

$$z = \frac{20 - 25}{5} = -1$$

$$z = \frac{30 - 25}{5} = 1$$

$$P(-1 \le z \le 1) = .3413 + .3413$$
$$= .6826$$

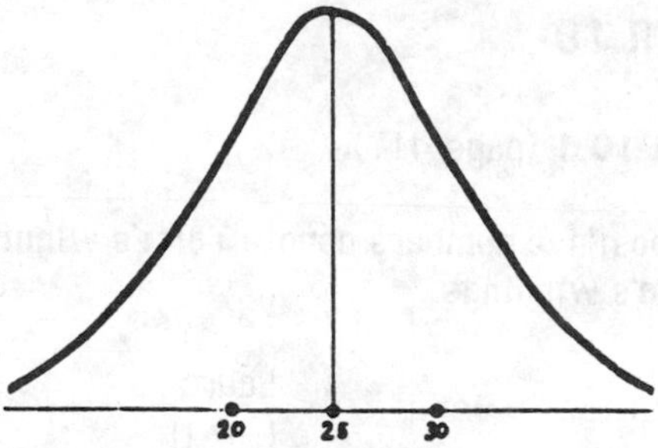

(b) $z = \dfrac{35 - 25}{5} = 2$

$$P(z > 2) = .5 - .4772 = .0228$$

10. (a) $\sigma = 1.25$

$$z = \frac{10.33 - 14}{1.25} = -2.933$$

$$P(z < -2.933) = .5 - .4983 = .0017$$

Approximately .2% of all dogs.

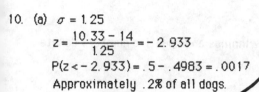

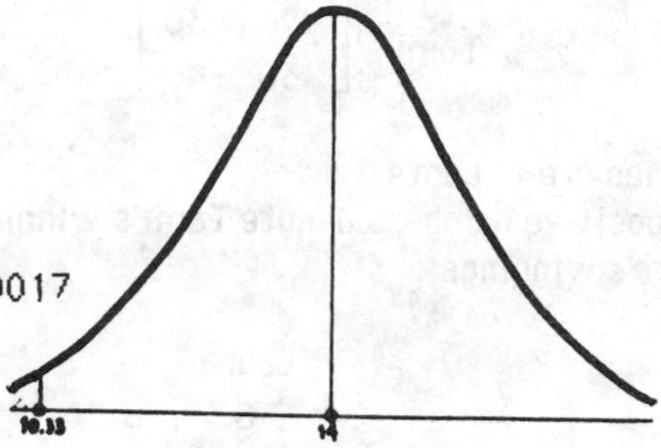

12. $z = \dfrac{89 - 79}{5} = 2 \qquad z = \dfrac{79 - 72}{3.5} = 2$

He ranked the same in both classes.

14. (a) $\bar{X} = 75, \ \sigma^2 = 25$

$$P(65 \le x \le 85) = P\left(\frac{65 - 75}{5} \le \frac{x - 75}{5} \le \frac{85 - 75}{5}\right) = P(-2 \le z \le 2)$$
$$= 2P(z \le 2) = 2(.4772) = .9544 = 95.44\%$$

(b) $P(75 - 5 \le \bar{X} \le 75 + 5) = .9$

$$P\left(\frac{70 - 75}{5/\sqrt{n}} \le \frac{\bar{X} - 75}{5/\sqrt{n}} \le \frac{80 - 75}{5/\sqrt{n}}\right) = .9$$

$$P(-\sqrt{n} \le z \le \sqrt{n}) = .9$$

$$P(z \le \sqrt{n}) = .45$$

$$\sqrt{n} = 1.645$$

$$n \approx 3$$

CHAPTER 10

Exercise 10.1 (page 417)

2. Let positive numbers denote Tami's winnings and negative numbers denote Laura's winnings.

$$\text{Tami}\ \begin{array}{c} \\ \text{I} \\ \text{II} \end{array}\!\!\begin{array}{c} \text{Laura} \\ \begin{array}{cc} \text{I} & \text{II} \end{array} \\ \begin{bmatrix} -20 & 30 \\ 30 & -40 \end{bmatrix} \end{array}$$

Entries are in cents.

4. Let positive numbers denote Tami's winnings and negative numbers denote Laura's winnings.

$$\text{Tami}\ \begin{array}{c} \\ 3 \\ 6 \\ 8 \end{array}\!\!\begin{array}{c} \text{Laura} \\ \begin{array}{ccc} 3 & 6 & 8 \end{array} \\ \begin{bmatrix} -60 & 90 & 110 \\ 90 & -120 & -140 \\ 110 & -140 & -160 \end{bmatrix} \end{array}$$

Entries are in cents.

6. Strictly determined; value = 0.

8. Strictly determined; value = 0.

10. Not strictly determined.

12. Strictly determined; value = 2.

14. Not strictly determined.

16.

$$\begin{bmatrix} a & a \\ b & c \end{bmatrix}$$

If $b \le a$, a is a saddlepoint in column 1. If $c \le a$, a is a saddlepoint in column 2. Otherwise, $a < b$ and $a < c$. If $a < b \le c$, b is a saddlepoint. If $a < c < b$, c is a saddlepoint.

Exercise 10.2 (page 420)

2. $P = [.3 \quad .4 \quad .3]$, $Q = \begin{bmatrix} .5 \\ .5 \end{bmatrix}$

The expected payoff is

Chapter 10 - p.105

$$[.3 \quad .4 \quad .3]\begin{bmatrix} 3 & -1 \\ -2 & 1 \\ -1 & 0 \end{bmatrix}\begin{bmatrix} .5 \\ .5 \end{bmatrix} = .25$$

4. $E = \begin{bmatrix} \frac{1}{2} & \frac{1}{2} \end{bmatrix}\begin{bmatrix} 4 & 0 \\ 2 & 3 \end{bmatrix}\begin{bmatrix} \frac{3}{4} \\ \frac{1}{4} \end{bmatrix} = \frac{9}{4} + \frac{3}{8} = \frac{21}{8}$

6. $E = [0 \quad 1]\begin{bmatrix} 4 & 0 \\ 2 & 3 \end{bmatrix}\begin{bmatrix} 0 \\ 1 \end{bmatrix} = 3$

8. $E = \begin{bmatrix} \frac{1}{4} & \frac{3}{4} \end{bmatrix}\begin{bmatrix} 1 & -1 \\ -2 & 3 \end{bmatrix}\begin{bmatrix} \frac{1}{3} \\ \frac{2}{3} \end{bmatrix} = \frac{-5}{12} + \frac{16}{12} = \frac{11}{12}$

10. $E = \begin{bmatrix} \frac{1}{3} & \frac{2}{3} \end{bmatrix}\begin{bmatrix} 4 & -1 \\ 2 & 3 \end{bmatrix}\begin{bmatrix} 0 \\ 1 \end{bmatrix}\begin{bmatrix} \frac{2}{3} \\ \frac{1}{6} \\ \frac{1}{6} \end{bmatrix} = \frac{16}{9} + \frac{5}{18} + \frac{1}{9} = \frac{13}{6}$

Exercise 10.3 (page 427)

2. $E_I = 2p + 3(1 - p) = 3 - p$

$E_I = 4p - 2(1 - p) = -2 + 6p$

$3 - p = -2 + 6p$

$-7p = -5$

$p = \frac{5}{7}$

Optimal strategy for player I is

$\begin{bmatrix} \frac{5}{7} & \frac{2}{7} \end{bmatrix}$.

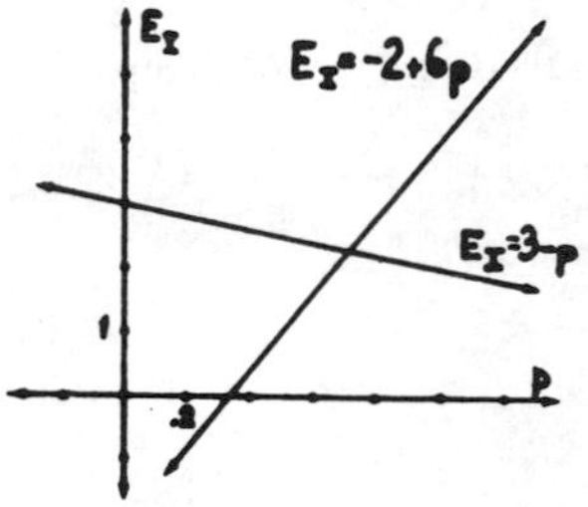

$E_{II} = 2q + 4(1 - q) = 4 - 2q$

$E_{II} = 3q - 2(1 - q) = -2 + 5q$

The optimal strategy for player II is

$$E = PAQ = \begin{pmatrix} \frac{5}{7} & \frac{2}{7} \end{pmatrix}\begin{bmatrix} 2 & 4 \\ 3 & -2 \end{bmatrix}\begin{bmatrix} \frac{6}{7} \\ \frac{1}{7} \end{bmatrix} = \frac{16}{7}$$

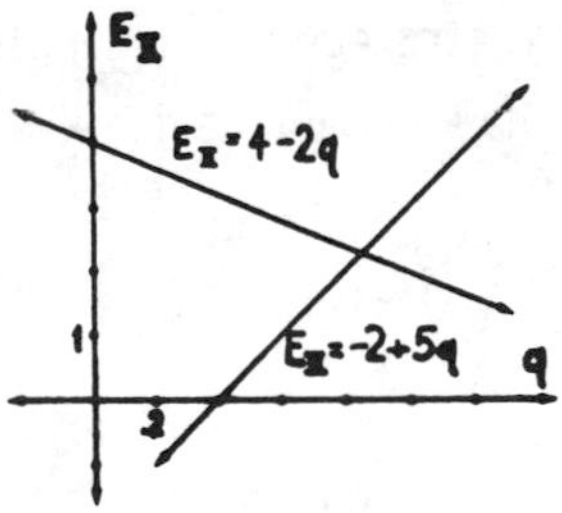

4. $E_I = 3p - (1 - p) = 4p = 1$

$E_I = -2p + 2(1 - p) = 2 - 4p$

Optimal strategy for player I is $\begin{bmatrix} \frac{3}{8} & \frac{5}{8} \end{bmatrix}$.

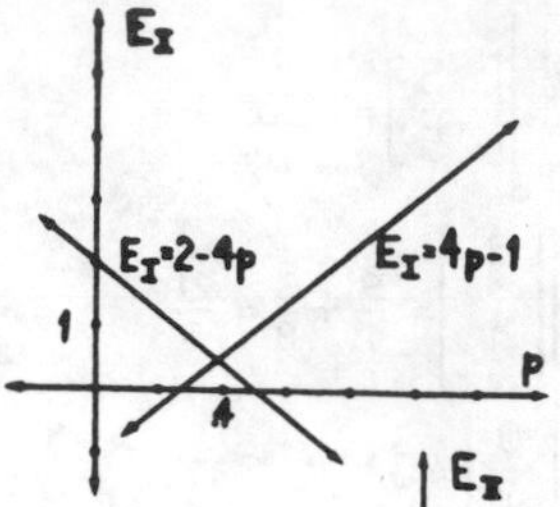

$E_{II} = 3q - 2(1 - q) = 5q - 2$

$E_{II} = v - q + 2(1 - q) = 2 - 3q$

Optimal strategy for player II is $[.5 \quad .5]$. The value of the game is

$$E = PAQ = \begin{bmatrix} \frac{3}{8} & \frac{5}{8} \end{bmatrix} \begin{bmatrix} 3 & -2 \\ -1 & 2 \end{bmatrix} \begin{bmatrix} \frac{1}{2} \\ \frac{1}{2} \end{bmatrix} = \frac{1}{2}$$

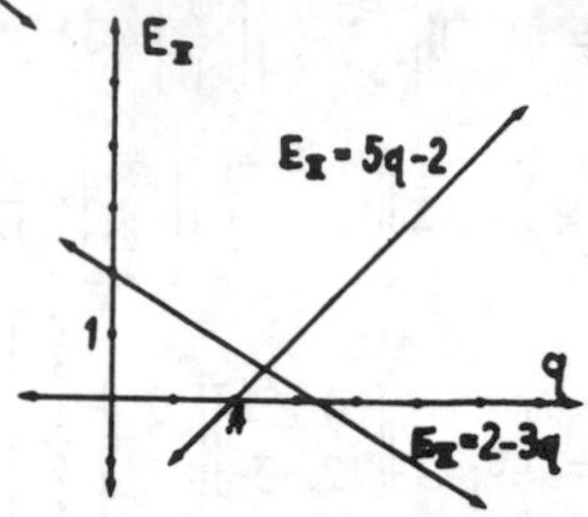

6. $\left. \begin{array}{l} E_I = 5p - 3(1 - p) = 8p - 3 \\ E_I = 4p + 7(1 - p) = 7 - 3p \end{array} \right\} \quad p = \frac{10}{11}$

The optimal strategy for player I is $\begin{bmatrix} \frac{10}{11} & \frac{1}{11} \end{bmatrix}$.

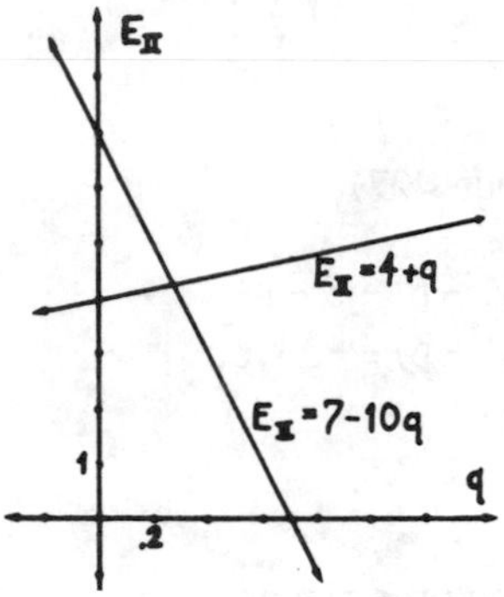

$E_{II} = 5q + 4(1 - q) = 4 + q$

$E_{II} = -3q + 7(1 - q) = 7 - 10q$

The optimal strategy for player II is $\begin{bmatrix} \frac{3}{11} & \frac{8}{11} \end{bmatrix}$. The value of the game is

$$E = PAQ = \begin{bmatrix} \frac{10}{11} & \frac{1}{11} \end{bmatrix} \begin{bmatrix} 5 & 4 \\ -3 & 7 \end{bmatrix} \begin{bmatrix} \frac{3}{11} \\ \frac{8}{11} \end{bmatrix} = \frac{47}{11}$$

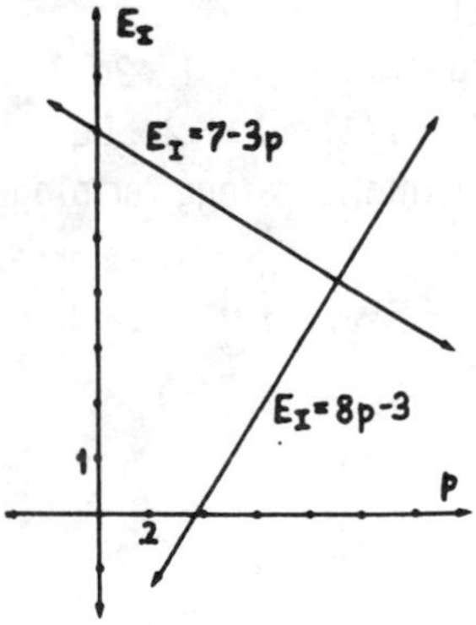

8.

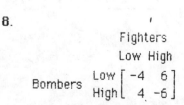

		Fighters Low	Fighters High
Bombers	Low	−4	6
	High	4	−6

$$p_1 = \frac{-6-4}{-4+(-6)-6-4} = \frac{-10}{-20} = \frac{1}{2}, \qquad p_2 = \frac{1}{2}$$

$$q_1 = \frac{-6-6}{-4+(-6)-4-6} = \frac{-12}{-20} = \frac{6}{10} = \frac{3}{5}, \qquad q_2 = \frac{2}{5}$$

The value is 0. The bombers can decide to fly high or low by flipping a fair coin. The fighters can decide whether to fly high or low by using an urn with 3 black and 2 white balls. If a black ball is drawn, they should fly low.

10. If

$$E_1 = a_{11}p_1 + a_{21}(1-p_1) = (a_{11} - a_{21})p_1 + a_{21}$$

and

$$E_1 = a_{12}p_1 + a_{22}(1-p_1) = (a_{12} - a_{22})p_1 + a_{22}$$

then

$$(a_{11} - a_{21})p_1 + a_{21} = (a_{12} - a_{22})p_1 + a_{22}$$

$$(a_{11} - a_{21} - a_{12} + a_{22})p_1 = a_{22} - a_{21}$$

$$p_1 = \frac{a_{22} - a_{21}}{a_{11} + a_{22} - a_{21} - a_{12}}$$

which is the first part of formula (3).

$$1 - p_1 = \frac{a_{11} - a_{12}}{a_{11} + a_{22} - a_{21} - a_{12}}$$

which is the second part of formula (3).
Similarly, if

$$E_{II} = a_{11}q_1 + a_{12}(1-q_1) = (a_{11} - a_{12})q_1 + a_{12}$$

and

$$E_{II} = a_{21}q_1 + a_{22}(1-q_1) = (a_{21} - a_{22})q_1 + a_{22}$$

then formula (4) is true.

Exercise 10.4 (page 437)

2. Let player 1 play row 1 with probability p. Hen then plays row 2 with probability (1 - p). Player 2 has 3 choices. The expected earnings for player 1 for each of the choices are

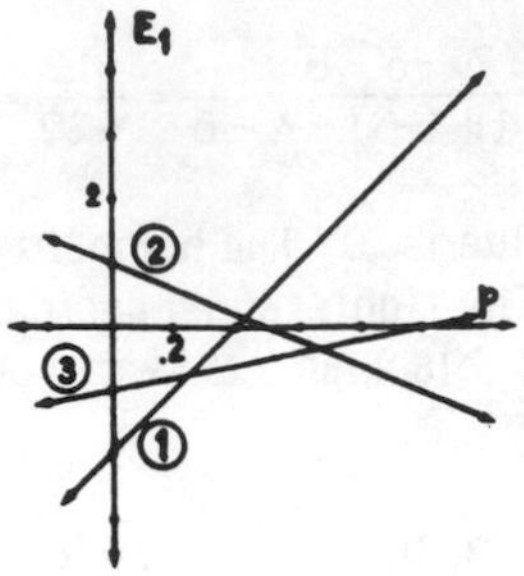

1. $E_1 = 3p - 2(1 - p) \quad E_1 = 5p - 2$
2. $E_1 = -1p + 1(1 - p) \quad E_1 = -2p + 1$
3. $E_1 = 0p - 1(1 - p) \quad E_1 = p - 1$

the graphs of these equations shows that the intersection of lines 2 and 3 yields the optimal strategy for player 1.

$$-2p + 1 = p - 1$$
$$p = \frac{2}{3}$$
$$1 - p = \frac{1}{3}$$
$$v = E_1 = \frac{2}{3} - 1 = -\frac{1}{3}$$

Eliminating column 1, the reduced matrix is:

$$\begin{matrix} 2 & 3 \end{matrix}$$
$$\begin{bmatrix} -1 & 0 \\ 1 & -1 \end{bmatrix}$$

thus $q_1 = 0$,

$$q_2 = \frac{1-0}{-1-1-1-0} = \frac{1}{3},$$
$$q_3 = \frac{2}{3}$$

Player 1 should select row 1 with probability $\frac{2}{3}$ and row 2 with probability $\frac{1}{3}$. Player 2 should not select column 1. Player 2 should select column 2 with probability $\frac{1}{3}$ and column 3 with probabililty $\frac{2}{3}$. The value of the game is $\left(-\frac{1}{3}\right)$.

4. Let player 2 choose column 1 with probability of q, column 2 with probability (1 - q). Depending on which row is chosen by player 1, the expected values are

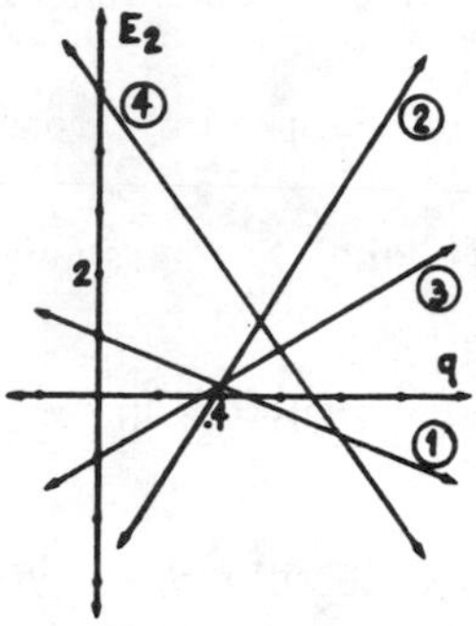

1. $E_2 = -q + (1 - q) = 1 - 2q$
2. $E_2 = 5q - 3(1 - q) = 8q - 3$
3. $E_2 = q - 2(1 - q) = 3q - 1$
4. $E_2 = -2q + 5(1 - q) = 5 - 7q$

The graph shows that the intersection of lines 2 and 4 gives the optimal choice of q for player 2:

$$q = \frac{8}{15}, \quad (1 - q) = \frac{7}{15}$$

Eliminating rows 1 and 3 from the matrix and setting $p_1 = p_3 = 0$, the reduced matrix

$$\begin{matrix} 2 & 4 \end{matrix}$$
$$\begin{bmatrix} 5 & -3 \\ -2 & 5 \end{bmatrix} \text{gives } p_2 = \frac{7}{15} \text{ and } p_4 = \frac{8}{15}.$$

Player 1 should never select row 1, select row 2 with probability $\frac{7}{15}$, never select row 3, and select row 4 with probability $\frac{8}{15}$. Player 2 should select colulmn 1 with probability $\frac{8}{15}$ and column 2 with probability $\frac{7}{15}$. The value of the game is $5-7\left(\frac{8}{15}\right) = \frac{19}{15}$.

6. Player 1 chooses row 1 with probability p, row 2 with probabilty (1 - p). Depending on which column is chosen by player 2, the expected values are:

1. $E_1 = 3p - (1 - p) = 4p - 1$
2. $E_1 = -2p + (1 - p) = -3p + 1$
3. $E_1 = 2p + 0(1 - p) = 2p$

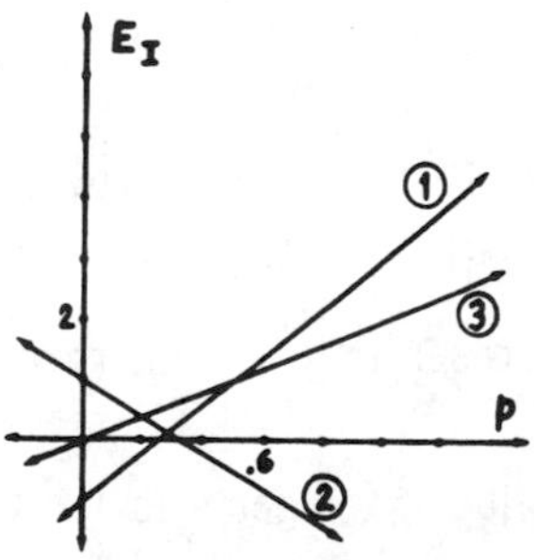

The intersection of lines 1 and 2 yields the optimum strategy for player 1:

$$4p - 1 = -3p + 1, \qquad p = \frac{2}{7}, \quad 1-p = \frac{5}{7}$$

Eliminating column 3, the reduced matrix

$$\begin{bmatrix} 3 & -2 \\ -1 & 1 \end{bmatrix} \text{ yields } q_1 = \frac{1+2}{3+1+1+2} = \frac{3}{7}, \quad q_2 = \frac{4}{7} \quad (q_3 = 0)$$

Player 1 should select row 1 with probability $\frac{2}{7}$ and row 2 with probability $\frac{5}{7}$. Player 2 should select column 1 with probability $\frac{3}{7}$, column 2 with probability $\frac{4}{7}$, and never select column 3.

The value of the game is $\frac{8}{7} - 1 = \frac{1}{7}$.

8. 1. $E_1 = -5p + 3(1 - p) = 3 - 8p$
2. $E_1 = -4p + 2(1 - p) = 2 - 6p$
3. $E_1 = -3p + (1 - p) = 1 - 4p$
4. $E_1 = = 2p - 2(1 - p) = 4p - 2$
5. $E_1 = 3p - 4(1 - p) = 7p - 4$

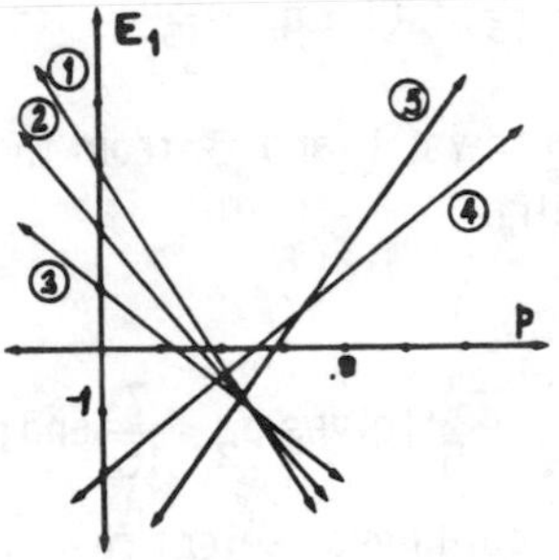

The intersection of lines 3 and 5 gives the optimum strategy for player 1.

$$1 - 4p = 7p - 4, \qquad p = \frac{5}{11}, \qquad 1 - p = \frac{6}{11}$$

Eliminating all the columns except 3 and 5, we get

$$\begin{bmatrix} -3 & 3 \\ 1 & -4 \end{bmatrix}, \quad q_3 = \frac{-4-3}{-3-4-1-3} = \frac{7}{11}, \quad q_5 = \frac{4}{11}$$

3 5

$$(q_1 = q_2 = q_4 = 0)$$

Player 1 should select row 1 with probability $\frac{5}{11}$ and row 2 with probability $\frac{6}{11}$. Player 2 should never select rows 1, 2, or 4, select row 3 with probability $\frac{7}{11}$ and row 5 with probability $\frac{4}{11}$.

The value of the game is $1 - 4p = -\frac{9}{11}$.

10. Player 2 chooses column 1 with probability q, column 2 with probability (1 - q). Player 1 has 5 choices. The expected earnings are

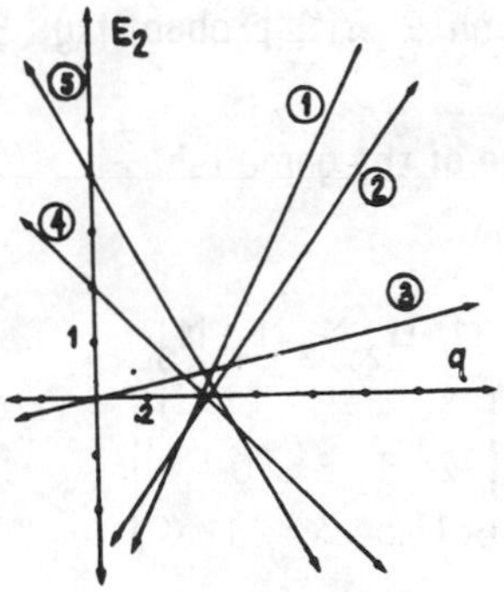

1. $E_2 = 6q - 4(1 - q) = 10q - 4$
2. $E_2 = 4q - 3(1 - q) = 7q - 3$
3. $E_2 = q - 0(1 - q) = q$
4. $E_2 = -3q + 2(1 - q) = 2 - 5q$
5. $E_2 = -5q + 4(1 - q) = 4 - 9q$

The graph shows that the intersection of lines 3 and 5 yields the optimum strategy for player 2.

$$q = 4 - 9q, \qquad q = 0.4, \qquad 1-q = 0.6$$

Eliminating all rows except 3 and 5:

$$p_1 = p_2 = p_4 = 0, \qquad p_3 = 0.9, \qquad p_5 = 0.1$$

Player 1 should never select rows 1, 2, or 4, select row 3 with probability 0.9, and row 5 with probability 0.1. Player 2 should select column 1 with probability 0.4 and column 2 with probabiltiy 0.6.

The value of the game is 0.4.

12.

$$\begin{bmatrix} 3 & 2 & 0 \\ 1 & 5 & -2 \\ 0 & 1 & 1 \end{bmatrix}$$

Note that column 3 dominates column 2, and after eliminating column 2, row 1 dominates row 2. Thus, the reduced matrix is:

$$\begin{bmatrix} 3 & 0 \\ 0 & 1 \end{bmatrix}$$

Applying formulas (3) and (4):

Player 1's optimal strategy is to choose row 1 with probability $\frac{1}{4}$ and row 2 with probability $\frac{3}{4}$.

Player 2's optimal strategy is to choose column 1 with probability $\frac{1}{4}$ and column 2 with probability $\frac{3}{4}$.

Value of the game is $\frac{3}{4}$.

14.

	M_1	M_2	M_3	M_4	M_5
A_1	.3	.4	.5	1	0
A_2	.2	3	.6	0	1
A_3	.1	.5	.3	.1	0

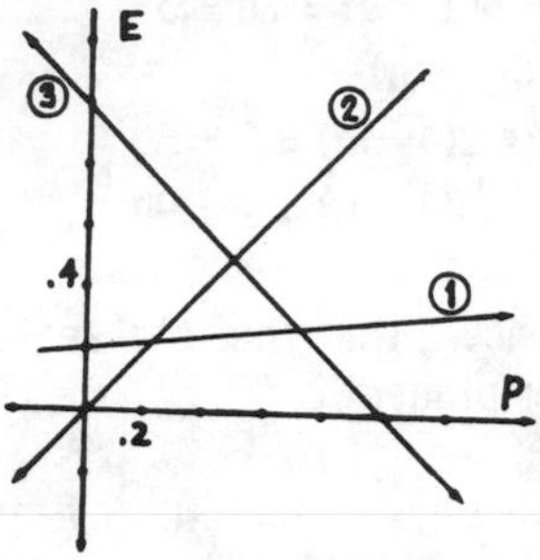

Column 1 dominates columns 2 and 3. The reduces matrix is

	M_1	M_4	M_5
A_1	.3	1	0
A_2	.2	0	1
A_3	.1	.1	0

Row 1 dominates row 3. The reduced matrix is

	M_1	M_4	M_5
A_1	.3	1	0
A_2	.2	0	1

Let antibiotic A_1 be a fraction p of the mixture. Antibiotic A_2 is then $(1 - p)$ of the mixture. The expected probabilities for destroying each of the 3 bacilli are

1. $E = .3p + .2(1 - p) = .1p + .2$
2. $E = p$
3. $E = 1 - p$

The intersection of lines 1 and 3 gives the optimum mixture:

$$.1p + .2 = 1 - p$$
$$p = \frac{8}{11}$$
$$1 - p = \frac{3}{11}$$

Thus, antibiotics A_1 and A_2 should be used in the ratio of 8 to 3. Antibiotic A_3 should not be used.

Review Exercises (page 441)

2. (a) $V = \begin{bmatrix} \frac{1}{3} & \frac{2}{3} \end{bmatrix} \begin{bmatrix} -1 & 1 \\ 1 & -1 \end{bmatrix} \begin{bmatrix} 1 \\ 0 \end{bmatrix} = \frac{1}{3}$

(b) $V = \begin{bmatrix} 0 & 1 \end{bmatrix} \begin{bmatrix} -1 & 1 \\ 1 & -1 \end{bmatrix} \begin{bmatrix} \frac{1}{2} \\ \frac{1}{2} \end{bmatrix} = 0$

(c) $V = \begin{bmatrix} \frac{1}{2} & \frac{1}{2} \end{bmatrix} \begin{bmatrix} -1 & 1 \\ 1 & -1 \end{bmatrix} \begin{bmatrix} \frac{1}{2} \\ \frac{1}{2} \end{bmatrix} = 0$

4. $\begin{bmatrix} 0 & 1 & 2 \\ -1 & -2 & 3 \\ -2 & 2 & -3 \end{bmatrix}$ This matrix has a saddle point ($a_{11} = 0$) but no dominant rows or columns.

6. (A non-zero-sum game.)

Number of plugs	Cost per plug	Selling price	Profit
1000	1.00	.60	\$400
2000	.70	.40	\$600
300	1.00	.60	\$120
1300	.70	.40	\$390

Retailer I plays rows in Matrix A; retailer II plays rows in matrix B. (U = usual price, D = discount price.)

$$A = \begin{array}{c} \\ \end{array}\begin{matrix} U & D \end{matrix} \qquad\qquad B = \begin{matrix} U & D \end{matrix}$$

$$A = \begin{bmatrix} 400 & 120 \\ 600 & 390 \end{bmatrix} \begin{matrix} U \\ D \end{matrix} \qquad B = \begin{bmatrix} 400 & 600 \\ 120 & 390 \end{bmatrix}$$

If there were collusion between the two retailers, they would agree always to sell at the usual price and both make a profit of \$400 per month. Since there is not, the best strategy for each is to choose row 2. The saddle pair (a_{22}, b_{22}) yields a profit of \$390 per month for each.

CHAPTER 11

Exercise 11.1 (page 450)

2. It is not a stochastic matrix; the sum of the first row is > 1.
4. (a) If the system is in State 2, it has probability 0.4 of changing to State 1 in one step.
   (b) $[1 \quad 0]\,p^2 = [.37 \quad .63]$
   (c) $[0 \quad 1]\,p^2 = [.36 \quad .64]$
6. $[.25 \quad .25 \quad .25]\,p = [.525 \quad .15 \quad .325]$
8.

$$p = \begin{bmatrix} \frac{1}{3} & \frac{1}{3} & \frac{1}{3} & 0 \\ \frac{1}{3} & \frac{1}{3} & 0 & \frac{1}{3} \\ \frac{1}{3} & 0 & \frac{1}{3} & \frac{1}{3} \\ 0 & \frac{1}{3} & \frac{1}{3} & \frac{1}{3} \end{bmatrix} \qquad p^2 = \begin{bmatrix} \frac{1}{3} & \frac{2}{9} & \frac{2}{9} & \frac{2}{9} \\ \frac{2}{9} & \frac{1}{3} & \frac{2}{9} & \frac{2}{9} \\ \frac{2}{9} & \frac{2}{9} & \frac{1}{3} & \frac{2}{9} \\ \frac{2}{9} & \frac{2}{9} & \frac{2}{9} & \frac{1}{3} \end{bmatrix}$$

$$\begin{bmatrix} \frac{1}{2} & 0 & \frac{1}{2} & 0 \end{bmatrix} p^2 = \begin{bmatrix} \frac{5}{18} & \frac{2}{9} & \frac{5}{18} & \frac{2}{9} \end{bmatrix}$$

10. (a) The probability that a commuter will choose one mode of transportation or the other depends only on which mode he used the previous week.
    (b)

$$\begin{array}{c} \\ R \\ C \end{array} \begin{array}{c} \begin{array}{cc} R & C \end{array} \\ \begin{bmatrix} .9 & .1 \\ .2 & .8 \end{bmatrix} \end{array} = p$$

   (c) $p^2 = \begin{bmatrix} .83 & .17 \\ .34 & .66 \end{bmatrix}$ (d) $p^3 = \begin{bmatrix} .781 & .219 \\ .438 & .562 \end{bmatrix}$

12. (a) The probability that the mouse is in a given room depends only on which room he was in previously.

(b)

$$\begin{array}{c} \\ 1 \\ 2 \\ 3 \\ 4 \\ 5 \\ 6 \\ 7 \\ 8 \\ 9 \end{array} \begin{array}{c} \begin{array}{ccccccccc} 1 & 2 & 3 & 4 & 5 & 6 & 7 & 8 & 9 \end{array} \\ \begin{bmatrix} 0 & \frac{1}{2} & 0 & \frac{1}{2} & 0 & 0 & 0 & 0 & 0 \\ \frac{1}{3} & 0 & \frac{1}{3} & 0 & \frac{1}{3} & 0 & 0 & 0 & 0 \\ 0 & \frac{1}{2} & 0 & 0 & 0 & \frac{1}{2} & 0 & 0 & 0 \\ \frac{1}{3} & 0 & 0 & 0 & \frac{1}{3} & 0 & \frac{1}{3} & 0 & 0 \\ 0 & \frac{1}{4} & 0 & \frac{1}{4} & 0 & \frac{1}{4} & 0 & \frac{1}{4} & 0 \\ 0 & 0 & 0 & 0 & 0 & 1 & 0 & 0 & 0 \\ 0 & 0 & 0 & 0 & 0 & 0 & 1 & 0 & 0 \\ 0 & 0 & 0 & 0 & 0 & 0 & 0 & 0 & 1 \\ 0 & 0 & 0 & 0 & 0 & 0 & 0 & 0 & 1 \end{bmatrix} \end{array}$$

14. This is a Markov process because the probability that the professor walks, or that he drives, depends only on what he did the day before. The transition matrix is

$$P = \begin{array}{c} \\ W \\ D \end{array} \begin{array}{c} \begin{array}{cc} W & D \end{array} \\ \begin{bmatrix} \frac{1}{2} & \frac{1}{2} \\ 1 & 0 \end{bmatrix} \end{array}$$

16. If A is a transition matrix, so are $A^2, A^3, \ldots, A^n$ for all n. The entry $a_{ij}^{(n)}$ in row i and column j of A^n is the probability that, if the system is initially in state i, it will be in state j after n steps.

Exercise 11.2 (page 461)

2. Not regular; every power of P will have a 0 in row 2 column 1.

4. Regular; $P^2 = \begin{bmatrix} \frac{7}{9} & \frac{2}{9} \\ \frac{1}{3} & \frac{2}{3} \end{bmatrix}$

If $\begin{bmatrix} t_1 & t_2 \end{bmatrix} \begin{bmatrix} \frac{1}{3} & \frac{2}{3} \\ 1 & 0 \end{bmatrix} = \begin{bmatrix} t_1 & t_2 \end{bmatrix}$ and $t_1 + t_2 = 1$, then

$$\left(\tfrac{1}{3}\right)t_1 + t_2 = t_1$$

$$\left(\tfrac{2}{3}\right)t_1 = t_2 = 1 - t_1,$$

so $t_1 = \frac{3}{5}$, $t_2 = \frac{2}{5}$. $\begin{bmatrix} \frac{3}{5} & \frac{2}{5} \end{bmatrix}$ is the fixed vector.

6. Regular; $p^2 = \begin{bmatrix} \frac{7}{16} & \frac{3}{16} & \frac{3}{8} \\ \frac{1}{8} & \frac{7}{8} & 0 \\ \frac{1}{2} & 0 & \frac{1}{2} \end{bmatrix}$ $p^3 = \begin{bmatrix} \frac{13}{64} & \frac{45}{64} & \frac{3}{32} \\ \frac{15}{32} & \frac{3}{32} & \frac{7}{16} \\ \frac{1}{8} & \frac{7}{8} & 0 \end{bmatrix}$

$$p^4 = \begin{bmatrix} \frac{103}{256} & \frac{62}{256} & \frac{45}{128} \\ \frac{21}{128} & \frac{101}{128} & \frac{3}{64} \\ \frac{15}{32} & \frac{3}{32} & \frac{7}{16} \end{bmatrix}$$

If $[t_1 \quad t_2 \quad t_3]\,p = [t_1 \quad t_2 \quad t_3]$ and $t_1 + t_2 + t_3 = 1$, then $[t_1 \quad t_2 \quad t_3] = \begin{bmatrix} \frac{4}{13} & \frac{6}{13} & \frac{3}{13} \end{bmatrix}$ = fixed vector.

8. If $[t_1 \quad t_2 \quad t_3] \begin{bmatrix} .9 & .10 & .00 \\ .85 & .05 & .10 \\ .50 & .10 & .40 \end{bmatrix} = [t_1 \quad t_2 \quad t_3]$ and $t_1 + t_2 + t_3 = 1$, then

$$.9t_1 + .85t_2 + .50t_3 = t_1$$
$$.10t_1 + .05t_2 + .10t_3 = t_2$$
$$.10t_2 + .40t_3 = t_3$$
$$t_2 = 6t_3$$
$$t_1 + 3t_3 + t_3 = 60t_3; \quad t_1 = 56t_3$$

$t_1 = \frac{56}{63} = \frac{8}{9} \approx .8889$; $t_2 = \frac{6}{63} \approx .0952$; $t_3 = \frac{1}{63} \approx .0158$

10.

$$p = \begin{array}{c} \\ A \\ B \\ C \end{array} \begin{array}{c} \begin{array}{ccc} A & B & C \end{array} \\ \begin{bmatrix} 0 & 1 & 0 \\ \frac{3}{4} & 0 & \frac{1}{4} \\ \frac{3}{4} & \frac{1}{4} & 0 \end{bmatrix} \end{array}$$

If $[x \quad y \quad z]\,p = [x \quad y \quad z]$ and $x + y + z = 1$, then

$$\left(\tfrac{3}{4}\right)y+\left(\tfrac{3}{4}\right)z=x$$
$$x+\left(\tfrac{1}{4}\right)z=y$$
$$\left(\tfrac{1}{4}\right)y=z$$
$$y=4z,\quad x=\left(\tfrac{15}{4}\right)z,\quad \left(\tfrac{15}{4}\right)z+4z+z=1$$
$$z=\tfrac{4}{35},\quad y=\tfrac{16}{35},\quad x=\tfrac{15}{35}=\tfrac{3}{7}$$

In the long run, she buys A 3 times out of 7, B 16 times out of 35, C 4 times out of 35.

12. No. If $\left[\tfrac{1}{3}\ \ 0\ \ \tfrac{1}{3}\right]p=\left[\tfrac{1}{3}\ \ 0\ \ \tfrac{1}{3}\ \ \tfrac{1}{3}\right]$, then we must have

$$p_{21}=p_{23}=p_{24}=0$$

and the same is true of any power of p. Thus p cannot be regular.

14. (a) $p=\begin{bmatrix} .8 & .18 & .02 \\ .4 & .5 & .1 \\ .2 & .6 & .2 \end{bmatrix}$ (b) $p^2=\begin{bmatrix} .716 & .246 & .038 \\ .54 & .382 & .078 \\ .44 & .456 & .104 \end{bmatrix}$

The probability is .716

(c) The probability is .038.

(d) $[.3\ \ .4\ \ .3]\begin{bmatrix} .716 & .246 & .038 \\ .54 & .382 & .078 \\ .44 & .456 & .104 \end{bmatrix}=[.5628\ \ .3634\ \ .0738]$

(e) $\left[\tfrac{83}{131}\ \ \tfrac{39}{131}\ \ \tfrac{7}{131}\right]$, or approximately 64.9% college, 29.8% high school. 5.3% elementary.

Exercise 11.3 (page 470)

2. Absorbing, in state 1. **4.** Not absorbing. **6.** Absorbing, in state 3.

8. Rearrange the matrix to obtain

$$\begin{array}{c} \\ C \\ A \\ B \\ D \end{array}\begin{array}{c} \begin{array}{cccc} C & A & B & D \end{array} \\ \left[\begin{array}{c|ccc} 1 & 0 & 0 & 0 \\ 0 & \frac{1}{3} & \frac{1}{3} & \frac{1}{3} \\ \frac{1}{2} & 0 & \frac{1}{4} & \frac{1}{4} \\ 0 & 0 & \frac{1}{2} & \frac{1}{2} \end{array}\right] \end{array}$$

then

$$T = \left[\begin{pmatrix} 1 & 0 & 0 \\ 0 & 1 & 0 \\ 0 & 0 & 1 \end{pmatrix} - \begin{pmatrix} \frac{1}{3} & \frac{1}{3} & \frac{1}{3} \\ 0 & \frac{1}{4} & \frac{1}{4} \\ 0 & \frac{1}{2} & \frac{1}{2} \end{pmatrix}\right]^{-1} = \begin{matrix} \\ A \\ B \\ D \end{matrix}\begin{matrix} A \quad B \quad D \\ \begin{bmatrix} \frac{3}{2} & 2 & 2 \\ 0 & 2 & 1 \\ 0 & 2 & 3 \end{bmatrix} \end{matrix}$$

$$TS = \begin{bmatrix} \frac{3}{2} & 2 & 2 \\ 0 & 2 & 1 \\ 0 & 2 & 3 \end{bmatrix}\begin{bmatrix} 0 \\ \frac{1}{2} \\ 0 \end{bmatrix} = \begin{matrix} C \\ \begin{bmatrix} 1 \\ 1 \\ 1 \end{bmatrix} \end{matrix}\begin{matrix} \\ A \\ B \\ D \end{matrix}$$

10. No answer:

$$TS = \begin{bmatrix} .75 & .4 \\ .60 & .3 \\ .15 & .15 \end{bmatrix}$$

which is not a stochastic matrix.

12. (a)

$$p = \begin{matrix} D \quad F \quad G \quad S \\ \begin{bmatrix} 1 & 0 & 0 & 0 \\ .25 & 0 & 0 & .75 \\ 0 & 0 & 1 & 0 \\ .10 & 0 & .9 & 0 \end{bmatrix} \end{matrix}\begin{matrix} \\ D \\ F \\ G \\ S \end{matrix}$$ is the transition matrix.

(b) Two states are absorbing. (Namely, D and G.)

(c)

$$T = \left(I - \begin{bmatrix} 0 & .75 \\ 0 & 0 \end{bmatrix}^{-1}\right) = \begin{matrix} F \quad S \\ \begin{bmatrix} 1 & .75 \\ 0 & 1 \end{bmatrix} \end{matrix}\begin{matrix} \\ F \\ S \end{matrix}$$

(d) (.75)(.90) = .675

14.

$$\begin{matrix} \\ 0 \\ 1 \\ 2 \\ 4 \end{matrix}\begin{matrix} 0 \quad 1 \quad 2 \quad 4 \\ \begin{bmatrix} 1 & 0 & 0 & 0 \\ .5 & 0 & .5 & 0 \\ .5 & 0 & 0 & .5 \\ 0 & 0 & 0 & 1 \end{bmatrix} \end{matrix} \qquad \begin{matrix} \\ 0 \\ 4 \\ 1 \\ 2 \end{matrix}\begin{matrix} 0 \quad 4 \quad 1 \quad 2 \\ \left[\begin{array}{cc|cc} 1 & 0 & 0 & 0 \\ \underline{0} & \underline{1} & \underline{0} & \underline{0} \\ .5 & 0 & 0 & .5 \\ .5 & .5 & 0 & 0 \end{array}\right] \end{matrix} \qquad S = \begin{bmatrix} .5 & 0 \\ .5 & .5 \end{bmatrix}$$

(The number of each state denotes Marsha's fortune in thousands of dollars.)

$$Q = \begin{bmatrix} 0 & .5 \\ 0 & 0 \end{bmatrix} \qquad T = (I - Q)^{-1} = \begin{bmatrix} 1 & .5 \\ 0 & 1 \end{bmatrix}$$

(a) The expected number of wagers is 1.5.

(b) $$TS = \begin{array}{c} \begin{array}{cc} 0 & 4 \end{array} \\ \begin{bmatrix} .75 & .25 \\ .5 & .5 \end{bmatrix} \end{array} \begin{array}{c} \\ 1 \\ 2 \end{array}$$

The probability of being wiped out (going from state 1 to state 0) is 0.75, and

(c) The probability of winning (going from state 1 to state 4) is 0.25.

16.

$$\begin{array}{c} \\ 0 \\ A \\ B \\ C \\ AB \\ AC \\ BC \\ ABC \end{array} \begin{array}{c} \begin{array}{cccccccc} 0 & A & B & C & AB & AC & BC & ABC \end{array} \\ \begin{bmatrix} 1 & 0 & 0 & 0 & 0 & 0 & 0 & 0 \\ 0 & 1 & 0 & 0 & 0 & 0 & 0 & 0 \\ 0 & 0 & 1 & 0 & 0 & 0 & 0 & 0 \\ 0 & 0 & 0 & 1 & 0 & 0 & 0 & 0 \\ \frac{1}{6} & \frac{1}{6} & \frac{1}{3} & 0 & \frac{1}{3} & 0 & 0 & 0 \\ \frac{1}{18} & \frac{5}{18} & 0 & \frac{1}{9} & 0 & \frac{5}{9} & 0 & 0 \\ \frac{1}{12} & 0 & \frac{5}{12} & \frac{1}{12} & 0 & 0 & \frac{5}{12} & 0 \\ 0 & 0 & 0 & \frac{2}{9} & 0 & \frac{2}{9} & \frac{5}{18} & \frac{5}{18} \end{bmatrix} \end{array}$$

(a) There are 8 states. (b) 4 absorbing states.

(c)

$$Q = \begin{bmatrix} \frac{1}{3} & 0 & 0 & 0 \\ 0 & \frac{5}{9} & 0 & 0 \\ 0 & 0 & \frac{5}{12} & 0 \\ 0 & \frac{2}{9} & \frac{5}{18} & \frac{5}{18} \end{bmatrix}$$

$$T = (I - Q)^{-1} = \begin{bmatrix} \frac{3}{2} & 0 & 0 & 0 \\ 0 & \frac{9}{4} & 0 & 0 \\ 0 & 0 & \frac{12}{7} & 0 \\ 0 & \frac{9}{13} & \frac{60}{91} & \frac{18}{13} \end{bmatrix}$$

The expected number of rounds is $\frac{9}{13}+\frac{60}{91}+\frac{18}{13}=\frac{249}{91}$

(d)

$$TS=\begin{bmatrix} \frac{3}{2} & 0 & 0 & 0 \\ 0 & \frac{9}{4} & 0 & 0 \\ 0 & 0 & \frac{12}{7} & 0 \\ 0 & \frac{9}{13} & \frac{60}{91} & \frac{18}{13} \end{bmatrix}\begin{bmatrix} \frac{1}{6} & \frac{1}{6} & \frac{1}{3} & 0 \\ \frac{1}{18} & \frac{5}{18} & 0 & \frac{1}{9} \\ \frac{1}{12} & 0 & \frac{5}{12} & \frac{1}{12} \\ 0 & 0 & 0 & \frac{2}{9} \end{bmatrix}$$

$$= \begin{array}{c} \begin{matrix} 0 & \quad A & \quad B & \quad C \end{matrix} \\ \begin{bmatrix} \frac{1}{4} & \frac{1}{4} & \frac{1}{2} & 0 \\ \frac{1}{8} & \frac{5}{8} & 0 & \frac{1}{4} \\ \frac{1}{7} & 0 & \frac{5}{7} & \frac{1}{7} \\ \frac{17}{182} & \frac{5}{26} & \frac{25}{91} & \frac{40}{91} \end{bmatrix} \end{array} \begin{matrix} AB \\ AC \\ BC \\ ABC \end{matrix}$$

Since the system starts in State ABC, the probability that A survives is $\frac{5}{26}$.

Exercise 11.4 (page 475)

2. (a)

$$P = \begin{matrix} & \begin{matrix} D & H & R \end{matrix} \\ \begin{matrix} D \\ H \\ R \end{matrix} & \begin{bmatrix} 1 & 0 & 0 \\ \frac{1}{2} & \frac{1}{2} & 0 \\ 0 & 1 & 0 \end{bmatrix} \end{matrix}$$

Note: P(D|D) = P(AA|AA + AA) = 1,
P(D|H) = P(AA|AA + Aa) = .5,
P(H|H) = P(Aa|AA + Aa) = .5,
P(H|R) = P(Aa|AA + aa) = 1

(b) P is not regular, but there is a unique fixed probability vector, namely [1 0 0]. In the long run, this means that genotypes H and R will tend to extinction.

(c)

$$T=\left[\begin{pmatrix} 1 & 0 \\ 0 & 1 \end{pmatrix}-\begin{pmatrix} \frac{1}{2} & 0 \\ 1 & 0 \end{pmatrix}\right]^{-1} = \begin{matrix} & \begin{matrix} H & R \end{matrix} \\ \begin{matrix} H \\ R \end{matrix} & \begin{bmatrix} 2 & 0 \\ 2 & 1 \end{bmatrix} \end{matrix}$$

(d) If the unknown genotype is R, the expected number of stages is 3. If it is H, the expected number is 2.

Review Exercises (page 476)

2. A matrix may be said to be a regular transition matrix if it is the transition matrix for a regular Markov chain. thus, it is a square matirx with no negative entries, the sum of each row is 1, and some power has no zero entries.

$\begin{bmatrix} .5 & .5 \\ 1 & 0 \end{bmatrix}$ Is a regular transition matrix; $\begin{bmatrix} .5 & .5 \\ 0 & 1 \end{bmatrix}$ is not.

4.

$$P = \begin{array}{c} \\ A \\ B \\ C \end{array} \begin{array}{c} \begin{array}{ccc} A & B & C \end{array} \\ \begin{bmatrix} .50 & .20 & .30 \\ .40 & .40 & .20 \\ .50 & .25 & .25 \end{bmatrix} \end{array} \qquad P^2 = \begin{bmatrix} .48 & .255 & .265 \\ .46 & .29 & .25 \\ .475 & .2625 & .2625 \end{bmatrix}$$

$[.25 \quad .25 \quad .5]\,P^2 = [.4725 \quad .2675 \quad .260]$

Thus, after 2 years, A has 47.25% of the market,
B has 26.75%,
C has 26%.

The fixed vector $T = [t_1 \quad t_2 \quad t_3] = TP$ is $\left[\frac{80}{169} \quad \frac{45}{169} \quad \frac{44}{169}\right]$. Thus, in the long run, A's share of the market is about 57.34% $\left(\approx \frac{80}{169}\right)$, B's share is about 26.63% and C's share is about 26.04%.

6.

$$P = \begin{array}{c} \\ F \\ S \end{array} \begin{array}{c} \begin{array}{cc} F & S \end{array} \\ \begin{bmatrix} .7 & .3 \\ .6 & .4 \end{bmatrix} \end{array} \qquad P^2 = \begin{bmatrix} .67 & .33 \\ .66 & .34 \end{bmatrix} \qquad P^3 = \begin{bmatrix} .667 & .333 \\ .666 & .334 \end{bmatrix}$$

The probability of a fat father being the great-grandfather of a fat great-grandson is .667. the fixed probability vector is $\left[\frac{2}{3} \quad \frac{1}{3}\right]$, thus the long-run distribution will be $\frac{2}{3}$ fat, $\frac{1}{3}$ skinny. This does not depend on the initial distribution.

CHAPTER 12

Exercise 12.1 (page 484)

2. Proposition 4. Not 6. Not 8. Not
10. The outlook for bonds is good.
12. Mike is not selling his apartment and his business.
14. Some people have no television set.
16. Jones is not permitted not to see that all votes are not counted.
18. John is an economics major or a sociology minor.
20. John is not an economics major.
22. John is a sociology minor. (or, "It is not the case that John is not a sociology minor.")

Exercise 12.2 (page 492)

2.

p	q	~p	~q	~p v q
T	T	F	F	F
T	F	F	T	T
F	T	T	F	T
F	F	T	T	T

4.

p	q	~p	~p v q
T	T	F	F F
T	F	F	F F
F	T	T	T T
F	F	T	T F

6.

p	q	~q	~p	p v ~q	(p v ~q) ∧ ~p
T	T	F	F	T	F
T	F	T	F	T	F
F	T	F	T	F	F
F	F	T	T	T	T

8.

p	q	~q	~p	p v ~q	q ∧ ~p	(p v ~q) ∧ (q ∧ ~p)
T	T	F	F	T	F	F
T	F	T	F	T	F	F
F	T	F	T	F	T	F
F	F	T	T	T	F	F

Chapter 12 - p.123

10.

p	q	~q	q ∨ ~q	p ∧ (q ∨ ~q)
T	T	F	T	T
T	F	T	T	T
F	T	F	T	F
F	T	T	T	F

12.

p	q	~q	~p	p ∧ ~q	q ∧ ~p	(p ∧ ~q) ∨ (q ∧ ~p)
T	T	F	F	F	F	F
T	F	T	F	T	F	T
F	T	F	T	F	T	T
F	F	T	T	F	F	F

14.

p	q	r	p ∧ q	p ∧ r	(p ∧ q) ∨ (p ∧ r)
T	T	T	T	T	T
T	T	F	T	F	T
T	F	T	F	T	T
T	F	F	F	F	F
F	T	T	F	F	F
F	T	F	F	F	F
F	F	T	F	F	F
F	F	F	F	F	F

16.

p	q	r	~p	~r	~p ∨ q	(~p ∨ q) ∧ ~r
T	T	T	F	F	T	F
T	T	F	F	T	T	T
T	F	T	F	F	F	F
T	F	F	F	T	F	F
F	T	T	T	F	T	F
F	T	F	T	T	T	T
F	T	T	T	F	T	F
F	T	F	T	T	T	T

18.

p	q	$p \vee q$	$q \vee p$	$p \wedge q$	$q \wedge p$
T	T	T	T	T	T
T	F	T	T	F	T
F	T	T	T	F	F
F	F	F	F	F	F

$p \vee q \equiv q \vee p$ $\qquad p \wedge q \equiv q \wedge p$

20.

p	q	r	$q \wedge r$	$p \vee (q \wedge p)$	$p \vee q$	$p \vee r$	$(p \vee q) \wedge (p \vee r)$
T	T	T	T	T	T	T	T
T	T	F	F	T	T	T	T
T	F	T	F	T	T	T	T
T	F	F	F	T	T	T	T
F	T	T	T	T	T	T	T
F	T	F	F	F	T	F	F
F	F	T	F	F	F	T	F
F	F	F	F	F	F	F	F

$p \vee (q \wedge r) \equiv (p \vee q) \wedge (p \vee r)$

p	q	r	$r \vee q$	$p \wedge (r \vee q)$	$p \wedge r$	$p \wedge q$	$(p \wedge r) \vee (p \wedge q)$
T	T	T	T	T	T	T	T
T	T	F	T	T	F	T	T
T	F	T	T	T	T	F	T
T	F	F	F	F	F	F	F
F	T	T	T	F	F	F	F
F	T	F	T	F	F	F	F
F	F	T	T	F	F	F	F
F	F	F	F	F	F	F	F

$p \wedge (r \vee q) \equiv (p \wedge r) \vee (p \wedge q)$

22.

p	q	p v q	~ (p v q)	~p	~q	~p ∧ ~q
T	T	T	F	F	F	F
T	F	T	F	F	T	F
F	T	T	F	T	F	F
F	F	F	T	T	T	T

~ (p v q) ≡ ~p ∧ ~q

p	q	p ∧ q	~ (p ∧ q)	~p	~q	~p v ~q
T	T	T	F	F	F	F
T	F	F	T	F	T	T
F	T	F	T	T	F	T
F	F	F	T	T	T	T

~ (p ∧ q) ≡ ~p v ~q

24.

p	q	~q	q ∧ ~q	p v (q ∧ ~q)
T	T	F	F	T
T	F	T	F	T
F	T	F	F	F
F	F	T	F	F

p ≡ p v (q ∧ ~q)

26. See problem 18.

28.

p	q	p ∧ q	(p ∧ q) v p
T	T	T	T
T	F	F	T
F	T	F	F
F	F	F	F

30.

p	q	r	~p	~q	~p ∧ ~q	~p ∧ ~q ∧ r	p ∧ q ∧ r	(~p ∧ ~q ∧ r)∨(p ∧ q ∧ r)
T	T	T	F	F	F	F	T	T
T	T	F	F	F	F	F	F	F
T	F	T	F	T	F	F	F	F
T	F	F	F	T	F	F	F	F
F	T	T	T	F	F	F	F	F
F	T	F	T	F	F	F	F	F
F	F	T	T	T	T	T	F	T
F	F	F	T	T	T	F	F	F

32. $p \wedge q = q \wedge p$: Smith is an exconvict and Smith is rehabilitated is equivalent to Smith is rehabilitated and Smith is an exconvict.

$p \vee q = q \vee p$: Smith is an exconvict or Smith is rehabilitated is equivalent to Smith is rehabilitated or Smith is an exconvict.

34. $(p \vee q) \wedge r \equiv r \wedge (p \vee q)$ commutative law
$\equiv (r \wedge p) \vee (r \wedge q)$ distributive law
$\equiv (p \wedge r) \vee (q \wedge r)$ commutative law

36. If the actor is intelligent but untalented, a is true while b is false.

Exercise 12.3 (page 500)

2. Converse: $\sim q \Rightarrow \sim p$
Contrapositive: $q \Rightarrow p$
Inverse: $p \Rightarrow q$

4. Converse: $\sim q \Rightarrow p$
Contrapositive: $q \Rightarrow \sim p$
Inverse: $\sim p \Rightarrow q$

6. Converse: If it is raining, it is cloudy.
Contrapositive: If it is not raining, it is not cloudy.
Inverse: If it is not cloudy, it is not raining.

8. Converse: If it is not raining, it is not cloudy.
Contrapositive: If it is raining, then it is cloudy.
Inverse: If it is cloudy, then it is raining.

10. The statement is equivalent to: If it is cloudy then it is raining.
See problem 6.

12. $p \to q \equiv \sim p \vee q$ Table 6

$\equiv q \vee \sim p$ commutative law

$\equiv \sim q \to \sim p$ Table 6

14. (a)

p	q	r	p ∧ q	p ∧ q → r	~p	~q	~r	p ∧ ~r	p ∧ ~r → ~q
T	T	T	T	T	F	F	F	F	T
T	T	F	T	F	F	F	T	T	F
T	F	T	F	T	F	T	F	F	T
T	F	F	F	T	F	T	T	T	T
F	T	T	F	T	T	F	F	F	T
F	T	F	F	T	T	F	T	F	T
F	F	T	F	T	T	T	F	F	T
F	F	F	F	T	T	T	T	F	T

Since column 5 and column 10 are identical,
$(p \wedge q) \to r \equiv (p \wedge \sim r) \to \sim q$ is true.

(b) $(p \wedge q) \to r \equiv \sim(p \wedge q) \vee r$

$\equiv \sim p \vee \sim q \vee r$

$\equiv \sim p \vee r \vee \sim q$

$\equiv \sim(p \wedge \sim r) \vee \sim q$

$\equiv (p \wedge \sim r) \to \sim q$

16.

p	q	~p	p ∨ q	~p ∧ (p ∨ q)
T	T	F	T	F
T	F	F	T	F
F	T	T	T	T
F	F	T	F	F

18.

p	q	~q	p ∨ q	(p ∨ q) ∧ ~q
T	T	F	T	F
T	F	T	T	T
F	T	F	T	F
F	F	T	F	F

20.

p	q	$p \vee q$	$p \vee q \Rightarrow p$
T	T	T	T
T	F	T	T
F	T	T	F
F	F	F	T

22.

p	$\sim p$	$p \wedge \sim p$
T	F	F
F	T	F

24.

p	q	$p \Rightarrow q$	$p \vee (p \Rightarrow q)$
T	T	T	T
T	F	F	T
F	T	T	T
F	F	T	T

26.

p	q	r	$q \vee r$	(A) $p \vee (q \vee r)$	$p \vee q$	(B) $(p \vee q) \vee r$
T	T	T	T	T	T	T
T	T	F	T	T	T	T
T	F	T	T	T	T	T
T	F	F	F	T	T	T
F	T	T	T	T	T	T
F	T	F	T	T	T	T
F	F	T	T	T	F	T
F	F	F	F	F	F	F

Since column (A) has exactly the same entries as column (B), $p \vee (q \vee r) \Leftrightarrow (p \vee q)$ r is always true.

28.

p	q	$p \wedge q$	$p \vee (p \wedge q)$	$p \vee (p \wedge q) \Leftrightarrow p$
T	T	T	T	T
T	F	F	T	T
F	T	F	F	T
F	F	F	F	T

30. $\sim p \wedge q$ **32.** $\sim p \wedge q$ **34.** $p \Rightarrow q$

Exercise 12.4 (page 507)

2. p: I go to work. q: I go fishing.

Given: $\sim p \Rightarrow q$
$\sim q$
Prove: p.

Direct: Since $\sim p \Rightarrow q$ is given, the contrapositive $\sim q \Rightarrow p$ is true. Thus p is true by the law of detachment.

Indirect: Assume p is false. Then ~p is true. I Since $\sim p \Rightarrow q$, then q is true, but ~q is true, and we have a contradiction.

4. p: Katy is a good girl. q: Mike is a good boy. r: Danny cries.

Given: $p \vee q$, $r \Rightarrow \sim p$, ~q.

Prove: r or ~r

Direct: Since ~q is true, then p ;is true (since $p \vee q$ is true). The contrapositive of $r \Rightarrow \sim p$ is $p \Rightarrow \sim r$. Hence ~r is true. (So Danny does not cry.)

Indirect: Asume r is true. Then ~p is true; hence q is true, which is a contradiction.

6. Not valid. Suppose Danny is affluent, a snob, and not a hypocrite. Then both parts of the hypothesis are true, but the conclusion is false.

Exercise 12.5 (page 510)

2.

p	q	~p	~q	$\sim p \wedge \sim q$	$p \vee (\sim p \wedge \sim q)$	$p \wedge [p \vee (\sim p \wedge \sim q)] \wedge q$
C	C	0	0	0	C	C
C	0	0	C	0	C	0
0	C	C	0	0	0	0
0	0	C	C	C	C	0

Current flows if and only if p and q are both closed.

4.

p	q	~p	~q	p∧q	~p ∧ q	p∧~q	(~p ∧ q)∨(p ∧ ~q)	(p∧q) ∨ [(~p ∧ q)∨(p∧ ~q)]
C	C	O	O	C	O	O	O	C
C	O	O	C	O	O	C	C	C
O	C	C	O	O	C	O	C	C
O	O	C	C	O	O	O	O	O

When p or q or both are closed.

6.

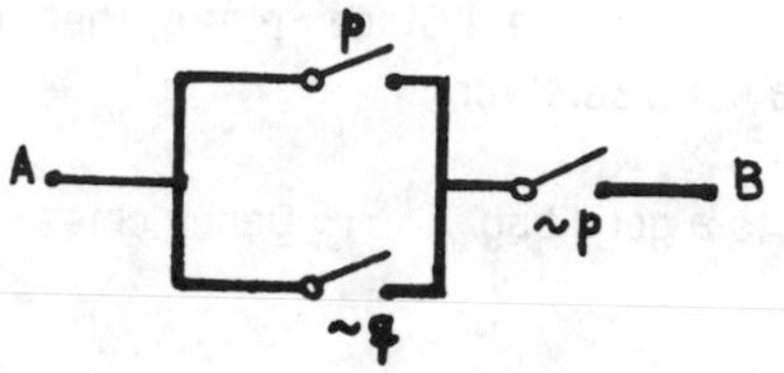

8.

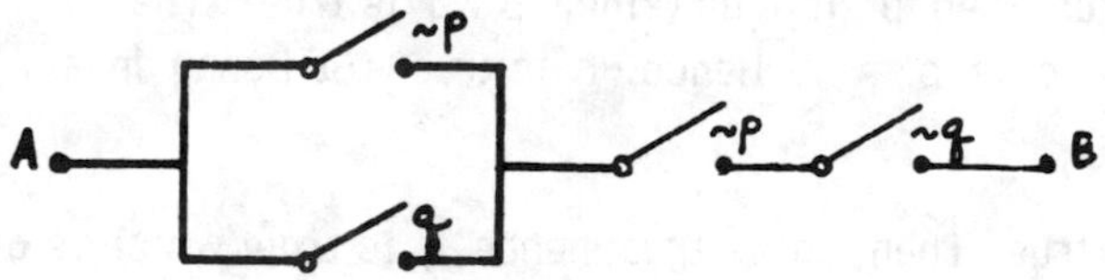

10. (a)

(b)

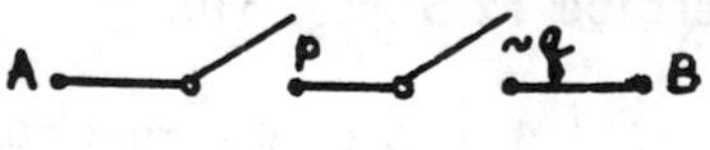

12.

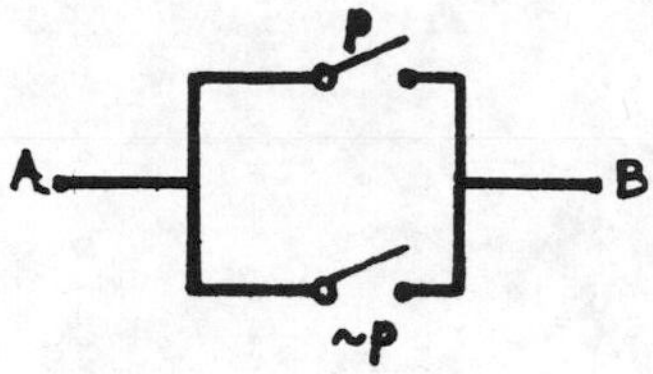

or A- ______ -B

14.

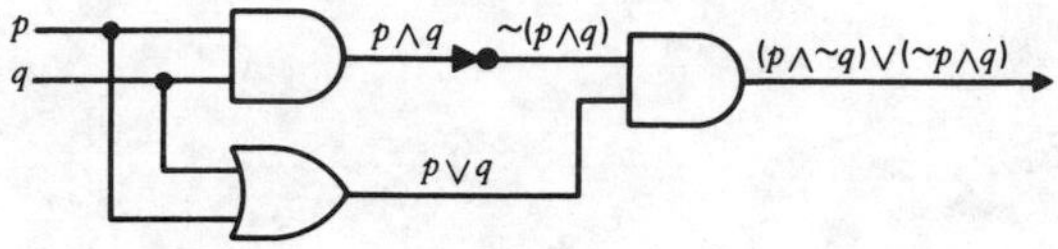

16. (a)

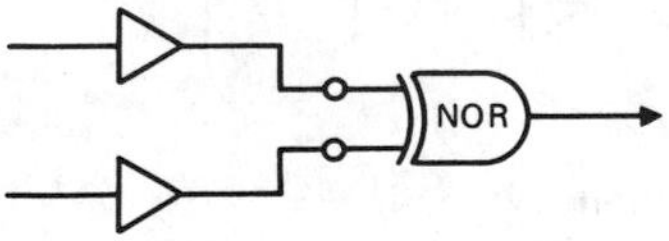

(b)

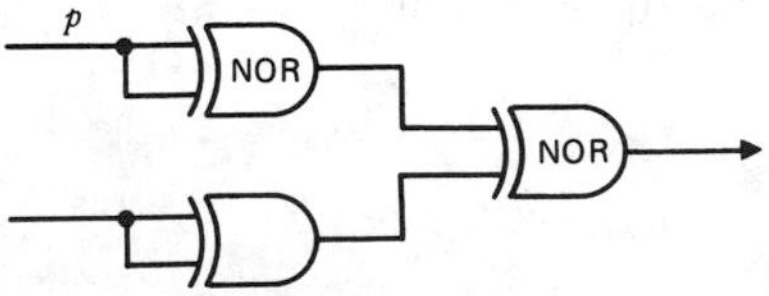

18. Since $p = (p \oplus r)(p \oplus \sim r)$ for all p,

$(p \oplus q)(p \oplus r)(q \oplus \sim r)$

$= (p \oplus q \oplus r)(p \oplus q \oplus \sim r)(p \oplus r)(q \oplus \sim r)$

$= (p \oplus q \oplus r)(p \oplus r)(p \oplus q \oplus \sim v)(q \oplus \sim r)$

$= (p \oplus r)(q \oplus \sim r);$

$(p \oplus r)(q \oplus \sim r) = (p \oplus r)\, q \oplus (p \oplus r)(\sim v)$

$= (pq) \oplus rq \oplus p\,(\sim v) \oplus (r)(\sim r)$

$= pq \oplus rq \oplus p(\sim r)$

$= qr \oplus p(\sim r)$, from #17

Review Exercises (page 513)

2. (a), (c)

4. (a)

6. Some people are not rich.

8. Mike is big or katy is big.

10.

p	q	p ∨ q	(p ∨ q) ∧ p
T	T	T	T
T	F	T	T
F	T	T	F
F	F	F	F

12.

p	q	~p	p ∨ q	~p ⇒ p ∨ q
T	T	F	T	T
T	F	F	F	T
F	T	T	F	F
F	F	T	F	F

14. $p \Rightarrow q$

16. Converse: If it is cold, then it is not sunny.
Contrapositive: If it is not cold, then it is sunny.
Inverse: If it is sunny, then it is not cold.

18. Danny is not crying, so Mike is a bad boy. If Mike is a bad boy, Katy is not a good girl. Thus, Katy is not a good girl.

20. They are logically equivalent.

$$(p \Rightarrow q) \wedge (\sim q \vee p) \equiv (p \Rightarrow q) \wedge (q \Rightarrow p) \equiv p \Leftrightarrow q$$

22.

CHAPTER 13

Exercise 13.1 (page 520)

2. True, false, true, false, true, false, true, false, true.
4. {(Apple II), (TRS, 1000), (IBM, 370), (Atari, 800)}
6. True, false, true, false, true, false, true.
8. (b) {2,2), (5,2), (5,4)}
(c) R is a subset of A X B
10. {(aa,ba), (ba, aa), (aa,bb), (bb,aa), (ab,ba), (ba,ab), (ab,bb), (bb,ab)}
12. !, &, ', 0, r, }
14. {(1,1), (1,3), (1,5), (2,2), (2,4), (2,6), (3,3), (3,5), (4,4), (4,6), (5,5), (6,6), (3,1), (5,1), (4,2), (6,2), (5,3), (6,4)}
16. {(0,0), (0,00), (00,0), (1,1), (1,01), (01,1), (1,10), (10,1), (00,00), (01,01), (10,10), (01,10), (10,01), (11,11)}
18. {(0,0), (0,1), (1,0), (1,1), (00,00), (00,01), (00,10), (00,11), (01,00), (10,00), (11,00), (11,11), (000,000), (000,010), (000,1000), (000,011), (010,000), (100,000), (011,000), (000,101), (000,110), (000,111), (101,000), (110,000), (111,000), (010,010), (010,100), (010,011), (010,101), (010,110), (010,111), (100,010), (011,010), (101,010), (110,010), (111,010), (100,100), (100,101), (100,011), (100,101), (100,110), (100,111), (101,100), (011,100), (101,100), (110,100), (111,100), (101,101), (101,011), (101,110), (101,111), (011,101), (110,101), (111,101), (011,011), (011,111), (111,011), (110,110), (110,111), (111,110), (111,111)}
20. {(1,3), (2,4), (3,5)}
22. {(0,0), (1,1), (4,2), (4,-2), (1,-1)}
24. {(a,a), (b,a), (a,b), (c,b)}
26. "≥"
28.

Variable Name	Value
I	1
B[I]	10
I	2
B[I]	20
I	3
B[I]	30
I	4
B[I]	40
I	5
B[I]	50

30. Not reflexive, since a number cannot be less than itself. Not symmetric, since if $a < b \Rightarrow b < a$ only if $a = b$. Transitive, since if $a < b$ and $b < c$ then $a < c$.

32. Reflexive. Not symmetric, since if a is a factor of b (where $a \neq b$) then b cannot be a factor of a. Transitive, because if a is a factor of b and b is a factor of c, then a is a factor of c. Symbolically, if $b = m \cdot a$ and if $c = n \cdot b$, then substituting $m \cdot a$ for b gives $c = n \cdot m \cdot a$. This shows that a is a factor of c.

34. Reflexive, symmetric, transitive.

36. Not reflexive because (1,1) and (3,3) $\notin$ R. However, R is both symmetric and transitive.

38. (i) through (iiii) : reflexive, symmetric, and transitive.

Exercise 13.2 (page 527)

2. 1, 10, 100 . Domain = {0,1,2}, range = {1, 10, 100}.

4. $\frac{1}{3}, \frac{1}{2}$, 1, –1. Domain = $\mathbb{R} - \{1\}$, range = $\mathbb{R}$

6. Yes, f defines a function.

8. Does not define a function, because f asigns two different values (2 and 3) to y.

10. Yes, f is a function.

12. No, f is not a function.

14. 1000010, 0101100, 1100100, 0101010, 1011100, 0110010, 0100100, 1000000.

16. 3, 3, -1, -10, -2, 1641

18. X1 = 43219.658; x2 = 43219; TRNCX = 4321.9

20. No. f is not unique because f(01) = 0 and f(01) = 1.

22. 2, 0, 2, 3, 1

24. Not one-to-one, but onto, therefore, not bijective.

26. Bot one-to-one and onto, therefore, bijective.

28. By inspection CHR is one-to-one and onto. Smae is true for ORD.

30. Let u and v be two binary words of length n. Then H(u,v) can at most be n. Thus, if we pick the value n + 1 in the range, it cannot be the image of any H(u,v) where both u and v are of length n. This shows that H is not onto.

32. (a) c,b,a (b) f is both one-to-one and onto, therefore, it is bijective.

34. 1,2,3,4

36. $(f^{-1} o f)(x) = f^{-1}[f(x)] = f^{-1}(x + 1) = (x + 1) - 1 = x$

and

$(f o f^{-1})(x) = f[f^{-1}(x)] = f(x - 1) = (x - 1) + 1 = x.$

Exercise 13.3 (page 532)

2. $1, -\frac{1}{2}, \frac{1}{3}, -\frac{1}{4}, -\frac{1}{100}$

4. (a) $0, -\frac{1}{2}, -\frac{2}{3}, -\frac{3}{4}, -\frac{4}{5}, -\frac{5}{6}$

(b)

$$n=0,\quad b_1 - b_0 = -\frac{1}{2} - 0 = -\frac{1}{2}$$

$$n=1,\quad b_2 - b_1 = -\frac{2}{3} + \frac{1}{2} = -\frac{1}{6}$$

$$n=2,\quad b_3 - b_2 = -\frac{3}{4} + \frac{2}{3} = -\frac{1}{12}$$

6. $0, \frac{1}{2}, \frac{1}{4}, \frac{1}{8}, \frac{1}{16}, \frac{1}{32}, \frac{1}{64}, \frac{1}{128}$

8. 1,2,5,10,17,26,37,50,65,82

10. $M_0 = \begin{bmatrix} 1 & 0 \\ 0 & 1 \end{bmatrix}, \quad M_1 = \begin{bmatrix} 1 & 1 \\ 1 & 1 \end{bmatrix}$

$M_2 = \begin{bmatrix} 1 & 4 \\ 2 & 1 \end{bmatrix}, \quad M_3 = \begin{bmatrix} 1 & 9 \\ 3 & 1 \end{bmatrix}$

12. $M_0 = M_1 = M_2 = M_{100} = \begin{bmatrix} 1 & 0 \\ 0 & 1 \end{bmatrix}$

14. $(-1)^{n-1} + 1, \ n = 1,2,3,\ldots$

16. $(5)^n, \ n = 0,1,2,\ldots$

18. $\left(\frac{1}{3}\right)^n, \ n = 0,1,2,\ldots$

20. $s_1 = \binom{1+1}{2} + 1 = \binom{2}{2} + 1 = 1 + 1 = 2$

$s_2 = \binom{2+1}{2} + 1 = \binom{3}{2} + 1 = 4$

$s_3 = \binom{3+1}{2} + 1 = \binom{4}{2} + 1 = 7$

$s_4 = \binom{4+1}{2} + 1 = \binom{5}{2} + 1 = 11$

Exercise 13.4 (page 537)

2. x = 25, y = 5

4. Algorithm SQRSUM

```
    Sum : = 0
        x : = 1
    Dowhile (x ≤ M)
        Input N(x)
        N square : = N(x) * N(x)
        Sum      : = Sum + Nsquare
                x : = x + 1
    End of While
End of SQRSUM
```

6. Algorithm EVENSUM

```
    Sum : = 0
        x : = 2
    Dowhile (x ≤ M)
        Input N(x)
        Sum : = Sum + N(x)
                x : = x + 2
    End of While
End of EVENSUM
```

8. Algorithm EMPLOYEE

```
    Sentinel : = 'xxx'
    Input name, wage
    Dowhile (name ≠ 'xxx')
        If (wage ≥ 7.5)
        Then output name, wage
        Input name, wage
    End of While
End of EMPLOYEE
```

10. Algorithm SOUP_DE_JOUR

```
    Input day
    If (day = 'Monday')
      Then output 'onion soup'
    Else If (day = 'Tuesday')
            Then output 'split pea soup'
        Else If (day = 'Wednesday')
                Then output 'lentil soup'
            Else If (day = 'Thursday')
                    Then output 'liver dumpling soup'
                Else If (day = 'Friday')
                        Then output 'clam chowder soup'
```

```
                    Else If (day = 'Saturday')
                        Then output 'vegetable soup'
                       Else If (day = 'Sunday')
                            Then output 'chicken noodle soup'
   End of SOUP_DE_JOUR
```

12.
```
Algorithm NUMBER
     Input N
     If (N < 0)
       then output 'Number is negative'
     Else output 'Number is positive or zero'
End of NUMBER
```

14.
```
Algorithm SALARY
     Input hours
     Input wage
     If (hours > 40)
       Then overtime = (hours - 40) * wage * 1.5
       Regular_pay, 'With overtime
     Else pay = hours * wage
       and output 'No overtime'
End of SALARY
```

Exercise 13.5 (page 544)

2. (a) $1 \cdot 2 = \frac{1(1+1)(1+2)}{3}$ which is true.

(b) $1 \cdot 2 + 2 \cdot 3 = \frac{2(2+1)(2+2)}{3}$ which is true.

(c) $1 \cdot 2 + 2 \cdot 3 + 3 \cdot 4 + \ldots + k \cdot (k+1) = \frac{k(k+1)(k+2)}{3}$

(d) $1 \cdot 2 + 2 \cdot 3 + 3 \cdot 4 + \ldots + (k+1)[(k+1)+1]$

$= \frac{(k+1)[(k+1)+1][(k+1)+2]}{3}$

4. (a) $\frac{1}{1 \cdot 2} = \frac{1}{1+1}$ which is true.

(b) $\frac{1}{1 \cdot 2} + \frac{1}{2 \cdot 3} + \frac{1}{3 \cdot 4} = \frac{3}{3+1}$ which is true.

(c) $\frac{1}{1 \cdot 2} + \frac{1}{2 \cdot 3} + \frac{1}{3 \cdot 4} + \ldots + \frac{1}{k(k+1)} = \frac{k}{k+1}$

(d) $\frac{1}{1 \cdot 2} + \frac{1}{2 \cdot 3} + \frac{1}{3 \cdot 4} + \ldots + \frac{1}{(k+1)[(k+1)+1} = \frac{(k+1)}{[(k+1)+1]}$

6. (a) $-1 = \frac{(-1)^1 - 1}{2}$ which is true.

(b) $-1 + 1 = \frac{(-1)^2 - 1}{2}$ which is true.

(c) $-1 + 1 - 1 + 1 \ldots + (-1)^{100} = \frac{(-1)^{100} - 1}{2}$ which is true.

(d) $-1 + 1 - 1 + 1 - \ldots + (-1)^k = \frac{(-1)^k - 1}{2}$

(e) $-1 + 1 - 1 + 1 - \ldots + (-1)^{k+1} = \frac{(-1)^{k+1} - 1}{2}$

8. Since $1^2 = \frac{1(1+1)(2+1)}{6}$ then S(1) is true. Thus, Condition I is true. Assume S(k) is true. Show that S(k + 1) is true. S(k + 1) states:

(1) $1^2 + 2^2 + 3^2 + \ldots + (k+1)^2 = \frac{(k+1)[(k+1)+1][2(k+1)+1]}{6}$

Using the assumption that S(k) is true the left hand side of (1) is then

$$\frac{k(k+1)(2k+1)}{6} + (k+1)^2 = \frac{k(k+1)(2k+1) + 6(k+1)^2}{6}$$

$$= \frac{(k+1)[k(2k+1) + 6(k+1)]}{6} = \frac{(k+1)(2k^2 + 7k + 6)}{6}$$

$$= \frac{(k+1)(k+2)(2k+3)}{6} = \frac{(k+1)[(k+1)+1][2(k+1)+1]}{6}$$

which is the right hand side of (1). Thus, S(k + 1) is true. So Condition II is true.

10. Since $2 = 1 \cdot (1 + 1)$ then S(1) is true. Thus Condition I is true. Assume S(k) is true. Show that S(k + 1) is true. S(k + 1) states:

$$2 + 4 + 6 + \ldots + 2(k+1) = (k+1)[(k+1)+1] \qquad (1)$$

Using the assumption that S(k) is true the left hand side of (1) is then

$$k(k+1) + 2(k+1) = (k+1)(k+2) = (k+1)[(k+1)+1]$$

which is the right hand side of (1) and thus S(k + 1) is true. So, Condition II is true.

12. Since $1 < 2^1$ then S(1) is true and thus Condition I is satisfied. Assume S(k) is true. Show that S(k + 1) is true. S(k + 1) states:

$$k + 1 < 2^k + 1 < 2^k + 2 \text{ (since } 1 < 2)$$

$\leq 2^{k+1}$ which is the right hand side of (1).

Thus S(k + 1) is true and so Condition II is satisfied.

14. $100 + 99 + 98 + \ldots + 2 + 1 = \frac{100 \cdot (100+1)}{2} = 5050$

16. $\frac{1}{1 \cdot 2} + \frac{1}{2 \cdot 3} + \ldots + \frac{1}{99 \cdot 100} = \frac{99}{100}$

18. $1^2 + 2^2 + 3^2 + \ldots + 100^2 = \frac{100(100+1)(200+1)}{6} = 338{,}350$

Exercise 13.6 (page 550)

2. $s_0 = 1$, $s_1 = s_0 + 1 = 2$, $s_2 = s_1 + 2 = 3$, $s_3 = s_2 + 3 = 6$, $s_4 = s_3 + 4 = 10$,
$s_5 = s_4 + 5 = 15$

4. $s_0 = -1$, $s_1 = s_0 + 2 = 1$, $s_2 = s_1 + 2^2 = 5$, $s_3 = s_2 + 2^3 = 13$, $s_4 = s_3 + 2^4 = 29$,
$s_5 = s_4 + 2^5 = 61$

6. $s_0 = 1$, $s_1 = s_0 + 1^2 = 2$, $s_2 = s_1 + 2^2 = 6$, $s_3 = s_2 + 3^2 = 15$, $s_4 = s_3 + 4^2 = 31$,
$s_5 = s_4 + 5^2 = 56$

8. $s_0 = 1$, $s_1 = -1$, $s_2 = 2s_0 + s_1^2 = 3$, $s_3 = 2s_1 + s_2^2 = 7$, $s_4 = 2s_2 + s_3^2 = 55$,
$s_5 = 2s_3 + s_4^2 = 3{,}025$

10. $s_0 = 3$, $s_1 = 6$, $s_2 = (s_0 + s_1)^{\frac{1}{2}} = 3$, $s_3 = (s_1 + s_2)^{\frac{1}{2}} = 3$
$s_4 = (s_2 + s_3)^{\frac{1}{2}} = 6^{\frac{1}{2}} = \sqrt{6}$, $s_5 = (s_3 + s_4)^{\frac{1}{2}} = (3 + \sqrt{6})^{\frac{1}{2}} = \sqrt{3 + \sqrt{6}}$

12. $s_0 = 2$, $s_1 = 1$, $s_2 = 1$, $s_3 = s_2 + s_1 - 2s_0 = -2$
$s_4 = s_3 + s_2 - 2s_1 = -3$, $s_5 = s_4 + s_3 - 2s_2 = -7$

14. $s_0 = 1$, $s_1 = 1$, $s_2 = 1$, $s_3 = (-1)^3 s_2 + 3s_1 + 3^2 s_0 = -s_2 + 3s_1 + 9s_0 = 11$,
$s_4 = (-1)^4 s_3 + 4s_2 + 4^2 s_1 = s_3 + 4s_2 + 16s_1 = 31$,
$s_5 = (-1)^4 s_4 + 5s_3 + 5^2 s_2 = -s_4 + 5s_3 + 25s_2 = 49$,

16. 63, 127, 255, 511

18. (a) The word that contains no bits is of length 0.
This word does not contain the patern 11.
The words 0 and 1 are of length 1 and do not contain the pattern 11.
The words 00,01,10 are of length 2 and do not contain the pattern 11.
The words 000,001,010,100,101 are of length 3 and do not contain the pattern 11.
The words 0000,0001,0010,0100,1000,1001,1010,0101 are of length 4 and do not contain the pattern 11.

(b) Recurrence relation $s_n = s_{n-1} + s_{n-2}$ with $s_0 = 1$ and $s_1 = 2$ as initial conditions

20. (a) \$2000, \$2110, \$2226.05, \$2348.48, \$2477.65

(b) $A_n = A_{n-1} + 0.055A_{n-1}$ (recurrence relation)
$A_0 = 2{,}000$

22. (a) N = 0, F = 1; N = 1, F = 1 · 1 = 1; N = 2, F = 2·1 · 1 = 2;

N = 3, F = 3 · 2 · 1 · 1 = 6; N = 4, F = 4 · 3 · 2 · 1 · 1 = 24;

N = 5, F = 5 · 4 · 3 · 2 ·1 · 1 = 120

(b) The factorial of N where $N \geq 0$.

Chapter Review (page 552)

2. $R^{-1} = \{(1,1), (2,8), (3,27)\}$

4. A = -1, B = -1

6. Algorithm AGEGROUP

```
    Input age
      If (age < 18)
        Then output 'minor'
     Else if (age ≤ 65)
           Then output 'adult'
         Else output 'senior citizen'
End of AGEGROUP
```

8. S(1) : $1 = \frac{1}{2}(3 - 1) = 1$, thus S(1) is true

S(2) : $1 + 3 = \frac{1}{2}(3^2 - 1)$

$4 = 4$, thus S(2) is true

S(3) : $1 + 3 + 3^2 = \frac{1}{2}(3^3 - 1)$

$13 = 13$, thus S(3) is true

To prove it in general we assume that S(k) is true. Note S(k) states:

$$1 + 3 + 3^2 + 3^3 + \ldots + 3^k = \frac{1}{2}(3^{k+1} - 1).$$

We must show that, based on this assumption, S(k + 1) is also true.
S(k + 1) states:

(1) $$1 + 3 + 3^2 + 3^3 + \ldots + 3^{k+1} = \frac{1}{2}(3^{[(k+1)+1} - 1)$$

Since S(k) is true (by assumption), then left hand side of (1) becomes

$\frac{1}{2}(3^{k+1} - 1) + 3^{k+1} = \frac{1}{2}3^{k+1} - \frac{1}{2} + 3^{k+1}$

$= \frac{3 \cdot 3^{k+1}}{2} - \frac{1}{2} = \frac{3^{k+2}}{2} - \frac{1}{2} = \frac{1}{2}(3^{k+1} - 1)$

$= \frac{1}{2}(3^{[(k+1)+1]} - 1)$ which is the right hand side of (1). Thus, S(k + 1) is true and so Condition II is satisfied.

10. $s_0 = 1$, $s_1 = 0$, $s_2 = (2 - 2)s_0 + s_1 = 0$
$s_3 = (3 - 2)s_1 + s_2 = 0$, $s_4 = (4 - 2)s_2 + s_3 = 0$
$s_5 = (5 - 2)s_3 + s_4 = 0$.

12. Let r_n be the number of pairs at the end of the nth month. Then we have:
$r_0 = 1$, $r_1 = r_0 + 0 = 1$
$r_2 = r_1 + 0 = 1$
$r_3 = r_2 + 0 = 1$
$r_4 = r_3 + 1 = 2$
$r_5 = r_4 + 0 = 2$
$r_6 = r_5 + 1 = 3$
$r_7 = r_6 + 0 = 3$
$r_8 = r_7 + 2 = 5$
$r_9 = r_8 + 0 = 5$
$r_{10} = r_9 + 2 = 7$

CHAPTER 14

Exercise 14.1 (page 560)

2. Vertices: $v_1, v_2, v_3, v_4, v_5, v_6, v_7, v_8, v_9, v_{10}$.
   Edges: $e_1, e_2, e_3, e_4, e_5, e_6, e_7, e_8, e_9, e_{10}, e_{11}$

4.

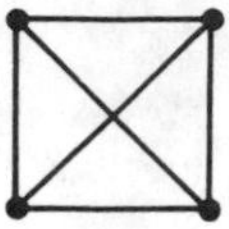

6. No. Sum of degrees of vertices is 35 which is not even.

8. (a) No. Sum of degrees of vertices is 9 which is not even.
   (b) No. Sum of degrees of vertices is 7 which is not even.
   (c) Yes,

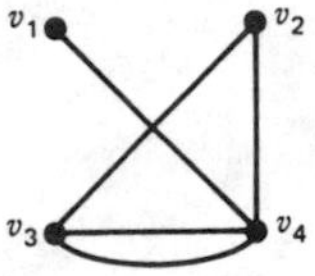

10. (a) No, because graph must have parallel edges thus it will not be simple.
    (b) No, because graph must have a loop thus it will not be simple.

12.

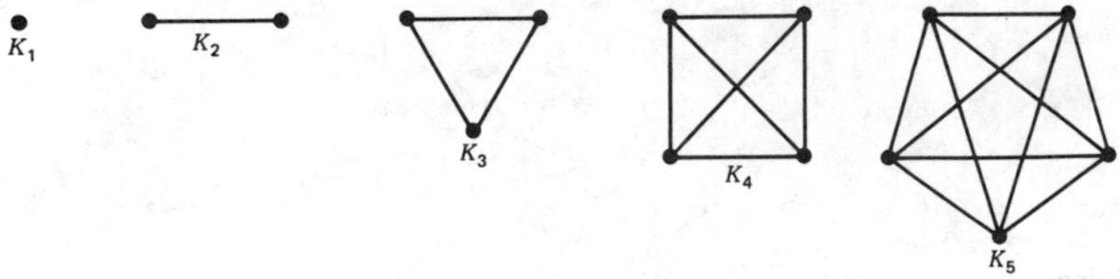

14.

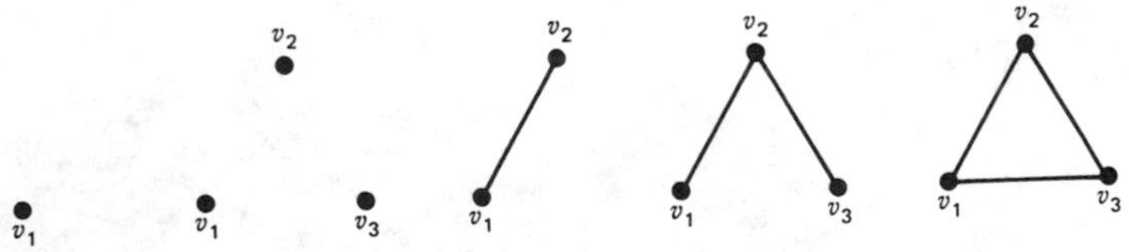

16.

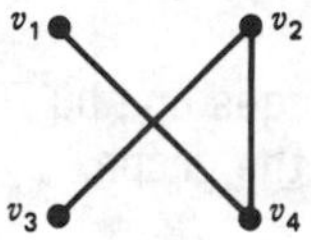

18.

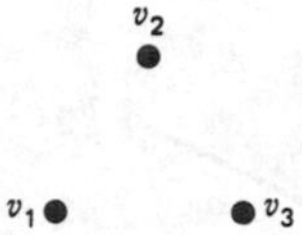

Exercise 14.2 (page 563)

2. (a) Simple circuit
(b) Simple path
(c) Circuit, but not a simple circuit.

4. (a) Simple circuit
(b) Path, but not a simple path

6. $v_1e_1v_2e_2v_3e_3v_4$;
$v_1e_1v_2e_7v_6e_8v_3e_3v_4$;
$v_1e_1v_2e_2v_3e_8v_6e_5v_5e_4v_4$;
$v_1e_6v_6e_5v_5e_4v_4$;
$v_1e_1v_2e_2v_3e_9v_5e_4v_4$;
$v_1e_6v_6e_7v_2e_2v_3e_3v_4$.

8. There are 6 such simple circuits. Here they are:
$v_1e_6v_6e_5v_5e_4v_4e_3v_3e_2v_2$;
$v_1e_1v_2e_7v_6e_5v_5e_4v_4e_3v_3$;
$v_1e_1v_2e_2v_3e_8v_6e_5v_5e_4v_4$;
$v_1e_6v_6e_7v_2e_2v_3e_9v_5e_4v_4$;
$v_1e_1v_2e_7v_6e_5v_5e_9v_3e_3v_4$;
$v_1e_1v_2e_7v_6e_8v_3e_3v_4e_4v_5$;

$v_1e_6v_6e_7v_2e_2v_3e_3v_4e_4v_5$;
$v_1e_1v_2e_2v_3e_3v_4e_4v_5e_5v_6$.

10.

12. No, the deletion of one edge will leave (n - 1) edges and by Theorem 1 the graph will be connected. For example consider the graph:

The deletion of one edge will not disconnect the graph.

14.

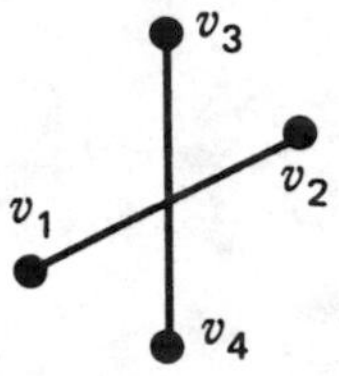

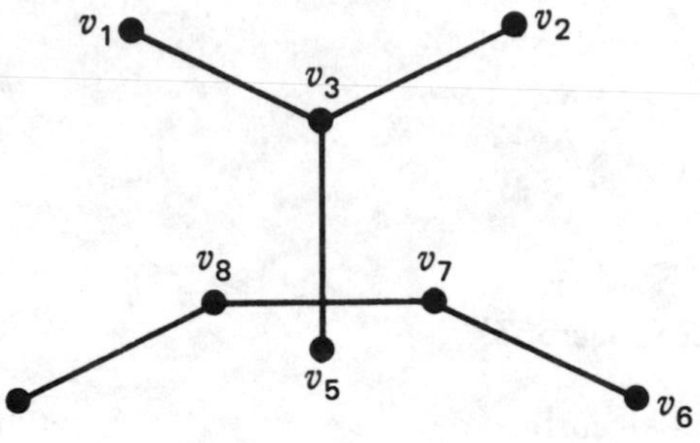

Exercise 14.3 (page 570)

2. No, not all vertices have even degree. Indeed none has even degree.

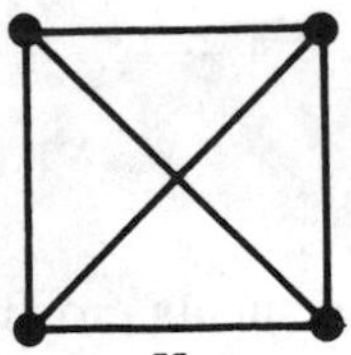

K_4

'6 A wm 9

'4 B wm 5

$10\left(\frac{9}{14}\right)$ ~~&~~ $10\left(\frac{5}{14}\right)$

$\frac{90}{14}$ 14)90.0 = 6.43
84
60
56
40

$\frac{50}{14}$ 14)50.00 = 3.57
42
80
70
100

B A

$4\left(\frac{5}{14}\right) - 6\left(\frac{9}{14}\right)$

$\frac{20}{14} - \frac{54}{14} = \frac{-34}{14}$

$5\left(\frac{7}{12}\right) + (-7)\left(\frac{5}{12}\right) = 0$

$$\frac{12}{52} \times 40 + \frac{3}{52} \times 50 + \frac{1}{52} \times 90$$

52

$$\frac{480 + 150 + 90}{52} = \frac{720}{52} - \frac{780}{}$$

$$\begin{array}{r} 520 \\ 280 \\ \hline 800 \end{array}$$

$$-\frac{60}{52} = -1\frac{8}{52} = 1\frac{2}{13} = 1.26$$

$$\frac{3}{13}(40) - \frac{3}{13}(15) + \frac{3}{52}(50) - \frac{3}{52}(15) + \frac{1}{52}(90) - \frac{1}{52}(15)$$

$$+ \frac{9}{13}(-15) - \frac{9}{1}(15)$$

$$\frac{3}{13}(40) + \frac{3}{52}(50) + \frac{1}{52}(90) - \left(\frac{3}{13} + \frac{3}{52} + \frac{1}{52} + \frac{9}{13}\right)(-15)$$

$$12 + 3 + 1 + 36$$

$$\frac{3}{13}(40) + \frac{3}{52}(50) + \frac{1}{52}(90) - 15$$

$\frac{1}{4} \times 2 + \frac{1}{2} \times 1 + \frac{1}{4} \times 0 = \frac{1}{2} + \frac{1}{2} = 1$ = Yes = 0

$.01 \times 78 + .99 \times 0 = .78$ No

$\frac{1}{4} \times 1 + \frac{1}{2} \times 0 + \frac{1}{4} \times (-1) = 0$

$.01 \times 75 + (.99 \times -1) = .75 - .99 = -.24$

$\frac{5}{14} \cdot 6 + \frac{9}{14}(-4) = \frac{50-36}{14} = \frac{14}{14} = 1$

$\frac{30-36}{14} = -\frac{6}{14}$

$\frac{50}{14} = 3\frac{8}{14} - 4 = -\frac{6}{14}$

$$y = e^{-\frac{z}{\pi}\left(\frac{\bar{X} - x}{\sigma}\right)^2}$$

$$y = e^{-kz^2}$$

$$\int_{-\infty}^{\infty} e^{-kz^2}\, dz = 1$$

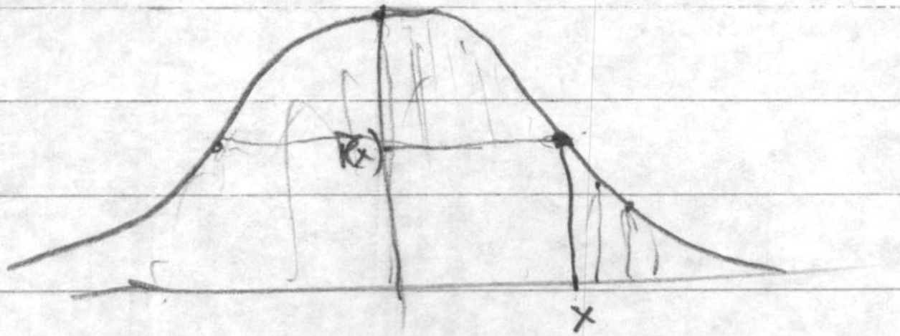

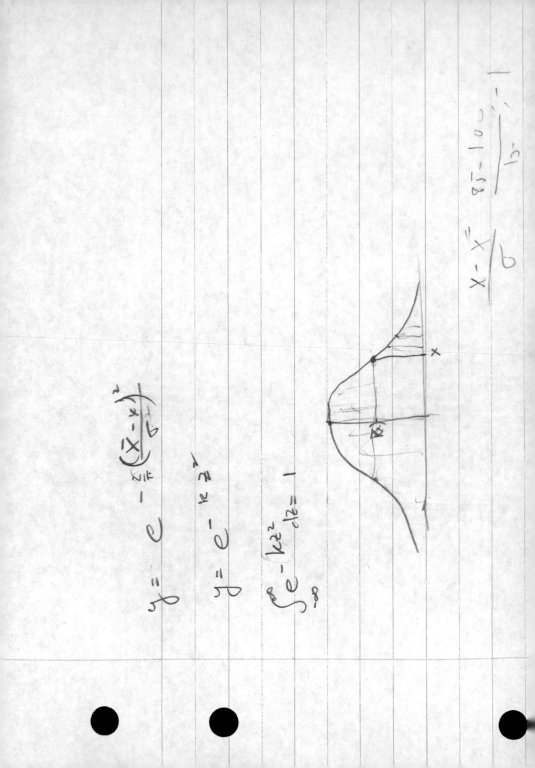

$$\frac{x - \bar{x}}{\sigma} \quad \frac{85 - 100}{15} = -1$$

4. If n is odd then every vertex in K_n is connected to (n - 1) vertices which is even. Thus, every vertex is of even degree, hence K_n, n odd, has an Eulerian circuit. If n is even then every vetex in K_n is connected to (n - 1) vertices which is odd. Thus every vertex is of odd degree and K_n, n even, has no Eulerian circuit.

6.

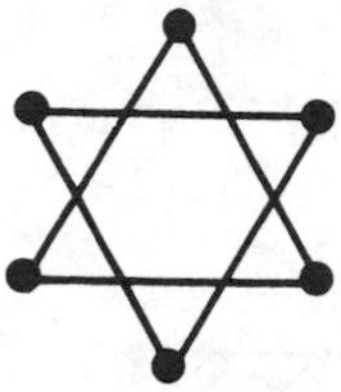

This graph has every vetex of even degree yet it has no Eulerian circuit because the graph is not connected.

8. Yes, because the graph in the figure which represents the house floor has every vertex of even degree. Therefore, it has an Eulerian circuit. One such circuit is ABCEFGHEDIA.

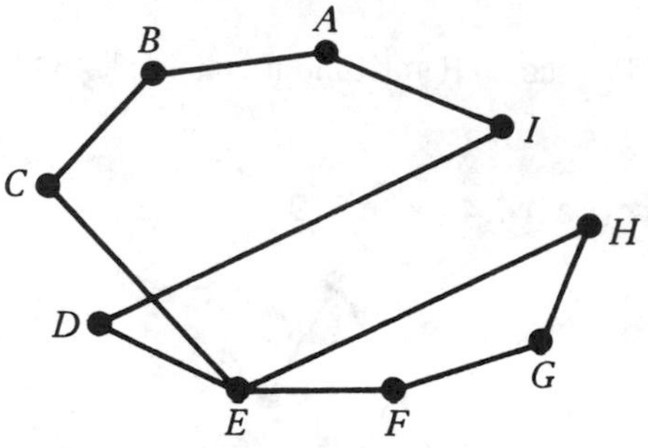

10. Yes, the route is (omitting the edges):

$v_1v_2v_3v_4v_5v_{14}v_{13}v_{12}v_{11}v_{10}v_9v_8v_7v_{16}v_{17}v_{18}v_{19}v_{20}v_{15}v_6v_1$.

12. (a) Yes, the Hamiltonian circuit is (omitting the edges):

$v_1v_2v_3v_4v_5v_7v_6v_1$.

(b) No, since, by Theorem 2, $\deg(v_1) + \deg(v_7) = 4 < 6$, number of vertices.

(c) Yes, the Hamiltonian circuit is (omitting the edges):

$v_1v_4v_3v_2v_6v_7v_8v_5v_1$.

(d) Yes, the Hamiltonian circuit is (omitting the edges):

$v_1v_2v_3v_4v_5v_1$.

14. The graph

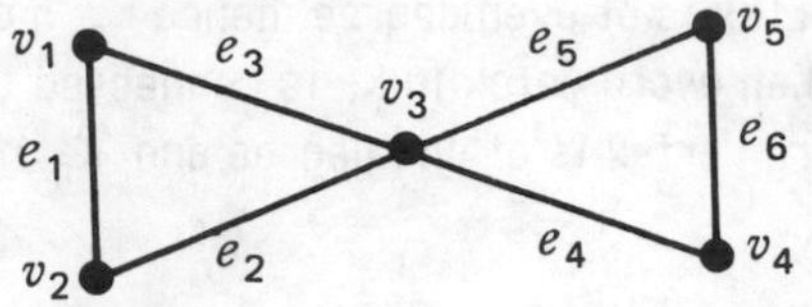

has no Hamiltonian circuit. It has the following Eulerian circuit.
$v_1e_1v_2e_2v_3e_5v_5e_6v_4e_4v_3e_3v_1$

16.

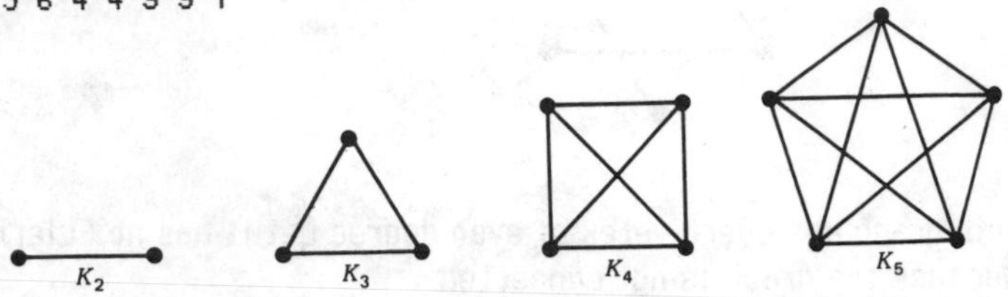

K_2 has no Hamiltonian circuit, K_3 and K_n, $n > 3$, have Hamiltonian circuits.

Exercise 14.4 (page 579)

2.

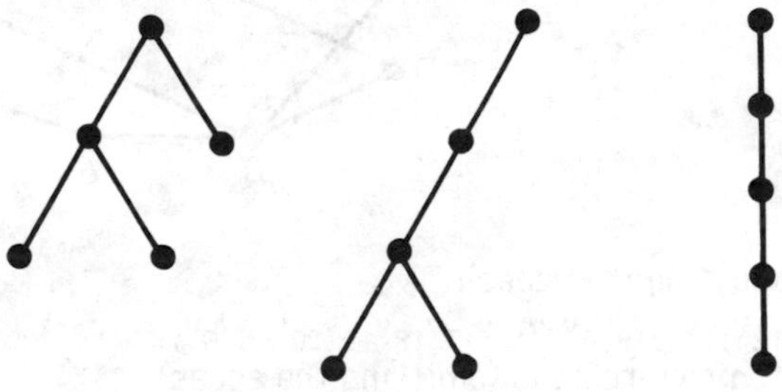

4.

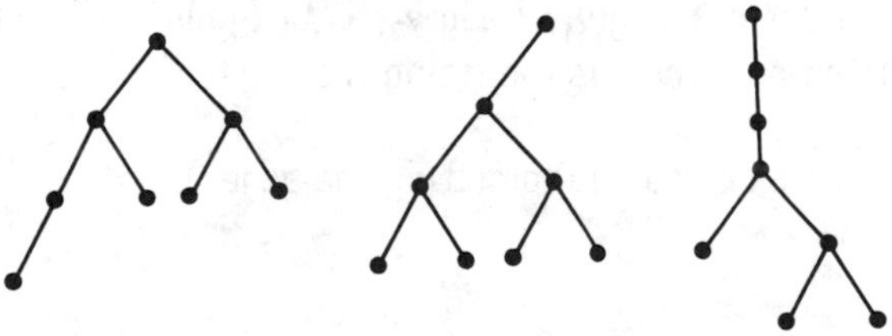

6.

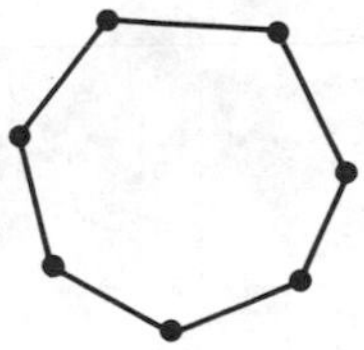

8. (a) Does not exist since for such a tree to exist there must be 5 edges.
(b) Does not exist since one of the vertices will be isolated.

10. Does not exist. Number of edges here exceeds 9.

12. Does not exist. Too many vertices.

14. No, in a tree an edge connects exactly two vertices.

16.

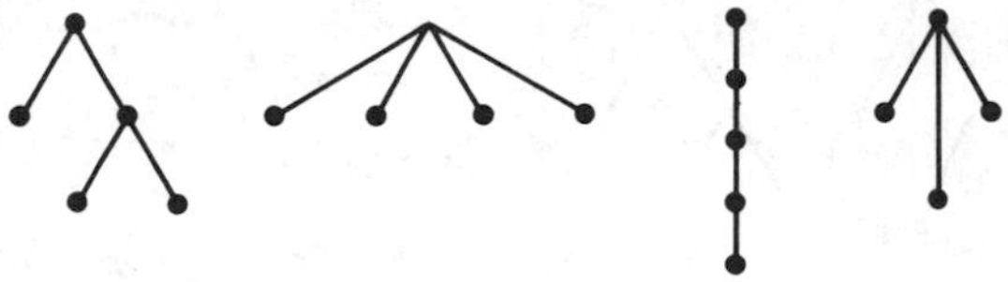

18. Leaves: $v_1, v_{13}, v_{12}, v_9, v_6, v_7$
Internal vertices: $v_2, v_{14}, v_3, v_4, v_5, v_{11}, v_{10}, v_8$

20. No, by definition an internal vertex must have a child.

22. (a) a,u,v,b,h are the descendants of x.
f,g,e,d are the descendants of y.
(b) vertex x: left subtree is

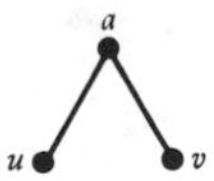

right subtree is

vertex y: left subtree is

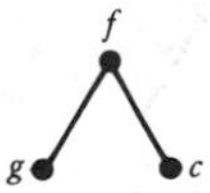

right subtree is 

(c)

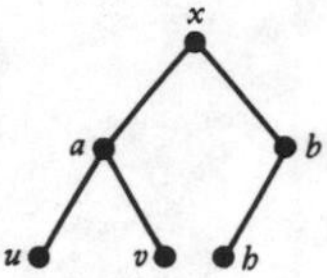

24. The trivial tree

26. $(a - b)^3$

28. [(a + b) * c - 5] + [(x + 1)/(y - 2)]

30.

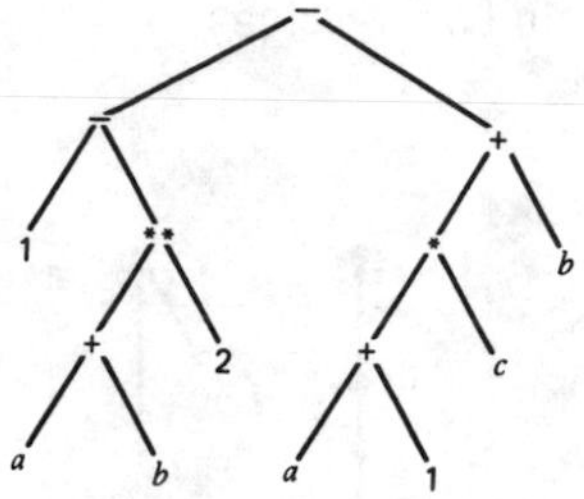

32. Begin with, say, 112:

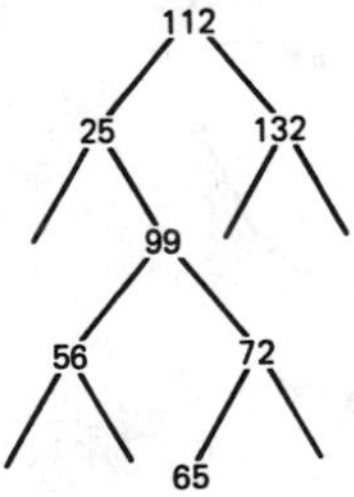

34.

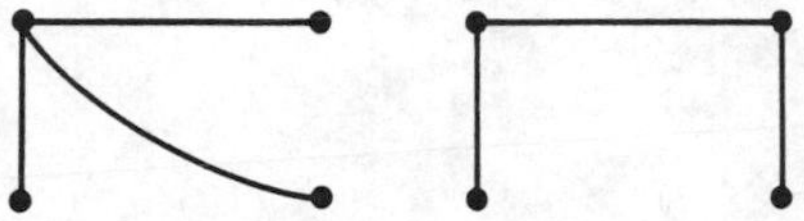

Exercise 14.5 (page 587)

2. (a)

Arc	Initial point	Terminal point
e_1	a	a
e_2	a	b
e_3	b	c
e_4	c	d
e_5	e	d
e_6	f	e
e_7	f	b
e_8	d	f
e_9	d	b

(b)

Vertex	Indegree	Outdegree
a	1	2
b	3	1
c	1	1
d	2	2
e	1	1
f	1	2

4.

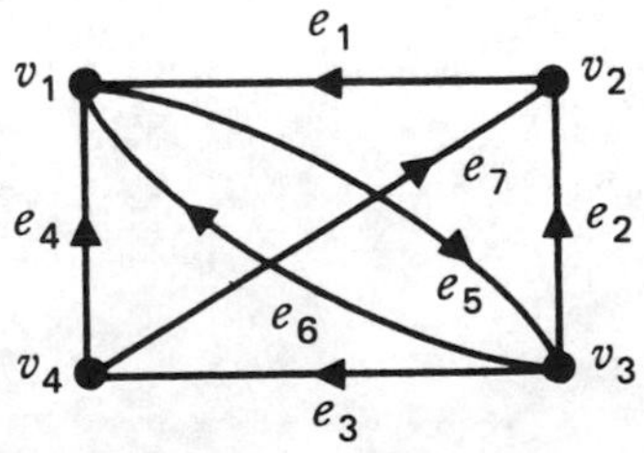

6.

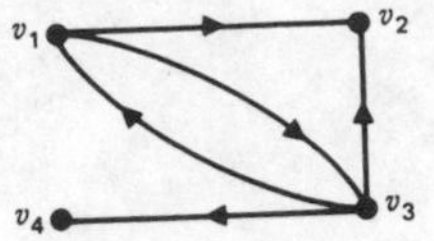

8.

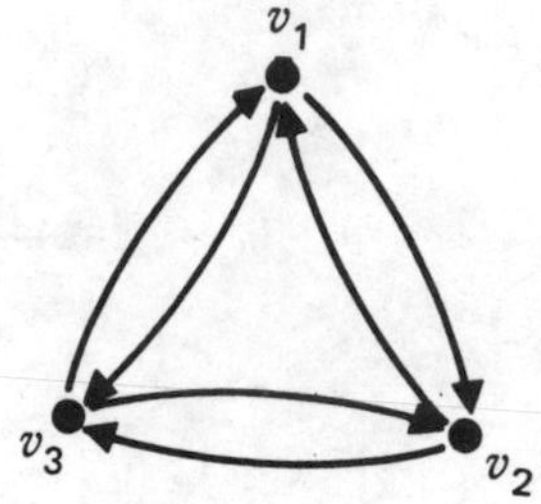

10. (a) Yes. $v_1v_2v_4v_5$ is a directed path from v_1 to v_5.
(b) Yes. $v_5v_3v_2v_4v_1$ is a directed path from v_5 to v_1.

12. Yes. Every vertex is reachable from any other.

14. (a) Vertex d has outdegree = 3 the highest of all outdegrees in the graph. This means d won the highest number of games.
(b) a b d e c

16.

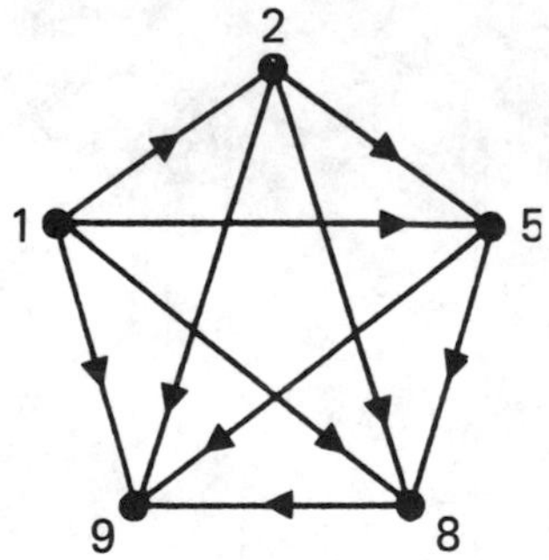

18. Graph is connected and contains no bridges. Therefore, it is strongly connected. The desired oriented graph is the following:

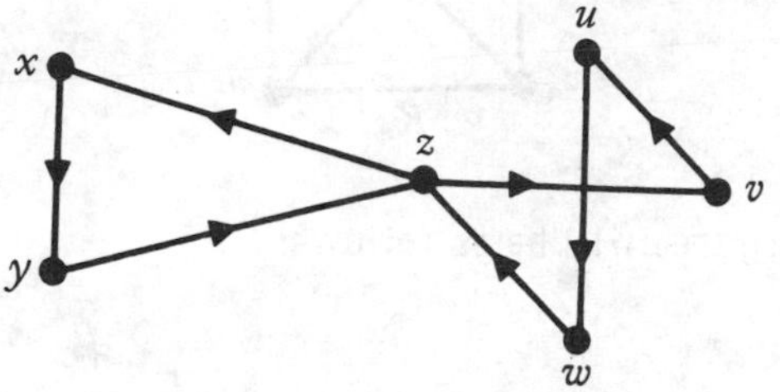

20. Graph is connected and has no bridges. Thus it is strongly connected. An orientation is given as follows:

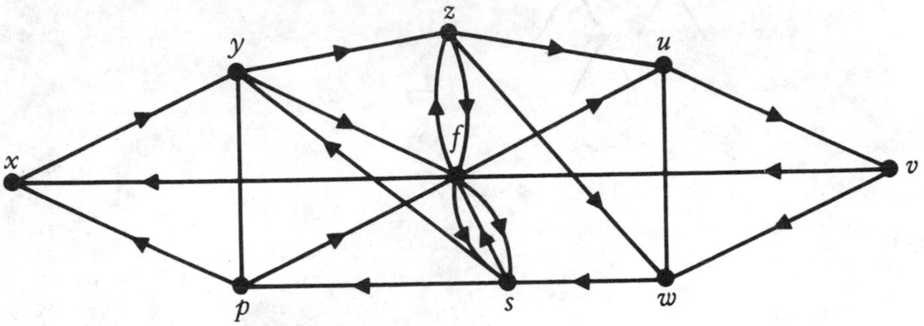

Review Exercises (page 590)

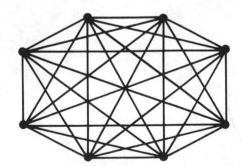

2.

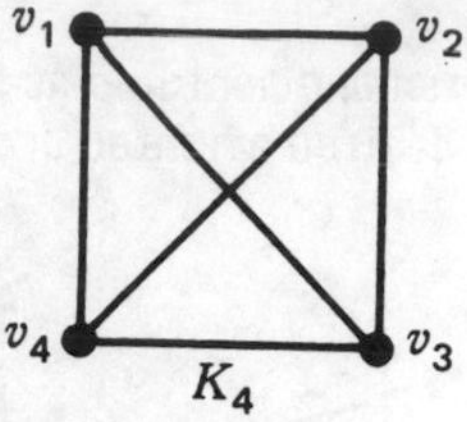

4. Two from each vertex. Total of eight. For example if we start at v_1, the two simple circuits (omitting edges) are:
$v_1v_2v_3v_4v_1$ and $v_1v_3v_2v_4v_1$

6. No. v_1 must be repeated.

8. Say we start at four. A binary tree will be as follows:

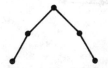

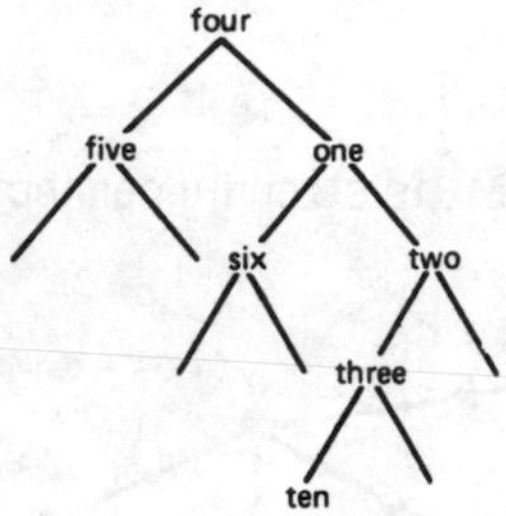

10.

12.

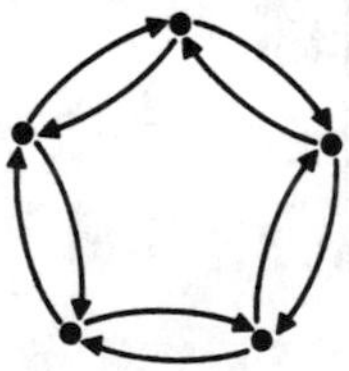

14. Since the graph has no bridges and is connected, then it is orientable. One way to orient it is given in the following graph:

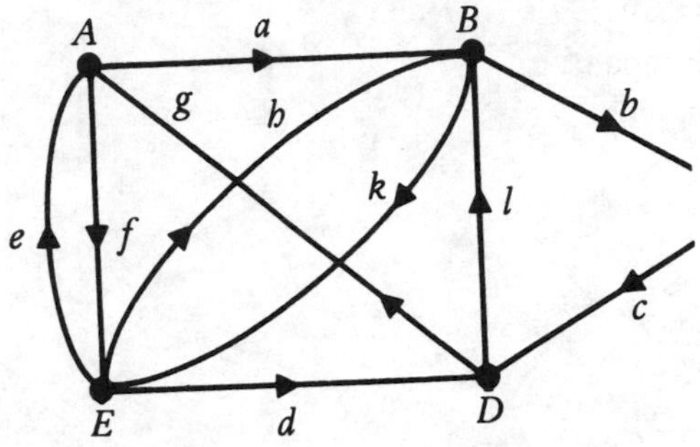

APPENDIX

OTHER BOOKS OR ARTICLES

OTHER BOOKS OR ARTICLES

CHAPTER 2 - MATRICES

Anton, H., Elementary Linear Algebra, 4th Ed., Wiley, 1984

Crandall, J.S. and Cedercreutz, M., "Preliminary cost estimates for mechanical work," Building Systems Design, Oct. - Nov. 1976, 73, p.35-51.

Isard, Walter and Kaniss, Phyllis, "The 1973 Nobel Prize for Economic Science," Science, (November 9, 1973)

Kolata, Gina, "Solving Linear Systems Faster", Science (June 14, 1985)

Leontief, Wassily W., "The Choice of Technology," Scientific American, June, 1985, pp. 37-45.

Leontief, Wassily W., The Structure of American Economy, 1919 - 1935, Oxford University Press, 1951.

Morris, Carl, "Breaking Deadlocks in Hockey: Prediction and Correlation" in Statistics by Example, F. Mosteller et. al. ed., Addison Wesley, 1973

Noble, B. and Daniel J., Applied Linear Algebra, Prentice-Hall, 1977

Rice, John R. Matrix Computations and Mathematical Software, McGraw-Hill, 1981

Rorres, C. and Anton, H., Applications of Linear Algebra, Wiley, 1984

Tuchinsky, Philip M., "General Equilibrium: Simple Linear Models," UMAP Module 208, COMAP, Inc., Lexington, Mass., 1986

OTHER BOOKS OR ARTICLES

CHAPTER 3 – LINEAR PROGRAMMING PART 1: Geometric Approach

Adams, F. Gerard, and James M. Griffin, "Economic Linear Programming Model of the U.S. Petroleum Refining Industry," J. Amer. Stat. Assoc. 67 (September 1972) pp. 542 - 551.

Allman, William P., "An Optimization Approach to Freight Car Allocation Under Time-Mileage Per Diem Rental Rates," Manage. Sci., 18, 10 (June 1972), pp. B567 - B574.

Broaddus, A., "Linear Programming: A New Approach to Bank Portfolio Management," Fed. Reserve Bank Richmond: Mon. Rev., 58, 11 (November 1972), pp. 3 – 11.

Carroll, T. Owen, "Modeling Tomorrow's Energy System: Applications of Linear Programming", UMAP Expository Monograph Series, COMAP, inc., 1985

Cohen, K.J., and F.S. Hammer, "Linear Programming and Optimal Bank Asset Management Decisions," J. Finan., 22 (May 1967), pp. 147 - 165.

Crandall, Robert H., "A Constrained Choice Model for Student Housing, "Manage Sci., 16, 2 (October 1969), pp. B112 - B120.

Dantzig, George, "Reminiscences about the Origins of Linear Programming," Operations Research Letters, Vol. 1, No. 2, April 1982.

Hanssmann, Fred, and Sidney W. Hess, "A Linear Programming Approach to Production and Employment Scheduling," Manage. Technol., 1 (January 1960), pp. 46 – 51.

Kohn, Robert E., "Application of Linear Programming to a Controversy on Air Pollution Control," Manage. Sci., 17, 10 (June 1971), pp. B609 - B621.

Lee, Sang M., and Edward R. Clayton, "Goal Programming Model for Academic Resource Allocation," Manage. Sci., 18, 8 (April 1972), pp. B395 - B408.

Loucks, Daniel P., Charles S. Revelle, and Walter R. Lynn, "Linear Programming Models for Water Pollution Control," Manage. Sci., 14, 4 (December 1967), pp. B166 - B181.

Markland, Robert E., and Robert M. Nauss, "Improving Transit Check Clearing Operations at Maryland National Bank", Interfaces 13 (February 1983), pp. 1 – 9.

Thomas, Harold A., Jr., and Roger Revelle, "On the Efficient Use of High Aswan Dam for Hydropower and Irrigation," Manage. Sci., 12, 8 (April 1966), pp. B296 - B311.

Wardle, P.A., "Forest Management and Operations Research: A Linear Programming Study," Manage. Sci., 11, 10 (August 1965), pp. B260 - B270.

CHAPTER 4 - LINEAR PROGRAMMING PART II: The Simplex Method

Adams, F. Gerard, and James M. Griffin, "Economic Linear Programming Model of the U.S. Petroleum Refining Industry," J. Amer. Stat. Assoc., 67 (September 1972), pp. 542 - 551.

Allman, William P., "An Optimization Approach to Freight Car Allocation Under Time-Mileage per Diem Rental Rates," Manage. Sci., 18, 10 (June 1972), pp. B567 - B574.

Angier, Natalie, "Folding the perfect corner: a young Bell scientist makes a major math breakthrough," Time, December 3, 1984, p. 63.

Aronofsky, J.S., Dutton, J.M., and Tayyabkhan, M.T., Managerial Planning with Linear Programming, Wiley, New York, 1978.

Broaddus, A., "Linear Programming: A New Approach to Bank Portfolio Managaement," Fed. Reserve Bank Richmond: Mon. Rev., 58, 11 (November 1972), pp. 3 - 11.

Cohen, K.J., and F.S. Hammer, "Linear Programming and Optimal Bank Asset Management Decisions," J. Finan., 22 (May 1967), pp. 147 - 165

Dantzig, George B., Linear Programming and Extensions, Princeton University Press, Princeton, N.J., 1963.

Gaber, P. Donald, and Gerald L. Thompson, Programming and Probability Models in Operations Research, Brooks/Cole, Monterey, Ca., 1973.

Gleick, James, "Breakthrough in Problem Solving," New York Times, November 19, 1984.

Graves, Stephen C., "Reflections on Operations Management in Shanghai," Interfaces, March - April 1986, p. 10 - 17.

Hanssmann, Fred, and Sidney W. Hess, "A Linear Programming Approach to Production and Employment Scheduling," Manage. Techn., 1 (January 1960), pp. 46 - 51.

Kozlov, Alex, "The Karmarkar Algorithm: Is It for Real?," SIAM News, Vol. 18, No. 6, Nov. 1985.

Kozlov, Alex and Black, L.W., "Berkeley Obtains New Results with the Karmarkar Algorithm," SIAM News, Vol. 19, No. 3, May 1986.

Lane, Kenneth and Goulet, John, "The Karmarkar Algorithm: New Issues in the Computational Complexity of Linear Programming," UMAP Journal, Vol. VI, No. 3.

Leff, S.H., Magbook, D. and Graves, S., "An L P Planning Model for a Mental Health Community Support System," Management Science, Vol. 32, 1986, pp. 139 - 155.

Murty, K.G., Linear and Combinatorial Programming, Wiley, New York, 1976.

Chpt. 4 - Other Books or Articles

Samuelson, Paul, Robert Dorfman, and Robert Solow, Linear Programming and Economic Analysis, McGraw-Hill, New York, 1958.

Sonderman, David and Abrahamson, Philip, "Radiotherapy Treatment Design Using Mathematical Programming Models," Operations Research, 33, 1985, pp. 705 - 725.

Thomas, Harold A., Jr., and Roger Revelle, "On the Efficient Use of High Aswan Dam for Hydropower and Irrigation," Manage. Sci., 13, 8 (April 1966), pp. B296 - B311.

Wardle, P.A., "Forest Management and Operations Research: A Linear Programming Study," Manage. Sci., 11, 10 (August 1965), pp. B260 - B270.

OTHER BOOKS OR ARTICLES

CHAPTER 6 - Sets; Counting Techniques

Benson, Oliver, "The Use of Mathematics in the Study of Political Science," paper presented to a symposium sponsored by the American Academy on Political and Social Science, Philadelphia (June 1963).

Coolidge, J.L., "The Story of the Binomial Theorem," American Mathematical Monthly, Vol. 56, 1949.

Golomb, Solomon, "A Mathematical Theory of Discrete Classification," Information Theory, Fourth London Symposium, Butterworths, London, 1961.

Mallows, C.L. and Sloane, N.J., "Designing an Auditing Procedure, or How to Keep Bank Managers on Their Toes," Mathematics Magazine, Vol. 57, 1984.

Reingold, E.M., Nievergelt, J. and Deo, N., Combinatorial Algorithms: Theory and Practice, Prentice-Hall, 1977.

Richbart, Lynn A., "Exotic Horse-Race Wagering and Combinatorics," The Mathematics Teacher, 1984, pp. 35 - 36.

Riker, William H., "Voting and the Summations of Preferences," Amer. Political Sci. Rev. 55 (1961), pp. 900 - 911.

Rudestam, Kjell Erik, and Bruce John Morrison, "Student Attitudes Regarding the Temporary Closing of a Major University," Amer. Psychol., 26, 5 (May 1971), pp. 519 - 525.

Slapley, L.S., and Shubik, M., "A Method for Evaluating the Distribution of Power in a Committee System," Amer. Political Sci. Rev., 48 (1954), pp. 787ff.

Tucker, Alan, Applied Combinatorics (2nd ed.), John Wiley, 1984.

CHAPTER 7 – INTRODUCTION TO PROBABILITY

Bello, Anthony, "A Papal Conclave Testing the Plausibility of a Historical Account", Mathematics Magazine 55, 1982, pp. 230 - 233.

Berlekamp, E.R. "The Technology of Error-Correcting Codes", Proc. IEEE, 68 (1980), pp. 564 - 593.

Deutsch, Karl W., and William G. Madow, " A Note on the Appearance of Wisdom in Large Bureaucratic Organizations," Behav. Sci., 6 (1961), pp. 72 - 78.

Downs T., D.C. Gilliland and L. Katz, "Probability in a Contested Election," American Statistican 32, (1978), pp. 122 - 125.

Duncan, David R. and Bonnie H. Litwiller, "A Question of Coincidences", Mathematics Teacher, May 1985, pp. 381 - 384.

Gelfand, Alan E., and Herbert Solomon, "Modeling Jury Verdicts in the American Legal System," J. Amer. Stat. Assoc., 69 (March 1974), pp.32 - 37.

Horvath, Frank S., and John E. Reid, "The Reliability of Polygraph Examiner Diagnosis of Truth and Deception," J. Crim. Law, Criminol. Police Sci., 62, 2 (1971), pp. 276 - 281.

Kalisch, B.J. and P.A. Kalisch, "An analysis of the impact of authorship on the image of the nurse presented in novels," Research in Nursing and Health, 6:1 (March 1983), pp. 17 - 24.

Meyer, Walter "Huffman Codes and Data Compression," UMAP Journal, Vol. 5, No. 3, 1984, pp. 277 - 296.

Mizrahi, A. and M. Sullivan, <u>Mathematics for Business and Social Science</u>, 3rd Ed., Wiley, New York, 1983.

Mosteller, F., and D.L. Wallace, <u>Inference and Disputed Authorship: The Federalist</u>, Addison-Wesley, Reading, Mass., 1964.

Mosteller, F., and D.L. Wallace, "Deciding Authorship," in Judith M. Tanur, ed., Statistics: A Guide to the Unknown, Holden-Day, San Francisco, 1972, pp. 164 - 175.

Overall, John E., and Clyde M. Williams, "Conditional Probability Program for Diagnosis of Thyroid Function," J. Amer. Med. Assoc., 183, 5 (February 2, 1963), pp. 307 - 313.

Pascal, Gerald R., and Barbara Suttell, "Testing the Claims of a Graphologist," J. Pers., 16 (1947), pp. 192 - 197.

Pless, Vera, <u>Introduction to the Theory of Error-Correcting Codes</u>, Wiley-Interscience, 1982.

Smith, Paul F., "Measuring Risk on Consumer Installment Credit," Manage. Sci., 11, 2 (November 1964), pp. 327 - 340.

Chpt. 7 - Other Books or Articles

Warner, Homer R., Alan F. Toronto, L. George Veasey, and Robert Stephenson, "A Mathematical Approach to Medical Diagnosis," J. Amer. Med. Assoc., 177, 3 (July 22, 1961), pp. 177 - 183.

___________, "Trial by Mathematics," TIME, April 26, 1968, p. 41.

OTHER BOOKS OR ARTICLES

CHAPTER 8 – ADDITIONAL TOPICS IN PROBABILITY

Coughlin, Mary and Carolyn Kerwin, "Mathematical Induction and Pascal's Problem of the Points; Mathematics Teacher, May 1985, pp. 376 - 380.

Dyer, J.S. and Shapiro, R.D., Management Science/Operations Research: Cases and Readings, 1982, Wiley, New York, 1982.

Gass, Saul, ed., Operations Research: Mathematics and Models, Proceedings of Symposia in Applied Mathematics, Vol. 25, American Mathematical Society, 1981.

Graves, Stephen C., "Reflections on Operations Management in Shanghai," Interfaces, March - April 1986, pp. 10 - 17.

Hillier, F.S. and G.J. Lieberman, Introduction to Operations Research, 3rd ed., Holden-Day, San Francisco, Ca., 1980.

Keeney, Ralph L. and Robert L. Winkler, "Evaluating Decision Strategies for Equity of Public Risks," Operations Research 33, 5 (1985) pp. 955 - 970.

Lucas, William F., "What is Operations Research?," UMAP Journal, Vol. IV, No. 4, 1983.

Mizrahi, A., and M. Sullivan, Mathematics for Business and Social Science, 3rd ed., Wiley, New York, 1983.

Schwartz, W.B., Gorry, G.A., et al., "Decision Analysis and Clinical Judgement," The American Journal of Medicine, Vol. 55, 1973, pp. 459 - 472.

Sullivan, W.G. and W.W. Claycombe, "The Use of Decision Trees in Planning Plant Expansion," Advanced Management Journal, Vol. 40, No. 1, (Winter 1975), pp. 29 - 39.

Wakin, Shirley, "Expected Value at Jai Alai and Pari-Mutuel Gambling", UMAP Module No. 631, COMAP, Inc., 1986.

CHAPTER 9 - STATISTICS

Hoel, P.G., Elementary Statistics, 4th Ed., Wiley, New York, 1976.

Mosteller, Frederick, William H. Kruskal, Richard F. Link, Richard S. Pieters, and Gerald R. Rising, eds., Statistics by Example, Addison-Wesley, Reading, Mass., 1973.

Sincich, T., Statistics by Example, Dellen, San Francisco, 1982.

Tanur, Judith M., Frederick Mosteller, William H. Kruskal, Richard F. Link, Richard S. Pieters, and Gerald R. Rising, eds., Statistics: A Guide to the Unknown, Holden-Day, San Francisco, 1972.

Tanur, Judith M., Frederick Mosteller, William H. Kruskal, Richard F. Link, Richard S. Pieters, Gerald R. Rising, and E.L. Lehmann, eds., Statistics: A Guide to Business and Economics, Holden-Day, San Francisco, 1976.

OTHER BOOKS OR ARTICLES

CHAPTER 10 - APPLICATIONS TO GAMES OF STRATEGY

Bennion, Edward G., "Capital Budgeting and Game Theory," Harv. Bus. Rev., 34, 6 (November - December 1956), pp. 115 - 123.

Blackett, D. W., "Some Blotto Games," Nav. Res. Logist. Q., 1 (1954), pp. 55 - 60.

Buchler, Ira, and Hugo Nutini, Game Theory in the Behavioral Sciences, University of Pittsburg Press, 1969.

Caywood, T. E., and C.J. Thomas, "Applications of Game Theory in Fighter versus Bomber Combat," Oper. Res., 3 (1955), pp. 402 - 411.

Friedman, Lawrence, "Game-Theory Models in the Allocation of Advertising Expenditures," Oper. Res., 6 (1958), pp. 699 - 709.

Gould, Peter R., "Man Against His Environment: A Game Theoretic Framework," Ann. Assoc. Amer. Geogr., 53, 3 (September 1963), pp. 290 - 297.

Haywood, O.G., Jr., "Military Decision and the Mathematical Theory of Games," Air Univ. Q. Rev., 4 (1950), pp. 17 - 30.

Haywood, O.G., Jr., "Military Decision and Game Theory," Oper. Res., 2, 4 (November 1954), pp. 365 - 385.

Jones, A.J., Game Theory: Mathematical Models of Conflict, Wiley, New York, 1980.

Kaplan, Martin, and Nicholas Katzenbach, The Political Foundations of International Law, Wiley, New York, 1961.

Luce, R. Duncan, and Howard Raiffa, Games and Decisions, Wiley, New York, 1957.

Luce, R. Duncan, and Arnold A. Rogow, "A Game Theoretic Analysis of Congressional Power Distributions for a Stable Two-Party System," Behav. Sci., 1, 2 (April 1956), pp. 83 - 95.

McClintock, C.G., and D.M. Messick, "Empirical Approaches to Game Theory and Bargaining: A Bibliography," Gen. Syst., 11 (1966), pp. 229 - 238.

Mathematics in the Modern World, readings from Scientific American, Freeman, San Francisco, 1968, pp. 300 - 312.

Rapoport, Anatol, and Albert M. Chammah, "Sex Differences in Factors Contributing to the Level of Cooperation in the Prisoner's Dilemma Game," J. Pers. Soc. Psychol., 2, 6 (December 1965), pp. 831 - 838.

Shapley, L.S., and Martin Shubik, "A Method for Evaluating the Distribution of Power in a Committee System," Amer. Polit. Sci. Rev., 48, 3 (September 1954), pp. 787 - 792.

Shubik, Martin, "The Uses of Game Theory in Management," Manage. Sci., 2 (1955), pp. 40 - 54.

Thie, P.R., An Introduction to Linear Programming and Game Theory, Wiley, New York, 1979.

OTHER BOOKS OR ARTICLES

CHAPTER 11 - MARKOV CHAINS

Beekman, John A., "Several Demographic Projection Techniques," Rural Demography, 8 (1981), pp. 1 - 11.

Bower, Gordon H., "Application of a Model to Paired-Associate Learning," Psychometrika, 26, 3 (September 1961), pp. 255 - 280.

Cohen, Bernard P., "A Probability Model for Conformity," Sociometry, 21 (1958), pp. 69 - 81

Cohen, Bernard P., Conflict and Conformity: A Probability Model and Its Application, MIT Press, Cambridge, Mass., 1963.

Cybert, R.M., H.J. Davidson, and G.L. Thompson, "Estimation of the Allowance for Doubtful Accounts by Markov Chains," Manage. Sci., 8, 3 (April 1962), pp. 287 - 303

Harary, F. and B. Lipstein, "The Dynamics of Brand Loyalty: A Markov Approach," Operations Research, 10 (1962), pp. 19 - 40.

Hoffman, Hans, "Markov Chains in Ethiopia," in Paul Kay, ed., Explorations in Mathematical Anthropology, MIT Press, Cambridge, Mass., 1971.

Hunter, Albert, "Community Change: A Stochastic Analysis of Chicago's Local Communities, 1930 - 1960," Amer. J. Sociol., 79 (January 1974), pp. 923 - 947.

Kemeny, John G., and J. Laurie Snell, Mathematical Models in the Social Sciences, Blaisdell, New York, 1962.

Liebman, L.H., "A Markov Decision Model for Selecting Optimal Credit Control Policies," Management Science 18, 10 (June 1972).

Mosimann, J., Elementary Probability for the Biological Sciences, Prentice-Hall, Englewood Cliffs, N.J., 1968.

Styon, G.P. and H. Smith, "Markov Chains Applied to Marketing," Journal of Marketing Research 1 (1964), pp. 50 - 55.

Thie, Paul, Markov Decision Processes, UMAP Monograph Series, COMAP, Inc. 1983.

OTHER BOOKS OR ARTICLES

CHAPTER 12 - LOGIC

Hohfeld, W.N., Fundamental Legal Conceptions as Applied in Judicial Reasoning and Other Essays, Walter Wheeler Cook, ed., Yale University Press, New Haven, 1919.

Hohn, Franz, "Some Mathematical Aspects of Switching," The American Mathematical Monthly, 62 (1955), pp. 75 - 90.